CAMBRIDGE TEXTBOOKS IN LINGUISTICS

General editors: P. AUSTIN, J. BRESNAN, B. COMRIE, S. CRAIN,
W. DRESSLER, C. EWEN, R. LASS, D. LIGHTFOOT, K. RICE,
I. ROBERTS, S. ROMAINE, N.V. SMITH

Child Language
Acquisition and Growth

Child Language
Acquisition and Growth

BARBARA C. LUST

Cornell University

CAMBRIDGE UNIVERSITY PRESS
Cambridge, New York, Melbourne, Madrid, Cape Town, Singapore, São Paulo

Cambridge University Press
The Edinburgh Building, Cambridge, CB2 8RU, UK

Published in the United States of America by Cambridge University Press, New York

www.cambridge.org
Information on this title: www.cambridge.org/9780521449229

First published 2006
Reprinted 2007

Printed in the United Kingdom at the University Press, Cambridge

A catalogue record for this publication is available from the British Library

ISBN 978-0-521-44478-1 hardback
ISBN 978-0-521-44922-9 paperback

To Jim and the World of Nagaraj

Contents

List of figures

List of tables

Preface

This book grew out of many years of teaching an interdisciplinary survey course, "Language Development," at Cornell. Many generations of students and their persistent questions, challenges and insights have built the material on which this book is based.

Like the course it is based on the book is essentially interdisciplinary, on the assumption that only an interdisciplinary approach can begin to advance our understanding of the fundamental mystery we are concerned with, i.e., the nature of the competence of the human species for language. It addresses this mystery by attempting to convert it to issues which allow and support scientific inquiry. Thus it does not simply adopt one point of view; nor does it deny debates in the field. It does not simply adopt a "logical" or "empirical" approach to the study of language acquisition. Rather, in the interest of grounding scientific inquiry in this area, it attempts to represent opposing points of view and to articulate their premises and predictions. It combines both theoretical and empirical inquiries in order to ground scientific inquiry. Hopefully, on the basis of the articulation of theoretical premises and the summary of empirical evidence which is provided in this book, the field now will have strengthened foundation for future research, allowing the continual course of inquiry which will be necessary to resolve fundamental debates which characterize the field.

Acknowledgments

There are many people without whom this book would not exist. Stephanie Shattuck-Hufnagel began the Language Development course with me in the 1970s. Her intellectual vitality and acuity provoked both our enthusiasm for this course and the idea that a book could capture this course. Judith Ayling at Cambridge University Press propelled this idea into a proposed reality through Cambridge University Press in 1997. Over the years, as the course and its materials developed, individual manuscript sections developed. So did the field of language acquisition, broadening its investigations, reinventing its fundamental nature–nurture debates, and continually extending its empirical results through new methodologies for experimental research. When the vastness of these developments on all fronts and intensity of theoretical debates, combined with the demands of active research, appeared to challenge the tractability of this project, Christine Bartels of Cambridge University Press breathed crucial life support into the intellectual and practical challenges involved in this book. Andrew Winnard added continual practical, supportive guidance, combining the role of "provacateur" to a deadline with incredible patience.

Helen Barton shepherded the work through critical stages. Finally, without Neil Smith, it could be said that this book would not exist. He not only insisted on receiving preliminary manuscripts of each chapter, but read each chapter, providing line by line incisive, acute comments and corrections, often within hours of receiving these, and leading to continual rewriting.

With regard to manuscript preparation, I thank Margaret Collins for her assistance in final manuscript preparation, and Lesley Atkin for her brave copy editing and indomitable courage in capturing endless references. Bob Kibbee of Cornell University Library intervened at several times to insure the scientific validity of the references in this volume. I am endlessly indebted to him and his crucial help. Suzanne Flynn, Claire Foley and Katherine Demuth provided critical manuscript comments. I am very grateful to Soon Park for his work on the index.

Finally, I thank all the students, graduate and undergraduate who have contributed to this book, more than can ever be expressed. They are not students anymore, but teachers, as they always were.

Of course, without Jim Gair, nothing would exist. He read and challenged every word, providing constant sharpening of issues and argument, bridging linguistics and psychology, theoretical inquiry and empirical data, and combining criticism and support without seam between these.

Acknowledgments are also due to "Dr. Seuss" (Theodor Seuss Geisel) for his wonderful insights into language, and to Lewis Carroll (Charles Lutwidge Dodgson) and his "Alice in Wonderland" for his brilliant insights into the relations between language and thought.

Of course, in spite of all the work provided by so many, the errors remain my own; and the work remains only the basis for the future, hopefully a future more fully grounded for continuous scientific inquiry.

1   The growth of language

1.1   Introduction

The acquisition of our first language is a silent feat. Most probably, we have no recollection of it at all. In many respects, the feat is essentially accomplished by the time children are three years old. Yet it is "doubtless the greatest intellectual feat any of us is ever required to perform" (Bloomfield 1933, 29; cf. Gleitman et al. 1988). The purpose of this book is to (a) introduce the scope and nature of this "intellectual feat," and (b) highlight results from the last several decades from intensive scientific study of the mystery of its accomplishment.[1] In doing so, we will (c) attempt to articulate essential theoretical issues which concern the "explanation" of this mystery. Throughout, we will (d) develop the foundation for a theory of first language acquisition. This theory is fundamentally "rationalist," acknowledging the innateness of a powerful Language Faculty in the human species but integrating the role of constrained experience in the "growth of language" in order to explain language development. We will see that language acquisition is an inherently intellectual feat in that children do complex theory construction. The growth of language is mediated in the human species by complex symbolic computation.

Nothing is more specifically "human" than the knowledge of language. We have no firm means of scientifically determining how or when language originated in the human species. However, we witness this feat continually – in ourselves and in every child born.[2]

1.2   A logical-developmental perspective

The research for review here bears on an ultimate mystery: *the nature of development, specifically development of the mind.* Since development entails

---

[1] Intensive scientific study of language acquisition (empirical and theoretical) developed with the appearance of work by Roger Brown (e.g., 1973b) at Harvard, and Noam Chomsky (e.g., 1965) at MIT; Chomsky's famous critique of Skinner's (1957) book in 1959 confronted the problem of language acquisition directly. Lashley's "The Problem of Serial Order in Behavior" (1951) implicated language in cognitive science (Bruce 1994).

[2] Although "human beings were anatomically ready to speak more than 150,000 years ago . . . clear evidence that they were doing so does not appear for 100,000 years afterward" (Holden 1988, 1455; see also Lieberman 1992).

the creation of what is entirely new, it involves a compelling area of scientific inquiry. Knowledge of language, in turn, represents one of the most challenging areas of human development. This is not only because of the formal complexity and infinity of language knowledge, but also because we know that the acquisition of language cannot be derived by simple inductive theories of learning (in which we merely copy or imitate properties of our environment). This implies internal control of language acquisition.

Development of language reveals biological programming, suggesting "genetic control." Except under the most extreme conditions, one cannot help but acquire a language. A regular course of acquisition is generally followed, one not determined by changes in the environment, nor by "goal directed practice" or immediate "need" (Lenneberg 1966, 220; 1967). Given only minimal input, neither deafness nor blindness nor both combined need prevent it.[3] The lack of vocal production in the oral medium need not prevent it.[4] The lack of a good model need not prevent it.[5] Neither severe cognitive deficits nor severe intersocial and communicative deficits need prevent it.[6] Neither amoebae nor plants acquire it. Not even chimps or bonobos acquire it as humans do, although many species do have other marvelous means of communication.[7] In many ways, there appears to be a developmental program for language acquisition in the human species, which specifies sequence and timing of general developmental events as well as certain precise aspects of the "program."

Yet the "language program" cannot be completely innate. Children are not born pre-programmed to learn a *specific* language – any of the world's approximately 7,000 languages are equally acquirable,[8] but children not exposed to a language do not learn that language. This seemingly puzzling developmental issue provides the foundation for our investigation of first language acquisition.

Study of language acquisition today is characterized by distinct, and in some ways contradictory, approaches. At one extreme is "developmental" research, in which the course of acquisition over time is described empirically. At another extreme is a "logical" approach, in which the problem of language acquisition is analyzed formally, often independent of empirical observations of child language.

---

[3] Herrmann 1998; Keller 1999; Landau and Gleitman 1985; Meier and Newport 1990; Goldin-Meadow 2003.

[4] Kegl, Senghas and Coppola 1999; Lillo-Martin 1999.

[5] Feldman, Goldin-Meadow, and Gleitman 1978; Goldin-Meadow and Feldman 1977; deGraff 1999. Helen Keller, who ultimately accomplished language, was 19 months old when stricken by a fever leaving her blind, deaf and dumb (Hermann 1998).

[6] Smith and Tsimpli 1995 and Blank, Gessner and Esposito 1979, respectively.

[7] Hauser 1997; Hockett 1977; Marler in press; Terrace et al. 1980; Smith 1999.

[8] Grimes (1992) lists 6,703 languages, although she notes the difficulty in distinguishing "language" and "dialect," making it impossible to provide an exact number of existing languages. (See also Crystal 1997, especially pages 286–288.) Michael Krauss (1995), in a paper presented at an AAAS annual meeting (February 1995), estimates that humans probably spoke between 10,000–15,000 languages in prehistoric times; that the number is dropping and that 20–50 percent of the world's languages now are no longer being acquired by children (Gibbons 1995). Ladefoged (1997) estimates that only 3,000 languages will remain in 100 years time. Hale 1994 estimates that only a few hundred languages may be acquired in our great-grandchildren's time.

A related tension exists between developmental paradigms such as Piaget's (1983, 23), wherein the essence of understanding cognitive development lies in studying the "very process of its transformation," i.e., in the study of developmental change *per se* over time, and a paradigm such as Noam Chomsky's in which the most powerful approach to understanding in this area lies in a formal characterization of what he terms the "Initial State" (e.g., 1980).[9]

These approaches must be merged if the essential mystery of human language acquisition is ever to be solved. We will attempt to do so in this book both by providing a description of empirical facts of language development and linking these to important theoretical issues regarding the nature of language and the mind.

1.3   Current research questions

Our developmental survey of language acquisition allows us to address several questions regarding language development which researchers in many laboratories are actively pursuing. What is it about the human mind that makes it possible to acquire language? Which aspects of the language program are biologically programmed? What specifically linguistic knowledge is evident at early periods? What underlies apparent differences between language acquisition in children and adults? Is there a "critical period" for language acquisition that critically distinguishes first and second language acquisition? How does the acquisition of the "end state" of specific language knowledge arise on the basis of biological programming of the Initial State? How do children "project" from the finite data to which they are exposed out to the knowledge of the grammar? Are there *universal* specific stages in the acquisition of sounds and structures of language? What determines the change in children's linguistic knowledge as they develop?

1.4   Language acquisition, linguistic theory and cognitive science

Linguistic theory provides hypotheses regarding a biologically programmed Language Faculty (e.g., Chomsky 1986; 1988a, b; 1999; 2000). In Cognitive Science, "the fundamental design specifications of an information-processing system are called its architecture" (Simon and Kaplan 1989). We may assume that the linguistic theory of the Language Faculty is a theory of the cognitive architecture for language knowledge and acquisition.

If there is a Language Faculty, what is its precise content, and how is it represented in the mind and ultimately in the brain (e.g., Matthews 1991, Pylyshyn

---

[9] Piattelli-Palmarini (ed.) 1980 reflects this "Piaget–Chomsky" debate; see also Mehler and Dupoux 1994.

1991)?[10] How does this theory contribute to our understanding of language acquisition and development? To what degree is the architecture of the Language Faculty independent of other cognitive components, and to what degree is development of language independent of other aspects of cognitive development? How does the Language Faculty constrain and direct experience? Does the Language Faculty itself develop over time in the individual?

1.4.1   Competing models

We assume "cognition can be understood as computation" (Pylyshyn 1980, 111). Current representations of the Language Faculty of the Cognitive System are defined in terms of a central "computational component," i.e., C_{HL}, Computation for Human Language (Chomsky 1995, 225; Uriagereka 1998).

On the other hand, several other current proposals for cognitive architecture have begun an attempt to account for language acquisition without the assumption of a Language Faculty. These are often referred to as "connectionist" or "neural nets" models. Although these alternative models admit the computational nature of human cognition, many deny its specifically linguistic nature as well as its symbolic and representational nature.[11] They deny the "combinatorial structure in mental representations" (Fodor and Pylyshyn 1988).[12] Can these alternative views be defended in terms of empirical evidence?

1.4.2   Cognitive Science and language development

The research for review bears on fundamental issues of cognitive science that must be addressed in all models. How is the cognitive architecture for language knowledge and acquisition related to the biological architecture of the brain? Is the development of language knowledge the result of a simple biological unfolding or "maturation," with gradual change in the fundamental architecture for language knowledge?[13]

Pylyshyn (1986; 1999) proposed that issues of language development may lie generally outside the area of Cognitive Science, and that they may be reducible simply to biologically determined changes in cognitive architecture. We suggest instead that language acquisition is inherently computational and thus as central to Cognitive Science as Cognitive Science is to it. Language acquisition is not reducible to changes in fundamental cognitive architecture for language. One of the major results of our research review will be that, on the contrary, this architecture is "fixed." There is no such thing as a "prelinguistic" child.

---

[10] "The amount of detail incorporated in an architecture depends on what questions it seeks to answer, as well as how the system under study is actually structured" (Simon and Kaplan 1989, 7).

[11] Elman, et al. 1996 argue against what they term "representational nativism" (367).

[12] Proposals termed "connectionist" vary widely. We return to these issues in chapter 4.

[13] In Cognitive Science, "the components of the architecture represent the underlying physical structures but only abstractly" (Simon and Kaplan 1989, 7).

Results of research reviewed in this book bear on the disciplines central to cognitive science today, from linguistics to neuropsychology. In *linguistics*: how closely does the current theory of "Universal Grammar" (UG) articulate the "Language Faculty"? Although the science of linguistics, a central component of cognitive science, seeks to discover the core principles of all natural languages (which are hypothesized to constitute a Language Faculty), issues remain on how best to obtain empirical evidence for it (e.g., Schutze 1996), and there are issues surrounding the application of Chomsky's theory of UG to actual language acquisition, which takes place in real time.[14]

Children can assist us in this discovery of the degree to which UG articulates the Language Faculty. Our study of children's language acquisition allows us to test, verify and develop linguistic theory, and we can use linguistic theory to guide precise scientific hypotheses about the child mind.

The research results reviewed here also bear on questions in *epistemology*: how is it possible that the human mind comes to know so much, based on limited, diverse and unstructured evidence ("Plato's Problem"), and to what degree is "innateness" necessary to solve this problem; and on questions in *computer science*, the fundamental science of complex knowledge computation; in *psychology*, whose central goal is the characterization of human intelligence, asking if the mind is "modular" in organization, and to what degree the nature of "learning" in this area of knowledge acquisition is inductive or deductive; and in *cognitive development*. Finally, the results will bear on those areas of *biology* and *neuropsychology* that address the relationship between "brain" and "mind."

1.5   The structure of this book

This book will pursue these fundamental issues by providing an introductory survey of existent research results in each basic area of language knowledge and its acquisition. This review will be situated in an introductory investigation of basic theoretical approaches to the study of language acquisition, and of basic research results regarding both the underlying biological matrix for language acquisition and the nature of experience in the human species acquiring language.

It makes little sense to characterize the acquisition of a domain without a reasonably clear concept of what the structure of that domain is, i.e., the goal and outcome of the acquisition process. For that reason, we follow a somewhat unusual mode of presentation in this book. Before discussing what we know of the language acquisition process, we call on modern linguistics to characterize what we know about children's goals. This will allow the reader to evaluate what current language acquisition research tells us about the acquisition process, and where there are gaps in our knowledge.

[14] E.g., Chomsky 1999; Atkinson 1992; Cook 1988; Lust 1999; Wexler 1999, Drozd 2004 on Crain and Thornton 1998 and related commentary.

After introducing basic issues in the area of first language acquisition, biological foundations of language and the role of environmental input in children's acquisition of language, we will consider each of the subsystems of language knowledge which are acquired and which have been researched extensively. Within each specific linguistic subsystem of language knowledge (*phonology*, *syntax*, and *semantics*), we will explicate the problem and issues in terms of "what has to be acquired." Each chapter begins by summarizing what we know about children's goals in that component of language knowledge. This characterizes the "Projection Problem" that they must solve.

Analogous to Lenneberg's classic (1967) description of behavioral developmental milestones in motor and language development (Appendix 1), we will provide a series of appendices that describe early intellectual milestones in the development of each of the basic components of linguistic knowledge. These milestones underlie the development of perception and production of speech sounds, syntax and semantics.

We will concentrate on discovering the origins, or foundations, of language knowledge as we pursue the role of the Initial State in language acquisition. Our emphasis will include cross-linguistic evidence from the acquisition of languages other than English (where research is available). This is in order to more closely approximate a discovery of the universal aspects of the "Language Faculty" and of language acquisition, and thus to begin to factor out which components are under biological control.

1.6   Toward a more comprehensive theory of language acquisition

Although we will survey existing empirical research, in the end we will also sketch directions for a new approach to a more comprehensive theory of language acquisition, that is, one which seeks to link theoretical explanation with investigation of the real time development of language, and one which considers all aspects of language development, i.e., not only syntax, but phonology and semantics as well. We will continually assess hypotheses regarding a biologically programmed "Language Faculty" and its contribution to language development in conjunction with description of real time development of children's language in each of the subsystems of language knowledge.

The research results we review in each area of language knowledge provide support for biological programming in the human species of formal properties of a Language Faculty, termed "Universal Grammar" (UG), and they provide evidence for the fundamental cognitive architecture of language as continuous between child and adult. This architecture reflects universal formal properties of language. This is a "Strong Continuity Hypothesis" (SCH) of UG. With regard to "mechanisms" of language development, we will conclude that neither a simple "maturational" theory of language acquisition nor a non-linguistic non-formal approach is explanatory or empirically motivated (cf. Lust 1999). Current models of language acquisition, which do not admit the role of symbolic computation and of linguistic constraints on child language acquisition are insufficient.

Recent research shows that infants have a marvelous capacity for analyzing language input from birth. However, children's relation to input is always mediated by their grammatical knowledge. Their relation to input data is selective and constructive, and consequently indirect. We relate this paradigm to a proposal for "innately guided learning" (Gould and Marler 1987; Jusczyk and Bertoncini 1988; Marler 1991) which recognizes the dichotomy between "innateness" and "learning" but suggests that these are not mutually exclusive.

Unless somehow cruelly impaired, children everywhere, whether faced with Tulu in South India, Sinhala in Sri Lanka, !Xóõ in the Kalahari desert, or English in Manhattan or London, are endowed with a biologically programmed universal formal architecture for language. Because of this biological programming and a refined, almost indomitable "instinct to learn" (Marler 1991; Pinker 1994) and create, they construct vastly complex, infinitely creative and systematic symbolic theories of their own specific languages.

The intent of this book is to introduce fundamental questions and provide a theoretical and empirical framework within which more in-depth studies of the field can be subsequently conducted. Although we now better understand many properties of the foundations for first language acquisition than ever before, its essential mystery remains.

1.7   Supplementary readings

This book may be used in conjunction with a collection of classic readings in the field of language acquisition, Lust and Foley 2003, or with collections like Bloom 1996.

It may be used in conjunction with a general introduction to linguistics, e.g., Weisler and Milekic 2000; Aitchison, 2003b, Akmajian, Demers, Farmer and Harnish 2001; or Fromkin and Rodman 1998, Fromkin (ed.) 2000. *Language Files* (Jannedy, Poletto and Weldon 1994) provides a useful companion resource, as does Crystal's *Encyclopedic Dictionary of Language and Languages* (1992) and *The Cambridge Encyclopedia of Language* (1997). Smith (1989) provides a general introduction to the study of language. Frazier 1999; Gardner 1985; Karmiloff-Smith 1992; Fodor 1983; and Hauser, Chomsky and Fitch 2002 provide introductions to "modularity" in human cognition.

Other general introductions to the field of language acquisition include Aitchison 1998; Pinker 1994; Jackendoff 1994; Gleitman and Gleitman 1991; Cattell 2000; Barrett 1999; Foster-Cohen 1999; and Mehler and Dupoux 1994. Elman et al. 1996 present an opposing view to the one we present here. The CHILDES (Child Language Data Exchange System) website provides on-line databases for both research publications in specific areas of language acquisition as well as for child language researchers (http://childes.psy.cmu.edu). A recent film series, "The Human Language Series" (Searchinger) provides a compelling introduction to the field.

For more general introduction to cognitive science and its relation to language acquisition see *The MIT Encyclopedia of the Cognitive Sciences* (Wilson and Keil, eds., 1999). Fodor and Pylyshyn 1988; Pylyshyn 1980; Smolensky 1991; Chomsky 1968/1972; Osherson (ed.) 1995; and Gleitman and Liberman (eds.) 1995 provide more advanced related material.

2   What is acquired?

2.1   What is language?

> In this chapter, we, like children, seek ". . . the discovery of the place of human language in the universe."   (Hockett 1977, 163)

It is impossible to study the acquisition of language scientifically unless we address the question, "what is language?," i.e., "what is acquired?" (2.1 and 2.2). We sketch an overview of the linguistic computation children must acquire when they acquire a language, laying down a number of fundamental concepts and terms (2.3). We sketch the basic design of human language knowledge and the basic architecture of the human Language Faculty (2.4). We provide a framework for investigation into the nature of language acquisition. These foundations allow us to form the "essential questions of language acquisition" (2.5).

2.1.1   Attempting to define language

Language is first and foremost *symbolic*. Sounds, words and sentences represent and capture an infinity of possible meanings and intentions. We can produce, understand and think of an infinity of possible statements, questions, commands or exclamations. These may concern the future, the past, what has occurred and what has not, what is possible or impossible. Through language, we can tell the truth or lie, regret or hope. We can deploy an infinity of demands, requests, contradictions, ranging from poetry to propaganda. The next sentence we say or understand is almost certainly going to be one we have never heard or said before, suggesting that this symbolic capacity of language is in a real sense limitless.

This knowledge can be taken to superb heights of beauty and intellectual power, as in the writing of William Shakespeare or of Wallace Stevens, and to heights of charm and fun as in the writings of Dr. Seuss. What is language that it has this marvelous symbolic power?

1.   "Look at me now!" said the cat,
         "with a cup and a cake
         on the top of my hat!
         I can hold up two books!
         I can hold up the fish!

> And a little toy sheep!
> And some milk on a dish!"   (Seuss, 1957)

We will see that by about three years, children have acquired the foundations for this infinite symbolic power of language and through it can transcend immediate situations. The two-year-old speaking in (2) worked through his series of utterances to convince himself that an abstract painting of a mythical bird did not truly reflect a dangerous monster, and therefore shouldn't deter his walking past and up the dark staircase beyond.

2.   a. No it's too bad . . . looking . . .
    b. What's that one too bad looking?
    c. That's too bad looking . . . .
    d. They're 'caring me . . . . .
    . . . *pause* . . . . .
    e. I'm not 'cared of those things
    f. They're only nice birds . . .   (CLAL, BGO21097, 2yrs. 10 mos.)[1]

This child still did not include the initial "s" in certain consonant clusters as in the word "scared" (2d–2e), and still did not evidence full English relative clauses in (2b), where the intention was to question "the one that is very bad looking", and he did not have perfect mastery of the lexicon. However, he clearly had the essential knowledge leading to sentence formation, sentence variation by movement of elements (question formation), and several grammatical operations involved in the use of "only", "too" and present progressive verb inflection using "ing" as the verb ending, and he had the competence to map from form to meaning in new ways. What then has the child acquired?

Early in this century, we find the linguist Sapir's definition of natural language:

3.   "Language is a purely human and noninstinctive method of communicating
    ideas, emotions and desires by means of a system of voluntarily produced
    symbols. These symbols are, in the first instance, auditory and they are
    produced by so-called organs of speech" (Sapir 1921, 8).

This definition of language is not sufficient for our purposes. It appears to assume, not define, the essence of what language is. In addition, we now know from more recent studies that not only oral (auditory) but sign (visual) languages have similar structural properties and are acquired at similar developmental periods with similar developmental patterns.[2]

About mid-century, the linguist De Saussure, sought to separate "from the whole of speech the part that belongs to language" (1959, 11). De Saussure's image in Figure 2.1 suggests this analysis: As De Saussure reasoned, "psychological" concepts represented in the mind are linked to "linguistic" sounds which are reflected in a physiological process: "the brain transmits an impulse corresponding to the (sound) image to the organs used in producing sounds"; this

---

[1] CLAL is an abbreviation for Cornell Language Acquisition Lab, the source of the data.
[2] E.g., Jackendoff 1994, chapter 7; Bellugi 1988; Kegl, Senghas and Coppola 1999; Lillo-Martin 1999; Meier 1991; Pettito 1988.

Fig. 2.1 *"Place of language in the facts of speech" (De Saussure 1959, 11).*

is followed by conversion to the physical sound waves which in turn must be received by a hearer and, in reverse, converted to psychological concepts represented in the mind (1959, 11). Where in this process, however, does *language* lie so that we can study it?

Language does not lie in speech itself. De Saussure recognized that while speech is an "individual act," language lies in the "associative and co-ordinating faculty" which "plays the dominant role in the organization of language as a system" (1959, 13). He leads us to a new definition: "Language is a system of signs that express ideas . . . [B]eyond the functioning of the various organs there exists a more general faculty which governs signs and which would be the linguistic faculty proper" (16, 11). De Saussure's analyses anticipated current scientific approaches to the study of language, pointing us to the "fundamental system" that underlies language knowledge (e.g., Anderson 1985). They open the fundamental questions: where/what is the "co-ordinating faculty" which organizes language, i.e., the "linguistic faculty proper"? What is the nature of this system and how is it represented in the mind and brain?

2.1.2   Language and thought

Linguistic (word) meanings are distinct from thoughts or concepts related to these meanings. Aphasic patients with anomia often show an inability to access lexical items, but retain related concepts: e.g., a patient unable to retrieve the lexical item for "wallet" provides circumlocutions "describing the appearance or function of the target concept" (as in, "I lost my . . . I keep my money in it") (Goodglass 1993, 85) (see also chapter 5). In the case of a patient who has lost the ability for language, even simple sentences still may show complex causal reasoning including the ability to infer the mental states of others (to hold a "theory of mind"; cf. chapter 10) (Varley and Siegal 2000).

2.1.3   Language and communication

Use and knowledge of language are also not equivalent to knowledge of means of social communication. The language of the child in (2) more clearly reflects the thought of the child than his attempt to communicate with someone else. Neither is all communication equivalent to human language. Frogs speak with their ears, birds convey sexual messages with their trills, and bees communicate distance, location and quality of nectar with their dance (e.g., Hauser 1997; Von Frisch 1967). Monkeys have general symbolic abilities. They can learn that a triangle can be a sign for all the red objects in a set.[3] Some such forms of animal communication do share certain design features with natural language, like *displacement*: "Linguistic messages may refer to things remote in time or space or both, from the site of the communication," and they reveal "openness" or "productiveness" (i.e., "New linguistic messages are coined freely and easily"; Hockett 1977, 171). Bee dances do both.

Distinct from other animal communication systems, human language critically reveals "Duality of Patterning" (Hockett 1960). Through Duality of Patterning, permutations of units, which are themselves meaningless, link to distinct meanings at another level of representation. The words in (4) are distinct in meaning, but vary only in the order of the component digital meaningless sounds.

4. tack
    cat
    act

5. Duality of Patterning
    By virtue of duality of patterning, an enormous number of minimum
    semantically functional elements . . . can be and are mapped into
    arrangements of a conveniently small number of minimum meaningless but
    message-differentiating elements . . . No animal system known to the writer
    shows a significant duality.   (Hockett 1961; 1977, 171f)

Although animal sounds may "have symbolic meanings . . . there does not seem to be any recorded natural example of an animal unambiguously sequencing calls to make a sentence, where the sequence has a new meaning compiled from the meaning of its parts" (Marler 1998, 11).[4]

Even given this unique design feature, however, we still do not fully answer the question "What is language that we can study it?"

2.2   The discovery of the place of human language: in the mind

We must look into the human mind in order to discover the nature of natural language and to study it scientifically. Noam Chomsky moved linguistic inquiry to this next step (see chapter 4). The human mind has a generative system, a combinatorial system of computation, "a system that makes infinite use of finite means" (Chomsky 1987, 54, after von Humboldt).

---

[3] Harlow and Harlow 1965, Pennisi 1999; see the discussion of "referential signaling" in various animal species in Hauser 1997; see Stambak and Sinclair 1990, as well as de Loache 1995 and Bates 1979 for study of the development of *semiotic* competence in young children. (cf. chapter 10).

[4] On these issues, Savage-Rumbaugh et al.'s 1998 study of the Bonobo, Kanzi, is particularly interesting because it tests for evidence regarding Kanzi's possible comprehension of sequencing in signs, e.g., "Pour the lemonade in the coke" vs. "pour the coke in the lemonade." See Smith 1999 and Marler 1999b for discussion.

6.   At an intuitive level, a language is a particular way of expressing thought and understanding . . . a language is a particular generative procedure that assigns to every possible expression a representation of its form and its meaning.   (Chomsky 1991, 8)

Knowledge of this generative system enables us to understand and be charmed by *The Cat in the Hat* (Dr. Seuss) as in (1), and to talk ourselves out of the fear of a dark staircase, as in (2). Through it, we join sounds with meanings in potentially infinite ways.

2.2.1   A cognitive system: grammar

    The new focus for study of language has become internal, a mental system which creates infinite language: a "generative grammar." The term "grammar" refers to this mental system, and formalizes it so that we can study it precisely and scientifically. This notion of grammar in the mind is distinct from the "grammar" we were taught in school, which is a set of prescriptive rules (see Pinker 1994a, chapter 12). We do not need to be taught it.

We must account for how children acquire knowledge of this generative system which maps form to meaning and to sound (spatial form, in the case of sign language) infinitely.

> **GRAMMAR**: The system of rules and the principles in the mind/brain which generate a language. Grammar is the cognitive system that maps from form to meaning.

7.   Language seems to be best understood as a "cognitive system." (Chomsky, 1991, 17)

2.2.2   A formal distinction: I-Language versus E-Language

    In order to to capture this new approach to defining language so that we may study it, Chomsky made a distinction between *I-Language* and *E-Language*. I-Language is the internal system which creates the language in the mind of an individual; E-Language is the external reflection of language; "the E-language is a set of expressions" and appears impossible to capture (Chomsky 1991, 9, 13; Chomsky and Lasnik 1996, 15–17). Chomsky's question, and that of much current linguistics, is: what is the nature of I-Language?"

What is in the mind? What do we know when we know a language?

The linguistic system in the mind is *tacit*: we do not know consciously what we know when we know a language, or how our mind works when we know a language.[5] We know language with such apparent ease that unless we are linguists we are unaware of the complexities of what we know. The system appears "inaccessible to consciousness" (Chomsky 1993b, 25). How then can we ever study this knowledge scientifically, or hope to begin to understand how it is that children acquire this knowledge?

While linguistics, like all science, continues to develop, there have been fundamental discoveries regarding the nature of this hidden system which lies beneath our language knowledge.

2.3   The computational system

> "Language is, at its core, a system that is both digital and infinite."
> (Chomsky 1991b, 50)

2.3.1   From the finite to the infinite

Early discovery of the general design feature of "duality of patterning" in natural language has allowed us to anticipate core properties of the linguistic faculty of the human species. The essence of language knowledge consists of the representation of a finite set of discrete units at several levels (involving *sound*, *syntax* and *meaning*), their combination and sequencing at each level, and the mapping between the patterning at each of these levels. Each level involves a different way of representing an utterance.

This unit-based system reflects the "digital" nature of language and underlies its infinite productivity. Without it we would not understand our own thoughts, our next conversation or our poetry. Children could not imagine or comprehend Dr. Seuss's *Hop on Pop*:

8.   See. Bee. We see a bee.
         See. Bee. Three. Now we see three.
         Three. Tree. Three fish in a tree . . .   (Seuss, 1963, 18f.)

Dr. Seuss plays with these formal properties of language by using units of sounds and words combined and recombined in repeated and varied syntactic patterns, relating sound, form and meaning.

2.3.2   A digital system

Sounds are combined to form words, words are combined to form sentences. Each of these units is cognitively "discrete, invariant and categorical" (Liberman 1996, 32).[6]

---

[5] Philosophers distinguish "knowing how" from "knowing that" (Ryle 1979); although language seems to challenge such characterizations.

[6] Although the rendition of a unit will vary every time it is spoken, the cognitive entity of the unit is invariant. A "p" is a "p" regardless of variations in how it's produced (cf. chapter 8).

2.3.3 A combinatorial system

Even a small set of sounds can lead to a large set of words, and even a small set of words can lead to a large set of sentences. This is because language uses a "combinatorial principle" to build a "large and open vocabulary out of a small number of elements" (Liberman 1996, 32), and to serve the function of building an infinite set of sentences out of a small set of words.

2.3.4 The power of sequencing

If a language had only two units, e.g., "T" and "O," and strings of only two units were allowed in forming "words," then *variable sequencing* of these two units would provide the possibility for four different "words" (compare to (4)):

9.   TO
        OT
        TT
        OO

If strings of three units were allowed, this would provide exponentially more possibilities for sequencing the two units and consequently more words:

10.   TOT
        TOO
        OTT
        OTO
        TTT
        TTO
        OOT
        OOO

> The GENERAL RULE: m different atomic signals in sequences of length n provide m to the n different labels.   (G. Miller 1981, 73)

If the language allowed three units, e.g., "T," "O," "B," and strings of three units, then a vocabulary of twenty-seven words would be possible, and so on. The longer the sequence allowed, the larger the possible vocabulary.

Natural languages range widely in the number of sound units which function linguistically in their language. Hawaian, for example, has only eight contrasting consonants, as opposed to twenty-four in English or 117 in !Xoo; Swedish has nineteen vowels and Spanish only five; some languages have as few as three (Ladefoged 1996). All languages show the same infinite power based on the combinatorial principle and sequencing regardless of this variation in the number of their units.

Natural languages build on the power of sequencing. All natural languages reveal a basic "word order" or constituent order, although the order chosen varies across languages.[7]

CROSS-LINGUISTIC ORDER VARIATION[8]

SVO	*English*
	He gave a mango
SOV	*Tulu* (Somashekar 1999, 32; = 29)
	aaye kukku kor-y-e he mango give-past-3rdsgmsc (He gave a mango)
VSO	*Welsh*
	rhoddodd ef fango i give-past he mango (He gave a mango)

2.3.5   The recursive property

This combinatorial system is recursive, applying to its own output over and over again. As Dr. Seuss demonstrates in (11), units can be created of smaller units and these can be recombined by the *embedding* of one unit in another, e.g., a [tweetle beetle [battle]], *subordinating* one to another, e.g., [[When tweetle beetles . . . . . ,] it's . . . . . .], or *coordinating* one with another (e.g., by "AND"), or coordinating and embedding as in the complete example. There is in principle no limit to the output of this recursive combinatorial system that we are all capable of when we know language, and that children must acquire.

11.   "When tweetle beetles fight,
       it's called
       a tweetle beetle battle.
       And when they battle in a puddle,
       It's a tweetle
       beetle puddle battle.
       AND when tweetle beetles
       battle with paddles in a puddle,

---

[7] Lashley early (1951) recognized the significance of word order in natural language. He saw "the occurrence of predetermined orderly sequences of action which are unique for each language" (507) and wondered if the semantic "idea" behind the sentence could possibly determine the order. He saw that it cannot, as all languages reflect similar meanings with systematically differing orders (Lust and Foley 2003). Today we pursue this question through a study of syntax in linguistics.

[8] All six order permutations of S(ubject), V(erb) and O(bject) have been attested as basic orders (Lust in prep.).

they call it a tweetle
beetle puddle paddle battle.
AND . . .
When beetles battle beetles
in a puddle paddle battle
and the beetle battle puddle
is a puddle in a bottle . . .
    . . . they call this
a tweetle beetle
bottle puddle
paddle battle muddle.
AND . . .
When beetles
fight these battles in a bottle
with their paddles
and the bottle's
on a poodle
and the poodle's
eating noodles . . .
    . . . they call this a muddle puddle
tweedle poodle
beetle noodle
bottle paddle battle.
AND . . ."   (Seuss, 1965)

2.3.6   Constituent structure

The combinatorial system involved in language knowledge does not simply operate on a linear string like a sequence of arbitrary numbers. In natural language, every unit reflects a combination of smaller units. Every linear sequence can and must be described in terms of its "constituent structure," which linguists identify through the use of brackets. It is because of this internal structure, grouping of units within units, that language can attain its infinite creativity. It is because of this structure that we can understand 11, analyzing it as in (12):[9]

12.   They call this
        [a [tweetle beetle
        [bottle [puddle
        paddle battle [muddle]]]]] . . .

---

[9] Left and right brackets mark beginning and end of each constituent; when these are embedded in each other, the result is a series of brackets reflecting the inclusion of one constituent in another. The structure displayed in bracketing notation is equivalent to that displayed in a 'tree structure' notation, e.g., 13, which linguists use to display hierarchical structure grouping constituents one within the other. (See Weisler and Milekic 2000, 142–163 for introduction of the basic concepts of syntax assumed here.)

2.3.7   Hierarchical structure: the "secret skeleton"

Combining structure recursively leads to a "secret skeleton" that underlies every sentence we hear or speak.[10] Constituents must be organized hierarchically within each sentence. Children and adults must both generate and discover this skeleton for every sentence they hear or produce, as in (13).

13.   a. [[the beetle [in [the bottle]]] [came back [with [a poodle [in [a battle]]]]]]

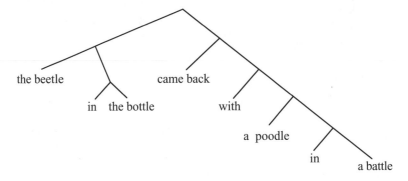

2.3.8   Discovery of syntax: special features of the system

Through study of *syntax*, linguists have now discovered specific properties of the human language faculty, i.e., of the computational system for human language.

2.3.8.1   Displacement

In natural language, sequences of units (more precisely, of constituent structures) can be permuted or "displaced." Order variation is productively possible, e.g., (14) or (16) in English, and (15) in Turkish.

14.   a. The Busy Beetle chased <u>the poodle</u>
       b. <u>The poodle</u>, the Beetle chased.

15.   (from Kornfilt 1994, 177, =8a–8c)
       a. Kopek butun gun kedi-yi kovala-dt
          dog whole day cat-Acc chase-past
          "The dog chased the cat all day long"
       b. Kedi-yi kopek butun gun kovala-dt
          cat-Acc dog whole day chase-past
       c. Kopek kedi-yi butun gun kovala-dt
          dog cat-Acc whole day chase-past

16.   a. Your tongue <u>is</u> numb
       b. <u>Is</u> your tongue numb?

---

[10] The use of the term "secret skeleton" is due to Brown in *Science* 1999, 283, 5 Feb. We use it throughout in a general sense to capture the underlying structure that characterizes every level of language knowledge.

If young children spoke only in static orders in repeated strings we would not say they had "acquired language." In a sense, they must not only acquire the basic word order of the language, but acquire a "moving" system. The child in (2) above already knows this basic property of language (e.g., compare (2a) and (2b)).

2.3.8.2   Missing elements

Natural language productively hides its units. It involves numerous devices for reducing redundancy.[11] Many sentence constituents are null (represented as "Ø").[12] They are part of our knowledge, even though they are not realized physically in the sequence of sounds which we hear.

17.   "We see a bee.
          Now we see three Ø"

          . . . .

          "Ø Eat a snack"   (Seuss, 1963)

In some languages, e.g., Chinese (18) or Spanish (19), null elements are more productive. (See Chomsky 1988a, 33; Huang 1984.)

18.   Question: Zhangsan kanjian Lisi le ma?
          (Did Zhangsan see Lisi?)
          Answer: Ø kanjian Ø le
                    Ø saw Ø
                    (He saw him)

19.   Ø Llega
          Ø arrives
          (He/she/it arrives)

Children must acquire a system whose elements are in some sense free to "disappear."

2.3.8.3   Pronouns

Pronouns provide another way for natural language to reduce redundancy.

20.   "*He* went into the tent"
          "*They* yelp for help"
          "*That one* is my other brother"   (Seuss, 1963)

21.   "Mr Fox, sir,
          I won't do *it*.
          I can't say *it*.
          I won't chew *it*"   (Seuss, 1965)

---

[11] "Redundancy offers protection against damage, and might facilitate overcoming problems that are computational in nature" (Chomsky, 1991, 50); yet natural language productively reduces redundancy, e.g., through pronouns and various forms of ellipsis.

[12] Here and throughout, we will use the symbol "Ø" to represent the fact that an element exists in our representation of an expression, but is not spoken (phonetically realized). The term "null sites" will be used to indicate their location.

Pronouns do not specify their reference and allow shifting reference. The duck and the mouse are confronted with this in *Alice in Wonderland*:

22.　　　"said the mouse," . . . " . . . the patriotic archbishop of Canterbury, found it advisable . . ."
　　　"Found what?" said the duck
　　　"Found it," the Mouse replied rather crossly: "of course you know what 'it' means",
　　　"I know what 'it' means well enough, when I find a thing," said the Duck: "it's generally a frog, or a worm. The question is, what did the archbishop find?"　　　(Carroll, 1998, 25)

The child in (2) has already acquired shifting reference with pronouns. (In fact (2)(a) through (2)(f) all involve pronouns.)

While "pronoun resolution" (determining the reference of a pronoun) remains one of the most challenging problems for formal machine-based computational approaches to "natural language processing" (NLP), it is one most naturally solved by anyone who knows a natural language. The language faculty of the human species appears to include particular facility for the special complex computation required by pronouns and null elements.

2.3.9　　Knowing the impossible

The infinitely productive special combinatorial system which under-lies our language knowledge is infinitely constrained. Without ever having heard either the possible or the impossible sentences in (23)–(27), we know which are and which are not possible. So do children who acquire the English language. Yet the number of "ungrammatical" constructions is infinite and so impossible to teach.

Constraints

Although infinite in capacity, combination and/or displacement in language is not always grammatical and thus not always possible. (23b) is not possible without changing the meaning of (23a) (in contrast to (15)). (23c)–(23d) in English are gibberish. Pronouns are not always possible with the same meanings, as in (24a) and (24b):

23.　　a. The poodle chased the beetle
　　　b. The beetle chased the poodle
　　　c. * Chased poodle the beetle the
　　　d. * Chased the poodle the beetle

24.　　a. The cat knew the boy liked *him* (= the cat)
　　　b. The cat liked *him* (not = the cat)

Constraints hold at every level (sounds, words, sentences), over all combinations of units. For example, we know which of the sound combinations in (25) are possible English words or not.[13] We tacitly know these constraints, which explains why we do not speak gibberish.

25.   ptak thole hlad plast sram mgla vlas flitch dnom rtut (Halle 1978, 294)

We know that while the combinations of morphemes in (26) appear to create possible words in English, those in (27) do not.

26.   a. overdose
         b. awesome
         c. downsize

27.   a. *underdose
         b. *bigsome
         c. *upsize

2.3.10   Finding the meaning

The formal computational system of language knowledge (syntax) must be integrated with other parts of human competence so that we, and children, can *say what we mean* and *mean what we say*.

Lewis Carroll confronted the complexities of this mapping between the form of language and its meaning in *Alice in Wonderland*:

28.   "Then you should say what you mean," the March Hare went on.
         "I do," Alice hastily replied; "at least – at least I mean what I say – that's the same thing, you know".
         "Not the same thing a bit!" said the Hatter. "Why, you might just as well say that 'I see what I eat' is the same thing as 'I eat what I see'!" (1998, 64)

Like us, Alice and the Mad Hatter must map the formal computational syntactic system of language to *meaning* and this meaning must be shared in order for communication to occur.

In part, the syntax of a sentence determines its meaning, as we can see simply by noting the difference between "I eat what I see" and "I see what I eat," varying only word order. Acquisition of syntax is fundamental to children's acquisition of meaning and avoidance of gibberish.

Not words alone. Not syntax alone.

As Alice discovered in her exchange with the Mad Hatter, words alone, even if we know their meaning and even if we organize them syntactically in sentences, are not enough.

29.   "What a funny watch!" she remarked. "It tells the day of the month, and doesn't tell what o'clock it is!"
         "Why should it? "muttered the Hatter. "Does your watch tell you what year it is?"

---

[13] As Halle 1978 suggests, speakers of English generally recognize "thole", "plast" and "flitch" as possible English words (294).

> "Of course not," Alice replied very readily: "but that's because it stays the same year for such a long time together."
> "Which is just the case with mine," said the Hatter.
> Alice felt dreadfully puzzled. The Hatter's remark seemed to her to have no sort of meaning in it, and yet it was certainly English. (65)

Alice most probably shares similar concepts related to the words ("watch", "year", "time") referred to, and she organizes her words in sentences, but she still does not fully share the meaning of her language with the Mad Hatter. We must also consult a theory of "pragmatics," i.e., "use of language" to explain Alice's challenge in Wonderland, and to fully comprehend what the child must acquire.

2.3.11   Closing in on the mystery: the hidden computational system

We can now begin to see fundamental properties of the hidden system which exists when we know a language, and which children must acquire, i.e., the C_{HL} (Computation for a Human Language). Children who acquire a language must acquire computation which allows productive sequencing and structuring of units and unit combinations according to a principled and constrained system. Their interpretation of any single linguistic expression requires that they go beyond the surface string and be able to relate moved or transformed orders to basic orders as well as to identify missing items or pronouns. In a sense, children must capture through computation an "underlying representation" for any sentence they hear, speak or think.[14]

2.3.12   Summarizing the basic properties of the hidden system

Natural language knowledge involves a system which is/has

a. symbolic
b. combinatorial and infinitely generative
c. based on units which are combined and sequenced, possibly in variable orders
d. structured hierarchically
e. recursive
f. constrained
g. specific formal linguistic properties, i.e., specific design features of human language, both allowing and constraining precise computation over missing and moved elements
h. instantiated in a human context of thought and interpersonal exchange

---

[14] We use the term "underlying representation" in a general sense to recognize that a representation of the surface string is insufficient. Another level of representation must exist for any linguistic expression. The question of how to characterize such underlying representation remains central to the field of linguistics today. Hockett 1958 coined the terms "surface and deep grammar" to distinguish between surface forms and underlying relations; although without the generative relation between them that Chomsky proposed.

In short, the system is representational and computational. Units must be represented in order for them to be computed over.[15] The formal computational system of language knowledge must be integrated with other parts of human competence so that children can "say what they mean" and "mean what they say."

"Hidden" to a large degree, the system can be clothed in the sounds (or signs) of many different languages, but it always exists if a natural language exists. It is hidden behind moving and reduced expressions. Its principles and constraints are never directly revealed through any particular linguistic expression or set of expressions.

2.4   Designing the architecture of the Language Faculty

We can now begin to uncover the design of the Language Faculty which must exist when children come to know a language, and to appreciate its power.

2.4.1   The basic design

Figure 2.2 sketches the basic design of the Language Faculty (adapted from Chomsky 1995). This overall architecture is necessary to generate *sentences* (*syntax*) and perceive and articulate the *sounds* of language (*phonology*)[16] in a way which has meaning (*semantics*), and to *use* that knowledge to proclaim, exclaim, argue or beg, to interact in the world socially or otherwise (*pragmatics*). Linguists differ in how they represent each of the components represented in this figure, and in how they represent the interrelation between the components, but the overall design must be accounted for in any theory of language knowledge and language acquisition.

In figure 2.2, the central component is the grammar, which provides a theory of how a language works: it relates *sound* (the *auditory interface*) and *meaning* (the *conceptual interface*). It is the core "computation for human language" or C_{HL} (Chomsky 1995), the essence of our "language faculty".

2.4.2   The interfaces

This Language Faculty coordinates – or "interfaces" – with other forms of cognition. *Sound* and *meaning* of language are both points of cognitive interfaces, acting as "modes of interpretation by performance systems" (Chomsky 1995, 171). Although they are given their "instructions" by the grammar, these

---

[15] See Larson and Segal 1995, 545f. and Pylyshyn 1999, 10f, for discussion of the term "representation" as it is used here.

[16] In sign languages, the interfaces will involve distinct visual and motoric modalities.

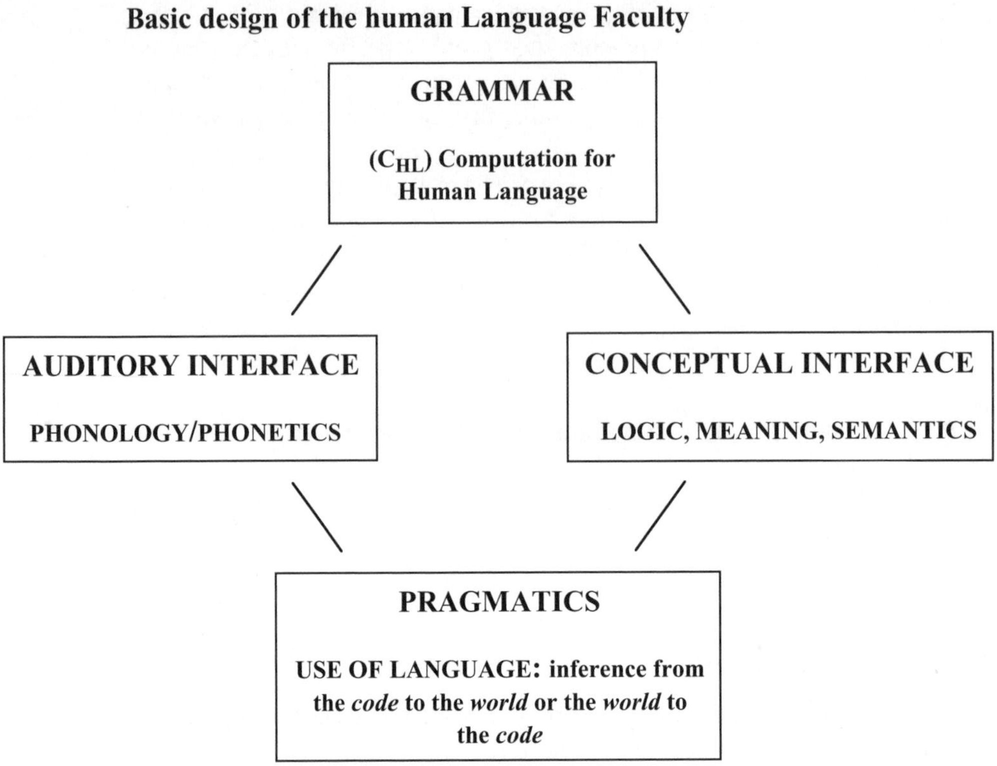

Basic design of the human Language Faculty

Fig. 2.2 *Basic design of the human language faculty.*

interfaces are "external to the computational system of language" (Chomsky 1995, 132, 168).[17]

> **The auditory interface: PF (Phonetic Form).** A formalization of the interface between the computational systems and sensorimotor systems involved in audition and articulation.
>
> **The conceptual interface: LF (Logical Form).** A formalization of the interface between the computational system and systems of conceptual structure and language use.

2.4.3   Levels of representation

As in figure 2.2, children must deal with several levels of representation at once so that these are interrelated and susceptible to computation. Units

---

[17] A critical and profound issue in linguistics and cognitive science today concerns the interrelations between the core computational and the interface components of the Language Faculty.

**Units at each basic level of representation
in language knowledge**

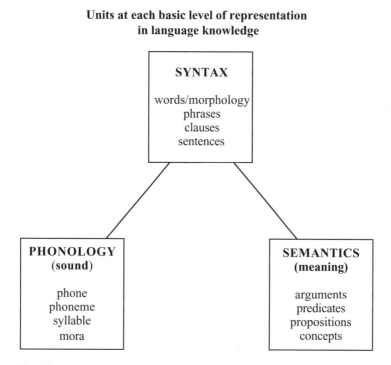

Fig. 2.3 *Units at each basic level of representation in language knowledge.*

must be discovered at leach level (figure 2.3).[18] The auditory and conceptual interfaces must be formalized so they can enter into the computation required by knowledge of a language. Thus linguists study "PF" (Phonetic Form) and "LF" (Logical Form) respectively in analyzing the interfaces of *sound* and *meaning* (Chomsky, 1995, 131).[19]

2.4.4   Relation of child language acquisition to linguistic theory

We look to linguistic theory for formulation of scientifically testable, theoretically based hypotheses regarding the exact nature of the architecture of the Language Faculty and of the adult end-state, i.e., what needs to be acquired when we acquire a language. At the same time, every normal child in normal circumstances will solve the problem which all linguists are pursuing, acquiring the "true" formal computational system for any and all possible languages (even for multiple languages at a time). We can only assume that children must know

---

[18] Chomsky's *Logical Structure of Linguistic Theory* (1975/1955) made this approach to the study of linguistic structure explicit. Levels of representation remain an essential component of generative grammar today, even though the exact form of levels remains debated; e.g., in current "minimalist" theory of generative grammar, previous "deep structure" and "surface structure" levels (Chomsky 1965) do not appear (see Chomsky 1995, 188, Lasnik 2002).

[19] Crystal 1997a, 82–83, provides a general introduction to the notion of linguistic "levels."

the "right" way to capture a language. We look to the child for empirical evidence regarding the Language Faculty.

2.4.5   Does the Language Faculty develop?

Every computer has an architecture built into it. Is the cognitive architecture of the Language Faculty, as sketched in figure 2.1, built into the child brain and in place from the beginning, or is it in some way developmentally acquired or constructed by children? Do infants begin solely with the pragmatic components of language use, and only later attain formal knowledge of the central computational system? Is development of general cognition, i.e., thinking and reasoning, and children's understanding of the world, a necessary precursor to significant development of the formal linguistic system, and perhaps a determinant of this formal system in some way? Are the components of the Language Faculty only assembled gradually?

Figure 2.1 suggests that the organization of this Language Faculty is "internally modular"; that is, the formal computational system C_{HL} is distinct from the conceptual and auditory components, although these interact. Is this "internal modularity" in place from the beginning? Do the basic components or "modules" of this faculty, i.e., knowledge of grammar (syntax), knowledge of the sound system (phonology) and knowledge of meaning (semantics) develop in parallel? Is development across these areas independent? Is development across the areas linked? What are the interactions among the internal modules?[20]

2.5   Conclusions

We now see more clearly the complexity of the "intellectual feat" which is involved in the acquisition of a natural language. Computation in every sentence must operate at once on each of the units at each of the levels of representation in language knowledge. The architecture of the Language Faculty must allow children to accomplish this complex computation naturally and without conscious effort. It provides the "coordinating faculty" that allows this computation. Because we apply a combinatorial system with its special design features, we are able to acquire language. Because we integrate this linguistic knowledge with our cognitive knowledge and understanding, we are able to use our knowledge of language.

We can now make more precise our fundamental questions in the study of language acquisition.

---

[20] The term "modularity" is used to refer to the general organization of the Language Faculty as distinct from the organization of other cognitive competencies *outside of* the Language Faculty, but also to specific organization of subcomponents *within* the Language Faculty as distinct from each other.

- How do children acquire the computational system which will provide *infinite new possibilities* for the combination of sounds, words, sentences and ideas, and at the same time rule out infinite ungrammatical possibilities?
- How does the Language Faculty guide and constrain this language acquisition?
- What are the relations between language development and other forms of cognitive development?

2.6   Supplementary readings

For recent studies of the "architecture of the language faculty" see Jackendoff 1997 and 2002, and Anderson and Lightfoot 2002.

3 What is the problem of language acquisition?

3.1 Getting started

In this chapter, we define essential aspects of the problem children face in language acquisition. We characterize the severity of a "Projection Problem" by an analysis of the types of evidence children might be expected to need in order to acquire a language. We see that not only is "negative evidence" generally not accessible to children, but also that "positive evidence" in the speech stream is fundamentally indeterminate with regard to the knowledge children must acquire. Both are always only "indirect." Given that the evidence available to children is fundamentally insufficient, we consider two possible approaches to "bootstrapping" from external (non-linguistic) evidence which they might alternatively try to solve the problem of language acquisition, and show that neither of these can solve the fundamental problem. We conclude that the evidence available to children can not in itself fully determine the linguistic knowledge they must acquire, and that no form of "bootstrapping" from solely extra-linguistic evidence can solve this problem. We therefore must look *within children*, beyond the input, for an explanation of language acquisition.

3.1.1 What evidence do children need?

We saw in chapter 2 that children must acquire a generative system which allows infinite possibilities in language, and also rules out infinite impossibilities. For this, we would expect them to need both positive and negative evidence.

3.1.1.1 Positive evidence

Children need experience of what *does* occur in a language, i.e., "positive evidence"; if they had never heard Hindi, Tulu or English, we would not expect them to acquire it. Speech streams constantly around infants, appearing to provide such evidence directly.

However, evidence presented to children (the "input") can only be effective if they process it correctly (cf. chapter 6). Even if they do attend to and parse input correctly, this evidence is finite; it will never fully determine the infinite expressions which are possible in a language. Adults do not introduce every possible lexical item in English which children will acquire (on average 50,000–250,000 words; Aitchison 2003). Adults cannot define what any particular expression will mean. While they can pick out and indicate an individual exemplar of a "dog" to a child, this positive evidence does not directly determine what the adult is referring to, e.g., some property of the situation containing the dog perhaps. It does not determine that the term will extend from "Snoopy" to a "chihuahua" (cf. chapter 10). Similarly, the input does not sort out for children the distinction between "grey tabbies" and "great abbeys."

Since the language learner must attain infinite generative capacity, at best, positive examples, demonstrating possible language, can lead children to a potential chain of inference.

3.1.1.2   Negative evidence

If we were learning chess, we would seek both positive and negative evidence. We would be taught not only specific moves which were possible, but those impossible. Certain formal languages have been shown to be unlearnable without negative evidence, on the basis of induction from positive evidence alone (Gold 1967; Kapur 1994).[1]

Parents may attempt to provide direct negative evidence by saying, "No that's not an apple" when a child refers to a pumpkin with the word "apple"; or "No, do not say 'flied'" to one who just said "he flied over the rainbow." However, children are not, for the most part, offered direct "negative evidence," and when it is offered, they frequently rebuff it (chapter 6). When corrections are attempted, parents tend to confront the meaning of an utterance, not its grammatical form – syntactic or phonological – as in (1a) and (1b) (Brown and Hanlon 1970, 49). Children too insist on relating the parent's comments to meaning, not form, as in the case of the noun case marking error in (1c);

1.   a. *Sarah*: "There's the animal farmhouse"
           Mother: "No, that's a lighthouse"
        b. *Eve*: "Mama isn't boy, he a girl"
           Mother: "That's right"
        c. *A three-year-old boy* : "Her is being mean"
           Mother: "No, SHE is being mean"
           Child: "Yea, that's right"

Perhaps parents provide "implicit" negative evidence to children by repetitions of their ungrammatical utterances, or by requests for clarification,[2] although whether children consult these adult behaviors in building their grammar remains doubtful (cf. chapter 6).

---

[1] The result in Gold 1967 depended on assumptions about inductive language learning, e.g., assuming a "conservative" learner, which did not change hypotheses unless contradictory evidence was available (Kapur 1994).

[2] E.g., Bohannon and Stanowicz 1988, Demetras et al. 1986, Hirsh-Pasek et al. 1984, Penner 1987.

3.1.1.3   Overgeneralization

If children must acquire language on the basis of positive evidence, what would keep them from overgeneralizing on the basis of the evidence received, and how do they come to eliminate or retreat from incorrect forms in favor of correct alternatives? Children do, in some cases over the first years of life, over-generalize, e.g., overregularizing verbs in (2), although such overgeneralizations appear to be limited (see later chapters, 6, 11). (See Marcus et al. 1992, Clark 1982, Bowerman 1988.)

2.   **Overgeneralization**
"His doggie bited him untied" (M, 5.10) – *Telling how "tied-up" man in a TV show was freed* (Bowerman 1988, 1982a, b).
"My teacher holded the baby rabbits and we patted them" (Cazden 1972).

3.1.1.4   Indirect negative evidence

A parent may simply "repair" a child's error by *not* using the child form, thus providing "indirect negative evidence." Most probably "bited" will not occur in a child's environment. While a child hears himself referred to as "John" or "Johnny" or "son," he is not likely to also hear himself referred to as "Sam."

However, children must be able to make use of such indirect *negative* information. What does not occur must first be perceived, and if it is *perceived* it doesn't necessarily constitute evidence that an expression *cannot* occur. Children who had never heard "The Cat in the Hat" would not be entitled to conclude that this expression was impossible. Presented with a new animal termed a "wug," they must be able to conclude that there can be several "wugs," even if they have never heard the plural form of this term before; and they do so productively (Berko 1958, Potts et al. 1979).

A learner must determine when non-occurrence matters. If we are stopped at a red light and the car in front of us does not turn right, this event may or may not be significant. This non-turning event could indicate that a right turn on red is not allowed in this state. It is only so significant, however, if we are interpreting this event with regard to a prior hypothesis about the possibility of right turns on red. Without the existence of this hypothesis, the event of a car stopped at a red light would mean nothing in particular. What does not occur is infinite. Not only is the car not turning right, but it is not making a U-turn, not going straight ahead, not blowing its horn, etc.[3] Non-occurrence is computationally intractable without a prior hypothesis or expectation that certain occurrences *are* possible in a particular situation.

If children do not hear (3a) or (3b), but do hear (3c), how do they know whether (3a), (3b) or both are significant negative evidence?

3.   a. Is the cat who is in the puddle in the hat?
         b. *Is the cat who in the hat is in the puddle?
         c. Is the cat who is in the hat in the puddle?

---

[3] Thanks to Guy Carden for the example.

Computing indirect negative evidence depends on pre-determined hypotheses regarding "possible" language (see in chapter 4 no. 16 [p. 58] on abduction). Yet this is what we are trying to explain: how do children come to know the significant hypotheses about their language?[4] (Cf. chapter 6.)

3.1.1.5   Primary linguistic data (PLD)

In the Initial State, infants for the first time hear sounds in the speech stream and begin to consult these physical phenomena in the process of language acquisition.[5]

Children born in the United States may hear an utterance like (4). Without knowledge of language, this corresponds simply to an acoustic stimulus, visually represented in (5); after phonetic analysis, it corresponds to (6). Children born in Sri Lanka may hear an utterance in Sinhala meaning (7), corresponding to an acoustic stimulus represented in (8), represented as (9) after phonetic analysis.

English

4.   This is a story about Cinderella

5.

6.   ðɪs ɪz ə storì əbawt sɪndərelə

Sinhala

7.   This is a story about mother.

8.

9.   me: katandəre: amma   gænə
          this story   mother about

We assume that all normal-hearing children, from birth or earlier, will be continually exposed to a wide range of ambient language (ranging from single word utterances to utterances more complex than [4] or [9]) not only between child and parent, but between adults and between other children, in all of the situations of children's normal life. In this sense, they are thoroughly "awash" in potential evidence.

However, the sound input, e.g., that corresponding to (4) or (7), recorded in (5) and (8), consists simply of "[v]ariations in air pressure in the form of sound waves" which "move through the air somewhat like ripples on a pond" (Ladefoged 1993, 160). The sounds themselves are "fleeting and transient . . . Even during the brief existence of a sound . . . there is nothing that can be seen; there is no visible connecting link between a speaker and listener. There is air around, but it

---

[4] See Kapur 1994 for analysis of indirect negative evidence and linguistic theory; Bowerman 1988; Marcus et al. 1992; Morgan and Travis 1989; Randall 1992.

[5] The term "Initial State" does not involve a temporal or age-based notion, but rather refers to the state of being *prior to experience*. For the adult acquiring a new language we may assume that the adult is once again in an Initial State (Flynn and Lust, 2002). See chapter 4.

is not normally possible to see any changes in the condition of the air when it is conveying a sound" (Ladefoged, 1996, 1).[6]

Phonetic analyses in (6) and (9) represent the linguist's transcription of this speech. The adult who knows either language – English or Sinhala – hears sound in (5) or (8), analyzes it, digitizes it (see chapter 2), remembers and reconstructs it according to adult "intuitions," exposing its units.[7] Unless we are bilingual, we can so transform the speech stream for only the language we know; the other remains just sounds. Children, initially, must find a way to map from (5) to (6), or (8) to (9), without knowing any language, without "adult intuitions," and without being taught any form for the representation of these sounds.

We speak of this initial input to the language learner such as (4)–(5) or (7)–(8), and the full range of ambient language in all contexts, as "primary linguistic data" (PLD). It is the grist for the mill of language acquisition.

10.   **Primary linguistic data** (PLD)
        The actual original finite language data to which children are exposed, and
        from which they must map to knowledge of a specific language; a
        combination of sound and extra-linguistic experience.

On the basis of such data, children must somehow eventually acquire a specific language. We call this the "Projection Problem."

11.   **The Projection Problem**
        The problem of mapping ("projecting") from the finite initial specific
        experiences of PLD to knowledge of a specific language.   (cf. Baker
        1979)

In general, children may be said to need to "crack the code" of the physical stimulus to which they are exposed, and project from the data to linguistic knowledge.

3.1.1.6   Cracking the code

To solve the Projection Problem, children must convert the acoustic stimulus from a continuous stimulus, e.g., (5) or (8), to a discontinuous or digital (unit-based) representation, e.g., (6) or (9). That is, children must discover the units that function in the language and their organization. We have seen that discrete units exist at several "levels of representation" in language knowledge (cf. figure 2.3).

---

[6] Spectrographs capture and display the acoustic energy of the input speech as a function of *time*, *frequency* and *amplitude* of the sound waves (Crystal 1997a, 136–137, and Ladefoged 1993, 191–214.)

[7] The linguist's phonetic transcription is used here in (6) or (9) to overcome the inconsistencies of spelling, and to capture the "real" sounds of the utterances. They use some version of a "phonetic alphabet" (e.g., some version of an International Phonetic Alphabet, IPA). The reader not familiar with this alphabet may consult Fromkin and Rodman 1998, Ladefoged 1993, Pullum and Ladusaw 1986, or Cipollone et al. 1998. Study of first language acquisition requires the adoption of a phonetic alphabet because it requires capture of the precise sounds of a child's utterance in an unambiguous way.

12.

⬇

[ ] [ ] [ ] [ ] [ ] [ ] [ ] [ ] [ ] [ ]

As in examples (5) and (8), children must discover the sounds (which combine into words), the words (which combine into phrases), the phrases (e.g., subjects and predicates which combine to form clauses), and the clauses and clause combinations (which form sentences) (chapter 2).

3.1.1.7 Summary

While both positive and negative evidence appear to be necessary for children to acquire a language, neither appears to be directly available to them.

3.2 The nature of the evidence: searching the speech stream for the units

3.2.1 The physical evidence

One might assume that the units may, even must, be discovered by careful analysis of the positive input data, i.e. the speech stream. However, the units do not actually exist there. This is, first, because the speech stream itself is *continuous*, as suggested in (12).

3.2.1.1 The continuous speech stream

Units of language, e.g., those revealed in (6) or (9), do not regularly correspond to "divisions" in the speech stream. Pauses or silences do not, in general, correspond to any of the requisite units. Essential units are merged, e.g., (13). The classic example (14) reflects the inherent ambiguity in mapping units to the continuous speech stream (cf. Searchinger film series, "*The Human Language Series*").

13.   *Wuddeesaay*? I didn't hear.
     Wuddeedo? He said he would do something.
     Jeatjet? Or would you like to go out to dinner?

14.   a. Mares eat oats
     b. Mairsy Doates

Careful fluent speech does not clearly mark either word boundaries or sound boundaries (Cole and Jakinik 1980). In languages like French, sounds and words will blend in "liaison" even more productively, e.g., "les#enfants," although not always; in "les#hotels" the words are separated. (In liaison, sounds are joined together as if one.) Infants learning French – or any other language – have to work backwards from PLD which may or may not contain liaison, determining when and where elision occurs, a problem which baffles most second language learners and linguists alike.

3.2.1.2   Finding the word units

Words are more difficult to perceive and are less clearly articulated in fluent speech than when isolated (Lieberman 1963; Pollack and Pickett 1964). A sentence of only about seven words can result in "millions of alternative possible word strings" (Jusczyk, Cutler and Redanz 1993; Klatt 1989). Parents do not first present all words individually to their children (Aslin 1993; Brent and Siskind 2001; cf. chapter 6).

3.2.1.3   Finding the sound units: the nature of speech perception

The linguistic units of sound which underlie words do not exist in the speech stream. Table 3.1 provides a list of critical results from the study of adult speech perception showing this. The continuous speech stream underdetermines the discovery of digital sound units (e.g., *i* and *ii* on table 3.1), much like a motion picture does not reveal individual images which compose it.

3.2.1.4   Opacity of the speech stream

In normal speech, the *same* sound is heard as *different* in certain cases (15a); in other cases, *different* sounds are heard as the *same* (15b), corresponding to *iii* and *iv* on table 3.1. Sound units may be null; e.g., in English pronunciation of "pants," the /t/ may have no phonetic realization.

15.   Opacity of the speech stream

    a.   [ ]   b.   [ ]   [ ]

          /   \   \   /

       [ ]   [ ]   [ ]

Given the facts summarized in table 3.1, there are not "criterial" acoustic invariants in the speech stream which regularly and necessarily correspond to the sound units which children must discover. Children make a fundamental conversion from a continuous speech stream to a discontinuous (digital) representation, schematized in (12). The evidence for the units is not direct, concrete or regular.

We do not perceive speech by analyzing individual segments sequentially, like beads on a string. How then *do* we perceive and understand speech?[8] Even more puzzling is the question: how can and do children come to discover the relevant

---

[8] These issues continue to pose a challenge to theories of speech perception. See Akmajian, Demers, Farmer and Harnish 2001 and Matthei and Roeper 1983 for general introduction ; and Klatt 1989, Remez et al 1994 for overviews. Liberman 1996 provides a solution in terms of a "motor theory of speech perception."

Table 3.1 *Critical results from the study of speech perception opacity of the speech stream*

i. The rate of transmission of relevant information in the speech stream is very fast (Liberman 1996, 32; Miller 1981, 75). 20–30 sound segments per second are possible (Liberman 1996), a rate faster than that at which we can reliably identify individual sounds in a sequence, i.e., 7–9 per second (Liberman 1970).

ii. Coarticulation. In production, "coarticulation folds information about several successive segments into the same stretch of sound" (Liberman 1996, 33). Coarticulation is necessary; consonants can not be identified without adjacent vowels for example (e.g., Delattre, Liberman and Cooper 1955; cf. Jusczyk 1997; Liberman 1996, 33). When sounds combine into larger units such as syllables or words, e.g, b – a – t [b a t], "the acoustic cues that characterize the initial and final consonants are transmitted in the time slot that would have been necessary to transmit a single isolated vowel" (Liberman 1996, 207, 223), reflecting what has been termed "parallel transmission" of the information regarding individual units and coarticulation of the combined units.

iii. The same phone (sound unit) may take on different properties in different environments. The same sound can be perceived differently depending on its context; e.g., [p] when clipped from [pi] and inserted before [a], as in [pa], is heard as [ka]. The same [p] when inserted before as in [pu] is heard as [pu]. Similarly, silence (75 msc of blank tape) inserted in "s#lit" is heard as split; inserted in s#ore is heard as store (Cooper, Delattre, Liberman, Borst and Gerstman 1952; Matthei and Roeper 1983; Akmajian et al. 1995, 407).

iv. Different phones (sound units) may appear the same in different environments. Adult speakers judge sounds to be identical which are distinct phonetically. For example, in many American English dialects, the unit [t] "has as many as eight distinct pronunciations," one of which may be complete silence (Kenstowicz 1994, 65). In many American English dialects, the /t/ in "write" and the /d/ in "ride" will appear as the same sound, a "flap", in "writer" or "rider".

units when cracking the code from the speech stream for the first time, without knowing a language? While adults can test hypotheses regarding the specific language they know, and can search the speech stream for cues to these relevant units, infants in the Initial State do not yet know a specific language and must *discover* these units when they do not actually exist directly in the data which they experience.

ACOUSTIC CUE: Some property of the physical embodiment of language may correlate with linguistic units, e.g., loudness or stress. For example, vowels are differentiated in terms of their formant frequencies (involving rate of variation in air pressure which correspond to shape and use of the vocal tract) (Ladefoged 1993, 2001).

3.2.1.5   Finding the cues

Cues lie in the speech stream; otherwise we could not accomplish a mapping from sounds to language. Yet how are children to know what constitutes a cue and which cues to use? The cues that indicate unit boundaries in different languages are "apt to be closely tuned to the underlying organization of the sound patterns for a particular language" and differ from language to language. "Consequently, among the things that one has to learn in order to speak and understand a native language is what the correct cues are for segmenting words from fluent speech in that language" (Jusczyk 1997a, 5).[9]

3.2.1.6   Confounding the search

Every time a word is uttered, e.g., "hat," it differs physically (acoustically). Variations in different speakers, genders and ages, amplitudes and tones add more variability. Whether the story in (4) or (7) is read by a man, woman or another child, in a soft or loud voice, in a lullaby or story-reading context, with varying intonation, the same segmentation must be captured. The same units must be discovered.

3.2.2   The linguistic evidence

3.2.2.1   Where are the words?

The same units which may be words in one language may be parts of words or multiple words in another. The Arctic Inuktitut language in (16) comes from the natural speech of a two-year-old; (17), from experimental studies.

In Inuktitut and other polysynthetic languages like it, the word, e.g., the verb in (16) or (17), is morphologically complex, capturing the information which might be represented primarily by isolated word units in a language like English. How are children in the Initial State to know which form of units to be searching for?[10]

16.   tamaaniiqujinngitualu
       ta – ma -ani -it -qu -ji -nngit -juq -aluk
       PRE -here -LOC -be -want -ANTP -NEG -PAR.3sS -EMPH
       He doesn't want (me) to be here (Juupi 2.0; Allen 1994, 133).

17.   Nattirmik qungutuqturmik quqhugturmiktikkuarit!
       Nattiq – mik qungutut- jug – mik quqhuqtuq – mik tikkuag – nit
       Point.to-IMP.25s
       Seal–INST.sg smile -NOM-INST.sg yellow -INST sg
       Point to the smiling yellow seal (Inuktitut, Parkinson 1999, p. 312).

---

[9] "Cue" is a "term of convenience, useful for the purpose of referring to any piece of signal that has been found by experiment to have an effect on perception . . . any definition of an acoustic cue is always to some extent arbitrary" (Liberman 1996, 22).

[10] Current research compares acquisition of Inuktitut and English: Allen 1996; Allen and Crago 1993a, b; Fortescue and Olsen 1992; Fortescue 1984/5; Parkinson 1999; Mithun 1989; Pye 1980, 1992.

3.2.2.2   Where are the sounds?

Children must be able to perceive the same sounds but categorize them differently, or perceive different sounds and categorize them similarly, depending on the "configuration" or "system" of the language being acquired.

Variations in aspiration [+h or −h] occur in English, e.g., distinguishing the acoustic properties of the [k] in the beginnings of words [+h] from those in the middle of words [−h], as (18a) and (18b) exemplify. (*Here 'h' signifies aspiration.*) We recognize a /k/ in each word, regardless of whether the sound involves aspiration. However, in Hindi, an aspiration distinction is linguistically significant ("contrastive") as in (19a) and (19b); new words result from this difference. In acquiring Hindi or English, children must consult acoustic variation in aspiration and categorize it differently, depending on the system (phonology) of the language.

18.   a. k^h it
             b. skit

19.   a. kal – yesterday, tomorrow
             b. k^h al – rogue

Children must discover a unit which categorizes all variations of a sound which are similarly significant in a language. The unit to be acquired, traditionally called a "phoneme,"[11] is not a physical but a cognitive unit. It is not a sound, but an abstract category of potential sounds.[12]

3.2.2.3   Discovering the system

Children cannot know *a priori* which sound variability is *phonemic* or significant in the system of their language. The number and nature of phonemes varies widely across languages, from eleven to over 100. English is generally thought to have thirty-five to forty-five, while Rotokas (Papua, New Guinea) only eleven (five vowels, six consonants; Comrie, Matthews and Polinsky 1996). Children must somehow discover how "sounds must be placed" in relation to each other according to "the inner configuration of the sound system of a language" (Sapir 1925, 25).

The child's task is not discovery of physical entities but discovery of a linguistic system. The linguist Sapir explicated this fact about language knowledge long ago: "phonetic phenomena are not physical phenomena *per se*, however necessary it may be to get at the phonetic facts by way of their physical embodiment" (1925, 25).

---

[11] The "phoneme" has been debated since its original discovery. Weisler and Milekic 2000, 41–44 introduce the concept.

[12] Phonetic forms corresponding to particular sounds are annotated in brackets (e.g., [k]), while phonemes, corresponding to the abstract linguistic category are annotated as /k/.

3.2.2.4   Making variability tractable: knowing the rules

We are not usually deceived by variability because we "know the rules" and "processes" which underlie speech sound alternations.[13]

PHONOLOGICAL PROCESSES AND RULES
A "phonological process" operates on sounds or features of sounds, changing them in certain ways, e.g., *assimilating* them to each other, *substituting* for them, *deleting* them. If such a process is regular, and generalizable, and we can specify the conditions (or contexts) under which it applies, we use the term "phonological rule."

The sound assimilation rule in (20) is an example where the plural /s/ appears in several forms depending on context. (*Here the notation '+/−V' refers to whether or not the sound' is voiced; cf. chapter 8*).

20.   Assimilation of sound features in English plural rule

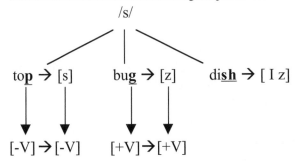

In any language, we know these rules and/or processes tacitly, only occasionally becoming conscious of them. The French second language learner of English may be recognized pronouncing words like "ten" because they may not demonstrate the aspiration rule which produces [tʰ] for [t] word initially in English.

21.   /t e n /

↓

[tʰ e n]

Phonological rules and processes provide a regular way of mapping from an "Underlying Representation" of what we know about the structure of the perceived word to the variable surface form.

---

[13] Halle and Clements 1983, 9–10, Weisler and Milekic 2000, 41–45; Cipollone et al. 1998; Kenstowicz 1994 introduces "phonological rules."

Even the preschool child productively applies the plural rule in (20) to nonsense words where these could not have been learned, as in a classic study which tested children on examples like (22).

22.   This is a wug.
           Now there is another one.
           There are two of them.
           There are two _____.

The preschoolers correctly provided the plural "WUG<u>Z</u>" in 76 percent of cases, and the plural "HEAF<u>S</u>" in 79 percent of cases (Berko 1958, 159; cf. Potts et al. 1979, Pinker 1999), unconsciously but regularly assimilating the sound of the plural /s/ to the sound of the final consonant of the word.

While adults know the rules specific to their language, and thus are not deceived by surface variations, children cannot start with language-specific rules. They must acquire them.[14] In Sinhala, for example, a plural form (23b) has a null inflection (with inanimate nouns), while the singular is inflected (23a).

23.   **a. Sinhala singular**
           poT∂   book
           kaduw∂   sword

       b. Sinhala plural
           poT   books
           kadu   swords

How do children come to know which sound changes are regular and systematic variations in their language? Should they attend to the beginning of the words, as necessary for Welsh (e.g., Meara and Ellis 1982), to the middle of words (e.g., in Inuktitut as in (16) or (17)), or to the ends of words, as necessary for English? When is a null form possible?

3.2.2.5   Relating levels of representation: phonology, morphology and syntax

As we saw in chapter 2, language knowledge involves digitization at several "levels of representation" and these levels must be related to each other (figure 2.2). Children must discover the units at each level – and the computation which relates them – in order to acquire a language. In (5) or (8), not only must sounds be grouped to words (e.g., to "Cinderella" or "amma"), but words to phrases, phrases to clauses, and clauses to complex sentences. Even if a language learner is able to determine the relevant phonological or sound units in the speech stream, they still must determine the structural relations among them: that "about Cinderella" modifies the "story" in (4), or that "nattiq" is the object of the verb "tikkuaq (point to)" in Inuktitut in (17). We can assume that the architecture of

---

[14] The surface form is opaque in another way: rules may interact and even contradict themselves in deriving the surface forms.

the Language Faculty must inform this computation, which must exceed either positive or negative evidence.

3.2.2.6   Summary

Direct negative evidence may not exist for children or have influence when it does; indirect negative evidence depends on reference to the learner's pre-existent hypotheses.

Positive evidence is available to the infant in the Initial State, but:

*   This evidence is variable and degenerate.
*   The speech stream is fundamentally opaque with regard to the units which must be discovered.
*   The stimulus provided to the infant is continuous, while language knowledge requires a digital representation.
*   There is cross-linguistic variation in the units which must be discovered and in the mode of their realization in the speech stream.
*   The units to be discovered are cognitive (linguistic), not physical, and they involve multi-level linguistic computation.
*   Children must discover the linguistic units by discovering the linguistic system for their language.
*   In order to discover the grammar, children must transform the PLD to which they are exposed. They must *create* a grammar.

3.3   How could the problem be solved?

Solving the Projection Problem seems similar to solving the problem of a linguist coming upon a new language and wishing to crack its code, to discover its grammar. The problem the infant faces, however, is more severe. Linguists setting out to discover a new language can access certain forms of evidence: (a) they already have a first language, allowing attempts at translation; (b) they will seek to find and use an "informant," a native speaker who can provide translations. The newborn infant has no first language to translate into.

Is it possible to "bootstrap" into the language system by initially leaning solely on non-linguistic information? Several forms of bootstrapping from external non-linguistic evidence have been hypothesized. If these involve a claim that children's initial knowledge is non-linguistic and this non-linguistic knowledge alone is the "source" of linguistic knowledge, then these proposals cannot succeed. There are several forms of each of these proposals: some assume a Language Faculty and may specifically compute over linguistic knowledge. Some may assume a "language of thought" which is "very like a natural language" although not identical (Fodor, 1975, 156). We'll consider only the strong forms of non-linguistic bootstrapping here, where no specifically linguistic knowledge provided by a Language Faculty is admitted.

3.3.1   Prosodic bootstrapping

The rhythmic structures, or prosody, of language have been argued to play a fundamental role in first language acquisition, perhaps helping children to crack the code and solve the segmentation problems we raised above, as in (24).

24.   **Prosodic Bootstrapping Hypothesis**
       Prosodic units which are acoustically signaled in the speech stream may provide critical perceptual cues by which children first discover the existence of linguistic units.[15]

Could such cues derive from general perceptual capacity, e.g., common to music and/or from other more general cognitive abilities? Certain prosodic features may correlate with constituent structure in language. For example, several acoustic features may mark the end of a unit of speech: (a) lengthening of the terminal segment; (b) fall in fundamental frequency; and (c) decrease in amplitude. Such prosodic markers can aid adults in the acquisition of an artificial language (Morgan, Meier and Newport 1987).[16]

Very young infants have demonstrated sensitivity to musical phrase structure. Presented with tapes of Mozart minuets, 4.5-month-old infants distinguished those sequences which were broken at well-formed musical phrase boundaries from those that were broken unnaturally within the phrase, listening longer to the well-formed musical phrases.[17] Rhythm perception has been attested in early infancy,[18] as well as numerous prosodic sensitivities (see chapter 8). Morgan 1996 argues for a "rhythmic bias in preverbal speech segmentation." Mehler et al. 1996 and Ramus, Nespor and Mehler 1999 propose that classifiable rhythmic properties of speech ground infants' first processing and representation of language.

In general, prosodic information in a language does not provide one-to-one mapping to linguistic units so that infants could directly and systematically infer linguistic structure from prosodic structure (see Lieberman 1996). This is because "many of the same acoustic changes that frequently coincide with important syntactic units in speech also occur in utterances for nonsyntactic reasons" (Jusczyk 1997a, 141). If listeners "were to rely on any one of these cues for information about grammatical units, they still would need some other mechanism to let them know when the cues were actually relevant to syntactic matters" (Jusczyk 1997a, 141). If a form of mapping from prosodic units to linguistic units is to be

---

[15] See Morgan and Demuth 1996, and Jusczyk and Kemler-Nelson 1997a for reviews; Gleitman and Wanner 1982, 26; Allen and Hawkins 1980.

[16] See Jusczyk 1997, 140, for review; Jusczyk et al. 1992 for experimental study. See Lieberman 1996 for review of language intonation and perception; Inkelas and Zec 1990 for cross-linguistic work; Nespor and Vogel 1986; Couper-Kuhlen 1993 on English speech rhythm. For general review combining adult prosody and child acquisition issues see Gerken 1996; Fowler 1977 for example of psycholinguistic work on speech production and serial ordering; Cooper and Paccia-Cooper 1980 for example of discussion of the relation between temporal effects and syntactic phrase structure and related psycholinguistic studies.

[17] Jusczyk and Krumhansl 1993; Krumhansl and Jusczyk 1990. Current research attempts to distinguish the precise acoustic cues which determine this effect; e.g., Jusczyk 1997, 146–147.

[18] Demorny and McKenzie 1977.

achieved, then it appears that the linguistic units must already be known; "language learners would already need to have a tacit understanding of the relation between prosodic cues and syntactic structure in order to reconstruct the speaker's intended bracketing" (Gerken 1996, 347).

Language-specific variation in prosodic units must be acquired. Tones, accents and stress vary from language to language. Stress may fall on inflection or on word stems. While English rhythmic structure involves alternating stresses on syllables which contrast by being either strong or weak, French rhythmic structure is "syllable-timed," where syllables tend to have equal timing. Knowledge of language-specific timing acquired in a first, native language, may persist in second-language acquisition.[19]

Children's control of prosody advances during the first twelve months, when integration of syntactic and prosodic units develops on the basis of specific language experience (Morgan 1994, 402; Jusczyk 1997a). As we will see, there is empirical evidence that children make use of prosodic factors in language acquisition, but prosody must integrate with other linguistic knowledge in order to be effective. "[Y]oung language learners use prosodic information to discover prosodic structure, not syntactic structure" (Gerken 1996, 348).

3.3.2   Phonological bootstrapping

The "prosodic bootstrapping hypothesis "– in its strong form – is actually a misnomer. "Most proponents of this view assume that learners are drawing on a range of information available in the speech signal that extends beyond prosody" (Jusczyk 1997a, 38). What has been described as a "prosodic bias" in language acquisition might be best categorized as a prosodic factor. "Prosodic bootstrapping" may be reformulated as "phonological bootstrapping" wherein it is recognized that "several forms of information are available in input speech – phonetic, phonotactic, prosodic, stochastic – and any or all of these could contribute to syntactically rich representations of input utterances" (Morgan and Demuth 1996, 2). Phonological bootstrapping reflects a type of potential "linguistic bootstrapping" wherein one form of linguistic knowledge may interact with and aid another (cf. chapter 11).

3.3.3   Semantic bootstrapping

Perhaps if language acquisition is not perceptually based, it is conceptually based. Could children *first* determine what the meaning of language is, and use this external knowledge to begin to crack the code of language? Could this meaning aid children in discovering the formal linguistic units and system? Could language acquisition initially result from a unidirectional mapping from meaning to form? Various forms of this hypothesis have been posed under the term "semantic bootstrapping", e.g., (25) or (26). Is language

---

[19] Cutler, Mehler, Norris and Segui 1986, 1992; Cutler 1994, 80.

acquisition based initially on children's ability to observe the world around them, and on the basis of this context, to induce meanings of words as well as grammatical knowledge?

25.   "The beginnings of language are learned ostensively. The needed stimuli are right out there in front, and mystery is at a minimum . . . Language bypasses the idea and homes on the object . . . we learn the language by relating its terms to the observations that elicit them."   (Quine 1973, 35–37)

26.   **Semantic Bootstrapping Hypothesis**
Initially, children do not have access to language form, but do have access to extra-linguistic forms of meaning. On the basis of these meanings, children "bootstrap" to formal knowledge of language, i.e., to its forms and its units.[20]

Under this hypothesis, children first observe "real world" situations and then use these observations to formulate word meanings and aspects of grammatical structure. Hearing the word "dog" in the context of dogs, or the word "push" in context of pushing will lead children to "induce" the meanings of these words; they will extract the relevant regularities from the contexts observed. In its strong form, this hypothesis also cannot provide a complete explanation for the language acquisition problem (cf. chapter 11).

3.3.3.1   Meaning is limitless

There is a limitless set of possible meanings in any particular context. Before knowing a language, how could a language learner possibly determine what meanings to assign?

3.3.3.2   Reference is inscrutable

The philosopher Quine explicated the problem here with a famous example (1960, 52), where the linguist goes out to the jungle to determine an unknown language. "A rabbit scurries by, the native says 'gavagai', and the linguist notes down the sentence 'rabbit' (or 'lo, a rabbit'), as tentative translation" (27), which he then subjects to further tests by asking the native to assent or dissent to possible translations. Any of an infinite set of possible meanings could exist and they would all trigger the native's assent under similar situations:

27.   Quine's reference to "*gavagai*":

stages or temporal segments of rabbit

an integral part of a rabbit

all and sundry undetached parts of rabbits

rabbit fusion of parts

the concept of rabbithood

the place where rabbithood is manifested

whole enduring "rabbit"

---

[20] See Grimshaw 1981 and Macnamara 1982 for early versions; Pinker 1987, 1984, 1989 for overview and summary; Bloom 1999.

Only on the assumption that the native performs the same translation as English could a shared meaning of "gavagai" be determined, e.g., "whole enduring 'rabbit,'" if this is in fact what the native had in mind. Quine terms this general problem "indeterminacy of translation." But this is what we are trying to explain: how do children acquire the correct translations for English, or any language? Children must face the problem of *"inscrutability of reference"*: the relation between the word and the thing it labels is complex, non-direct and indeterminate (Quine 1960, 80; 1971, 142).

Is it possible that, for children, pointing or gestural reference (i.e., a form of manual ostension) could determine reference and meaning? As Quine points out, "Point to a rabbit and you have pointed to a stage of a rabbit, to an integral part of a rabbit, to the rabbit fusion, and to where rabbithood is manifested" (52). Pointing alone does not in itself resolve the problem.[21]

If meaning is so indeterminate, how could it possibly be the source of children's ability to crack the code of the PLD? Even if linguistic units are already known, e.g., the word or sentence, the problem of determining meaning remains. "The difficulty is that neither words nor sentences, nor even propositions, are in any direct way encodings of scenes or situations in the world" (Gleitman and Wanner 1982, 9). When someone says "The cat is on the mat," (28) gives only a few of the possible meanings which this utterance could have.[22]

28.   Interpreting context
                A mat is supporting a cat
                A mat is under the cat
                The cat is ruining the mat
                The floor is supporting the mat and the cat
                The cat is sleeping
                The cat has come in again
                What a good bed that mat makes for the cat

How could children know which interpretation to choose?

In a large corpus of mother utterances to 13–23 month olds, out of 8,000 utterances which contained a verb, 3,000 did not refer to an ongoing event (Beckwith, Tinker and Bloom 1989). For the verb "open," only 37.5 percent of utterances actually involved the "here and now" (Gleitman 1994). Parents tend to use verbs in contexts like "Put it in here" or "Do you want to roll it to me," which are nonostensive (Tomasello, Strosberg and Akhtar 1996, 158).

In many adult utterances, the same event can be described by different verbs, e.g., "chase" or "flee" (Gleitman 1994). Many verbs cannot be based on observation, e.g., "think" (Gleitman 1994, 188). Even when contexts are ostensive in some way, the context in itself does not reveal word meaning. Adults were shown videotapes of mothers playing with their young infants (aged about 18 months),

---

[21] Blake 2000 provides discussion; Bruner 1974/64 is a classic study; Schick 2000 provides empirical study of pointing in hearing and deaf children.

[22] See Gleitman and Wanner 1982; Gleitman and Gleitman 1994; Gleitman and Gillette 1999.

with audio eliminated (Gleitman and Gillette 1999, 279). Even with leading information (that the mother is uttering a "target noun" when a beep sounds), adults were only correct in guessing this referent about 50 percent of the time on the basis of the observational context alone. Fewer than 10 percent of the verbs are identified correctly, even with only frequent child-directed verbs when the adults knew these in advance (281). Thus, even for an adult given leading cues, there is no determinate 1:1 mapping between observational context and word units.

Pinker (1984) suggests that a probabilistic word–world mapping would be possible for word learning if we assume children compute over several cross-situational contexts. Some such computation must be involved in the acquisition of concepts and word meaning. Consider the task of determining where the bull's eye is from a target punctured by arrow holes. One or two holes are not highly informative, but multiple holes may be.[23] However, the availability of multiple contexts does not in itself solve the essential problem we have raised here. As in the bull's eye example, if multiple contexts are to become informative for children, we must posit some form of hypothesis of what is being looked for, i.e., the bull's eye, and analysis of what is alike about these contexts so they can be compared (cf. abduction in chapter 4). How would children attain this initial hypothesis? Children's fast mapping of new word meanings (cf. chapter 10) also appears to challenge the degree to which cross-situational comparisons are necessary for initial acquisition.

3.3.3.3 Learning in non-ostensive contexts

Children do not depend on ostensive contexts for early word learning. They learn new words by overhearing them as well (Akhtar, Jipson and Callanan 2001). In some cases, young children learned a novel verb best when it was "said in anticipation of an impending event or action" (Tomasello 1995). Infants as young as 18 months were introduced to a new word for a new toy. In an "ostensive condition," the toy was immediately found by an adult as the word was introduced. In a "non-ostensive context," the adult first found an incorrect toy, frowned at it and replaced it, only eventually finding the correct toy. Children learned the new word equally well either way when tested in either comprehension (asked to select the toy) or production (asked to name the toy). Children learned a new word for an adult's intended referent which wasn't seen at all until a later comprehension test.[24] Joint attention between child and caregiver does not determine or explain infant word learning (Carpenter, Nagell and Tomasello 1998) (chapter 10).

3.3.3.4 Learning in the blind child

Children's lack of direct dependence on ostensive contexts for word learning is revealed also in the congenitally blind child. The blind child's

---

[23] Suggested by Neil Smith.

[24] Tomasello, Strosberg and Akhtar 1996; Akhtar and Tomasello 1996; Tomasello and Barton 1994; Baldwin 1993b, Baldwin et al 1996, Tomasello and Kruger 1992.

understanding of "look" and "see" develops similarly to that of the sighted child (Landau and Gleitman (1985)). Asked to make it so Mommy cannot "see" a toy, for example, a blind child put the toy in her pocket. Asked to "look behind you," she explored the area behind her with her hands (see also Gleitman and Gillette 1999, 283). The blind child's acquisition of reversible pronouns (I, you) was found to be no later than that of the sighted child's. Even color terms are acquired. This indirect relation between language, meaning and referential context form the basis for the development of an alternative "syntactic bootstrapping hypothesis" of acquisition of word meaning (see chapter 11).

3.3.3.5   Ontological primitives

Are human beings born predetermined to realize that certain meanings are possible and others not? Something like this must be true to some degree,[25] but it cannot alone solve the language acquisition challenge for children in the Initial State. We might consider certain concepts unnamable, e.g., a certain "arrangement of leaves on a tree," but as Chomsky (1975b, 44) argues, an artist could develop such a reference in his work, using it to connote, for example, serenity. It is not clear how and where meaning units can be presumed, nor which lexical mappings can be presumed. The term "concept" is notoriously difficult to define. It does not provide us with *a priori* units which link to the lexicon. Attaining a concept would not in itself fully determine the acquisition of word meanings (e.g., chapters 2 and 10). Languages differ in concept lexicalization. Consider words which we might consider to be among the most important possible meanings: "hope" or "love" or "tomorrow." Sinhala has no word for "hope." There is no direct way in Sinhala to say "*I hope* this book is in the library" (meaning "it is good to me if it were there"). Malayalam does not have a word closely corresponding to the English "love," but distinguishes types of love. In some African languages, the verb "defeat" is used to capture the meaning of "is bigger than." In many languages, the verb "smoke" is equivalent to the verb "drink" (Heine 1992). Children cannot assume, on the basis of general non-linguistic cognition alone, which concepts have been lexicalized in a language or how. Again, paradoxically, it appears that children must know the language in order to know the meaning.

3.3.3.6   Meaning is necessary

There may be something innate about the human assumption of a relation between linguistic form and meaning.[26] The evidence above suggests only that meaning in itself cannot be a unique and independent first step, independent of linguistic knowledge, which can solve the essential language acquisition problem

---

[25] Cf. Chomsky, 1975b, 44 and fn. 15; see also Fodor 1975 on a "language of thought."
[26] Blake and Fink 1987, 229 provide argument that infant babbling may involve "sound–meaning relations."

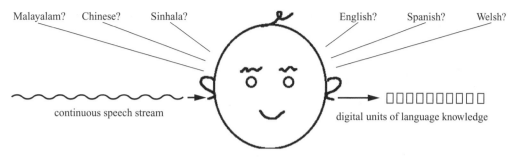

Fig. 3.1 *The child.*

for children in the Initial State. A relation between external context and linguistic form will not work unaided (Gleitman 1994, 188). In order to make specific forms of semantic bootstrapping work, the formal linguistic categories which are mapped to meaning categories would presumably have to be made available to children so that they could map to them. As Pinker (1987, 1984; 1989a, 361) suggests, "the syntactic nature of the rules acquired is the basis for the real power of the bootstrapping theory" (1987, 409) (cf. chapter 11).

3.4   Conclusions

Without knowledge of which properties of the speech stream to consider and how to evaluate them, children cannot determine which are the most significant units. Without a linguistic guide, children have no way of knowing which components of the data to use.

It appears that neither an approach of "looking really closely at the data" (its specific acoustic properties), nor "above the data" (its acoustic rhythms), nor of "looking outside of the linguistic data" (the context or the meaning) can alone solve the problem of language acquisition. If to "bootstrap" means to be able to arrive at an initiation of formal linguistic structure through solely language-external means, then it appears that there is no such bootstrapping available to children. This divorce between the data children have to work with externally and the nature of the knowledge which must be acquired is sometimes termed the "poverty of the stimulus" (Chomsky 1980, 34).

In philosophical terms, this problem of first language acquisition corresponds to the most fundamental problem of knowledge acquisition: it appears to be necessary for children to have some initial knowledge in order to even begin to make use of the PLD they are exposed to and thus to acquire new linguistic knowledge. The knowledge required for language, e.g., the units and their structured and sequential organization, must be imposed on the data. If the critical information is not in the input data, then we have only one place to look. We must look inside the child mind.

3.5   Supplementary readings

Halle 1997 presents an introduction to the non-physical nature of phonetic stimuli. Morgan and Demuth 1996 and Weissenborn and Hohle 2001 provide collections of recent studies relevant to the acquisition problem we raise here. Fodor 1998 discusses fundamental issues related to "concepts." Thomas 2002 reviews history of "poverty of the stimulus."

4   How we can construct a theory of language acquisition

Approaches to the study of language acquisition differ in their fundamental epistemological assumptions. These assumptions underlie the choice of which questions researchers ask, and which methodologies they choose. Approaches may provide (a) *developmental* descriptions, such as in the research paradigm initiated by Roger Brown at Harvard (1973b), (b) formal *logical* or mathematical analyses of the language acquisition problem, (c) *computational modeling* of various language acquisition behaviors, or (d) psycholinguistic studies of language acquisition led by specific hypotheses derived from linguistic theory. The tensions reflected here have interested philosophers for many centuries.

4.1   Theoretical approaches to the study of language acquisition

4.1.1   Classical approaches to epistemology

Table 4.1 summarizes basic properties of two classically opposed approaches to the representation and acquisition of knowledge. They differ in their views of: (a) the *ultimate source* of knowledge (either external and led by environmental input or internal, led by the structure of the mind); (b) *mechanisms* of acquisition; (c) *characteristics* of the Initial State, i.e., whether or not innate "knowledge" of some form exists. A *rationalist* perspective proposes some innate competence (thus the term "nativist" is often used). In a classical empiricist paradigm, "learning" based on input explains all knowledge; the Initial State therefore is a *tabula rasa*. (See Wilson 1999 for overview.)

These approaches differ in the form of reasoning which they recognize to underlie knowledge acquisition. *Induction* (building on direct experience of input data) is central to an empiricist paradigm; *deduction* (which does not depend on experience of data to confirm conclusions) to a rationalist paradigm (table 4.2).

4.1.2   The challenge of language acquisition to classical empiricist approaches

Acquisition of language is the "jewel in the crown" of cognitive science, "what everyone wants to explain" (Pinker, cited by Kolata 1987, 133),

Table 4.1 *Approaches to epistemology.*

Empiricism	Rationalism
(Locke, Berkeley, Hume; seventeenth century)	(Descartes, Kant; seventeenth, eighteenth centuries)
i. Knowledge is derived from experience of the "outside world."	i. Knowledge is derived from the structure of the human mind. "Anything intelligible to us must be made so by rules of the mind"; "appearances in general are nothing outside our representations" (Kant 1781, in Beardsley 1960, 439).
ii. Information is copied (by sensations and images), remembered, associated with other stored information. Complex ideas result from associating simple ideas.	ii. Many ideas, e.g., time, space, "or," God, mathematical concepts, infinity, truth, necessity, have nothing essentially sensory about them, and cannot be "copied." ". . . bodies are cognized not by the senses or by the imagination, but by the understanding alone" (Descartes, 1637 in Beardsley 1960, 40).
iii. Infant is born as a *"tabula rasa."*	iii. Infant is born with certain "innate" ideas; and an active mind which imposes a structure on experience; what is innate is a precondition of what is learned. "*a priori* knowledge . . . absolutely independent of all experience" (Kant, in Beardsley 1960, 376).

and challenges empiricist theories. Because of its infinite creativity, complexity and systematicity, knowledge of language cannot be based on simple "pick up," copy or association of input, and cannot be derived from simple forms of induction.

4.1.2.1   Serial order

Karl Lashley (1948/1951/1960) saw this early. He recognized a fundamental problem posed by language for empiricist approaches:[1] relations between units in a patterned sequence – steps of a horse, notes of music, words in a sentence – cannot be fully explained by local associations between any or every two elements in the series. Wherever there is serialization of units, the set of units must be organized: "What then determines the order?"[2] There must be a higher-order organizer and this requires a cognitive representation (Lashley

---

[1] See Bruce 1994 for discussion of historical relation between Lashley's and Chomsky's work.
[2] Piaget and his collaborators (Inhelder and Piaget 1964) also recognized the cognitive problem of serial order in a general sense. They directed crucial studies of "seriation" as a fundamental area of all logical thought, although they did not deal with language in this area.

Table 4.2 *Induction/deduction.*

INDUCTION	DEDUCTION
General inference is drawn from instances which are experienced.	Conclusions are drawn on the basis of premises already known.
	Transitive inference
Fido is a dog. Fido barks. Rover is a dog. Rover barks. Therefore: Dogs bark.	Sarah is shorter than Mary. Mary is shorter than Eve. Therefore: Sarah is shorter than Eve.
or: That swan is white. This swan is white. Therefore: Swans are white.	or: $2 + 2 = 4$ $3 + 1 = 4$ Therefore: $2 + 2 = 3 + 1$ Syllogism All men are mortal. Harry is a man. Therefore: Harry is mortal.
Properties	**Properties**
Synthetic truth: can be disconfirmed by experience.	Analytic truth: can not be disconfirmed by experience.
Conclusion can be rejected without rejecting the premises.	Can reject conlusions only by rejecting at least one of the premises
Often reasoning from particular to general.	Often reasoning from general to particular.

1948/1951/1960, 510).[3] Lashley struggled with this problem.[4] (See chapter 2, note 4, p. 12.)

4.1.2.2   Chomsky's review of Skinner

B.F. Skinner (1953) attempted to extend a classical behaviorist model of learning to language in his famous *Verbal Behavior*.[5] His goal was "to provide a way to predict and control verbal behavior by observing and manipulating the physical environment of the speaker" (1957, 547). In his review of this work, Chomsky (1959) showed that the Skinnerian concepts for learning (which included *stimulus*, *conditioned response* and *reinforcement*) do not apply to

---

[3] We use the term "cognitive" in a general sense to reflect all computation by the human mind; we consider specifically "linguistic" computation as one component of cognitive computation.

[4] "[T]he indications which I have cited, that elements of the sentence are readied or partially activated before the order is imposed upon them in expression, suggest that some scanning mechanism must be at play in regulating their temporal sequence. The real problem, however, is the nature of the selective mechanism by which the particular acts are picked out in this scanning process, and to this problem I have no answer" (Lashley 1951/1960, 522).

[5] On "behaviorism" see Boring 1950, Holyoak 1999.

language knowledge and behavior. No obvious concept of reinforcement appears to be relevant to language use or knowledge.

1.   Our capacity to generate language crucially determines our capacity to perceive language. It appears that we recognize a new item as a sentence not because it matches some familiar item in any simple way, but because it is generated by the grammar that each individual has somehow and in some form internalized. And we understand a new sentence, in part, because we are somehow capable of determining the process by which this sentence is derived in this grammar.   (Chomsky *1959*, 576)

      . . . a refusal to study the contribution of children to language learning permits only a superficial account of language acquisition."   (578)

4.1.2.3   Language acquisition vs. language learning

Chomsky's conclusion led to a distinction between "language learning" and "language acquisition," recognizing that language is not "learned" in any classical sense of the term but requires computation through cognitive structure. Addressing the question Lashley had struggled with for language, Chomsky identifies a "generative grammar," a component of the mind/brain, which provides syntax, central to language knowledge. Through detailed theoretical and empirical analyses in linguistics, he argued that knowledge of syntax determines the order of a sentence by generating its structure, i.e., its "secret skeleton."

4.2   Current approaches to the study of language acquisition

4.2.1   A rationalist approach

Chomsky's theory reflects a rationalist explanation of language acquisition: (a) The ultimate *source* of knowledge is the mind, not the external input. Grammar in the mind applies to, and to some degree determines, linguistic experience. (b) The essential *mechanism* of knowledge acquisition lies in the mind's ability to *generate* what is perceived as input, and to *deduce* new knowledge. (c) The Initial State is *biologically programmed* prior to experience in such a way that it makes linguistic experience possible and constrains its form.

4.2.1.1   The Language Faculty

Chomsky proposed and investigated a theory of the Initial State, i.e., the "Language Faculty" of the human species:

2.   "[T]here is a specific faculty of the mind/brain that is responsible for the use and acquisition of language, a faculty with distinctive characteristics that is apparently unique to the species in essentials."   (Chomsky 1987, 50)

This Language Faculty "serves the two basic functions of rationalist theory: it provides a sensory system for the preliminary analysis of linguistic data, and a schematism that determines, quite narrowly, a certain class of grammars" (Chomsky 1975b, 12). It involves an *innateness hypothesis* (1986, 60).[6]

---

3. **THE INNATENESS HYPOTHESIS**: "[I]t must be that the mind/brain provides a way to identify and extract the relevant information by means of mechanisms of some sort that are part of its biologically determined resources" (Chomsky 1988a, 15).

Linguistic analysis and computation must be, at least in part, distinct from other forms of cognitive computation (reflecting a *modular* theory of mind).

4.2.1.2   Content of the Language Faculty

Scientific study of the Language Faculty requires specification of its content. This has developed with the science of linguistics.

4.2.1.2.1   *Chomsky's LAD*

Chomsky's early formulation of a Language Acquisition Device (LAD) logically explicated the preconditions for acquiring linguistic knowledge on the basis of projection from input (Chomsky 1984, 30; Chomsky 1999, 43), thus beginning to formalize a solution to the Projection Problem raised in chapters 2 and 3 (Peters 1972, 173).

4.2.1.2.2   *Challenges to LAD*

Formulation of the LAD appeared to beg the issue of language acquisition. Component 3 was often interpreted as implying that a predetermined set of "specific language grammars" were innate (English, Swahili, Sinhala, Hindi, etc.) and that these merely needed to be "selected from," raising the question of how these grammars arise and how children judged whether the data were "compatible" with the grammar hypothesized (exemplifying the "evaluation metric" (component 5)) (Peters 1972, 179). The model in table 4.3 is a-temporal, consistent with an "instantaneous" view of language acquisition an assumption Chomsky realized is "obviously false" (1975, 119, 121).

4.2.1.2.3   *From LAD to UG*

Chomsky moved the theory of the Language Faculty from LAD to Universal Grammar (UG).

4.   "[U]niversal grammar is part of the genotype specifying one aspect of the initial state of the human mind and brain."   (Chomsky 1980, 82)

---

[6] See Chomsky 1975, 122 on interpretation of the innateness hypothesis.

Table 4.3 *Chomsky's early model: Language Acquisition Device (LAD)* *(Aspects of the Theory of Syntax, 1965; chapter 1, 30–31).*

Components of LAD	These components require
1. a technique for representing input signals	1. a universal phonetic theory that defines the notion "possible sentence"
2. a way of representing structural information about these signals	2. a definition of "structural description"
3. some initial delimitation of a class of possible hypotheses about language structure	3. a definition of "generative grammar"
4. a method for determining what each such hypothesis implies with respect to each sentence	4. a method for determining the structural description of a sentence, given a grammar
5. a method for selecting one of the (presumably, infinitely many) hypotheses that are allowed by 3, and are compatible with the given primary linguistic data	5. a way of evaluating alternative proposed grammars

The definition of UG is formal, general and abstract, no longer suggesting access to a list of pre-defined grammars. UG differs from LAD in its formulation of what is proposed to be biologically programmed. Consequently, it reassesses the relation between children and the PLD.

5.   "Universal grammar may be thought of as some system of principles, common to the species and available to each individual prior to experience" (Chomsky 1981b, 7).

UG is bidimensional, as in (6).

6.   **Universal Grammar**
  a. "Universal Grammar might be defined as the study of the conditions that must be met by the grammars of all human languages" (Chomsky 1968, 126, 62)
  b. "In a highly idealized picture of language acquisition, UG is taken to be a characterization of children's pre-linguistic initial state" (Chomsky 1981, 7) and of the "language faculty" (Chomsky 1981, 7).

If all natural languages follow a universal architecture, and the human species is so programmed, this would explain why universals of language exist and why any language is normally acquired in children's first years, escaping the epistemological dilemma seen in chapters 1–3.

4.2.1.2.4 *Armed for discovery*

Theoretical developments over the last several decades have progressively: (a) streamlined the theory of Universal Grammar;[7] (b) eliminated many "substantive" proposals and replaced them with more abstract "formal" universals, substituting general principles for specific "rules";[8] (c) shifted focus away from the question of how linguists or children analyze a sentence with a specific structure, and toward a focus on identifying and understanding the underlying architectural principles which converge to result in knowledge of specific constructions.

"Principles and Parameters" theory of UG defines both a set of universal *principles* which capture what underlies language structure everywhere, and a finite set of *parameters* to account for possible cross-linguistic variation.

4.2.1.2.4.1 Principles   The most fundamental principle of UG is "structure dependence."[9] Armed with it, children acquiring a language will not be thwarted by the continuous speech stream, but will impose linguistic units upon it. Children will never consider language data as simply linear "beads on a string," but will know that grammatical computation depends on structure.

7.   **Structure dependence**
      "The rules operate on expressions that are assigned a certain structure in terms of a hierarchy of phrases of various types" (Chomsky 1988a, 45).

This principle provides children with the foundation for discovering and building the secret skeleton that underlies every sentence. Neither will children be thwarted by the fact that linguistic elements move or disappear, since they now have the basis for tracking movement of units and knowing where they might or might not appear.

The principle of structure dependence rules out infinite possible false hypotheses regarding possible computations. In a classic example, Chomsky argues that without structure dependence and by induction ("analogy") alone on sentences like (8) in English or (9) in Spanish, a child might surmise a rule such as: delete the first "is" or "está" in the sentence; insert one of these at the beginning of the sentence; thus leading from examples like (8a) or (9a) and (8b) and (9b) to the ungrammatical (8c) or (9c) (Chomsky 1988a, 41f).

8.   English
      a. The man is in the house
         Is the man in the house?

---

[7] The acronyms TG (Transformational Grammar), GB (Government and Binding Theory) and P&P (Principles and Parameters Theory) reflect developing versions of Universal Grammar.

[8] The distinction between "substantive" universals and "formal" universals is difficult. The basic distinction intended is: universals that specify specific content, e.g., nouns or verbs vs. universals that refer to the architecture by which symbolic forms are generated and computed over.

[9] UG also would provide principles and parameters for the areas of semantics and phonology, although these areas have received less work in theory and in language acquisition.

b. The man is happy
   <u>Is</u> the man happy?
c. The man who is in the house is happy
   * <u>Is</u> the man who in the house is happy?

9.   Spanish
   a. Está el hombre en la casa?
      Is the man in the house?
   b. Está el hombre contento?
   Is the man happy?
   c. *Está el hombre que contento está en la casa?
      Is the man who happy is in the house?

Structure dependence constrains children's grammatical hypotheses so that they must analyze the structure (bracketed) in (10) and (11) before forming a question inversion rule and thus not first "consider the simple linear rule . . . then discard it" (Chomsky 1988a, 45). The structure-dependent rule comes first. Children's knowledge would be to a degree deductive; knowledge acquisition would be initially and continuously constrained.

10.   [The man[who is in the house]] <u>is</u> happy
         [El hombre [que está contento]] <u>está</u> en la casa

11.   Is [the man [who is happy]] at home?
         Está [el hombre [que esta contento]] en la casa?

4.2.1.2.4.2 Parameters   Parameters target critical dimensions for grammar building and constrain cross-linguistic variation along these dimensions.

---

12. **PARAMETER**: a principled dimension of language variation, which specifies predetermined values of this variation. Parameters provide the "atoms" of linguistic structure (Baker 2001).

In the strongest theory, parameters are minimal in number and binary valued. When set, parameters allow children to establish the basic forms of grammars and draw widespread deductive conclusions from this.

13.   **UG Parameters: A Switch-box Metaphor**
         "The initial state of the language faculty consists of a collection of
         subsystems, or modules as they are called, each of which is based on certain
         very general principles. Each of these principles admits of a certain very
         limited possibility of variation. We may think of the system as a complex
         network, associated with a switch box that contains a finite number of
         switches. The network is invariant, but each switch can be in one of two
         positions, on or off. Unless the switches are set, nothing happens. But when

the switches are set in one of the permissible ways, the system functions, yielding the entire infinite array of interpretation for linguistic expressions. A slight change in switch settings can yield complex and varied phenomenal consequences as its effects filter through the network . . . To acquire a language, children's mind must determine how the switches are set" (Chomsky 1988, 68).

Example parameters
Word order: head direction

One language may demonstrate word (and constituent) orders that reverse another language (cf. chapter 2). Through a "head direction" parameter, UG allows languages to vary order (chapter 9). This setting will generalize across various constituents. To a significant degree, children can then deduce basic aspects of their language.

Pro Drop

Romance languages, among many others, allow subject omission as in (14) (Haegeman 1991, Chomsky 1986) and are categorized "+Pro Drop," unlike English (15). Parameter setting of a language as (+) or (−) "Pro Drop" would direct children to this dimension of variation and allow cross-linguistic variation in a principled manner. If children set the Pro Drop parameter, they can, to some degree, determine grammatical consequences by deduction. For example, expletive "it" subjects, as in "it is raining", may occur in non-Pro Drop languages.

14.   a. Ø ha telefonato
         b. Giacomo ha detto che Ø ha telefonato

15.   a. John has telephoned
            * Ø has telephoned
         b. John has said that he has telephoned
            * John has said that Ø has telephoned

4.2.1.2.5 Summary

UG provides the basis for a more comprehensive theory than the classic formulation of the LAD, i.e., one which relates linguistic theory to language development in real time.

a.   Recognizing the necessity for biological programming of initial linguistic knowledge, UG does not propose that specific language grammars are innate, only the universal architecture for language.

b.   UG does not deny that other cognitive components are necessary to language acquisition. It is one "specific component of LT $_{(H, L)}$ (Learning Theory of a human for language) (Chomsky 1975b, 28).

c.   UG does not deny the role of experience. It proposes that abstract linguistic principles interact with experience and allow children to go beyond the limits of actual experience.

d.   UG eliminates an "evaluation metric" of the form in the original LAD
        (Chomsky 1996, 171). Principles and parameters direct and constrain
        children's experience so that their interaction with the PLD can deter-
        mine a language.[10]

e.   UG allows us to bridge deduction and induction through *abduction*.[11]
        "Abduction" refers to the analysis of observed fact against explanatory
        hypotheses. A model including abduction recognizes the necessity for
        children to use the input with which they are presented, but allows that
        they do so in a guided way (by the Language Faculty), going beyond
        the limits of induction alone. Peirce exemplifies this form of inference
        in (16) (1955, 151).

16.   Abduction
          i. A surprising fact, C, is observed.
         ii. But if A were true, then C would be a matter of course.
        iii. Hence, there is reason to suspect that A is true.

4.2.2   Challenges to the UG paradigm

Given the armamentarium of a Language Faculty, we must still ask:
(a) what is the relation of children to the input data and (b) what is the nature of
development? How are UG "principles" applied, and "parameters" set? What are
the "primitives" of the Language Faculty, and how are they realistically applicable
to children's input data?

How can children acquire a grammar or set a parameter without having a
grammar by which to process the input data? If children are to use input, they must
be able to parse it. Perhaps "parser failure" is informative, e.g., if the parser fails, it
tells children that the data are not compatible with their hypothesis. Here children
are assumed to be "error-driven." However, are there not "inherent limitations on
children's parser" (Valian 1990, 144)? If parsing is deficited, how can children
attain useful data? If parsing is determined by a grammar for a specific language,
then how can children begin the process of using input data or deal with data from
another language in order to set a parameter?[12]

4.2.2.1   How does parameter setting work?

Researchers have attempted to identify sentences which reveal a
grammatical parameter setting for a language – i.e., "triggers."[13] Triggering
input is generally untrustworthy, however. For example, with regard to the Pro

---

[10] As Chomsky 1996 notes, if parameter values have "marked" and "unmarked" settings, this would
   constitute "a last residue of the evaluation metric" (213, fn. 6).
[11] Peirce 1901; Chomsky 1980, 14; Bever 1992; Deutscher 2002.
[12] Valian 1990, 122; Kapur 1994, Crain and Thornton 1998, Mazuka 1998 for discussion. If numerous
   parameters exist, how should this parameter setting be ordered and what consequences will
   parameter ordering have? (See Clark 1994.)
[13] Gibson and Wexler 1994, Frank and Kapur 1996, Fodor 1998.

Drop parameter, children acquiring a non-Pro Drop language like English may encounter sentences like (17b) in the context of (17a) (Valian 1990, 140):

17.   a. She's there day and night
       b. Ø Runs the place with an iron hand.

If children don't already know English is a non-Pro Drop language, how will they be able to recognize (17b) as a non-trigger sentence? The evidence in (18) is consistent with parameter setting of a left-headed language like English, given its VO order:

18.   The baby likes ice cream.

It is also consistent with a V-2 language, such as German or Dutch, where verb movement allows or requires the verb to appear in second position in some conditions.[14]

One approach to triggering postulates that children's experience may be a sample of total linguistic experience, one which presumably matches the assumed "simple" nature of children's data analysis. Everything can be "learned from main clauses (degree-zero learnability) plus a little bit," i.e., with data input that includes no embedding, or just "the front of an embedded clause" (Lightfoot 1994, 1989 and discussion). However, there is no independent, theory-neutral definition of the term "simple" (Sober 1975), nor any *a priori* way to determine what is "simple" for a child; such proposals must be subject to empirical testing.[15]

Another approach holds that the classic switch-setting mechanism should be modified so that parameters come preset to one value ("unmarked") over another ("marked"). Hyams (1986, 1987) proposed this approach to the Pro Drop parameter (chapter 9), instantiating a "markedness" theory in parameter setting.

19.   **Markedness**
       "Markedness" is often used to describe a distinction between most "natural"
       (unmarked) and more "unnatural"(marked) knowledge. "Marked"
       phenomena are often characterized as less frequent, or as representing
       exceptions, difficult to learn or learned later.[16]

Parameter markedness results in new questions. How and why do children in a non-Pro Drop language reset the parameter to a marked value?[17]

---

[14] See Fodor 1998 for an attempt to reduce the ambiguity of triggers; Tesar 1998, 131, for another example.

[15] This follows an earlier proposal that "degree 2 learnability" (two levels of embedding) would provide sufficient input for children to determine grammatical knowledge (Wexler and Culicover 1980).

[16] The concept of "markedness" also occurs in studies of language change. Although recognized as a "genuine linguistic phenomenon," this concept has been notoriously difficult to define. It often "rests on a basis, however ill-defined, of relative production and perceptual ease" (Thomason and Kaufman 1988, 26). In general, "markedness" is not explanatory in itself, but must be explained. See Pinker 1989 and Gair 1988 for explication.

[17] See Lust et al. 1994, Hyams and Wexler 1993, Hyams 1994; Mazuka, Lust, Wakayama and Snyder 1986, 1995; Valian 1994; Bloom 1990; Smith 1990.

Table 4.4 *Beyond triggering: approches to modeling children's use of input data*

A probabilistic model of parameter setting
Children's use of the data is probabilistic with regard to any particular utterance. Indirect negative evidence is consulted. Children are not error driven. "Noisy" or misleading data are not devastating (Kapur 1994, Brill and Kapur 1997).

Cue-based parameter setting
A "cue-based learner follows an ordered path and looks for patterns, not individual forms or sentences to match" (Dresher 1999, 63; Dresher and Kaye 1990). Cues become increasingly abstract and "grammar-internal" (64) over development.

Robust interpretive parsing/constraint demotion algorithm
In "Optimality Theory" (Tesar and Smolensky 1998), in lieu of parameters, linguistic constraints must be evaluated and ranked by children in each specific language. Children consult both underlying and surface aspects of utterances. Their relation to input is mediated by their structural analysis of these data.

Recent approaches move beyond a triggering model of children's use of input data, e.g., table 4.4.

One proposal is that the parameters of UG actually constrain and determine parsing and do so even before specific language grammars are fully acquired (Mazuka 1996, 1998; Mazuka and Lust 1990). Acoustic cues in the speech stream assist initial parameter setting.[18] Another approach investigates the possible interaction between a pragmatic "Principle of Relevance" with specifically linguistic knowledge in children's parameter-setting experience. Perhaps children can avoid mis-setting of parameters by ignoring "the irrelevant stimulus" (Smith 1990, 287).

4.2.2.2   A separate learnability module?

Parameter-setting models must also confront the problem that knowledge of language requires knowing what is impossible, although negative evidence is not directly available to children, as we have seen. One approach to this problem is to supplement the Language Faculty: "Some aspects of language and its acquisition seem better stated not in linguistic theory, but outside it, in, say, a learning module" (Wexler and Manzini 1987, 41), which would add non-linguistic principles to the Language Faculty. Angluin (1980) proposed a "subset principle" (SP) in inductive machine learning. She showed that if the classes of languages to be learned were ordered in subsets like figure 4.1, and if learners followed (20) and never changed their guess without positive evidence, then learnability could be achieved through inductive inference on the basis of positive evidence alone.

---

[18] See also Crain and Fodor 1985. See Frazier and Rayner 1988 for an independent proposal linking parameters and parsing in the adult grammar.

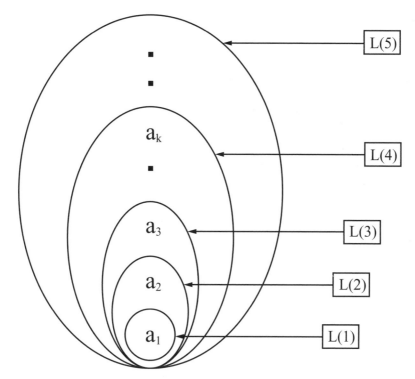

Fig. 4.1 *Languages in subset relation.*

20.   "If the learner begins by hypothesizing that the correct language is the
             smallest one" then the learner will not overgeneralize (Berwick 1985, 37,
             237; also 1982).

Application of the SP to natural language acquisition assumed that: (a) induction
is the basic mode of acquisition; (b) the relation of the input data to the grammar
in the mind of the learner is direct, simple and deterministic as it is in machine
learning; and (c) the relevant data are *extensional*, i.e., in figure 4.1 smaller sets
of sentences included in larger sets of sentences.[19] This proposal contrasts with
intensional approaches which propose that the grammar in the mind provided by
the Language Faculty (UG) restricts children's hypotheses.[20]

4.2.2.3   The nature of development

             Researchers also continue to debate the nature of real time develop-
ment in language acquisition, given a theory of UG.

---

[19] There is no necessary relation between size of language and restrictiveness of grammar, so these
   two approaches are not equivalent. (See Williams 1981a, Kapur et al. 1992, Lust 1986c, Wexler
   1993.)
[20] If parameters don't involve marked and unmarked settings, and don't provide an inclusion relation
   for sets of sentences generated in a language, then issues of extensional set size or of their inclusion
   relation need not arise. See chapter 11.

An instantaneous hypothesis

In one interpretation, UG principles would be instantly and continuously available to children, unchanging over time or with experience (e.g., Chomsky 1988, 73; Chomsky 1975b, 119). In the strongest form of this hypothesis, all developmental change in children's grammatical knowledge is denied.[21] Apparent differences between child and adult language are attributed to development in processing or performance, or to the effects of specific methodologies used to test child knowledge, not to change in grammatical knowledge itself. Children's knowledge (both UG and SLG, Specific Language Grammar) is assumed to match adults' at all times.[22]

Maturation Hypothesis (MH)

Another interpretation of the UG paradigm recognizes developmental change in children's grammatical knowledge. Some have argued that UG should be interpreted as "a genetic program (UG) guiding grammar growth" (Wexler 1999, 56; after Chomsky 1980, 245). UG should encode and determine developmental steps in the acquisition of grammatical knowledge.

21.   **Maturation Hypothesis**
        "This theory . . . does not assume that the formal principles available to
        children are constant through development. Rather, the assumption is that
        certain principles mature. The principles are not available at certain stages
        of a child's development, and they are available at a later stage" (Borer and
        Wexler 1987, 166).

Input would work differently at different times: "When maturation occurs, relevant positive evidence allows the reanalysis of . . . representations" (Borer and Wexler 1987, 166). Explanation for language development lies in brain development. UG is only fully realized at the end state.[23]

The Strong Continuity Hypothesis

Another approach, the Strong Continuity Hypothesis (SCH),[24] maintains UG as a model of the Initial State "prior to experience" and continuous throughout development. This SCH accords with a general "continuity assumption": "the null hypothesis in developmental psychology is that the cognitive mechanisms of children and adults are identical" (Pinker 1984, 7). Some versions

---

[21] Another interpretation of "instantaneous" holds only that the order of developmental stages is irrelevant to the end state.

[22] See Crain 1991, 1994; Hamburger and Crain 1982; Crain and Wexler 1999; Crain and Thornton 1998.

[23] While there is no question that maturation is involved in language acquisition in general, there is considerable debate regarding the MH, especially as applied to specific language grammar (SLG) knowledge (e.g., Lust 1999 and Wexler 1999) (chapter 9). Presently, theory of UG does not provide a specification of how UG should be fractionated over time or in what order. It does not provide an explanation for change from one stage of UG to another.

[24] Lust 1999, Boser et al. 1991, 1992, Whitman, Lee and Lust 1991 provide examples.

recognize and attempt to account for change in children's grammatical knowledge. Through a "Grammatical Mapping" paradigm, these locate grammatical development not in the development of UG, but in the development of Specific Language Grammar (SLG).[25]

4.2.2.4   Summary

Current approaches to a theory of language acquisition in a rationalist framework, having pursued a Language Faculty in the human species, now attempt to lay the foundations for a more comprehensive model of language acquisition which can be tested through empirical research. Current questions concern children's relation to the input, and the true nature of development of language knowledge.

4.2.3   Empiricist approaches to the study of language acquisition ▓

Empiricist theories (table 4.1) attempt to explain language acquisition without attributing to children abstract linguistic knowledge. Bates and MacWhinney (1989, 1987) propose a "Functionalism and Competition Model" (F&CM) of language acquisition, according with general "connectionist" modeling and with a "Language Making Capacity."[26] A "usage based account" hypothesizes that language acquisition is based on item by item imitative learning (Tomasello 2000a, b).

4.2.3.1   Functionalism and Competition Model (F&CM)

The F&CM proposes "that Universal Grammar can ultimately be explained without recourse to a special 'language organ' that takes up where cognition leaves off" (Bates and MacWhinney 1989, 7). It attempts to rectify a lack of emphasis on learning in the rationalist perspective. The source of knowledge is proposed to lie in the input, not in the mind. Discoveries are made "during processing of the structure inherent in the input" (Elman et al. 1996, 123). The mechanisms of acquisition lie in inductive learning. Language acquisition "is guided by form–function correlations" (Bates and MacWhinney 1989, 26). The relation between input data and the child mind/brain is direct and input-driven. The approach is founded on an interpretation of linguistic *functionalism*: "the forms of natural languages are created, governed, constrained, acquired and used in the service of communicative functions" (Bates and MacWhinney 1989, 3), which attributes a causal and reinforcing role to pragmatic factors in linguistic competence. Unlike earlier empiricist approaches, the F&CM does not deny that innateness is a prerequisite for the acquisition of language, although the term

---

[25] Lust 1999; Boser, Santelmann, Barbier and Lust 1995; Santelmann, Berk and Lust 2000. Several intermediate proposals have been entertained, e.g., Borer and Rohrbacher's 2002 "Full Competence Hypothesis".

[26] Slobin 1973, 1985; Elman et al. 1996 lay out the general perspective of this framework as "Rethinking Innateness."

is redefined; it now refers to "putative aspects of brain structure, cognition or behavior that are the product of interactions internal to the organism" (Elman et al. 1996, 23).[27] Symbolic rules, principles or constraints are replaced by physical architecture and its function. Symbolic representation of the input data and computation over this representation are bypassed initially, and only emerge as a "property of the network's functioning" (Elman et al. 1996, 124).

Language acquisition is viewed not as a cognitive problem, but as "a perceptual-motor problem" (Bates and MacWhinney 1989, 31). Language development involves "a process of emergence" from connections (Elman et al. 1996, 359), not a cognitive construction based on cognitive computation over symbolic representations; "something new seems to emerge from out of nowhere" (113) through a combination of biology and connectionism involving match and mismatch between inputs and outputs.

4.2.3.2   Connectionism

The term "connectionism" refers in general to a form of cognitive modeling wherein cognitive processing is represented in terms that can be implemented by a mechanical device, i.e., by a computer programmed to carry out the processes.[28] Current approaches to connectionism range widely in their technical properties as well as in their essential nature. Some explicitly recognize a linguistic symbolic component wherein "structured mental representations and structure-sensitive processes" are recognized (e.g., Smolensky 1991, 201). In contrast, Elman et al. (1996) adopt a strong form which does not recognize a linguistic symbolic component.[29]

The essential methodological assumption is: if computational modeling can be accomplished for the learning of a specific behavior, then it is possible that this modeling reflects the actual cognitive process involved in human learning and knowledge. In one classic example, Rumelhart and McClelland (1986) showed that it is possible for a computer learning network using "Parallel Distributed Processing" (PDP) to model a U-shaped developmental curve with regard to the acquisition of English verbal morphology (chapter 11). The network did not assume linguistic units such as "word" or "word stem" or "rules." Rather, "all that happens in learning is that the network compares its own version of the past tense form with the correct version provided by a 'teacher,' and adjusts the strengths of the connections and the thresholds so as to reduce the difference" (Prince and Pinker 1988, 195). In the machine's learning curve, "not only did overregularization of the past tense occur, but the patterns were strikingly like those that occur in children's speech" (Kolata 1987, 134). Rumelhart and McClelland conclude

---

[27] Elman et al. 1996 explicitly state "We are not empiricists" (357), presumably because they accept the necessity of some form of innateness in a comprehensive learning model.

[28] See Rumelhart and McClelland 1986, figure 7.3. MacWhinney 1989 views "connectionism" as a "way to formalize" the Functionalism and Competition Model (1989, 422). "Cue strength" is a "quintessentially connectionist notion" concerning "the weight on the connection beween two units" (Bates and MacWhinney 1989, 43).

[29] See Pinker and Prince 1988.

that "implicit knowledge of language may be stored in connections among simple processing units organized into networks" (1986, 195).

To date, this paradigm has not attempted to confront the full extent of grammatical knowledge which is involved in language acquisition (chapter 2); nor has it attempted to confront the indirect relation of the child to the data which we reviewed in chapter 3. Most principled and systematic aspects of syntactic knowledge appear to be considered merely as "structural eccentricities" (Elman et al. 1996; Smith 1997). This paradigm has recently begun to extend to other areas of language knowledge, e.g., vocabulary and syntax acquisition (Plunkett 1996), although no precise hypotheses are presented yet for why "mice do not become men, and vice-versa" (Elman et al. 1996, 361).[30]

Further evaluation of any particular application of the model will necessitate evaluation of the specific manipulations providing the machine with programming for its operation.[31] It will also require empirical validation of the psychological phenomena chosen for study.

4.2.3.3   Language Making Capacity

Slobin proposes a "Language Making Capacity" (LMC) (1973, 1985). Like Chomsky's Language Faculty, the LMC contains universal principles (table 4.5). Unlike the principles of Chomsky's Language Faculty, these are operating principles (OP), i.e., principles specifically for working inductively on the physical acoustic stimulus of a specific language to which children are exposed. The principles involve two types (i) Perceptual and Storage Filters and (ii) Pattern Makers (Slobin 1985, 1161). The early formulation of these operating principles in 1973 was generalized, specified and extended in 1985.

The formulation of an LMC considers that children must process specific language data in order to acquire a language, and takes a data-up approach. With a cross-linguistic approach, it attempts to provide "detailed examination of children's verbal interaction with others . . . across individual children and languages" in order to "begin to form hypotheses about the underlying capacities that may be responsible for language acquisition in general" (Slobin 1985, 1158). Accordingly, the LMC paradigm has provoked many studies of language acquisition across various languages and much description of the real time course of development in language acquisition. (See the Slobin 1985, 1992, 1997 collections.)

The OP propose that children are at first dependent on concrete, perceptually salient properties of the speech stream, presumably because this would aid their induction. Thus children are proposed to fail at first with abstract relations between underlying structures and surface strings, with order permutations, with empty

---

[30] The authors realize "we are probably going to have to work out a scenario involving constraints on architecture and timing" (Elman et al. 1996, 361).

[31] For example, Pinker and Prince 1988 argued that the original Rumelhart and McClelland results depended on the researcher changing the input to the computer in specific ways at specific times in order to result in the U-shaped developmental curve. They provided empirical evidence that in children's natural environment, irregular verbs are always more frequent.

Table 4.5 *The Language Making Capacity (LMC) (Slobin 1973, 1985)*

The **LMC** is "a set of procedures for the construction of language" (1985, 1159) "Clearly LMC must begin life with some initial procedures for perceiving, storing and analyzing linguistic experience, and for making use of capacities and accumulated knowledge for producing and interpreting utterances"

Two Types:
1. Perceptual and Storage Filters: "convert speech into stored data which the child will be able to use in constructing language" (1985, 1161)
2. Pattern Makers: "used to organize stored data into linguistic systems" (1985, 1161).

Operating Principles (1973)
A. Pay attention to the ends of words
B. The phonological forms of words can be systematically modified
C. Pay attention to the order of words and morphemes
D. Avoid interruption or rearrangement of linguistic units
E. Underlying semantic relations should be marked overtly and clearly
F. Avoid exceptions
G. The use of grammatical markers should make semantic sense

Supplemented and Developed in 1985
Perceptual and storage filters
OP (ATTENTION SOUND) Store any perceptually salient stretches of speech
OP (STORAGE: FREQUENCY) Keep track of frequency of occurrence of every unit and pattern that you store
OP (ATTENTION): END OF UNIT.
OP (ATTENTION): STRESS
OP (ATTENTION): BEGINNING OF UNIT

Pattern makers
Conceptual development provides starting points for grammatical marking (1985, 6).
Conceptual development determines order of emergence of grammatical forms (1985, 9).
Concepts are combined in grammatical morphemes according to semantic affinities.
Grammatical markers are placed according to principles of semantic relevance.

---

categories, with semantic synonymy or ambiguity, or with wherever "semantic relations" are not "marked overtly and clearly." Semantic bootstrapping appears to be assumed.

Bates and MacWhinney (1989, 72) propose that "work on operating principles can feed directly into work on the Competition Model," although this proposed relation is not spelled out. On the other hand, Slobin considers the growth of perceptual and information-processing capacities to be "operating in conjunction with innate schemas of grammar" (1985, 5). The OP could then be viewed as supplemental to UG principles.

Several, if not all of the proposed OP must be relevant to language acquisition in some way. However, the developmental status of the OP in language acquisition as "stand-alone" principles is not clear. Most of the OP apply to some linguistic "unit," e.g., word or syllable, which is assumed to pre-exist. Thus they assume that children have solved the initial foundations for language acquisition, i.e., discovering the units in the continuous speech stream (chapter 3). This would suggest that the proposed OP have an intermediate status in the course of language acquisition.

The operating principles are proposed to exist "in their initial form . . . prior to the child's experience with language" (Slobin 1985, 1160). The form of the OP themselves may develop over the course of language acquisition, presumably led by the development of grammatical knowledge of the language to be acquired. If so, the OP can be viewed as derivative of, or dependent on, grammatical knowledge. The OP must assume children's prior knowledge regarding the language being acquired. The original OP (A) could not have wide productive applicability to languages which are not suffixing, e.g., Algonquian languages such as Cree or Blackfoot or Inuktitut, or isolating languages such as Chinese. Similarly, "Universal (C3) must be limited to languages that rely heavily on word order to express semantics relations" (Slobin 1985, 1165, fn. 6). Grammatical markers in natural languages do not generally have a simple one-to-one relation to semantic or syntactic factors (cf. chapter 11). OP (A) was "derived from a widespread crosslinguistic finding that post-verbal and post-nominal locative markers were acquired earlier than pre-verbal and pre-nominal locative markers, holding semantic content constant" (Slobin 1985, 1164), but "holding semantic content constant" proves to be elusive; semantic content is language-specific to a significant degree. (See Slobin 1985, fn. 5 for discussion.)

Further analyses of the relation between OP and UG principles will be necessary to evaluate the status of OP and the LMC in language acquisition.

4.2.3.4 Usage-based item by item imitative learning

Another attempt to provide an alternative to the rationalist paradigm of a Language Faculty is currently being developed by Tomasello (e.g., 2000a, b).[32] Here, children at first "imitatively learn" specific "concrete linguistic expressions," without the aid of abstract specifically linguistic principles; then they use general "cognitive and social-cognitive" skills to "gradually and in piecemeal fashion" begin to "categorize, schematize and creatively combine these individually learned expressions and structures" (Tomasello 2000a, 156).

---

[32] Tomasello debates a particular interpretation of the Chomsky paradigm; he assumes that it proposes that "children have full linguistic competence at birth and need only to learn to express this competence overtly in performance" (2000a, 160).

In this view, early "grammars" are qualitatively distinct from those of the adult.[33]

Tomasello bases his proposal on certain observations of child language data and experimental studies intended to assess the nature of child language competence. In early periods of language acquisition, natural speech samples do not usually demonstrate complete verbal paradigms, nor wide numbers of verbs used across verb paradigms, but commonly evidence utterances with individual verbs used in particular instances, e.g., with certain inflectional endings and not others.[34] This result suggests to Tomasello that children follow an "item based" approach and he formulates a "Verb Island Hypothesis" wherein "each of their verbs forms its own island of organization in an otherwise unorganized language system" with no abstract categories (Tomasello 2000a, 157). Experimental studies tested 2–3 year olds on whether they take novel verbs and change them, e.g., from intransitive as in (22a) to transitive as in (22b).

22.   a. "The sock is tamming" (referring to a situation in which a bear was causing a sock to roll)
         b. "He's tamming the car" (e.g., when asked by the experimenter "What is the doggie doing" where the dog is causing the car to roll)

Tomasello and Brooks (1998) found that very few children produced a transitive sentence (like (22b)) with the novel verb in their experimental situation. This suggested to them that children lack abstract syntactic competence to generalize verbs to syntactic contexts they have not heard.

Since this model represents a relatively recent attempt to revive empiricist bases for language acquisition, its formulation is still at a preliminary stage. Before it can be fully evaluated as a viable and comprehensive alternative model, it must confront several issues: what are the specific "cognitive and social-cognitive" mechanisms by which children are proposed to convert from an individual item to a generalized pattern? What form do children's constructed "generalized patterns" take and how do they relate to the actual linguistic structure of the constructions? How do children determine "similarity" across constructions in order to know how to construct the proper generalization without linguistic analyses? What are the mechanisms by which children change from a non-grammatical to a grammatical form of knowledge? (In Tomasello's proposal, this developmental change occurs at about three years.)

Attaining critical evidence on this proposal will depend on resolving certain methodological issues and issues of interpretation;[35] and on consulting the wide amounts of data now available on early periods of language acquisition which

---

[33] Compare an earlier proposal of this type in Braine 1971 and discussion in Brown 1973 on "pivot grammars"; Pine and Lieven 1997.

[34] Pizzuto and Caselli 1992 for Italian, Gathercole et al. 1999 for Spanish.

[35] Since the intransitive–transitive verb alternation is lexically specific and language-specific, a conservative learner, either child or adult, may not be expected to overgeneralize this alternation on any account.

appear to document continuous, abstract and systematic knowledge in early language acquisition.[36]

4.2.4   Empirical rationalists and rational empiricists

Much research is conducted in intermediate paradigms. Jean Piaget, for example, offered an essentially rationalist perspective, documenting "the insufficiency of an 'empiricist' interpretation of experience" (Piaget 1980, 23) with a wealth of developmental evidence (see chapter 10). Work of the Roger Brown school and the Harvard Child Language Project generated countless discoveries regarding the structural knowledge of children at various points in development (see Brown 1973b, Kessel 1988). The work of Lois Bloom (e.g., 1970) provided the foundation for much current work on children's early grammars, as did that of Klima and Bellugi (1966).[37]

4.2.5   Resolving epistemological tensions

Before we attempt to formulate predictions for investigation of language acquisition, we must consider the meaning of the term "general learning mechanism." Since early learning theory, such as Skinner's, the concept has undergone revolutionary changes (e.g., Gallistel 1990).

Instinct to learn

We now know that it is not the case that any stimulus can be conditioned to any response at any time in any organism (see Marler in press a for review, and Garcia 1981). Organisms are guided in their learning "by innate learning predispositions" (Marler in press a, 4). "Organisms are preprogrammed to learn certain things in certain ways" (Gould and Marler 1987).

As Gould and Marler 1987 review, rats could not be trained to associate visual or auditory cues to foods that made them ill, although they could be trained to associate olfactory cues. Quail, on the other hand, could not be trained to olfactory or auditory cues, but could be trained to visual cues. Rats could be trained to press a bar to gain food, but not to avoid electric shock; they could be trained to jump to avoid shock, but not to obtain food. "[C]ues memorized, speed memorized and the way data are stored" has been found to be innate in bees, who in learning about flowers appear to hierarchically organize their cues. Different species of songbirds demonstrate different forms of interaction between biological programming and experience. The Eastern Phoebe produces the same song whether reared in isolation or not, in contrast to the Song Sparrow. Acoustic cues affect species differently: the male swamp sparrow focuses on the song syllable, while song sparrows with more complex songs focus on a number of syntactic

---

[36] See Fisher 2002 for discussion.

[37] Hirsh-Pasek and Golinkoff (1997) and Jusczyk (1997) provide overviews which explicitly attempt to integrate wide amounts of new research data across the paradigms we have formulated. Gomez and Gerken (2000) do the same with recent studies of infant artificial language learning.

features (Marler 1999a, 5–6; 1997; 1991). You "cannot design an organism that learns quickly and efficiently without including in the plans major elaborate genetic instructions that facilitate the emergence of certain kinds of environment-contingent variation in behavior" (Marler 1999a, 5). There is "no unitary learning process at the computational level of analysis" (Gallistel 1997, 82). Innateness, including specialized biological programming, is not dichotomous with learning, but may determine possible learning.

Our question then becomes not whether there is linguistically specific programming for natural language acquisition, but what it is precisely, and how it works; not whether some form of learning is involved in language acquisition, but how this works, and why it is so successful in the human species.

4.3   Toward a comprehensive and realistic theory of language acquisition

We may pursue a comprehensive theory of language acquisition by combining, not confounding, rationalist and empiricist foci.[38] We must integrate refined approaches to the study of what is termed "learning" with refined approaches to the formulation of the linguistic competence of the human species for language knowledge.

4.3.1   Predictions of a rationalist paradigm

If there were biological programming of a Language Faculty in the human species such as the theory of UG proposes, then children would:

a.   Perceive speech as special and discriminate language stimuli from other auditory and/or visual stimuli.
b.   Have an indirect relation to input data.
c.   Begin with some knowledge about the possible units in the continuous speech stream and impose these units from the beginning. Children would have a way to begin to "crack the code."
d.   Be constrained in language acquisition.
e.   Be "structure dependent" from the beginning, and attend to the parameters of language variation.
f.   Be creative, i.e., go beyond the stimuli, and not simply copy.
g.   Be systematic; acquisition would not be piecemeal or item by item.
h.   Show competence for abstraction from the beginning.
i.   Rapidly acquire new linguistic knowledge.
j.   Not offend universals shown across natural languages.
k.   Make errors, but these errors would not be a-grammatical in UG.

[38] Hirsh-Pasek and Golinkoff 1997 describe these as "inside out" and "outside in" theories respectively.

l.   In general, language acquisition would be characterized by modularity. Although the language faculty would interact with other cognitive modules, critical developments in language knowledge would occur to some degree independently of critical developments in general cognition.

4.3.2   Predictions of an empiricist paradigm

If there were no biological programming of a Language Faculty, and children had only general purpose learning mechanisms, then they would:

a.   Not treat speech or language stimuli differently from other physical stimuli.
b.   Have a direct relation to input data.
c.   Possibly perceive physical regularities in the input data although these may not be linguistically constrained.
d.   No universal linguistic constraints are predicted, e.g., no "structure dependence."
e.   Only randomly, if at all, attend to parametric variations of language.
f.   Not be creative but highly imitative; generalizations should only be based on perceived forms or analogy.
g.   Not build a grammatical system from the beginning; acquisition may proceed in piecemeal fashion.
h.   Proceed from concrete knowledge to more abstract knowledge only later. A discontinuous "tadpole to frog"-like development may exist.
i.   Have a long initial period of learning.
j.   Not evidence universal language principles or patterns.
k.   Critical developments in language acquisition should depend on critical developments in general cognition.
l.   Modularity of linguistic and other forms of cognitive knowledge should not be observed.

4.4   Conclusions

Current theories of language acquisition continue to reveal a tension between the philosophical paradigms of Rationalism and Empiricism. "Functionalist" and "usage based" models which have arisen in contrast to the leading Rationalist theory of Noam Chomsky reveal a central concern for understanding the interaction of children with the input data during the time course of language acquisition. This concern is also central to current studies of language acquisition in a linguistically based rationalist framework, although applications of these approaches differ critically in their proposals regarding the ultimate source and mechanisms of language acquisition.

Both rationalist and empiricist approaches must now be tested against the empirical facts of language acquisition. Neither logical analyses nor computational modeling alone will be conclusive in building a comprehensive theory of language acquisition unless supplemented by empirical research.

4.5   Supplementary readings

Wilson 1999 reviews philosophical paradigms in cognitive science; Pinker 2002 questions empiricist assumptions and Gardner 1985 provides general introduction to cognitive modularity.

For overviews of Chomsky's theory, see Smith 2004 and McGilvray 1999. Chomsky 1975b, 1986, 1988a, b, 2002 provide general introduction; Lasnik 2002 and Uriagereka 1998 review recent developments.

Hirsh-Pasek and Golinkoff 1996, chapter 2, and Foster-Cohen 1996 provide introductions to theories of language acquisition. Cook 1988 provides introduction to application of Chomsky's theory to language acquisition. For introductions to connectionism see: Elman et al. 1996; Fodor and Pylyshyn 1988; Hinton 1992; Kolata 1987; Lachter and Bever 1989; Marcus 1998; McClelland 2000; Prince and Pinker 1988; Ramsey 2000; Roberts 1989; Seidenberg 1994; Smith 1997.

For a survey of recent controversies in language acquisition see Cattell 2000. For debates regarding Chomsky's theory see a Special Issue of *The Linguistic Review* (Ritter 2002), including a lead article by Pullum and Scholz 2002 and reactions to it.

5   Brain and language development

5.1   Introduction

Both rationalist and empiricist perspectives on language acquisition make predictions regarding the nature of biological foundations for language knowledge. As we saw in chapter 4, Chomsky hypothesizes that the brain predetermines how language knowledge is acquired, and represents this knowledge as distinct from other cognitive knowledge, i.e., as modular.[1] In contrast, for empiricist perspectives, "distributed" representations of language knowledge in the brain are hypothesized to resemble "the organization of neural nets" (Bates and MacWhinney 1989, 33).[2] Both predictions provoke us to look carefully at brain structure and function, although neither paradigm yet precisely predicts how brain development underlies language development.

Such predictions may soon be addressed more precisely through recent technical advances in brain imaging methodologies. (See ERP, fMRI, MEG and electrical stimulation mapping in Glossary.) These new instruments will add evidence to decades of research on language pathologies caused by various forms of brain injury and allow us for the first time to study the normal brain engaged in normal language functions.[3] Some can be extended to the study of normal children (e.g., Posner et al. 2001; Molfese et al. 2001; Casey 2002).

Lenneberg 1967 laid foundations for scientific study of this area. His behavioral observations of "Developmental Milestones in Motor and Language Development" (appendix 1) implied a biological and maturational component in language development, similar to motoric development. Lenneberg began to formulate hypotheses in this area which could be subjected to empirical tests, although his premise was that in the search for "the biological basis of language capacities . . . the exact foundations are still largely unknown" (1967, viii).

In this chapter, we will briefly review fundamental discoveries regarding organization of language knowledge in the adult brain, identifying major

---

[1] See also Gazzaniga 1988, 448. Although Chomsky proposes that language knowledge is modular, this does not make specific predictions about brain organization, i.e., does not require any specific physical localization (Chomsky 1999, 39; 2000).

[2] Rumelhart and McClelland 1986; Bates and MacWhinney 1989; Elman et al. 1996; Hinton 1992, 145.

[3] See Kandel and Squire 2000, Baraniga 1997 and Toga and Mazziotta, 1996 for recent reviews.

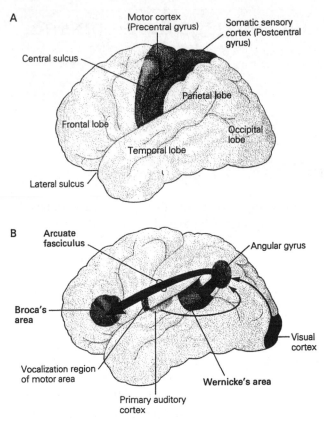

Fig. 5.1 *Major areas of the cerebral cortex*
From: Kandel, Schwartz and Jessell (eds.) (2000).

structure-function correlations, and then seek parallel discoveries regarding children. Research in this area is an exciting frontier, though fraught with disputes and uncertainties.[4]

5.2   The human brain

"... the most complex structure in the known universe."   (Fischbach 1992 and 1993, 2)

Size alone cannot account for the linguistic power of the human mind, since whales and elephants have large brains but not language as we know it. "The liver probably contains 100 million cells, but 1,000 livers do not add up to a rich inner life" (Fischbach 1993, 3, 1992; Hubel 1979).[5] We must investigate the

---

[4] To a large degree, linguistic and neuroscience expertise have not yet merged in this area.

[5] Adult brains typically weigh approximately 3lbs.

Table 5.1 *The human brain.*

i.   Estimated 10^{11} (a hundred billion) neurons in cerebral cortex; "about the same order of magnitude as the number of stars in the Milky Way" (Fischbach 1993).

ii. Approximately 100 trillion synapses, the mechanisms by which neurons communicate; reflect "structural and functional specialization between neurons where transmission occurs (excitatory, inhibitory, or modulation) using neurotransmitter substances" (Hendelman 2000, 235; Fischbach 1993).

iii. Electrical events by which neurons communicate occur in milliseconds, faster than available brain imaging techniques can measure.

iv. Thousands of synapses on each cell. One neuron generally is fed by hundreds or thousands of other neurons; it, in turn, feeds into hundreds or thousands of still other neurons.

v.   Both electrical and chemical signaling. Neurons generate "action potentials" (impulses) which move like waves down the cell's axon "and are converted to chemical signals at synapses" (Fischbach 1993, 6).

organization of the human brain in order to explain the capacity of the human species for language.

5.2.1   Cerebral cortex

The cerebral cortex, or "neocortex," the grey mantle which covers the two hemispheres of the brain, is the latest development in brain evolution; it is where higher cognitive functions, including language, are largely centered (Fischbach 1993, 5), although subcortical structures may also be implicated. Its hills and valleys create a convoluted appearance and allow increased space for cells. Its critical lobes (frontal, parietal, temporal and occipital) are separated by noticeable *sulci* (grooves) and *gyri* (crests) which provide reference points. For example, the Sylvian Fissure (lateral sulcus) divides the temporal lobe from parietal and frontal lobes (and centers the "perisylvian area"). The organization of language involves all the lobes and all their sub-areas.

In general, ". . . the brain is made up of discrete units rather than a continuous net" (Fischbach 1993, 3); it is "not made up of interchangeable parts" (1993, 4). The functioning brain involves multiple distinct sub-systems with ". . . precision and overall stability of the wiring diagram" (1993, 9). Distinct neural pathways for certain "higher functions have been precisely mapped" (Kandel et al. 2000, 9; Ojemann 1991).

Although distinct areas of brain subserve distinct functions, when one "functional region or pathway is damaged, others may be able to compensate partially for the loss, thereby obscuring the behavioral evidence for localization" (Kandel et al. 2000, 9). The term "plasticity" generally refers to this ability of various regions of the brain to assume functions as a result of experience when other regions have been damaged or lost.

Table 5.2 *Brain development.*

i.	"By the time a child is two years old, the brain will have more than tripled its mass and come close to its full size" (Springer and Deutsch 1993, 233).
ii.	The corpus callosum "is present at birth but appears disproportionately small in cross section when the brain of a newborn is compared with the brain of an adult" (Springer and Deutsch 1993, 243, after Wittelson et al. 1988).
iii.	Different cortical areas develop at different rates, e.g., aspects of frontal cortex are delayed (Huttenlocher et al. 1993, 1997)
iv.	Myelinization continues across two decades.
v.	Connections between neurons multiply in the form of synapses. Synaptogenesis peaks between 9 and 24 months of age, reaching approximately 150 percent of that of the human adult.
vi.	Synapses are lost; synaptic density begins to decrease after 2 years of age (e.g., Bourgeois et al, 1994; Huttenlocher 1990). Cell death begins in gestation and continues across the life span (Bates et al. 1992).
vii.	Fundamental frequency of brain waves is slower in children than in adults, increasing with development.
viii.	Metabolic activity of the human brain peaks around 48 months of age (Chugani et al. 1987).
ix.	Although it has been long assumed that no new neurons were formed after birth, some new research in the last few years is challenging this view (Kempermann and Gage 1999).
x.	Aspects of brain function for language may change with experience, e.g., acquisition of a second language. Brain maturation and language experience are confounded throughout development (e.g., Ojemann 1983).

5.2.2   Brain development

In general, the basic structure of the brain is in place at birth. Most, if not all, neocortical neurons and their location are generated prenatally, although cortical development is now under intense scrutiny (Rakic 1988, 1993, Huttenlocher 1993, Galaburda 1995, Johnson 1993).

General developmental changes are summarized in table 5.2. At present, we have no way of linking this set of general facts regarding brain development to specific facts regarding language development. We thus must look to more general correlations regarding the organization of brain and language.

5.3   Cerebral dominance

The two cerebral hemispheres are neither structurally nor functionally equivalent.[6] The organization of language in the brain involves asymmetric

---

[6] The LH is generally larger and longer than the right (particularly the temporoparietal, or TPT, area which may be ten times larger). Temporal lobe cortex (*planum temporale*), central to Wernicke's area, is asymmetrically larger in the LH in most adults (Galaburda 1995 and Eckert et al. 2001

relation between right and left hemispheres (Gazzaniga 1989 and 1998; Baynes and Gazzaniga 2000).[7] In the adult brain, the most fundamental set of structure–function correlations which has been discovered involves hemispheric dominance, or lateralization. In most individuals, the left hemisphere (LH) is dominant for language.[8]

1.   "Cerebral lateralization or cerebral dominance refers to the differential proficiency of the cerebral hemispheres for the acquisition, performance and control of certain specific neurological functions" (Galaburda et al. 1985, 1).

Damage to the left hemisphere often provokes *aphasia* (dysfunction in, or loss of, language due to neurological damage) whereas right-side damage does not (Springer and Deutsch 1993, 1). Direct electrical stimulation of the cortex confirms this (Penfield and Roberts 1959; Ojemann 1983, 1991).

In the dichotic listening task, subjects – presented with competing stimuli in each ear – are frequently more successful at reporting speech presented to the right ear (a "right ear advantage", or REA, with assumed privileged left hemisphere projections) than non-speech stimuli presented to the left ear. In the Wada test (anesthetization of one hemisphere by injection to the carotid artery), anesthetization of the left hemisphere interferes with language performance, e.g., counting out loud, while anesthetization of the RH may not (Iaccino 1993). Electrical stimulation studies provide converging evidence.[9]

In patients who have undergone commisurotomy, the left hemisphere may provide productive verbalization regarding a visual stimulus, such as describing "a woman talking on the telephone." In contrast, the right hemisphere may be mute; patients deny that they have seen anything, are unable to describe verbally what they have seen at all, or are extremely deficited in verbalization. At the same time, the right hemisphere (RH) may be able to draw (with the left hand) what has been seen, pick it out manually from a group of objects, or write the word for what has been seen, seemingly unconscious of why. The RH appears deficited in using grammatical factors, e.g., passive sentence operations, in comprehension.[10]

"Split brain" patients who, with their RH alone, write words for what they have been shown, do reveal some access to language, at least to vocabulary. Some can pick the name of an object presented to the RH from a list of names read aloud and the isolated RH of most split brain patients can comprehend written words (Baynes and Eliassen 1998; Beeman and Chiarello 1998, 4). RH

---

for review). There is greater LH branching in dendritic neurons. The Sylvian Fissure is longer and straighter on the left side (Geschwind and Galaburda 1987; Galaburda 1995).

[7]   Anatomical evidence is not explanatory in itself; we must know how anatomic asymmetries relate to functional asymmetries. Some aspects of the anatomical asymmetries are not uniquely human (e.g., Galaburda et al. 1985; Gannon et al. 1998). Some cellular differences across the hemispheres may exist (e.g., Buxhoeveden 2002).

[8]   Mayeux and Kandel 2000; Dronkers, Pinker and Damasio 2000.

[9]   Hirsch et al. 2000; Hirsch, Rodriguez-Moreno and Kim 2001.

[10]   Sperry 1961 and 1968, Gazzaniga 1989 and 1995b, Baynes and Gazzaniga 2000 for review.

language comprehension has been reported to be less impaired than production.[11] LH dominance for language does not mean that the RH is not involved at all.[12]

In brain damaged patients with localized right hemisphere injury, discourse-based uses of language have been damaged even when basic phonological and syntactic abilities remain intact. Deficits may include failure to integrate information across sentences, integrate information in making inferences, follow a storyline in a narrative, or fully understand jokes, sarcasm or prosody.[13]

5.3.1   Handedness

About 90 percent of individuals are right handed, suggesting left hemisphere control of motoric activity.[14] Does this mean that LH dominance for language is explained by motoric dominance? Left-handed individuals provide a critical population here. To test for the possibility of right hemisphere dominance for language in left handers, Satz 1979 surveyed the frequency of observed aphasia after unilateral brain damage in left handers compared to right handers. Cerebral dominance for language among LH individuals was estimated in (2):[15]

2.   **Estimated cerebral dominance for language among left-handed individuals**

Bilateral	LH	RH
.70	.15	.15

We conclude that strong right cerebral dominance "either does not exist or is rare . . . and in left handed, cerebral dominance for language is either left-sided or bilateral" (Geschwind and Galubruda 1987, 6).[16] Handedness and left-hemisphere dominance for language are to some degree independent.

5.3.2   Sign language

LHD (Left Hemisphere Damaged) signers perform more poorly on a number of linguistic measures (naming, fluency, comprehension of isolated

---

[11] Sperry, Gazzaniga and Bogen 1969; Baynes and Gazzaniga 1988 summarize RH language in commisurotomy patients.

[12] Some recovery of RH language production over time has been reported (Baynes and Gazzaniga 1988; Baynes et al. 1995b).

[13] Brownell et al. 1986; Wapner, Hamby and Gardner 1981; Beeman 1993; Joanette, Goulet and Hannequin 1990; Bloom et al. 1996; Calvin and Ojemann 1994, 65; Brownell and Stringfellow 1999; Beeman, Bowden and Gernsbacher 2000; Calvin and Ojemann 1994, 74; Milner 1958; Zaidel 1994.

[14] "Handedness" is complex and multifaceted (Peters 1995).

[15] Sodium amobarbital testing "has shown that over 95 percent of right handers have speech localized to the left hemisphere, with 70 percent of left handers showing the same pattern. Of the remaining 30 percent, most show evidence of bilateral speech representation" (Springer and Deutsch 1993, 137). Dichotic listening tasks "also suggest that the majority of left handers (a smaller majority than is the case for right handers) are left-hemisphere-dominant for language" (Peters 1995, 199).

[16] Mayeux and Kandel 2000, 691; Peters 1995; Penfield and Roberts 1959.

signs) when compared to RHD signers; at the same time, they frequently demonstrate competent motor control for non-linguistic gestures with hands and arms.[17] This confirms that left hemisphere dominance for language reflects linguistic knowledge, and not motoric dominance, oral production or auditory reception alone.

5.3.3   Development

Lenneberg hypothesized that cerebral dominance for language did not characterize the initial state of children, but developed gradually from about age two, complete only at puberty. This hypothesis accorded with suggestions (e.g., Penfield and Roberts 1959) that there was a "critical period" for language acquisition, which terminated about the time of puberty.[18]

3.   **Equipotentiality Hypothesis**
        "At the beginning of language development both hemispheres seem to be
        equally involved; the dominance phenomenon seems to come about through
        a progressive decrease in involvement of the right hemisphere . . ."
        (Lenneberg 1975, 15)

        ". . . lateralization is apparently a gradual process of differentiation
        (functional specialization) concomitant with brain maturation . . . As the
        growing child becomes capable of finer and finer intellectual operations
        (Inhelder and Piaget 1964) both structural and functional specializations
        occur in the neural substrate that polarize activity patterns, displacing those
        instrumental for language to the left and others, such as those involved in
        nonverbal processes, to the right" (Lenneberg 1975, 13)

Early clinical observations, which provided the basis for this hypothesis, suggested that there was similar incidence of aphasia from injury to either left or right hemisphere in childhood, relatively infrequent aphasia in the child, and a transitory nature of infant aphasia.

Current evidence, however, suggests that the Equipotentiality Hypothesis cannot be maintained in its strong form. Although there is some development in cerebral dominance, and remarkable recovery abilities have been noted in children, the child brain initially appears to involve hemispheric asymmetry. In this way, it is comparable to the adult brain and biological foundations for language development are consistent with the adult's.[19] Anatomical asymmetries characterize

---

[17] Hickok, Bellugi, Klima 1996 and 2001. RH damage can result in severe visuo-spatial disruption, but leave sign language intact. The Wada test (amytal injection) to the LH of a hearing signer resulted in aphasia in both English and ASL (Damasio et al. 1986). Studies are now investigating RH involvement in ASL . Like RHD hearing patients, RHD deaf show trouble with discourse organization (Hickok et al. 1999).

[18] Whether there is a critical period and whether cerebral dominance exists initially are to some degree independent questions.

[19] Early clinical observations were collected prior to antibiotics and may have involved spreading of injury or infection beyond initial lesion sites.

the newborn infant and the fetus;[20] functional asymmetries appear early.[21] Infants show a larger response in sucking (at about fifty days) with dichotic presentations of words to the right ear[22] and in heartbeat (at three months) (Best 1988). Infants as young as four days show a right ear advantage for syllables and a left ear advantage for musical sounds (Bertoncini et al. 1989, Corbalis 1991). There is some evidence of greater left hemisphere activity for speech sounds, and greater right hemisphere activity for nonspeech (noises, piano chords) in one-week to ten-month olds (Molfese et al. 1975). Dichotic listening tests with toddlers (as young as three years) have also shown a right ear superiority for speech.[23] In four-month-old infants, evoked potential recording confirms that "specialized modules are present within the auditory cortex very early in development" (Dehaene-Lambertz 2000, 449). Functional magnetic imaging suggests "precursors of adult cortical language areas" in infants three months old (Dehaene-Lambertz et al. 2002, 2013). In neuroimaging studies, infants (two to three months) listening to a female reading a children's book in their native language (French) showed activation of left hemisphere areas of the cerebral cortex, similar to adults, suggesting that a "preconstrained network" of cerebral organization is in place early to structure the course of language acquisition.[24]

Five to six-month-olds link production of sounds with their auditory perception (chapter 8) and may do so in a manner linked to the LH. Infants presented with videos of a woman articulating sounds, which were sometimes synchronized with an auditory stimulus and sometimes not (a woman's face articulating "lu lu" or "ma ma" was paired with either matched or mismatched sounds; figure 5.2), were able to recognize the intermodal match, looking significantly longer at the video where the woman's articulation matched the sound heard. They did so predominantly when looking at a right-sided video, suggesting a "predisposition of the LH to recognize the sensorimotor connections between the auditory structure of speech and its articulatory source" (MacKain et al. 1983, 1348). Videotapes of six- to twelve-month-old babbling showed greater left hemisphere control of babbling than of other sounds, with greater asymmetric mouth opening (favoring right side) during babbling (Holowka and Pettito 2002).[25]

[20] Eckert et al. 2001; Galaburda 1995; and Springer and Deutsch 1993, 238 for review. Chi, Dooling and Gilles 1977; Molfese, Freeman and Palermo 1975; Witelson 1977; Stiles 1998; Mehler and Christophe 1995 and Stromswald 2000 for review; Corbalis 1991, 301; Thatcher et al. 1987.

[21] Segalowitz and Berge 1995; Segalowitz and Gruber 1977.

[22] Entus 1977, cf. Vargha-Kadem and Corballis 1979.

[23] Springer and Deutsch 1993, 240; Corbalis 1991, 285. Additionally, "[i]nfants as young as seventeen days on average grasp objects for a longer time with the right hand than with the left (Caplan and Kinsbourne 1976; Hawn and Harris 1979), and the right arm tends to be more active than the left during the first three months of life (Hiscock and Kinsbourne 1995; Springer and Deutsch 1993, 239, Corbalis 1991, 284–285).

[24] Dehaene-Lambertz, Dehaene, Hertz-Pannier 2002; Souweidane et al. 1999. See also Molfese et al. 2001, Muller et al. 1998.

[25] Recent fMRI imaging studies have linked temporal lobe "planar asymmetry" to verbal ability, including phonological awareness skills, in eleven-year-olds (Eckert et al. 2001). Absence of early (twenty-eight to thirty months) asymmetry of ERP (with greater activity in the LH for responses to familiar words) may predict language delays observable at forty-two months (St. George and Mills 2001).

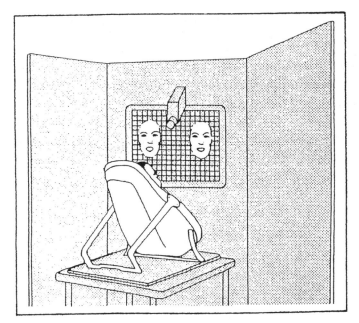

Fig. 5.2 *Infants' cross-modal speech perception*
Source: Kuhl 1987, fig 12.12, p. 380. "The special-mechanisms debate in speech research: Categorization tests on animals and infants." In Stevan Harnad (ed). *Categorical Perception* (Cambridge University Press), 355–386.

Research since Lenneberg has challenged many of the original observations which initiated the Equipotentiality Hypothesis. Given brain injury, aphasic symptoms occur in children aged two to fifteen years.[26] Although they may subside more quickly in children than adults, and clinically observed recovery may be remarkable, more subtle long-term deficits may result. Recovery is hardly ever complete.[27] Frequency of aphasia, given similar cortical lesions, is comparable between children and adults (Hecaen 1983; Eisele and Aram 1995 for review). Age at time of lesion is not a consistent predictor of recovery. Acquired aphasia occurs in children with left hemisphere damage with greater frequency than in those with right. In sixty-five children aged two to fourteen years, 73.5 percent of those with left-sided lesions suffered aphasia, compared to 6.9 percent of those right handed with right sided lesions (Woods and Teuber 1978).

Many studies of hemispherectomy have suggested an advantage of the left hemisphere (right hemispherectomy) in child language development.[28] A survey

---

[26] In "acquired aphasia," disorders of language due to cerebral lesions are acquired after (some or all) language has been acquired. Most common symptoms include mutism (often temporary), simplified "telegraphic" syntax, word finding difficulties, paraphasias, and reading and writing disorders.

[27] Fabbro and Paradis 1995; Woods and Carey 1978; Dennis and Whitaker 1976 and 1977; Aram et al. 1986.

[28] Stark et al. 1995. The right hemisphere has been found to support the development of some productive language in children, although this may never be fully normal (Stromswald 2000; St. James-Roberts 1981). Several variables confound comparison of adult and infant, including

of forty-three hemispherectomied children confirmed that left hemidecortication resulted in significantly lower "spoken language ranks" on children's spoken language several years postoperatively (Curtiss et al. 2001).[29] Dennis and colleagues argued that the RH does not support as complete a development of language knowledge as the LH especially when complex syntax is involved.[30] Three nine- to ten-year-olds (one right hemispherectomy, two left) did not differ in discrimination and articulation of speech sounds, or in producing and discriminating words. Left hemispherectomy children could accurately judge semantic anomalies, e.g., (4).

4.   My favorite breakfast is radios with ice cream

However, only the right hemispherectomy children gave correct grammaticality judgements on sentences like (5) or (6) which involve syntactic operations of word order related to the passive voice in (5) or embedding in (6). Dennis and colleagues concluded that the two hemispheres are not equivalent substrates for language acquisition, particularly syntax acquisition.

5.   a. *I paid the money by the man
         b. *I was paid the money to the lady
         c. I was paid the money by the boy

6.   a. Touch the yellow circle after you touch the blue circle
         b. Touch the yellow circle with the blue triangle

Linguistic analyses of speech of eight left and five right hemispherectomies (ranging from four to seventeen years old at testing) confirmed that left hemispherectomied children had greater error rates on syntax including inflection, e.g., (7), than did right hemispherectomied. Left hemispherectomies showed problems with auxiliaries, while right hemispherectomies were "almost error-free" in auxiliary use (Curtiss and Schaeffer 1997).[31]

7.   me go home (SM, aged 9.2, surgery at 4.0)
         I not tell a story (GG, aged 8.0, surgery at 6.2)

high post-surgery morbidity rate for adults and more limited recovery time (St. James-Roberts 1981).
    The study of hemispherectomy is complex, given differences in etiology (e.g., varying nature of prenatal or postnatal pathology), age of operation, and/or of seizure onset, as well as other experiential variables. Few studies have provided precise linguistic tests and analysis of language knowledge and processing before and after hemispherectomy. Most studies apply standardized tests of language knowledge which are descriptive of overt behaviors, e.g., single words or word combinations, often based on parental reports. Here "normal" language development generally refers to lack of clinical features (Curtiss, de Bode and Mathern 2001 provide review based on a survey of forty-three cases; St. James-Roberts provides interpretive critique).

[29] For hemispherectomies with developmental or prenatal etiology, the trend was in the same direction, although not significant.
[30] Dennis 1983, 198; Dennis 1980; Dennis and Kohn 1975; Dennis, Lovett and Wiegel-Crump 1981; Dennis and Whitaker 1976 and 1977; Hiscock and Kinsbourne 1995, 551.
[31] Two of eight left hemispherectomied children (one with early surgery, one with late) were striking exceptions, showing significantly correct inflection, and every child in the left hemispherectomied group, except one, used at least some correct inflection.

In studies of unilateral focal hemispheric damage,[32] LH lesions are linked to particular syntactic deficits in children (especially evident in production), and to delays in first word production and word combinations. RH lesions are linked to lexical comprehension deficits and to subtle semantic deficits (Eisele and Aram 1993a, b, 1994, 1995). In a study of 276 children and adolescents (eight to twenty-five years) with left hemisphere lesions, Woods and Carey (1979) found deficits in comprehension of sentences with syntactic embeddings, e.g., (8), in left lesion subjects.[33]

8.   a. [The boy [that built the boat]] went in for lunch
       b. [My [father's [sister]]] is my aunt

In sixteen children after early right and left hemisphere unilateral lesions, those with LH lesions performed significantly worse than a control group when compared to those with RH lesions (Aram, Ekleman and Whitaker 1986). Production of sentences like (9) showed significant deficits in the LL (Left Lesion) group (Eisele and Aram 1995 and 1994).[34]

9.   a. [The elephant hit the lion] and [he patted the hippo]
       b. [The lion scratched the hippo] and [–was chased by the dog]
       c. [The dog [that licked the hippo]] patted the elephant

When children with focal brain lesions required computation of *presupposition* and *implication* in complex sentences, LH lesioned children made significantly more errors than RH lesioned. Deficit in syntactic computation correlated with LH lesion, while deficit in lexical computation correlated with RH lesions (Eisele, Lust and Aram 1998). Error types differed across the lesion groups (see chapter 10).

One child, Alex, was left hemispherectomied at 8.6 (after chronic seizures affecting the left hemisphere). In contrast to "deficited" language comprehension and near mutism before surgery, Alex began to speak ten months post-surgery. The authors suggest that "clearly articulated, well structured, and appropriate language can be acquired for the first time as late as age nine years with the right hemisphere alone" (Vargha-Khadem et al. 1997, 159). Although these results do confirm that language can be subserved to some degree in the RH, this case is inconclusive. There do not appear to be tests of the child's receptive comprehension prior to surgery or of syntactic knowledge such as in (5)–(9) either pre- or post-surgery.[35]

---

[32] As Curtiss et al. 2001 suggest, interpretation of these cases is complicated by the possibility that performance can reflect the damaged hemisphere, or combination of hemispheres, as well as the non-damaged hemisphere.

[33] The effects were linked to those who had experienced the injury after one year of age, and were "recovered aphasic."

[34] Tests of comprehension of complex sentences usually did not reveal significant differences between lesion subjects and controls.

[35] Recent imaging study of recovery from aphasia and dyslexia in another eight-year-old boy was found not to be explained by right hemisphere take-over of language, but by LH organization (de Bleser, Faiss and Schwarz 1995).

Now, developmental studies must be framed without assuming the Equipoten-tiality Hypothesis and with assumptions of preconstrained cerebral organization for language. One current approach deriving from Helen Neville's lab, using electrophysiological techniques such as ERP with young children across early language acquisition, tests a "neo Lenneberg" hypothesis; it may cohere with the evidence for early cerebral organization, but allow a role for experience.

10.   **A neo-Lenneberg Hypothesis** (Neville and Bavelier 2000; St. George and Mills 2001)
    ". . . it is likely that language-relevant aspects of cerebral organization are dependent on and modified by language experience" (Neville and Bavelier 2000, 91); ". . . language experience determines the development and organization of language-relevant systems of the brain" (93).

In support of this hypothesis, Neville's lab reports analyses of ERP recordings from infants and toddlers at 20, 28–30 and 36–42 months as they listened to func-tion and content words (chapter 9). They argue that initially these "are processed by similar brain systems, and that these systems become progressively special-ized with increasing language experience" (Neville and Bavelier 2000, 95).[36] Although a left temporal site reflected differentiation of known and unknown words when infant (16 months) ERPs were recorded, none of the known versus unknown word effects in infants under sixteen months was exclusive to the LH.[37] Although left hemisphere advantage for response to a phonetic contrast (ba/ga) has been found in young infants,[38] left hemisphere advantage for non-linguistic stimuli was also observed, suggesting that left hemisphere dominance may not be specific to linguistic stimuli.[39]

In summary, developmental studies reveal early hemispheric dominance con-tinuous with adults, and continuous cerebral organization for language. At the same time, aspects of brain organization develop. The exact nature of this devel-opment is the focus of current research.

5.4   Dissociation: localization within the left hemisphere

    Based on discoveries of a basic cerebral organization for language in the infant in terms of hemispheric dominance, we can now consider more precise aspects of language knowledge and more precise aspects of its biological representation in development, e.g., its "localization."

---

[36] Mills et al. 1993, Neville and Mills 1997; Mills, Coffey-Corina and Neville 1997. Behavioral research suggesting early differentiation of these categories (chapter 9) must be coordinated with these findings; also Shafer et al. 1998.
[37] Molfese et al. 2001; Segalowitz and Berge 1995 provide review.
[38] Dehaene-Lambertz and Dehaene 1994; Dehaene-Lambertz 2000.
[39] Different neuronal components were involved in responses to linguistic and non-linguistic stimuli within the left hemisphere.

Table 5.3 *Examples of classical aphasia types: dissociations of components of language knowledge.*

	Clinician: What happened?
Broca's Aphasia	*Patient*: The brain is- see . . . headaches . . . first
Berko Gleason and Ratner 1993a, b	
	Clinican: Your baby?
	Patient: Yeah . . . [trIsm nts], uh one year ago . . . . s- Chrismonts day . . . died
Wernicke's Aphasia	*Patient*: I got it in the- in the- in the brain and they him
Berko Gleason and Ratner 1993a, b	him in here and they hit him over here and this one here, I figure the next time they hit this will knock this off [unintelligible].
	Patient (attempting to say "cushion"): "Oh, uh, uh,
Apraxia	/chookun/uh, uh, uh, /dook/ I know what it's called. It's
Dronkers 1996, 160	c-u, uh, no, it's, it's /chook/chookun/no"
	Patients with apraxia of speech do not consistently articulate words correctly, and they struggle for correct pronunciation.

11.   *Localization*
         Determination of restricted cortical areas which subserve specific
         components of language knowledge.

As we have seen, language knowledge involves several components corresponding to several levels of representation, which must be integrated (figure 2.1).
Processing of a word or a sentence involves complex orchestration of all of this
knowledge in very short time periods (Caplan 1992); this linguistic orchestration
must be constantly related to general cognition. The organization of this complex
computation in the brain is currently under investigation through several different
areas (5.4.1–5.4.5).

5.4.1   Language pathologies

Various components of language knowledge are revealed when they
are *dissociated*, i.e., when one component, (A), is lost, while another, (B), is
retained. Even stronger evidence is revealed when there is *double dissociation*:
(B) may also be lost, while (A) is retained. Such dissociations reveal separable
components of language knowledge; they provide clues as to how language is
built and which components are independent.

Numerous studies of aphasia have revealed that language knowledge and general cognitive knowledge, as well as various components of language, may become
dissociated when the brain is injured. Table 5.3 provides examples of several classical aphasia types (Caplan 1992, 1995; Goodglass 1993). They have evidenced

dissociation and *localization* of various specific language functions within the adult left hemisphere.[40]

5.4.2   Classic aphasias

Broca's Aphasia (agrammatism). In this aphasia type, patients with slow, labored speech and extreme difficulty in sentence construction often omit grammatical words and morphemes. The sentence, "no ifs ands or buts about it" is most difficult. This type of aphasia reveals a loss of structure building while other forms of language knowledge, e.g., vocabulary, are intact; basic aspects of general cognition may be maintained. Language loss is not simply due to motoric deficits; patients can often sing words that they can't speak or repeat. This syndrome reflects an injury in left anterior areas, including the inferior frontal lobe, adjacent to the motor cortex (see figure 5.1).[41]

Wernicke's aphasia (fluent aphasia). Patients talk fluently, even excessively, productively using sentence syntax. But their sentences make no sense. They produce circumlocutions and paragrammatisms (choosing wrong words or wrong phonemes within words). They cannot fathom the language they hear, although their hearing is unimpaired. Wernicke's aphasia is frequently observed in the elderly. In contrast to Broca's aphasics, these patients appear to have retained structure-building abilities for sentence syntax, but to have lost much comprehension and word level ability. This syndrome reflects injury in left posterior areas, in the rear temporal lobe, adjacent to the auditory cortex. (See figure 5.1.)

Both aphasias differ from apraxia (loss of motor ability).

5.4.3   Refining dissociations

Aphasic patients may show impaired processing of verb forms of words like "watch," "crack," or "dress," but not of their noun forms; other patients the reverse (Damasio and Tranel 1993). Patients with frontal lobe lesions may have more difficulty producing verbs, while those with temporal lobe lesions more difficulty with nouns. In one patient, ability to define "animals" was spared, while other categories were deficited; in another, the category of "animals" was disproportionately impaired (Hillis and Caramazza 1991).

Linguistic analyses of the speech of an Italian aphasic showed negligible *derivational* errors, but productive *inflectional* errors in morphology (Badecker and Caramazza 1989). Different neurological systems have been implicated for processing English regular and irregular verbs (Pinker 1991).

These "double dissociations" provide evidence for a modular and categorical representation of language knowledge. How does the brain organize this?

---

[40] Original studies in this area were conducted by observation and description of specific syndromes of language behavior, followed by post-mortem examination of brain damage.

[41] Broca's original patient suffered damage to a wide area including not only the lower rear portion of the frontal lobe, but portions of the parietal and temporal lobe (Calvin and Ojemann 1994, 43).

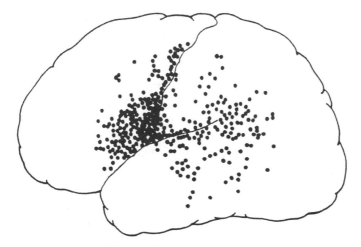

Fig. 5.3 *Mapping the left hemisphere*
Source: Wilder Penfield and Lamar Roberts 1959. *Speech and Brain Mechanisms* (Princeton, NJ: Princeton University Press), fig. vii-3, p. 122. Reprinted by permission of Princeton University Press.

5.4.4   Modeling the brain's organization

Aphasia studies led to a classic neurological model (Geschwind 1972, 5). Although this model has been extended and revised over time, it provides the foundation for more current modeling of brain organization for language.

5.4.4.1   The Wernicke Geschwind Model

According to the Wernicke Geschwind model (figure 5.1B), a word heard is processed in the Primary Auditory Area and passed to Wernicke's area, where it is understood. If a word is to be spoken, this is transmitted (by the connecting band of nerve fibers, the arcuate fasciculus) from Wernicke's to Broca's area, where its articulation is organized and passed to the motor area controlling muscles related to speech. When a word is read, the primary visual areas first pass it through the angular gyrus to Wernicke's area, where its auditory form and comprehension is aroused.

This model, based on focal localization of brain injury in each of several classic types of aphasia, proposed that a sensory–motor distinction and a comprehension–production distinction were fundamental to the brain's organization of language. Broca's aphasia was described as a production deficit; Wernicke's as a comprehension deficit. The model proposed a serial posterior–anterior process. It made a number of successful predictions regarding aphasia types (Geschwind 1972). In general, the classic Wernicke Geschwind model centralizes the perisylvian area, known through direct electrical stimulation to provoke interference with speech (arrest, slurring, repetition, anomia; figure 5.3), and generally coheres with results of direct cortical stimulation, concluding that "[L]anguage functions are discretely and differentially localized" in cortex (Ojemann 1983, 189).

5.4.4.2   Current modeling

Based on new brain imaging with normal subjects, new models of the brain's organization for language cohere with much of the Wernicke Geschwind model, but revise and extend it. The perisylvian area of the dominant left hemisphere remains central, and it continues to be recognized that "the cortical area dedicated to language is not unitary" (Ojemann 1991, 2281).

However, in contrast to the classic Wernicke Geschwind model, more recent research has revealed the brain's organization does not simply involve a production–comprehension or sensory–motor division. Broca's aphasia does not simply involve a deficit in language production, but comprehension is also deficited. When complex syntax was tested, a patient diagnosed with Broca's aphasia post-stroke, who demonstrated good vocabulary and good basic syntax in simple sentences, was unable to answer questions like "Who killed the leopard?" when given a sentence like (12) by Geschwind:

12.   The leopard was killed by the lion

The same patient had difficulty with interpreting the meaning of a sentence which had embedding, like (13). Broca's aphasics are deficited in certain grammatical knowledge necessary for language comprehension.

13.   That's [my [brother's [sister]]]

More sophisticated linguistic and psycholinguistic testing was necessary to discover these language deficits connected with brain injury (Zurif 1980 and 1983). Current research pursues an exact characterization of linguistic and processing deficits involved in different forms of aphasia.[42]

Current models of the brain's organization for language integrate cognitive psychology with neuroanatomy and physiology.[43] Using imaging methods, they provide more precise evidence on both localization and timing (within milliseconds) of various aspects of language processing during the complex orchestration of language use in real time (Posner 1997 and 1995). They find that incoming sensory stimuli leading to language production and comprehension are processed in more than one neural pathway (Posner et al. 1988). Different areas of left hemisphere cortex are revealed when *viewing* words than when *listening* to words,

---

[42] Broca's aphasia (Linebarger 1995; Mauner 1995; Grodzinsky 1990; Caplan 1992, 296f.); fluent aphasia (Caramazza, Papagno and Ruml 2000).

[43] Imaging studies allow researchers to begin to resolve indeterminacy surrounding interpretation of brain injury. For example, absence of a function which may correlate with a particular lesion site does not necessarily identify the location of the program underlying this function, any more than knocking out a light bulb on a car identifies the electrical system or program underlying the car's lighting (Ojemann 1991; Posner and Raichle 1994/1997; Caramazza 1997a; Caplan 1992).

although both visual and auditory pathways converge on Broca's area (Kandel et al. 2000, 14). Both parallel processing and serial processing are involved: accessing meaning activates an area of left frontal cortex as well as Wernicke's area (Posner and Raichle 1994, 115; Ojemann 1991, 2282). Current models consider parallel processes in addition to the serial processing involved in the Wernicke Geschwind model, and top–down as well as bottom–up processes (Posner and Raichle 1997, 111). Compartmentalization of perception and production is not the basis for brain organization of language. Cortical organization for language knowledge does not only involve sensory–motor components of language processing, but different knowledge components. The "functional role of the language-related areas is more accurately characterized in terms of linguistically relevant systems including phonology, syntax and semantics than in terms of activities such as speaking, repeating, reading or listening" (Posner et al. 2001, 297).[44]

Mapping language knowledge to its biological foundations is complicated by many factors.

5.4.5   Individual variance

No two brains and no two brain injuries are identical. Substantial individual differences exist in the exact localization of language functions within the dominant left hemisphere, within and around the perisylvian area, e.g., differences in localization of naming (Ojemann 1991). Factors such as attention and practice can affect patterns of cortical activity (Posner 1995).

5.4.5.1   Gender differences

Basic cortical organization for language does not appear to differ fundamentally across male and female brains; although some sex differences have been noted in electrophysiological tests of language processing.[45] Macaulay 1977 challenged the "myth of female superiority in language" on the basis of a review of the literature, concluding that "the evidence of consistent sex differences in language development is too tenuous and self-contradictory to justify any claims that one sex is superior to the other" (361). When infants between eight and twenty months were tested for their comprehension of words in a visual preference task, there was "no total difference in comprehension for boys and girls" (Goldfield and Reznick 1990, 163).[46]

---

[44] One example of how combining new imaging methods with sophisticated linguistic design of stimulus sentences and precise experimental methods has led to new precision in our understanding of the neural basis of sentence processing is Friederici 2002.

[45] Kimura 1992; Shaywitz et al. 1995; Segalowitz and Berge 1995.

[46] Tomlin 1999 reports that boys may be more likely to show behavioral problems connected with language disorders, and thus be identified more readily.

5.4.5.2   Multilingualism

Bilinguals, like monolinguals, demonstrate left hemisphere dominance for language knowledge.[47] But intraoperative direct cortical stimulation of bilinguals has suggested some dissociated sites across multiple languages, i.e., cortical stimulation at a particular point may interfere with naming in one language, but not the other (Ojemann 1983, 189), and aphasia types in multilinguals may dissociate languages (Paradis 1990). Study of the brain's representation of multiple languages and their acquisition remains a central area of research inquiry today (Kim et al. 1997).[48]

In summary, new brain imaging methods are empowering new more precise models for the brain's processing of language.

5.5   Brain imaging in language development

Many current brain imaging methods are not widely applicable to the study of children during critical periods of language acquisition (0–3 years),[49] making study of brain organization in development especially difficult. A small set of groundbreaking studies now exists.[50]

As a result, modeling biological foundations for language development still must rest to a large degree on behavioral studies such as those cases where language does not develop normally.

5.6   Language development and dissociations

Dissociations in language knowledge are revealed in disorders which affect language development.

5.6.1   Developmental disorders

The term "language disorder" (or developmental dysphasia) has been used to refer to "any disruption in the learning of a native language" (Bloom and Lahey 1978, 290). Such disorders may involve a breakdown in the (a) form,

---

[47] Vaid and Hall 1991; Paradis 1990.

[48] Researchers are attempting to evaluate the role of a learner's *proficiency* in their second language as well as other factors (Perani et al. 1996; Weber-Fox and Neville 1996; Perani et al. 1998). See Danesi 1994 and Obler and Gjerlow 1999 for reviews of neuroscientific second language acquisition research.

[49] FMRI is not generally applicable to infants awake at these ages, if simply because of the mechanical requirements, which require no movement.

[50] Molfese et al. 2001 provides review of electrophysiological studies of infants from birth through the first few years of age; see also Friederici and Hahne 2001; Neville and Bevalier 2000; Neville, Nicol, Barss and Forster 1991; Shafer et al. 2000; Neville and Mills 1997; Hahne and Friederici 1999; Friederici and Hahne 2001; Ojemann 1991; Ojemann et al. 1989; Shafer et al. 1998; Mills et al. 1997.

(b) content or (c) use of language, each leaving the others intact (see Bloom and Lahey 1978, 289–303).

5.6.2   SLI (Specific Language Impairment)

Specific Language Impairment (SLI) may occur, revealing the existence of language disorder or delay which is apparently uncorrelated with general cognitive deficits. Children showing SLI may develop normally in many ways but show linguistic deficits.

SLI children may have delayed language onset, articulation difficulties and problems with grammatical aspects of language such as tense and inflection, as in (14), or (15) where children acquiring Zulu overgeneralize "i" forms for noun class prefixes and subject agreement markers.

14.   *Samples of SLI from affected members of a three-generational family (linguistically mature adults in English) (Gopnik 1994)*
"Then the branch fall off"
"He did it then he fall"
"The boy climb up the tree and frightened the bird away"

15.   *Child at 2.7 years acquiring Zulu and evidencing SLI (Demuth and Suzman 1997)*
"It drinks"   iya-phuza   (adult target: I-ya-phuza)
"He drinks"   iya-phuza   (adult target: U-ya-phuza)

SLI covers a heterogeneous sample of deficiencies, which may explain why there are several hypotheses regarding its nature and etiology, ranging from hypothesized deficits in morphosyntactic knowledge including the representation of tense,[51] to deficits in auditory processing,[52] to specific syntactic deficit,[53] to more widespread grammatical deficit,[54] to specific cognitive deficits related to verbal knowledge, e.g., sequential verbal memory/processing.[55] The study of SLI promises to provide information on the biological foundations of linguistic knowledge as well as the organization of language knowledge. It is currently under intense scrutiny by researchers.

Several behavioral genetic studies suggest a familial and genetic component in SLI (5.9.2).[56] At least some SLI children "reflect aberrant functional lateralization for language, with language present either bilaterally or predominantly in the right hemisphere," and possible lack of normal hemispheric asymmetry anatomically (Stromswald 2000, 917).

---

[51] Gopnik and Crago 1991.   [52] Tallal et al. 1996.
[53] Van der Lely 1998; Bishop 1997; Rice and Wexler 1996.   [54] Demuth and Suzman 1997.
[55] Kushnir and Blake 1996; Stromswald 2000; Bishop 1997; Curtiss and Tallal 1991; Leonard 1998.
[56] Fisher et al. 1998; Gopnik and Crago 1991; Pinker 2001 for discussion.

5.6.3   Special cases

Double dissociation of language knowledge components is also revealed in a cluster of "special cases" which have been studied in some detail (Curtiss 1988).

Williams Syndrome

Children with Williams Syndrome (WS), a rare genetic disorder involving deletion of portions of chromosome 7, may show an unusual command of language, including exceptional vocabulary as in (16) and good general syntax as in (17). They also show surprising musical, visuospatial and number competence. At the same time, they may demonstrate low IQs and selected language deficits, e.g., gender as in the Italian example in (18) (Stromswald 2000).

16.   (From Reilly, Klima and Bellugi 1990)
       Asked to name all the animals they could think of:
       brontosaurus, tyranadon, hippopotamus, ibex, whale . . .

17.   (From Bellugi et al. 1992)
       "You're looking at a professional book writer. My books will be filled with drama, action and excitement. And everyone will want to read them"
       (age 15)

18.   (From Volterra et al. 1996)
       Target: "L'elefante *lo* tansporta" (the elephant carries *it*)
       Child: Points incorrectly to the picture where the elephant carries *her*.

Laura

Laura, diagnosed as mentally retarded, continuously functioned at a pre-kindergarten cognitive level. She could not read, tell time, give her age, count or do simple problem solving. Relational concepts such as same/different, big/little were problematic. Yet her language was well-developed syntactically, revealing complex sentences with multiple embeddings, e.g., (19), with passives and complex vocabulary, although this language was often inappropriate.

19.   (From Yamada 1990, 29)
       He was saying [that I lost [my battery powered watch [that I loved]]]. I just loved that watch.

In summary, with various aphasia types in the adult (5.4), various developmental language disorders (5.6) also reveal dissociations not only of language and thought in general, but also of various specific components of language knowledge.

5.7   Plasticity

A model of the biological foundations of language knowledge and development can be informed by study of the degree to which various language disorders can be overcome at various points of development.

The "ability of the brain to recover or compensate after injury early in life is often regarded as nothing short of miraculous" (Johnson 1994, 703). The neurological mechanisms for this "plasticity" in children as well as adults, its extent and its limits are now being pursued, both during their initial development and during their modulation later in life (Posner et al. 2001). We still do not fully understand the biological foundations of plasticity. "Environmental factors and learning bring out specific capabilities by altering either the effectiveness or the anatomical connections of existing pathways" (Kandel, Schwartz and Jessell 2000, 1277).[57]

5.8   Critical Period

Are there perhaps specific biological foundations for language acquisition which are linked to a particular period of time during brain development (a "critical" or "sensitive" period), analogous to some species of bird song acquisition? (e.g., Marler 1987).

20.   **Critical Period**
        A period of time with a distinct onset and offset during which experience
        can lead to learning by an organism; assumed to be innately programmed
        and irreversible.

Puberty has sometimes been posed as "offset" time for language acquisition, potentially linked to development of hemispheric dominance.[58]

Given the findings above (5.3.3), there is not a simple basis for a clear biological definition of a Critical Period for language acquisition in terms of hemispheric asymmetry and lateralization. To test the hypothesis of a critical period, researchers may look for cases where language experience has not occurred until post-puberty. Several relevant cases exist, such as Genie (Curtiss 1977).[59] These cases may involve extreme deprivation and are complex and confounded. Another form of evidence would involve adults acquiring a second language later in life.[60] In keeping with the hypothesis of a Critical Period for human language acquisition, some researchers have proposed that:

21.   ". . . adults no longer have access to UG for the second language acquisition
        process" (Schacter 1990).

None of these forms of evidence are conclusive, however.

[57] See Kolk 2000 for review of "multiple routes" to brain plasticity. There are limits to plasticity: Curtiss et al. 2001; St. James-Roberts 1981; Gazzaniga 1977.

[58] See Lenneberg 1967, 158; Penfield and Roberts 1959. There is considerable disagreement as to hypothesized time of offset. Lenneberg's early hypothesis does not refer to the ability to acquire language knowledge, but rather to the physiological components connected with "verbal behaviour" (1967, 158).

[59] Also: Chelsea (Curtiss 1977), Isabelle (Brown 1958), EM (Grimshaw et al. 1998).

[60] Mayberry 1993; Newport 1990. Hypothesis of a critical period for language acquisition is more complex than first appears. If the human brain is biologically programmed to include a Language Faculty, this may exist continuously once formed, as does the brain's biologically determined faculty for vision. A critical period is not necessary for bird song acquisition; some species can repeat the song learning process indefinitely as adults (Brainard and Doupe 2002).

5.8.1   Genie

The tragic case of "Genie" is important to these issues because of the relatively precise and extensive linguistic and cognitive analyses which it has received (Curtiss 1977, Curtiss et al. 1974).

Born in 1957, Genie experienced extreme deprivation beginning at about twenty months of age when she was confined to a dark room in the back of a house, harnessed to a potty seat by day and strapped in a sleeping bag in a caged crib at night, until she was discovered in 1970 at the age of 13.9. She was exposed to little or no auditory stimulation during confinement, and beaten when she made sounds. Genie's language experience during confinement was thus thought to be minimal to non-existent.[61] Her father barked and growled at her; her mother, going blind, was allowed minimal contact with her children. When discovered, Genie appeared to be about six or seven years old, weighed 59 pounds, was malnourished, incontinent, had difficulty standing and walking, could not chew solid food, and never spoke. She appeared to understand only a few words.

With physical nourishment and various attempts at personal, social and cognitive nourishment, Genie's physical development quite quickly brought her into puberty. Her general cognitive development reached the six- to eight-year level by the next year, when she was fourteen. At the same time, Genie's language development, particularly its syntax, appeared extremely deficited. After five months she began to use single words and her vocabulary grew quickly. Her first words were often cognitively complex, e.g., color and number words and superlatives. Two words were combined and then three to four words, e.g., (22); after about two years, attempted recursion appeared, e.g., (23).

22.   want milk
        Genie love Curtiss
        big elephant long trunk

23.   ask [go shopping]
        tell [door lock]

However, a complex of coherent linguistic deficits continuously characterized the syntax of Genie's language (table 5.4). The nature of these deficits suggests the absence or malfunction of a Language Faculty. They all reflect incompetence for relating a surface form with an underlying form, i.e., to relate distinct levels of representation in ways required by natural language (chapter 2). Accordingly, Genie's language lacks structure dependence; attempts at recursion in her language are deviant, as in (24a)–(24b).

---

[61] Little is known of Genie's history before her confinement. Medical records exist for a blood transfusion at birth during a Caesarian birth, and a normal birth rate of seven pounds. However, her mother reported that she did little cooing or babbling and showed certain developmental lags. Records also indicate a splint for congenital hip dislocation at four months, a weight of only fourteen pounds at six months, and only seventeen pounds at eleven months, and at fourteen months an acute illness involving fever, unresponsiveness and "possible retardation."

Table 5.4 *The case of Genie: a complex of linguistic deficits (derived from Curtiss 1977).*

- Word order problems
  Inability to deal with *word order variation* in production and comprehension
  "There are no rules permuting sentence constituents" (196)
- Failure with *question formation*; "where cracker" (163)
  No subject–aux inversion, as in "Do you have a cracker"
- No *contractions*
- No *auxiliaries* in Inflectional Phrases of sentences: "I *do* have a candy"
- *Irregular and optional application of inflectional endings*: both "Curtiss is dance" and "Curtis is dancing"
- Difficulty with *pronouns* of all forms

24. a. I want mat is present (19 March 1975)
     b. Father hit Genie cry long time ago (2 May 1975)

In these constructions, the linear series of one proposition is simply juxtaposed with that of a second. A single noun functions both as the object of the first, and the subject of the second proposition, without embedding.

25. a. S - V - O - V - O
     b. Father hit [Genie] cry long time ago

Genie predominantly used her right hemisphere for language (and, to a lesser degree, for non language).[62]

One possible explanation for Genie's failure with language is that after a critical period the left hemisphere can no longer control language acquisition, ". . . accounted for by a kind of functional atrophy of the usual language areas, brought about by disuse (due to inadequate stimulation) or suppression" (Curtiss 1977, 216). Another possibility is that Genie's brain function is related to brain damage which may have at least in part existed prior to her confinement. In the absence of full medical records, it is not possible to conclusively choose between these. This, plus the massive damage caused to all aspects of Genie's development by her horrendous confinement, make it difficult to view this case as conclusive in evaluating a Critical Period Hypothesis for language development.

Genie's case does provide converging evidence on the internal modularity of language organization, however. Genie's relatively fast development of complex lexical knowledge, combined with her fundamental deficits in syntactic knowledge, once again demonstrate the dissociation of these components.

---

[62] This was determined through dichotic listening, tachistoscopic tests and ERP analyses (Curtiss 1977, 213). In many ways, Genie's language is consistent with the language of RH adults: commisurotomy and/or hemispherectomized (Curtiss 1977).

5.8.2   Second language acquisition

The proposal in (21) remains the center of intense debate.[63] Clearly, there are differences between child and adult learners of a language. Yet age alone does not necessarily involve loss of ability to acquire another language. In some cultures, adult acquisition of second languages is commonplace.[64] (a) A substantial proportion of adults do acquire accent-free speech when acquiring another language, (b) while some child learners do show an accent. (c) Adults can be trained on foreign phonological distinctions; (d) some non-native sound distinctions are maintained while others are lost. Difficulties with specific types of sounds or sound distinctions in a second language may relate to the grammatical system of the L1, not to a global loss of ability. (e) Fundamental UG components, viz., linguistic principles and parameters, have been found to constrain adult second language acquisition as they do first. (f) Experience and age must be dissociated in comparing first and second language acquisition.[65]

In order to evaluate the role of early language experience in later language learning, a recent study compared later language acquisition of American Sign Language (beginning between ages of 9 and 15) by two groups of subjects who had not been exposed to sign language at early ages. One group was born deaf and one was lately deafened, having experienced spoken language early in life. The group without early language experience showed low levels of performance with ASL, contrasting with the lately deafened. The researchers then compared three groups of adults on late acquisition of English: the first, born profoundly deaf, with little exposure to language before ASL exposure in school; the second, born profoundly deaf but with experience in ASL in infancy; and the third, born hearing but having learned a language other than English in childhood. Whether deaf or hearing, exposure to a language, whether sign or oral, resulted in superior performance on the late-learned language (English). The authors conclude that "the ability to learn language arises from a synergy between early brain development and language experience, and is seriously compromised when language is not experienced during early life" (Mayberry, Lock and Kazmi 2002, 38).

In summary, if there is a critical period for language acquisition, then its nature remains to be discovered. It very likely involves complex interactions between cerebral foundations and experience.

---

[63] Epstein et al. 1996 and related commentary; Singleton 1989 for review; Flynn and Manual 1992, Birdsong 1992, 1999; Newport 1990; Flynn 1996; White 1996.

[64] Singleton 1989 for review; Snow and Hoefnagel-Hohle 1978; Slavoff and Johnson 1995.

[65] (a): Seliger, Krashen and Ladefoged 1975; (b): Asher and Garcia 1969; White and Genesee 1992; (c): Best et al. 1988; Flynn and Manuel 1991; (d): Best et al. 1988; (e): Flynn 1996; White 1996; Martohardjono 1993; Flynn and Martohardjono 1994; Epstein et al. 1999; (f): Vinnitskaya, Foley and Flynn 2001.

5.9   Creating a theory

5.9.1   Where is the Language Faculty?

As we have seen, evidence exists for dissociation of components of language knowledge. These dissociations cohere with the architecture of the language faculty and with the multiple levels of representation in language knowledge (chapter 2). These suggest modular organization of language knowledge. Evidence has demonstrated, for example: dissociation of general cognition from language knowledge, of syntactic knowledge from semantic/comprehension knowledge (Broca's vs. Wernicke's to some degree; and severely demented Alzheimer's patients), of certain semantic components from others, and dissociation of phonetic or phonological production from certain semantic and syntactic components. Dissociation of various components of language knowledge is also revealed through brain imaging methods which reveal neural maps underlying language processing.[66]

Evidence suggests that the modular organization of language knowledge maps to its biological representation in the brain, mediated by organization involving left hemisphere dominance, and interaction of both hemispheres and of various intrahemispheric areas. No single area explains the complex organization of language knowledge. These discoveries have led at least one researcher to conclude that models of language representation in the brain cannot be based on anatomy alone (Ojemann 1991, 1983): "The functional unit that constitutes a system is still under investigation" (2282).

5.9.2   Is there a language gene?

While it is clear that there is a genetic component to language acquisition, no single gene bears sole responsibility for language. A genetic component is indicated in studies of "specific language impairment" and in twin studies.[67] Recent research resulting from the Human Genome Project has located a small segment of chromosome 7 in the British family where about half the members over three generations are affected by SLI, studied by Gopnik and Crago 1991 (Lai et al. 2001). However, several different genes have been implicated in various forms of language knowledge and development. We are still far from understanding how specific aspects of the genetic code translate to knowledge or acquisition of language.[68]

---

[66] Friederici 2002; Caramazza 1997; Uttal 2001.

[67] A review of more than 100 studies seeks to dissociate genetic factors by a comparison of monozygotic (MZ) and dizygotic (DZ) twins: Stromswald 2000, 2001.

[68] Pinker 2001 for discussion; Wagner 2002. Although we still do not know how many genes compose the human species, it is now believed to be a much smaller number than previously believed; somewhere over 30,000, only half again as large as the roundworm C. elegans. This small number of genes confounds a reductionist view wherein "one item of code (a gene) ultimately

5.10   Conclusions

- Children begin first language acquisition on the basis of biological programming of brain structure and function which in many fundamental ways is continuous with that of the adult.
- In adults, the left hemisphere is privileged in language knowledge and processing. The perisylvian areas in the left hemisphere are crucial. In children, hemispheric asymmetry and left hemisphere specialization for language is evidenced as early as birth. The two hemispheres are "not equivalent substrates for language acquisition" (Dennis and Whitaker 1997, 102–103). An initial form of cerebral dominance underlies and constrains normal language development and constrains plasticity of the brain's organization for language. This disconfirms a strong form of Lenneberg's equipotentiality hypothesis, although there is evidence for further development of inter-hemispheric organization over the first years of life.
- Although the left hemisphere is privileged for language, it does not exclusively serve as the substrate for language knowledge and language development in adult or child. "[T]he direction of future research in lateralization of function lies in exploring how the hemispheres act as complementary processing systems and integrate their activities" (Banich and Heller 1998, 2). Neither does any one area of anatomic localization alone exclusively subserve language.
- Studies of the deaf and of acquisition of sign language suggest that speech and hearing are not necessary conditions for the emergence of language capabilities in the left hemisphere. Cerebral dominance is not simply determined by motoric dominance.
- Studies of adult aphasias have confirmed that the representation of language knowledge is organized in terms of the various subcomponents of the Language Faculty. Syntax, semantics, phonology as well as general cognition can be dissociated through brain damage, as can more specific categories of linguistic knowledge.
- In children, various forms of developmental disorders in language development also reveal dissociations of these subcomponents of the Language Faculty. This suggests an essential continuity in the biological foundations for language knowledge between children and adults.

mak[es] one item of substance (a protein), and the congeries of proteins mak[es] a body" (Gould 2001, A21). A simplistic model of one gene–one trait can no longer be maintained in order to explain the immense cognitive and linguistic complexity of the human species in contrast to other species; ". . . the key to complexity is not more genes, but more combinations and interactions generated by fewer units of code – and many of these interactions (as emergent properties, to use the technical jargon) must be explained at the level of their appearance, for they cannot be predicted from the separate underlying parts alone. So organisms must be explained as organisms, and not as a summation of genes" (Gould 2001, A21).

The nature of developmental language pathologies and a cluster of special cases reveal that the components of language knowledge may dissociate during language development, just as they may come apart during brain injury to the adult. In general, these dissociations suggest that the organization of language in the normal case reflects the basic architecture of the Language Faculty (figure 2.2). When this architecture is broken, components of language knowledge may develop independently, one without the other. These facts cohere with a continuous modular organization of a cognitive faculty for language, and with its modular internal organization.[69]

- Through new brain imaging techniques, modeling the brain's organization for language knowledge and processing is quickly developing. The classic model of brain organization for language (e.g., the Wernicke–Geschwind model) is being refined and revised.

- There is evidence not only for the modular organization of language knowledge but also for modular organization of the human cortex. Various components of language processing are both temporally and spatially localized.

- Brain activity across widespread cortical areas coheres. An interactive organization which combines distributed and modular aspects must be identified. The dynamic nature of linguistic information processing must be identified and accounted for. Current models of the brain organization for language reveal a complex multi-site, precisely timed organization, rather than a simple "localization" model.

- We no longer search for a single, specific localization for language in terms of a discrete cortical space, but for an organization of a system. We no longer search for a single gene as an explanation for language acquisition, although the relation between the genetic code, brain structure and function, and development of language knowledge must be related in a full theory of language acquisition.

- We still do not understand how one modular organization (the mental representation involved in linguistic knowledge) maps onto another modular organization (the cortical organization of the brain). We "are still far from having detailed neural theories of language" knowledge, i.e., theories that would allow us to represent linguistic principles and parameters such as involved in syntactic knowledge (Caramazza 1997a, 150).

- The extent and limits of plasticity in child and adult brains remain the center of active inquiry.

- The issue of whether a Critical Period exists for language acquisition, and of what it consists, remains debated. Neither the case of Genie nor

---

[69] On relations between language pathologies and modularity, see Levy's 1996 argument that the facts do not necessitate a modular representation of knowledge, but a modular representation of "access" to various language components.

the study of second language acquisition in the adult resolves these debates.

• The superb ability of young children to learn a language (or many) remains to be explained. If brain maturation does not simply explain this, what does?

5.11   Supplementary readings

For a basic introduction to neural science: Kandel, Schwartz and Jessell 2000, including chapter 59. *Language and the Aphasias* by Dronkers, Pinker and Damasio. Gazzaniga 2000 provides an introduction to cognitive neuroscience. Fischbach 1992 and 1994 present a brief overview to issues relating to *mind and brain*. For an introduction to basic discoveries linking cognitive science to neural science and brain imaging: Posner and Raichle 1994/1997. Obler and Gjerlow 1999 provide general introduction. *The Whole Brain Atlas* presents a web site of brain images on CD-ROM. For a general introduction to the neuropsychology of language, see Caplan 1992. Johnson 1993 provides a collection of studies of brain development.

For an overview of results of recent research involving the developing brain, including language development: Posner et al. 2001. Neville and Bavelier 2000 and Stromswald 2000 link neuroscience and language development. Bates et al. 1992 provide an initial attempt to link brain development to basic milestones of language development. Nelson and Luciana 2001 provide a *Handbook of Developmental Cognitive Neuroscience*, including a set of chapters involving language. A film, *The Secret Life of the Brain* (Grubin, 2002; Restak, 2001) documents brain development including language development.

For an overview of brain imaging methodologies: Toga and Mazziotta 1996; Jezzard, Matthews and Smith 2001, Brown and Hagoort 1999. For general overview of functional neuroimaging for word learning, see Price 2000 and for language more generally, see Binder and Price 2001.

6 The nature of nurture

Full knowledge of any specific-language grammar is not biologically programmed; the theory of Universal Grammar does not propose that it is. The *input* of specific language data must interact with whatever biological programming exists within children.

In this chapter we first review empirical evidence that experience is necessary, but suggest that widely varying forms of experience allow language acquisition (6.1). We then review evidence for the infant's remarkably rapid knowledge about first language input (6.2). We consider evidence for the claim that a specialized form of input is provided to infants as a "Baby Talk Register" (6.3–6.4), then evidence regarding the nature of children's relation to the input to which they are exposed (6.4–6.5), concluding (6.6) that children's use of this data is *indirect*, *selective* and *reconstructive*. The structure of the organism – the child mind – continually determines and mediates (a) what data are used and (b) how they are used by children in language acquisition.

6.1   Is experience necessary?

6.1.1   The "royal" experiments

What would happen if children were given no experience of a specific language? Herodotus describes an experiment conducted by two kings who isolated two infants from all language input to discover which language, Phrygian or Egyptian, would emerge as "the first of all languages on earth" (Feldman, Goldin-Meadow and Gleitman 1978, 354).[1] Although the royal experiments cannot, thankfully, be conducted anymore, several alternative forms of scientific evidence exist now regarding the role of experience in language acquisition and its precise nature.[2]

6.1.2   Lack of overt practice

In an infant tracheotomized at six months of age for an eight-month period, Lenneberg (1966, 233) showed that the child's progress (beginning a day

---

[1] Campbell and Grieve 1982; Bonvillian et al. 1997. We must doubt the scientific value of any such reported isolation experiments.
[2] See also Lenneberg 1967, 141–142 on "wolf children".

after removal of a tube which had been inserted in the trachea) suggested that normal overt practice of vocalizations appeared not to be necessary for language development during this period. Some form of experience of a model occurs for these children, as long as their hearing is intact, but it is not overt production.[3]

6.1.3   Oral babbling in deaf children

While hearing children follow a regular course of development of babbling during the first twelve months (see chapter 8), oral babbling for deaf children may continue for at least six years (Locke 1983, 27), presumably because of the lack of a model.[4]

6.1.4   Language acquisition without a language model

Over the last two decades, research has led us to question the degree to which a conventional model with well-formed input is necessary for language knowledge (Meier 1991).

6.1.4.1   "Beyond Herodotus"

Researchers found that a form of creative signing ("Homesign") appears to develop spontaneously in deaf children who are not exposed to a conventional model of either oral or sign language.[5] Ten deaf children (ranging in age from 1.4–4.1 at first interview, and 2.6–5.9 at final interview) were videotaped in their homes.[6] Even without a model, the children "combine[d] their gestures into strings that functioned in a number of respects like the sentences of early child language" (Goldin-Meadow and Mylander 1990a, 334). These followed a pattern similar to children learning languages from conventional language models: first single gestures, then combinations into two-gesture sentences, and finally complex sentences (Goldin-Meadow and Mylander 1990a, 339).

"Homesign" revealed systematic structural properties shared with natural language developed from a conventional model.[7] It showed categorization of types of signs (*referential* and *predicative*) and systematic combinatorial phenomena involving order. Signs are distinguished as nouns or verbs,[8] e.g., "[O]ne child produced a pointing gesture at a bubble jar (representing the argument playing the patient role) followed by the . . . gesture 'twist' (representing a predicate)

---

[3] Results from a large survey of tracheotomized children suggest an effect of timing of the treatment during language acquisition (Locke 1993). See Lenneberg 1967 for studies of anarthria and other pathological cases; Bishop 1988; Locke and Pearson 1990 and Locke 1993.

[4] Lenneberg 1964a; 1967, 139–140; Oller and Eilers 1988, 441; Mogford 1988.

[5] These children have severe hearing losses, but have not been exposed to conventional manual languages. Although they were being trained to lipread, they "had made little, if any significant progress in their oral training" (Goldin-Meadow 1987, 108). Approximately 90 percent of deaf children are born to hearing parents.

[6] Goldin-Meadow and Mylander 1990; Goldin-Meadow and Feldman 1977; Feldman, Goldin-Meadow and Gleitman 1978.

[7] See Feldman et al. 1978 and Goldin-Meadow and Mylander 1990 for review of research methods.

[8] Goldin-Meadow et al. 1994.

to request that the experimenter twist open the bubble jar" (Goldin-Meadow and Mylander 1990, 334).[9]

Homesign showed complex sentence formation (involving two or more propositions), including evidence of recursion and redundancy reduction corresponding to "syntactic deletion" and the mapping of underlying structure to a distinct surface structure (Goldin-Meadow and Mylander 1990a, Goldin-Meadow 1982, 1987). Combinatorial structure was also revealed in homesign morphology: handshape and motion combinations "formed a comprehensive matrix for virtually all of the spontaneous gestures for each child" (Goldin-Meadow, Mylander and Butcher 1995) and included inflection (Goldin-Meadow and Mylander 1995). Semantically, communication extended beyond the "here and now" to displaced reference (Morford and Goldin-Meadow 1997). Deaf children in Taiwan (aged 3.8–4.11) provided cross-cultural replication.[10]

The children produced more combinations and used them earlier than their parents did. While the mothers were "prolific producers of single gestures, they were not prolific producers of gesture strings" (Goldin-Meadow and Mylander 1983; Goldin-Meadow and Mylander 1990a, 344), and the mothers' strings "did not show the same structural regularities as their children's" (1990a, 344).[11] There was a "striking qualitative distinction . . . between the signs of mothers and children" (Feldman, Goldin-Meadow and Gleitman 1978, 378), with the mothers frequently using objects as props in their signed actions while the children appeared to use signs more independently.

While the children did not create their homesign language "in a vacuum," the deaf children went beyond their input, "contributing linearization and componentialization to the gestures they received as input from their hearing mothers" (Goldin-Meadow and Mylander 1990a, 345). Yet, when one of the homesigning children, David, was studied again when he was 9.5 years old with little exposure to a conventional sign language, he had made little progress. He had developed a system "as consistent within his own system as native signers are within theirs,"[12] but it remained simple. It may be that "complexity can be introduced into a linguistic system only if the system is used by a community of signers who transmit the system from one generation to the next" (Singleton et al. 1993, 698).[13]

---

[9] A website accompanying Goldin-Meadow 2001 provides examples: www.psypress.com/goldinmeadow.

[10] In both English and Taiwanese, "gesture production was high and equal for intransitive actors and patients, and low for transitive actors" (280). Objects tend to be ordered before transitive verbs (OV) as are intransitive actors, while transitive actors are often deleted (Goldin-Meadow and Mylander 1990b and 1998 relate this to a possible "ergative" language-like pattern).

[11] Chinese mothers' gestures appeared to resemble their children's more than US mothers' did, e.g., in the linear order of sign combinations produced (Goldin-Meadow and Mylander 1998).

[12] The authors used a *Verbs of Motion Production* (*VMP*) test (Supalla et al. 1993, 688) in which subjects were shown short videos designed to elicit motion verbs, allowing "subject's control of individual morphemes and morpheme categories" to be evaluated, e.g., motion, location and handshape of signs.

[13] This simplicity contrasted with the case of Simon, a deaf child near David's age, who was presented with ASL in a degraded form by his late-learner parents and is reported to have gone beyond the degraded input in constructing a system with the full complexity of ASL (Singleton and Newport 1993).

These results confirm the indomitable drive to create language in the human species, and the inherent capacity of the mind/brain to impose structure on this language, given wide variation in amount and nature of input. They suggest that children are predisposed to create language out of whatever input they receive and do so at more than one level of representation, reflecting the structure of the Language Faculty.[14]

6.1.4.2   A creative deaf community

In Nicaragua, we find deaf children creating their own sign language in a situation allowing shared communication.[15] Although no pre-existing sign language was available in Nicaragua, individual deaf children came together each with their own homesign, and "immediately the children began to sign with each other" (Senghas 1995b, 36) demonstrating "one of the first documented cases of the birth of a natural human language," Nicaraguan Sign Language (Kegl et al. 1999, 179). We find here the development of linguistic complexity over time that was missing in David's homesign, even though there is still no conventional model (Kegl et al. 1999, 201; see Kegl 1991).

Both Homesign and Nicaraguan Sign Language have shown that "[a]ll children have a special inborn ability not only to learn language, but to surpass the language of the environment when it is weak, and to create a language where none existed"; "the source of language is within us but . . . the conditions for its emergence depend crucially upon community" (Kegl et al. 1999, 223).

6.1.4.3   Creoles

Further evidence in support of language creation without the positive evidence of a conventional language model, but with the presence of a community, is suggested by studies of the creation of Creoles, i.e., pidgin languages which become the native language of a community.[16]

6.1.5   Language acquisition without communication

Normally, acquisition of language and acquisition of communication appear to develop hand in hand, but this convergence is not necessary. For instance, "John," at age 3.3, showed a divorce between his knowledge of language, which was normal, and his knowledge of interpersonal communication, which was "almost nonexistent" (Blank, Gessner and Esposito 1979, 329, 350). John refused to speak with other children and teachers. His "verbalization was irrelevant to what the parent had just said" (344). When his mother asked: "Are

---

[14] David was retested as an adult at age twenty-three, after having been first exposed to ASL at age nine and then attending a college program for deaf students for two years (Morford, Singleton and Goldin-Meadow 1995).

[15] Kegl 1994, Senghas 1995a, b; Kegl, Senghas and Coppola 1999, Senghas and Coppola 2001. A postrevolutionary literacy campaign in 1980 brought large numbers of deaf children (over 500 children over the first few years) together for the first time in public schools (Kegl et al. 1999).

[16] See Crystal 1997 for introduction, and the papers in deGraff 1999, including Bickerton 1999.

you going to go in and say hi to daddy?", John replied "OK, here we are in the garage" (344). 30 percent of the time he ignored what his parents had said.

Christopher, in his thirties, was severely deficited in non-verbal IQ: he was unable to find his way around or look after himself, didn't conserve number, and showed severe visuo-spatial deficits (Smith and Tsimpli 1995). At the same time, "Christopher's linguistic abilities [were] exceptional both in the *speed* with which he acquire[d] new languages and in his *fluency* in those languages he already [knew]" (80). He could read and write any of fifteen to twenty languages (1) and showed a "remarkable ability to translate" these (12). He showed "an attention bordering on obsession with the orthographic form of words and their morphological make-up" (82). At the same time, he had "somewhat impoverished conversational ability" (169), including a "tendency to monosyllabicity and a reluctance to initiate exchanges" (171).[17]

Another case, Clive, exemplifies double dissociation by revealing non-reluctant communication, but deficited grammatical knowledge. He demonstrates desire to communicate while he reveals grammatical deficit, as in: "They mean. Cold bath-ice in it. They do all the kids" (Smith 1989, 167–177). Here we see in several ways that language and communication "may have different and independent sources" (Blank et al. 1979, 351).[18]

6.1.6   Language acquisition without direct perceptual input

As we saw in chapter 3 (3.3.3.4), the young blind child Kelli (24–36 months) acquired and distinguished the terms "look" and "see" (Landau and Gleitman 1985). Young children both deaf and blind can also acquire language, through vibrotactile information provided to face and neck (Chomsky, 1986 on the Tadoma method; Smith 2002a). Here we again see language acquisition which cannot be based on children's direct perception of their environment.

6.1.7   The inscrutability of rate of language acquisition

There is considerable variability in the rate of language development among children.[19] Some of this difference in rate may be related to aspects of input (e.g., Potts et al. 1979), but rate differences occur in highly enriched environments as well as in more deprived ones. Although orphanage children with limited language input often suffer developmental delays, it is not clear to what degree these involve language development; "catch up" mechanisms may apply regardless of such variations.[20]

---

[17] Not all communicative ability was missing; Smith and Tsimpli 1995, 184. Not all grammatical knowledge was attained.

[18] Rees 1978; Bloom and Lahey 1978.

[19] Mogford and Bishop 1988, 22; Fenson et al. 1994. Consider Roger Brown's chart (chapter 7, p. 000) showing the course of development (in MLU) of Adam, Eve and Sarah.

[20] Skuse 1988, 30–31 for review.

6.1.8   Summary

While there can be no doubt that experience is necessary for language acquisition, the form of experience can vary widely. The genesis of a new language appears to require the existence of a community, but the ontogenesis of a first language in children can involve different amounts and types of communicative interaction. All normal children appear to contain within themselves the ability to create a language in spite of wide variations in experience.

6.2   When does linguistic experience begin?

Hearing infants, surrounded by oral language in the natural environment, seem to pounce on this input immediately and analytically long before they use language in communicative situations.

6.2.1   Before birth?

External auditory stimulation is available to the fetus, although attenuated (Armitage, Baldwin and Vince 1980, 1173). "Mother's voice is a prominent sound in the amniotic environment"; "experience with sounds begins prior to birth" (Fifer and Moon 1989, 175, 184).[21]

6.2.1.1   Speech is special

Newborns appear to distinguish speech from birth, and to be drawn to language. They orient to sound (Muir and Field 1979, 435), showing a preference for speech and voice or song over other stimuli (e.g., instrumental music) and prefer to listen to words over other sounds (Colombo and Bundy 1983).[22] For infants five to fifteen weeks old, speech sounds act as reinforcing stimulation (Trehub and Chang 1977).

6.2.1.2   Language is special

A newborn younger than three days "can not only discriminate its mother's voice but also will work to produce her voice in preference to the voice of another female" (DeCasper and Fifer 1980, 1175). Infants tested in a nonnutritive sucking experiment and given differential feedback in terms of whether the infant's mother or another female read Dr. Seuss's "To think that I saw it on Mulberry Street" sucked significantly more with the maternal voice, suggesting the role of auditory experience before birth (1176).

In a later experiment, women were asked to read particular stories aloud during the last six weeks of pregnancy, "two times through each day when you feel that your baby (fetus) is awake" in a quiet place (135). Newborns were then tested

---

[21] Lecanuet and Granier-Deferre 1993; de Boysson-Bardies 1999; Kisilevsky et al. 2003.
[22] See deVilliers and deVilliers 1978, 24; Moon, Bever and Fifer 1992; Cooper and Aslin 1990, Morse 1972.

on this story or another, matched in basic characteristics. For example, the first twenty-eight paragraphs of *The Cat in the Hat* were compared to *The Dog in the Fog*. The newborns showed a significant preference for the target story over the new story, in contrast to control subjects whose mothers had not participated in the study. They even did so with a change in speaker (DeCasper and Spence 1986). When the story was read backwards, the effect disappeared (Mehler et al. 1978).

6.2.1.3   Is one language enough?

Many, if not most, infants are exposed to more than one language. An important series of research studies now confirms that "a few days after birth, infants are able to tell apart two different languages, even when neither of them is present in their environment; moreover, they already show a preference for their maternal language" (Mehler and Christophe 1995, 947). Infants are not confused by exposure to more than one language, and seem to know very early which language is "going to be their maternal language" (948; see appendix 4).

Mehler et al. (1988) tested four-day-old French infants and two-month-old American infants on whether they could distinguish languages. A French–Russian bilingual woman and an Italian–English bilingual woman each recorded a narrative in their two languages. French infants showed a greater arousal to French than to Russian. American infants distinguished English and Italian.[23] Two-day-olds whose mothers were either English or Spanish monolinguals, tested with audio recordings of monolingual speakers of Spanish or English, "activated recordings of their native language for longer periods than the foreign language" (Moon, Cooper and Fifer 1993, 495).

When two-month-old English infants were tested on sentences half in English and half in Japanese (recorded by four female native English speakers and four female native Japanese speakers), they distinguished their mother tongue and the foreign language; language change had a significantly greater effect than speaker change (Hesketh, Christophe and Dehaene-Lambertz 1997). Similar results were found with French three-day-olds (Nazzi et al. 1998). Five-month-old infants responded to new utterances in a new language significantly more than to new utterances in the same language, as with English compared to Spanish (Bahrick and Pickens 1988). Infants thus not only discriminate, but categorize sounds by language.

More recent research has confirmed that neonates (at four days) can discriminate "two unfamiliar languages without any difficulty" (Mehler and Christophe 1995, 946).[24] French newborns distinguish English and Italian or English and

[23] Although the American infants did not show a significant preference for the English sample in this early research, subsequent research confirmed this preference (Mehler and Christophe 1995 reporting research by Lambertz).

[24] The results of the Mehler et al. 1988 study at first suggested that infants were not able to distinguish unfamiliar languages, and that familiarity with one language was necessary in order to achieve this effect. Mehler and Christophe 1995 report a reanalysis of the original data and disconfirm this.

Table 6.1 *Language discrimination by infants (neonates to four to five months)* (*=no discrimination).

Neonates	Language Contrast	Reference
(French)	French–Russian	Mehler et al. 1988
	English–Japanese	Nazzi et al. 1998
	*English–German	Nazzi et al. 1998
	*English–Dutch	Nazzi et al. 1998
(English)	English–Italian	Mehler et al. 1988
	English–Spanish	Moon et al. 1993
(Spanish)	English–Spanish	Moon et al. 1993
2 months		
(English)	*French–Russian	Mehler et al. 1988
	English–Italian	Mehler et al. 1988
4–5 months		
(English)	English–Dutch	Nazzi et al. 1998
(Spanish, Catalan)	Spanish–Catalan	Bosch and Sebastian-Galles 1997
(Spanish–Catalan bilinguals)	*Spanish–Catalan	Bosch and Sebastian-Galles 1997

Japanese (Nazzi et al. 1998). However, two-month-olds have been found *not* to make some distinctions between two unfamiliar languages – which the newborn does – although they continue to differentiate their native language from others. Two-month-old American infants appear not to distinguish French and Russian, although neonates do (Mehler et al. 1988). Older infants may "already concentrate on utterances that share a structure corresponding to the maternal language and neglect utterances that do not . . . by the age of two months the infant has set the first values to individuate the structure of the maternal language" (947).

Bilingual infants

Infant discrimination varies with whether the child is in a monolingual or bilingual environment. Four-month-old monolinguals (either Spanish or Catalan) were found to distinguish Catalan vs. Spanish (Bosch and Sebastian-Galles 1997, 37). However, infants being raised in Catalan–Spanish bilingual environments showed no preference for either of the familiar languages, but did distinguish a foreign language (e.g., English or Italian).

Table 6.1 summarizes language discrimination results in infants from birth to four to five months of age.

What are the mechanisms by which the infant makes such early distinctions between languages? Several of the infant discriminations persist with low-pass filtered stimuli (where only low frequency, e.g., less than 400 HZ, is available), eliminating much of the segmental information and leaving suprasegmental prosodic features. Suprasegmental (e.g., rhythmic or prosodic) characteristics of the languages thus appear to affect the infant's discrimination. Although French newborns discriminate British English and Japanese, which differ in certain rhythmic properties, they do not discriminate British English and Dutch, which share them (Nazzi et al. 1998). If speech is played backwards, these discriminations disappear. (See Ramus et al. 1999 for a comprehensive study of this issue.)

These facts led to new hypotheses regarding the linguistic features used by infants when they represent language at early periods (Ramus et al. 1999), targeting selected prosodic properties in the infant's initial representations.[25] However, the Spanish–Catalan distinction made by four-month-old infants would require recognition of lower level units, since these are "both Romance languages which present differences at the segmental level and at the syllable level, but have important similarities concerning prosodic structure" (Bosch and Sebastian-Galles 1997, 61).[26]

Non-human primates (cotton-top tamarin monkeys) have also distinguished Dutch and Japanese language stimuli, suggesting that this discrimination may at least partially involve "general processes of the primate auditory system" (Ramus et al. 2000). However, it is not necessary that human and non-human primates accomplish this cross-language discrimination in the same way, i.e., by using the same cues. Human infants' distinct capacity may lie precisely in the ability to integrate a rhythmic sensitivity with other aspects of language knowledge. (See Werker and Vouloumanos 2000 for discussion.[27])

6.2.2 Summary

Regardless of the precise mechanisms used, human infants show a marvelously quick, differentiated, effective approach to experience of language, one which may begin even before birth. Infants show an initial powerful discrimination of, and classification of, the continuous speech stream.

The results above are consistent with the first priorities of an innate Language Faculty; i.e., infants have the initial means to discriminate language from non-language stimuli, and an initial way of "representing input signals" of language (cf. chapter 4). The infants "form a representation of one language and compare results from the new language with their representation" (Ramus et al. 1999, 280). The results show how marvelously tuned to linguistic data infants are, and how easily linguistic experience can have an effect.

6.3 What is the nature of the input?

Is it possible that the language input to which newborns are so finely tuned is actually more structured than we might think?

---

[25] A "Time and Intensity Grid Representation" (TIGRE) has been proposed for initial infant speech perception as a "first order filtering device" (Mehler et al. 1996, 113).

[26] See Lieberman 1996 for argument that low-pass filtering may not eliminate all segmental information.

[27] Evaluation of the Language Faculty will require further comparing the infant and non-human primate (e.g., monkeys, unlike infants, failed to distinguish language change more than speaker change).

6.3.1   Baby Talk Register (BTR)

Presented with an infant, adults will often change their manner of speaking, adopting "Baby Talk" (BT), sometimes called "Motherese" (Snow 1972). The linguist Charles Ferguson speculated in an early survey of twenty-seven languages that "in every speech community people modify their speech in talking to young children, and that the modifications have an innate basis" (1977, 203). He proposes a core set of properties of a "Baby Talk Register" (BTR), which, he speculated, might be universal.

It has been suggested that:

> [E]vidence of BT. . . refutes overwhelmingly the rather off-hand assertions of Chomsky and his followers that the preschool child could not learn language from the complex but syntactically degenerate sample his parents provide without the aid of an elaborate innate component . . . it has turned out that parental speech is well formed and finely tuned to the child's psycholinguistic capacity. The corollary would seem to be that there is less need for an elaborate innate component than there at first seemed to be.   (Brown, 1977, 20; see also Snow and Ferguson 1977)

Infants are sensitive to high frequency sounds, and some studies have argued that they "prefer to listen to motherese" when given a choice experimentally (e.g., Fernald 1985; cf. Cooper et al. 1997). Could it be that the BTR is designed to meet requirements of infants and thus structure language teaching for them, and that children actually use it in a privileged way for language learning?

1.   **Motherese Hypothesis**
      "Those special restrictive properties of caretaker speech play a causal role in language acquisition."   (Newport, Gleitman and Gleitman 1977)

We know now that BTR (table 6.2) is not universal. We also know more about the nature of BTR and its use by children. These results challenge the Motherese Hypothesis, suggesting a more general role for the BTR in adult–infant interaction, linking it to culture and to affective interaction rather than to language teaching per se.

We also know logical reasons for questioning the Motherese Hypothesis. (a) Children could not learn adult language if it were restricted to the BTR. (b) The properties attributed to BTR would not solve the essential problems we raised in chapter 3. For example, slowing down a continuous speech stream does not automatically evidence the requisite linguistic units; "bat" might be rendered as "b∂-ae-t∂" if the sounds were separated. (c) The transformations in the BTR are not clearly rule bound (see Ferguson 1977), and do not conform to a general notion of "simplicity." Although one might assume that [ch] as in "church" is less simple than [s], in Hindi baby talk the adult will often substitute [ch] for [s] as in "Chona" for the name "Sona" (Smith 1989, 143). (d) How do we know that adults are not imitating children rather than vice versa? (e) Infants hear *all* audible language in the environment, meaning we cannot separate experience of BTR from experience

Table 6.2 *Essential Properties of "Baby Talk Register"*

PROSODY
1. high pitch
2. exaggerated contours
3. slow rate

SYNTAX
4. short sentences
5. parataxis
6. telegraphic style
7. repetition

LEXICON
8. kin terms and body parts
9. infant games
10. qualities
11. compound verbs
12. hypocorism

PHONOLOGY
13. cluster reduction
14. liquid substitution
15. reduplication
16. special sounds

DISCOURSE
17. questions
18. pronoun shift

EXTENDED USES
19. child speech
20. animals
21. adult intimacy

Source: Ferguson 1978, 214

of normal language. (f) The putative simplification of language in the BTR allows children a wider range of potential hypotheses (Smith 1989, 142–155). (g) The fact that a high-pitched stimulus may attract their attention does not necessarily mean that children need this for language acquisition[28] (see Lieberman 1996).

There are also empirical reasons to question the universality of BTR and its (causal) significance in language acquisition. Clifton Pye studied language acquisition and parental input in the subsistence farming community of Zunil, a small village in the Western Highland regions of Guatemala. He analyzed the speech of adults to children and compared it to speech to other adults in order to evaluate

---

[28] Methodological issues characterize some of the cited experiments. In the Fernald 1985 study, infants were placed in a situation where contrasting stimuli were presented on two sides. A side bias interacted.

Ferguson's list of proposed BTR properties, adding acoustic analysis of collected speech. In Zunil, most houses had dirt floors and adobe walls, and people had few material possessions. Babies were kept close to their mothers, either strapped to their backs or nearby, and accompanied them on daily activities, but "vocal interaction between infants and parents [was] minimal" (Pye 1986, 86); the child was "most often ignored and conversation revolve[d] around matters of interest to the adults or older children" (87). Mothers "frequently reduced their voice so much that it became a whisper. At the same time, the speech rate continues at a normal pace or may even be increased slightly" (88). Mothers' speech to children did not have high pitch or exaggerated contour or slow rate, and was "about equal in morphological complexity, MLU [Mean Length of Utterance] and amount of repetition" (94). The complex system of verb terminations in this language was preserved, as in "k-o-e-in-k'am-a:"/aspect-object-go-subject-root-termination/ ("I'll go and bring it"), spoken by a mother to a 1.10 year-old child with a lexicon of fewer than fifty words (92). Several of the proposed BTR features from table 6.2 did hold; motherese involved special words for qualities, special sounds and repetition. However, "not only does Quiché speech to children lack many of the simplifying features found in other communities, it also contains features which increase its complexity: special sounds, a special verbal suffix, few overt noun phrases, diminutives" (Pye 1986, 98), or additional instructions frequently added to the end of sentences. These results mean "it no longer seems possible to maintain the strong version of the Motherese Hypothesis, which predicts that the features of speech to children play an essential role in language acquisition . . . It would appear that no single feature need be present in the input for children to acquire language" (98).[29]

In their analyses of the effects of English motherese, Newport, Gleitman and Gleitman (1977) reached converging conclusions. They found that although mothers' speech to children was simple in certain ways (e.g., mothers tended not to talk in long complex sentences with subordinate clauses), it was in other ways more complex than that addressed to adults. It had more transformed utterances, fewer declaratives (87 percent to adults, 30 percent to infants), more imperatives and more questions; in general, a wider range of constructions and more inconsistency of types. (Imperatives and questions both involve null sites, e.g., "Ø stop that", and questions involve both null sites and displacements, e.g, "What do you want Ø"; cf. chapter 2.)

6.3.2   How does experience work?

6.3.2.1   Is BTR a language-teaching mechanism?

Newport, Gleitman and Gleitman 1977 provided scientific test of the motherese hypothesis to address this question. Recognizing that mothers vary in the degree to which they use BTR, they reasoned that if a mother shows a greater

---

[29] See Ingram 1995 for discussion, Schieffelin 1979 for study of the Kaluli in Papua New Guinea.

amount of motherese, then, following (1), the child should show faster language acquisition. They also tested a "Fine Tuning Hypothesis": if a mother is acting as teacher, then as the mother's speech grows in complexity, then so should the child's (Gleitman, Newport and Gleitman 1984; Valian 1999 for discussion).

Fifteen American mother–daughter pairs in three age groups were studied (12–15, 18–21, and 24–27 months), with children's MLUs ranging from 1.00 to 3.46 (mean 1.65). The pairs were interviewed twice, six months apart. Both times, adult speech was recorded, analyzed and coded for various specific measures: e.g., for specific measures of length, complexity, utterance type, and repetition, as was child speech (Newport, Gleitman and Gleitman 1977, 116–118, tables 5.1 and 5.2). Correlations were then computed between every property of maternal speech and growth in child language on relevant measures (132, table 5.3).[30]

Results showed that the vast majority of properties of maternal speech did not correlate positively with developing complexity in child speech. The length or complexity of a mother's utterances did not correlate with the same features in the child's language; nor did amount of repetition by the mother correlate with any form of growth measured. Growth of complex sentence structures in the child's speech did not correlate with any property of maternal speech.

Only two correlations were significant: (a) the number of yes/no questions in the mother's speech (e.g., "Do you want to take a bath now?") correlated with the development of overt auxiliaries in the verb phrases of child speech (e.g., "I will jump"), although absolute amount of auxiliaries used in mother's speech did not; and (b), noun phrase inflections (e.g., plurals) in the child developed in correlation with amount of deixis (e.g., "That's a dog") in the mother's speech. A Fine Tuning Hypothesis was not supported. Mothers' MLU was found to correlate with age, but not with language development in children.

These findings disconfirm a strong form of the Motherese Hypothesis, although they do not suggest that children cannot or do not attend to specific properties of the input. They suggest a "semi autonomous unfolding of language capabilities." Effects of maternal input are those which match the biases of the learner, which act "as a filter through which the linguistic environment exerts its influence" (137). These results begin to factor out which properties of the input infants may select. The input is not the primary determinant of the universal aspects of language knowledge, e.g., those involved in complex sentence formation, but it may affect language specific factors which require induction, e.g., the lexical form of the auxiliary verb used in English, or the morphology involved in English pluralization.

---

[30] These researchers realized that finding simple positive correlations would not suffice to confirm either the Motherese or the Fine Tuning Hypothesis. "Basic Motherese may be used more when the child is least sophisticated linguistically, but also the child may grow the fastest the less his linguistic sophistication, i.e., the more he has left to learn" (Newport, Gleitman and Gleitman 1977, 133), thus providing the spurious result that more growth correlated with more Motherese. To correct this, the researchers partialled out variance due to the child's age and language level.

Do mothers need to provide "super vowels"?

In another study of BTR, mothers' speech to their two- to five-month-olds in three countries (USA, Russia and Sweden) was subjected to spectrographic analysis and showed that "mothers addressing their infants produced acoustically more extreme vowels than they did when addressing adults" (Kuhl et al. 1997, 684). The researchers concluded that "language input to infants provides exceptionally well-specified information about the linguistic units that form the building blocks for words" (1997, 684). In all countries, when the mothers' vowels, /a/, /i/ and /u/, were measured in terms of vowel formant frequency, fundamental frequency (pitch) and duration, not only was there an increase in duration and fundamental frequency, but the vowel triangle was found to be "stretched."[31]

We do not know if such phenomena are influential in language acquisition, nor how universal they are (e.g., Quiché Mayan). Acoustic exaggeration of a vowel space would not alone provide the information to determine the phonemic contrasts of a language.[32] In Swedish, children must distinguish at least sixteen variations within this vowel space corresponding to different vowels, while in English they must distinguish nine, and in Russian only five. As we have seen, linguistic units do not exist in the acoustic information.[33] Yet children must discover these, including the contrasts which create them, and the system which relates them.[34]

Kuhl et al. suggest several ways in which vowel space expansion might "enhance learning" (1997, 684). (a) The three vowels may be more easily perceived because they are "more distinct" from each other. However, as we see in chapter 8, infants make very fine distinctions in the speech stream, even more so the younger they are (see chapter 8). Thus infants appear not to need acoustic expansion, or hyperarticulation, for initial speech perception. (b) "[E]xpanding the vowel triangle allows mothers to produce a greater variety of instances representing each vowel category without creating acoustic overlap between vowel categories. Greater variety may cause infants to attend to non-frequency-specific spectral features that characterize a vowel category, rather than to any particular set of frequencies the mother uses to produce a vowel" (Kuhl et al. 1997, 685). If so, some form of linguistic unit must guide analysis so that variety is not a hindrance to categorization.[35]

---

[31] The "vowel triangle" is a schematic representation of the range of tongue positions possible within the human oral tract. This BTR effect appears to be linked to content rather than function words (van de Weijer 2001).

[32] For treatment of "vowel systems" across languages, see Hockett 1955, 83f, and Ladefoged 2001.

[33] Even phonetic units do not "exist" in an expanded vowel space without further analysis on this space.

[34] With an expanded triangle, there are more sound possibilities, each of which may or may not be significant.

[35] Kuhl et al. 1997 provide an analysis of their acoustic data in a form that corresponds to compact–diffuse and grave–acute distinctions, linguistic features which were proposed by Jakobson to innately guide language acquisition (chapter 8).

6.3.2.2   Statistical learning

Could it be that although infants are not generally dependent on a specialized form of restricted linguistic input (e.g., BTR), they still are input-driven, perhaps in even more subtle ways? Words reflect sound combinations which occur more probably than sound combinations across words, e.g., the syllables "pre-ty" or "ba-by" appear more productively together, since they form a word; as opposed to "-ty ba-" as in "pretty baby," which occur across words. Earlier linguistic research suggested that observation of such phoneme distributions could possibly lead to "the discovery of morpheme-like segments" (Harris 1955, 212). Recent experimental studies with eight-month-olds have now documented infants' impressive computational ability to differentiate auditory stimuli in terms of probability of sound combinations (Saffran, Aslin and Newport 1996).

Saffran, Aslin and Newport's experiment 1, using a "familiarization preference" procedure (Jusczyk and Aslin 1995), presented eight-month-old infants synthesized speech with sequenced sounds created by consonant–vowel combinations (without any acoustic cues such as intonation or pauses normally associated with natural speech), e.g., "*bidakupadotigolabubidaku.*"[36] Four combinations of 3 CV (consonant–vowel) units, corresponding by hypothesis to "statistical words," were repeated in random order (e.g., *golabu, tupiro*) (forty-five tokens of each). Infants were then tested on either the sequences that appeared in the familiarization phase, or on new combinations with the same CV combinations in different orders, corresponding by hypothesis to "statistical part-words," to see if the infants would distinguish these. After only two minutes of exposure to the first familiarization string, the infants showed significantly longer fixation/listening time to the three sound sequences which they had not heard (the statistical "part-words"), presumably recognizing them as novel, compared to those they had heard (the statistical "words").

In a second experiment, the authors confirmed that infants consulted relative frequency of co-occurrence of these sound units. The CV sequences which had occurred less frequently were fixated on by the infant longer than those more frequent. The authors suggest that this contrast can be represented in terms of the differences in "transitional probabilities" (TP) between the CV combinations;[37] "infants can use simple statistics to discover word boundaries in connected speech" (Bates and Elman 1996, 1849).

Saffran et al. suggest "infants possess experience-dependent mechanisms that may be powerful enough to support not only word segmentation but also the acquisition of other aspects of language"; they motivate "innately based statistical learning mechanisms . . . rather than innate knowledge" (1996, 1928) operating on

---

[36] Web sites of Saffran and Aslin provide exposition and examples of the stimuli used in this experiment: http://whyfiles.org/058language/baby_talk.html http://www.bcs.rochester.edu/bcs/research/LIS/lis.frameset.html.

[37] "Transitional probabilities" were 1.0 in the case of the target sequences, as opposed to .33 for the others.

"statistical properties of the language input" (1926) in order to allow the child to induce linguistic knowledge. Some have concluded: "Chomsky and his followers have underestimated the power of learning and thereby overestimated the need to build language-specific knowledge into the organism in advance" (Elman and Bates 1997, 1274).[38]

While these experimental results do provide additional evidence on children's remarkable computational abilities to detect distributional facts and co-occurrence regularities in input, they do not solve the language acquisition problem we introduced in chapter 3, nor do they eliminate the necessity for guiding linguistic knowledge. The experiments assume that infants have already decoded sound and syllable units from the continuous speech stream. There is no evidence that the specific information which infants extract from the input in these experiments leads to any form of specific linguistic knowledge, e.g., knowledge of words, without some form of linguistic knowledge and linguistic computation. As we see in the following chapters, an impressive amount of linguistic knowledge is evident even before infants are eight months old, leading to the possibility that linguistic knowledge constrains their induction from input during this period. If infants are looking for possible words, i.e., if they hold the prior hypothesis, presumably linguistically determined, that sequences of certain auditory stimuli might correspond to the linguistic category "word," it is possible that they could use frequent co-occurrences of particular sounds to perform the right induction, possibly exemplifying a form of "abduction" (cf. chapter 4).[39]

Infants must discover word boundaries in a categorical and deterministic fashion which must override statistical probabilities. They must be able to distinguish "about the flu" from "a bout of the flu," for example, or "your" from "you're." They must realize that "walked," "walks," and "will walk" involve the same word. In some languages, "intra word" and "inter word" probabilities may provide significantly less information regarding word boundaries; e.g., in the Bantu language, Bukusu (Western Kenya), "omundu omuleeyi" (a tall person) reveals an "across word" sequence of "u-o" which is not less common inside words.[40] In languages with subject or topic marking, children cannot take frequent occurrence of the particle sound with prior sounds as "word," e.g., "boku#wa" ("as for me" in Japanese).[41] If children were merely consulting various observed sound combinations and computing their relative frequency and transitional probabilities, we would expect them to be widely misled by their very fine analysis of

---

[38] See Pinker 1999 and a collection of responses in *Science*, vol. 284, April 16, 1999 and in vol. 276, May 23, 1997 ("Letters" 1177–1276) for discussion.

[39] See Di Sciullo and Williams 1987 for example of linguists' attempts to capture and define "word."

[40] Aggrey Wasike, personal communication.

[41] It is not clear how "statistical probabilities" should be computed in order to determine "word," a categorical concept; i.e., how much more probable does a sound combination have to be in order to be considered a "word"? To deal with such problems, Saffran et al. define Transitional Probability as =(frequency of Y given X)/frequency of X). Presumably the frequency of "wa" with many forms would override the induction that "boku wa" was a word. The wide-ranging predictions made by this form of computation remain to be tested.

the speech stream. Children's interpretation of the statistical information in the speech stream cannot be arbitrary.

6.3.2.3   Beyond transitional probabilities

Infants have remarkable abilities to derive patterns that go beyond statistical computing and include linguistic properties of the natural speech stream. As we have seen, even before infants are a year old, they know something of the sound combinations which distinguish their language from other languages at a prosodic level of representation. Infants as young as 7.5 months detect and remember repeated words in fluent speech, and use word stress patterns as well as distributional information when they do so (chapters 8 and 10). These word segmentation abilities develop between 6 and 7.5 months.

Johnson and Jusczyk 2001 showed that Saffran et al.'s (1996) results replicate with eight-month-olds when synthesized speech stimuli are replaced by natural speech. They tested whether natural speech cues (e.g., word stress or coarticulation between syllables) would be consulted and/or favored by infants more than statistical regularities. In one experiment, the first syllable of each "part-word" was replaced with a stressed version. In another experiment, they replaced the "part-word" combinations with their coarticulated counterparts in natural speech. Results confirmed that eight-month-olds rank such speech cues "more heavily than a statistical cue regarding the transitional probabilities of certain syllable sequences" (565).

Other research has documented that seven-month-olds also consult a higher level of abstract representation of the speech stream; they "represent, extract, and generalize abstract algebraic rules" (77) from input corresponding to an "artificial language" constructed to reflect either ABA or ABB patterns (Marcus et al. 1999, Marcus 2004). At a still more abstract level of representation, infants (about twelve months) learn and generalize from sound strings they hear to new strings based on patterns derived from a finite state grammar (controlling for a change in vocabulary) (Gomez and Gerken 1999). After less than two-minute exposures to an artificial grammar, the infants showed evidence of abstracting these patterns, confirming that "they were extracting information in the form of larger units, perhaps involving second-order dependencies or series of first-order dependencies, but not limited to isolated word pairs" (Gomez and Gerken 1999, 130).

While statistical information may potentially be a powerful asset in word segmentation, infants use multiple forms of information.

6.3.2.4   Cross-cultural differences

Even though, in general, there are no major cross-linguistic differences in language acquisition (in that by three years normal children appear to complete the foundations of language acquisition), some cross-cultural differences exist.

In a cross-language study of infants' late babbling and first words in French, English, Japanese and Swedish, Japanese children produced their first words two

Table 6.3 *Mean age (months) of subjects in four languages at four language milestones.*

	0 words	4 words	15 words	25 words
French	10	12	15	16–17
English	9–10	11–2	14	16
Japanese	13	14	17–18	19
Swedish	9	11–12	15–16	16–17

Source: After de Boysson-Bardies et al. 1991.

to three months later than children in the other cultures. Age of attainment of first twenty-five words was also later for them (de Boysson Bardies et al. 1991).

Japanese and American mothers' speech to their children differ: American mothers provide object labels more often in their interchange with children, while Japanese mothers more often use objects to engage the child in social routines (Fernald and Morikawa 1993). The differences in child language such as in table 6.3 may thus reflect differences in parental and cultural input.[42]

6.3.3   What is the nature of experience?

6.3.3.1   Direct negative evidence

It is remarkable that when children are provided with direct negative evidence, whether the intended correction concerns phonology (2), syntax (3) or semantics (4), adult attempts to force direct negative evidence on the child are frequently rebuked.

2.   (Neil Smith, 1973)
        Child: There's a fiss in there
        Father: You mean there's a fish in there
        Child: Yes, there's a fiss
        Father: There's a fiss in there?
        Child: No, there's a **FISS** in there.

3.   (Bever 1975, 72)
        Child: Mommy goed to the store
        Father: Mommy goes to the store?
        Child: No, Daddy, I say it that way, not you.
        Father: Mommy wented to the store?
        Child: No
        Father: Mommy went to the store
        Child: That's right. Mommy wen . . . Mommy goed to the store.

---

[42] We don't know if the difference in productivity between Japanese and other infants involved a difference in comprehension.

4.   (CLAL, ENG, BGO22897; 1,9.15)
          Mother: This is a duck
          Mother: Say "duck"
          Child: "doggie"
          Mother: say "duck"
          Child: "doggie"
          Mother: What is this?
          Child: "doggie"

6.3.3.2   Indirect positive evidence

The examples above not only show the futility of "direct negative evidence," but also to some degree the futility of "direct positive evidence." The "correct" modeled form is only accepted by children when they are ready to accept it.

6.3.3.3   Non-effects of repetition

Repetitions have often been found to be ineffective in language acquisition (e.g., Newport, Gleitman and Gleitman 1977). In one study, when the modal "could" was modeled by numerous repetitions (360 times over a six-week period) this produced no significant advances over a control group of two-year olds (Shatz, Hoff-Ginsberg and MacIver 1989).

6.3.3.4   Non-effects of relative frequency

Infants' early discrimination of sounds within the speech stream is not determined by relative frequency of their occurrence in the input (see chapter 8). 4.5 month olds don't show longer listening times to common words, e.g., "baby" or "mommy," than to uncommon words, like "hamlet" and "kingdom" (Jusczyk 1997, 131). What children do *not* produce in early language (e.g., frequent overt determiners or auxiliaries are often missing in early child English), or what they *do* produce (e.g., the child who says "this is for mine" [CLAL, ENG, BGO 22897; 2 yrs.], or "Who be's in this game?") does not correlate with frequency with which forms have been heard.[43]

Non-effects of frequency are also shown in cross-linguistic studies of children's morphological overregularizations of irregular verbs, e.g., he "breaked" for "he broke" in English (cf. chapter 11). In English, most verbs are regular (although irregulars comprise a large proportion of the most commonly used verbs, e.g., "get/got," "go/went," etc.). However, in German, regular patterns are not statistically dominant (Marcus et al. 1995). Children acquiring German demonstrate a default inflection of German participles, adding the -t suffix, "despite the fact that the -t affix does not apply to the majority of German verbs" (Marcus et al., 1995; Pinker 1999, 215–228). With German noun plurals, the German child shows the affix -s as a default, despite its low frequency (Marcus 1995). Overregularizations

---

[43] An "order" of fourteen morphemes in English language acquisition has been proposed (e.g., Brown 1973b) and debated (Moerk, 1980, Pinker 1981).

in English child language also occur with nouns; e.g., "my pantses." Although the English plural system is predominantly regular, it behaves similarly to the English past tense, which has a much greater number of irregular words. "The findings from English plurals (almost all regular) on the one hand and German plurals (almost all irregular) on the other, strongly suggest that regular inflection is independent of frequency" (Marcus 1995, 456–457; see also Clahsen 1999).[44]

Frequency certainly may have effects. For example, Gathercole (1986) found Scottish children use a present perfect construction more frequently than children acquiring English; presumably Scottish adults do so also. What needs to be explained is why some frequent things are "picked up" by children while others are not, at particular times.

In summary, children are selective in their choice of input, whether direct or indirect, whether positive or negative, whether frequent or infrequent.

6.3.3.5   Fast mapping

In fact, much of child language acquisition involves a remarkable "fast mapping"; minimal exposure to a model is sufficient. In the area of word meaning, this term refers to a quick formation of an initial hypothesis after limited exposure to input (chapter 10, 10.3.3). The mechanisms of "fast mapping" are currently under investigation (e.g., Wilkinson and Stanford, 1996).

6.3.3.6   Imitation

Children may spontaneously repeat utterances they hear, varying widely in the degree to which they do so. Can children imitate a structure for which they do not already have the essential grammatical competence?[45] Is imitation a cause or a result of language acquisition? As we will see in chapter 7, imitation of language appears not to be a direct passive rote copy of the input, but requires analysis and reconstruction of the input. In a comprehensive study intended to explore the role of imitation in language development, Bloom, Hood and Lightbown (1974) analyzed over 17,000 utterances in six children aged eighteen to twenty-five months of age, with MLU from 1.0 to 2.0, over a six-month period. They found (a) significant individual differences, with two children barely imitating at all; (b) when multiword utterances were imitated, there was a tendency for them to be present in spontaneous speech as well; (c) there was some tendency for individual words to be imitated and then become spontaneous. Therefore imitation is not necessary in language acquisition, and there is no evidence, particularly at the level of syntax, that it plays a significant causal role.

---

[44] Marchman, Plunkett and Goodman 1997 challenge the Marcus claim that these effects are independent of frequency.

[45] In studies of the development of imitation (Piaget 1951), children were found to imitate actions already in their repertoire, but not to imitate complex coordinative actions which were not directly in their repertoire, i.e., if the requisite cognitive computation was not there. Later studies of neonate imitation (e.g., of tongue protrusion) (Meltzoff and Moore 1977) can be similarly analyzed.

6.3.3.7   Experience without feedback

A classic experiment documents the indirectness of the role of experience in language acquisition. Cromer (1987) studied the acquisition of structures like those in (5) and (6), known to be late developing in English language acquisition (Chomsky 1969). In comprehension tests, young children do not distinguish between these two structures in terms of who bites and who gets bitten. Doing so requires not only knowing where the empty categories exist in the structures, e.g., (5b) vs. (6b), and which antecedents bind these, but doing so differently for the lexical items "glad" vs. "fun".

5.   a. The wolf is glad to bite
       b. The wolf is glad to Ø bite

6.   a. The wolf is fun to bite
       b. The wolf is fun to bite Ø

Cromer asked children (7–9 years) to interpret the two structures in an act-out task every three months over a period of one year. No feedback was given to the children as to whether or not they were correct. Half of the sentences required the named doll to be the actor, e.g., (5); the other half, a non-named doll, e.g., (6). Pretraining exposed children to both act-out possibilities. This non-corrective experience resulted in significant improvement, leading to levels of performance "by nine years of age that not only were significantly improved but also are not typically found until age ten or eleven in cross-sectional studies" (415). Mere exposure was sufficient for growth and change. Cromer concluded that "experience stimulates language organizational processes and that these affect other linguistic structures that are internally related" (412). The children appeared to be building their own grammars in their own way, without direct positive or negative evidence as to what was right or wrong.

6.4   Conclusions

We saw in chapter 3 that the information required to solve the Projection Problem and crack the code of language acquisition is not directly in the data. We saw in chapter 4 (cf. chapter 11) that in many cases children must come to know what is *not* possible in their language where the only evidence lies in the non-occurrence of these phenomena. Now we see that children are not "data driven," in the sense that they are not trying to solve the problem by simply "looking very closely at the data" and "picking up" knowledge from it. Rather, children are considering the input and imposing structure on it. They are building a theory about the language to be acquired. Input must fit their theory. Children are *selective* and *reconstructive* in use of input data. We can only explain when and where input is either quickly absorbed or resisted by children by consulting their internal state.

The relation of children to the language input, i.e., their language experience, is *indirect*. It is mediated by the computation of the child mind, which is preprogrammed to be highly sensitive to aspects of input language data that correspond closely to internal organizing principles. Why are children as impervious as they are to so many aspects of input at the same time that they are so marvelously sensitive to so many other aspects? When it comes to language acquisition, they know best. "One generalization that appears to cover all the studies is that situations that encourage the child to filter the input through her grammar will facilitate language development more than situations that do not" (Valian 1999, 524).

Children will operate on any amount and any form of available language data in a creative manner, led by internal linguistic biases and supported by strong computational abilities allowing quick, effective use of input. Experience in a general sense "legitimizes" and fosters the natural creation of language, as does a communicative context. The best environment appears to be the richest natural productive interactive one.[46]

6.5   Supplementary readings

Valian 1999 provides a comprehensive survey and critique of research on language input in child language acquisition. Bornstein et al. 1992a, b, Camaioni et al. 1998 provide empirical studies of cross-cultural variation in input.

---

[46] Huttenlocher et al. 2002 provide recent study of effects of experience.

7 How can we tell what children know? Methods for the study of language acquisition

7.1 Introduction

We need to know what children know and don't know about the grammar for their language along the course of language development. How can we do so? We must enter, with a developmental perspective, the domain of *psycholinguistics*, the study of how the mind represents and processes language, based on behavioral studies of language use.

7.1.1 Knowing vs. doing

We need to assess what children *know* about language on the basis of how they *use* language, i.e., how they *speak* and *understand* language, or make *metalinguistic judgments* about it. However, when we observe a child speaking, interpreting or judging any particular utterance, this single behavior will never reveal the child's knowledge.

If Mary utters a sentence like (1a), Jessica may answer with (1b). We can't estimate Jessica's knowledge on the basis of her utterance in (1b) alone. If we did, we could mistakenly think that Jessica doesn't know how to inflect verbs for tense, or doesn't know that English requires overt subjects in sentences. Our data must expand beyond observations of single sentences.

1.   a. *Mary*: What do you want to do now?
        b. *Jessica*: Go home

We must also discover what children do *not* do in principle. If Jessica randomly produced not only (1b) but also (2) at other times, this would suggest that, for Jessica, word order was random. We need to know that (2) does *not* occur while (1b) *does*, in related contexts.

2.   Home go

If children behave appropriately given sentence (3), we don't know whether they have fully analyzed the structure of the utterance in order to understand it, parsing it (into its bracketed units with embedding), or whether they have simply

Table 7.1 *Competence/Performance*

Competence	Performance
Tacit knowledge of the generative grammatical system that underlies language.	Behavior with language, e.g., *speaking, comprehending* or making *judgments* about language in real time.

understood individual lexical items, e.g., "Daddy" and "slipper", and inferred the rest of the meaning from context, independent of syntax.[1] How then do we link our data and our analyses in a scientific way?

3.   I'm home now. [Would [you [please _ [go [get [Daddy's [slippers]]]]]]].

7.1.1.1   Competence and performance

On the basis of children's *performance* with language, we must infer their *competence* (table 7.1). To justify our inference, we must dissociate various factors which interact with children's expression of linguistic knowledge in their performance. The researcher chooses experimental designs, methods, tasks and modes of analysis which allow him/her to constrain this inference. (7.1.1.2–7.1.1.4 summarize these factors.)

7.1.1.2   Language processing

The researcher consults both current linguistic theories of grammatical competence, and also current models of "language processing." The latter attempt to formulate how tacit mental computation activates and relates each form of linguistic representation (cf. chapter 2) in the various modes of behavior with language, e.g., speaking, hearing, judging, reading, writing.[2] Every behavior with language which we observe in children involves this computation as well as their linguistic knowledge.[3]

7.1.1.3   Language knowledge and pragmatic factors

The researcher's job is made even more complex when we realize that every act of speaking or understanding language which we observe in children involves their use of language in a particular time and place. Children may adopt certain "strategies." When asked to interpret sentences such as "The red truck is pushing the green truck," they respond quickly and with more ease if the green truck, not the red truck, is already placed on the track; i.e., if the truck children have to place is the subject of the sentence. For passive sentences, like "The green

---

[1] Shatz (1978) has documented tendency of the young child to respond to many sentence types with action responses, even when an action is not called for by the sentence itself.
[2] See Caplan 1992, Garrett 1990, Garman 1990 for review; Cooper and Walker 1979, Levelt 1991.
[3] For attempts to factor out possible developments in language processing from developments in language knowledge see Mazuka 1998; Valian 1993; Tyler and Marslen Wilson 1978, 1981; Bates and MacWhinney 1989; Trueswell et al. 1999.

truck is pushed by the red truck," children respond more easily if the truck to be placed is the logical subject, i.e., the red truck.[4]

Young children may adopt an "order of mention" strategy (a "comprehension strategy"). In Ferreiro's 1971 study, 130 French speaking children (aged 4–10) were shown a girl doll wash a boy doll's face and then the boy doll go upstairs. Then they were asked to start a sentence describing the event with "the boy." Instead of easily generating "order reversals" allowed by natural language ("the boy was washed by the girl after . . ." or "Before the boy went upstairs, the girl . . ."), they generated numerous contortions, like: "The boy, he washed his hands, and then the girl went upstairs" (trans. from the French; Ferreiro 1971, 112), trying to make the order of the extralinguistic context cohere with the order of the sentence. (See also Clark 1993, 61; 1973a.)

The cognitive content of a sentence can also affect performance with language. For example, for 4–5 year olds, the number of animate nouns referred to in a sentence increases the complexity of cognitive computation, consequently decreasing performance in an act-out test of comprehension on sentences like (4a) as opposed to (4b) (Goodluck and Tavakolian 1982).

4.   a. The <u>dog</u> kicks the <u>horse</u> that knocks over the <u>sheep</u>
        b. The <u>dog</u> kicks the <u>horse</u> that knocks over the table

Pragmatic factors such as number of horses available (a plural reference set or a singular one) may also interact with performance on sentences like (4) (Hamburger and Crain 1982 propose a concept of "pragmatic felicity").[5]

7.1.1.4   Language acquisition and performance factors

Children's behavior with language is also affected by numerous "performance factors", e.g., their *memory* and ability to deal with *length* of linguistic utterances. The relation between these factors and linguistic knowledge is complex.

Children's ability to remember what they hear is to some degree determined by their ability to structure it. Given a random list of terms like (5a), memory is likely to be deficient when compared to memory for the same list structured, e.g., (5b) (Epstein 1961).

5.   a. brillig slithy toves gyre gimble wabe
        b. 'twas brillig, and the slithy toves
           did gyre and gimble in the wabe. (Lewis Carroll, 15, TLG)

Earlier research has shown that memory and cognition are not independent in the child. Piaget and Inhelder argued that "the most important factor in the

---

[4] Huttenlocher and Weiner 1971; Huttenlocher, Eisenberg and Strauss 1968; Huttenlocher and Strauss 1968; Bloom 1974, 307.

[5] Relatively few studies of language acquisition have investigated precise interactions between developing linguistic and pragmatic knowledge in order to account for child language behaviors and to determine what aspects of children's knowledge may be developing. See Blume 2002; Kaufman 1994; Grimshaw and Rosen 1990; Boser 1995; Austin et al. 1998; Foster-Cohen 1990; Clark and Grossman 1998; Crain and Thornton 1998; Drozd 2004.

development of memory . . . is its gradual organization" (Piaget and Inhelder 1969, 80, 1973).[6]

Recent research suggests that "infants' memory processing does not fundamentally differ from that of older children and adults" (Rovee-Collier 1999, 80; 1997; Rovee-Collier, Hartshorn and DiRubbo, in press; Rovee-Collier and Gerhardstein 1997c, 32–33). Numerous experiments have evidenced infants' remarkable capacity for memory of language stimuli (e.g., Jusczyk 1997, 124–125). At two months, they have been shown to remember a set of three different syllables, enough to detect a change in a single phonetic feature after a two minute delay, e.g., [si][ba][tu] when [ba] was changed to [da] (Jusczyk 1997, 125). At eight months, they recognized words from a story read to them two weeks earlier (Hohne, Jusczyk and Redanz 1994; Jusczyk and Hohne 1997). While infants' memory surely affects their linguistic behaviors, it is also to some degree determined by their linguistic knowledge.[7]

Children's ability to deal with long utterances may also relate to their ability to structure these. Early speech is characterized by a *universal length constraint* (e.g., Brown 1973c) which is gradually overcome, as in the progression from (6a) to (6d) (Bloom 1970a).

6.   a. go#   (G, age 19.1, MLU 1.12, Bloom 1970, 11)
           car#ride
        b. Mommy jacket (G, age 20.2, MLU 1.34, Bloom 1970a, 93)
           Lois baby record
        c. no open the wallet (G, age 23.3, MLU 1.79, Bloom 1970a, 184)
        d. no man ride this tank car (G, age 25.2, MLU 2.30, Bloom 1970a, 161)

One young child's multisyllabic vocabulary was largely produced as one syllable until the age of eighteen months, e.g., [po] for "piano" and [kiz] for "candies" (Johnson, Lewis and Hogan 1997). In Finnish, where the proportion of multisyllabic words is higher, children at early stages appear not to produce longer than disyllabic forms, e.g., [api] for "apina" (monkey) (Kunnari 2002, 128).

Length constraint on early language has led to a general developmental measure termed Mean Length of Utterance (MLU; after Brown 1973c and Cazden 1968). This descriptive measure of early speech counts the number of morphemes in each utterance, sums over the utterances, and then divides by the number of utterances in the sample, as in (7).[8]

7.   **Computing MLU**
        dat bunny   2
        dat bunny get juice on it   6
        sloppy bunny   2
        bunny hops   3
        Total: 13/4 = 3.25 MLU

---

[6] See Kail 1997 and Cowan 1997 for collected readings on the development of memory in childhood.
[7] Gathercole and Baddeley 1989 and Gathercole 1999 argue that phonological short-term memory in four- and five-year-olds may correlate with development of vocabulary.
[8] No precise definition of "morpheme" was provided.

MLU is widely used for describing general language development, especially up to MLU 3.5, when embedding, coordination and recursion are first observed (Brown 1973c).[9] Different children overcome the length constraint at different rates. Figure 7.1 reveals normal variation in release of the length constraint in English acquisition among six children: the Harvard children, Adam, Eve and Sarah (Brown 1973c), and the children studied by Lois Bloom (1970a), Kathryn, Eric and Gia. Age and MLU do not correlate consistently and/or directly, especially within the first two years when MLU is often most quickly expanding.[10]

Although useful in a general sense for estimating general developmental levels of early language acquisition, MLU is a superficial measure which does not inform us directly of children's grammatical knowledge. We still do not understand the source of the length constraint, how it is overcome, or how it interacts with grammatical knowledge.[11] Cross-linguistically, we still do not have a universal typology of morphology, and the MLU measure is not comparable across languages (e.g., Hickey 1991, Dromi and Berman 1982).

Just as we cannot explain language development in terms of memory development, we cannot explain it in terms of length development. We must factor out the effects of a length constraint from developing grammatical knowledge.

Brown (1973c) suggested that development of a child's MLU was an "excellent simple index of grammatical development because almost every new kind of knowledge increases length" (53). MLU does appear to be superior to age as a general descriptor for language development (e.g., Shipley, Smith and Gleitman 1969, 342; Lust 1977a).

However, the development of MLU does not correlate with grammatical "stages" in the full sense of the term, e.g., (8) (cf. Brown 1973c, 58). It does not appear to precisely correlate with grammatical development.[12]

8.   **Basic properties of a "stage"**
    a. Distinct onset and offset time
    b. General organization of the underlying grammatical system is distinct during that time
    c. Widespread related unique characteristics characterize all structures during a distinct period of time

---

[9] UB (Upper Bound) is another descriptive measure: the longest utterance in a child's observed speech sample.

[10] Conant 1987; Klee and Fitzgerald 1985; Miller and Chapman 1981.

[11] Lois Bloom (1970) suggested that the length constraint "reflected an inability to carry the full structural load of the underlying representation. Limitations in linguistic operations appear to interact with limitations in cognitive function to influence linguistic expression in an as yet unspecified way" (169). It has been suggested that the length constraint on words may reflect ". . . a limitation in the processing capacity required to retrieve and hold a lexical item, translate the auditory code to a sequential set of motor plans, and execute these plans" (Johnson, Lewis and Hogan 1997, 339, 347; see also Salidis and Johnson 1997).

[12] See Piaget 1983 and Gruber and Voneche 1977 on prerequisites for "stage" in cognitive development.

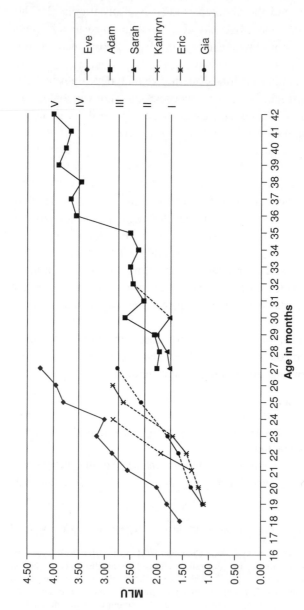

Fig. 7.1 *Variation across children in MLU development*

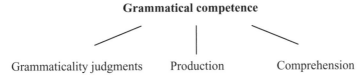

Grammatical competence

Grammaticality judgments   Production   Comprehension

Fig. 7.2 *Grammatical competence*

In summary, assessing grammatical development requires dissociation of children's linguistic competence from various factors involved in their performance with language, and application of the science of Linguistics in the context of the science of Psycholinguistics as well as Developmental Psychology. The researcher may do so through systematic application of a range of methods and measures.

7.2 Typology of methods

Three modes of performance with language can be tested (figure 7.2). Each of these reflects children's linguistic knowledge as well as processing and performance factors.[13]

Each can be studied either naturalistically or experimentally. Table 7.2 summarizes the range of methodologies available for the study of language acquisition in each mode, and examples.[14]

7.2.1 Grammaticality judgments

Linguists' primary method of assessing language knowledge rests on "grammaticality judgments," where adult speakers are asked to judge whether sentences with various structures and operations are possible or not. These kinds of judgment involve a type of performance invoking *metalinguistic* knowledge.

Grammaticality judgments are not a perfect measure of grammatical competence, especially when the informant is not a linguist; many factors other than grammatical knowledge enter into a person's judgment about a sentence; the possible source for a "yes/no" response to a sentence is not explicit. Judgment can be made on the basis of semantic or pragmatic factors as well (e.g., Levelt 1974a, 14f.; Schutze 1996; Eisele and Lust 1996). Judgment is confounded when this type of performance is requested of children, e.g., (9).

---

[13] We concentrate on methods used in primary research on children's language development, rather than standardized "tests" of language acquisition, or assessments like the MacArthur Communicative Development Inventory (Fenson et al. 1994), which are based on parent interpretations and reports.

[14] Table 7.2 reflects an idealization. Most, if not all, methods require some cross-modal component.

Table 7.2 *Methods for the study of language acquisition*

Types of language performance	Types of method and example	
	Naturalistic	**Experimental**
Metalinguistic/grammaticality judgment	Sinclair et al., 1978; Gleitman, Gleitman and Shipley 1972 *Self-initiated corrections* Clark and Anderson 1979	McDaniel and Cairns 1996 *Jokes* Hirsh-Pasek et al. 1978
Production Spontaneous speech and elicited production	*Natural speech* Roger Brown 1973; Stromswald 1996; Demuth 1996 CHILDES: Child Language Data Exchange System (computerized databank of child language corpora) MacWhinney and Snow 1985, 1990; MacWhinney 1991 *Triggered natural speech* Berk 1996	*Elicited production* Thornton 1996, Crain and Thornton 1998 *Picture – question* Fraser, Brown and Bellugi 1963; Leonard and Dromi 1994; Donahue 1984 *Modified cloze procedure* Potts et al., 1979
Imitation	*Spontaneous imitation* Bloom et al., 1974 Ervin-Tripp 1964	*Elicited imitation* Slobin and Welsh 1973 Lust, Flynn and Foley 1996
Comprehension Commands	*Natural Commands* Smith 1970 Shipley, Smith and Gleitman 1969; Gleitman et al. 1978	"Simon Says" (Chien and Wexler 1987b, 1990)
Act-out (toy moving)		*Free Act-Out* Piagetian Labs (e.g., Ferreiro et al. 1976, Beilin 1975); Goodluck 1996; Lust 1986d *Structured Act-Out* "Big Bird's ice cream" (Foley et al. 1997, 2003); "The Party Game" (Chien and Wexler 1990)
Question/answer Picture-choice		Chomsky 1969; Roeper and deVilliers 1994 Garman 1974; Fraser, Bellugi and Brown 1963; Gerken and McIntosh 1993
Truth value judgment		Crain and McKee 1985; Chien and Wexler 1990; Chien and Li 1998; Eisele 1988; Eisele and Lust 1996; Grimshaw and Rosen 1990; Gordon 1996
Infant head turn /Preferential looking techniques		Hirsh-Pasek and Golinkoff 1996; Jusczyk 1997a

9.   (Jessica, age 5; Shattuck-Hufnagel and Long 1977, personal
       communication)
       Here's another sentence Jessica. Could you say "John went home and Mary
       went home"?
       J: John and Mary went home
       No, I didn't mean you had to say it. I wanted you to tell me whether or not
       that was an OK sentence. "John went home and Mary went home". Is that
       OK?
       J. It's worse
       Why is it worse?
       J: Because I'm laughing
       . . . .
       Suppose I say this sentence, "Jessica is a sister." Is that an OK sentence?
       J: What?
       Suppose I say . . . well, let me say now, suppose I say "Jessica is a girl." Is
       that an OK sentence?
       J: No, say what you said before
       Jessica is a sister
       J: That's the worst one, because I don't have a sister or a brother.
       What if I say "Jessica is a girl." Is that OK?
       J: No, I'm a boy!
       What if I say "Jessica are a girl"
       J: Well, I don't like you (wailing)

When children do give metalinguistic judgments, it is often for reasons other
than grammar. For a "long word," young children have suggested "newspaper"
because it has a lot of written things in it (Berthoud-Papandropoulou 1978, Papandropoulou and Sinclair 1974).[15]

There is naturalistic evidence that children discriminate well-formed from non-
well-formed utterances, e.g., (10) (See Clark and Clark 1977, 384–386; Clark and
Anderson 1979). Some researchers do report success in eliciting grammaticality
judgments with young children (McDaniel, McKee and Cairns 1996). Questions
persist as to what development is necessary before children are capable of performing such judgments in a manner which targets specific aspects of grammatical
knowledge.[16]

10.   Father: Say "jump"
       Son: [d∧p]
       Father: No, "jump"
       Son: [d∧p]
       Father: No, "jummmp"
       Son: Only daddy can say [d∧p]   (Smith 1973, 101)

---

[15] For studies of development of metalinguistic knowledge, see Clark 1983; Gleitman, Gleitman
and Shipley 1972; Hirsh-Pasek et al. 1978; Sinclair et al. 1978. A number of tests to assess
metalinguistic knowledge have been developed, e.g., Ferreiro 1978; Liberman et al. 1977; Bruce
1964, Read et al. 1986, Goswami and Bryant 1990.

[16] Smith 1973 (136) suggests that the young child in (14) may have recognized his own phonological
deformations on a tape recording when he was still producing them, but not later.

7.2.2   Assessing language production

7.2.2.1   Natural speech sampling

One prominent method of studying young children's language knowledge involves studying their language production through the recording and transcription of natural speech (see Demuth 1996a). This uses "rich interpretation." If a child utters "mommy sock," the researcher consults the context in which children and hearer are communicating to determine what the syntactic form alone does not, e.g., whether the utterance corresponds to "[mommy's sock]" or "[mommy [please [put [on [my sock]]]]]" (Bloom 1970a).

Natural speech sample analyses confront all the challenges of creating a valid transcription of speech involved in the transcription of adult speech (Edwards 1992a, b) and have the added difficulty of capturing the particular properties of early child speech, e.g., "abbreviation" and distinction from adult speech models, including possible phonetic deformation (Ochs 1979, Demuth 1996a, Edwards 1992b).[17]

In order for data to be comparable across natural speech samples from different children, principles of data collection, transcription and coding must be consistent and systematic. Many specific decisions need to be made: "which utterances from which subjects' utterances will be examined, what criterion will be used for acquisition, how error rates will be calculated" (Stromswald 1996, 50). Different transcription systems exist.[18]

Systematic analysis of natural speech, assessing both grammatical forms of utterances and contexts in which they occur, can maximize the possibility of the researcher's discovery of children's grammatical system at any particular time. Longitudinal analysis of a child's speech, combined with systematic linguistic analyses, can reveal developmental change in this system over time (e.g., Smith 1973). One can measure age of first occurrence of a grammatical form, or productivity at a particular time. Measure of productivity can assess: (a) if a form occurs in obligatory contexts (Brown 1973c); (b) how often the form occurs or is absent in these contexts; (c) if a constituent occurs in several forms, e.g., the same verb in several conjugations (Gathercole et al. 1999).[19] Estimates of a grammatical

---

[17] As Edwards notes, "transcription has become such a commonplace tool that it is easy to forget that it is an artifact. The transcript is necessarily selective and interpretive, rather than exhaustive and objective" (1992a, 367).

[18] Samarin 1967; Ingram 1989; Blake and Quartaro 1990; Klee and Paul 1981; Edwards and Lampert 1993; some allow computer access, e.g., the CHAT system developed in connection with CHILDES databank. See Pye 1994, Edwards 1992b and MacWhinney and Snow 1992; the Linguist's SHOEBOX (Davis and Wimbish 1994 or Wimbish 1989); COALA (Pienemann 1991); SALT (Miller and Chapman 1983); or the Data Transcription and Analysis (DTA) tool of the Cornell Language Acquisition Lab (CLAL).

[19] Cross-lab and cross-linguistic calibration of natural speech data collection, transcription, and coding remains to be achieved. Stromswald (1996) reviews issues surrounding analyses of natural speech samples to determine when a child has mastery of (a particular component of) grammar (44f.). See also Blake, Quartaro and Onorati 1993.

system can search for evidence of specific linguistic operations, e.g., question formation or relative clauses.

Different forms of data sharing are possible. For example, CHILDES (Child Language Data Exchange System; MacWhinney and Snow 1985 and 1990) maintains copies of various researchers' transcripts of child speech samples and distributes them (by internet and CD-ROM).[20] Scholars may access these transcripts from this databank and either derive secondary research from them, or test the generalizability of their own primary research results against them.[21]

Natural speech samples can provide rich sources of evidence on children's language knowledge, but they are inherently limited. Specific constructions may not occur in a particular child's language sample simply because the pragmatic or cognitive context of the situation hasn't motivated them.[22]

7.2.2.2   Elicited Production (EP)

Experimental methods can elicit language production in ways which allow the researcher to target particular aspects of linguistic knowledge, and do so in controlled fashion.

In one type, the experimenter tries to provide children with a standardized context which would motivate children to select a sentence which the researcher is interested in; e.g., (11a) tries to provoke children to give a response like (11b), with an inverted question (Thornton 1996):

11.   a. Experimenter: In this story, the crane is tickling one of the zebras.
                     Ask the puppet which one.
        b. Model Child: Which zebra is getting tickled by the crane?

This method, like natural speech sampling, can provide rich examples of children's ability to create and structure language.[23] Another EP method provides initial structure from which children can be "led" to the particular form the researcher is studying. This "cloze procedure" is exemplified in (12) (Potts et al. 1979, 132), in study of relative clauses. Here a child is asked to complete the experimenter's sentence (in the presence of picture contexts):[24]

---

[20] CHILDES is centered at Carnegie Mellon University: http://www.childes.psy.cmu.edu
[21] Where researchers work on transcripts from CHILDES, they usually accept the transcript provided by the original researcher. In some cases, audio recordings are available and transcripts can be analyzed against these.
[22] Some researchers have taken steps to insure productivity of targeted structures. In order to generate an array of questions from a child, Berk (1996) devised a "triggered natural speech" technique in which she eliminated pages from a story book, thus disrupting the story line, and successfully provoked children to produce full-formed questions by answering every single-word "Wh" question from children (e.g., "why?") with a follow up question, "Why what?"
[23] Children may not produce the particular structure which the researcher is interested in, e.g., in response to (11a), one could simply ask "who?" or "which one?"
[24] The cloze procedure is not directly applicable to languages which do not have a left–right subject–predicate order, and is not equally suited to all constructions in English.

12.   Experimenter: Some children walk to school and some children ride the
           bus. These are children . . . (*who ride the bus, that ride . . .*).

7.2.2.3   Elicited Imitation (EI)

An Elicited Imitation task requests children to imitate a sentence or set
of sentences which have been specifically designed and controlled to test specific
structures or operations and the principles which underlie them (Lust, Flynn and
Foley 1996). In this case, the researcher knows the structure that the children
are attempting to produce, can analyze children's reproduction for matches and
mismatches to the adult structure, and can link these to a theory of linguistic
structure in order to make inferences regarding children's theory of language.
There appears to be an innate ability for imitation in the human species, making
the EI method accessible to young children (Piaget 1962; Meltzoff and Moore
1983). Use of EI depends on a remarkable and fundamental fact about language: it
appears to be virtually impossible for children (or for the adult) to passively copy
a sentence and to repeat it without analyzing and reconstructing it.[25] Production
therefore reflects this active analysis.

Errors. In EI and other production tasks, analyses of children's "errors" may
reveal their linguistic computation.[26] An early anecdotal study of elicited imitation
observed (13) from a two-year-old child, Echo. (Lust 1977a provides experimental
test of related structures using EI and converging evidence.) (13a) shows the child
maintaining the *meaning* while abandoning the form of the model; i.e., relative
clause embedding is converted to a coordinate structure. (13b) shows the child
maintaining *the form*, while abandoning the meaning of the model. (13c) shows
the child interpreting and expanding *gaps* (or null sites corresponding to ellipsis)
in the model, while (13d) shows the child reducing redundancy to *create such
ellipsis*. (13e) compared to (13f) shows that length of utterance is not the primary
determinant of the fullness of a child's imitation; the grammar of the sentence
interacts with its length in determining EI.

13.   Slobin and Welsh 1973
           a. Experimenter: [Mozart [who cried]]came to my party
              Echo: [Mozart cried] and [he came to my party]
           b. Experimenter:[[The blue shoes] and [blue pencils]] are here
              Echo: [blue pencil are here] and [a blue pencil are here]
           c. Experimenter: [The pencil and some paper are here]
              Echo: [some pencil here] and [some paper here]
           d. Experimenter: [Here is a brown brush and here is a comb]
              Echo: Here's a [brown brush and a comb]

---

[25] This issue remains to be evaluated more thoroughly in pathological populations, e.g., Caplan
1992. This may be true of word repetition as well (e.g., Leonard et al. 1979). This result confirms
an early speculation by Chomsky (1964, 39) as well as early conclusions by Piaget.

[26] The term "error" usually refers to any mismatch between children's production and the model
sentence.

e. Experimenter: The pencil is green
   Echo: pencil green
f. Experimenter: The little boy is eating some pink ice cream
   Echo: little boy eating some pink ice cream

In summary, children analyze different components of linguistic knowledge and resynthesize these in order to map from form to meaning in their language production. Several methods are available to the researcher in order to elicit and assess language production data.

7.2.3   Assessing comprehension

Although various EP methods also tap comprehension to some degree, they often do not provide direct evidence on particular aspects of sentence interpretation. For example, if we want evidence on how children interpret a pronoun like "she" or "herself," we want a more direct test of a child's comprehension. Several different methods are available for this, as in table 7.2.

7.2.3.1   Act out / toy-moving task

The "act out" method is useful for testing language comprehension because of its simplicity and its gamelike quality (e.g., Goodluck 1996). It can be applied cross-linguistically with standardization (e.g., Ferreiro et al. 1976). A sentence designed to vary factors of interest can be tested by asking children to "show the story" in a model sentence with a set of dolls. Stimulus sentences similar to those used in production methods can provide converging evidence. The task can also be used to test for children's obedience to certain linguistic constraints. It can be manipulated in terms of the context presented to children, and the nature of the activity required (e.g., Foley et al. 1997, 2003; Chien and Wexler, 1990).

7.2.3.2   Truth Value Judgment Task

While production methods require children to mediate their knowledge through vocal motor production systems, and act-out tests of comprehension require children to mediate their knowledge through motor actions of toy-moving behavior, some tests of comprehension reduce the amount and type of overt behavior required. In various types of "Truth Value Judgment Task (TVJT)," the adult may perform an act-out situation or provide a picture showing a particular action, and children can be simply asked to judge whether this is a possible interpretation for a particular sentence, which the experimenter reads, by answering "yes" or "no." Like act-out tasks, the TVJT can test for possible constraints on interpretation, but more directly. Children can be presented with various interpretations which do or do not abide by a hypothesized constraint (see Crain and McKee 1985; Chien and Wexler 1990; Eisele and Lust 1996). The Truth Value Judgment

Task provides data which are quickly and easily summarized, although the actual source of yes/no responses can only be indirectly inferred.[27]

7.2.4   Summary

All tests of comprehension or production tap complex linguistic and non-linguistic processes in children's minds. Choice of method depends on the particular aspect of linguistic knowledge being studied.

7.3   Methods before the first words

In the last decades, a revolution occurred in experimental methods used to study very young infants and toddlers, even newborns. These now allow testing of what infants know about language even before they speak by inducing simple non-linguistic behaviors (sucking, looking, listening) in response to language stimuli. With careful design of language stimuli, the researcher can infer children's ability to detect, discriminate and categorize them; with infants and toddlers these methods can begin to measure the origins of language discrimination and comprehension (Jusczyk 1997a, for review; chapter 5, figure 5.2 for example).

These methods (which modify those used to study the development of visual perception in infants) have documented that infants show not only sensitivities to fine distinctions in linguistic stimuli but also preferences. Infants appear to distinguish, and prefer to listen to, language stimuli which are natural or familiar for them (cf. fn. 28 below). Because they are applicable to infants even a few days old, these methods allow us to begin mapping a continuous developmental course in language knowledge from birth.

7.3.1   High Amplitude Sucking (HAS)

One widely used method for study of language acquisition in the first few months of life is a technique based on changes in infant sucking rate, which is monitored and measured statistically – the infant sucks a nipple which is connected to a computer ("non-nutritive sucking"). It is based on the infant establishing a baseline of sucking. Then a measure of sucking is developed in conjunction with a particular sound stimulus (familiarization phase) followed by a period of satiation or habituation (decreased sucking as the infant becomes less attentive to repetition of the same sound). Each suck by the infant beyond the baseline rate activates a sound. By shifting the stimuli presented to the infant in comparison to continual presentation of the same stimulus and measuring shift

---

[27] Both adults and children are influenced by pragmatic contexts of the scenes and sentences presented in these tasks (e.g., Eisele and Lust 1996).

or lack of shift in sucking rate, the researcher can infer whether the infant has discriminated the changed stimulus. If infants perceive a sound as different, they begin to suck vigorously again (see de Boysson-Bardies 1999, 20–22).

7.3.2   Head turn techniques

Several other methods, frequently used with infants aged six to twelve months, measure head turn response to various auditory and/or visual stimuli (these may be combined with measures of children's visual fixation time or listening time in conjunction with a head turn).

In a version of this technique, "visually reinforced infant speech discrimination" (VRISD), the infant sits on a parent's lap and is presented with repeated sounds in a three-sided chamber; the infant is conditioned to expect that when a sound changes, an interesting event will occur near a loudspeaker to one side, e.g., an animated dancing bear. The infant is trained to produce a head turn response toward the loudspeaker with the visual reinforcer when they perceive a sound change. Sounds can then be varied by the experimenter to test the infant's generalization of the initial sound distinctions. If the infant perceives a sound change, a head turn toward the expected toy is predicted. Both discrimination and categorization can be tested (see Werker et al. 1981).

In another version, infants are presented with different stimuli from loudspeakers to the right or left (e.g., "baby talk" or adult directed speech, or natural or unnatural speech samples). After infants are familiarized with which type of sounds occur on which side, they are tested for their head turn preference for one side or the other. Presentation of a speech sample is contingent on the infant's head turn. Looking and listening time can be measured in conjunction with direction of head turn.

An intermodal "preferential looking paradigm" presents the infant with a choice between visual images in the presence of an auditory linguistic stimulus. The rationale is "that infants will prefer to watch the screen that matches the linguistic stimulus more than the screen that does not" (Hirsh-Pasek and Golinkoff 1996, 61; Golinkoff et al. 1987). For example: one video screen shows a woman kissing a ball; the other screen shows the woman kissing keys; the infant is presented with "Hey, she's kissing the keys"; infant preference for looking at the matched versus the mismatched screen is assessed. This method can be used with older infants, including two-year-olds.[28] In one variation of this method – "split screen preferential looking" – an infant may be positioned in the middle of a split screen presenting two options. If infants comprehend the auditory stimulus, they are expected to differentiate the two visual stimuli accordingly.

---

[28] Because this method is based on an assumption of the infant's preference for matched auditory and visual stimuli, it differs from intramodal tasks, where response may be increased in the face of "novelty." Infant visual looking time is generally found to increase to novel visual stimuli. (See Hirsh-Pasek and Golinkoff 1996, 61–62 for discussion.)

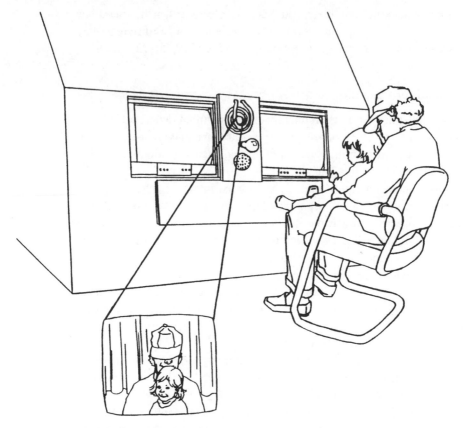

Fig. 7.3 *Preferential looking.*
From: Naigles, L. and Kako, E. 1993. *"First Contact in Verb Acquisition: Defining a role for syntax." Child Development,* **64**: 1665–1687 (figure on p. 1670). Reprinted by permission of the Society for Research in Child Development.

7.4   Comparing methods

7.4.1   Naturalistic vs. experimental

Naturalistic studies provide an important resource for the study of language acquisition primarily because very young children often resist controlled experimental procedures.[29] They also may allow children to reveal their knowledge with minimal adult influence.[30]

Although theoretical explanations can be developed on the basis of naturalistic observations, they must always be *ad hoc*. We can never fully test for the

---

[29] Even in the extremely "natural" sucking environment, "attrition rates of 50 percent or higher are not uncommon" (Aslin, Jusczyk and Pisoni 1998, 154).
[30] This is the principal component of Piaget's "clinical method."

existence of a constraint on the basis of natural speech alone; especially since, as we have seen, there is no guarantee that the pragmatic context or the cognitive state of children will be sufficient to trigger an utterance with a particular structure, not to mention to trigger it productively. One can never be certain, when analyzing natural speech samples, what representation children are attempting to approximate. Combining naturalistic and experimental data can provide stronger evidence regarding language knowledge.

7.4.2   Comprehension vs. production[31]

Smith demonstrated that children's perception may surpass their production, e.g., (14) (1973, 137; see our chapter 8). For this child, "mouse" and "mouth" were both produced as [maus]:

14.   NVS: What does [maus] mean?
             A: Like a cat
             NVS: Yes: what else?
             A: Nothing else
             NVS: It's part of you
             A [disbelief]
             NVS: It's part of your head
             A [fascinated]
             NVS: [touching A's mouth] What's this?
             A: [maus]

"Only after a few more seconds did it dawn on him that they were the same" (137). The same child picked out the correct picture or toy when asked to show the "jug" or the "duck," both produced as [gˆk] (134).

Eight-month-olds without overt language production or comprehension discriminated passages containing words they had been familiarized with from those containing non-familiar but similar words (Jusczyk and Aslin 1995). Eighteen- to twenty-three-month-olds who were presented with sentences containing words which were either correctly pronounced or mispronounced in the presence of two pictures, one of which was the referent of the sentence "Where's the **b**aby? Can you find it?" or "Where's the **v**aby? Can you find it?", recognized the correct picture significantly more successfully when the word was correctly pronounced (Swingley and Aslin 2000; White, Morgan and Wier 2004).

These results do not allow us to determine conclusively that children's underlying representation for the language they recognize is identical to the adult's, or even that the nature of children's comprehension is identical to the adult's; however, they do suggest that children's representation of the input is significantly

---

[31] If comprehension were fully divorced from production, and both reflected children's grammar, then a dilemma arises: how could different grammars co-exist; do children not have only one grammar? (e.g., Smolensky 1996).

well specified and close to the adult's, and they show that this representation is not dependent on children's "correct" production.

To test whether comprehension surpassed production, children (eighteen to thirty-two months) demonstrating primarily "holophrastic" or one-word speech (MLUs between 1.06 and 1.16) were compared to children demonstrating "telegraphese" (MLUs 1.4–1.85) to see if their comprehension would be superior when adult commands were given in a form which either closely matched or exceeded the children's production (Shipley, Smith and Gleitman 1969). Both groups were tested for their comprehension of commands which varied, (15), as: (a) single words, (b) telegraphic or (c) full adult-like forms.

15.   a. Ball (Noun)
       b. Throw ball (Verb Noun)
       c. Throw me the ball (Verb–function words–Noun).

For both groups of children, comprehension appeared superior to production, but not by much. The holophrastic group whose natural speech corresponded most closely to (15a) responded most successfully to the telegraphic form (as in (15b)), while the telegraphic group with speech resembling (15b) responded most successfully to (15c). The authors concluded that "competence, as well as performance, seems to change and grow. Not only speech, but the perception of what is well formed, changes with increasing verbal maturity" (337).[32]

In certain cases, children's production may appear to be in advance of their comprehension (Dale 1976, 115). With respect to word order, Wetstone and Friedlander (1973) showed that children may respond correctly to "where's the truck" only to respond in the same way to "truck the where is", while using consistent well-formed word order in speech (see also Chapman and Miller 1973).

Experimental evidence from the study of syntax acquisition shows that children's grammatical knowledge may be reflected in both comprehension and production data, although the nature of the evidence differs.[33] Tests of comprehension and production differ at least partially in how they access and reveal grammatical competence.[34] These may be more closely related in language development than previously recognized.

7.5   Conclusions

In order to discover the nature of children's knowledge about language and its development, we must make complex inference from their behavior with language. We must attempt to dissociate various factors involved in children's

---

[32] In this study, correct comprehension needed to involve only some form of obedience to the command, such as touching the object referred to.

[33] See Lust et al. 1986, Cohen Sherman and Lust 1993a, Eisele and Lust 1996 for examples.

[34] Direct comparison of results across imitation, comprehension and production tasks proved impossible (Fraser, Bellugi and Brown 1963; Bloom 1974; Baird 1972; Fernald 1972).

performance from factors involved in their knowledge. Performance factors such as memory and length of utterance may reflect linguistic knowledge. Inferences must continually factor out children's knowledge of principles and parameters of UG from their knowledge of components of the language-specific grammar, as well as from other cognitive factors. A strong form of analysis of child-language data will not only consider knowledge at particular points in time, but constraints over the time course of language acquisition.[35] Certain errors may never occur due to such constraints. The researcher must also search for an abstract form of evidence by assessing what children do *not* do as well as what they *do* do systematically. Children's "errors," or mismatches to adult forms, are as important as correct adult-like utterances since they may reflect children's grammatical system.

Various forms of child behavior with language provide data by which to investigate components of language knowledge. Each technique may be applied either naturalistically or experimentally. The strongest methodology involves "converging evidence," combining and comparing different forms of performance; although comparisons across these methods may involve complex and abstract analyses. This assists us in separating effects of performance from effects of knowledge or competence. Valid assessment of grammatical competence should replicate across various performance types.

Currently researchers are working to establish shared "best practices" in the field for language study (e.g., Simons and Bird 2003a, b; Lust, Blume and Ogden in preparation), as well as for calibrated data preservation and dissemination through an Open Language Archives Community (e.g., Bird and Simons 2003).[36]

7.6   Supplementary readings

For introduction to psycholinguistics, see Garman 1990; Clark 1999; Gernsbacher, ed., 1994; Berko, Gleason and Ratner 1993; Fodor, Bever and Garrett 1974; Foss and Hakes 1978.

Menn and Bernstein-Ratner 2000 provide a general introduction to methods assessing language production. McDaniel, McKee and Cairns 1996 provide chapters on each of several methods to test children's knowledge of syntax, as do Crain and Thornton 1998. McKee 1994 provides an overview of interactive factors in assessing children's language knowledge; Lust, Chien and Flynn 1987 provide an overview of foundations of scientific methods and issues in the study of language acquisition. Crain and Wexler 1999 and Lust et al. 1999 present opposing views. See also Ingram 1989 and Drozd 2004 and related commentary.

---

[35] Some approaches evaluate whether constraints may be variable under certain conditions; i.e., whether the relation between constraints changes over time, e.g., "constraint ranking" in Optimality Theory (see chapter 8).

[36] See http://www.language-archives.org/

Infant speech perception methodologies are described in: Jusczyk 1997a, appendix 233–250; Kuhl 1985; Aslin, Pisoni and Jusczyk 1983, 576–585; and Aslin, Jusczyk and Pisoni 1998, 153–156. Hirsh-Pasek and Golinkoff 1996 provide an overview of the use of the Intermodal Preferential Looking Paradigm with infants and toddlers, and Kuhl 1985, 1987b and Kemler-Nelson et al. 1995 explicate head turn techniques.

8   The acquisition of phonology

8.1   Introduction

We saw in chapters 2 and 3 that newborns must convert a continuous speech stream into units of sound which provide a *digital* representation of language, and must create a representation of how these units are sequentially and systematically related. This analysis of the speech stream and a "combinatorial principle" which applies to the sound units are necessary for children to both produce and perceive any of an infinite number of possible new words and sentences, e.g., (1).

1.   We like to hop on top of pop. Stop. You must not hop on Pop. (Seuss, 1963).

> **CRACKING THE CODE:** Discovering the essential units of the sounds of a language and their system of combination, i.e., the *phonology* of a language, is a necessary and primary step in "cracking the code" of the language surrounding the child.

Over the past several decades, research on development of both *speech perception* and *speech production* in young children has exploded with new scientific evidence (see 8.5). In this chapter, we will summarize highlights of research results in this area. Appendices 2a, 2b and 3 summarize developmental results for infant speech perception and production. Appendix 7 provides some common notational conventions in this area.[1]

8.1.1   What must children acquire?

Children must:

(a)   Discover the units required[2] in order to map from the continuous acoustic stimulus to a digital knowledge of language.

---

[1] See footnote 7, chapter 3 regarding the International Phonetic Alphabet.

[2] Linguists are not agreed on which units most fundamentally characterize the knowledge of a sound system of a language. Some have characterized phonemes as "bundles of distinctive features" (Halle and Clements 1983, 3), abstract properties of sounds which have linguistic significance. These features (about twenty total) are hypothesized to be sufficient to characterize all the significant sound distinctions of the world's languages, to differentiate and classify them. Linguists vary in their exact formulation of these features and in the number proposed and some do not admit them at all. Some propose that features are not simply grouped in bundles, but are hierarchically organized in a multi-tiered structure, organized into subgroups with their own geometry (Clements 1999).

(b)   Make fine distinctions in both perception and production. If they do not distinguish the initial sounds in "bop" and "pop", for example, "Bop the pop" will be indistinguishable from "Pop the bop." For this, infants must distinguish specific features of sounds, e.g., the "+/− voice" feature which, in English, makes [p] and [b] discrete.

(c)   Discover which differences are linguistically significant and which are not, i.e., which are *contrastive* in their language(s).

(d)   Know when to dismiss insignificant sound variations and to treat sounds as equivalent even though they may differ. Since every time a sound or stream of sounds is uttered it differs, and since covariation and phonological rules continually modulate sounds in the speech stream (cf. chapter 3), it is as important for children to dismiss variation as to attend to it. Otherwise, every "pop" could be treated like a different word.

(e)   Discover the *phonological* and *phonotactic rules*, which provide the forms of words. This involves creating an Underlying Representation (UR) for the sounds of words in the language and a systematic way of mapping from this UR to a representation of their surface forms, or Surface Representation (SR).

(f)   Combine sound segments into larger phonological units, i.e., "suprasegmental units," sequencing them. In this way, acquiring knowledge of phonology can be viewed as acquiring "an orchestral score" (Anderson 1985, 348). This "score" allows us and the child to realize the rhyme in (2), where word pairs match syllable structure and meter as well as subtle sound substitutions.

2.   A Simple Thimble
                  or
              a Single Shingle?
       (Seuss, 1979)

(g)   Confront suprasegmental units and systems of their organization. For example, in Berber (Morocco), syllables need not have vowels; utterances like "tsqssft stt" ("you shrank it") are "quite unexceptional" (Clements 1999, 639). Words in English, Dutch and Sesotho are productively *trochaic* in metrical structure; the hierarchical "word tree" is frequently strong–weak in foot structure, whereas Quiché Mayan is iambic (weak–strong).[3] Infants must determine whether the language is "syllable-timed" like the Romance languages (organized temporally on the basis of syllables) or, like English, organized with regard to stress.

---

[3] Jusczyk suggested that approximately 90 percent of content words in English conversations begin with a stressed syllable, cf. Cutler and Carter 1987.

(h)   Relate the score and the notes, discovering what we might call the "secret skeleton" which relates these.[4] One representation of this is sketched in (3).

3.   A Secret Skeleton (Clements and Keyser 1983)

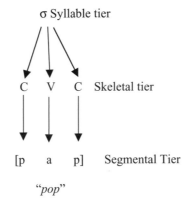

σ Syllable tier

C   V   C   Skeletal tier

[p   a   p]   Segmental Tier

"pop"

(i)   Discover what sound combinations are *not* possible in their language.
(j)   Relate speech perception and production.
(k)   Map from acoustic "cues" in the speech stream in order to accomplish (a–j).
(l)   Discover which speech cues are critical in the language and how (cf. chapter 3).

8.1.2   What are the challenges?

As we saw in chapter 3, the speech stream does not directly provide the units or the system for organizing them. In the absence of perceptual invariants, children must create invariant contrasts and categorize sounds, acquiring and integrating a set of levels of representation: the sound categories (phonemic units), the linguistically distinctive features which characterize and distinguish these units, and the syllable and word units. Computation must combine segmental and suprasegmental dimensions in order to derive the "score" of the language. Length, stress and tone which shape words and word combinations must be considered. Children must acquire the rules and processes which relate the levels of representation across a hidden skeleton in a constrained but invisible manner, as suggested in figure 8.1.

---

[4] Suprasegmental phonological structure includes a temporal level of representation (e.g., the foot, syllable or mora). A "hidden skeleton" can capture this, providing "slots" or a "template" to which segments can be associated. Research is pursuing various theories of this skeleton (Kenstowicz 1994). In "non linear" phonology, different units may be represented on separate parallel levels (or tiers) in what is called an "autosegmental" representation. Some have proposed a Prosodic Hierarchy (Selkirk 1984; Nespor and Vogel 1986).

Phonological knowledge

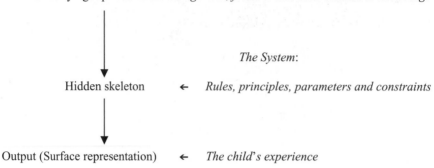

Underlying representation: *Categorical, featural and other structural knowledge*

The System:

Hidden skeleton   ←   *Rules, principles, parameters and constraints*

Output (Surface representation)   ←   *The child's experience*

Fig. 8.1 *Phonological knowledge*

8.1.3   Leading questions

- When do children perceive and produce the fine sound distinctions of language? How and when do children differentiate the contrastive sound categories (the phonemes) of language?
- When do children categorize sound distinctions?
- Are children's speech perception mechanisms qualitatively different from adults'?
- Do children's auditory or motoric abilities change over time and determine acquisition of phonology?
- Do relations between speech perception and speech production change with development?
- Does children's early phonology first reflect input-determined, language-specific structure before universal structures, or do universal structures lead?
- Is the basic architecture of the Language Faculty operative in the Initial State and continuously through development, or are there qualitative changes? Is there a "prelinguistic" stage in children's early sound perception and production? Is the course of acquisition marked by a passage from "phonetics" to true "phonology" only later (e.g., Vihman and Velleman 2000)? What is the nature of *change over time* in the course of language acquisition of phonology?
- How do children use the input at the Initial State and over time? For example, how are URs determined from exposure to input data?
- Are children's perceptions of adult words and their URs for these similar to adults' (e.g., Smith 1973; Menn and Matthei 1992), or qualitatively different?[5] (Contrast Figures 8.2a–8.2b.)

[5] Ingram 1976; Braine 1976; Macken 1979; Vihman 1982; Fee 1995.

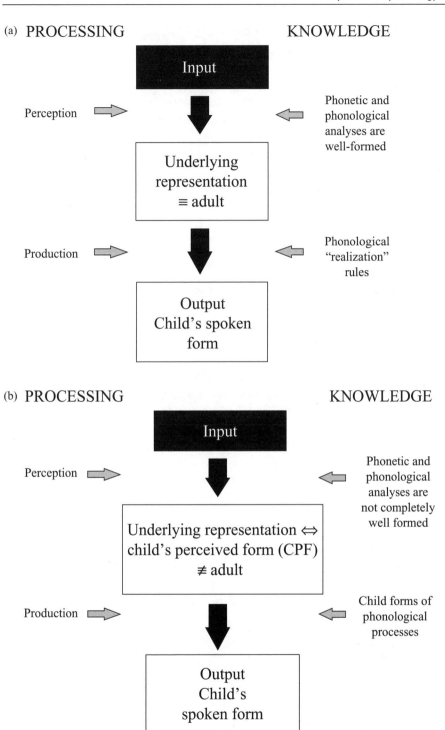

Fig. 8.2 a, b *Two models of the child's relation to the input in acquisition of phonology*

8.2   How do children meet the challenge? Laying the foundations: the first twelve months

Biology immediately provides infants with fundamental auditory ability, and with the basis for motoric ability within the first few months of life.[6] Language development during the first twelve months lies neither in the auditory system nor in the vocal tract, but in the cognitive (linguistic) computation that relates one to the other and to the phonological grammar of the specific language being acquired.[7]

Newborns immediately begin solving both the challenges of speech perception (8.2.1) and of speech production (8.2.2), as well as their integration (8.2.1.4).

8.2.1   Development of speech perception

8.2.1.1   Categorical perception

Psycholinguists made a major discovery of the fundamental cognitive mechanism for speech perception: *categorical perception*. Given categorical perception, we do not perceive the speech stream as continuous; we automatically categorize speech sounds. Our ability to identify speech sounds (e.g., as /p/ or /b/) appears to regulate our ability to discriminate them.[8]

Infants only a few hours old also perceive the speech stream in a categorical manner. In a classic study, one- and four-month-olds in an English environment heard tokens of stimuli along a synthetic /b/–/p/ continuum (as in syllables [ba] and [pa]) in a HAS (High Amplitude Sucking) paradigm (Eimas et al. 1971; Moffitt 1971). Six stimuli were created (varying in 20msc intervals) along a Voice Onset Time (VOT) continuum from −20 msc to +80 msc. Infants at one and four months categorized the speech sounds. This was shown by the fact that intra-category changes of 20 msc in VOT between two stimuli labeled by the adult as /b/ (e.g., −20 vs. 0) did not cause infants to dishabituate, while a change of the same absolute amount between stimuli did so when it crossed the adult's /b/–/p/ (25 msc) boundary (20 ms vs. 40 msc).

Infants categorize sounds in spite of widespread variability in natural speech (Eimas, Miller and Jusczyk 1987, 161); one- to four-month-olds discriminated a contrast (e.g., between [a] and [i]) even when there was continuous variability

---

[6] Infants' auditory system appears basically functional at birth (Trehub and Schneider 1985; Aslin et al. 1983; Fifer and Moon 1989; see Aslin 1987, Eisenberg 1976 and Mehler and Dupoux 1994 for review); but the vocal tract changes length and diameter quite rapidly during the first year of life (Crelin 1969; Oller 1981, 87; Boysson-Bardies 1999, 16–17; Vihman 1996). The larynx and tongue root lower, the tongue lengthens, the pharynx opens. Several aspects of the infant's vocal tract resemble the Neanderthal (Miller 1981, 46; Lieberman 1975). Essential motor control for speech production is near complete by six months (Boysson-Bardies, Sagart and Durand 1984; Koopmans-van Beinum and van der Stelt 1979; Boysson-Bardies 1999; Smith and Oller 1981).

[7] Certain "older, severely retarded children, who had shown normal growth of the vocal tract, were, at three to four years of age, still producing primitive sounds" of a kind characteristic of the first six months of life (Stark 1981, 122).

[8] Liberman 1996 for review; Crystal 1997, 147l, for introduction.

in pitch of speaker's voice (Kuhl 1976; Kuhl and Meltzoff 1982). Two-month olds detected change between words like "bug" and "dug" across speaker variability (Jusczyk 1997, 68).

8.2.1.2   Discrimination of speech sounds

As appendix 2b[9] suggests, infants not only categorize sounds, but show a remarkable sensitivity to a wide set of speech distinctions along the major dimensions of variation which characterize phonetic and phonemic function in languages of the world, i.e., variations in *manner*, including voicing, and in *place* of articulation. Infants distinguish and categorize sound variations that do not occur contrastively in their own native language. African infants distinguish a +V/−V (+ voiced/−voiced) distinction which is contrastive (phonemic) in English, but not in their native African language, Kikuyu (Aslin et al. 1981; Streeter 1976).

Category boundaries recognized by infants do not always match those of the adult model. Along the VOT continuum, infants from a Spanish-speaking environment (which does not include the prevoiced–voiced distinction and where the voiced–voiceless distinction lies at a different location from English) discriminated both Thai and English contrasts, but not the Spanish contrast (Lasky, Syrdal-Lasky and Klein 1975; Aslin et al. 1998, 149).

How does development proceed?

Unless they're native speakers of the language in question, adults tend to find cross-linguistic sound distinctions difficult, if not impossible, to detect (e.g., Flege 1995). This was seen when English-speaking and Hindi-speaking adults and English-learning infants aged six to eight months were tested on two Hindi contrasts: [ʈa]–[t̪a] (*retroflex vs. dental unaspirated stop consonant*), where the critical distinction is in "place" of the two sounds (the contrast is relatively rare across languages); and on /tʰ/- vs. /dʰ/- (*voiceless aspirated dental stop vs. breathy voiced dental stop*), where a difference in voicing (VOT) is the critical distinguishing feature. They were tested on an English place distinction (which is approximated also in Hindi), /ba/–/da/ (Werker 1994, 96; Werker et al. 1981; Werker and Tees 1983). All groups discriminated the /ba/–/da/ contrast, but only the six- to eight-month-old English-learning infants and the Hindi-speaking adults distinguished the Hindi contrasts. Among English-speaking adults, only 40 percent discriminated the Hindi /tʰ/–/dʰ/ contrast and only 10 percent the [ʈa]–[t̪a] one.

Similarly, when a glottalized velar versus glottalized uvular stop distinction, /k'i/ – /q'i/ (in Thompson/Salish [Nthlakampx], a Northern Canadian language) was tested with Nthlakampx-speaking adults, English-learning infants aged six to eight months, and English-speaking adults, it was found once again, that infants

---

[9] Many of these distinctions have been shown to be perceived categorically, although not all have been tested for categorical perception. Infants have also been shown to form equivalence classes between sounds based on consonant and vowel information (e.g., Eimas, Miller and Jusczyk 1987, 163–164; Kuhl 1987a).

and native-speaking adults made the distinction, but English-speaking adults did so only rarely.

English-speaking twelve-, eight- and four-year-olds performed as poorly as English adults on the Hindi distinctions (Werker and Tees 1983). To determine when change occurred, both the Hindi retroflex/dental and Nthlakampx glottalized velar/uvular contrasts were tested with English-learning infants aged six to eight, eight to ten, and ten to twelve months. Most six- to eight-month-olds made the distinctions, but by eleven to thirteen months had largely stopped doing so (Werker and Tees 1984a, b; Best 1994 replicated developmental change between six and twelve months). Discrimination responses therefore decrease between six and twelve months.

Development was not equivalent across all sound distinctions, however. The Hindi /tʰ/ and /dʰ/ voicing distinction was more accessible for English-speaking adults than the dental/retroflex distinction. While all six eight- to ten-month-old American children responded to the Hindi [ʈa]–[ʈa] retroflex–dental distinction, only three distinguished the Nthlakampx contrast (Werker and Tees 1984). Distinction in German vowels made by four-month-old English-learning infants significantly decreased at six months, suggesting that rate of change may be accelerated in vowels as opposed to consonants (Polka and Werker 1994).

"*The native language magnet.*" Recent research has confirmed that "linguistic experience in the first half-year of life alters phonetic perception" and pursues the mechanisms which underlie this (Kuhl 1993, 264; Kuhl et al. 1992). Infants have demonstrated a "magnet effect" for a "prototype" of vowels in their native language. Six-month-olds from the US and Sweden listened to prototypes and variants of an American English /i/ (the front unrounded vowel in the word "fee") and a Swedish /y/ (the front rounded vowel in the Swedish word "fy"). Infants were less able to tell the difference between their native language prototype and its variants than between the non-native language prototype and its variants. The native language prototype appears to act like a "magnet" which pulls the variants to itself and makes close sounds less discernable ("magnet effect").

PHONETIC PROTOTYPES: "speech sounds that are identified by adult speakers of a given language as ideal representatives of a given phonetic category" (Kuhl et al. 1992, 255); "centers of speech categories" (Kuhl 1993, 262).

These results all suggest that a mapping to the specific language phonology is occurring by six months, and that changes in speech perception continue to develop over the the infant's first year of life.

8.2.1.3   Suprasegmental structures

Sensitivity to suprasegmental units also develops over the first year. Newborns (mean age fifty-one hours) acquiring English sucked more to activate their mother's voice when canonical syllables like "pæt" or "tæp" signaled her voice than when non-canonical ones like "pst" and "tsp" did (Moon, Bever and Fifer 1992). Dutch infants at nine months distinguish between phonologically legal and non-legal clusters at the beginning of words (Friederici and Wessels 1993). Infants as young as four days are sensitive to differences between bisyllabic and trisyllabic items (Bijeljac-Babic, Bertonciji and Mehler 1993). French infants distinguish stimuli with the same phonetic content, differing only in prosodic factors (e.g., stress, accent) corresponding to word formation, e.g., they distinguish [mati] appearing in the French forms, "panora<u>ma ty</u>pique" and "mathé<u>mati</u>cien" (Christophe et al. 1994). Two-month-olds distinguish bisyllables with initial stress from those with final stress, e.g., **'ba**da, vs. ba'**da**. American infants (nine months) acquiring English distinguish stress patterns across words, listening longer to a strong–weak (trochaic) pattern (Jusczyk, Cutler and Redanz 1993; Turk et al. 1995). American six-month-olds distinguish between a list of English and a list of Norwegian words (all of which are low frequency and abstract, e.g., "withering" vs. "pragmattsk"), and listen longer to the English words. English and Norwegian words differ in prosody in certain ways. Infants acquiring English also use prosodic differences to distinguish lists of words from two non-native languages, e.g., Dutch and French (Tucker, Jusczyk and Jusczyk 1997).

Suprasegmental sensitivities develop over the first twelve months. Although six-month-olds distinguished English and Norwegian words, they did not distinguish English and Dutch words (which do not differ in the same prosodic factors) until nine months (Jusczyk et al. 1993).

8.2.1.4   Intermodal integration

Infants are also capable of intermodal linking of auditory and articulatory information regarding speech very early. Infants (eighteen to twenty weeks) shown videos of two women producing one sound or another (e.g., /a/, vs. /i/, as in "pop" or "peep") looked longer at the video corresponding to the sound heard.[10] (See figure 5.2.) Infants (five to six months) showed a similar correspondence between acoustic and optic stimuli with disyllables (e.g., /mama/ or /zuzu/).[11]

8.2.1.5   Summary

Infants share with adults basic mechanisms and organization of speech perception. They not only reveal categorical perception, but an ability for intermodal connection of articulatory and auditory information regarding speech.

[10] Kuhl and Meltzoff 1982; also Kuhl and Meltzoff 1984. There was a greater tendency of the infants to imitate the vowel than a pure tone.

[11] MacKain, Studdert-Kennedy, Spieker and Stern 1983. Cf. chapter 5, figure 5.2. Such intermodal integration underlies what has been termed "the McGurk effect" in adult speech perception (McGurk and MacDonald 1976). When presented with sight of a face articulating a syllable and an auditory stimulus of a syllable, adult perception of the sound appears to combine properties from both the optical and the auditory information (Massaro and Stork 1998, 237; Jusczyk 1997a, 60–65).

Infants perceive a wide array of linguistically relevant sound distinctions (varying in *place* and *manner* features), extending beyond those which are significant in the native language. Earliest effects of specific language grammars on infant speech perception are experimentally demonstrated by about six months, and increasingly evident between six and twelve months. During this time, infants' responses to sound variations which are not contrastive in their language are continually and gradually eliminated.

Researchers now debate what the initial unit of analysis is for children: segment, syllable, phoneme or word.[12] They ask: How abstract are infants' initial representations? When does a representation involve contrastive features and how does it come to do so? Although there has been little research to answer this question, infants are forming such abstract representations at least by nine months (e.g., Jusczyk et al. 1999, Maye and Gerken 2001).

8.2.2   Development of speech production

At the same time that infants' speech perception is developing over the first twelve months, so is their speech production.

Infant vocalizations during the first year normally proceed as in appendix 3. Although vocalizations before the first words have sometimes been dismissed as "wild sounds," unlinked to the onset of words and language, we now know that these behaviors are steps in language acquisition. Reflexive and vegetative sounds appear within the first six weeks, "cooing" around six weeks, "babbling" at six to seven months. An early period of marginal babbling develops to canonical babbling, then variegated babbling (ten to fourteen months), followed by first words (twelve months). This development is not in clear stages but continuous, with overlapping forms occurring even between babbling and words.[13] Wide variation in age occurs normally: the onset of canonical babbling has been reported from eighteen to forty-eight weeks.

8.2.2.1   What's in a "coo"?

In cooing,[14] increased control over voicing and the vocal tract reflects an integration of previous vocalization types (a *vocalic* mechanism in crying and a *consonantal* mechanism in vegetative sounds) in a first structure allowing a consonant–vowel like configuration of the "coo" (Stark 1978).

---

[12] Mehler and Christophe 1995. These researchers do not regard the phoneme "as the necessary and unique device to represent the speech stream" (950), and consider the syllable as an alternative and primary form of segmentation.

[13] Normal infants may evidence "jargon babbling" until late in the second year of life, after they have already thirty words in their vocabulary, and may produce 50 percent babbling with 50 percent words (Blake and Fink 1987).

[14] In "cooing" (six weeks), the infant starts and stops phonation within a single breath unit, moving beyond reflexive and vegetative productions (Koopmans-van Beinum and Van der Stelt 1998, 122; Oller 1981).

8.2.2.2   What's in a "babble"?

Infants (seven to fifty-three weeks) show more spontaneous vocalization when alone than when with others (Locke 135, 1993), suggesting that babbling is internally driven. There are several hypotheses for why.

(a) Babbling might constitute a form of "*vocal play*," including "exercise of the organs of speech" (Kent 1981, 113), a purely motoric exercise. If so, a random cacophony of all possible wild sounds might be expected.

(b) Babbling might reflect *biological maturation* of a brain-based language capacity (e.g., Locke 1983; 1993). This would predict a general developmental course in types of articulation in babbling, independent of the ambient language.

(c) Finally, although biologically determined, babbling may actually play a *linguistic role* in infants' mapping to the phonetic and phonemic properties of the language system they are acquiring. If so, we would expect to see a form of "babbling drift" (e.g., Locke 1983).

BABBLING DRIFT HYPOTHESIS: infant babbling differs in specific ways which reflect the specific language being acquired.

Although biological constraints and maturational determinants exist (cohering with hypothesis (b)), so does essential linguistic computation reflected in infants' babbling and its development over the first twelve months, cohering with the hypothesis in (c).

A biological foundation for babbling is evident in its regular emergence at similar ages and through similar stages regardless of language and culture and in the fact that oral babbling emerges in deaf children. Order of sound development in babbling from back to front of the mouth (glottal to velar to alveolar to labial) is shared between hearing and deaf children to some degree (Locke 1993, 187; 1983). Yet infant babbling does not demonstrate all possible sounds. Rather, the "infant has a segmental repertoire that is phonetically highly patterned and selective" (Locke 1983, 5).

Deaf children in an oral-language environment begin oral babbling later (twelve to twenty-six months), show a slower attainment of canonical babbling, a reduced repertoire which lessens over time, and may continue to babble until six years (Locke 1993, 191). At the same time, deaf infants exposed to American Sign Language (ASL) as their first language demonstrate the onset and development of *manual babbling* like children exposed to oral language do with oral babbling. "Phonetic units" characteristic of ASL, e.g., handshapes, movements, locations and palm orientations vary in this manual babbling; by seven to ten months "syllabic" manual babbling is observed, and a "jargon" form of babbling at about twelve to fourteen months (Petitto and Marentette 1991).

Experimental studies of adult perception of cross-linguistic infant babbling have provided evidence (even at six months) that babbling does reflect increasing "drift" to the language being acquired. French adults were presented with babbling samples from infants in three languages: Chinese/Cantonese, French, and Arabic (Boysson-Bardies, Sagart and Durand 1984). Pairs of babbling samples came from infants from different countries (pairs were French and either Arabic or Chinese). Adults were asked "which sample of a pair they thought came from a French infant" (6). Stimuli included "long and coherent intonation patterns" of babbling (1984, 1) in 15 second segments, from infants at six, eight and ten months of age in each language. With eight-month-old babbling, adults were able to correctly identify the French in French–Arabic (75.8 percent) and in French–Cantonese (69.8 percent) comparisons. With six-month-olds, French–Arabic samples were distinguished reliably by phoneticians (68 percent) only. Acoustic analyses confirmed differences between French, Arabic and Cantonese babbling and suggested that suprasegmental factors critically differentiate them.

French, Cantonese and Algerian infant babbling has also been found to differ in the form of its vowels (Boysson-Bardies et al. 1989), and suprasegmental units (e.g., rhythmic and prosodic patterns). Acoustic and perceptual analyses of French and English infant babbling (between five and twelve months) revealed differences in fundamental frequency and syllable-timing patterns as well as in length of prosodic utterances (e.g., Levitt 1993, 385; Whalen, Levitt and Wang 1991; Levitt and Utman 1992).

Another study compared development of infant vocalizations from babbling to first words in each of four languages (French, English, Japanese and Swedish) (Boysson-Bardies, Vihman and Vihman 1991). Infants' vocalizations were analyzed over time (from nine months to sixteen to nineteen months) for *consonantal place* and *manner* features in comparison to the adult target. Although there were certain common general tendencies across babbling in the languages, e.g., a high percentage of labials and dentals in all four languages, these common tendencies were modulated by the target language. As seen in figure 8.3, there was a much higher percentage of labials in French babbling; the cross-language ranking in frequency of labials corresponded closely to that in target adult words, indicating that children were making a phonetic selection from the linguistic environment (1991, 297).

As figure 8.3 suggests, phonetic properties of infants' late babbling cohere with those of their first words (Boysson-Bardies, Vihman and Vihman 1991). Both show more singleton consonants than consonant clusters and more initial than final consonants (Oller et al. 1976). The distribution of consonants, vocalization length and phonotactic structure in babbling across languages shows "striking parallelism between babbling and words" within each child (Vihman et al. 1985).

8.2.2.3   Summary

Infant babbling reflects neither simple "motoric play" nor simple biological maturation alone, but a continuous mapping to the phonology of the language being acquired, whether the phonology is expressed orally or visually (sign language). Earliest evidence of cross-linguistic variation in babbling has been found at six months. Approximation to the adult model appears over the second half of the first year. Late stages of babbling reflect the ambient language at both

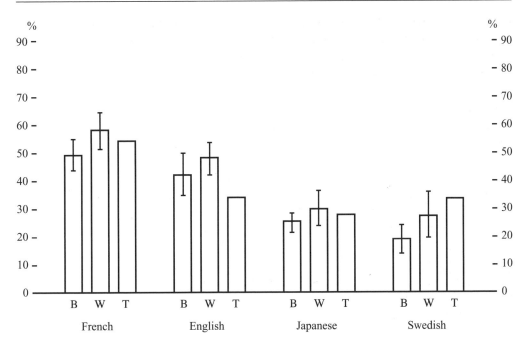

Fig. 8.3 *Cross-linguistic variation in babbling: distribution of labials in babbling, infant words and target words.*
From: B. de Boysson-Bardies, B. Vihman, M. Vihman. 1991. "Adaptation to Language: Evidence from Babbling and First Words in Four Languages." *Language* **67**(2), 297–319. (Figure is on page 310.)

segmental and suprasegmental levels. There is continuity between babbling and first words, including some language-specific phonetic and suprasegmental properties. Thus, babbling provides one "mechanism by which infants discover the map between the structure of language and the means for producing this structure" (Petitto and Marentette 1991, 1495). It allows children to explore the linguistic properties of the language surrounding them and to relate these properties to their own productions.

8.2.3   Linking perception and production

Developments of infants' speech perception and speech production correlate; both reveal infants mapping to the sound system of the ambient language during the first twelve months; both reveal cross-linguistic evidence of specific language grammars by six months, increasing thereafter.

8.3   First words and beyond

8.3.1   Early phonological deformations

It would seem that in many ways, children have "cracked the code" of the speech stream before speaking a first word. Yet their first words (about

Table 8.1 *First twenty-five recorded forms of four normal children, based on published diary information in Velten 1943, Menn 1971, Leopold 1947 and Ingram 1974a*

Joan Velten		Daniel Menn*		Hildegard Leopold		Jennika Ingram	
	0;10		1;4		0;10		1;3
up	[ap]	*byebye*	[bab]	*pretty*	[prəti]	*blanket*	[ba]
bottle	[ba]		[bæ bæ]	*there*	[dɛi]		[babi]
	0;11		1;6			[dti]	*byebye*	[ba]
bus	[bas]	*hi*	[hæ]		[de:]		[baba]
put on	[baza]		[haj]		0;11	*daddy*	[da]
that	[za]		1;7	*pretty*	[prɪti]		[dada]
	1;0	*no*	[Oⁿo]	*there*	[dɛ:]		[dadi]
down	[da]		[no]	*ticktock*	[tak]	*dot*	[dat]
out	[at]		[nu]		1;0		[dati]
away	[ba·ˈba]	*hello*	[hwow]	*ball*	[ba]	*hi*	[hai]
pocket	[bat]	*squirrel*	[gæ]	*Blumen*	[bu]	*mommy*	[ma]
	1;1		[gow]	*da*	[da:]		[mami]
fuff	[af]		1;8	*opa*	[pa]		[mama]
	[faf]	*nose*	[o]	*papa*	[pa-pa]	*no*	[no]
put on	[badaˈ]	*ear*	[iJ]	*piep*	[pi]	*see*	[si]
	1;2		1;9		[pip]	*see that*	[siæt]
push	[bus]	*boot*	[bu]	*pretty*	[prti]	*that*	[da]
dog	[uf]	*nice*	[njaj]	*sch-sch*	[ʃʃ]		1;4
pie	[ba.]		[njajF]	*ticktock*	[tˈɪtˈa]	*hot*	[hat]
	1;3	*light*	[aj]		[tˈatˈ-tˈ]	*hi*	[hai]
duck	[dat]		1;10		1;1		[haidi]
lamb	[bap]	*car*	[gar]	*ball*	[ba]	*up*	[ap]
	1;4	*cheese*	[džiF]	*bimbam*	[bt]		[api]
M	[am]	*Stevie*	[i:v]	*da*	[da]	*no*	[nodi]
N	[aṇ]	*egg*	[egY]	*Gertrude*	[dɛɛ:da]		[dodi]
in	[ṇ]	*apple*	[æp]		[də:di]		[noni]
	1;5–1;7	*kiss*	[giF]	*kick*	[ti]		
doll	[daʼ]	*up*	[ʌf]	*kritze*	[tttsə]		
S	[as]	*mouth*	[mæwf]				
O	[uʼ]	*eye*	[aj]				
R	[a]						
nice	[nas]						

*·*Note*: If sound was indeterminate, Menn would use a capital letter, e.g. F means fricative of some kind.

Source: D. Ingram (1976). *Phonological Disability in Children*. London: E. Arnold. Reprinted by permission of Hodder Arnold.

Table 8.2 *Speech sample from CLAL*

Child: **oh! man!**
Child: ə **fix it**

Adult(BL): You fixed it? Let me hear. Did you fix it? Let me see. Is it fixed?
Child: **yea, ə fix**
Adult: you fixed it?
Child: **bwok**
Adult: It broke?
Child: ə **bwokt**
Adult: It broked?
Child: **See (ovə) fire**
Adult: Is that for the fire? Is that for the electricity? (referring to cord)
Child: erɛksi
Adult: Where's the fire?
Child: ə **han(t/d)**
Adult: In your hand, there's fire? I don't see any fire. Do you feel it?
Child: ə **feel it**
Child: **Ow! Ih bwokt**
Adult: It broked. That's terrible. Did your finger break?
child: **oh, Ih bwokt**

Adult: Oh no, don't burn your finger
Child: ə **fire**
Child: **han(t/d)**
Adult: Is a fire in your hand?
Child: ə **hurt**
Adult: Oh no, That's terrible.
Child: ə **hurt**
Child: ə **hurt**
Child: ə **hurt**

---

* *Note: This sample (CLAL, BGO 2 28 97, 2.2) involves a discussion of electronic equipment in a living room (the "fire" and "hurt" are imaginary). At this time, this child is often holophrastic, but does create two or three-word utterances.*

twelve months) and sentences (over the first three years) demonstrate many months of phonological development before production closely resembles that of adults. Table 8.1 shows a set of first words (Ingram 1976, 17), and table 8.2 early sentences.[15]

Several phonological "processes" frequently deform the child's early productions, e.g., table 8.3.[16] Many sounds are *omitted* or are *substituted* by others.

---

[15] From the Cornell Language Acquisition Lab [CLAL].
[16] The term "deformation" here is used to refer to the production of a word which does not match the adult form.

Table 8.3 *Phonological processes in early child language*[*]

Deletion/Omission
Consonant cluster reductions
    e.g., 'broke' → bok
Final consonant deletion
    e.g., 'it' → ɪ-h
Unstressed syllable deletion
    e.g., 'banana' → ˈnaenə
Assimilation
Regressive assimilation
    e.g., 'duck' → gʌk
    'doggy' → goggy
    'nipple' → mibu
Progressive assimilation
    e.g., 'kiss' – gik
        'cloth' → gʌk
Reduplication
    e.g., 'daddy' – dada
    e.g., 'stomach' → ˈtum tumˈ
Substitution
Gliding
    e.g., substitution of [w] or [y] for liquids
        'broke' → bwok
        'rabbit' → wabbit
Fronting
    e.g., substitution of front consonants such as [t] or [d] for
back such as velars [k] [g]
        'kitty' → ditty
Stopping
    e.g., substitution of stop consonants for fricatives and affricate
        'shoes' → tuid
Voicing
    e.g., voicing word initial consonants
        'pie' → bie
        'pocket' → bat
Devoicing
    e.g., devoicing final consonants
        'knob' → nop

---

[*]*Note*: See Ingram 1976

Sounds are *assimilated* to each other (made to become similar in pronunciation, either completely or partially). Assimilation operates on adjacent or non-adjacent sounds, causing them to share some or all features, e.g., *place* and/or *manner* features. An earlier sound in the word may be assimilated to one which follows it (regressive assimilation) or a later sound may be assimilated to one which precedes it (progressive assimilation). Syllables may be repeated (*reduplication*) (e.g., Fee and Ingram 1980).

Speech comprehension also develops. Infants (fourteen months) were taught to link two nonsense labels with two different brightly colored moving clay objects, where these labels differed only in a single phonetic (place) feature in the initial consonant, e.g., "dih" versus "bih". The infants did not notice a switch in word–object pairings, e.g. the "dih" referent now called "bih", but did notice this switch when "lif" changed to "neem" and when "bih" and "dih" were related to two different graphic displays – checkerboard patterns. These results suggested that although there is not a general loss of perceptual ability at fourteen months, word learning is still developing. Surprisingly, eight-month-olds did notice the "bih"–"dih" switch (in a simplified procedure), suggesting that there is development between eight and fourteen months and that some "functional reorganization" occurs about this time (Stager and Werker 1997, 382).[17]

How do we explain this apparent relapse in perception and production, following the accomplishments during the first twelve months? A learning theory which operated simply in terms of *frequencies* of sounds children hear could not work. The phoneme /ð/ (voiced "th" as in "that"), for example, is one of the most frequently occurring word-initial consonants in English; yet children acquiring English frequently deform it (Pye, Ingram and List 1987, 183f.). Although [s] is highly frequent, children acquiring English often substitute other sound for it.

There are several possible types of explanation, which may operate alone or together.

- Are children biologically *pre-ordained* to produce deformations?
- Do children suffer from "*mushy mouth*" or "*mushy ear*," i.e., an inability to motorically produce or to perceive the sound combinations necessary?
- Are children confronting a task of *Grammatical Mapping* by which the phonological system of their language must be created?

8.3.2   Is acquisition of phonology pre-ordained?

If acquisition of phonology were biologically pre-ordained, then children in all languages would evidence similar deformations and universal order in development.

Roman Jakobson (1941/1968; 1971/2004) provides a prototype biologically determined "maturational theory."[18] Here, the structure of linguistic knowledge is viewed as correlating with the structure of language acquisition, mediated by

---

[17] See Shvachkin 1948 and Garnica 1973 for earlier behavioral studies related to the child's perception of distinctive features after the first words.

[18] Jakobson's theory has not been fully explored as a language acquisition model. Acquisition orders predicted by Jakobson's theory to some degree "depend on the target language because that's what's being learned – so the maturation is into the particular properties of that language

Jakobson's Hierarchy of Development

cooing and babbling period   indeterminate sounds
(neither consonant nor vowel)

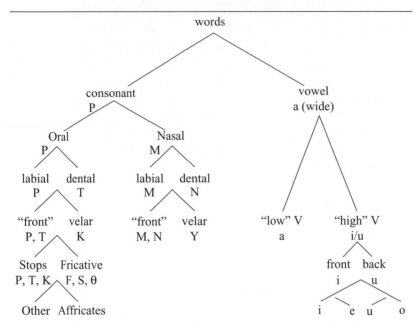

Fig. 8.4 *Jakobson's implicational hierarchy*

biological programming in the human species (Jakobson 1980). This provides an early example of a proposal for Universal Grammar: "the first attempt within modern linguistics to create a genuinely explanatory theory of linguistic systems by establishing logical and empirical connections between the data of linguistic analysis per se and other, independent domains" (Anderson 1985, 129).

Jakobson's theory viewed first words as the onset of a linguistic dimension of language acquisition, since words provide first overt evidence of "linguistic contrast." Babbling was viewed as "wild sounds," with children "capable of producing all conceivable sounds" unrelated to linguistic knowledge. Following first words, Jakobson proposed a universal course of development, based on a finite set of binary *Distinctive Features* (DF) underlying all possible phonemes of the world's languages, which were *arranged in a hierarchy*, from those which characterized all languages of the world down to the most rare, as schematized in figure 8.4. Those requiring combinations of features, e.g., affricates, were lower on the hierarchy and predicted to be acquired later. This predicted a "regular succession of acquired phonemic oppositions" (1941/1968). What was "unmarked"

. . . [T]o predict what is learned first, you have to know which is the distinctive feature in the language and whether it's acting alone or in syncretism with [an] other" (Waugh personal communication 5 March 2001). When these details are articulated, the theory may approximate a form of "grammatical mapping" (cf. chapter 12).

characterized all languages of the world, and was first and most easily acquired by children.

> **IMPLICATIONAL UNIVERSALS:** if a contrast lower on the hierarchy appears, then the higher contrasts must exist. For example, if a contrastive affricate appears, then contrasts higher on the hierarchy, e.g., involving stops, should exist. If a lower contrast did not exist, children would be expected to substitute earlier (higher) contrasts.

Jakobson's hierarchy progressed from "maximal contrasts" (Jakobson 1990a); its highest node reflects a distinction between a consonant and a vowel. Children would begin with simple CV syllables, as in an utterance like [pa], which involves /p/, a labial stop consonant where the vocal tract is closed maximally, and an undifferentiated /a/, where the vocal tract is opened as widely as possible. An utterance like [pa] combines two extremes, the "optimal consonant" and the "optimal vowel" in a maximal contrast.[19] Next consonantal opposition would involve a nasal stop contrasting with an oral labial (e.g., mama/papa), followed by an opposition between labials and dentals, e.g., mama/dada.[20]

Many phonetic dimensions underlying Jakobson's theory are significant in languages of the world; some implicational universals appear to hold.[21] Children do begin with a limited inventory of segments in early productions. Early productivity of labials appears across languages (e.g., Boysson-Bardies, Vihman and Vihman 1991, and figure 8.3). Early consonantal inventories in Swedish, Estonian and Bulgarian children reveal a common early occurrence of nasal [m] and stop [p] or [b] (Ingram 1992). Certain productions which would be considered complex on Jakobson's hierarchy appear later in acquisition, e.g., the affricate or retroflex. Across child languages, some common substitutions are observed, e.g., in (4), where a "velar" [k] or [g] is replaced by an alveolar [t] consistent with figure 8.4.

4.   *Common substitutions*
        kaka → tata (Serbian child, 1 year; Swedish child)
        kopf → topf (German child)
        garçon/cochon → tosson (French child)
        cut → tut (English child)

---

[19] Jakobson's axis of development included features such as "grave" "formed with a relatively large, undivided oral resonant cavity, resulting in a relatively low frequency region of prominence in their acoustic spectrum" grouping labial and velar (e.g., [p] and [k]) vs. "acute," formed with an oral cavity "divided into two smaller resonators" such as dentals and palatals (Anderson 1985, 120); and "compact" vs. "diffuse" (corresponding to higher and lower tonality). Both of these axes corresponded to acoustic features and therefore to perceptibility.

[20] In "Why Mama and Papa" (1990), Jakobson notes the remarkable similarity and productivity of "nursery forms" used by adults across the world, which involve a simple CV structure, and a nasal or stop: Welsh "mam," Sinhala "amma," African Baga "ma," for "mother" (see also Ingram 1991). He attributes this to the principle of "maximal contrasts."

[21] Anderson 1985, 127, 132; Macken and Ferguson 1981; Macken 1995, 675–677.

In general, Jakobson was correct in proposing independence of motoric ability from development of phonology; "children are not acquiring isolated phonetic segments, but rather a set of systematically related phonological categories" (Pye, Ingram and List 1987). However, we saw above that "babbling" is not discontinuous with first words as Jakobson had proposed. Cross-linguistic investigation now reveals the necessity for a broader range of oppositions in language typology and in language acquisition than Jakobson defined (Anderson 1985, 125) and acquisition evidence challenges aspects of Jakobson's universal hierarchy.

The early productivity of labial sounds among first words is modulated by language and by individual development (as we saw in figure 8.3, for example). Cross-linguistic differences in early productions reveal that children can produce and substitute a wide range of sounds; they demonstrate different paths of development, depending on the phonological system of the language being acquired (see table 8.4). Ingram (cf. table 8.1) suggested that the first word for four children acquiring English involved a labial (e.g.[ap]-up; [bab]-byebye; [ba]-blanket, [prəti]-pretty). However, another child produced an alveolar [d] as a stop sound in his first words, e.g., [dn]-down; [dædæ]-bye bye (Menn 1975). One child substituted an early glottal stop for /k/ and /t/ (Labov and Labov 1978). Joan Velten's (in Ingram 1976) first words involved a labial at ten months, and nasal sounds not until sixteen months, long after fricatives (see Macken 1980). The adult model and children's own creativity modulate their early productions from the beginning, frequently vitiating the hierarchy in figure 8.4. Maturation alone does not determine order of acquisition.[22]

8.3.3   "Mushy Mouth–Mushy Ear" Hypothesis

Children's motor control for a wide repertoire of sounds is evidenced during babbling. Further evidence of their articulatory abilities is found in "regressions," e.g., Hildegard, who first produced the word "pretty" without deformation, later deformed it, and subsequently reproduced the adult-like form.

5.   Regression (Leopold's Hildegard)
          Target: "pretty"
          10–16 months [prɪti]
          18 months [bɪdi]
          18 + months [prɪti]

---

[22] Since Jakobson's theory concerns *contrasts*, it is not easily testable. Simply observing a sound produced or not by a child is inconclusive regarding the child's knowledge of contrast (see Kiparsky and Menn 1977). Suprasegmental processes such as initial word voicing and final word devoicing may interact with segmental production, necessitating tests in different positions of the word. A child may show well-formed production in one position, e.g., maintain a /p/ word finally (as in [ap] for "up"), but not in another, e.g., word initially (as in [baza] for "put on") (table 8.1). forty-five Dutch children (1.3–4.0) produced an early labial, i.e., [p], in both word initial and final position, but nasals were several months delayed in final position (Fikkert 1998, citing Beers 1995). A child's perception as well as production must be tested. Absence in production may provide evidence of contrast. One child produced only coronals as initial stop consonant, e.g., [d], and avoided words containing either labials or velars, suggesting some knowledge of contrast between /b/ and /d/ (Menn 1976).

Table 8.4 *Cross-linguistic differences in early word production*

Quiché Mayan	In a study of five children between ages 1.7 and 3.0, the two most common sounds were the affricate [ts] and the liquid [l], which are frequently later acquisitions in English, and both of which are lower on the Jakobsonian hierarchy (Pye 1980). Whereas children acquiring English frequently replace [ts] with a stop, or [l] with a "j" or a "w", the Quiché Mayan children frequently changed /s/ to [ʃ] or /ʃ/ to [s] and they substituted [l] for /r/ (Pye, Ingram and List 1987).
English	Children frequently substitute a stop such as [d] or [t] for [ð]
Spanish	Children may substitute [ð] by [l] and sometimes [r]. In Spanish, [l] is relatively early, as is [s] or [tS] (Macken 1980, 149, 1986; after Stoel 1974; Eblen 1982). The Spanish speaking child may substitute a stop with a fricative, as in "dedo" (finger/toe) → [zezo] (Serra et al. 2000).
Greek	Children may also use [l] for [ð] (Hinofotis 1976; Drachman and Malkouti-Drachman 1973).
Hindi	Children "normally substitute [l] for [r]," e.g., "gira:" (fell down) is pronounced "gila:" at sixteen months (Srivastava 1974, 114).
Sinhala	Similar to Hindi: e.g, "arə'" (that) as "alə'" (Karunatillake, personal communication).
Bulgarian, Estonian and Swedish	While the fricative [v] is frequently late in English, here we find it early in certain positions (Ingram 1998, 1992).
Taiwanese or Cantonese	[ts] may be substituted for [s], e.g., [pa tsi] for /pa si/ (So and Dodd 1995), unlike the "stopping" process in English, e.g., [tɪp] for "chip".
Oriya	Dentals have been earlier than labials, e.g., a child produces "tata" at eleven months (for "tai dai" = curd), and "papa" and "mama" only later at age 1.1 (Mohanty, nd)

Children's deformations are not due simply to inability to articulate. This is confirmed in "The Puzzle–Puddle phenomenon," discovered by Smith. Here a young child deforms "puddle," but produces "puzzle" as "puddle" (6) (Smith 1973, 55, 149). If a child *can* produce "puddle", why is it not produced when it is the target?

6.   **Puzzle–puddle phenomenon**

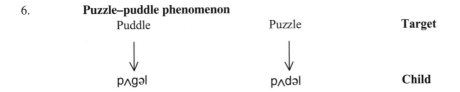

Puddle	Puzzle	**Target**
pʌgəl	pʌdəl	**Child**

Similarly, a young child's production of "thick" as [fɪk] might suggest an inability to produce /θ/. However, the same child produces "sick" as [θik], disconfirming this hypothesis (Smith 1973, 150).

Is it possible that the child's perception of the adult model is faulty? This would be surprising, given the fine perceptual sensitivity we have seen during the first twelve months. Evidence against it is exemplified in the "fiss phenomenon" (7):

7.   Child: There is a fis in my pail
         Adult: There is a fis in the pail?
         Child: No, not fis, FIS'.

Likewise, the child who was producing both "mouth" and "mouse" as "maus" was not misled by his own deformation, as he correctly picked out their referents, e.g., chapter 7, (14) (Smith 1973, 137). A child may also correctly discern the deviance of his/her own form (8) (Smith 1973, 136):

8.   NVS: What's a [sip]? ("for ship")
         A: When you drink [imitates]
         NVS: What else does [sip] mean?
         A: [Puzzled, then doubtfully suggests "zip," though pronouncing it
             quite correctly]
         NVS: No, it goes in the water.
         A : a boat
         NVS: Say it.
         A: No, I can only say [sip]

The example (8) implies "that the adult form is not only available to the child as his phonological representation of the word, but also that the adult form has priority in some way" (Smith 1973, 137). "Mushy mouth" or "mushy ear" hypotheses can not alone explain children's deformations.

8.3.4   Grammatical mapping: continuity of the Language Faculty ▬

The linguistic computation performed between the input (adult model) and children's productions – not articulatory or perceptual deficit – explains early deformations. The relation between the adult target and children's productions is complex and indirect because of this.

Systematic analysis of children's deformations of the adult target, e.g., *metathesis* (where order of sounds is changed) as in (9a)–(9c) or *epenthesis* (where successive sounds become separated by sound insertion) as in (10a)–(10d), reveals this linguistic computation.

9.   Children's *metathesis*
         a. **English** (Smith 1973)
            ask → aːks (2 years. 247–256 days)
            elephant → ɛfələnt (2 years. 300–312 days)

   b. **Spanish**
      elefante (elephant) → [efélante] (Serra et al. 2000)
   c. **Greek** (Kappa 2001)
      tubes (somersault) → [pude] (2.4.11)
      skupa (broom) → [puka] (2.8.17)

10.   Children's *epenthesis*
      a. **English**
         blue → belu (Locke 1983)
      b. **Spanish**
         flor (flower) → ['falo] (Serra et al. 2000)
      c. **Telugu**
         ya:tra → ya:ttala (child Swati 2.0) (Nirmala 1981)
         padmam → padamam (child Kalyani 2.2) (Nirmala 1981)
         pa:rk → pa:ruku (child Madhavi 3.3) (Nirmala 1981)
      d. **Dutch** (Kehoe and Stoel Gammon 1997, 123, Demuth 1996c, after Fikkert 1994)
         balloon → /bəlún/ [balúnjə]
         melk (milk) → ['mɛɪək]
         bal (ball) → ['balə]

8.3.4.1   Neil Smith and Amahl

For study of a child's linguistic computation, *Acquisition of Phonology* (Neil Smith 1973) is unparalleled. It includes systematic investigation of data collected from Amahl, aged 2.2–4.0. The grammatical system underlying the child's speech is studied through linguistic analysis. Lexical formations and deformations are completely reported across twenty-nine developmental sessions. Like Jakobson, Smith proposes a UG-determined model of language acquisition. Unlike Jakobson, his is not a maturational model, but recognizes the child mapping to the adult target. In spite of widespread deformations (e.g., words of more than two syllables cause problems early and even one syllable words may be "deformed" [Smith 1973, 101]), a principled system was found to underlie the child's productions.

The child's computation is analytic, appearing to operate on Distinctive Features (DF) of the underlying lexical representation. At one point in Amahl's language, all *coronals* (articulated with the tip or blade of the tongue raised towards the teeth or alveolar ridge) underwent a common stopping process as in (11a), while non-coronals did not, as in (11b):

11.   Change referring to Distinctive Feature
      a. [+ coronal] feature in initial consonant
         shut – ḍ ʌt
         touch – ḍ ʌt
         yes – ḍɛt
         yawn – ḍɔ:n

Table 8.5 *Universal constraints on early phonological rules*

1. Vowel and consonant harmony
2. An ideal CVCV canonical form
3. Systematic simplification
   (limiting the inventory of elements)
4. Grammatical simplification
   (simplifying the child's phonological system)

Source: Smith, 1973, 206; 1975, 57.

b. [-coronal] feature in initial consonant
   wet – wɛt
   cat – g̊æt
   bite – b̥ait

If children's deformations make reference to abstract features, such as "+/– coronal," we can explain why they treat certain sets of sounds as identical and differentiate others, e.g., (11a) as opposed to (11b) (Smith 1973, 185f.).

"Realization rules" appeared to underlie Amahl's grammatical system at each point of development, revealing analytic mapping from the phonemic structure of the adult form to the child form "prior to the application of phonetic rules," and accounting for deformations (1973, 13). One such rule, (12), reveals the source of the child's changes of the adult form in contexts involving consonant clusters with nasals. Another, (13), accounts for widespread (regressive) *assimilation* of consonant features and resultant "consonant harmony", e.g., (14).[23]

12.   **Realization Rule 1**
       A nasal consonant is deleted before any voiceless consonant

13.   **Realization Rule 19**
       Alveolar and palato-alveolar consonants harmonize to the point of
       articulation of a following consonant; obligatorily if that consonant is velar,
       optionally if it is labial.

14.   **Consonant Harmony** (Amahl, English)
       dark – g̊aːk
       stuck – g̊ʌk
       singing – g̊iŋiŋ
       knife – maip

Universal constraints (table 8.5) underlie realization rules. According with Constraint 2, consonant cluster reduction evidenced in Amahl's speech and cross-linguistically (e.g., (15)) creates canonical form.

---

[23] The term "consonant harmony" generally refers to non-adjacent units, while "assimilation" may refer to adjacent units. This distinction is not applied consistently in child language analyses, where assimilation can apply to non-adjacent units.

15.   Consonant cluster reduction: cross-linguistic
     a. **Spanish** (Serra et al. 2000)
        flor (flower) → [fo] or [for]
        plato (saucer) → [pato]
     b. **Telugu** (Nirmala 1981)
        gu:rkha → ku:ka (child Swati 1.7)
        simham → simam (child Pavan 2.9)

Assimilation of features of one consonant to those of another reveals consonant harmony (Constraint 1), accounting for a large proportion of the changes by Amahl and children acquiring other languages, e.g., (16).

16.   Consonant harmony: cross-linguistic
     a. **Spanish** (Serra et al. 2000)
        comprar (to buy) → [pom'pa]
        araña (spider) → [a'nana]
     b. **Hindi**
        Sangya: (girl's name) → gangya: (Srivastava 1974)
        dhaagaa (thread) → daadaa (13-24 mos) (Sharma 1973; Bai and Nirmala 1978)
     c. **Telugu** (Nirmala 1981)
        sa:ndilsu → [ta:ndittu] (1.8)
        ceckram → cekkam (3.1)
     d. **Dutch** (Fikkert 1998)
        brood/bro:t (bread) → [bo:p]
        bed/bɛt (bed) → dɛt

Vowel harmony is also attested, although less common than consonant harmony.

17.   Vowel harmony
     a. **English** (Smith 1973)
        little → ḍidi:
        broken → ḅugu:
     b. **Telugu** (Bai and Nirmala 1978)
        puucii (insect) → piitii (Chetan)
        roTTe (roti/bread) → atta (Swati)

Consonant and vowel harmony are also attested cross-linguistically in the form of reduplication:

18.   Reduplication
     a. **English**
        helicopter → [ægəgəgə] (Smith 1973, 164)
     b. **Spanish**
        patata (potato) → [pa'pa pa] or [ta'ta ta] (Serra et al. 2000)

8.3.4.2   Explaining children's "deformations"

The mysterious "puzzle–puddle" phenomenon is now explained. Distinct rules operate on the input, "puddle" (19a), and on the input, "puzzle" (19b), leading to distinct outputs.[24]

19.   a.

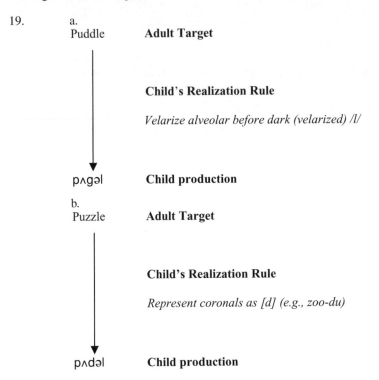

Puddle   **Adult Target**

Child's Realization Rule

Velarize alveolar before dark (velarized) /l/

pʌgəl   **Child production**

b.

Puzzle   **Adult Target**

Child's Realization Rule

Represent coronals as [d] (e.g., zoo-du)

pʌdəl   **Child production**

In this theory, the underlying form and structure of rules does not change. Rules need to be eliminated and/or restricted. Children are continually mapping to the adult target through a well formed system which is consistent with basic universal structures and principles of adult grammar (Smith 1973, 206).[25]

8.3.4.3   Natural Phonology

Smith's paradigm converges with "Natural Phonology" (Stampe 1969). Here also children are viewed as biologically programmed with universal

---

[24] Rule ordering is also postulated.

[25] Certain phonological changes in Amahl's early phonology were "across the board" and not simply linked to individual lexical items. When he overcame the omission of post consonantal liquids in consonant clusters such as (i) (2 yrs, 189–196 days), he overcame them in all such contexts almost simultaneously.

　　i. Bread – bɛd → blɛd

　　　Black – bæk → blæk

　　　Blow – bu → blu:

If the child is acquiring a system, we would expect to see evidence of such generalization in developmental change, although not all changes are abrupt, and numerous factors (e.g., phonetic and articulatory) interact to determine a child's production (cf. Smith 1973, 140–143).

linguistic processes, and their early perception of adult forms is assumed to be well formed. Development involves limitation and ordering of an innately available set of linguistic "natural processes," affected by experience with a specific language. It includes "suppression" of those which are not required by the language being acquired, or which conflict with others which are. For example, *assimilation* of features involved in consonant harmony must be retained in English for pluralization (cf. chapter 3), but lost in many other contexts. Reduplication must be retained in Japanese, (20), or Indonesian, (21), but suppressed in English. Final devoicing must be retained in adult German.[26]

8.3.4.4   Continuity of child and adult grammars

If acquisition of phonology is UG-constrained continuously, then we would expect commonalities between child language acquisition and the structure of natural languages and language change.

Assimilation (e.g., English pluralization) is one of the most fundamental phonological processes in languages across the world, as well as in language change (Hock 1991). Both *loss* (segments are deleted) and *epenthesis* are common (Hock 1991, 117f.). *Metathesis* occurs; e.g., compare Old English and modern English "bridd→bird" (Hock 1991). Final *devoicing* is common, e.g., Polish, Russian or Tamil as well as German. *Reduplication* is fundamental morphologically and syntactically, e.g., Japanese subordination, (20), Indonesian pluralization, (21), or Indo-Aryan nominalization (Abbi 1992).

20.   tabe (eat)
         tabetabe (while eating)

21.   Ibu (mother)
         ibuibu (mothers)

Vowel harmony (feature assimilation across non-adjacent vowels in neighboring syllables) is common across languages, and in language change. Although *consonant harmony* (feature assimilation across non-adjacent consonants) is relatively rare in adult languages and more restricted than in child language, it does occur in adult grammars and grammatical change.[27] Apparent inconsistency between child and adult (with the child grammar showing productive consonant harmony and less vowel harmony and the adult grammar showing productive vowel harmony and less consonant harmony) deserves further study, but it lies in the amount, not the nature, of the process.[28]

---

[26] Kiparsky and Menn 1977; Ingram 1989, 386–392; Macken 1995.

[27] Note the pre-Latin to Latin change due to consonant harmony (Hock 1991, 63)
   pre-Lat *penkwe → *kwenkwe → *Lat* quinque (five)
            *pekwo → *kwekwo → *Lat* coquo (I cook)
   Hock notes that such consonant harmony does not typically lead to regularization, and may remain lexically specific (1991, 64).

[28] Vowel production may be more difficult to characterize in featural terms in general; acoustic analyses may be necessary to identify them.

8.3.4.5   Variation

While UG can determine principles and constraints of language structure, it cannot determine the actual experience (including the specific words or
phonological systems) which confronts children.

Different "styles" of child phonology have been observed, e.g., "cautious system builders," or more loose and variable ones.[29] Variation within child production
can and does exist. While Amahl appeared to be applying a velarization rule to
"puddle" in (19a) as well as to other words which shared the defining context
for the rule, he made certain *lexical exceptions* (Macken 1980, 9). One child
demonstrated eight different versions in his attempt to produce "boat" during a
twenty-minute session (Macken and Ferguson 1981, 123).[30]

Another young child (studied over five and a half months at about age 2, Fey
and Gandour 1982) attempted to capture a "voiced/voiceless" contrast in stops in
word final position by creating a new "postnasalization" rule not attested in the
adult language. For words such as those in (22a) with a word final voiceless stop,
the child consistently produced them without voicing. However, words with final
voiced stops the child "consistently produced with voicing, and with a distinctive
nasal release," e.g., (22b). This new *postnasalization rule* was stable over several
months and productive in new words as they entered the child's vocabulary.[31]

22.   a. drop → [dap^h]
           eat → [it^h]
           broke → [bok^h]
       b. lightbulb → [jajt^h-babm]
           stub → [dabm]
           dad → [dædn]
           feed → [vidn]

Another child (aged 2.9) in (23) created a rule apparently for the purpose of eliminating word initial fricatives, while maintaining the fricative phoneme elsewhere
in the word (Leonard and McGregor 1991):

23.   soap → aps
          saw → as
          school → kus
          snoopy → nupis
          fall → af

In both cases, the children share with Amahl a veridical perception of (distinctive
features in) the representation of the target word, propensity to create a productive

---

[29] Ferguson 1986; Macken and Ferguson 1983; Ferguson and Farwell 1975; Schwartz and Leonard 1982; Peters and Menn 1993.

[30] Apparent exceptions to generalizations in child grammar can sometimes reflect a systematic source under comprehensive and systematic analyses (e.g., Smith 1973).

[31] The rule appeared to reflect the child's unique way of maintaining both veridical phonological contrasts (i.e., [+/−V] and [−continuant] or stop features) of the target and an independent phonetic constraint which appeared to require release of all word final stops.

rule-based generalization, and individual creation of the sound system of the target language.

If children attempt to match the grammatical system being acquired, cross-language variation in early deformations is also expected. Accordingly, choice of distinctive features assimilated in consonant harmony in child language appears to vary across languages, as does execution of consonant cluster reduction. Assimilation to nasals, marginal in English (Smith 1973, 15), is common in Hindi child language (Srivastava 1974) and Telugu (Nirmala 1981; Bai and Nirmala 1978).

24.   **Hindi**
ni:d (slumber) → nandi:/nind: (22 months)
sa:bun (soap) → mammun (24 months)

25.   **Telugu**
ba:wundi → na:ni
taNNi (water) → nanni
miida(up) → miina

A velar feature may be a common assimilation target in English, as in (19a), but Telugu child language such as in (26) shows not only assimilation of the dental [d] stop to a nasal, but also assimilation of the velar /k/ to a dental.

26.   **Telugu** (Bai and Nirmala 1978)
kinda (below) → tinna

Hindi child language, (27), provides another example of nasal assimilation, and the consonants in the adult form which are velar are represented as dental in the child's production.

27.   **Hindi** (Sharma, 1969; Bai and Nirmala 1978)
kanghi (comb) → danni

In English child language, consonant cluster reduction may result in voicing voiceless stops, especially word initially (29), while in Telugu it does not, even with borrowed vocabulary (29) (Nirmala 1981, 72):

28.   spoon → bu:n
stop → dap
please → bis

29.   spoon → [pu:n]
please → [pi:s]

Adult-like voice onset time productions in Spanish and in Hindi are significantly delayed (after age of four), while in English their acquisition nears age two (Macken and Barton 1980; Davis 1995).

Variation in phonological deformations in early child language then appears to reflect both the child's creativity and their analysis of the phonology of the specific language being acquired.

8.3.5   Suprasegmental dimensions[32] ▬▬▬▬▬▬▬▬▬▬

Development of suprasegmental aspects of a language's phonology occurs hand in hand with the development of segmental aspects seen above. It also reveals children's linguistic computation.

8.3.5.1   Acquisition of prosody

While some aspects of linguistic prosody develop until adolescence, others appear early.[33] This development also reveals children's continuous linguistic computation and mapping to the target grammar.

Children organize around a rhythmic template in their early word production. Early deformations reveal children operating on syllable units, e.g., in *unstressed syllable omission* (30).

30.   a. **English**
            banana → ['nænə]
        b. Spanish
            pelota (ball) → [ota]

Although stressed syllables, because of their increased duration, amplitude and pitch, may be viewed as more accessible to perception, experimental work documents that children perceive unstressed syllables which they omit in their speech production (e.g., Gerken et al. 1990). In Quiché Mayan, where stress on the verb shifts with linguistic context, children at different times produce different parts of the verb when they omit unstressed syllables.[34] For example, a young child (aged 2.9) produced (31a), but a week later (31b) for the same verb where it was in utterance medial position (Pye 1983, 594).

31.   a. kach'a:wik (It's talking)
            wik (**child**)
        b. kach'a:w taj (It's not talking)
            chaw taj (**child**)

Since this varying production involved the same verb, the child's perception must involve more than shown in their production at any one time.

If children were not aware of unstressed syllables, e.g., suffering a perceptual deficit, and if their syllable omission were not linguistically constrained, we could

---

[32] Research on prosodic structure development has exploded over the last decade (e.g., Gerken 1996b, c; Kehoe and Stoel-Gammon 1997).

[33] Crystal 1979 for early review.

[34] When the verb was clause medial and primary stress was on the verb stem, the child produced it. When it was not, and the single stressed final syllable on that verb involved a functional category (e.g., a clausal termination or transitivizing suffix), he produced this.

not explain why all unstressed syllables are not omitted or all stressed syllables retained equally (e.g., Echols 1993). Data from eleven children (up to age 2.6 in Czech, English, Estonian, German, Slovenian and Spanish) show productive initial unstressed syllable deletion, and far less final unstressed syllable deletion (Vihman et al. 1998). Syllable omission in child language thus not only reflects children's access of the syllable unit, but also includes prosodic organization.

In general, children's early deformations may represent the overall sound pattern of a word.[35] The "minimal word" (a binary foot) may provide a fundamental "prosodic unit to which different prosodic and morphological processes apply" (Demuth 1996c, 176). Early productivity of disyllabic words provides evidence such as in (32) (Demuth 1996c, 172–173).

32.   a. **English** (Echols and Newport 1992)
               elephant → ɛlfʌn
          b. **Dutch** (Winjen et al. 1994)
               olifant (elephant) → 'oːxant
               andere (other) → 'Anʀə /'Anə
          c. **Sesotho** (Demuth 1996c)
               n.ta.te (father) → ta.te
               ma.-sim.ba (chips) → tim.pa

In addition, early words appear "constrained by the prosodic realization of foot structure in the language being learned" (Demuth 1996b, 10). For example, early child productions in English often reflect a strong–weak trochaic foot, predominant in English (Jusczyk et al. 1993; Gerken 1994a,b).

33.   Adult target: e̲ra̲ser
          Child: [raisə] (Echols and Newport 1992)

Dutch children add material to transform early words into disyllabic, trochaic feet (Demuth 1996c, 172).

34.   Adult target: ziekenhuis (hospital)
          Child: ['sikhʌys]
               jurk (dress) → ['joeʀək]
               bal (ball) → ['balə]

Again, child language appears to reveal linguistic analyses. Children may initially build on a core syllable, then equate the phonological word with a fundamental rhythmic unit, the foot (consisting minimally of a binary foot), and then follow a Prosodic Hierarchy in development (Demuth 1996c, 14; Vihman et al. 1998, 936). A "metrical production template" may explain why children acquiring English eliminate pretonic unstressed syllables more than posttonic ones: banana → ['nænə], not *[bə'næn].

---

[35] Ferguson and Farwell 1975; Macken 1979, 1986 and 1992; Menyuk and Menn 1979; Waterson 1971; Demuth 1996c.

8.3.5.2   Integrating segmental and suprasegmental dimensions

"Before children can talk, they must learn to sing" (Pye, 1983, 599).

Segment–prosody interactions appear to account for a number of children's word deformations. These interactions again show the child's linguistic computation. Not only are children operating at once on segmental and suprasegmental representations of the language they are acquiring, but they are integrating these.

Truncations may combine segmental features from the beginning and end of a word, as in (35), demonstrating "conflation effects" (Kehoe and Stoel-Gammon 1997, 141)

35.   CHIMpanZEE
         Child: [tSi:]

In Sesotho, the preverbal subject marker "ke-" and the future tense marker "-tla-" frequently surface as one syllable, "ka-," where the onset consonant from the first syllable is joined with the vowel nucleus from the second (Demuth 1996c, 6). In Dutch, similar "syllabic merger" effects occur, e.g., (36) (Winjen, Kirkhaar and den Os 1994, Demuth 1996c):

36.   microfoon (microphone) → [mi'kʀon]

The child's integration of language-specific properties of segmental and suprasegmental units develops over the first twelve months of life. Experiments have shown that when infants (six and nine months) were presented with a sequence of syllables which varied in (a) syllable order and (b) rhythmic properties independently (e.g., with or without a trochaic stress pattern), six-month-olds represented these as a unit when they correlated with rhythmic regularity, regardless of syllable ordering (Morgan and Saffran 1995). Nine-month-olds represented these as a unit only when syllable ordering and rhythmic regularity correlated.

Comparative research has now begun on children's developing integration of suprasegmental and segmental phonology.[36] Researchers have compared acquisition of French, which involves dominant iambic rhythm, to English. Four of five French infants in the late single-word period (aged 1.1–1.8) produced primarily iambic structures, e.g., (37), while a comparable group of nine children acquiring American English used both trochaic and iambic patterns (with individual variation). This provides evidence for the early role of the ambient language in determining a rhythmic template. It does not support a "universal trochaic constraint" on early child language.

37.   French iambic patterns in early words (Vihman et al. 1998, 937)
         chapeau (hat) → [bo'lo]
         lapin (rabbit) a'pa
         poupee (doll) a'pa

---

[36] Infants must learn how syllable weight is realized in a given language and thus assign stress patterns of the language; e.g., in English, they have to learn that only syllables with branching coda, e.g., CVCC, are "heavy" enough to influence stress placement (Demuth 1996c, 10).

Further evidence that children very early consult suprasegmental aspects of the target language comes from analyzing variations in children's first words. For example, these are monosyllabic in Quiché Mayan, e.g., (38a) (Pye 1992, 303–304; Demuth 1996c) while typically disyllabic in Sesotho, e.g., (38b) (as in Dutch above):

38.   a. **Quiché Mayan** first words (Pye's examples)
          jolom (head) → lom
          wa'ik (eat) → 'ik
      b. **Sesotho** (Demuth 1996 citing Connelly 1984)
          n.ta.te (father) → ta.te
          ma.-sim.ba (chips)?→ tim.pa
          che.le.te (money) → tee.te

French children at early periods produce as many multisyllabic (three or more syllables) as monosyllabic words (Vihman et al. 1998, 936), differing from English (with frequent monosyllables or disyllables in earliest child speech). Children acquiring Spanish show earlier development of word structures with an initial weak syllable, infrequent in languages like English and Dutch until after the age of two (Gennari and Demuth 1997).

Further evidence that children are analyzing and mapping the target language is shown by the fact that young bilingual children differentiate their early word patterns according to the language they are speaking. A young Italian–English bilingual produced more monosyllabic utterances in English and more polysyllabic in Italian (Ingram 1981/2). An Indian child acquiring both Hindi and English produced first English words as dominantly monosyllabic (a CVC type), and first Hindi words as dominantly disyllabic (a (C)VCV type), with frequent initial consonant deletion in Hindi, e.g., [ro:ti] (unleavened bread) → [o:ti]; or [pa:ni] (water) → [a:ni] (Nair 1991).

8.3.6   Summary

Children's first word deformations reveal their linguistic computation. Children are continually integrating universal principles with language specific grammars at both suprasegmental and segmental levels and gradually integrating these. Even when child productions appear to reflect deformations or "errors," they reveal general and universal properties of adult language systems and language change. Children are continually operating on the specific grammatical system of the language they are acquiring.

8.4   Conclusions

The first year prepares children for first words and beyond. During a child's first twelve months, they categorize sound immediately and can even detect speech distinctions corresponding to contrasts which do not exist in their native language. "[T]he most important factor controlling the young infant's . . . speech . . . appears to be a basic set of innate perceptual mechanisms rather than exposure to specific types of early linguistic experience" (Aslin, Pisoni and Jusczyk 1983 and 1998, 642). The wide array of non-native and native sound distinctions of which infants are capable (appendix 2b) has suggested that:

39.   a. "[I]nfants can without prior exposure discriminate contrasts relevant to any particular language" (Trehub 1976).
       b. They initially "discriminate many, if not all, phonetic contrasts regardless of the linguistic environment in which they are reared" (Kuhl 1987a).

Although it is not yet possible to identify a universal phonetic repertoire with a universal set of category boundaries which subsequently get extended or reduced in an individual language,[37] we can conclude that infants appear to be preprogrammed to distinguish sound variations along every major dimension of speech-sound variation which any language of the world may potentially involve. These facts provide a basis for solution of the problem of language acquisition raised in chapter 3: infants do not need to search the speech stream to perceive acoustic invariants and thereby discover units. Categorical perception allows them to assign units immediately.

Both speech perception and production reveal continuous linguistic mapping to the phonology of the language being acquired, and developments of perception and production are linked. Effects of the language-specific target on both are first detected about six months. Sensitivity to general prosodic properties of the language, evidenced shortly after birth, develops continuously thereafter. Developments in speech perception and speech production converge on the child's production of first words at about twelve months.

Consistent with Jakobson's theory, acquisition of phonology after the first twelve months represents a linguistic, not merely a motoric, challenge for children. They gradually extend their phonetic repertoire; many of the fundamental phonetic dimensions Jakobson identified may guide the course of this language acquisition. Although there appear to be general constraints at work on children's acquisition of phonology, such as early sensitivity to given phonetic dimensions of variation and early limitation to simple (CV-based) word forms, as well as other markedness constraints, there appears to be no universal order of acquisition of sounds (or phonemes) that is revealed across all children independent of the language being acquired.

Development over the first twelve months in acquisition of phonology does not simply reflect maturation, since it differs from language to language. It also does not cohere with a simple "learning theory"; i.e., more experience producing

---

[37] Given the possibility for up to seventy or more phonemes in a language, no infants have been tested for the full range of possible contrasts. The boundaries of phonemic categories vary across languages, e.g., along the VOT continuum, as in English vs. French or Spanish. We assume that the infant cannot be born with all boundaries for all contrasts.

proportionately more learning, and thus more knowledge. Instead, during the first year, we see a gradual elimination of response to excess distinctions, resembling a narrowing or "fine tuning" to those which characterize the target language.

The gradual elimination of children's responses to certain sound distinctions is not due to general decline in perceptual abilities. (a) Infants maintain a sensitivity to sound distinctions where phonemic contrasts based on this distinction exist in the native language. (b) Adults can discriminate non-native sound distinctions when a more sensitive procedure is used and can train to discriminate nearly any non-native contrast (Pisoni, Lively and Logan 1994). (c) Adults can discriminate acoustic cues differentiating non-native contrasts even without training (Werker and Pegg 1992). (d) Some non-native contrasts remain more accessible in adulthood, e.g., certain Zulu clicks (which "are not at all assimilable to English," Werker 1994, 108; Best, McRoberts and Sithole 1988). The facts reviewed above suggest that development involves neither simple *addition*, nor *loss*, but the gradual *organization* of a specific phonological system (Werker and Pegg 1992, 297). The construction of this grammatical system determines how speech input is perceived. It begins to do so before the infant speaks a first word (Werker 1994 and Best 1995).

After the first year, children master language-specific word and phrase structures, integrate segmental and suprasegmental units and levels of representation, coordinate the "notes" and create the "score" of their language's phonological system. Constraints are continually modulated by the specific language being acquired. Development involves an increase in language-specific linguistic computation.

8.4.1   Toward an explanation

Because early phonological competencies do not depend on experience of a specific language, they suggest an innate component as their source.[38] Because children demonstrate these very early, before lexical learning or meaning or linguistic communication are developed, they appear modular. Do these results reflect an innate "Language Faculty" (e.g., Aslin, Pisoni and Jusczyk 1983, 642)?

Categorical perception characterizes other cognitive areas[39] and non-human species (e.g., chinchillas, crickets), and is thus not specific to the Language Faculty.[40] However, biological programming may provide a general (cross-species) auditory/acoustic structure which is co-opted by the Language Faculty. Since non-human species do not develop language, it must be that this auditory/acoustic structure is differentially "connected" for the human species to

---

[38] It is not clear how a model could be developed which allowed the opposite of the empirical facts: how could one learn that speech perception should be categorical?

[39] E.g., perception of color and music (Harnad 1987).

[40] These cross-species behaviors require thousands of training trials, differing from the human infant who demonstrates sensitivity to the distinctions within the first few minutes of testing (e.g., Jusczyk 1997, 57f.). Some infant abilities appear not to generalize across species, e.g., Kuhl 1987b.

language acquisition ability, a human Language Faculty. If a linguistic module does characterize infant knowledge, co-opting general auditory abilities immediately, then an explanation exists for: (a) why the wide range of phonetic abilities exists in infants without experience; (b) why infants demonstrate a continuous mapping to language specific phonologies beginning so early during the first twelve months; (c) why we find early (even during the first twelve months) convergence between infant language perception and production; (d) why certain specialized speech processing mechanisms (e.g., "duplex perception") appear to hold for the infant's sound perception (Eimas and Miller 1992). One intriguing hypothesis regarding formulation of this linguistic module is provided by the Motor Theory of Speech Perception (MTSP).[41] (See Liberman 1996, Best 1995.)

> **MOTOR THEORY OF SPEECH PERCEPTION:** listeners perceive speech in terms of their articulatory movements or organization thereof.

8.4.2   Linguistic theories

We may ask how these results bear on linguistic theories in phonology. Smith's 1973 study (and Stampe's 1969) was framed in terms of an early theory, *Sound Pattern of English* (Chomsky and Halle 1968). While it was the rigor of this paradigm which allowed their discoveries, further theoretical developments now allow further articulation of the cohesive systematic properties underlying a child's Language Faculty and their computation. Recent phonological theory helps us to integrate our understanding of suprasegmental components and the skeletal structure which may unify different levels of representation of phonological knowledge (e.g., Spencer 1986), and to formulate principles and constraints affecting these components.[42]

In common with "natural phonology," *Optimality Theory* (OT) assumes that a preexisting set of well-formedness constraints characterizes the Language Faculty and is available to children, although it shifts the paradigm to a universal set of *constraints* rather than *rules*, or processes, principles or parameters (table 8.6). A specific grammar to be acquired consists of a set of "constraints arranged in a strict domination hierarchy" (Prince and Smolensky 1997, 1604; Tesar and Smolensky 2000, 48). Different ordering of constraints allows any one constraint to range in a language from absolute to nil. An optimal grammar violates the fewest constraints.

---

[41] Several versions of a motor theory of speech perception exist (see Fodor, Bever and Garrett 1974, 309; Liberman 1996).
[42] Consonant harmony, widespread in child language, involves spreading of one or more features from one consonant to another in non-linear phonology. Certain synchronic changes in Amahl's phonology can be unified in a principled way if autosegmental representation is adapted (e.g., the interdependence of the loss of labial attraction and cluster acquisition) (Spencer 1986, for example).

Table 8.6 *Universal constraints in Optimality Theory*

STRUCTURE CONSTRAINTS (SC)	*Markedness constraints* which concern the "complexity" of a structure. For example: NO CODA constraint on syllables is violated by a closed syllable. Marked structures violate SC.
FAITHFULNESS CONSTRAINTS (FC)	An input and an output should be identical in a certain respect. For example: PARSE – every segment of the input must appear in the output FILL – new material should not be added which is not present in the input

Language-specific grammars involve a competition between SC and FC. In OT, children's early word structures are viewed as "the result of competing phonological constraints" (Demuth 1996, 113).[43] Child grammar evolves toward the adult by re-ranking constraints. Constraint ranking is proposed to apply differently to speech production (where SC outrank FC) and speech perception (where FC outrank SC) (Prince and Smolensky 1997, 1609; Tesar and Smolensky 2000). FC "gradually become more highly ranked over time" and Structural Constraints are demoted (table 8.6; Demuth 1996b, 123).

8.4.3   Open questions

While the postulation of an innate linguistic module described by linguistic theory can help to explain the basic structure, guidance, constraint and motivation for acquisition of phonology, the exact mechanisms of the child's use of input data in such a way as to converge on the target grammatical system remain elusive.[44] In the first twelve months, some form of infants' experience adjusts initial category boundaries and eliminates response to categories not needed in a language. It does so before children know words and/or can test for minimal pairs of contrasts as the linguist can (see Jusczyk 1997, 74, for discussion). How can this experience work? This problem was posed almost a century ago, (40), and it remains a challenge today, (41).

40.   It is time . . . . to face the question, "How can a sound be assigned a 'place' in a phonetic pattern over and above its natural classification on organic and acoustic grounds?" . . . "The answer is simple. A 'place' is intuitively found for a sound (which is here thought of as a true 'point in the pattern', not a mere conditional variant) in such a system because of a general feeling of its phonetic relationship resulting from all the specific phonetic relationships (such as parallelism, contrast, combination, imperviousness to combination, and so on) to all other sounds."   (Sapir 1925, 23)

---

[43] See Demuth 1995, 18; 2001 and 1997.
[44] Menn 1976 proposes an "interactionist-discovery" theory.

41.   **How does experience work?**

"Let us consider the phrase 'experience with speech sound contrasts of the infant's language community.' This definition entails that the infant's perceptual/cognitive system SEGMENTS the speech stream into phonetic units and registers the relation between members of the two phonetic categories such that the two sounds are experienced AS A CONTRAST. To claim that sound contrasts are 'experienced' and that such experience enhances sensitivity to the perceptual cues that separate phonetic categories for adults of that community, we must attribute to the infant the processes by which such experience could affect subsequent discrimination performance. That linguistic experience has such an effect presupposes that infants have accomplished at least all of the following: (1) segmented the speech stream into discrete units; (2) recognized that the sounds to be contrasted vary along some underlying perceptual continuum(s); (3) ignored covarying redundancy information; (4) identified variations along certain continuum(s) as perceptually equivalent (perceptual consistency); (5) recognized that these instances along the continuum(s) separate into contrasting categories; (6) recognized that these instances have occurred before (such that current experience is identified with previous experience); and (7) accounted for the frequency with which such instances have occurred" (MacKain 1982, 534–535).

How do children acquire the correct representation of the adult form?[45] What is the true cause of development of children's rules? What makes children eliminate false rules or re-rank constraints? In the acquisition of phonology, as in the acquisition of the other areas of language knowledge, mechanisms of knowledge development remain mysterious.

8.5   Supplementary readings

For a general introduction to Phonetics/Phonology in Cognitive Science, see Keating, Kenstowicz and Clements, all in Wilson and Keil 1999. Chapter 2, "Sounds," in Weisler and Milekic 2000, provides an introduction to basic terms and concepts, with interactive demonstrations and lab exercises available on CD.

Ladefoged 2001 provides an introduction to the field of phonetics, with CD demonstrations. Ian Smith 1999/2001 provides "Higgins the phonetics tutor" on CD.

A conceptual introduction to the field of phonology is provided by Bromberger and Halle 2000.

---

[45] How can we be certain that the child's underlying representation is identical to the adult's, and is it always so? (Macken 1980, Braine 1974, 1976 for discussion.) Macken 1980 argues that the true source of the "puzzle" deformation by Amahl may be a perceptual error.

An introduction to phonology in generative grammar can be found in Kenstowicz 1994; to non-linear phonology, in the introductory chapter to van der Hulst and Smith 1982, and Goldsmith 1990, 1995, 1999. Many papers in the area of OT and a bibliography are available at the Rutgers Optimality Archive: *http://ruccs.rutgers.edu/roa.html.*

A distilled version of Jakobson's proposal, "The Sound Laws of Child Language and Their Place in General Phonology," appears in Waugh and Monville-Burston 1990, 294–330). Reviews and critiques of Jakobson's theory can be found in Anderson 1985, Kiparsky and Menn 1977, Ingram 1989, Macken 1995, and Garnica 1975.

Development of Speech Perception. Jusczyk 1997a (also 1986) provides an important summary and critique. See also Aslin, Jusczyk and Pisoni 1998, 1983, and Werker and Tees 1999; Eimas, Miller and Jusczyk 1987; Werker 1994; Best 1994.

The development of Speech Production. Boysson-Bardies 1999, Vihman 1996 and Locke 1993 and 1983 provide review. Description of phonatory and articulatory aspects of early vocalizations is given by Koopmans-Van Beinum and Van der Stelt 1998.

Formal Learnability Problems in acquiring phonology are surveyed in Dresher 1999.

Examples of current research applying theoretical paradigms to empirical language acquisition data: Archibald 1995. Fikkert 2000 provides general overview of the "state of the art"; and Macken 1995, general overview.

A collection which links early speech perception and production to other aspects of language acquisition and to general issues in the area of language acquisition is Morgan and Demuth 1995.

9 The acquisition of syntax

Introduction

Through knowledge of syntax, children can relate the sounds of language to thought, and can produce and comprehend unlimited new sentences with unlimited recursion, e.g., Dr. Seuss's *"When* tweetle beetles *fight . . ."* (chapter 2 (11)).

For syntax as for phonology, children must discover the relevant units, then categorize and combine them. They must link distinct levels of representation and do so in a systematic, productive, but constrained manner. As we saw in chapter 2, children must know the special design features of natural language, i.e., units may move (*displacement*) or combine through operations on them, and many may be null or "empty." Appendices 4 and 5 summarize milestones in infants' early acquisition of syntax revealed through their perception and production of language.

9.1.1 What must children acquire?

Table 9.1 summarizes what children must know minimally in order to acquire the syntax of language, i.e., the epistemological primitives of syntactic knowledge.

On the basis of these primitives, children must discover (A) – (G).

(A) *The units*
Children must discover syntactic units: sentences (or clauses) and phrases, i.e., the smaller units which combine to form sentences. These compose the "constituent structure" of a sentence. All syntactic operations and computations make reference to the clause, the essential syntactic unit.

A CONSTITUENT: A sequence of one or more items that functions as a single unit in a sentence.

[Poodles] battle
[The poodles] battle
[The poodles in the puddle] battle
[The poodles [the tweetles follow]] battle

Table 9.1 *Foundations of syntax*

1. Constituent structure
2. Order
3. Operations[a]
   – movement leading to *displacement* of elements
   – coordination, adjunction and embedding leading to recursion whereby one unit is *merged* with another[b]
4. Computation
   – anaphora (e.g., pronouns, empty categories or ellipses)
   – morphosyntax (e.g., inflection and agreement between units possibly distant from each other in a sentence)

[a] In earlier linguistic theory, "transformations" had been defined in terms of specific rules, e.g., "passive transformation." Current theory seeks to define fundamental operations which underlie all these specific rules (cf. chapter 4).
[b] The operation "merge" in current linguistic theory involves the creation of phrase structure. It joins two constituents to form a new constituent (cf. Lasnik 2002). Linguists now pursue the degree to which "merge" and "move" could be reduced to a single operation.

(B) *The hidden skeleton*

   Children must discover the secret skeleton, or "configuration," that underlies every sentence. Constituents are arranged in hierarchical structure through this skeleton, e.g. 2.3.7 and figure 9.1.

   When children can map words and morphemes to this skeleton, they can parse seemingly incomprehensible strings of words, e.g., (1) (Pinker 1994, 212), and can resolve unlimited ambiguities, e.g., (2).

1.   a. Police police police police police
        b. [[[Police [police police]] police police]]
          [[[N   [N V]]]$_{]NP}$ V   N   ]$_{VP}$]$_S$

2.   The mouse and the cat in the basket
        a. The mouse and [the cat[in the basket]]
        b. [[The mouse and the cat] in the basket]

(C) *Categorizing the units*

   Children must make a basic distinction between "functional" and "content" categories (sometimes termed "lexical" categories), and relate each to the sentence skeleton.[1]

[1] The terminological distinction between "functional" and "lexical" categories is misleading, since both functional and content categories involve the lexicon. The distinction represented in table 9.2 is not simple. Functional categories often involve semantic content, e.g., inflection may represent time; and there may be many FC in a language, depending on whether one counts each potential inflection. We must also distinguish between FC as characterizing a type of lexical item, versus FC as heads of phrase structure where lexical items may be associated. While we can hypothesize that children may initially know abstract principles of phrase structure involved with functional heads, we would not hypothesize initial knowledge of the associated lexicon, which must be learned for each language.

Table 9.2 *Category types and English examples*

Functional categories	Generally serve a grammatical role, with little or no semantic content
	A "closed" class: a small, finite number of items
	Complementizers (COMP) and conjunctions (CONJ): e.g., "that," "and"
	Inflectional markers: e.g., "AUX" ("do", "will")
	e.g., Determiners: e.g., "a," "the"
Content categories	Generally convey meaning
	An "open" class: an infinitely expandable set of items
	e.g., Nouns, verbs, adjectives, adverbs

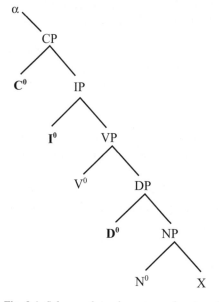

Fig. 9.1 *Schema of simple sentence functional architecture: English order.*

Functional categories (FC) mark and head each of the basic constituents of a sentence. They reflect the "joints" in the secret skeleton.

Basic FC heads

Head of sentence or clause	**C** heading CP (Complementizer phrase)
Head of predicate	**I** heading IP (Inflectional phrase)
Head of noun phrase	**D** heading DP (Determiner phrase)

The FC heads provide a structure to "hold" the content words, and create the basis for displacements of units in sentences, providing targets or landing sites to which constituents may move. They create the basis for recursion. (See Hoekstra 2000.)

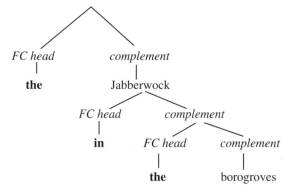

Fig. 9.2 *Parsing "Jabberwocky."*

Figure 9.1 provides the secret skeleton for a simple sentence, showing its basic functional category heads (in bold) and its hierarchical structure.[2] This skeleton is in principle unlimited. In the figure, "Alpha" suggests that one could always add to any clause another, such as "I know [that . . . . " or "I know [that you think [that . . .", etc. Here the complementizer "that" which heads the clause reflects sentence recursion. A conjunction like "and" in English does the same (2.3.5). Every clause or noun phrase referred to can be recursively expanded.

Functional categories provide a critical mechanism by which we map the speech stream to the secret skeleton, just as we do for "Jabberwocky," e.g. (3). Here, the function words that convey syntactic knowledge are represented (bold and underlined), but the content words that have substantive meaning are replaced by nonsense, e.g., figure 9.2.

3.   "Jabberwocky" (*Through the Looking Glass*, 1964, 15)[3]
                'T**was** brillig **and the** slithy tove**s**
                Did gyre **and** gimble **in the** wabe:
                All mimsy **were the** borogrove**s**,
                And the mome rath**s** outgrabe.

Children must link content words to the skeleton. As Alice in Wonderland remarks, with only syntax and no words which have substantive meaning, Jabberwocky "[s]omehow . . . seems to fill my head with ideas — only I don't exactly know what they are!" (17). When words are linked to the skeleton, children can label phrases; e.g., nouns will head noun phrases, verbs will head verb phrases.

---

[2] We purposely simplify here. Linguists debate whether there is a universal set of functional categories, and how many there are, e.g., whether Inflection is split to several heads (tense, agreement, etc.) each with their own phrasal projections (Thrainsson 1996). We choose the minimal assumption for the Initial State: C, I and D, which correspond to both the fundamental syntactic architecture of a sentence and its fundamental semantic units, i.e., to its propositional and predicate–argument structure. See Bai and Lakshmi 1996–1997 for acquisition evidence on this issue.

[3] Noun inflection provides an additional functional element in Jabberwocky.

a. <u>Left heads</u>   b. <u>Right heads</u>

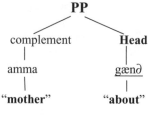

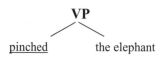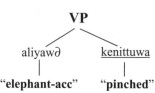

Fig. 9.3 *Ordering the units.*

4.   a. NP – [**poodles** [in the bottle]]
          VP – [**fight** [the battle]]
          PP – [**with** [their paddles]]
          AP – [**gluey** [with the goo]]

      b. DP – [**the** [poodle]]
          IP – [**will** [battle]]
          CP – [**that** [the poodle will battle]]

(D) *Ordering*

Children must discover the basic constituent order of their language and link it to the sentence skeleton.

(E) *A different order for each language*

They must do so for any language they acquire, whatever its order, whether like Sinhala (9.3b) or English (9.3a).

(F) *Operations and computation*

Children must discover what movements the language allows, creating displacements where allowed (2.3.8.1) and computations where required, e.g., interpreting null elements and pronouns in the right manner (2.3.8.2).

(G) *Constraints*

Children must discover how operations and computations are constrained both within and across languages (2.3.9). Seemingly small offenses, e.g., the order variation in (5), can crash the output.

5.   *Fight tweetle beetles when called is it

Summary

Children must be able to generate the underlying skeleton of every sentence, and the system which operates on this skeleton, in every language they acquire.

Onto this skeleton they must map the fundamental syntactic units, i.e., the clauses and the phrases which are the constituents of the clause. Words must be mapped to these units. Children must know that constituent structure and order may be transformed; yet the system is always constrained.

9.1.2   What are the challenges?

The PLD (see p. 32) does not directly expose syntactic units or computational knowledge (Chapters 2, 3, 4 and 6). The speech stream includes null elements (chapter 2) and both combinations and displacements of units. Words jump from category to category, nouns become verbs and vice versa. Similar structures may relate to different meanings and similar meanings may relate to different structures. No evidence directly demonstrates the syntactic constraints which make a sentence ungrammatical, nor the rules or operations which make it grammatical.

9.1.3   Leading questions

We saw in chapter 4 that the theory of Universal Grammar (UG) provides leading hypotheses regarding child language acquisition in the face of indeterminate evidence, in opposition to several empiricist models. Debates between models raise several questions.

- When do children evidence knowledge of the foundations of syntax? (table 9.1)
- When do children distinguish Functional and Content categories?
- When do children become capable of categorizing syntactic units?
- When does the recursive property of natural language syntax appear?
- Does children's early syntax reveal universal principles and parameters such as provided by a Universal Grammar (cf. chapter 4)?
- Does children's early syntax reveal universal properties before language-specific properties or the opposite?
- Is there a "pre-syntactic" stage in which children are without the benefit of grammar, or with a deviant or incomplete grammar? Do children perhaps start with content "words," without functional structure?
- Is the course of syntax acquisition continuous or discontinuous?
- What is the nature of change over time in children's knowledge of the syntax of their language? Is there evidence for or against a maturational theory of development of syntactic knowledge (chapter 4)?

9.2   How do children meet the challenge? Laying the foundations: the first twelve months

Although we are concerned with children's *knowledge* of syntax, we must once again derive our evidence from study of their *perception* (9.2.1) and *production* (9.2.2) of language. While much early research on the acquisition of syntax focused on study of children's production of their first sentences, the new methods which assess infant perception (cf. chapter 7) have made it possible to begin to assess the origins of syntactic knowledge even earlier in development.

9.2.1   Perception

We saw that shortly after birth infants recognize and categorize certain language types (appendix 4; chapter 6), suggesting that at the same time that they are working on the acquisition of phonological knowledge, they are also sensitive to larger units. Now we will see that children are also sensitive to the epistemological primitives of syntax – *order* and *constituent structure* – prior to speaking or understanding their first words.

9.2.1.1   Linear order

Infants with a mean age of two months were tested in a habituation paradigm using sentences read by a female speaker which varied in order, e.g., (6) (Mandel, Kemler-Nelson and Jusczyk 1996).

6.   a. Cats <u>jump wood</u> benches
        b. Cats <u>would jump</u> benches

After being habituated to one of these sentence types, e.g., (6a), these infants recovered from habituation when hearing the other type, e.g., (6b). Infants in a control group who had not heard either sentence previously, did not. Since this differentiations of sentences like (6a) and (6b) occurs without lexical comprehension, we may assume that order variation is the source of the infants' discrimination. The sentence unit was essential carrier of the order information, since order variations in fragments, e.g., (7), were not distinguished.

7.   a. Cats jump. Wood benches.
        b. Cats would. Jump benches.

In another study, ten-month-olds listened longer to grammatical sentences with well-formed word order, such as (8a) over (8b), showing that they distinguish order variation and do so with functional categories (determiner phrases) as well (Shady, Gerken and Jusczyk 1995).

8.   a. She knew <u>her brother's</u> tiny hungry meows.
        b. * She knew <u>brother's her</u> tiny hungry meows

Word order sensitivities appear to characterize language acquisition continuously through development. By 2.4 years, children may still not be producing long multiword combinations. Yet given an opportunity to watch two videos, each showing one of the scenarios in (9), they look longer at the one that matches the sentence they hear (Golinkoff et al. 1987), showing that they are able to consult

Table 9.3 *Experimental stimuli: the clause*

Natural clause breaks	Cinderella lived in a great big house./ but it was sort of dark/ because she had this mean, mean, mean stepmother./ And, oh, she had two stepsisters that were so ugly./ They were mean too.
Unnatural breaks	. . . in a great big house. but it was/ sort of dark because she had/ this mean, mean, mean stepmother. And, oh, she/ had two stepsisters that were so/ ugly. They were mean,/ too. They were . . .

Source: *The Cinderella Experiment* (Hirsh-Pasek et al. 1987, 273)
Note: slashes indicate pause insertion

the word order differences in these sentences. Infants sixteen to eighteen months, some of whom have only one or two words in their productive vocabularies, do so also (Hirsh-Pasek and Golinkoff 1993 and 1996; Naigles 1998).

9.   a. Cookie Monster is tickling Big Bird
         b. Big Bird is tickling Cookie Monster

9.2.1.2   Constituent structure

In processing the speech stream around them, infants also appear to continuously consult constituent structure, another epistemological primitive of syntactic knowledge.

9.2.1.2.1   The clause

As early as 4.5 months, infants are sensitive to clausal units in the speech stream. Hirsh-Pasek et al. (1987) found that infants (six to ten months) oriented longer to passages of a woman reading a Cinderella story to a child where one-second pauses corresponded to clausal units than to those where pauses unnaturally broke those clausal units, e.g., table 9.3. They did so even when intonation involving length and frequency of pauses was controlled. Jusczyk 1989 replicated this result with 4.5-month-olds. Infants prefer the natural ("coincident") version of speech which corresponds to well-formed clausal units.. A version of the "click experiments" (Fodor, Bever and Garrett 1974), which demonstrated clause structure processing in adults, has also been conducted with infants using a head turn paradigm. It provides converging evidence of infants' sensitivity to clause structure. Infants better detected an extraneous noise when it occurred at clause unit boundaries rather than within the clause (Morgan, Swingley and Miritai 1993).

In another study, Nazzi et al. (1998) also found that six-month-olds better detected and remembered clauses which were prosodically well formed in passages of continuous speech, e.g., they remembered sequences of words (underlined) from (10a) in contrast to (10b).

Table 9.4 *Experimental stimuli: the phrase*

Natural phrase breaks	The little boy at the piano/ is having a birthday party. All of his friends/ like to sing. Many different kinds of animals/ live in the zoo. The dangerous wild animals/ stay in cages . . .
Unnatural breaks	The little boy at the piano is having/ a birthday party. All of his friends like/ to sing . . . Many different kinds/ of animals live in the zoo. The dangerous/ wild animals stay in cages. Some/ of the animals . . .

Source: Jusczyk et al. 1992, 268

10.   a. John doesn't know what rabbits eat. <u>Leafy vegetables taste so good</u>. They don't cost much either.
      b. Many animals prefer some things. Rabbits eat <u>leafy vegetables. Taste so good</u> is rarely encountered.

This study not only confirmed infant clause detection, but confirmed that the overall context of a clause aids other aspects of linguistic processing, e.g., memory for word sequences.

These results suggest that infants have very early ability to parse the speech stream into the most fundamental syntactic unit, the clause, and to use this unit for linguistic organization. Even earlier, two-month-olds tested with the HAS procedure made phonological distinctions in a sentence context but not in a citation list context with which they had been familiarized.[4] They detected change of a single segment (e.g., [k] vs. [r]) in one word among a group of words, e.g., "the **c**at chased white mice" vs. "the **r**at chased white mice," when they heard the words in sentences, but not when they heard them read as a list (where the overall durations of the list sequences were equated to the comparable sentences) (Jusczyk 1997a, 53).

The fundamental syntactic unit, the clause, thus appears to be consulted by infants very early, and to aid the child's segmental distinctions as well.

9.2.1.2.2   *The phrase*

Experimenters have also investigated whether infants would also be sensitive to smaller syntactic units, i.e., phrases.[5] They artificially segmented speech samples at linguistically natural phrase boundaries, or unnatural ones (table 9.4). Although at six months, infants did not distinguish the samples, at nine months they did, preferring to listen to English speech which was segmented at the major phrase boundary, just before the verb phrase. Some aspects of phrase structure thus also appear to be accessible early in language acquisition (nine months), but after the clause (4.5 months).

Converging evidence was found when nine-month-olds were presented with a contrast between phonologically identical sequences, one of which was a well

---

[4] Mandel, Jusczyk and Kemler Nelson 1994; Jusczyk 1997, 153.   [5] Jusczyk et al. 1992.

formed subject NP and one of which involved fragments of phrases (NP and VP), as in (11). Here, the well-formed sequences are italicized and the fragmented sequences are underlined (Soderstrom et al. 2000).

11.   a. At the discount store, *new watches for men* are simple and stylish. In fact some people buy the whole supply of them.
       b. In the field, the old frightened gnu watches for men and women seeking trophies. Today, *people by the hole* seem scary.

Infants listened significantly longer to the sequences with well-formed NP boundaries, again showing sensitivity to phrase structure.

In summary, infants even before twelve months show sensitivity to constituent structure, to both clausal and phrasal constituents, in the speech stream around them. Detection of well-formed phrasal constituents develops after the basic syntactic unit, the clause.

9.2.1.3   Mapping to the speech stream

Researchers have begun to ask how infants accomplish these early structural distinctions when mapping to the speech stream.

Hirsh-Pasek et al. (1987) tested six-month-olds on stimuli, such as in table 9.3, when they were low-pass filtered, eliminating much of the segmental features but leaving components of the prosody intact.[6] They reasoned that if infants still recognized well-formed constituents, this would indicate that they must be using suprasegmental information in the speech stream. They found that infants continued to prefer the samples with the natural clause boundaries, even when low-pass filtered. This indicated that the infants' detection of and preference for well-formed constituent structure involves suprasegmental or prosodic components. Prosodic packaging is also implicated in the infant's phrasal detection through similar experiments (Soderstrom et al. 2000). Rhythmic properties of the speech stream, which correlate with constituent structure, appear to facilitate the child's structuring of the speech stream. This hypothesis is consistent with other research findings showing that infants are sensitive to well-formed musical phrasing (chapter 3). It is also consistent with research suggesting that children use rhythmic properties to distinguish between languages at very early ages (cf. chapter 6).

Infants thus appear early to link a grammatical unit (clause or phrase) to an acoustic unit in the speech stream, even as both units are developing.

9.2.1.4   Structural variability

At the same time that infants show early sensitivity to constituent structure, they also appear thirsty for variable syntactic experience. They don't simply prefer to listen to repeated units. When nine-month-olds were given a

---

[6] Certain prosodic markers may correlate with clause units, e.g., falling intonation contours, pausing, duration at boundaries (Jusczyk 1997, 142f. for review; and our chapters 3 and 6); these correlations are not necessary.

chance to listen to pairs of sentences which either shared the same syntactic structure, e.g., (12a) or varied ((12b) where the complementizer "that" signals an embedded sentence), they listened longer to the sentence set with structural variability and did so even when lexical variation was controlled. This suggests not only that infants are sensitive to differences in structural organization of sentences, but that they prefer such variation (Jusczyk and Gerken 1996, 398f.; also Jusczyk, Gerken and Kemler Nelson 2002).

12.   a. The farmer's wife heard the devout man in church
         The bus driver saw the big truck on the curb
       b. The farmer's wife saw the big truck on the curb
         The bus driver heard <u>that</u> the brown cow escaped

9.2.1.5   Across languages

Although all languages involve clauses as syntactic units, they vary in how they reflect them prosodically and syntactically. Although there is still only a small amount of cross-linguistic investigation of infants' sensitivities to the epistemological primitives of order and constituent strcture, some study was initiated by Peter Jusczyk. When infants in Buffalo, NY, who were acquiring English were tested in Polish on passages like those in the Cinderella story (read by a Polish woman), 4.5-month-olds recognized the difference between the natural and unnatural versions of Polish clauses and listened longer to the natural ones. However, six-month-olds did not. By six months, it may be that infants are affected by specific language differences between Polish and English, and already more attuned to English clausal structure (Jusczyk 1989).[7]

As in acquisition of phonology, acquisition of syntax may reveal children's mapping specific-language variation by six months of age.

9.2.1.6   Functional Categories (FC)

Not only do children show early sensitivity to syntactic order and constituent structure, they appear to use Functional Categories to map the speech stream to the hidden skeleton of sentences, long before their productive speech. When newborns (one to three days) were tested in a HAS procedure with lists of function words (e.g., *in*, *the*, *you*) and content words (e.g., *toy*, *chew*, *chair*) which had been taken from mothers' speech, they differentiated and categorized these types of words. Infants dishabituated to shifts across these lists, but not to shifts within each list (Shi, Werker and Morgan 1999). Other experiments found that 10.5-month-olds learning English demonstrated a preference for passages that contained natural unmodified function words (e.g., (13a)) over those that involved unnatural modification of these function words (e.g., (13b)), even when these were phonologically similar, showing very early sensitivity to these FC (Shady 1996). Modification of content words revealed no such differentiation.

---

[7] This seminal research deserves replication and expansion with both infants and adults. Adults may also distinguish foreign language clausal structure (e.g., Pilon 1981; Wakefield et al. 1974).

This sensitivity to FC developed, however. Only at sixteen months did infants distinguish grammatical from ungrammatical function morphemes, as in (14a) vs. (14b).

13.   a. There **was** once **a** little kitten who **was** born in **a** dark cozy closet. She knew
           how **the** light . . . . .
        b. There [haI] once [Ih] little kitten, who [haI] born in [Ih] dark cozy closet.
           She knew how [gIh] light . . . . .

14.   a. **This** man **has** bought two cakes. **A** cake **was** purchased by his wife . . . .
        b. *__Has__ man **this** bought two cakes. **Was** cake **a** purchased . . . . .

A brain imaging study measuring ERP also suggested development in the area of FC. It revealed that eleven-month-olds, but not ten-month-olds, distinguished passages with modified and unmodified function words (Shafer et al. 1998).

Young children have also shown early sensitivity to relations between FC, involving linguistic computation. They have revealed early perception of relations between functional elements which are discontinuous within a sentence, e.g., (15a) vs. (15b), although this also develops (Santelmann and Jusczyk 1998). For example, infants distinguished passages with a well-formed dependency between the auxiliary verb "is" and a main verb ending in "ing" (e.g., (15a)) from passages with an ungrammatical combination of a modal "can" and main verb ending in "ing" (15b).

15.   a. At the bakery, everybody <u>is</u> bak<u>ing</u> bread . . .
        b. * At the bakery, everybody <u>can</u> bak<u>ing</u> bread . . . . .

Eighteen-month-olds looked significantly longer toward the source of the grammatical passages, although fifteen-month-olds did not.

Infants thus are sensitive to the distinction between functional and content categories, and to subtle differences among functional categories; they "first begin to track the phonological characteristics of function morphemes sometime during the first year of life" and over time become aware of "their relations within sentences" (Shady 1996, vi). At least by eighteen months, infants "can track relationships between functor morphemes" (Santelmann and Jusczyk 1998, 105).

9.2.1.7   Summary

During their first year, infants' perception of language suggests that they have competence for the epistemological primitives of syntax, i.e., precisely those factors which will be necessary for the acquisition of a language: *structure* and *order*.

Infants, long before their first words, can parse the speech stream into the essential syntactic unit, the clause; and parsing phrases develops over the first year. Beginning a few days after birth, they not only can differentiate languages and language types but they can categorize types of words in terms which involve their syntactic roles, e.g., distinguishing functional categories from content categories. The universal syntactic unit, the clause, appears to be distinguished by infants within the first few months of life. Language-specific clausal and phrasal structures develop with time and experience. First evidence for gradual language-specific variation appears by about six months.[8]

9.2.2   Production

Children's knowledge of syntax can be studied more directly and in more detail when children begin production of first words and word combinations, about twelve months and beyond.

9.2.3   Perception and production

Given the infants' syntactic sensitivities seen above, we can assume that infants' developing perception of their language during the first year underlies the onset of productive syntax through their first words at about twelve months.

9.3   First words and beyond

9.3.1   The development of production

As appendix 5 suggests, children's first sentences over the next two years seem to demonstrate slow development (cf. chapter 7). First utterances may be limited to single words, leading to the term historically used for them, "holophrastic utterances." Early multiword sentences frequently deviate from the adult model, leading to the term historically used for such language, "telegraphic speech" (Brown 1973), e.g., (16). These phenomena cross languages, as seen in the Tamil and French child language in (17).

16.   "no dirty"
         "Me like coffee"
         "pull hat"
         "mommy go store" (Bloom 1970)
         "Mommy fix" (Eve 1, Brown 1973, 205)

17.   **Tamil** (aged 1.9, PS,040396, Lakshmanan 2000a, b)

         KuD-cu   [adult: kuDi-kkir-e]
         drink-verbal participle   drink-PRES-2S
         ((you) are drinking (tea))
         tuuk   [adult: train-ai tuuk-kar-een]
         lift (BARE STEM)   train-ACC lift-PRES-IS
         ((I) am lifting (the train))

---

[8] See Hirsh-Pasek and Golinkoff 1993, 1997 for related review.

French (Pierce 1992)
MangE le chien
Eat-E the dog[9]

For months, the child's speech is often short and may omit subjects and other arguments as well as nominal and verbal inflection.[10] Functional Categories are frequently absent or diminished. Even the single word period appears to involve several developmental steps between twelve and about twenty-eight months of age (Bloom 1973).[11] In spite of the foundational knowledge about language that infants demonstrated during the first twelve months, they now appear to be remarkably "unaccomplished."

However, much research now provides evidence that children's grammatical knowledge greatly exceeds their seemingly simple productions. Children's sensitivities to the syntactic foundations of order and constituent structure, as well as to Functional Categories, appear to be continuously at work during language development during this time.

9.3.1.1   Linear order

It has long been observed that children's first sentences generally respect the basic word order of their language, whether SVO, SOV, VSO or other.[12] Hypotheses that children may begin with a false word order, or begin with a general non-linguistic "cognitive" based order, have not been confirmed. Not only simple sentence order, but adjunction order in complex sentences, appears to be known very early, as we see below (9.3.2.2.1).

The acquisition of word order is especially interesting in languages such as German, where main and subordinate clauses reflect different orders. The subordinate clause is verb final, but the main clause verb second (V-2). Early hypotheses held that the child acquiring German would first show an extended period of verb-final sentences (e.g., Clahsen 1982; Mills 1985). Subsequent work, however, confirmed that children have early accurate knowledge of German order. They know the relation between main and subordinate clauses, a relation that has been represented in terms of "verb raising."[13] They know very early that the verb is

---

[9] The "E" in the notation "MangE" is intended to capture the indeterminacy of this form: e.g., "manger" = infinitive or "mangé" = past participle (cf. Dye, 2005a; Dye, Foley and Lust in preparation).

[10] These phenomena replicate both in natural speech and in experimentally elicited child speech.

[11] The true explanation for "holophrastic speech" remains a mystery. As Bloom 1973 shows, neither lack of motor control, lack of vocabulary, nor lack of cognitive complexity can fully explain it.

[12] Brown 1973, 156f.; Bowerman 1973 for Finnish; Weist 1983 for Polish; Kornfilt 1994 for Turkish; Barbier 1995, 1996, and Neeleman and Weerman 1997 for Dutch.

[13] Boser 1992, 1997, Boser et al. 1991, provide detailed cross-sectional and longitudinal study of thirty German children (0.21–2.10). Also Weissenborn 1990, Poeppel and Wexler 1993 and related studies of verb-raising in Dutch (Barbier 1995) and Swedish (Santelmann 1995). Meisel 1992 and Lust, Suñer and Whitman 1994 provide review and debate.

final in subordinate clauses, but not in main clauses. Accordingly, negation occurs correctly in constituent order, e.g., (18).[14]

18. Da brauchst du auch nicht zur Jule gehen
     Then need you also not to Jule go (2.7, CLAL Boser corpus, Boser et al. 1995).
     (Then you don't need to go see Jule also)

In addition, syntactic properties such as finiteness correlate with syntactic verb order in early child German, demonstrating that the child's grammar not only consults order but integrates order with abstract linguistic computation. The generalization in (19) has been found to characterize early child German.[15]

19. *Verb position and finiteness correlate. V-2 is always finite.*
     A nontensed verb never appears in a V-2 position.

Children have also been shown to have an early knowledge of displacement of elements (cf. 2.3.8.1).[16] They know order can and does permute. Where order may vary, children use variable orders. Knowledge of syntactic "scrambling" has been attested,[17] although acquisition of specific forms of scrambling may differ with differences in the adult grammar.[18]

In addition, experimental study suggests that displacement in child language respects constituent structure. In Japanese, where eighty-one children (aged 2.5 to 5.9) were tested on standard order sentences such as (20) compared to dislocated sentences such as (21), children not only productively reconstituted the basic order for dislocated sentences, but did so in a manner which respected constituent structure (Lust and Wakayama 1981).

20. **[S+S] V**
     Sumire-to tanpopo ga saku
     Violet and dandelion bloom

     S [V+V]
     Sakana wa oyogu-shi hane-ru
     Fish swim and jump

---

[14] See Deprez and Pierce 1993; Barbier 1995 for review and debate. The position of negation is important because it reflects the underlying constituent structure and order of FC heads.

[15] Boser 1997; Boser et al. 1991; Poeppel and Wexler 1993. While there is some evidence of non-adult-like verb placement in early child German, researchers debate how these can and should be explained; Boser 1995 for example, argues that examples like (i) can be explained in terms of deficiency in pragmatic knowledge corresponding to felicitous use of verb initial utterances in German (Boser et al. 1991; also 9.3.1.3.3).

i.   hat der papa fort (Ellen, 2.0; Boser corpus)
       has papa away (Papa has gone away)

[16] These facts mean that it can be difficult to evaluate a child's early knowledge of word order; e.g., a "groping strategy" such as suggested by Braine (1971) may reflect the child's experimenting with possible variations in word order and/or distinctions in meaning.

[17] Japanese (Otsu 1994), Turkish (Kornfilt 1994) and Dutch (Schaeffer 1997; Barbier 1995).

[18] German, Dutch and Swedish are compared in Boser et al. 1995.

21.   **V [S+S]**
           Hashiru-yo, usagi-to kame-ga
           Run, rabbit and tortoise

           [V+V] S
           Aruku-shi tobu-yo, kotori-wa
           Walk and fly, bird

Certain order errors, such as (22), have not been attested in children's natural speech, again suggesting that displacement, although possible, is constrained in child grammars (Neeleman and Weerman 1997; cf. Smith 1999).

22.   * didn't have today a nap (English)
           *ik wil de yoghurt even pakken (Dutch)
           (*I want the yoghurt quickly get*)

In summary, studies of children's early language production (both in natural speech and experimentally elicited) suggest that children very early know not only basic word and constituent order in their language, but also the essential syntactic property of displacement. Their grammars reveal early linguistic computation linking order and other linguistic properties, e.g, finiteness.

9.3.1.2   Recursion

The child's knowledge of order and constituent structure provide the foundations for knowledge of recursion, an essential design feature of natural language (cf. chapter 2).

By the time MLU reaches about 3.5 (cf. figure 7.1) in child language, recursive sentences are evident. Coordination, including clausal coordination, e.g., (23), is obvious then in the child's natural speech and elicited production.[19]

23.   [There Barbara] and [that cold] (mean age 2.2, MLU 2.36, Lust and Mervis
           1980)

Early forms of embedding are also evident

24.   I want to go (Limber 1973, age 1.11–2.5)
           That my did it (Hamburger 1980, age 2.0)

There appears to be no measurable period where this essential design property of natural language is missing from children's knowledge.[20]

---

[19] Brown 1973b; Lust 1977; Lust and Mervis 1980. English full coordinations require minimum length 3.5, e.g., [N&N]V, or N[V&V]. 63 percent of a group of children (2.0 to 2.4; MLU 1.97 to 2.91) produced some form of coordination in short samples of their natural speech (Lust and Mervis 1980).

[20] We assume we cannot measure recursion if length does not allow it, e.g., one- or two-word utterances.

9.3.1.3   Functional Categories and constituent structure

In spite of the foundational knowledge of essential syntactic properties which children demonstrate early, we still must ask how adult-like children's grammars can be, especially when we notice the frequent absence of Functional Categories in child language like (16) and (17).

If FC were missing in children's grammatical knowledge, not just in their productions, this could signal that their grammar is qualitatively distinct from adults'. It could motivate a "discontinuity" theory of development, where "maturation" of grammatical knowledge (brain maturation), learning or some other developmental force was necessary (cf. chapter 4) before children's grammar achieved Functional Categories. Some researchers have hypothesized (25).

25.   **A Maturational Hypothesis** (Radford 1990)[21]
       The child proceeds through a set of biologically determined stages in
       grammatical development:
        (I) Precategorical Stage: one-word period, no grammatical categories
        (II) Lexical Stage: Content Categories, e.g., Nouns and Verbs
        (III) Functional Stage: Function Categories finally appear

In contrast, others have hypothesized that children's knowledge surpasses what is overt in their early productions, e.g., (26).

26.   **Functional Projection Hypothesis**[22]
       Accurate representations of children's early sentences include Functional
       Categories and/or their projections; these may be phonetically null.[23]

In support of (26), researchers have noted that although children may omit functors in production they know these exist and are aided in production and comprehension by FC, even when they omit them. In early studies of children's natural speech using "rich interpretation" of their intended meanings, Bloom (1970) had found evidence for elements in the underlying representation (UR) of children's sentences, even when not overt in early utterances. The same utterance, e.g., "Mommy sock," may map onto different interpretations, and therefore different underlying representations (e.g., a subject–predicate relation such as "Mommy has a sock" or an attributive relation like "Mommy's sock"). Bloom argued for a "reduction operation" in child grammars which mapped from the UR to production under a length constraint. She noticed that children frequently produced various parts of a sentence, showing that they had the competence for each of the parts, while they rarely produced these together in a single utterance, e.g., "make ə block" (VO), as opposed to "Kathryn make ə house" (SVO). When one item (an extra argument) was included, another (a verb) might be deleted, as in "∅ raisin ∅ grocery store." Operators in the internal syntax of a sentence, e.g.,

---

[21] Radford 1994b modifies this proposal.   [22] Whitman, Lee and Lust 1991; Boser et al. 1992.

[23] This FC Projection Hypothesis leaves open whether the initial set of FC involves mainly the abstract phrase structure heads, C, I and D, as in figure 9.1, or additional categories and nodes as well (cf. fn. 3 and 4).

Table 9.5 *Testing functors*

	Content	Function	
i.	English	English	Pete push<u>es the</u> dog
ii.	English	Nonsense	Pete push<u>o na</u> dog
iii.	Nonsense	English	Pete baz<u>es the</u> dep

Source: Gerken, Landau and Remez 1990

predicate negation, appeared to trigger reductions (e.g., "Daddy like coffee," but "Lois . . . no coffee"), as opposed to operators that were clause external, e.g., anaphoric negation (as in "No Lois do it") (It is not the case that Lois did/will do that).

Experimental methods have since been used to examine the underlying representations of children's early sentences, confirming Bloom's early hypotheses. Experiments tested children's (aged 1.11 to 2.6) elicited imitation of sentences which varied in content words and/or functors (verb inflection and determiners); these were English or non-English (nonsense), e.g., table 9.5. If children do not "perceive" and/or process functors, then they should not notice deviations in them, although they may notice the content words, and they should omit both English and nonsense functors equivalently.

Results showed that functors were frequently omitted in children's productions, e.g., "Pete push dog," but English functors were omitted significantly more than nonsense ones, evidencing that children were in fact sensitive to the properties of functors; they are encoded.[24] In another experiment, three- to five-year-olds found it more difficult to repeat sentences with missing or ungrammatical functors than those with grammatical functors, even though they frequently deleted functors (Egido 1983). This suggests that the functors facilitated children's construction of the sentence, even if omitted.[25]

Two-year-olds performed better in a picture identification task when the target was described in terms which included grammatical as opposed to ungrammatical functors (determiners), e.g., "Find <u>the</u> bird for me," vs. "Find <u>was</u> bird for me," or "Find <u>gub</u> bird for me" (Gerken and McIntosh 1993). This suggests not only that young children are sensitive to function morphemes they may omit in their own speech, but that they actually use these morphemes in comprehension.[26] Other research provided evidence that two-year-olds taught to refer to objects (either animal or block-like toys) as "a DAX" or simply "DAX" used the syntactic difference between these (the presence or absence of the determiner, "a") to acquire the meaning of the word (cf. chapter 11).[27] Three- to four-year-olds use

---

[24] This result replicated even when synthetic speech controlled for intonation and stress variations.
[25] Freedle, Keeney and Smith 1970 for converging evidence with four- to six-year-olds.
[26] For recent converging evidence using an infant preferential looking task, see Kedar, Casasola and Lust 2004.
[27] See also Shipley, Smith and Gleitman 1969.

Table 9.6 *Cross-linguistic variation in early Functional Categories*

KOREAN (Choi and Gopnik 1995, 98)	Pap mek-<u>ess-ta/e/ci</u> Rice eat-past-suffix (somebody ate)
"from the single word period, the Korean children . . . spontaneously used verb-ending suffixes appropriately"	
QUICHE MAYAN (Pye 1983, 594) Child (AC 2.9)	**Adult: Kach a:<u>wik</u> (It's talking)** Child: <u>Wik</u>
In this polysynthetic language, children used certain terminal functional categories "correctly in over 86 percent of their first verbs" (583), at the same time that they reduced morphology and consulted stress.[a]	**Adult: kacha:w <u>taj</u> (It's not talking)** Child: Chaw <u>taj</u>
HINDI (Varma 1979)	Pani accha <u>hai</u> Water good is
Child (1.4 to 1.10), MLU below 2	Ye Daddy <u>ka hai</u> This Daddy's is 'This is daddy's'
TAMIL (Raghavendra et al. 1989)	amma kaTTa-<u>TTum-a:?</u> mother show may INT particle' 'Might mother show (it)?'
Children age 2.0	
ITALIAN (Hyams 1984)	Io vad<u>o</u> fuori I go-1p sg outside Tu leg<u>gi</u> il libro (You-2p sg read-2ps sg the book)
Children aged 1.10 to 2.4	Dorm<u>e</u> miao dorm<u>e</u> (Sleeps-3p sg cat sleeps)
SPANISH (Blume 2002, 4, ex. 3) Child JP, aged 2.00, MLU 2.97	IYooo! Quier<u>o</u> este I-1p sg want -1p sg this
SESOTHO (Demuth 1990; Connelly 1984)Child 1.9 years	<u>ma</u>-kwenya <u>a-ka</u> 6-fat-cakes 6-POSS-my (My fat-cakes)

[a] In Quiché Mayan, the FC is stressed in clause-final position, the verb stem in clause-medial position.

syntactic information including FC to assign word meaning, e.g., distinguishing between the adjective in "This is a red one" and the noun in "This is Mr. Red" (Hall et al. 2003).

Cross-linguistic evidence   In many languages, overt FCs appear earlier and more productively than in English, as the examples in table 9.6 and related literature suggest; (FC underlined).

This cross-linguistic evidence disconfirms the hypothesis of a biological limitation on children's competence for FC (e.g., (25)) and suggests that acquisition of FC must be linked to acquisition of specific language grammars.

Summary

These results disconfirm a maturational theory that the child is biologically limited at early periods to a grammar without FC. Lack of production of overt FCs does not mean that child grammar does not include FCs and/or that there are biological limitations on child competence for them. Cross-linguistic differences in early child language suggest that absence of FCs in children's early productions must be related to the specific language which the child is acquiring, not to biological limitation.[28]

Researchers now ask not whether children have grammatical competence for Functional Categories, but which FC they control initially, what features may specify them even when they may be null, and what relation morphological affixes have to structural projections in the secret skeleton.[29] Numerous studies are investigating syntactic operations in child grammar in order to evaluate if and how each of the critical functional heads in the sentence skeleton may work in children's grammatical computation.

9.3.1.3.1 DP (Determiner Phrase)

Each of the fundamental FC in figure 9.1, which provide essential sentence skeletal structure, have been investigated, i.e., DP, IP and CP, in child language and grammar.

Many of the results in 9.3.1.3 suggest children's early knowledge of the functional category, D-zero, including determiners, even when these are not overt.[30] Supporting evidence comes from early child productions such as (27) or (28), where the possessive ('s) has a determiner function.

27. That Daddy's (Kendall; MLU 1.48; Bowerman 1973, 242; Whitman et al. 1991)

28. Mami sis (J, 1.07) (Penner and Weissenborn, Bernese Swiss German, cited in Powers and Lebeaux 1998, 39)
     Mother its :NEUT:SGL:NEUT:SGL
     (Mother's)

In Sesotho there is evidence for overt Determiners before the age of two (table 9.6; Demuth 1990). Penner and Weissenborn have hypothesized that DP structure is universally available in early language acquisition (1995, 1996).

---

[28] Some researchers suggest that children may omit FC in language production because of a speech production constraint linked to prosody or metrical structure of the language. See Gerken et al. 1990; Gerken 1996; Gerken and McIntosh 1993. See also Demuth 1994, 1996c for a Metrical Model of Production which consults language-specific word structure and Pye 1983 for a theory that intonation interacts with FC production.

[29] Tesan 2003, Borer and Rohrbacher 1997, Smith 1999, 124–125, Dye et al. 2004.

[30] A "Universal Determiner Requirement Hypothesis" has been proposed, suggesting that the phrase marker of all nominals (non-vocative) includes a determiner head throughout the course of language acquisition (Penner and Weissenborn 1996; see also Powers and Lebeaux 1998, and Schaeffer and Kedar 2002 for Hebrew).

9.3.1.3.2   IP (Inflectional Phrase)

The IP in the secret skeleton of a sentence, headed by the FC I-zero, provides the backbone for the predicate of the sentence, as well as knowledge concerning the predicate, e.g., (29).[31] Within the IP, the verb's inflection and related verbal elements, e.g., auxiliary verbs, may express the *time* of the predicate referred to (present, past, future), the *aspect* (perfective or non), and the *modality* (e.g., "can" vs. "should" vs. "might"), possibly adding clues as to who is being referred to (as the subject of the predicate) through agreement.

To acquire verbal inflection in a language, children must know a set of FF (formal features) and how to map these to the lexicon and verbal morphology in their language. This mapping varies: in English, verb paradigms are limited, compared, for example, to Spanish (Blume 2002), Italian or a polysynthetic language. In addition, children must know how to distribute the FF in the phrase structure. In English, either an AUX (auxiliary verb) – a functional category associated with the I-zero projection – or the main verb or both may carry the FF, as in (30), while in Basque, inflection is mainly represented on an AUX (Austin 2001). In British English, "do" is often overt, e.g., (31), where it is null in American English, while in Chinese, there is little verbal morphology representing tense.

29.

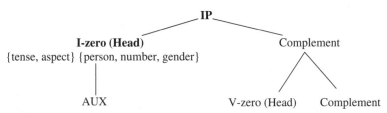

30.   She laugh<u>s</u>
        She <u>does</u> laugh
        She <u>is</u> laugh<u>ing</u>

31.   British: Will you repair this? Might <u>do</u>.
        American English: I might Ø

While the I-zero head of IP and basic IP structure may be determined by UG, knowledge of the specific ways that inflection is instantiated in a language is not. The development of inflection appears to be slow and gradual. Not only do children often use only a certain subset of verbs as they begin to learn the lexicon of the language, and express these verbs in only certain inflections (e.g., Gathercole et al. 1999), but various forms of inflection error occur (both omission (16)–(17) and commission errors (32)).[32] In (32a), children acquiring English overmark both the AUX and main verb (32ai, ii, iv), or move (33aiii) inflection. In (32b), German children overmark tense (32bi, ii) or mistake number features (32biii).

---

[31] See Smith 1989, chapter 10 for introduction. Linguists study the mechanism by which verbal inflection and the IP phrase structure are related; e.g., by movement or checking.

[32] Generally, omission errors are more frequent than commission.

32.   a. **English** (Santelmann et al. 2000)

          i. <u>Does</u> Pardita chas<u>ed</u> a pu . . . puppy? (3.0)

          ii. Mickey Mouse <u>is</u> open<u>s</u> a present (3.8)

          iii. Bunn<u>y's</u> touch a carrot (2.3)

          iv. Where <u>does</u> this go<u>es</u>? (CV, 3.4)

      b. German (Boser 1997, 166)

          i. da ich <u>hab</u> das lauft (Ter, 2.0)

            there I have that walked (gelauft, past participle)

            (I made it walk)

          ii. ein Turm <u>ist</u> umfaellt (Julia, 2.7)

            a tower is falled-down (umgefallen, past participle)

            (a tower fell down)

          iii. Was <u>sind</u> der (VG 1.11)

            What are he?

            (What are they?)

At the same time, in certain ways, this aspect of language acquisition shows remarkable abstractness, accuracy and constraint, and does so in a way which links to the FC head of IP.[33]

Acquisition of AUX   For example, Stromswald 1990 analyzed natural speech from fourteen young children (aged 1.2–7.10) for use of auxiliary verbs. She found children's inflection distinguished the AUX from main verbs very early, confirming an early distinction between function and content words (e.g., over-regularization of inflection occurred for main verbs – "doed" – never for AUX).[34] In spite of the fact that "There are about twenty-four billion logically possible combinations of auxiliaries (e.g., "have might eat"), and only about 100 are grammatical, Stromswald found no such errors in the children's AUX combinations" (Pinker 1994, 272). Children's early knowledge of the role of AUX in syntactic computation also excels. In English, children show early knowledge that auxiliaries invert in questions, inverting the AUX "do" about 95 percent of the time, while they do not demonstrate this inversion with main verbs (Stromswald 1990). Auxiliaries are remarkably correct in their association of finiteness and verb position. In German, the AUX demonstrated an early correlation between finiteness and verb position in a study of thirty German children's language (aged 0.21–1.10) (Boser et al. 1991; 1992; Boser 1997).

---

[33] Where children do show slow development in verb inflection, attempted explanations range from theories that posit no linguistic abstract knowledge (e.g., Tomasello 2000b), to various accounts recognizing linguistic analysis (chapter 4). Some posit deficits within UG (e.g., Wexler 1994, 1999) or outside of UG, in discourse and pragmatics (e.g., Borer and Rohrbacher 2002; Blume 2002), in accessing morphological knowledge (Phillips 1995), or in constructing language-specific knowledge through Grammatical Mapping (Santelmann et al. 2000; Boser et al. 1995; Boser 1997; Whitman et al. 1991; Lust 1999; see also Schutze 1997). Others propose a role for markedness (Roeper 1993; Hollebrandse and Roeper 1996), or a cognitive relation between *aspect* and *tense* (Shirai and Anderson 1995).

[34] cf. Valian 1992. This result is particularly impressive, given that AUX and main verbs may be homonymous, e.g., "do" or "have" or "be."

33.   AUX always appears in V-2 position, never V-finally, and AUX is always tensed

Thus, certain mistakes are not attested, e.g., (34).

34.   *Das Kind auf die Strasse kann
The child on the street can
(The child can go on the street)

AUX Insertion
Children have been observed to insert the AUX, "do," even when not required by the adult model, as in (35) (Roeper 1991).

35.   I do wash my hands

Dutch children have also spontaneously produced (36a) and (37a) in contrast to adult forms in (36b) and (37b).[35]

36.   a. ik doe ook praten (S, 2.5)
I do also talk
    b. Adult: ik praat ook
I talk also

37.   a. wat doe jij zeggen?
What do you say
    b. Adult: wat zeg jij?
What say you

German children in an imitation task inserted a form of AUX even when this did not appear in the elicitation model (38) (Boser 1989).

38.   Model: Suzanne warf den Ball als Manfred den Schneeball warf
Suzanne threw the ball as Manfred the snowball threw
Child: Suzanne tat den Schneeball werfen
Suzanne did the snowball throw (3.5)
(Suzanne threw the snowball)

The "Null AUX Hypothesis"
Boser (1997a, b; Boser et al. 1991, 1992), as well as others, has found evidence that even when the auxiliary is null in a child's language, there is evidence that the child knows about it. Through natural speech analyses, she found German child language alternates null with lexical auxiliaries, consults discourse context, and generates German participle forms which imply an auxiliary.[36] By this hypothesis, ostensibly simple utterances such as (39a)–(41a) actually have representations such as in (39a)–(41b), where AUX is present although phonetically null.

---

[35] Evers and van Kampen 1995, 25 ex. 2a, b; 28, 6a, b. In adult Dutch, a restricted form of "do insertion" appears mainly in topicalization contexts.

[36] See also Ingram and Thompson 1996; Guasti and Rizzi 1996 and Dye et al. 2002 for related studies.

39.   a. der eine Hose anziehen (GM 2.4; Boser 1997a, Boser et al. 1991, 55)
            he a pants on-put (-fin)
            (He puts on a pair of pants)
          b. der (hat) eine Hose anziehen
            he (has) a pants put on (+fin)

40.   a. Mommy go store
          b. Mommy (can/will/did) go store

41.   a. Where Daddy go?
          b. Where (did) Daddy go?

Speaking in infinitives?

One contrasting hypothesis – which has attracted considerable debate – holds that at early ages, children's biological programming involves a deficit in the knowledge that declarative utterances must be propositional and finite: therefore, children at first optionally allow declarative sentences to be infinitives. Under this hypothesis, children's utterances with verbs lacking overt inflection, e.g., (15), contain not bare morphological stems but infinitive forms, i.e., "root infinitives" (RI). Children not only lack essential knowledge requiring semantic and pragmatic properties of a sentence to correlate with its syntax (i.e., propositional semantics and sentence syntax cohere), but do "not know values of T. T to this child is essentially pleonastic" (where T refers to "Tense") (Wexler 1994, 342). Children during this period are proposed to be in an "Optional Infinitive Stage" (OI), and thus to have grammar qualitatively distinct from adults.[37]

OPTIONAL INFINITIVE STAGE HYPOTHESIS (Wexler 1994, 311, #7):
There is an early "optional infinitive stage" in which:

          a. finite and non-finite forms are in free variation; and
          b. the finite forms have moved to their correct position

---

The OI hypothesis has been challenged. Cross-linguistic differences in adult grammars reveal that morphology underspecified for tense need not connote non-finiteness (Schutze 1997, Klein 1998, Dye 2004, 2005a, b). Many utterances which have been analyzed as infinitives in child language (e.g., 16 or 17) are subject to the "null Aux" hypothesis (e.g., 39–41), and thus would be finite (Boser et al. 1991, 1992). Others are licensed by context, as in (42) (e.g., Blume 2002). Cross-linguistic variation in ostensibly OI structures[38] and acquisition in bilingual children[39] implicate the adult grammar rather than biological limitation in explaining children's productions which lack overt tense inflection.

---

[37] This OI hypothesis is very restrictive in its claims about children's grammatical deficit, since children are proposed to abide by "a" in this hypothesis at the same time that they abide by "b," without contradiction.

[38] E.g., Phillips 1995; Gathercole 1986; Dye 2005a, b.

[39] E.g., Austin 2001; Paradis and Genesee 1997.

42.   What do you want to do now?
           Go home

In the acquisition of inflection, development does not appear to concern the fundamental architecture of UG or fundamentals of linguistic computation. Rather, the I-zero head of IP, represented by AUX, appears to provide a continuous foundation for the construction of the language-specific grammar, including the development of the morphology of verbal inflection.

9.3.1.3.3 CP (Complementizer Phrase)

The highest FC node in the sentence skeleton, the C (Complementizer), is perhaps most elusive in children's early language production. Generally, it requires complex sentences or some form of transformation before becoming lexically overt, even in adult language. Yet numerous lines of evidence suggest that this FC (COMP) is also present and accessible initially and continuously, even when children omit it in production.

The general structure of children's first attempts at complex sentences may reveal evidence for underlying COMP heads, even when these are not overt, e.g., in German (43):

43.   Adult: Was will er tun? Ein Apfel essen?
                  (What does he want to do? Eat an apple?)
           Child: nein . . . will nich . . . traurig ist (Sebastian, 1.5, Boser)
                  No want not sad is
                  (No, he doesn't want to, **because** he is sad)

In (43), the child's word order, with the verb "be" appearing at the end of its clause, indicates that the COMP has a role in its representation even though it is null.[40] The child distinguishes main and subordinate clauses in word order, presumably by consulting the CP structure these involve.

Children also sometimes insert complementizers even when these are not modeled directly. In Korean, children's early relative clauses productively insert a "kes" complementizer, e.g., (44), although adult language obligatorily lacks them.[41]

44.   [[Mok-ey]$_{NP}$ [e]/ ke-nun] kes] ya? (S.P., 2.3, Lee)
           neck-on   wear-pres comp be-Z
           (Is it what you wear on your neck?)

Evidence for knowledge of COMP exists, even when complementizers are null, whenever operations move elements to the COMP position or through it, e.g., topicalization or question formation. Both of these operations occur very early in child grammar. Extensive evidence for this exists in natural speech studies of

---

[40] In German, verb-final order correlates with the presence of COMP heading subordinate clauses.

[41] Lee 1991; Whitman, Lee and Lust 1990. Demuth 1990 presents evidence for COMP in Sesotho acquisition at least by age 2.6.

child Swedish (Santelmann 1995) and German (Boser 1997a; Boser et al. 1991). Children's knowledge of German word order also suggests knowledge of COMP since German main clause order is thought to involve the verb moving to COMP in these clauses. Early recursive structures in child language (9.3.1.2) also suggest the role of COMP.[42]

Experimental tests have elucidated early sensitivity to COMP. In one experiment, children (3.5–6) were tested on sentences which do (46) or do not (45) involve an overt element in COMP (underlined) (deVilliers et al. 1990, Roeper and deVilliers 1994).

45.   When did the boy say – he hurt himself – ?
        a. when he said it
        b. when he hurt himself

46.   When did the boy say **– how** he hurt himself?
        a. when he said it
        b. *when he hurt himself

If children are sensitive to the role of overt COMP in syntax, then they should realize that (46) blocks one possible interpretation – (46b) – which is available in (45). Results confirmed this prediction, showing that children's question formation (Wh-movement) is significantly constrained by the intervening COMP.

Another experiment tested children (2.2– 4.5) on sentences involving a coordination (involving "and") (47a) or a subordination (with a subordinating connective, "when") (47b). If children distinguish these structures in terms of the differences between their complementizers and corresponding structures, then like adults they should allow a null subject in the coordinate structure, (47b), but not in the subordinate structure (48b). Even the youngest children obeyed this structural distinction (Nuñez del Prado et al. 1993)

47.   a. Bunny jumps up and Bunny falls down
        b. Bunny stands up and he/0 falls down

48.   a. Oscar whistles when Oscar jumps up
        b. Oscar whistles when he/*0 jumps up

9.3.1.4   Summary
Children's early language production converges with their early perception (9.2). Both reveal abstract linguistic knowledge. The basic sentence skeleton, including the three foundational functional categories (D, I and C), appears to be basically in place even during earliest language productions.[43] Functional elements in this skeleton may provide abstract linguistic structure by which children create the grammar for their language.

---

[42] See Hyams 1992 for overview.
[43] See Somashekar 1999 for study of the structure of DP in Tulu acquisition and for discussion of possible relations between DP and CP in Tulu early child language.

9.3.2   Principles and parameters

With child grammars armed for discovery of language, we can now test hypotheses regarding higher order abstract principles and parameters of grammar. We can evaluate children's expanding language.

9.3.2.1   UG Principle of Structure Dependence

We saw in chapter 4 that a rationalist theory of the Language Faculty (Chomsky) proposed that certain principles and parameters of linguistic knowledge were biologically programmed and enabled language acquisition, e.g., the basic principle of Structure Dependence. Evidence for children's sensitivity to DP, IP and CP (9.3.1.3) suggests that they are armed for this principle.[44] There are many ways in which knowledge of this principle can be tested (4.2.1.1), since any grammatical computation must consult it.

Researchers tested children (aged 3–5) on sentences with questions resembling Chomsky's original examples (cf. chapter 4):

49.   Ask Jabba if the boy who is watching Mickey Mouse is happy.
       Ask Jabba if the boy who is unhappy is watching Mickey Mouse.
       Ask Jabba if the boy who can see Mickey Mouse is happy.

Although children sometimes generated ungrammatical questions, e.g., (50), they did not generate forms which offended structure dependence, e.g., (51), suggesting that even if aspects of grammar are still developing, this development is constrained (Crain and Nakayama 1987).

50.   Is the boy who's watching Mickey Mouse is happy?

51.   a. *Is the boy who watching Mickey Mouse is happy
       b. *Can the boy who see Mickey Mouse is happy?

Structure dependence is also evident in subtle distinctions children make across different types of sentences differing in their underlying configurations (e.g., 47–48) and involving anaphora (chapter 2 and 9.3.4). In English, children (aged 3–8) have been found to differentiate sentences like (52a–52b), which differ in the structure of the embedded clause, i.e., either a finite tensed clause with a pronoun subject (52a) or a nonfinite clause with a null subject (52b), and they differentiate both of these from coordinate sentences, e.g. (47).[45]

52.   a. Oscar promises/tells Big Bird [that he will drop the block]
       b. Oscar promises/tells Big Bird [to Ø drop the block]

Children tend to choose the subject "Oscar" as antecedent for the pronoun subject "he" in the embedded clause in (52a), but the object "Big Bird" for the embedded clause in (52b); here, Big Bird drops the block. When given pragmatic lead, such as

---

[44] We assume that children's sensitivity to D, I and C underlie sensitivity to the functional projections, DP, IP and CP (although cf. fn. 3 and 22).
[45] Cohen Sherman 1983; Cohen Sherman and Lust 1986, 1993a, b; Cairns et al. 1993.

"this is a story about 'Oscar,'" they let this influence their interpretations in (52a) significantly more than in (52b). Therefore, children differentiate these structures and appear to know that the null subject in the nonfinite embedded clause in (52b) (termed a "control structure") is "bound" (cf. 9.3.4), differing from the pronoun subject in the finite embedded clause in (52a).[46] Children, like linguists and adult speakers, determine bound anaphora with relation to the structure in which it occurs.

> **BOUND ANAPHORA:** Interpretation of a proform is obligatorily determined by an antecedent within the sentence; not subject to free interpretation.

This structural distinction has also been attested in the acquisition of other languages, even those where subjects are null in both finite and nonfinite embeddings, e.g., Japanese and Chinese, or Sinhala in (53). Here, children differentiate their interpretation of two null sites depending on which structure they occur in, even where there is no overt lexical difference between the proforms – both are phonetically null. Only the structure of the sentences could determine the distinction.

53. a. wandura boole ahuləpuwaamə Ø appudigahanəwa
       monkey ball   pick up (when) Ø hand claps
       (When the monkey picked up the ball, Ø claps hands)

    b. wandura keselgediyə   ahul21a   Ø at wanənəwa
       monkey   banana   (having) picked up Ø hand waves
       (When the monkey picked up the banana, Ø waves the (his) hand)

Studies of 169 children (aged 2–6) in Sri Lanka acquiring Sinhala investigated both their production and comprehension of sentence types like (53a)–(53b). (53a) involves the "aamə" connective and a finite adjunct clause, while (53b) involves a "la" connective and a non-finite control structure (cf. English (52b)). For a non-finite embedding like (53b), children provided more interpretations of the empty category based on the antecedent within the sentence (coreference interpretations), consistent with bound anaphora; for a "free" pronominal like (53a) they made more external interpretations (disjoint reference interpretations). While children allowed a pragmatic lead to affect their interpretation of the (free) empty category in the "aamə" clause types, they restricted its effects on the (bound) "la" type, in keeping with its structure (Gair et al. 1998).[47]

---

[46] If a pronoun is "free" in interpretation, its reference can be determined by an antecedent in the sentence, or one outside of it. See also Goodluck 1991.

[47] For experimental study in Japanese, see Oshima and Lust 1997; Lust et al. 1985; Lust in preparation. For study showing that children distinguish Chinese control structures from coordinate and embedding structures in their interpretation of empty categories, see Chien and Lust 1985; Lust, Mangione and Chien 1984. Recent studies suggest that early verbal morphology is also structure dependent. Study of the acquisition of several forms of Tulu relative clauses showed that children (2–6) omit inflection and agreement features not in main clauses or in finite adjunct clauses, but predominantly in non-finite Verbal adjective clauses (Somashekar 1999, 272; see also Foley et al., submitted).

The UG principle of structure dependence thus appears early and cross-linguistically, applying across different structures and operations, and constraining the child's linguistic computation, such as in anaphora.

9.3.2.2   Parameters

As we saw, language acquisition requires not only knowledge of universal principles such as structure dependence, but also requires principled knowledge of how languages vary. We saw that parameters of language variation have been hypothesized to guide language acquisition (e.g., chapter 4). Two parameters have received substantial testing in language acquisition.

9.3.2.2.1   Head Direction/Branching Direction

If the Language Faculty is parameterized by Head Direction/Branching Direction, and children are guided by this parameter, then they will have the means to acquire the hierarchical structure for any language, whether left-headed and right branching like English or right-headed and left branching like Sinhala (figures 9.3 and 9.4). Children need only switch set head direction/branching direction in a grammar in order to classify types of languages (cf. chapter 4).[48] Many aspects of constituent order would follow by deduction, as would other facts about a language that correlate with this structural distinction.

Results from matched experiments in English, Arabic, Japanese, Sinhala, Chinese and Hindi language acquisition suggest early sensitivity to this parameter in children aged 2–6.[49] Children's early competence with sentence order (9.3.1.1) may reflect this parameter setting.

9.3.2.2.2   Pro Drop

Effects of a Pro Drop parameter on early language acquisition were investigated in a classic study, Hyams 1986, which has led to much related research.[50] As we saw in chapter 2, languages vary in terms of whether and how subjects may be null. Noticing that children's first utterances in English often omitted subjects (e.g., (16)), Hyams hypothesized that children may not only have consulted a Pro Drop parameter in their early grammar construction,

---

[48] It is necessary to define the notion "head"; e.g., lexical or functional. "Principal Branching Direction" focuses on the Complementizer head of the clause and the recursion direction of the language. Lust in preparation provides a fuller analysis of this parameter and its role in a theory of language acquisition, as well as relevant data from cross-linguistic study of language acquisition. Flynn 1987 assesses it in second language acquisition, Mazuka 1998, in language processing. Some versions of current "Minimalist" theories of UG hypothesize that the head direction parameter can be eliminated (Kayne 1994), where alternative triggers for systematic order reversals across languages would have to be identified (see Saito and Fukui 1998 for discussion). Formulation of this parameter must recognize that languages may not vary in order consistently: e.g., Chinese shares the SVO word order of English, but subordinate clause order/Branching Direction of Sinhala or Japanese.

[49] Lust and Chien 1984; Gair et al. 1998; Flynn and Lust 2002; Lust and Mangione 1983 and Lust in preparation.

[50] Papers collected in Lust, Hermon and Kornfilt 1994 provide review.

English Type

Left Headed and Right Branching

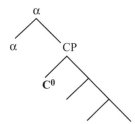

Sinhala Type

Right Headed and Left Branching

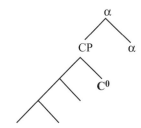

Fig. 9.4 *Head direction/branching direction parameter.*

but that they may begin with an *unmarked setting* for it; they may universally first believe that their language is +Pro Drop, deduce consequences from this, and then eventually reset this parameter if necessary for their language (cf. chapter 4).

Research comparing children's null subjects across languages subsequently confirmed early sensitivity to the Pro Drop dimension of language variation in early child language, but suggested that children are not universally constrained by an unmarked setting of this parameter. Rather, they seem to effectively correctly set the Pro Drop parameter very early. Children acquiring English (−ProDrop) were found to provide lexical subjects about twice as often as Italian (+ Pro Drop) children at similar early periods (Valian 1991). Spanish child language also differs from English at these times in accord with variation in the adult language (Austin et al. 1997).

Evidence from children's earliest productive language then suggests that early setting of both parameters, Head Direction/Branching Direction and Pro Drop, constrains the course of language acquisition.[51] These results raise the issue of

---

[51] Although researchers continue to debate the proper formulation of each of these parameters, and even their existence, these results from language acquisition suggest that some form of these grammatical parameters is at work in the Language Faculty very early.

how and when parameter setting has occurred. Mazuka (1996) provides initial investigation of how the infant may use cues in the speech stream to accomplish this even during the first twelve months, before first productive words.[52]

9.3.3   Operations

As table 9.1 suggested, knowledge of the foundations of syntax also involves knowledge of linguistic operations and computations.

Occurrence of recursion in child language (9.3.1.2) suggests that children are capable of *merging* constituents early. We saw that children appeared to show evidence of knowledge of *displacement* early (9.3.1.1). However, a classic study of language acquisition suggested that children might begin the language acquisition process without the competence for operations of *displacement*, which move constituents; it was hypothesized that they lacked competence for inversion of subject–verb order in English question formation. If so, children would begin language acquisition without an essential component of the Language Faculty. Children were proposed to go through a staged progression of development summarized in (54).

54.   **Staged Acquisition of Movement** (Klima and Bellugi 1966)
  i. yes/no questions appear with only rising intonation, no inversion
  ii. *Wh* questions begin to appear; no inversion
  iii. Inversion only in yes/no questions
  iv. Adult-like inversion on both yes/no and *Wh* questions

This proposal had consulted observations of children's early natural speech including utterances like (55).

55.   That a doggie?
        Where milk go?

As we know now, apparently deviant forms of children's utterances need not accurately reveal the knowledge that underlies them (9.3.1). Because the examples in (55) involve no overt auxiliary, it is not possible to determine where the auxiliary is. The classic proposal in (54) has now been widely challenged.[53]

One recent experimental study of children's acquisition of English yes/no questions factored out children's knowledge of inflection from their knowledge of inversion. Sixty-five children (2–5) were tested on matched declaratives and questions. Some questions required only inversion, e.g., (56a), others required not only inversion but knowledge of the English inflectional system of "do support," e.g., (56b) (Santelmann et al. 2002).

---

[52] There is some evidence that the two parameters, Head Direction/Branching Direction and Pro Drop, may be linked in children's early computation (Mazuka et al. 1995, Mazuka et al. 1986, Bloom 1990).

[53] Labov and Labov 1978; Stromswold 1998, 1990; Valian 1992; Erreich 1984.

56. **Declaratives**   **Questions**
     a. Kermit is eating a cookie   Is Kermit eating a cookie?
        Jasmine can hug a teddy bear   Can Jasmine hug a teddy bear?
     b. Mickey Mouse opens a present   Does Mickey Mouse open a present?

Although performance on both sentence types improved with development, there was not significantly more difficulty for questions over declaratives in (56a), while there was in (56b). This suggests that knowledge of inversion is available initially; development lies in the area of language-specific processes of inflection, not in knowledge of inversion.[54]

New issues now arise: when do children become capable of long distance movement (e.g., (57a) and what grammatical constraints do they obey (de Villiers 1995)? Even when children provide "errors" in such cases, e.g., (57b) (Thornton 1990, Crain and Thornton 1998), these appear to evidence options that UG allows. (57b) resembles a question form in dialects of German (McDaniel 1986).

57.   a. Adult: <u>What</u> do you think pigs eat ___?

         b. Child: What do you think what pigs eat?

9.3.4   Computation: anaphora

We can test children's knowledge of linguistic computation through analysis of their knowledge of anaphora, where various proforms must be related to antecedents within the sentence, under various constraints. We can test whether children's grammars consult structure dependence through study of anaphora, since anaphora can vary in directionality but at the same time is structurally constrained (see Lust 1986b for early review). Pronouns can occur either after their antecedents (forward anaphora) as in figure 9.5 (1) or (3), or before their antecedents (backward anaphora) as in figure 9.5 (4). They may be either coreferent with their antecedents (where "Sarah" and the pronoun "she" corefer) or disjoint in reference (where the pronoun "she" does not refer to "Sarah").

If children's grammars are constrained by structure dependence, children will know where anaphora is not allowed. If the pronoun is subordinate, as in figure 9.5 (4), then backward anaphora is possible; but if it is higher in the tree than the main clause, e.g., figure 9.5 (2), it is not.[55] They may also know where forward anaphora is not allowed, e.g., (58) (Lust and Clifford 1986).[56]

---

[54] Early knowledge of verb movement (9.3.1.3.2) in children acquiring German or Swedish suggests that knowledge of inversion is available in children's earliest productive grammars. Debate on these issues continues, e.g. Rowland and Pine 2000.

[55] Linguists use the term "c-command" to describe this configurational relation. After Reinhart 1983, a node A c-commands a node B if A and B do not dominate each other, and the first branching node dominating A also dominates B.

[56] Guasti and Chierchia 1999/2000 provide converging evidence for Italian. For sentences such as (58) with blocked forward anaphora, if the anaphora is blocked because of the configuration of the sentence, then the subject pronoun in these sentences is in some way higher in the tree than the preceding name.

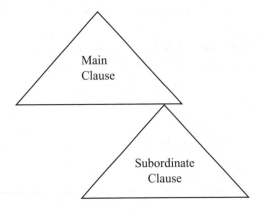

1. *Sarah* listens to music [when *she* reads poetry].
2. **She* listens to music [when *Sarah* reads poetry].

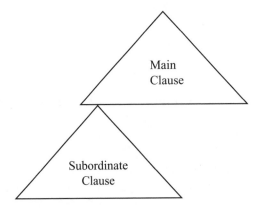

3. [When *Sarah* listens to music] *she* reads poetry.
4. [When *she* listens to music] *Sarah* reads poetry.

Fig. 9.5 *Structure and order in pronoun interpretation.*

58.   On the top of <u>Oscar's</u> head, <u>he</u> rubbed the donut
                     ____X_____↑

          On <u>Cookie Monster, he</u> quickly dropped the choo-choo train
                     ____X____↑

    Many studies have now confirmed that: (a) directionality affects children's pro-
noun interpretation. In English acquisition, forward anaphora (figure 9.5 (1)) is
most productive and preferred compared to backward anaphora like figure 9.5 (4);
children more productively choose an anaphoric interpretation in sentences with
forward than with backward anaphora. (b) At the same time, this directionality
effect is structure dependent. Children give significantly fewer coreference judgments in structures where anaphora is blocked grammatically, whether backward

(e.g, figure 9.5 (2)) or forward, in (58).[57] The directionality effect is also related to the grammatical structure of a language. In left branching languages such as Chinese or Japanese or Sinhala, backward anaphora is as productive and in some cases more productive than forward anaphora in related structures.[58]

Binding Principles

In addition to structure dependence, linguists have attempted to formulate specific linguistic principles for anaphora computation, creating a "Binding Theory" in UG to explicate when a proform may be *bound* or *free*, and to formulate constraints on anaphora (see chapter 4). Psycholinguists have tested young children for their knowledge of these principles (Binding Theory Principles A, B and C).

BINDING PRINCIPLES:
  A: Anaphors (e.g., reflexives) are locally bound
  B: Pronouns are locally free
  C: Referring expressions (e.g., nouns) are free everywhere

Binding Principle B

Using different methods to test Binding Principle B, they found that children frequently interpret the pronoun "her" in (59) as though it were the anaphor "herself" (Chien and Wexler 1987; Wexler and Chien 1985). They allow Mama Bear to be touching herself.

59.   This is Mama Bear; this is Goldilocks. Is Mama Bear touching her?

The Binding Theory (Principle B) would rule out this interpretation of the pronoun "her" which involves binding by a local antecedent; adult interpretation would involve Mama Bear touching Goldilocks.[59] This error has been interpreted as involving deficits in pragmatic knowledge or in various types of grammatical knowledge.[60] Others view it as structure dependent, proposing that children are correctly consulting UG, but are not distinguishing the lexicon: the pronoun "her" is not differentiated from "herself."[61] In acquisition of Dutch,[62] Spanish,[63] and Chinese,[64] as well as English, this error persists; full acquisition of the pronoun-reflexive distinction is not achieved until between five and ten years of age.[65]

  Once again, this children's "error" is consistent with UG. Children's interpretations of pronouns like (59) are grammatical in various languages (cf. chapter 11).

---

[57] Lust, Eisele and Mazuka 1992 for review, Eisele and Lust 1996; Guasti and Chierchia 1999/2000.
[58] Lust and Mazuka 1989; Lust et al. 1996; O'Grady, Suzuki-Wei and Cho 1986 and Carden 1986, Lust in preparation.
[59] Here the antecedent is 'local' because it does not go out of the clause.
[60] Grimshaw and Rosen 1990; Kaufman 1994; Jakubowicz 1993.
[61] Lust et al. 1989; Mazuka and Lust 1994; Kapur et al. 1993.
[62] Deutsch, Koster and Koster 1986; Koster 1994.
[63] Padilla 1990.   [64] Chien and Wexler 1987.
[65] Further tests of this phenomenon which have quantifier subjects have provoked superior results (Chien and Wexler 1990).

Binding Principle C

Binding Theory Principle C depends critically on structure, e.g., ruling out 9.5 (2) but allowing (4). It does not depend on a lexical distinction between pronouns and anaphors, and has independently been found to characterize a wide set of languages.[66] It has now been found early in language acquisition, documented by converging evidence across a variety of methods.[67] Recent studies have suggested that the strongest indication of Principle C may be evidenced in younger children. Somashekar (1995; Somashekar et al. 1997) found, in a study of Indian children acquiring Hindi sentences corresponding to those in figure 9.5, that younger children (mean age 3.07) revealed the Principle C constraint more fully than older children. She hypothesized that with the course of language acquisition, and concurrent pragmatic development, other factors come to be integrated with the universal syntactic principle.[68]

Integrating linguistic knowledge: VP ellipsis

Children bring their knowledge of phrase structure and anaphora to bear not only on sentences with pronouns but on those with ellipsis, which provide little or no overt evidence for the computation required for their production and interpretation. For example, in (60) (with VP ellipsis), the second clause provides no evidence for what Ozzie does; only linguistic computation can provide this. The predicate in the second clause (What Ozzie does) is phonetically null.

60.   Fozzie Bear rubs his foot and Ozzie does too

In experiments to test their comprehension, children as young as two years have demonstrated the constrained and linguistically sophisticated knowledge required by the interpretation and the production of VP ellipsis (Foley et al. 2003).[69] Children have shown they understand both the ambiguity of these structures and their grammatical constraints.

9.3.5   Summary

Even children's apparently primitive first sentences involve abstract linguistic knowledge and linguistic computation. Children create underlying sentence skeletons for their language, including its critical functional category nodes. Their early language shows evidence for constraint by a principle of structure dependence and by parameters of Pro Drop and head direction/branching direction, which may act like switches; they appear to be correctly set before first

---

[66] Lust et al. 1999.

[67] Crain and McKee 1985; Lust, Eisele and Mazuka 1992 for review, and Eisele and Lust 1996. In current linguistic theory of UG, the nature of Principle C, and of Binding Principles in general, remains debated.

[68] For review of research on acquisition of the Binding Principles in several East Asian languages, see Nakayama et al. forthcoming and Li et al. forthcoming.

[69] Guo et al. 1996 for Chinese; Koster 1994, 1993 for Dutch; Thornton and Wexler 1999 for studies integrating Binding Theory with VP ellipsis.

words. Knowledge of basic syntactic operations, e.g., *merge* and *move*, appears to be accessible initially and throughout development, as does knowledge of complex computation across distant constituents in a sentence, e.g., *anaphora*. Aspects of child grammar develop over the first years but even "errors" during this time respect universal constraints.

9.4   Conclusions

The epistemological primitives of syntactic knowledge – sensitivity to linguistic *structure* and *order* – appear to operate as soon as they can be measured in the first year, and to apply throughout the course of acquisition. The mapping from general to specific language syntax begins in the first year, even before the child speaks or understands language.

By the time children are about to produce first words and simple sentences, they have already begun to crack the code of the language to which they are exposed, with regard to syntax. They have realized the basis of the secret skeleton of the sentence – order and constituent structure, including Functional Categories – even though the phonetic realizations of this knowledge may often be null and even though they still do not, for the most part, understand the meaning of language.

Beyond the first year, there is no evidence for a stage in which children do not have fundamental competence for grammatical structure or linguistic computation. Children are enabled continuously to analyze sentence structure in terms of functional categories. Their sensitivity to linear order is linked to their sensitivity to grammatical structure. The special design properties of natural language involving empty elements and displacements are accessible from the first measurable periods. There is no evidence for a stage in which children do not know the basis for linguistic operations, such as *move* or *merge*. Recursion appears as soon as children control the minimal length required.

9.4.1   Toward an explanation

If a Language Faculty is present in the initial state, then we would have an explanation for how and why the epistemological primitives of language knowledge occur so early, and for why principles and parameters of syntax appear to guide early language development.

Children appear predisposed to analyze the speech stream in order to discover critical syntactic units. Acoustic patterns appear to assist the infant's analysis of the speech stream (as suggested by low-pass filtering experiments, 9.2.1.2.3). However, infants appear biologically predisposed to analyze these acoustic properties in just the right way for syntax acquisition.

Children's grammar is continuously constrained. A universal principle of structure dependence guides the acquisition of grammar, ranging over many domains, including those with empty elements. Developmental delays in certain forms of syntactic knowledge may reflect areas of necessary inductive learning, e.g., the lexicon, morphosyntax involved in specific language inflectional realizations, or specific lexical distinctions between anaphors and pronouns (cf. chapter 11).

9.4.2   Open questions

Debates about the course of syntactic development and the nature of developmental changes continue.[70]

9.5   Supplementary readings

Suggested readings in chapters 1 and 4 provide general background for study of the acquisition of syntax. For general overviews: Cook 1994; Cook and Newson 1996; Weisler and Milekic 1999 (chapter 4); O'Grady 1997; Goodluck 1991 (chapter 4); Pinker 1984. For overviews in a generative tradition: Atkinson 1992; Guasti 2002. Crain and Thornton 1998, and Crain and Lillo-Martin 1999 provide specific proposals in this tradition. For general introduction to the area of syntax, see Adger 2004, Radford 2004.

For review of research on the origins of syntactic knowledge in the infant: Hirsh-Pasek and Golinkoff 1997; Jusczyk 1999; Morgan 1986; Gleitman, Gleitman, Landau and Wanner 1988.

For collections of research in specific areas of syntax acquisition: Lust et al. 1994 (vols. I and II); Dittmar and Penner 1998; Meisel 1992. Tomasello 1992 provides a case study in a verb-based paradigm.

---

[70] Grimshaw 1994; Frank 1991; Lebeaux 1990; Lust 1999.

10 The acquisition of semantics

10.1 Introduction

As we saw in chapter 2, unless children can "say what they mean" and "mean what they say" they have not acquired language. Children must bring all their computational power for syntax and phonology to bear on the expression and comprehension of a potentially infinite set of thoughts, beliefs, hopes and desires. In formal terms, the Language Faculty must include a "conceptual interface" (figure 2.1). Our investigation must include *semantics*: the study of meaning which is linguistically encoded. It must include study of how children link cognitive concepts and ideas (both their own and those of others) to those meanings which are linguistically coded.[1] This linking requires "powerful inferential capabilities" involving *pragmatics*, the study of language use. (Carston 2002 provides overview.)

Meanings are not provided by the environment (chapter 3); children must create them. Unlike the acquisition of syntax and phonology, the acquisition of the semantic dimension of language knowledge will continue throughout life (see appendix 6 for summary of developmental milestones).

10.1.1 What must children acquire?

Children must:

(A) Discover the units, not only breaking the speech stream into words, e.g., (1), but interpreting them. Although (1) is parsed into units, and it isolates potential words in (a) and words and functional categories in (b), it remains meaningless.[2]

1.   a. FAX BOB TOD GAXZAB TA MOX BIXGAB
       b. The FAX BOBed a TOD while TAing . . . . .

Children must acquire word meaning, achieving by adulthood a continually expanding "mental lexicon" of hundreds of thousands of words which are stored in the mind and continually accessible (Aitchison 2003). Also, children must discover larger semantic units: those composing propositions underlying

---

[1] We can think many thoughts that we cannot or do not linguistically encode, and any linguistic encoding in a word or sentence never alone fully expresses our complete thoughts. Thus the study of cognitive conceptualization and linguistic semantics must be recognized as distinct, but interactive.

[2] See Jusczyk, Luce and Luce 1994 for discussion of mapping to words in the mental lexicon.

sentences, e.g., predicates and arguments as in (2a); and those combining sentences as in (2b).

2.　　　a. [The FAX [BOBBed [a TOD]]]
　　　　b. [The Fax will bob a tod] and/or [the Mox will Bixgab]

(B) Categorize. Know that a word, e.g., "dog," does not only refer to any particular physical object, e.g., the child's pet, but to the category of dogs, allowing potentially infinite variation in color, size or type and potentially infinite membership.

(C) Link thought to language. Since concepts are distinct from word meanings (they can be retained in pathological cases while word meanings are lost;[3] see chapter 2), children must link concepts, ideas and word meanings. This linguistic computation will take time – mastery of color words may come years after the capacity for color discrimination, color sorting and induction based on color (Soja 1986; Miller and Johnson-Laird 1976). Deaf children may confuse signs for "I" and "you" even though the sign itself points to the referent, and the child understands the basic concepts (Petitto 1987).

(D) Know that words and sentences can be *ambiguous* (both lexical and structural ambiguity must be recognized). Even apparently simple words, e.g. "hit," may convey indefinitely many concepts (e.g., "Sam hit Bert," "This soup hits the spot," "The ball hit the wall").

(E) Acquire a mental representation (intension) which allows determination of the meaning and reference of words. Through this mental representation, children must become able to pick out a potentially infinite set of exemplars: any possible dog.

INTERNAL STRUCTURE OF WORDS
Intension
The properties which are mentally represented and by which we can pick out exemplars, e.g., whatever makes a dog a dog

Extension
The exemplars or real world objects which exemplify the word, e.g., every "dog" you may ever see, hear or know

---

Children must also acquire a mental representation (Logical Form) which allows multiple interpretations of sentences, such as those with quantifiers such as "some" and "every" in (3a)–(3b).

3.　　　　Some girl pulled every dog's tail
　　　　a. There is a girl x such that, for every dog's tail y, x pulled y
　　　　　　[some girl [every dog's tail [x pulled y]]]

---

[3] For discussion of the relation between concepts and word meanings, see Aitchison 2003 and Miller and Johnson-Laird 1976. On "concepts" see Hampton 1999; Keil 1999; Keil 1994; Keil et al. 1998.

b. For every dog's tail y, there is a girl x such that x pulled y
   [every dog's tail [some girl [x pulled y]]]

(F) Compute sentence meaning by combining the meanings of the parts of a sentence and *composing* the meaning of the proposition.

COMPOSITIONALITY: "The meaning of an expression is a function of the meanings of its parts and of how they are syntactically combined" (Partee 1999, 739).

This computation involves computing the *scope* of logical elements. For example, "think" is negated in (4b) but not in (4a), where the embedded clause is negated instead.

4.   a. I do <u>not</u> think [that <u>the Red Sox will win</u>]
         b. I do <u>not</u> think

(G) Understand relations among words as well as between words and the world, e.g., which words mean the same (synonymy: "couch" and "sofa") or sound the same and mean differently (homonymy: "bank"). *Basic level* categories like "dog" must be related to *hypernyms* (or *suponyms*) corresponding to *superordinate* categories (animal) and to *hyponyms* ("poodle") corresponding to specific subtypes; they must be related to other semantically related words, e.g., "cat" or "wolf" (Miller 1978).

(H) Determine referential relations between words and the world (Devitt 1999). Children must determine the referent for "dog" as opposed to "cat" or "wolf" in spite of physical variation among the exemplars of each of these. Words themselves do not "refer"; mental computation must relate intension and extension in order to establish reference.

(I) Conduct extensive and complex computation of the context of every word and utterance to determine how words and sentences are used, since any word's meaning will be determined to some degree by linguistic context as well as by communicative context. Comprehension involves inference: "words are used as pointers to contextually intended senses"; concepts must be constructed on the spot in every individual use of language ("ad hoc concepts") (Sperber and Wilson 1998, 200).

Children must link each sentence heard or spoken to a *speech act*. Neither the syntax nor the semantics of a sentence alone can determine what speech act is intended. For example, (5) can function as a question, an observational declarative statement or an exclamation, depending on context.

5.   Aren't you a nice baby

Children must also interpret and produce utterances according to their *communicative relevance* (Sperber and Wilson 1995), and ascertain that speaker and hearer share reference. The acquisition of semantics and pragmatics must thus be linked. Some researchers have hypothesized that specific pragmatic principles may guide this process, e.g., a Communicative Principle of Relevance (Sperber and Wilson, 1998, 192).

10.1.2   What are the challenges?

Children cannot know which meanings are lexicalized and which are not, since various concepts may or may not be lexicalized in a language (cf. chapter 3). Even presumably "simple" words may vary in their extensions. "Mother" ("amma" in Sinhala or Tamil) may extend in some languages (Sinhala and Tamil) to older women, and to children as a form of endearment (Tamil). "Tree" ("gaha" in Sinhala) may refer also to blades of grass, strands of hair or stalks of lemon grass.[4]

As we have seen in chapter 3, the meanings of words of a language are not directly evident through context (e.g., Gleitman 1994; cf. Bloom 2000, 2001) due to "inscrutability of reference." For any possible new word there will be an indefinite number of possible hypotheses. The evidence underdetermines the possible hypotheses. Accordingly, children do not depend on ostensive context in acquisition of word meanings (cf. 3.3.3.3).

Most – perhaps all – words do not allow a simple or direct definition (Putnam 1975; Fodor 1975). This is true even of an apparently simple word like "bird" or "game." Scientists continue to debate whether the archaeopteryx is a dinosaur or a bird.[5] What then is the mental representation for word meaning, and how do children acquire it? These challenges have led to many proposals by linguists and philosophers, including the proposal that children must be born with an innate inventory of word-like units (Fodor 1975).[6] Yet children solve this problem unaided by our ruminations.

Once again, in the acquisition of semantics, as in the acquisition of phonology and syntax, children must accomplish complex linguistic computation involving more than one level of representation. For example, concepts must be related to linguistic forms, intension to extension in word meaning, logical forms which represent propositional meanings must be related to word meanings, the representation of contexts of use of language must be related to computation of word and sentence meaning. The knowledge children must create is underdetermined by the data; they must infer the knowledge.

---

[4] This cross-linguistic variation has correlates in English, e.g., "father" used also for Catholic priests.
[5] The archaeopteryx had feathers and wings but lived mainly on the ground.
[6] Fodor's 1975 proposal raises many issues, e.g., regarding how many such units exist, how cross-linguistic variation in similar and dissimilar units are composed (Sterelny and Devitt 1999).

10.1.3   Leading questions

- How does children's general cognitive development interact with the development of language (word meanings and higher semantic computation)?
- When do children first understand words?
- Are children's word meanings qualitatively different from adults'? For example, are children's meanings characterized first by concrete features, and only later by definitions? When are children's word meanings categorical? If most words do not allow distinct definitions, how do children represent their meanings?
- Are children at first limited to the present or the "here and now" in word meanings, and incapable of semantic displacement, i.e., incapable of representing what is possible but not evident?
- How do children create the infinite set of meanings possible through natural language? How do they use the input to determine word meanings and resolve the indeterminacy of reference?
- How do children constrain infinite possibilities for meaning?
- Is child acquisition of word meanings continuous with adult acquisition of word meanings?
- What are the relations between children's acquisition of semantics and their acquisition of language in general? Does children's acquisition of syntax interact with acquisition of semantics and vice versa? Do formal properties of semantic representation, e.g., scope in Logical Form, have correlates in development of syntactic representation?

10.1.4   Language and thought

The Chomsky–Piaget Debate

In a lifetime of research on cognitive development across numerous domains, Piaget, like Chomsky (cf. chapter 4), argued that Cognitive Structure determines knowledge and knowledge acquisition.[7] Like Chomsky, he provided evidence in each of these domains that "knowledge does not result from a mere recording of observations without a structuring activity on the part of the subject" (Piaget 1980, 23). Like Chomsky, he held that "the empiricist assumptions are fundamentally wrong, as a matter of empirical fact" (Chomsky 1988b, 53). The debate between Piaget and Chomsky centered around two specific issues: modularity and innateness (cf. chapter 4).

Although Piaget did not deny that some specifically linguistic module might exist (a "noyeau fixe"), and that some form of innateness was necessary to explain language acquisition, he focused on the relation between language and other

---

[7] The term "cognitive structure" is used in a general sense here (see Piaget 1983).

s of symbolic representation, under a general area he framed as "semiotic
ion". He traced linked developments in the child's competence for "object
permanence," "symbolic play" and "deferred imitation" – culminating at about
eighteen months – as a general period of intense language acquisition.[8]

> **SEMIOTIC FUNCTION:** the general function of signifying something (e.g.,
> object, event, concept) by virtue of some form of signifer (e.g., language, mental
> imagery, symbolic gesture).

He focused on issues of development rather than innateness:

6.   "... the real problem is not to decide whether such a fixed nucleus or other
          cognitive structures are innate or not; the real question is: what has been
          their formation process? And in the case of innateness, what is the
          biological mode of formation of that innateness ..." (Piaget 1980, 60)[9]

Piaget and Hermine Sinclair provided several arguments that language development does not determine cognitive development.[10] In experiments they showed
that teaching linguistic terms such as "more" and "less" or "thinner," for example, did not affect children's cognitive performance on conservation tasks where
children were asked to reason about abstract quantities in the face of perceptual
variation (Sinclair 1967). The existence of specific classificatory terms in a language did not determine earlier development of classification ability in children
than in other languages (Opper 1977).

Linguistic determinism

Contrary to Piaget, one hypothesis has posited that language may indeed fundamentally affect thought (7).

7.   The "Sapir–Whorf" Hypothesis[11]
          "... every language is a vast pattern-system, different from others, in which
          are culturally ordained the forms and categories by which the personality
          not only communicates, but also analyzes nature, notices or neglects types
          of relationship and phenomena, channels his reasoning and builds the house
          of his consciousness" (Whorf 1956, 252). Different societies, speaking
          different languages, inhabit distinct conceptual, perceptual and emotional
          worlds; our language acts to segment and structure our world.

Research has tested various forms of this hypothesis, which has come to be
termed *linguistic determinism*. Would the Dani, who have only two words for

---

[8] See Chandler 2002 for the area of semiotics.

[9] Piaget's question here is complementary to Chomsky's, which focused on defining the content of
the Initial State (cf. chapter 4).

[10] Piaget did not work directly on language acquisition. This research area was directed by Hermine
Sinclair.

[11] The proposals of both Sapir and Whorf are more complex than suggested by the general statement
of their hypothesis. See Lucy 1992b; Gumpertz and Levinson 1996 and Bowerman and Levinson
2001.

color, perceive color differently? Would Chinese speakers not show counterfactual reasoning because their language doesn't explicitly express it as English does (Au 1983; Bloom 1984)? This research generally suggests that a strong form of the Sapir–Whorf Hypothesis does not hold; language at best reflects rather than causes cognitive and perceptual representations.

Research and debate continues today on a potential weak form of the Sapir–Whorf Hypothesis: language structure may influence expressibility even if it does not determine fundamental forms of perception or cognition (Boroditsky 2001; Li and Gleitman 2002; Lucy 1992a, b; Mazuka and Friedman 2000). Recent cross-linguistic studies are now pursuing these issues in early language acquisition.[12]

LINGUISTIC DETERMINISM: Language Structure determines cognitive structure
LINGUISTIC RELATIVITY: Cognitive Structures differ depending on language of speaker

---

10.1.5   Relating language and cognition

Much of the research in a Piagetian mode has sought evidence for effects of cognitive development on language development. Years of research on relations between cognitive development and language development have generally revealed only imprecise and non-necessary links between specific forms of cognitive development and specific forms of language development (Corrigan 1978; Harris 1982 for review). Even when developmental parallels are found, it is not possible to attribute causality, i.e., to conclude that a specific aspect of cognitive development determines a specific aspect of linguistic development. For example, knowledge of logical classification operations such as set intersection, and linguistic control of logical connectives such as "and" and "or," do develop in parallel, but developmental studies do not necessarily imply causality between them (Beilin 1975). Such comparisons are confounded by the continuity of language development (which we have discovered in both phonology and syntax), which makes it difficult to determine a particular "point in time" at which correlations between certain forms of cognitive development and language development should or could be tested.[13]

These results combine with a wide array of results which have suggested modularity of language development and independence of language development and general cognitive development. In the "one word" stage children are willing and eager to express cognitive concepts for which they do not have language (Bloom

---

[12] E.g., Bowerman 1996; Gopnik and Choi 1990; Imai and Gentner 1997; Mazuka and Imai 2000.
[13] Researchers also continue to debate potential continuity in various forms of cognitive development (Gelman and Baillargeon 1983).

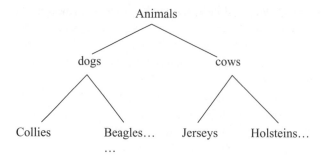

Fig. 10.1 *Class inclusion*

1973). "Special cases" of language development dissociate language development and cognitive development as do various language pathologies (chapter 5).
Bilingual children also provide evidence for an independence of general cognitive
development and language. For example, before two years of age, two children
acquiring both Hungarian and Serbo-Croatian were productively and appropriately using directional and locative expressions in Hungarian while failing to
do so in Serbo-Croatian. Since Serbo-Croatian grammar for these expressions is
more complex than that of Hungarian, we may assume that linguistic computation, not cognitive concepts alone (directional and locative), are determining rate
of language development in this area (Slobin 2004; Mikes 1967).

Relations between language and cognition may be subtle and complex (see
Sinclair 2004a, b). In classic experimentation, Inhelder and Piaget tested children
on reasoning involving "class inclusion," i.e., hierarchical relations between sets
and subsets. When given sets of objects (four cows and two horses), children
(before six to eight years) report that they are "all animals" and may count "six
animals." Yet when asked, "Are there more animals or more cows," children
claim "there are more cows." Inhelder and Piaget argued that this behavior fundamentally reflects limitations on cognitive computation over a hierarchical class
inclusion structure, e.g., figure 10.1. Children are not computing the simultaneous positive and negative relations involved in the hierarchy. (The cows are both
more than the horses when comparing subsets, but less than the animals when
comparing supersets in the hierarchical relation.) Children fail to hold the abstract
"animals" superset constant while relating the subsets.[14]

This cognitive phenomenon certainly involves a relation between thought
and language, but need not necessarily reflect a specifically linguistic development. Kang 2001 assesses children's responses to sentences involving quantifiers
as in (8) in an attempt to assess the cognitive, linguistic and pragmatic factors
involved (see Guasti 2002 for discussion). Children may, for example, demonstrate "*quantifier spreading*," answering "no" when asked "Is every boy riding a
pony?" if an extra pony is present in the reference set, a response which resembles the cognitive phenomenon discovered by Inhelder and Piaget in their class

[14] Inhelder and Piaget's (1964) argumentation involved empirical and theoretical analyses of
widespread effects of the same underlying cognitive structure across different cognitive domains.

inclusion tests, because of the general cognitive development Inhelder and Piaget described.[15]

8.   Every boy is riding a pony (Philip 1995)

Theory of mind

Another area which involves subtle relations between cognitive development and language development concerns what has been termed children's "theory of mind," or their ability to think about thinking and about the content of thoughts. Under four years of age, children have been found to do poorly on tests of "false belief," i.e., tests which require thinking about beliefs counter to facts. In a seminal study, children were exposed to an "unexpected transfer" of chocolates. A story recounts that a young boy, Maxi, places chocolates in a cupboard in his kitchen. After he leaves the kitchen, his mother moves the chocolate to another cupboard. Children are asked to predict where Maxi would look for his chocolates on his return. Less than half the younger children tested predicted that Max would look in the original hiding place, while almost all children aged six and seven did so, suggesting that younger children do not yet control "theory of mind," i.e., they do not acknowledge Maxi's false beliefs (Wimmer and Perner 1983; Johnson and Maratsos 1977).[16] Researchers currently debate the degree to which children's language development may be related to this cognitive development.[17]

We conclude that cognitive development and linguistic development are basically independent, when we consider formal computation of the linguistic system. At the same time, they cannot be totally independent when we consider the acquisition of semantics and pragmatics. Children must continuously link language development with cognitive development over the course of language acquisition.

THEORY OF MIND: the representation of a person's beliefs or thoughts, independent of reality; implies the ability to impute mental states to oneself and others (see Dennett 1978).

10.2   How do children meet the challenge? Laying the foundations: the first twelve months

10.2.1   Perception

We have seen (chapters 6 and 8) that word segmentation develops during the first twelve months. Infants at 7.5 months, but not at six months, listened

---

[15] For further study of the acquisition of quantification see Hanlon 1988; Chien 1994.
[16] For review of research in this area and its potential interpretations see Mitchell 1996.
[17] Astington and Jenkins 1999, deVilliers and deVilliers 2000 and Garfield et al. 2001 suggest a correlation between language development and Theory of Mind development, while Charmon and Baron-Cohen 1992 and Peterson 2002 suggest a dissociation. Development of certain semantic concepts such as involved in "deontic" and "epistemic" uses of modals (e.g., "must") may be linked to development of Theory of Mind (Papafragou 1998).

longer to passages that contained words which they had been familiarized with and remembered abstract words (which they could not understand) from stories heard two weeks earlier.[18] Children very early appear capable of parsing strings like (1). But how do these come to be meaningful?

Numerous research studies, using methods of studying infant perception (cf. chapter 7), are now revealing the infant's (during the first twelve months) knowledge of the foundations for linguistic computation required for acquisition of semantics.

Categorical from the start

In a "novelty preference" procedure, infants were presented with different toys from a given category, one at a time, in a familiarization series. Then they were presented with either another object from the same category or a new category. If infants consult categorization, then they should notice change in category and increase attention to the novel object, while attention to the familiar category should wane (Waxman and Markow 1995). Thirty-two infants (mean age 13.5 months) were tested with either basic categories (car vs. airplane) or superordinate categories (animals vs. vehicles). The experimenter introduced objects during the test phase with a noun, e.g., "[Infant's name], look an 'animal'," or no word, "[Infant's name] look." Infants in the noun condition in superordinate contrasts preferred the novel object, while those with no word did not. The authors conclude that "labels focus attention specifically on categories of objects" (275; see also Balaban and Waxman 1997, 1999). These results suggest not only that children bring categorical computation to bear on earliest words, but that they begin with an assumed link between word and category (Waxman and Markow 1995; Xu and Carey 1995; Xu et al. 1995; Xu 2002).

Infant categorization does not only apply to nominals. Six- and ten-month-olds have been shown to form an abstract category of "containment" as opposed to "support" (relevant to English prepositions "in" vs. "on"), and by eighteen months to categorize these in opposition to "tight fit" (relevant to the Korean postposition "kkita") (Casasola, Cohen and Chiarello 2003, Casasola and Cohen 2002, Casasola, Parramore and Yang in press.)

10.2.2   Production

Although the child's production of meaningful language must in general await first words, generally after twelve months of age, relations between "babbling" and meaning have been studied even during the first twelve months of the infant's life (Blake and Fink 1987). A relation between language production and meaning may exist even prior to first words.

---

[18] Jusczyk and Aslin 1995; Jusczyk and Hohne 1997; Jusczyk 1993, 1997; Jusczyk, Houston and Newsome 1999.

10.2.3　Perception and production

Bases for understanding word meaning appear to be available to infants during the first twelve months, as shown in infant perception studies (10.2.1; appendix 6). They appear to provide the foundations for the onset of first words produced about twelve months and thereafter.

As we saw in chapter 8 (8.3), links between speech perception and reference are developing between eight to fourteen months (Stager and Werker 1997; cf. chapter 8).

10.2.4　Summary

Over the first twelve months, children have accomplished discovery of word units (as well as larger sentential units, cf. chapter 9), have begun to link these to abstract categories as well as to reference, and demonstrate continual interaction between language and thought. At this point they are poised to realize overtly what has been described as "momentous":

9.　　"There is no step more uplifting, more explosive, more momentous in the history of mind design than the invention of language. When Homo Sapiens became the beneficiary of this invention, the species stepped into a slingshot that has launched it far beyond all other early species in the power to look ahead and reflect . . ." (Dennett 1996, 147).

10.3　First words and beyond

The first twelve months have prepared children for the momentous acquisition of first words. Yet, as in the acquisition of syntax and phonology, the first twelve months have only begun a long course of discovery and linguistic creation in the area of semantics. This course is marked by creativity and abstract construction by the child.

10.3.1　Creativity

From the beginning, universally, children creatively confront the acquisition of word and sentence meaning. Once again we see that what may look like deformation in the child's early productions, in their early word meanings, actually indicates the child's linguistic competence. For example, although specific innovations in the child's first words, as in table 10.1, may be "illegal" in specific contexts, denominalizations exemplified in table 10.1 are required in general in English (e.g., "shovel the snow"), and across languages. Such "lexical innovation" persists to adolescence as well as adulthood.

Table 10.1 *Early creativity in the lexicon.*

	Instrument verbs	Locatum verbs
English	You have to <u>scale</u> it first (2.4) Don't <u>broom</u> my mess (2.11)	Mummy <u>trousers</u> me (2.3) <u>Pillow</u> me (2.6) [in pillow fight]
French	C'est <u>deconstruit</u>, c'est <u>bulldozé</u> (2.0) "It's unbuilt, it's bulldoz(er)ed"	Je vais me <u>pantoufler</u> dedans (4.5) "I will slipper myself inside"
German	Leitern (1.11) [about climbing something with] "to ladder" Schnuren (1.11) [about tying something with] "to cord"	Reinspitzen [about poking] "to put the point in"

Source: Clark 1982

10.3.2   Semantic displacement

Infants do not seem to be constrained by the "here and now." Although early communication may often be linked to the present context, analysis of child early speech with precise analyses of context also reveals competence for reference to "possible worlds." For example, Kulikowski 1980 provides an analysis of a young child, Shannon's (1.11), early two-word speech, where reference to the concrete context, "Mama coffee," was replaced with "Mama tea, Shannon coffee," etc., revealing that the child was not simply extensional in first semantics, but intensional (able to adapt different reference points) (cf. Weir 1970).

10.3.3   Fast mapping

Between thirteen and eighteen months, children are capable of "fast mapping" between words and meanings. In one experiment, thirteen- and eighteen-month-olds were shown two objects, a large plastic paper clip and a small plastic strainer, each in several colors, and the experimenter said about one of the objects, "That's a toma. See, it's a toma. Look it's a toma" (nine times during three to five minutes). When tested in a multiple choice situation both age groups showed comprehension of the new word after twenty-four hours (Woodward, Markman and Fitzsimmons 1994; also Schafer and Plunkett 1998).

With only a few minutes of exposure, infants at fourteen months "rapidly learn associations between words and objects" (Werker et al. 1998, 1289). Infants in this series of experiments were shown moving objects (dog or truck) paired with the sounds of nonsense CVC words ("neem/liff") and were then tested on the same, switched or different (new object and new word) trials.[19] With only one exposure to a new word, eighteen-month-old infants "readily establish a mapping between the word and its appropriate referent, and extend this new word to a

---

[19] In this study, eight-, ten- and twelve-month-olds did not show this effect (cf. 8.3.1).

reasonably appropriate set of exemplars" (Nelson and Bonvillian 1973; Baldwin et al. 1996, 3136).

Fast mapping continues through a period of high vocabulary growth. Three-and four-year-old children were introduced through brief exposure to a new color word, "chromium," in a nursery school. Their teacher simply said "You see those two trays over there. Bring me the chromium one. Not the red one, the chromium one" (Carey and Bartlett 1978; Bartlett 1978). A week or more later, children were tested on their understanding of the new word. Many of the children showed they had learned something about the new word, e.g, that it referred to color, even after this brief one-time exposure.[20] Subsequent research has confirmed the effect with two-year-olds in domains other than color (Heibeck and Markman 1987).

The continuous mechanism of fast mapping must help explain children's productive new word acquisition over the coming years (appendix 6).

10.3.4 Overextensions

While infants are remarkably competent to acquire new words, they also demonstrate some remarkable phenomena, like "overextension" (OE), the use of words whose extension ranges beyond that of the adult. A child might call a whole set of different animals by the term "doggie," or a whole set of fruits and vegetables by the term "apple."

It has been estimated that between ages 1 and 2.5 (the period of earliest word acquisition), over one third of child vocabulary may involve overextensions (Rescorla 1980). Some overextensions have been found to increase past age 5 (Carpenter 1991). They co-occur with other lexical items which appear to be used correctly, and with "underextensions," e.g., the word "roof" used only for peaked structures, not for flat ones (Reich 1976; Kay and Anglin 1982). They occur with both nouns and verbs (Bowerman 1978) as well as with classifiers in languages like Chinese and Thai (Carpenter 1991).

The "process of overextending a word is strikingly similar regardless of the language being acquired" (Clark 1983; 1973b). Among a child's first fifty words in Telugu, 16 percent were overextended, e.g., "Pa:Pa" (baby girl) for both girls and boys, baby and non baby; "pu:u:" (flower) for flower, coconut, mango, leaf, vegetables (Srinivas and Mohanty 1995; see Dromi 1987 for Hebrew).

Fremgen and Fay (1980, 205) suggested that "children never overextend in comprehension when tested properly," even if they do so in production. They tested sixteen children (1.2–2.2) on comprehension of words they had overextended in production, with four pictures (a correct exemplar, e.g., "dog"; an incorrect exemplar, e.g., "cat"; and two irrelevant examples, e.g., "car" and "vase"). "Never once" did a child select an incorrect exemplar. Research using a preferential looking paradigm (children with mean ages 1.9 and 2.3) also reported that

---

[20] See Wilkinson and Stanford 1996, Dockrell and Campbell 1986 for follow-up studies.

differences in OE status in production did not map on to differences in comprehension" (Naigles and Gelman 1995, 40). Such results suggest that the OE phenomenon does not reflect a qualitative limit on children's semantic theory. However, there is evidence that some errors of comprehension do exist when children overextend in production (e.g., Mervis and Canada 1983).

Several theories attempt to explain why the overextension phenomenon occurs. Some suggest constraint on the child's semantic or conceptual knowledge,[21] while others suggest lexical retrieval failure,[22] constraints on linguistic performance or a communicative strategy.[23] The fact that overextensions are not necessarily linked to age and can be linked to particular elements in different languages (e.g., Thai classifiers vs. English nouns) suggests that "they are better characterized as stages of organizing knowledge rather than as maturational stages defined by age" (Carpenter 1991, 109).

The overextension phenomenon, still a mystery, reveals general properties of language acquisition: children are selective and reconstructive, and resistant to adult correction to their chosen words and referents (chapter 6). Children are initially categorizing, never simply "labeling" distinct objects, but creating and following a controlling intension. The task of development is to converge intension and extension in a way which coheres with the surrounding community.

10.3.5   Categorical throughout

Children appear to rely continuously on category membership more than on perceptual appearances when inferring meanings for new words. This was shown in an experiment in which three-year-olds were taught a new fact about a target object, e.g., a "cat" "can see in the dark." They were then presented with choices between items which varied in category (cat, skunk or dinosaur) and/or in perceptual appearances (a cat with skunk stripes, a cat with differing appearance, or a skunk similar in appearance to the cat). Children were then asked "This one's an X [where X was the label, e.g., cat, skunk or dinosaur]. See this X? Do you think it can see in the dark, like this cat?" Three-year-olds drew more such inferences to pictures with the same label but different appearance than to pictures of similar appearance but different label (Gelman and Markman 1987). 2.5-year-olds showed similar results (Gelman and Coley 1990). Children as young as two years also bring their categorical knowledge to bear on compound noun formation, establishing the modifier–head relation in "banana-box" (Clark, Gelman and Lane 1985; Berman and Clark 1989).

These results contrast with earlier views that children begin with concrete details of their specific experience, and that a "characteristic-to-defining" shift characterizes development of word meaning (Vygotsky 1962; Keil and Batterman

---

[21] Semantic feature theory, Clark 1973b.

[22] Aitchison and Straf 1982; Huttenlocher 1974; Thomson and Chapman 1977; Gershkoff-Stowe and Smith 1997; Fremgen and Fay 1980.

[23] Clark 1978, McShane 1979, Bloom 1973. Hoek et al. 1986, Dromi 1987 and Clark 1973b and 1993 provide overviews.

1984).[24] They show that children "understand that some categories reflect more than a superficial set of features, and include deeper, nonobvious properties as well" (Gelman and Markman 1987, 1540).

10.3.6   Theories of the acquisition of word meaning

Theories attempting to explain how the child solves the language acquisition problem – with regard to the acquisition of word meanings – have developed over time; changing from theories that the child was mainly dependent on perception to ones which view the child as involved in abstract linguistic computation.

10.3.6.1   Early theories of the acquisition of word meaning

One early theory, Semantic Feature Theory (Clark 1973b; Locke 1968/1690), explored the possibility that the child's acquisition of word meaning could be explained in terms of gradual addition of a universal set of discrete criterial perceptually based features. Perhaps "bird" is represented as a set of binary features such as: [+ has wings][+flies][+lays eggs][+animal], or "tall" as: [+spatial dimension, +polar, +vertical]. Children's word meanings then could at first consist of only one or more of these features, possibly the most general ones, potentially explaining overextensions; word relations such as *synonymy* and *antonymy* could be easily computed.

Feature theory foundered when researchers realized that it was not possible to establish a set of defining features for any word, no way to limit their number or nature, and each feature itself appeared to need further decomposition (e.g., "has wings") in a potentially infinite regression.

Prototype Theory (Anglin 1977; Rosch 1973; Rosch and Mervis 1975) attempted to resolve these difficulties. Perhaps the mental representation for word meanings is not organized around a categorical set of distinctive features, but in terms of "family resemblances" which grade off from a central exemplar (*prototype*) which has most or all of a set of privileged features, to other more distant exemplars, sharing few of the relevant features. Mental representation of "bird" might involve a robin as a prototype, owls less, and ostriches least "birdy." Experience with specific exemplars leads to generation of a prototype around which a non-categorical family resemblance structure is generated. "Bird" or "birdiness" does not involve a categorical representation (+/− bird) but a graded concept with fuzzy edges. Experiments with both adults and children confirm that (a) they typically rank exemplars of many concepts along such a scale (e.g., "apple" is a "prototype" fruit and "most fruity," while "olive" is least "fruity") and (b) show quicker reaction times in a verification task the more "prototype"-like a concept is, e.g., verifying "The apple is a fruit" more quickly than "The olive is a fruit").[25]

---

[24] These earlier proposals become more questionable when the absence of accepted definitions for words is recognized.

[25] If prototypes (and stereotypes) exist, they are presumably part of encyclopedic knowledge.

Prototype theory also foundered. It too assumed a set of ill-defined criterial features by which "more or less prototype-like" was defined. One critical experiment clarified the nature of prototype effects and confirmed that it does not provide a theory of word meaning. Armstrong, Gleitman and Gleitman 1983 tested prototype effects (exemplariness ranking and verification times) with sets of exemplars of well-defined or categorically defined concepts, e.g., even and odd number. They tested adults' responses to: 4, 8, 10, 18. . . .34, 806, as exemplars of "even number." Surprisingly, adults demonstrated prototype-like responses resembling those they gave to fruits and vegetables. The even number 4 was ranked very high as an even number, and was most quickly judged to be an even number, while 806 was ranked lower and more slowly judged. Since we must assume that the meaning of "even number" is categorical and not graded, these results showed that prototype effects must reflect something other than the "intension" or meaning of the words. They must apply to how extensions are computed.

Another study did not support either the feature or prototype theories of acquisition of word meaning. In one study, children (three to five years old) were shown drawings of sets of three objects, e.g., figure 10.2, and tested on their conception of the meaning of the word "tall" for these sets. Children judged the tallest of a set of objects differently depending on how it was named. They gave different judgements of which was the "tallest" when a set of objects was called "houses" one day from when it was a week later called "arrows." Similar results occurred when another set was called "mountains" one day but "blankets" another (Keil and Carroll 1980). What children think about meaning determines their judgments about a word's reference. Children determine the extension of words in terms of their ideas regarding the word and the world.

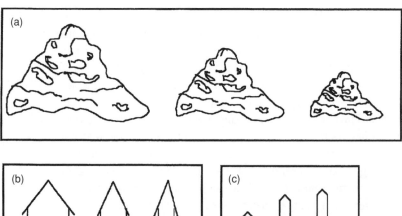

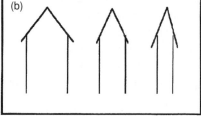

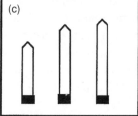

Fig. 10.2

Table 10.2 *Semantic constraints on acquisition of word meaning*

Constraint	Mutual Exclusivity	Whole Object	Taxonomic
Source(s)	Markman 1984, 1987, 1989; Markman and Wachtal 1988 Also: Principle of Lexical Contrast, cf. Clark 1988; 1993; 2003; 1997 Also: Uniqueness Principle, Pinker 1984	Carey 1978 Mervis 1987	Markman and Hutchinson 1984
Child constrained to:	construct mutually exclusive extensions for new words assume different words have different meanings	treat novel terms as labels for whole objects	assume labels refer to categories
Prediction:	assume a novel name applies to a novel exemplar rather than to one with a known label	assume a novel word applies to an object rather than to a part or property of the object	assume a word (e.g. "dog") refers to objects of the same type, not to thematically related objects (e.g., "bone")

10.3.6.2   Semantic Constraints

More recent theoretical approaches to explaining how infants converge on "correct" hypotheses regarding word meaning hypothesize that *semantic constraints* – presumably biologically determined – may constrain children's hypotheses and determine that they will not try all potential false hypotheses when acquiring word meanings. Three of these proposed constraints are summarized in table 10.2 (Markman 1994 for review). These would act like syntactic constraints on the acquisition of syntax.

Unlike syntactic constraints, semantic constraints are proposed to apply to children only, not adults; unlike syntactic constraints which rule out ungrammatical forms, they may rule out possible well-formed word meanings at early stages of language acquisition.[26] For example, Mutual Exclusivity would eliminate *synonymy* in early child language, *superordinate* terms and *pronouns*; the Whole Object constraint would eliminate reference to *properties or parts* of objects.

---

[26] The Taxonomic Constraint differs from the others in table 10.2 in that it would be expected to be continuous with adults' knowledge and to eliminate non-well-formed meanings (e.g., one label referring at once to both a dog and a bone as a thematic association for dog).

In a classic test of the proposed Mutual Exclusivity constraint, children (3.2–4.2) were presented with pairs of objects, one familiar and one not (Markman and Wachtel 1988). They were asked: "Show me the Zav." Coherent with a Mutual Exclusivity constraint, children showed "a striking tendency to select the novel object as the referent for the novel term" (128), not the object for which they already had a name. They did so significantly more than a control group which had simply been asked "show me one."

Subsequent research pursued several potential explanations for children's behavior in this experiment other than a Mutual Exclusivity constraint on word meaning: perhaps they were filling lexical gaps, or had inferred "what else could the experimenter be asking me" (making the behavior an experimental artifact). Further research which allowed children to first familiarize themselves with both objects in a similar experiment showed that a Mutual Exclusivity type of response was only developmentally achieved, increasing between two and five years (Merriman and Bowman 1989). Adults also show the effect. Bilingual children may override it, as well as children in other experimental situations, as when offered another label for basic level category terms already known.[27] When given appropriate pragmatic directions, children use more than one term for the same object, construct novel words to mark alternate perspectives and shift perspective when asked (e.g., "cat" to "animal"); they readily learn new terms for already labeled kinds (Clark 1997).

Similarly, with regard to the proposed Whole Object constraint, two-year-olds learned a novel part name of an unfamiliar object when the experimenter demonstrated an action on this object (Kobayashi 1998). Thus the hypothesized constraints, Mutual Exclusivity and Whole Object (table 10.2), may at best be viewed as "tendencies" regarding the use of language rather than as semantic constraints on word meaning (see Bloom 2000 for discussion). Other formulations are being considered now: a "principle of contrast" where "[s]peakers take every difference in form to mark a difference in meaning" (Clark 1993, 64; 2003, 144; 1997). This pragmatic principle, not a semantic principle constraining word meanings, is proposed to apply to adults as well as children and allows "lexical overlap," i.e., words may share meaning.

10.3.6.3   Ontological constraints

Another type of word acquisition constraint involves concepts regarding ontology (the nature of being). Infants have been tested to determine if their initial hypotheses about word meaning consult whether words refer to objects which *count* versus those which are *mass*, e.g., "a block"/one block/another block, vs. "some clay"/more clay. Introduced to an object with "This is my blicket" or to a substance (Dippity-do) with this is "my stad" and then asked to choose "which is the blicket" or "which is the stad," two-year-olds distinguished words referring to solid objects which can be individuated versus those referring to substance which

---

[27] Au and Glusman 1990; Mervis, Golinkoff and Bertrand 1994; Clark and Grossman 1998; Waxman and Hatch 1992; Gelman, Wilcox and Clark 1989.

can not (Soja, Carey and Spelke 1991, 1992; Gordon 1985). Chinese children also make this count–mass distinction in spite of the fact that this factor is not explicitly reflected in their language (Chien et al. 2003).

10.3.6.4 Theory construction

Recent research suggests that children construct theories during the acquisition of word meaning. They have "top down abstract expectations about what sorts of features will be causally central to a domain" (Keil 1994, 193), i.e., which features are most likely to be relevant in instantiating a concept, and build word meanings around these expectations. In one series of experiments, three- and four-year-olds were presented with novel names and items which were introduced as belonging to four categories: artifact, plant, animal, or non-living natural kind. Children differentiated the categories, using color in deciding on non-living natural kinds, but shape in deciding on living kinds and artifacts (Simons and Keil 1995). A wide set of studies suggest that preschoolers "see living kinds as having their own causal patternings distinct from physical mechanics and social behavior."[28]

10.3.6.5 Pragmatics

Very early, perhaps initially, children can shift perspective and consult a speaker's intentions as well as other pragmatic cues to determine word meaning and reference (e.g., Clark 1997; Clark and Svaib 1997; Tomasello 1995, 1992), although it will take years before these complex mechanisms are fully established (e.g., Piaget 1959). Infants (eighteen to nineteen months) "spontaneously check and follow a speaker's line of regard, and link the label with the object of the speaker's focus," suggesting that they are consulting the "speaker's intent" (Baldwin 1991 and 1993; Baldwin et al. 1996, 3136); "infants take an active part in establishing joint reference when attentional discrepancies occur" (Baldwin et al. 1996, 3137). These results suggest that infants have the foundations for establishing interpersonal inference and for understanding social criteria necessary for establishing the relevance of what they say and hear (Baldwin et al. 1996).

Infants appear to know that "signs of referential intent are criterial for the establishment of word-world relations" which they must compute (Baldwin et al. 1996, 3137). Infants (eighteen to twenty months) looking at a new toy heard a novel word as label, e.g., "A toma! There's a toma!", under two conditions. In one (decoupled), the word was uttered by someone who was out of sight of the child and known to have been in telephone conversation with another speaker. In the other (coupled), the word was uttered by an adult jointly involved in attention to the new toy which the child was inspecting. Infants were then tested on their comprehension of the new word ("Where's the toma?"). They systematically linked the new word to the toy to a significantly higher degree in the coupled

---

[28] Keil 1992; Inagaki and Hatano 2003; Hatano et al. 1993; Gelman and Gottfried 1993; Keil 1994, 181.

condition, suggesting that "infants understand the critical significance of cues to referential intent" (Baldwin et al. 1996, 3138).

Children's computation thus mediates between the development of word meaning and their experience of the world around them. Inference about a speaker's intentions mediates children's use of this experience. Pragmatic principles (cf. 10.1.2) may guide this inference.

10.3.7   Higher order semantics

The fundamental competencies and developments reviewed above prepare the way for the child's acquisition of higher order semantics, i.e., for semantic computation required for composition of propositions and propositional relations (cf. 10.2). Children work to integrate semantic, syntactic and pragmatic factors for years to come. The child is struggling with this integration with sentence syntax in (10), and with the lexicon (the verb "promise") in (11).

10.   RCS, about three years, pc
        "I picked up everything that my Dad said no to"
        = Everything that I picked up (while shopping), my father told me I
        couldn't have

11.   Child aged 3.6 (Cohen Sherman and Lust 1993a)
        E: Did you ever promise your Dad that you'd do something for him? What
        did you promise him?
        C: I promised him to um uh to make a wooden sword for me. He made one
        for my sister too.
        E. So did he promise you to make a wooden sword for you?
        C: No, I can't make one! He did it with a saw!

In their subsequent development, children's interpretation of sentences must go beyond interpretation of words and logical operators (e.g., quantifiers or logical connectives) in order to compute the truth of a proposition and of a sentence's *implications* and *presuppositions*. This computation must integrate syntactic structure (*syntactic knowledge*) and lexical meaning, including verbs and negatives (*semantic knowledge*), with pragmatic knowledge. For example, in either (12a) or (12b), it is *presupposed* that Max in fact did lock the door – we judge (12bii) to be true. Even when Max did "not remember" in (12b), we assume that he did lock the door.[29] In contrast, in (13a) and (13b), we can't be totally sure whether Max did or did not lock the door. Although it is implied that he did so in (13a), it is implied that he did not in (13b). We are more likely to judge (13bii) to be false. The subtle differences in interpretations and understanding of the truth of sentences like (12) with presupposition, and (13) with implication, depend on syntactic analysis that consults the difference between the finite tensed clause in (12) and the nonfinite non-tensed clause in (13), a syntactic factor involving sentence embedding and determining the scope of negation. This knowledge

---

[29] The maintenance of truth under negation is a leading diagnostic for the existence of presupposition.

must be integrated with understanding of the verbs as well as the meaning of the negative in order to compute what the sentences mean, imply and presuppose. In order to acquire this area of language, many areas of knowledge must be brought together: general cognition, linguistic analyses of syntax and semantics and pragmatics. (See Eisele, Lust and Aram 1998 for investigation of biological foundations of the knowledge required in (12) and its development.)

12.   Finding the meaning and judging truth (Eisele, Lust and Aram 1998)
       a. Max remembered [that he locked the door]
        i. Max remembered = T
        ii. Max locked the door = T (a fact)
       b. Max did **not** remember [that he locked the door]
        i. Max remembered = F
        ii. Max locked the door = T

13.   a. Max remembered to lock the door
        i. Max remembered = T
        ii. Max locked the door = T (perhaps)
       b. Max did **not** remember to lock the door
        i. Max remembered = F
        ii. Max locked the door = F (perhaps)

10.3.8 Summary

Children do not appear qualitatively different from adults in methods of word acquisition. They are capable of semantic displacement (not solely "concrete" in perception and reasoning) and always capable of categorical thought. Children construct theories of word meaning through linguistic computation and pragmatic reference. Once again, children are involved in creative theory construction. Ontological constraints may guide this theory construction. Children's use of their environment is indirect and constructive; they are creative and systematic.

"Feature" theory or "prototype" theory are insufficient (for adult and child) as models of word meaning (as a word's intension). There are prototype effects but these are related to selection of exemplars in the world, not to the word meaning or intension itself. Proposed semantic constraints such as Mutual Exclusivity or Whole Object are not equivalent to syntactic constraints. They do not necessarily constrain children's acquisition of semantic representations or word meanings, i.e., the mental representations which constitute the "intension" in word meaning.

10.4 Conclusions

In the acquisition of semantics, we again see continuity of the fundamental architecture of the Language Faculty between child and adult. We see the development of the Conceptual Interface in this Language Faculty (figure 2.1). Once again, we see abstract and complex linguistic computation occurring in the child's language acquisition.

Although language and non-linguistic cognition are basically independent in their development, they must be related continuously. Many current studies are investigating this relationship. Cognitive development is not the fundamental "cause" of language development, nor is language development the fundamental "cause" of cognitive development.

10.4.1   Toward an explanation

Psycholinguists pursue implications of developmental facts for models of the acquisition of semantics, debating associative empiricist approaches as opposed to rule- and principle-based ones (Keil et al. 1998). Investigation of the acquisition of higher order semantics has barely begun, an area that will require subtle studies of interactions between the acquisition of syntax and semantics as well as pragmatics.[30]

Even explanation for development in the area of word meaning alone may require more complex theory construction than yet exists, and more empirical research. Much evidence suggests that the underlying mental representation of word meaning does not change qualitatively; rather, development may involve "increasing elaboration of explanatory beliefs that are able to interpret a larger and larger percent of the tabulated information" as well as "shifts in which explanatory system is deemed most relevant to understanding members of a category"; young children may have "less detail in some of their explanatory systems" (Keil 1994, 193). While "childlike" explanations for word meanings exist early, e.g., (14), they may in fact reflect adult-like constraints. Even (14) may reveal the child's realization that "adaptive or design explanations provide . . . a distinct form of explanation linked to the biological sciences" (Keil 1994, 181).

14.   Worms don't eat because they cannot have feelings of hunger and desires for food like humans (Carey 1985).

10.4.2   Open questions

Researchers continue to debate:

*   Whether the acquisition of word meaning involves linguistically specific principles or constraints, and if so, what they are. Just as philosophers continue to debate specific ontological constraints on word

---

[30] For some initial studies of language acquisition which bear on children's competence for logical form and on relations between children's syntactic knowledge and the conceptual interface related to semantics and pragmatics, see van Kampen and Evers 1995; Foley et al. 2003; Thornton 1995; Papafragou 1998.

meanings, researchers in language acquisition continue to seek potential cognitive bases for concepts and their relation to word meanings and their acquisition.

- What is the nature of word meaning, or intension? What form does this representation take, if definitional theories of word meaning are impossible?
- Do these representations change over time during the child's language acquisition, and if so, how?
- How precisely does Fast Mapping occur and what is its early content?
- Why are overextensions universal in language acquisition? Perhaps because they are virtually necessary for adults as well as children (cf. (10.3))? What role do they play? How are they related to a theory of word meaning in adults? Developmentally, what leads children to overcome overextensions?
- How does development in children's word meanings proceed, or change occur?

10.5   Supplementary readings

Partee 1999 and Weisler and Milekic 2000 (chapters 5 and 3) introduce the study of meaning in language, as does Jackendoff 2002 (part 3); Fromkin 2000 (part 3); Larson and Segal 1995; Chierchia and McConnell-Ginet 1990. For introduction to pragmatics, see Carston 2002. For "logical form" see May 1999 and Stanley 1999.

On acquisition of words, see Bloom and Gleitman 1999, Bloom 2000, 2001 and related discussion in *Behavioral and Brain Sciences* 2001, 6, Clark 1993, and Golinkoff et al. 2000, Smith and Locke 1988, Gleitman and Landau 1995, Dromi 1987. Gleitman and Gleitman 1991 provide introduction. For acquisition of verbs, Tomasello and Merriman, 1995; Golinkoff et al. 1995, 1996. For introduction to acquisition of higher order semantics, see Crain 1999.

For introduction to language–thought relations, see Sterelny and Devitt 1999 and Crystal 1997b; Piatelli-Palmarini 1980 for the Piaget–Chomsky Debate.

On acquisition of pragmatics, see Clark 2003, Ninio and Snow 1999, Foster-Cohen 1990; for introduction to Relevance Theory in acquisition, Foster-Cohen 1990, 2000a, b.

11   On the nature of language growth

We have seen that aspects of phonology, syntax and semantics develop separately and in parallel, beginning in the first twelve months of life, appearing to cohere with the architecture of the Language Faculty in figure 2.2. The development of language and the development of thought appear to proceed independently, though interactively. We have also seen that many questions remain regarding how different components of knowledge interact in language acquisition as it proceeds over time. *How does language "grow" over time?* Debates persist: does language development involve qualitative changes in the structure of children's language knowledge or in their computational mechanisms, e.g., is language acquisition analogous to a discontinuous "tadpole-to-frog"-like development, or do children continuously employ formal analyses?

This chapter will focus on mechanisms of developmental change especially after the first twelve months. It will briefly introduce several areas where significant cross-linguistic variation in adult grammars exists and where language development is delayed; here language acquisition must involve some induction. It will briefly introduce several proposed mechanisms of growth. If language acquisition involves continuous linguistic computation, as previous chapters have suggested, then such mechanisms of growth will involve continuous linguistic computation by children. If the architecture of the Language Faculty is in place continuously, then children will not be forced to resort solely to general non-linguistic conceptual means, even at early periods.[1]

11.1   Formal analyses from the start: "Frogs all the way down" (*Levy 1983b*)

11.1.1   Grammatical categories[2]

There is evidence of children's ability to construct syntactic classes efficiently, e.g., nouns and verbs, as in "Give me [that shovel]$_{NOUN}$" or "Please

---

[1] Alternatively it has been hypothesized that "infants learn their language by first determining, independent of language, the meaning which a speaker intends to convey to them, and by then working out the relationship between the meaning and the language . . . the infant uses meaning as a clue to language, rather than language as a clue to meaning" (MacNamara 1972; cf. chapter 3).

[2] For research on the acquisition of grammatical categorization of words (e.g., as noun or verb), see Tomasello and Kruger 1992; Golinkoff et al. 1996; Choi 2000; and Goldfield 2000.

[shovel]$_{\text{VERB}}$ the path."[3] Grammatical operations, rather than semantic distinctions, are "clearly at the heart of providing the differentiations among categories" (Maratsos 1982, 250). Rather than conceptual knowledge being the basis of development, "category knowledge can be seen as a prerequisite for representing semantic roles in speech" (Valian 1991, 572).

Children do not mistakenly take any word conveying action and assume that action words are verbs. For example, they do not freely construe action-like adjectives, e.g., "nasty" or "noisy," as verbs, e.g., (1). They do not confuse formal categories as in (2) (Maratsos 1982, 246).[4]

1.   *The turtle nastied the frog
         *The drum noisied the room

2.   *big he
         *the go is fast
         *the follow is bad

Children inflect noun forms appropriately even if they are not semantically based in any obvious way, as in (3).

3.   man sit blocks (Bloom 1990)
         not go shops
         birdies flying
         touch heads

Children compute syntactic operations of agreement in early sentences across a wide array of semantic relations (e.g., Italian in (4)); their early forms of agreement occur across varied semantic types, including non-agentive subjects, as in (4c)–(4d). "In short, agreement holds between what is traditionally referred to as 'subject' and 'verb'" (Hyams 1984, 60).

4.   (Hyams 1984)
         a. Tu leggi il libro
            "You (2p.sg.) read the book"
         b. Io vado fuori
            "I go (1p.sg.) outside"
         c. Gira il pallone
            "The balloon turns (3p.sg.)"
         d. Dorme miao dorme
            "sleeps (3p.sg.) the cat sleeps"
         e. A'cola perche bimbi piangono?
            "At school why do the babies cry (3p.plu.)?"

Determiners, e.g., "a" or "the" in English, appear with a variety of nouns which do not fall into any apparent semantic pattern (Ihns and Leonard 1988, 677).

---

[3] How words are categorized differs across languages and must involve some language-specific learning (Baker 2003).

[4] Maratsos and Chalkley 1981; Valian 1986.

Children do make mistakes in specific forms of inflection and in specific forms of agreement, e.g., (5), as we saw in chapter 9, but these mistakes do not appear to involve absence of knowledge of the grammatical categories involved.[5]

5.   a. That's the tires and wheels are on it (Valian 1986, 570)
      b. I see a bears, I say hi to them (Valian 1986, 569)

In (5), the pronoun ("them") substitutes for the noun ("bears"), documenting the grammatical NP status of the elements referred to by the pronoun ("a bears"), even though the article "a" lacks plural features.

Nouns before verbs?

It has often been assumed that first words consist mainly of nouns (e.g., Gentner 1982). Some researchers have suggested that there is a universal acquisition order: nouns before verbs.[6] If so, this might suggest that child language is first based on non-formal and referential concepts, possibly devoid of formal grammatical analysis.

Much of children's early vocabulary is indeed nominal, reflecting a prolific outburst of new word learning, including naming, which characterizes the onset of productive language. However, the assumption that children were initially limited to nouns was largely based on parental reports of their words. In a study designed to test this assumption in English, Bloom, Tinker and Margulis (1993) analyzed monthly vocabulary growth in fourteen children (aged 0.9–2.0) with assessment of both onset and achievement in vocabulary learning. Their results disconfirmed the traditional assumption: object names constituted on average less than 40 percent of the new words children learned from one month to the next, and made up less than half of the words in children's vocabularies at any time.

Usage depends on the language being acquired. Korean children consistently use verbs over the course of acquisition, and for many of them a "verb spurt" in vocabulary development occurs before a "noun spurt" (Choi and Gopnik 1993, 1995; Gopnik and Choi 1995). In Mandarin Chinese, children produce more verbs than nouns in their early vocabularies (Tardif 1995, 1996), and "relatively fewer nouns and more verbs than English-speaking children" (Tardif, Gelman and Xu 1999, 620).

Although explanation for such cross-linguistic differences remains a matter of current research and debate, these results confirm that there is no cognitive bias that necessarily privileges nouns in children's early language to the exclusion of other formal categories, such as verbs; in this way, there appears to be no significant qualitative difference between children and adults.[7]

---

[5] As we saw in chapter 10, children do modify grammatical categories; e.g., children's creation of denominal verbs, like "Don't broom my mess" (2:11) (Clark 1982, 402). Here rather than leaning solely on the meanings of words, we see children creatively adapting the semantics to the formal (inflectional) structure of the language.

[6] e.g., Golinkoff, Hirsh-Pasek and Nandakumar 1996; Gentner 1982.

[7] Issues of methodology are involved, e.g., noun use is predominant in book-reading contexts (Tardif, Gelman and Xu 1999).

Getting started on verbal inflection

If children were operating not on a formal "verb" category, but on the semantic concept of "action" alone in their first hypotheses, then we would predict that they might first inflect verbs only if they were active (corresponding to actions), but not stative (Brown 1973). We now know, however, that children's early inflections are not so limited. In English, "children produce overregularizations such as *thinked, knowed, feeled, heared* and *seed* with reasonable readiness" (Maratsos 1982, 261).[8] In Inuktitut, children apply verbal inflection processes across grammatically different verb types (Allen and Crago 1993). In the polysynthetic agglutinating language Quiché Mayan, two-year-olds not only differentiated and contrasted verbal inflection across grammatical categories, e.g., verbs opposed to other classes, but also transitive opposed to intransitive verbs. Even though the inflectional mappings "encode a complex set of semantic features," the children "worked with the form-meaning combinations the adult language presented to [them] rather than relying exclusively on the meanings of the items as the primary basis for formal analyses" (Pye 1992, 252). The semantic diversity of the verbs used in the children's early inflection argued against the hypothesis that they "originally recognized the class of verbs on the basis of some type of prototypical action schema" (Pye 1992, 251).

Children's efficient acquisition of grammatical categories in their language appears to be guided by grammatical analyses, not by word meanings or general cognitive concepts alone.

11.1.2   Grammatical case[9]

In exceptionally complex computation, children must also map verbs to their *arguments* (e.g., *agents* or *experiencers*) and to their *grammatical relations* in sentences (e.g., sentence subjects or objects) which involve transitivity or intransitivity of the verb, and then map these to *case systems* for their specific language (e.g., assigning Nominative case to sentence subjects in English and Accusative case to objects, as in "he likes him," not "*him likes he"). Once again, languages vary in what computation will be required. Finnish demonstrates fifteen cases; Inuktitut eight; Modern English only three ("he," "his," "him"). In some languages, morphology marks case prolifically: on nouns as well as pronouns, and on adjectives and/or determiners which may agree with the nouns they modify (as in German).

---

[8] Both children and adults in English have shown a preference for producing regular inflection on verbs (and nouns) with novel meanings (e.g, "The batter flied/*flew out to centre field,") when a new meaning of the verb is intended (e.g., "to be put out by hitting a fly ball that is caught" in a baseball game). It is argued that their usage is based on dominant grammatical knowledge of verb inflection (Kim et al. 1994). Shirai (1997) suggested that semantic/functional factors may also be involved if "speakers avoid the use of irregular forms to avoid conveying the conventional meaning associated with the irregular form" (495); see also Bloom et al. 1980.

[9] Regarding acquisition of case, see Bai 1984 for cross-linguistic work and discussion; Austin 2001; Powers 1995, Vainikka 1993 and Schutze 1997; Pinker 1989 and Van Valin 1992 for discussion of the acquisition of ergativity and papers in Slobin 1992.

Computation must be mediated by children's understanding of the meaning of verbs and the semantic roles the nouns play relative to them. However, semantic relations alone cannot determine case marking. For example, in English, the mapping of semantic relations to surface case can be reversed, as in (6). The semantic "theme" and grammatical object of the verb "likes" in (6a) surfaces as the grammatical subject of the verb "pleases" in (6b), and the "experiencer" subject of the verb "likes" surfaces as a grammatical object of the verb "pleases" in (6b), causing case changes of the object referred to accordingly. Grammatical subjects receive Nominative case in both conditions.

6.   a. He likes him
        b. He pleases him

In some languages, the grammatical subject of a sentence regularly requires non-Nominative case, e.g., a Dative marker, and a grammatical object may take Nominative marking, e.g., Hindi in (7):[10]

7.   siitaa-ko raam pasand hai
        Sita -DAT Ram-NOM liking is
        (Sita likes Ram)

Here the Dative case marker may carry a range of semantic relations to the verb (e.g., recipient, experiencer, benefactive, possessor). In Sinhala, sentence subjects may occur with a range of case markings, dependent partially on semantics and partially on verb form and other factors (Gair 1998). In some languages termed "ergative" (e.g., Inuktitut [Allen and Crago 1993] or Basque), subjects of intransitive sentences share the same case as the object of a transitive verb, while the subject of transitive sentences bears a distinct ergative case, e.g., the Basque examples in (8a)–(8b) (from Austin 2001, 14):[11]

8.   a. Ni-k liburu-a-Ø irakurri dut
           I-ERG book-det-ABS read AUX-3sgABS-1sgERG
           (I have read the books)
        b. Ni-Ø eseri naiz
           I-ABS sit AUX-1sgABS
           (I have sat)

In knowing how to case mark, a language learner must link overt case marking, grammatical relation in the sentence, syntactic position, word order, and the lexicon and morphology, as well as certain aspects of cognitive roles, e.g., "agent" or "theme." The learner must attend to the semantics of the sentence, but be able

---

[10] Verma and Mohanan 1990; Gair 1991/1998; Davison 1999.
[11] In Basque, two classes of intransitive verbs exist. For those which allow agent subjects, often involving volition ("Unergative Verbs" like "talk," "run," "dance," "sleep"), the subject case resembles the transitive subject – not the intransitive. For other verbs, often involving subjects which are themes and which may involve change of state ("Unaccusative Verbs" like "arrive," "go," "fall," "sit," "come") the subject case follows the Ergative pattern (Austin, 2001).

to know how semantics is or is not relevant.[12] These facts have provoked the linguist to develop theories of "case" (e.g., Haegeman 1991, 141f.). They lead us to inquire how children discover the systems which underlie them and to ask again whether children begin this complex learning with general cognitive concepts alone or with formal linguistic analyses.

It has been suggested that a mechanism for acquisition of grammatical case may lie in innate "linking rules" which build a direct relation between children's semantic and formal grammatical concepts. If it were possible to formulate such rules, e.g., (9), and they were a primary mechanism in language acquisition, then once children could determine thematic roles of arguments, these could provide a possible explanation of how children begin to acquire basic grammatical relations (e.g., what constitutes the subject of a sentence) and appropriate case.[13]

9.   "Link the first argument of 'cause' (the agent) to: the SUBJ function
            (LFG)/external argument (GB)" (Pinker 1989, 74).[14]

LINKING RULES: "Linking rules are regular ways of mapping open arguments onto grammatical functions or underlying syntactic configurations by virtue of their thematic roles; they are the mechanisms that create the syntactic argument structure associated with a given thematic core" (Pinker 1989, 74).

If certain linking rules were predetermined, this would predict that certain forms of linking would have priority in acquisition, both within a language and across languages; they would be "canonical." For example, *agent* subjects might be acquired first with proper case marking, and Nominative–Accusative systems might be earlier acquired than either Ergative or Dative case-marking systems. Ergativity provides a "most blatant counterexample" to proposed "semantic linking" rules, since "patients, not agents, are linked to the subject role, and transitive agents, not patients, are linked to the object role" (Pinker 1989, 251). Ergative systems might be predicted to be late in acquisition. Although children do show developmental delay in acquisition of case marking, initial cross-linguistic studies challenge these predictions.

Initially, overt case marking may be null in child language. In a study of the acquisition of Telugu by four children in India, early speech was "marked by the absence of case inflection" (Nirmala 1982, 118; cf. Bai 1983, 1984). In young bilingual children acquiring Basque and Spanish simultaneously, Ergative case marking on nouns is frequently null in early periods of Basque (Austin 2001). And in Japanese, "there is a period in which children never use any case marker in their

---

[12] In languages with "split Ergative" systems, e.g., Hindi, whose case marking is sensitive to tense and aspect, this learnability problem appears especially severe (e.g., Davison 1999). Several mixed types of ergativity exist (See Comrie 1981 for review). Presumably, substantial positive evidence will be available to children in these cases.

[13] See Pinker 1987, 408, table 1 for an articulation of a full theory here.

[14] "LFG" refers to "Lexical Functional Grammar," a linguistic theory of grammatical relations linked to the lexicon.

sentences" (Ito 1988, 51; see also Miyahara 1974, Miyata 1993). Children err in case marking, e.g., (10) in English, or (11) in Tamil, where children overgeneralize Dative for Locative, as underlined in (11), or Locative for Dative (Bai 1984, 89; Nirmala 1982.

10.   a. Her curl my hair (Sarah, from Brown and Hanlon 1970, table 1.12)
       b. Me sawed her (12.36mos., MLU 2.78) (Rispoli 1995, =8, 238)
       c. This is for mine (=This is mine) (BG, 2, CLAL)
       d. Catch it to me (=Throw it to me) (BG, 3.0, CLAL)
       e. I want they (4.29mos., MLU 2.02) (Rispoli 1995, =4, 237)
       f. Can me eat this in the living room? (2.35mos., MLU 4.19) (Rispoli 1995, =13, 238)

11.   bablu <u>viiTuku</u> aanTi illa (Bai 1984, 89)
       Bablu house to aunt not there
       (Auntie is not in Bablu's house)

Linking rules do not explain early child case marking acquisition or errors.[15] In English, for example, "canonically linked verbs are no easier for children than non-canonically linked verbs" (Bowerman 1990, 1267). Some of the earliest verbs are noncanonical, e.g., "gots bottle" (age 1.8) and "stay home baby" (age 1.8). "There is no advantage for prototypical agent-patient verbs" (Bowerman 1990, 1275). In general, "no support is found for the hypothesis that knowledge of linking is innate" (1253; Pinker 1989 for discussion). These rules themselves need to be acquired for each specific language, and often for individual constructions within a language.

In Inuktitut, children produced Unaccusative verbs as well as Unergative verbs from earliest periods (Allen and Crago 1993; see our fn. 11). In Telugu, children appear to systematically map various forms of arguments to Dative case from the beginning of the course of acquisition (Rani 1999), e.g., (12).

12.   a. neenu waaDi-ki pennu icceenu
          I   he-DAT   pen gave
          (I gave a pen to him)
       b. aame-ku baagaa jwaram waccindi
          she-DAT high   fever came
          (She has high fever)

Two Tamil–Telugu bilingual children showed from the time they began combining words (age 1.7 and 1.3), they "could comprehend . . . agent, dative (recipient), object, locative and possessive roles" (Bai 1984, 81), even when missing in their

---

[15] To test for the existence of predetermined linking rules, we may investigate children's novel verbs, e.g., denominal verbs (e.g., to "broom" the sidewalk = "sweep," Bowerman 1990, 1261), or investigate how children treat nonsense verbs introduced by an experimenter with noncanonical mappings (e.g., Marantz 1982; Tomasello 2000b; Tomasello and Brooks 1998; Maratsos 1982); or one might investigate how children acquire actual verbs of their language with noncanonical mappings in contrast to those with canonical mappings (which can be mapped directly by a linking rule). See Pinker 1984, Bowerman 1990.

early speech. The first overt case relation to be marked was "Dative" for both children, e.g., (13) (Bai 1984, 84, =#39), or (14) (Bai 1984, 84, =#41).[16]

13. Telugu:
     naaki toocaa
     to me dosa
     (Give me dosa)

14. Tamil:
     annaaku naanaa
     to elder brother water
     (The water is for elder brother)

In Quiché Mayan, children show early awareness of the Ergative/Absolutive case distinction, "neither overgeneralizing the ergative marker of transitive subjects to intransitive subjects nor overgeneralizing the absolutive marker of intransitive subjects to transitive subjects in any consistent way" (Parkinson 1999, 107, referring to Pye 1992). In Samoan, while Ergative case marking "rarely appears in the speech of 2–4 year old children," "evidence suggests that Samoan children encode ergative distinctions through word order" (Ochs 1982, 646). Ergative case marking is attested in early Inuktitut (Allen and Crago 1993, 21, =37c). Two- to three-year-olds who were acquiring both Basque, an Ergative case language, and Spanish, a Nominative–Accusative case language, followed different patterns of development of case and inflection in the two languages (Austin 2001). First case agreement produced in Basque was Absolutive, followed by Ergative (marked on the verb in (15a)), and then Dative; in Spanish it was Nominative, then Accusative, then Dative (marked on noun and verb in (15b)).

15.   a. Basque
         zergatik Peter Pan hegan egiten du
         because Peter Pan (no ERG marking) fly do-IMP Aux-3sgERG3sgABS
         (Because Peter Pan flies . . .)

      b. Spanish
         pero yo tengo otro
         but I-NOM have-1sgNOM another
         (but I have another)

Thus, across languages and even within the same child, the link between grammatical case marking and semantic roles can be reversed in accord with the formal grammar of the languages involved.[17]

---

[16] The children made "clear cut distinction between the different semantic roles of dative" even when they did not produce the Dative marking for all roles (Bai 1984). For one child, first semantic roles to receive overt Dative case marking included "recipient"; for the other, "early dative forms typically expressed the experiencer role" with mental state verbs, e.g., "like" and "want" (Bai 1984, 85, =#48,49).

[17] See Goldwin-Meadow, Yalabik and Gershkoff-Stowe 2000 for evidence of early Ergative-like relations in Homesign.

The acquisition of case marking, then, cannot be directly explained in terms of selected concepts like "agent" which link in some privileged way to selected grammatical concepts, e.g., sentence subject or object, through innate linking rules. Whether children begin by representing Nominative/Accusative, Dative/Nominative, or Ergative case systems appears to depend on the formal grammar of the adult language being acquired. Children's formal analyses of this grammar of the language appears to guide the linking of case marking to semantic concepts, rather than vice versa.

11.1.3   Grammatical gender[18]

For children learning a first language, as for the adult learning a second language, grammatical gender is another hurdle, since it requires a complex and often arbitrary integration of both formal (syntactic and phonological) and general cognitive factors related to meaning and reference, as well as wide cross-linguistic variation. While in a language like English gender is minimally represented, in other languages all nouns must be inflected for gender, e.g., Hebrew, French or German. Swahili has six genders, Fula twenty-six.[19] While some languages involve mainly natural gender (i.e., the form is predicted by the nature of the referent, as in Dravidian languages), in many others gender is largely grammatical. For example, in French, "the moon" ("la lune") is feminine while "the sun" ("le soleil") is masculine, but in German it's the reverse, and in Hindi both are masculine. In French, two synonyms for "bicycle" ("velo" and "bicyclette") differ in gender (see Karmiloff-Smith 1979). In German, "cabbage" ("der Kohl") is masculine while "girl" ("das Mädchen") is neuter. Formal cues may be essential. In Hebrew, all nouns are marked for gender through the phonology of the final syllable of the word. In French, "le can**ton**" (district), "le bis**on**" (buffalo) and "le cit**ron**" (lemon) are all masculine, showing phonological and morphological conditioning.

We may wonder if children at early periods would base their initial hypotheses on the concepts involved in word meanings, rather than on formal properties. The "egg–tadpole–frog" hypothesis which proposes that children's language organization changes qualitatively from non-formal to formal can be tested here (Levy 1983b, 75). Will children first generalize from the phonology of "le citron" in French? Will children begin by first establishing natural gender where there is a consistent correlation with meaning, but be delayed where formal properties such as phonology are involved?

Although children show developmental delays in acquisition of grammatical gender, they appear to learn it as a linguistic system consulting formal cues, with

---

[18] On the acquisition of grammatical gender across languages: Levy (1983a and 1997) provides review of Polish, Russian, German, French and Hebrew.

[19] In languages where numerous noun classes exist, going beyond the gender and classifier systems discussed above (e.g., Bantu has sixteen "genders") (see Comrie, Matthew and Polinsky 1996 for an introduction), research on language acquisition suggests that children are choosing formal bases for language development (e.g., Demuth 1987, Suzman 1980).

little or no tendency to base their early hypotheses on the extralinguistic cognitive concepts related to natural gender. A series of experimental studies of the acquisition of French gender (341 monolingual French children between the ages of 3.2 and 12.5) revealed that children as early as three to four years constructed a very powerful, implicit system of phonological rules which concerned phonological changes in word endings in order to determine gender (Karmiloff-Smith 1979, 167; see also Clark 1985). Studies of the acquisition of Hebrew (both longitudinal and cross-sectional) evaluating young children's natural speech from two years of age also suggested that there was no point where children were basing their hypotheses solely on generalizations from semantic concepts related to gender. Rather, "formal rule based generalizations were observed as early as 2.0," an age at which there is a "lack of cognitive clarity and cognitive salience of gender" (Levy 1983a, b, 91, 1997, 669).

11.1.4   Classifiers[20]

Classifiers form yet another domain of cross-language variation that challenges the language learner. In many languages, including various Asian languages and sign languages, classifiers denote a semantic feature of nouns. Chinese has roughly 150 classifiers, e.g., (16), differentiated by semantic features; Korean around 290; Thai about forty frequently used and twenty less so (Cheng and Sybesma 1998). Classifier systems vary across languages: they may involve basic semantic features such as animacy, humanness, or cultural attributes (e.g., distinguishing "man made" from other objects), or honorific or religious properties.

16.   a. san ge ren
           three CL people
           (three persons)
        b. san zhi bi
           three CL pens
           (three pens)
        c. san ben shu
           three CL book
           (three books)

Although the classifiers represent a closed class of items, and thus may be considered "functional categories," their acquisition requires a complex mapping of semantic features and categories to a special lexicon; and this lexicon must be integrated with syntax, e.g., word order of the determiner phrase and phrase structure in each language. In Chinese, the classifier appears after a quantifier

---

[20] For studies of acquisition of classifiers in Japanese, see Yamamoto and Keil 2000, Matsumoto 1985, 1987; for Chinese, Erbaugh 1986, Chien, Chiang and Lust 2003; for Thai, Carpenter 1991; for Korean, Lee 1997.

and before the noun (*Det-quantifier-classifier-noun*) in a noun phrase, e.g., (16), while in Thai, the usual word order is *Noun-quantifier-classifier*, e.g., (17).

17.   Thai (Carpenter 1991, 94)
        phu: jin   s :n **khon** phu: chaj **khon** diaw
        people female two   CL   people male CL   single
        (Two girls and just one boy)

Do children first attempt to extract semantic generalizations suggested by the classifiers? Do they learn item by item, fastening on to specific exemplars of the classifiers? If so, are these determined, at least initially, by mere frequency or perceptual saliency of use?

In all Asian languages which have been studied, evidence suggests that children appear to determine syntactic position, correct word order and syntactic structure of the classifiers very early. A generalized classifier appears to hold the phrase structure position of the functional category head of the phrase syntactically for children. Children appear to acquire the syntactic aspects of classifiers very early, while mapping between the formal syntactic structure to semantics and pragmatics takes time; "the role of meaning increases rather than decreases" (Carpenter 111, 1991).

There is developmental delay in acquisition of classifiers. Full acquisition of a classifier system for a language proceeds slowly, persisting into the elementary school years. Numerous semantic mistakes include overextensions[21] and under-extensions.[22] Frequency alone does not determine the course of acquisition. For example, young Thai children (about age 2yrs. 11mos.) rarely use the classifier for elephant (in a ceremonial function) /chyag/, despite its frequent modeling in school, but rather use /tua/, a classifier used by adults more consistently with snake, and they use /chyag/ with other nouns which are long, thin and flexible (see Carpenter 1991, 107 for discussion).

Children's early language production does not start with selection of a specific classifier with salient semantic–perceptual features, but with a more general classifier, as in Chinese, Thai or Japanese, e.g., (18). This generalized classifier, correctly positioned syntactically, is used even in conditions where it would be ungrammatical for an adult (Carpenter 1991, 104). Comprehension tests of eighty children acquiring Chinese confirmed that classifiers applying to restricted items are not acquired first (Chien, Lust and Chiang 2003).

18.   a. **Chinese** (Erbaugh 1986, 415)
           *peng, dao le yi <u>ge</u> kaishui
           (bumped into a boiling water)
        b. **Thai** (Carpenter 1991)
           One three-year-old used "tua" to "classify all twenty-one nouns he was tested on, resulting in correct classifications for elephant, snake and shirt,

---

[21] E.g., Hu 1993, Sanches 1977, Carpenter 1991.   [22] Loke 1991. See our chapter 10.

but incorrect classifications of airplane, banana and balloon, among others" (103).

c. **Japanese** (Matsumoto 1985, 1987)

"[T]he child studied used 'tsu' instead of the correct classifier ri/-nin' for babies, suggesting that the contrast of tsu and ri/-nin had not yet been acquired" (240).

When Japanese children begin to categorize the classifiers semantically, they do so in terms of more abstract categories first, e.g., +/− animal (Yamamoto and Keil 2000). Development proceeds by differentiation from a more abstract category to finer distinctions. Development in Thai coheres (Carpenter 1991).

The acquisition of classifiers is led by grammatical analyses, and not solely by general cognitive concepts related to meaning alone.

11.1.5   Summary

Across areas of language knowledge which require inductive learning – identification of grammatical categories, grammatical case, grammatical gender and classifier systems, all of which involve significant cross-language variation and certain arbitrariness in mapping to individual language grammars and lexicons – children do show developmental delay. In each of these areas, however, the growth of language knowledge over time appears led by formal grammatical analyses. Integration with semantic concepts related to word meaning takes time. It is a result of, rather than a sole cause of, development.

11.2   Mechanisms of growth

11.2.1   Do the mechanisms of language acquisition change?

It is commonly accepted that language acquisition may occur in three stages, dependent on qualitative differences in the mechanisms which apply at each stage; e.g., (19).[23]

19.   1. Learn examples by rote
       2. Extract rules and begin to generalize
       3. Constrain these rules

Evidence which appears to support this proposal includes the observation of Leopold Hildegarde, whose initial pronunciation of "pretty" appeared to be correct, /prIti/; an "incorrect" form, "bidi," appeared later, followed still later by the correct form again, /prIti/ (cf. chapter 8). In acquisition of morphology, it is often held that children first use irregular verbs correctly ("swam"), then overgeneralize ("swimmed") before finally using the correct form ("swam"). Some attempts to

---

[23] See Kiparsky and Menn 1977 on the acquisition of phonology.

mathematically model specific aspects of language acquisition, e.g., verb inflection, assume that such a "U-shaped developmental curve" generally characterizes child language acquisition.[24]

We now know that the "U-shaped developmental curve" does not accurately describe discrete or age-based stages of child development.[25] Systematic study of children's acquisition of English verb inflection and the overregularization phenomenon has now been conducted, challenging this (Marcus et al. 1992). In natural speech samples of eighty-three children acquiring English, all verbs from every available speech sample over the first five years were measured, and amount of overregularization was calculated.[26] Results showed that: (a) amount of overregularization of irregular verbs differed significantly across children (ranging from 0–24 percent); (b) often, children produced both overregularized and non-overregularized forms of the same verb in the same speech sample; (c) individual verbs differed: while some verbs showed initial overregularization followed by correct forms, followed again by overregularization (e.g., the verb "eat" for Abe); others were always overregularized at early periods for certain children (e.g., the verbs "draw" and "win"); others remained correct with rare overregularization (e.g. "say" for Abe) (Marcus et al. 1992, 38–39, figures 3–6).

Following these results, a model posing that at a particular developmental period a child's mechanisms for acquisition are generally limited to an initial rote form is not supported.[27] A capacity for generalization and rule formation is always present in children.

11.2.2   Eliminating false hypotheses

When children make "errors," they appear to be holding false hypotheses about how language works. How and why do children eliminate such false hypotheses? Even if children are not wildly productive of such errors, and even if such errors are limited in type, we must explain how they come to be abandoned.[28] If "swimmed" seems right to children at one time, then how and why do they change this hypothesis? As we saw in chapter 6, direct negative evidence in general does not exist, and when attempted, is frequently rebuffed by children.[29]

---

[24] Rumelhart and McClelland 1986.

[25] Cf. chapter 7 for definition of developmental "stage." Although a U-shaped developmental curve may serve as a descriptive device for certain forms of data, it does not directly describe a child learner as an organism.

[26] Marcus et al. 1992 measured "overregularization rate" in terms of number of overregularization tokens over number of overregularization tokens plus number of correct irregular past tokens (29).

[27] See Marcus et al. 1992 for discussion; Pinker 1999.

[28] When systematic studies of children's natural speech are conducted, the amount of such overregularization has been found to be much less productive than originally thought, showing "consistently low rate of overregularization across children, ages, and commonly used verbs" (Marcus et al. 1992, 59). For a set of twenty-five children, the mean rate of overregularization was only .042. In another study, Marcus reports 8.5 percent overregularization of nouns in a set of English children's natural speech (e.g., *foots, mans*) (Marcus, 1995; see Marchman et al. 1997 for discussion).

[29] It has been shown that the nature of the adult input to children does not explain children's overregularization errors (Marcus et al. 1992).

There is no simple way that we can look to "input" to directly explain children's retreat from overgeneralization. Several models look *within* the child.

11.2.2.1   A separate learnability module?

One approach has postulated a separate "learnability module" with separate inductive learning principles, e.g., a "subset principle" (or SP), to supplement the Language Faculty and constrain the order of children's hypotheses. Working only with positive evidence, it would prevent overgeneralization by determining that children's first hypothesis would generalize only from a "subset" of the data, which would be "unmarked" and acquired first; a marked hypothesis would be adopted only on the basis of additional positive data – a superset (Berwick 1985; also see chapter 4, p. 61).

Application of the SP to natural language acquisition has been challenged on theoretical grounds. At the same time, several empirical tests of predictions made by the hypothesis of an SP have now been conducted in various areas of language acquisition. Results generally disconfirm it.[30]

Languages which do not allow null subjects (i.e., −Pro Drop) allow a smaller set of sentences (those without null subjects) than languages which do (+Pro Drop), and thus may be viewed as forming a subset. Languages like Spanish that allow sentences with null subjects also allow those without them. If the SP constrained children's hypotheses, their initial hypothesis would be that languages are "−Pro Drop" until additional positive evidence provided information to the contrary. Children would not make errors (allowing null subjects) which would need correction subsequently in a non-Pro-Drop language. As we saw in chapter 9, however, children's initial hypotheses across languages appear to allow null subjects. In addition, evidence reviewed in chapter 9 suggested that children set either plus (+) or minus (−) Pro-Drop settings for language very early.[31]

The SP has also been tested with regard to children's hypotheses regarding anaphora across languages (chapter 9). In English, reflexives do not normally occur in binding relations beyond the clause, e.g., (20), while in many languages, e.g., Japanese (21), Chinese and many South Asian languages, a reflexive can occur with such "long distance" relations. This cross-linguistic variation can be viewed as composing a subset relation.[32] If the SP applied, children should initially hypothesize only the English type "local" forms of anaphoric binding and not allow long-distance binding.

20.   a. *Father$_i$ grilled the fish when himself$_j$ opened the window
       b. Father$_i$ saw himself$_j$ in the mirror

---

[30] Test of SP predictions is not straightforward. The data to which children refer must be arranged in a subset relation, e.g., there must be parameters with marked and unmarked values, where each value corresponds to languages whose sentence sets can be arranged in a subset relation. It is not clear how children could compute such subset relations (Joshi 1994, Kapur 1994 for discussion).

[31] Issues also arose as to how children could shift hypotheses from subset to superset (cf. chapter 9).

[32] Jakubowicz 1984, Berwick 1985, Manzini and Wexler 1987.

21.   Papa-ga$_i$ sakana-o yaku toki zibun-ga$_i$ mado-o aketa
            Father-NOM fish-ACC grill when self-NOM window-ACC opened
            (When Papa grilled fish, he (himself) opened the window)

However, Japanese children treat the reflexive in a manner which differs qualitatively from English, converting the reflexive to an emphatic adjunct, e.g., (22),
consistent with the adult grammar (Mazuka and Lust 1994). Children thus appear
to consult the grammar of the language rather than the size of the sentence sets
in those languages, when forming early hypotheses in language acquisition.

22.   Papa-ga sakano-o yaku toki **Ø zibun-de** mado-o aketa (ML #19,163)
                            [Ø self-by]
            (When Papa grilled fish, he opened the window by himself)

Similarly, in Chinese, the antecedent for a reflexive pronoun must be the subject in
a sentence like (23), and cannot include the object (the "Subject Orientation Property" of "the Chinese Reflexive Ziji"). In (23), "self's picture" refers to Howhow's
picture, and cannot refer to Garfield's picture. This differs from English, e.g., (24),
where the antecedent may be either the subject or the object: either Howhow's
or Garfield's picture could be referred to. Chinese appears to provide a subset
of the possibilities allowed in English. The SP predicts that the Chinese child,
like the English child, would begin by choosing only subjects as antecedents
for the reflexive pronoun. Subsequently, children would, on the basis of positive
evidence, move to the option for object antecedents as well (Chien, Wexler and
Chiang 1995).

23.   Howhow$_i$ gei Jiafeimao/i yi-zhang ziji-de$_{i,*j}$ zhaopian (=CWC 1,75)
            Howhow give Garfield one-CL self's picture
            (Howhow gave Garfield a picture of self)

24.   Howhow$_i$ gave Garfield$_j$ a picture of himself$_{i,j}$

Experimental tests of Chinese-speaking children's (three to eight years) interpretation of sentences like (23) found that (unlike Chinese-speaking adults), children
accepted both subject and object antecedents. It was adults who demonstrated the
more restricted hypothesis (the subset), not children (Chien and Li 1998; Chien
and Lust forthcoming).[33]

Such evidence suggests that a "subset principle" does not guide or constrain
natural language acquisition in the child. Constraints on induction which are
defined in terms of subsets of input data do not accurately describe or explain the
course of language development.

---

[33] In another, perhaps the most developed form of a proposal for a subset principle in language
acquisition, pronouns and anaphors (reflexives) were hypothesized to have opposite markedness
values because of the size of the sets in which they occur. This prediction was also challenged
(Manzini and Wexler 1987, Kapur et al. 1993; Lust et al. 1989; Wexler 1993; Fodor 1994; Chien
and Li 1998).

11.2.2.2   Blocking and retrieval

In another attempt to explain how the child overcomes overgeneralizations, Marcus et al. (1992) propose that children's overregularizations of verb forms may be eliminated by a cognitive mechanism summarized in (25). This proposal derives from a theory that regular and irregular verb forms have distinct forms of cognitive representation in the brain. While regular forms reflect "rules," irregular forms reflect associative learning and rote memory (Pinker's "Hybrid Theory," 1991). This reflects an attempt to formulate precisely a psychological mechanism of computation integrating both positive and negative evidence.

---

25. BLOCKING PLUS RETRIEVAL FAILURE: "As children's experience of irregular verb forms increases, the efficient retrieval of these forms from memory increases. Efficient retrieval of irregular verb forms blocks the regular form. The generation of forms by rule persists for all verbs until the time when blocking occurs." (Marcus et al. 1992)

While (25) remains possible, it remains to be seen how this mechanism (a) can deal with cross-linguistic acquisition where regular and irregular verbs are not neatly categorized; (b) can be generalized to more general aspects of language acquisition; and (c) how a "blocking" function can work – e.g., how can children allow synonyms and still apply a blocking principle?

11.2.2.3   Indirect negative evidence

In another approach to limiting false hypotheses in the child during language acquisition, it has been hypothesized that the Language Faculty may allow children to consult *indirect* negative evidence in the creation of a language-specific grammar. This would work in those areas in which UG does not directly provide a language-specific constraint or principle. As we have seen, UG does not directly provide specific morphological case markings, particular classifier systems or verb inflection paradigms, even though it may provide general abstract principles regarding these in any natural language. When such forms are creatively generated or overgenerated by children and then overcome, it must sometimes be because children have recognized their nonexistence. When children acquiring English eliminate "dived," leaving only "dove," indirect negative evidence can contribute to this elimination: "dived" does not occur in their dialect.[34]

UG must not prevent this overgeneralization. "Dived" does occur in some English dialects and did occur in Old English. Similarly, we have seen that children at early periods overgeneralize their interpretation of reflexives to pronouns in certain local domains (chapter 9). While in modern English, a sentence with a pronoun like "The father likes him" is normally not possible with a meaning like "The father likes himself," in Old English, pronouns normally could and did

---

[34] This computation may work even without "blocking" (cf. 11.2.2.3).

occur with such readings; as they do in several South Asian languages. Children today must observe not only that "The father likes himself" does occur with this interpretation, but that "The father likes him" does not.

There has been little empirical study of mechanisms of computation of indirect negative evidence, and its success depends on strong leading hypotheses (cf. chapter 4).[35]

11.2.3   Summary

Children's grammatical analyses continually lead the growth of their language. A separate inductive "learnability module" does not appear to be motivated. Researchers now look within children to discover computational mechanisms of growth, attempting to account both for children's creative generalizations and their retreat from overgeneralizations. Both indirect positive and indirect negative evidence are implicated in this computation.

11.3   Syntactic bootstrapping

If children's grammatical analyses lead their language acquisition, then we may expect to find examples of "linguistic bootstrapping," i.e., where one dimension of language knowledge "bootstraps" another. For example, it is hypothesized that children may "use their syntactic knowledge of categories and distributional regularities to learn how to express their concepts in language. Syntax might help in the acquisition of semantics" (Valian 1991, 572). This speculation is consistent with a Syntactic Bootstrapping Hypothesis:

> **SYNTACTIC BOOTSTRAPPING HYPOTHESIS:** "[L]earners perform a sentence–world pairing rather than a word–world pairing, taking advantage of the clues to interpretation that reside in the structure of the sentence heard" (Gleitman and Gleitman 1994, 294; see also Gleitman 1990; Naigles, Gleitman and Gleitman 1993).

As we saw in "Jabberwocky" (chapter 9), the syntax of sentences can assist in determining meaning. Although sentence syntax does not provide the full meaning of words, it can "narrow the search space for the correct mapping between the word and the world"; "the structure of the sentence that the child hears can function like a mental zoom lens that cues the aspect of the scene the speaker is describing" (Gleitman 1994, 294). If a verb occurs in a syntactic context like (26a), we may

---

[35] This paradigm also makes predictions regarding the course of development and the ordering of hypotheses. The experience necessary for computing indirect negative evidence would take time. This paradigm predicts that developmental delays in acquisition will be found where indirect negative evidence is necessary. Lust, Mazuka, Martohardjono and Yoon 1989 develop an initial proposal.

Fig. 11.1 *"Sibbing" example.*
From: Gleitman and L. Gleitman 1991. *Psychology* (W. W. Norton & Co.)
(Figure is on p. 371; based on original paper by Roger Brown, 1957. "Linguistic
determinism and the part of speech." *Journal of Abnormal and Social
Psychology* **55**:1–5.)

expect that it has a different possible set of meanings than if it occurs in a context
like (26b). In (26b), one can "biff" someone/something else (a transitive action),
whereas in (26a), the action can be a solo type with a single subject argument (an
intransitive action); just so for the word "bark" in (27a) and the word "bite" in
(27b).

26.   a. The dog was biffing (*intranstive*)
         b. The dog was biffing the cat (*transitive*)

27.   a. The dog was barking (*intransitive*)
         b. The dog was biting the cat (*transitive*)

A series of studies provide empirical evidence in support of a syntactic bootstrapping hypothesis. In an early seminal study, Brown (1957) presented three-
to five-year-olds with situations like that shown in figure 11.1.

When asked to find "*sibbing*," the children pointed to the hands; when asked to
find "*a sib*," they pointed to the bowl; when asked to find "*any sib*," they pointed

to the confetti contents of the bowl. The children used the syntactic frames in which "sib" appeared to determine word classes as well as word meaning and reference.

Later researchers named dolls with syntactic expressions, like "Look what I've brought you. This is **a zav**" or "This is **zav**." When asked to perform actions on "a zav" or "zav," children (aged seventeen to twenty-four months) differentiated their reference. They more often chose the particular doll seen initially when the introductory expression had the form of a proper noun, without the determiner "a" (Katz, Baker and Macnamara 1974). A further study replicated this result with stronger experimental controls, concluding that "linguistic form class is a powerful source of information for children acquiring new words" (Gelman and Taylor 1984, 1539).

Recently, using a "Preferential Looking" task (figure 7.3), researchers taught young children (mean age 2.1) a new verb, "gorping," in varied syntactic contexts to test the role of these contexts in children's determination of word meaning. Children were presented with video portrayals of complex actions such as shown in figure 11.2, and the new verb was introduced: "Look! The duck is gorping the bunny" (frames 5 and 6). Other children were shown the same video, with the new verb presented in an intransitive syntactic context: "Look! The duck and the bunny are gorping." The video action allows the verb to have either a transitive (duck acting on the bunny, pushing it down) or an intransitive meaning (both duck and bunny are circling their arms in the air). If the children use the syntactic context in which the new verb appears to begin to create a meaning for the verb, then they should look at one part of the action or the other when asked "Where's gorping now?" (frames 9 and 10). Infants looked significantly longer at the video that matched the syntax of the sentence which had introduced the new word. "Those who heard the transitive sentence apparently concluded that *gorp* means 'force to squat.' Those who heard the intransitive sentence decided that *gorp* means 'wheel the arms'" (Gleitman 1990, 43).[36]

If syntactic bootstrapping provides an essential growth mechanism, we can explain how the blind child so quickly learns the meanings of words like "look" and "see" even in the absence of direct perception of visual context (chapter 3, Landau and Gleitman 1985). We can begin to explain how children acquire verbs like "know" and "think" that can not be derived from observation. Children can learn from a relatively small data base, i.e., a limited number of sentence frames, consistent with "fast mapping" in early word learning (chapter 10). Children and adults would share similar word-learning mechanisms.

Further research must test the extent and nature of syntactic bootstrapping, and determine its prerequisites.[37] Further research is required on the interaction of children's semantic concepts with their syntactic bootstrapping (e.g., Marantz

---

[36] See Naigles and Kako 1993 for further research in this paradigm.

[37] Is it necessary for children to have a prior knowledge of nouns or selected functional categories?

Video 1	Audio	Video 2

5

Look! The duck is gorping the bunny!

Black

6 Black

Look! the duck is gorping the bunny!

7

Look! the duck is gorping the bunny!

8

Oh! They're different now!

9

Where's gorping now?

10

Find gorping!

Fig. 11.2 *"Gorping" example*
From: Naigles (1990). "Children use syntax to learn verb meanings." *Journal of Child Language* **17**: 357–374.

1982; Fisher et al. 1994). Research must also be directed towards the role of indirect negative evidence which the paradigm requires.[38] Cross-linguistic studies must inquire into which formal syntactic analyses are available universally to early word learning and which are language specific. Typological studies of what syntax–semantic correlations may be universal in natural language will be critical.

---

[38] In the Naigles experiment (1990), if "biffing" appeared in *both* transitive and intransitive syntactic frames (as occurs with a verb like "eat" in English and with most verbs in Chinese), the syntax then would not appear to provide an initial distinctive categorization of verb meaning type. Only if "biffing" appears in one context and *not* the other, and children know this, can it do so. See also figure 11.2.

11.4   Conclusions

Children are conducting formal analyses of language data from the start and throughout periods of developing productive language acquisition. Rather than non-formal factors grounding the development of formal computational knowledge of language, and children transforming from tadpole to frog as they acquire their language, their competence for formal computation appears to underlie the acquisition and development of language from the beginning.

There is no evidence for any general age-based change in this formal approach, e.g., U-shaped course of development, wherein children's earliest approaches to language data are not formal and analytic. According with evidence in chapter 3, there is no period of non-linguistic "bootstrapping" during which children are forced to work without formal analyses of the language data surrounding them, e.g., to depend solely on general cognitive concepts. There is no evidence for a non-linguistic external "learning module" which determines extrinsically how children use evidence. "Linguistic bootstrapping" is evident, e.g., syntactic bootstrapping. Here the fundamental components of the architecture for language knowledge are mutually supportive.

11.5   Supplementary readings

There have been relatively few studies which pursue the exact form of the psychological computation involved in developmental change in children's syntactic knowledge. See Randall's "catapult theory," 1990, 1992; Bowerman 1987 on "mechanisms of change," Brown and Hanlon 1970 on "Cumulative Complexity". Clark 1994 seeks to formulate principles of language change and language acquisition where parameter setting is involved. See also works on "language learnability": formal analyses in Wexler and Culicover 1980, studies in collections of Lust, Suñer and Whitman and Lust, Hermon and Kornfilt 1994 and Legendre and Smolensky forthcoming for approaches within an Optimality Theory framework; Kapur 1994, Kapur and Bilardi 1992a, b, Lasnik 1990 for study of the role of indirect negative evidence.

12 Conclusions: toward integrated theory of language acquisition

Are you having trouble
in saying this stuff?
It's really quite easy for me.
I just look in my mirror
and see what I say,
and then I just say what I see.   (Seuss, 1979)

12.1   Introduction

Our review of research in the basic areas of language acquisition has led us to several conclusions regarding our fundamental question: *how does a child acquire language?*

They lead us to overturn several common myths about language acquisition. While they do not directly provide us with a full theory of language acquisition, they allow us to lay the foundations for a future theory, one which can link both linguistic and developmental approaches. In this chapter, we will first summarize fundamental generalizations that emerge from the research we have reviewed; next, we will identify remaining open questions and sketch a framework which we consider promising for future research.

12.2   Conclusions

(A)   We have seen that the course of language acquisition begins at birth, if not before, and proceeds continuously through the first few years of life. There is no "prelinguistic" stage. Although language acquisition is commonly thought to begin with children's first produced words, we have seen that the first words are the culmination of previous, complex language development. Contrary to a common assumption, words are not the "building blocks" of language acquisition, but develop in parallel to acquisition of the formal system of language, and in part as a result of this.

(B)   Language acquisition proceeds in parallel across all the fundamental levels of representation necessary to knowledge of language:

phonology, syntax and semantics. There is no stage when any level of representation is absent. For example, there is no evidence for a stage during which only "words" are available to children. At the same time that children are extracting words from the speech stream, or even before, they are performing formal analyses on the speech stream around them with regard to every level of representation necessary for language knowledge.

(C)   Across all dimensions of language knowledge, children appear to be accessing and developing formal representations even before they have access to meanings of these forms.

(D)   Across all dimensions of language knowledge, children are continually applying linguistic principles and constraints. Developmental change moves from more universal to more language-specific patterns.

(E)   In every area of language knowledge – syntax, semantics or phonology – children's relation to input data is highly indirect (chapter 6). Language acquisition – and the child's use of input data – is continuously guided by the child's linguistic computation in every area of language knowledge.

12.3   Toward a theory of language acquisition

The facts in 12.2 lead us to conclude that a basic Language Faculty is at work initially and continuously through language acquisition, providing the basic architecture, principles and parameters required for the creation of a language. They lead us to pursue a comprehensive theory of language acquisition that considers both precise theories of linguistic competence and precise descriptions and theories of developmental change. They suggest a theory of language acquisition which reverses commonly held views, e.g., that infants begin with semantically or contextually determined "meanings" and must bootstrap from these to become linguistic individuals.

12.3.1   Linguistic bootstrapping

The developing dimensions of language knowledge seem to support rather than precede one another. For example, developing phonetic and prosodic knowledge assists in the discovery of words (Jusczyk 1999; Jusczyk, Houston and Newsome 1999) as well as in the discrimination and categorization of languages (Ramus et al. 1999). The development of words feeds back on the development of the realization of phonemic contrasts and phonotactic contrasts (e.g., Brent, Gafos and Cartwright 1994). Sentence units appear to aid phonological acquisition (see chapter 9; Mandel, Jusczyk and Kemler Nelson 1994; Jusczyk 1997, 153). Syntactic structure appears to aid the development of semantics, e.g., word meaning, and vice versa (Gleitman 1994; see chapters 3 and 11). This suggests that infants are continuously integrating different forms of linguistic knowledge (see Jusczyk 1997, 157 for speculation on how this relation may work).

12.3.2 Strong continuity of the Language Faculty

Children continuously demonstrate formal analyses of the input. For example, in the acquisition of phonology, we saw evidence of infants' fine discrimination and categorization of universally available phonetic and intonational distinctions from the earliest periods we could measure, soon after birth. This developed over the first twelve months in a manner which demonstrated continuous mapping by children to the specific language phonology being acquired. In the earliest periods of acquisition of syntax, we found infants discriminating and categorizing syntactic units as well, beginning with the most universal and fundamental unit of syntax, the clause, and proceeding to phrasal units by nine months. In each of the areas we reviewed, children first evidenced the influence of a specific language grammar (SLG), as well as guidance by Universal Grammar, within the first twelve months of life.

If children were solely dependent on non-formal, non-linguistic analyses of the language surrounding them, it is not clear how we could account for these facts. It is difficult, if not impossible, to see how children at these early periods could be building on non-linguistic forms of meaning in order to acquire aspects of the formal system of language knowledge. Even infants' segmentation of words from the speech stream is to a degree accomplished independently of word meaning. Integration of the formal word unit with word meaning was found to be a long, complex process (chapter 10). Although children are clearly using acoustic properties of the speech stream in mapping to linguistic units, we must account for why they are making use of these properties in just the right way for linguistic creation, and how they are so successfully reducing the hypothesis space. A Strong Continuity Hypothesis of the Language Faculty is confirmed by the finding that there was no testable time when children were not "structure dependent" in their early hypotheses about language.

If the formal architecture which defines the Language Faculty were in place in the Initial State (figure 2.1) and throughout the course of language acquisition, it would provide children with a coherent and continuous formal structure for building the grammar of their specific language. This appears to be the case.

12.3.3 Reviewing Universal Grammar

These results lead us to better comprehend the theory of Universal Grammar as a model of the Language Faculty and of the Initial State. UG articulates the essential architecture, the epistemological primitives necessary to each level of linguistic representation, and the linguistically specific computational system for combining multiple levels of representation. In this sense, we view

Universal Grammar as a "theory of innate mechanisms, an underlying biological matrix that provides a framework within which the growth of language proceeds" (Chomsky, 1980, 187).)

12.3.4   The growth of language

The results we have reviewed lead us to qualify existing views of language development. Lenneberg held that children "are endowed with an innate propensity for a type of behavior that develops automatically into language" (Lenneberg 1964, 589). If "automatic" here refers to children's nearly indomitable drive to create language, then this statement is verified. However, in a more specific sense, language acquisition is not automatic, but rather the result of several years of complex formal computation in which children are gradually mapping from a biologically programmed Language Faculty to the specific language grammar (SLG) of the language to be acquired. Children are discovering the language of their world by creating it, or more specifically, by creating its grammar, on the basis of the input they receive.

Innateness and learning are not contradictory, but complementary in language acquisition. This is consistent with an acquisition model which involves an "instinct to learn" (e.g., the Gould and Marler paradigm in chapter 4; Jusczyk 1997; Jusczyk and Bertoncini 1988 for discussion).)

12.4   The open questions

12.4.1   The mystery remains

If the basic architecture of the Language Faculty is in place continuously, then what exactly is the nature of the change in children's language acquisition and what causes the change?

- What are the precise mechanisms of linguistic computation and its interaction with input data?
- If direct positive and negative evidence does not neatly determine children's use of input (chapter 6), then how does indirect negative evidence work?
- What are the precise mechanisms of grammatical mapping?

In every area we reviewed – phonology, syntax and semantics – we evaluated the development both of children's *perception* and *production* of language in order to derive evidence about their *knowledge* of language. In each area, perception and production were seen to develop in parallel, often closely synchronized.[1] We can assume that development in knowledge underlies this common development.

---

[1] Although development of language perception and language production are not specifically identical (chapter 7), these demonstrated general and remarkable commonality in developmental changes.

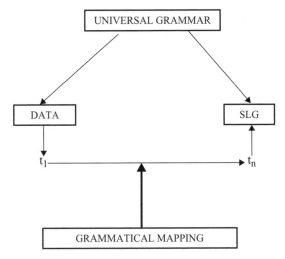

Fig. 12.1 *The grammatical mapping paradigm*

Fundamental computational mechanisms of development may be linked to the integration of perception and production yet to be discovered.[2]

Discovery of fundamental developmental mechanisms will depend upon findings regarding the true nature of Universal Grammar. Given that there is evidence for the Language Faculty over the course of development, it will be essential to dissociate what knowledge the Language Faculty provides and what aspects of grammatical knowledge develop over time. This cannot be accomplished without precise specification of the content of UG as a model of the Language Faculty. By working together both linguists and developmental psychologists can advance this quest.

12.4.2   A suggested framework

A framework we consider useful for guiding future research involves what we have referred to as "grammatical mapping" (chapter 4), e.g., figures 12.1 and 12.2. In this paradigm, children use UG to confront the data of the speech stream around them and to create developmentally the Specific Language Grammar (SLG) of their language.

12.5   Toward the future

12.5.1   Cross-linguistic data

As the reader must have noticed, there remains a dearth of cross-linguistic data in the field of language acquisition. Factoring out the content of

---

[2] If so, Dr. Seuss's "Oh Say Can You Say" is prescient.

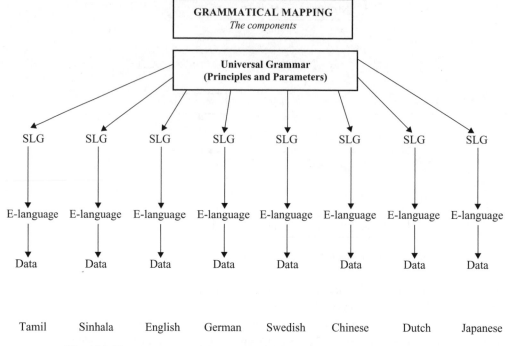

Fig. 12.2 *The components of the grammatical mapping paradigm*

UG from the content of Specific Language Grammar, and factoring out what is biologically programmed from what is learned, requires expansion of the cross-linguistic data base, especially if cross-linguistic data is collected in a theoretically guided form and uses scientific methods allowing calibration of comparable data across languages.

12.5.2   Pragmatics

The persistent mystery of language acquisition becomes even more compelling when we realize that the acquisition of language, assuming all its formal computational properties, must be integrated with the acquisition of pragmatics, a topic we have not directly addressed here. Unless children can embed the knowledge of language in a social system of shared and exchanged knowledge and reference, they cannot be said to have "acquired language." This area, one that involves its own cross-linguistic variation, may be the most difficult aspect of language knowledge for children to master (e.g., Paradis 2003). If pragmatic principles, such as "Principles of Relevance," are themselves deemed to be innate, then further research must link these principles to the Language Faculty.[3]

---

[3] Sperber and Wilson 1995; Smith 1982; Foster-Cohen 2000, 1994; Kempson 1988.

12.5.3   Multilingualism

The mystery of language acquisition deepens when we realize that humans are capable of acquiring more than one language at once.[4] Simultaneous acquisition of more than one language, even languages which differ in basic parameters, can be achieved by the infant in about the same time as the acquisition of one language alone.[5] Questions regarding how the child sorts and stores the input data to which they are exposed become more gripping when one realizes that children can and do do so for more than one language at a time. Profound issues persist regarding the role of the Language Faculty in language acquisition later in life (e.g., Epstein et al. 1996 and related commentary; Flynn and Martohardjono 1994).

The early and continuous language acquisition we have seen in infants raises the question of how this early experience may be effective if a young child suddenly changes language environment, perhaps during or after the first three years of life. Recent research suggests that early language experience does indeed have effects on later acquisition of a new or recalled language.[6]

12.5.4   Brain imaging

As we saw in chapter 5, recent advances in brain imaging technologies provide us with new promise for understanding links between the biological foundations of language knowledge and language acquisition. However, only through interdisciplinary collaborations – integrating strong theory, both linguistic and psycholinguistic, and scientifically sound behavioral evidence – can we now pursue this promise.

While we have now advanced our understanding of the fundamental nature of language acquisition through decades of research, and while we can now look forward to the future for further advances, it is still only the child who possesses the answer to its fundamental mystery.

---

[4] For further readings in the area of bilingualism/multilingualism see: Bialystok and Hakuta 1994; Nicol 2001; Bhatia and Ritchie 1996, 2004.
[5] E.g., Petitto et al. 2001; Genesee 2002; Lakshmanan 1995.
[6] Au et al. 2002; Sebastian-Galles and Soto Faraco 1999; Slobin et al. 1999.

Appendix 1   Developmental milestones in motor and language development (adapted from Lenneberg 1967, 128–130)

	MOTOR DEVELOPMENT	VOCALIZATION AND LANGUAGE
YEAR I		
0–6 months		
3 months	Supports head when prone	Less crying than at 8 weeks; smiles when talked to; *cooing*
4 months	Plays with rattle; head self-supported	Responds to human sounds more definitely
5 months	Sits with props	Cooing begins to be interspersed with more consonantal sounds; all vocalizations are very different from the sounds of the mature language of the environment
6–12 months		
6 months	Sitting; bends forward and uses hands for support; cannot yet stand without help; no thumb apposition	Cooing changing into babbling resembling monosyllabic utterances; neither vowels nor consonants have very fixed recurrences
8 months	Stands holding on; grasps with thumb apposition	Reduplication frequent; intonation patterns distinct; utterances can signal emphasis and emotions
10 months	Takes side steps, holding on; pulls to standing position	Vocalizations are mixed with sound-play such as gurgling or bubble-blowing; tries unsuccessfully to imitate sounds
12 months	Walks when held by hand; walks on feet and hands, knees in air; seats self on floor	Identical sound sequences replicated with higher relative frequency of occurrence and words are emerging; definite signs of understanding some words and simple commands
YEAR 2		
18–24 months		
18 months	Grasp, prehension, and release fully developed; gait stiff, propulsive, and precipitated; creeps downstairs backwards	Has a repertoire of three to fifty words; babbling now of several syllables with intricate intonation pattern; little ability to join any of the lexical items into spontaneous two-item phrases; understanding is progressing rapidly

24 months	Runs, but falls in sudden turns; can quickly alternate between sitting and stance; walks stairs up or down, one foot forward only	Vocabulary of more than fifty items; begins to join items into two-word phrases; all phrases appear to be own creations; increase in communicative behavior and interest in language
30 months	Jumps into air with both feet; stands on one foot for about two seconds; takes few steps on tiptoe; can move digits independently; manipulation of objects much improved	Fastest increase in vocabulary; no babbling; utterances have communicative intent; frustrated if not understood by adults; sentences and phrases have characteristic child grammar; intelligibility not very good; understands what is said
Year 3	Tiptoes well; runs smoothly with acceleration	Vocabulary of some 1,000 words; about 80 percent of utterances are intelligible even to strangers; grammatical complexity of utterances is roughly that of colloquial adult language
Beyond 3	Jumps over rope; hops on dominant foot; catches ball in arms; walks line	Language is well-established; deviations from adult norm tend to be more in style than in grammar

Note: We now know there are wide variations in precise ages at which a normal child reaches a "milestone." However, the sequence of milestones and their correlations remains Lenneberg's major point. Within a single child, there do not seem to be necessary causal links between motor development and language development (Bates et al. 1979; Menyuk 1995; Bloom 1993).

Appendix 2a Developmental milestones in infant speech perception

YEAR 1

0–2 months   Distinguishes maternal voice, speech and non-speech

Evidences Categorical Perception (Eimas et al. 1971; Jusczyk 1997, 1986; Aslin, Pisoni and Jusczyk 1983; Aslin, Jusczyk and Pisoni 1998)

Perceives wide set of sound distinctions corresponding to possible phonetic contrasts along many major dimensions of phonetic variation (appendix 2b)

Discriminates between different numbers of syllables (Bijeljac-Babic, Bertoncini and Mehler 1993/1992)

Discriminates canonical and non-canonical syllables (Moon et al. 1992)

Discriminates certain prosodic differences in stress and accent (Christophe et al. 1994)

2–3 months   Discriminates certain allophonic variations between sounds, e.g., the allophones of [t] and [r] in "night rate" vs. "nitrate" (Hohne and Jusczyk 1994)

Distinguishes bisyllables with initial stress from those with final stress, e.g., "**ba**da" from "ba**da**" (Jusczyk and Thompson 1978; Spring and Dale 1977; Jusczyk, Cutler and Redanz 1993)

Compensates for changes in speaking rates (Eimas and Miller 1980)

4 months   Prefers to listen to words over other sounds (Colombo and Bundy 1983)

"Duplex Perception" is evident (Eimas and Miller 1992)

5 months   Capable of linking auditory and articulatory information (Kuhl and Meltzoff 1982, 1984)

6–7 months   Pair of syllables recognized as unit when "supported by rhythmic familiarity" regardless of syllable ordering (Morgan and Saffran 1995)

When acquiring English, distinguishes English words compared to Norwegian words, but not compared to Dutch (Jusczyk, Friederici et al. 1993); infant appears to know some aspects of possible patterns of words in specific language

First evidence that early perception of sound distinctions is being narrowed to more closely reflect the Specific Language Grammar being acquired; certain distinctions weaken or disappear when not in the specific language being acquired (Werker and Lalonde 1988; Polka and Werker 1994)

"Magnet Effect": recognition of specific language "prototype" vowel sounds (Kuhl et al. 1992)

Word segmentation skills apparent: infant recognizes words in sentences which were heard in isolation (monosyllabic words like "dog" or bisyllabic words like "doctor") and recognizes words in isolation which were heard in sentences (Jusczyk and Aslin 1995)

Recognizes recurrence of a three-sound sequence of continuous synthesized speech (Saffran, Aslin and Newport 1996)

8 months   Recognizes words from stories read two weeks earlier (Jusczyk and Hohne 1997)

Recognizes phonotactic patterns of specific language, e.g., strong–weak patterns in English, and listens longer to these (Jusczyk, Cutler and Redanz 1993)

9 months   Distinguishes English from Dutch words (Jusczyk, Luce and Luce 1994)

Uses phonotactic information to segment speech into words (Mattys and Jusczyk 2001)

Prefers language-specific phonotactically well-formed strings (Friederici and Wessels 1993; Jusczyk et al. 1993; Jusczyk, Luce and Charles-Luce 1994)

Integration of segmental and suprasegmental information in recognition of units (Morgan and Saffran 1995)

Distinguishes passages with pauses between words from those with pauses within words (Myers et al. 1996)

Integrates multiple sources of information to locate word boundaries in fluent speech, phonotactic and prosodic (Aslin et al. 1998; Jusczyk 1997)

10–11 months Uses context-sensitive allophones in segmenting words (Jusczyk, Hohne and Bauman 1998)

Loses response to distinctions of some allophonic sound variations (Pegg 1995)

12 months   Retains discrimination of phonetic contrasts which are phonemic in the infant's native Specific Language Grammar; but has ceased to demonstrate discrimination of many, if not most, others (Werker 1994; Werker and Tees 1984a, b; Best 1994)

Onset of first words in production (appendix 3)

Year 2

14 months   Does not use phonetic detail in a task requiring the pairing of words and objects, suggesting "functional reorganization" (e.g., /bih/ vs. /dih/) (Stager and Werker 1997; Schvachkin, 1973; Garnica 1973)

Appendix 2b Examples of sound distinctions perceived by infants

Distinction	Examples	Sources
1. VOT (−V/+V)	pa/ba	Eimas et al. 1971
	Guatemalan infants acquiring Spanish show English type contrast, not Spanish	Lasky et al. 1975; Aslin and Pisoni 1975
	African Kikuyu infants 2 months old show (+/−V); (Kikuyu has no V/−V; only pre-V/V) Infants from English-speaking environments also distinguish −V vs. +V as well as pre-V	Streeter 1976 Aslin et al. 1981 Werker et al. 1981
	tha/dha (breathy voiced vs.voiceless aspirated dental stops e.g. Hindi)	Werker 1994
2. Place features	ba/ga bæ/dæ dæ/gæ	Moffitt 1971; Morse 1972; Eimas 1974; Bertoncini et al. 1987
	ma/na fa/θa va/ða	Eimas and Miller 1980; Holmberg et al. 1977; Levitt et al. 1988
	ta/t (Hindi dental vs. retroflex)	Werker 1994
	glottalized velar vs. uvular: /k'i/ vs. /q'i/ Salish/Nthlakampx /s/ vs. /ʃ/	Werker and Tees 1984 Kuhl 1980, Holmberg et al. 1977
3. Manner features	oral/nasal consonants ba/ma	Eimas and Miller 1980; Miller and Eimas 1983
	Stridency with the consonant /r/ (Czech); falling and rising intonation (ba+)(ba−)	Trehub 1976; Morse 1972
Liquids	/r/ and /l/ (2–3 month old American; 6–8 month old Japanese)	Eimas 1975 Tsushima et al. 1994

4. Vowels	/a/ vs. /i/, /i/ vs. /u/ /Y/ Vs. / ʊ / (lax high front rounded vs. lax high back rounded)	Kuhl and Hillenbrand 1979; Polka and Werker 1994; Trehub 1973; Swoboda et al. 1976
Oral/nasal vowel distinction (as in Polish, French)	/pa/ /pã/	Trehub 1976

Appendix 3 Developmental milestones in infant speech production

YEAR I

   0–1.5 months   Reflexive and vegetative sounds (Stark, Rose and McLagen 1974)

— cry

— vegetative sounds (coughing, burping, swallowing, glottal catches, grunts, sighs)

— discomfort sounds (fussing)

Vocal tract not developed; high larynx. Primitive reflexes: e.g., tongue in apposition with soft palate. Child unable to control tongue, lips, jaw muscles.

"Vocal contagion" (Piaget 1962/1945)

   1.5–3 months   "Cooing" and laughter

Maturation of vocal tract

Comfort sounds: produced in pleasurable interaction

"The new combination of the features of voicing, egressive breath direction and consonant like results from the overlap of a period of acquisition of control over the larynx with the reflexive activity of the vocal tract which has not yet been suppressed" (Stark et al. 1978)

Beginning babbling periods: vocalization containing "articulated and identifiable sounds and syllables"

   4 months   Vocal play

   5 months   Expansion, exploratory mapping of sounds

Playful use of behaviors like squealing, yelling, nasal murmurs

Terminates in "marginal babbling": consonantal and vocalic elements are combined in novel ways; consonantal and vocalic elements both occur, but may not resemble syllables of adult speech in their durational aspects or other articulatory features

Produce sounds after short-term exposure (Kuhl and Meltzoff 1996); elaborate reproductions possible (Uzgiris 1993; de Boysson-Bardies 1999)

6–12 months

   6–10 months   Canonical babbling, including Reduplicated babbling. Canonical syllables found for first time. Two or more syllables with two or more articulatory movements combined (Koopmans-van Beinum and Van der Stelt 1998); adult-like timing develops (Vihman 1996)

	Properties of babbling distinguishable in terms of infant's language vs. other language (e.g., French first vs. Arabic) by phoneticians, at 6 months (de Boysson-Bardies et al. 1984)
10–14 months	Variegated babbling: variation in C and V within a series; V, VC, and CVC syllables in addition to CV
	Greater variety of intonation and stress pattern
	Babbling shows evidence of specific properties of infant's language which are continuous with first words and detectable by untrained adults (e.g., de Boysson-Bardies, Vihman and Vihman, 1991, Oller et al. 1976; Vihman et al. 1985)
	Some evidence of sound-meaning correspondences in babbling (Blake and Fink 1987; Blake and de Boysson-Bardies 1992)
	Onset of first words

Year 2 +

	Multisyllabic vocabulary may be pronounced as one or two syllables, reduced in length (Johnson, Lewis and Hogan 1997) and structure
	Common "deformations" of the adult target reflect universal structures and organizing principles
	Mastery of language-specific phonologies through integration of segmental and suprasegmental units may develop for years

Appendix 4 Developmental milestones in infant syntax: perception

Year 1

0–2 months Infants know a few days after birth "which language is going to be their maternal language" (Mehler and Christophe 1995, 948): they distinguish their own language from others; e.g., French newborns distinguish French from Russian and prefer French; infants in Spanish-speaking environments distinguish Spanish from English and prefer Spanish (Mehler et al. 1988; Moon et al. 1993).

"Infants are able to tell apart two different languages, even when neither of them is present in their environment" (Mehler and Christophe 1995, 947). They distinguish foreign languages from each other – French infants distinguish Italian and English (Mehler and Christophe 1995; Mehler et al. 1988), or English and Japanese (Nazzi et al. 1995, 1998). They respond more to a change in language than to a change in speaker (Nazzi et al. 1998).

Newborns discriminate lists of *lexical* and *functional* ("grammatical") words (e.g., "chew, chair, find" from "it's, the, in, your") (Shi, Werker and Morgan 1999).

2 months Infants continue to discriminate their native language from other languages, but may no longer respond to distinction between two foreign languages. Infants may have already "set the first values to individuate the structure of the maternal language," beginning to tune out other variations (Mehler and Christophe 1995, 947; Mehler et al. 1988).

". . . [A]ble to remember the order of spoken words when they are embedded within the coherent prosodic structure of a single well formed sentence" (Mandel, Kemler Nelson and Jusczyk 1996)

4 months Continue to respond to a change in language (native language vs. foreign language), but not to a change in sentences uttered within a language (Bahrick and Pickens 1988).

Show evidence of ability for clausal segmentation in their native language and in some foreign languages as well. However, English learning infants do not do so in Japanese (Mandel, Jusczyk and Mazuka 1992; Jusczyk, Mazuka et al. 1993).

5 months Still discriminate languages from different rhythmic classes; e.g., American infants distinguish English and Japanese or Italian and Japanese, but not within two foreign languages which share "rhythmic class" (e.g., Italian versus Spanish).

Distinguish two "similar" (stress-timed) languages if one is the native language, e.g., American infants distinguish English and Dutch (Nazzi and Jusczyk 1999).

6–12 months

6 months   Clausal segmentation becomes more language specific. For example, infants acquiring English continue to prefer well-formed clausal segmentation in English, but no longer distinguish well-formed from non-well-formed segmentation of clauses in Polish (Jusczyk 1989).

Detect clauses in fluent speech (Nazzi et al. 2000).

Infants do not distinguish phrasal segmentation as well formed or not (Jusczyk et al. 1992).

7 months   Detect abstract "algebraic" patterns in sound sequences generated by artificial grammar (Marcus et al. 1999).

9 months   Distinguish phrasal segmentation as well formed or not in their native language (Jusczyk et al. 1992).

In speech processing, phonological packaging into "major prosodic units" overrides syntactic units in phrasal units (for example, subject–predicate sentences with pronoun subjects do not show the same preference effects as those with non-pronoun subjects) (Gerken, Jusczyk and Mandel 1994).

10 months   Sensitive to grammatical function morphemes versus phonologically dissimilar nonsense morphemes (Shady 1996).

11 months   Notice violations of grammatical morphemes in novel sentences (Shady 1996; Shafer et al. 1998; Gomez et al. 1999, 133)

12 months   Infants detect abstract patterns generated by a finite state grammar and generalize to change of vocabulary (Gomez and Gerken 1999). Parameter setting may be accomplished before the first words (Mazuka 1996).

Year 2

18 months + Language-specific syntax becomes increasingly evident.
Infants learning English are shown to be sensitive to discontinuous elements involving agreement, e.g., "is–ing" (Santelmann and Jusczyk 1998).

Year 3   Comprehension of basic operations of complex syntax and knowledge of ambiguity becomes evident, e.g., as in VP ellipsis (Foley et al. 2003).
Comprehension of basic grammatical operations becomes evident by start of third year: simple sentences, as well as coordinate and adjoined or embedded sentences.

Year 3+   Development of semantic scope operations in syntax is gradual, as well as some language-specific syntax.
Development continues for operations involving integration of language-specific lexicon and syntactic computation, e.g., "promise/tell" alterations in control structures in English (e.g., Cohen, Sherman and Lust 1993; Chomsky 1969), or Spanish lexical control variations (Padilla Rivera 1990; Cromer 1987).
Language-specific pragmatic principles continue to develop.
Lexical, semantic and pragmatic knowledge continue to develop in language-specific interaction with the syntax of the language.

Appendix 5 Developmental milestones in infant syntax: production

YEAR I

        12 months   First words.

YEAR 2

        14 months   Average about ten words in production (Benedict 1979), often single word utterances.

        15 months   Combinations appear, e.g., "Dada widə" (Bloom 1973).

        17–19 months   Successive single word utterances (Bloom 1973).
Beginning of sentence construction.
Early language-specific constraints on word order and structure are evident, although utterance length is constrained.
Gradual release on length constraint as words begin to be combined into sentences.
Early word combinations, "wiping baby chin" (Bloom 1973; 1970).
Often missing overt inflection, with cross-language differences in how much, and which, inflection is missing.

2 YEARS   Complex syntax, with various forms of embedding and transformations, becomes evident as early sentences grow in length.
Morphosyntax continues to grow.

YEARS 3+   The essential syntax of a grammar for the language is evident.
Certain language-specific properties of grammar, syntax/semantics interactions, and lexicon/syntax interactions continue to develop.

Appendix 6   Developmental milestones in infant semantics

YEAR 1
0–6 months

Beginnings of word recognition, e.g., "mommy" and "daddy" or infant's own name (Tincoff and Jusczyk 1999; Huttenlocher 1974; Nelson et al. 1993; Mandel, Jusczyk and Pisoni 1995).

6–12 months

7.5–8 months   Remembers and detects words in fluent speech (Jusczyk and Aslin 1995). Remembers words from stories heard two weeks earlier (Jusczyk and Hohne 1997).

9 months   Labeling facilitates categorization (Balaban and Waxman 1997).

10.5 months   "Earliest evidence of recognitory comprehension" (Oviatt, 1980; Benedict 1979; Huttenlocher 1974).

11 months   Developing receptive lexicon (Halle and de Boysson-Bardies 1994); ability to actively seek a named object for frequent words.

12 months   Kind concepts like a "cup" or "ball" are acquired. Uses property or kind properties (e.g., "dog" versus "ball") to differentiate and quantify objects (Xu and Carey 1995; Xu et al. 1999; Xu 2002; Wilcox and Baillargeon 1998; Spelke et al. 1995); linkages between words and categories are made (Waxman and Markow 1995).

YEAR 2
12–24 months

12–13 months   Distinguishes novel words categorically (count nouns versus adjectives; link nouns and object categories) (Waxman 1999).
Rapid increase in receptive lexicon (Benedict 1979).

14 months   "[C]an rapidly learn associations between words and objects" with only a few minutes of exposure (Werker et al. 1998, 1289).
Understands as many as fifty words (Benedict, 1979; Snyder, Bates and Bretherton, 1981).
Discriminates between two different words for a single action (e.g., "push" and "pull"), and between two different actions, but shows "a difficulty in processing language labels and actions simultaneously," thus not linking specific words to specific actions (Casasola and Cohen, 2000).

15–16 months   "word spurt" in comprehension (Casasola and Cohen, in press).

18 months   One trial learning is sufficient for initiation of new words (Nelson and Bonvilian 1973).

Links words with speaker related referents (Baldwin 1991, 1993b; Baldwin et al. 1996).

Able to form an association between a nonsense language label and a causal action within minutes (e.g., "push" and "pull") (Casasola and Cohen, 2000).

Symbolic competencies are fully developed for: object permanence, deferred imitation, symbolic play (Piaget 1983).

New words proliferate; estimated vocabulary 10–220 (Fenson et al. 1994).

2 YEARS+

May understand and produce 50–1,000 words (Fenson et al. 1994).

3 YEARS+

Estimated vocabulary of 5,000–10,000 words by 5 years (Anglin 1993). By 6 years the child may control 14,000 word meanings; by adult, 50,000–300,000.

Development of theory of mind and communicative intentions relevant to language (Mitchell 1996; Sabbagh and Callanan 1998).

Higher order semantics (e.g., logical connectives and quantifiers) continue to develop.

Integration of pragmatic, semantic and syntactic factors continues to develop.

Appendix 7   Abbreviations and notations

A. General

UR: Underlying representation
SR: Surface representation

C: consonant
V: vowel

+V: plus voicing (plus value of a voice feature)
−V: voiceless (minus value of a voice feature)

B. Phonetic Symbol Guide

Authors vary in the symbols they use for phonetic transcription, although most aspire at least in part to some form of the IPA (International Phonetic Alphabet), shown below. (Ladefoged 2001, for example. See also Pullum and Ladusaw 1996 and Cipollone, Keiser and Vasishth, (eds.) 1998, *The Language Files.*)

British and American scholars may vary in their notations, as do authors working across languages, e.g., in India. In this book, we have attempted to maintain each author's transcription system for the sounds they are representing. This has resulted necessarily in variation across notations.

Some common variations:

For Neil Smith, a dot above or beneath a consonant, e.g., [g] or [b] indicates a voiceless, lenis articulation. (See Smith 1973, viii for this and other conventions.)

For Indic scholars, a capital letter or a letter with a tail or a dot beneath it may indicate retroflex.

[CHART OF THE INTERNATIONAL PHONETIC ALPHABET (REVISED 1993, UPDATED 1996)

CONSONANTS (PULMONIC)

	Bilabial	Labiodental	Dental	Alveolar	Postalveolar	Retroflex	Palatal	Velar	Uvular	Pharyngeal	Glottal
Plosive	p b			t d		ʈ ɖ	c ɟ	k ɡ	q ɢ		ʔ
Nasal	m	ɱ		n		ɳ	ɲ	ŋ	N		
Trill	B			r					R		
Tap or Flap				ɾ		ɽ					
Fricative	ɸ β	f v	θ ð	s z	ʃ ʒ	ʂ ʐ	ç ʝ	x ɣ	χ ʁ	ħ ʕ	h ɦ
Lateral fricative				ɬ ɮ							
Approximant		ʋ		ɹ		ɻ	j	ɰ			
Lateral approximant				l		ɭ	ʎ	L			

Where symbols appear in pairs, the one to the right represents a voiced consonant. Shaded areas denote articulations judged impossible.

CONSONANTS (NON-PULMONIC)

Clicks		Voiced implosives		Ejectives	
ʘ	Bilabial	ɓ	Bilabial	ʼ	Examples:
ǀ	Dental	ɗ	Dental/alveolar	pʼ	Bilabial
ǃ	(Post)alveolar	ʄ	Palatal	tʼ	Dental/alveolar
ǂ	Palatoalveolar	ɠ	Velar	kʼ	Velar
ǁ	Alveolar lateral	ʛ	Uvular	sʼ	Alveolar fricative

VOWELS

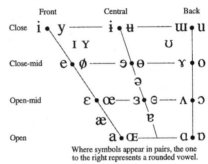

Where symbols appear in pairs, the one to the right represents a rounded vowel.

OTHER SYMBOLS

ʍ	Voiceless labial-velar fricative
w	Voiced labial-velar approximant
ɥ	Voiced labial-palatal approximant
H	Voiceless epiglottal fricative
ʕ	Voiced epiglottal fricative
ʡ	Epiglottal plosive

ɕ ʑ Alveolo-palatal fricatives

ɺ Alveolar lateral flap

ɧ Simultaneous ʃ and x

Affricates and double articulations can be represented by two symbols joined by a tie bar if necessary.   k͡p t͡s

SUPRASEGMENTALS

ˈ	Primary stress	
ˌ	Secondary stress	ˌfoʊnəˈtɪʃən
ː	Long	eː
ˑ	Half-long	eˑ
̆	Extra-short	ĕ
ǀ	Minor (foot) group	
ǁ	Major (intonation) group	
.	Syllable break	ɹi.ækt
‿	Linking (absence of a break)	

DIACRITICS   Diacritics may be placed above a symbol with a descender, e.g. ŋ̊

̥	Voiceless	n̥ d̥	̤	Breathy voiced	b̤ a̤	̪	Dental	t̪ d̪
̬	Voiced	s̬ t̬	̰	Creaky voiced	b̰ a̰	̺	Apical	t̺ d̺
ʰ	Aspirated	tʰ dʰ	̼	Linguolabial	t̼ d̼	̻	Laminal	t̻ d̻
̹	More rounded	ɔ̹	ʷ	Labialized	tʷ dʷ	̃	Nasalized	ẽ
̜	Less rounded	ɔ̜	ʲ	Palatalized	tʲ dʲ	ⁿ	Nasal release	dⁿ
̟	Advanced	u̟	ˠ	Velarized	tˠ dˠ	ˡ	Lateral release	dˡ
̠	Retracted	e̠	ˤ	Pharyngealized	tˤ dˤ	̚	No audible release	d̚
̈	Centralized	ë	̴	Velarized or pharyngealized	ɫ			
̽	Mid-centralized	e̽	̝	Raised	e̝ (ɹ̝ = voiced alveolar fricative)			
̩	Syllabic	n̩	̞	Lowered	e̞ (β̞ = voiced bilabial approximant)			
̯	Non-syllabic	e̯	̘	Advanced Tongue Root	e̘			
˞	Rhoticity	ɚ a˞	̙	Retracted Tongue Root	e̙			

TONES AND WORD ACCENTS

LEVEL			CONTOUR		
e̋ or ˥	Extra high		ě or ˄	Rising	
é ˦	High		ê ˅	Falling	
ē ˧	Mid		e᷄ ˄	High rising	
è ˨	Low		e᷅ ˄	Low rising	
ȅ ˩	Extra low		e᷈ ˄	Rising-falling	
↓	Downstep		↗	Global rise	
↑	Upstep		↘	Global fall	

Glossary

The index to this book will serve as a glossary wherever terms are defined within the text. In addition, this glossary may be used in conjunction with Matthews 1997 and Aitchison 2003, as well as: http://www.sil.org/linguistics/ GlossaryOfLinguisticTerms/Index.htm

Abduction: the analysis of observed fact against explanatory hypotheses

Alienable (vs. inalienable): a separable versus an inherent property, e.g., a possessed object versus a body part

Allophone: phonetic variants of a single phoneme

Anaphor: used to refer to certain types of proforms which must be bound, e.g., reflexive pronouns such as "herself"

Anaphora: relation between a proform such as a pronoun or reflexive and another term (often called its "antecedent") in the sentence or in another sentence, whereby the interpretation of the proform is determined by the interpretation of its antecedent; e.g., "Mary said she was proud of herself" or "Mary said that she liked squash"

Anomaly: an item, event, term, result, etc., that is contrary to expectations or inappropriate, e.g., "the table read the book"

Aspiration: a period of voicelessness (marked by a burst of air resulting from a build-up of air pressure) after the articulation of a consonant and before the articulation of a following sound; this property may be contrastive in some languages while not in others

Assimilation rules: cause a sound to become similar to a neighboring sound with respect to some phonological feature

Attrition rate: rate of loss, e.g., among subjects in a research study, possibly due to sickness or inattention

AUX (Auxiliary): a type of supporting verb which occurs with another verb and which may carry features such as TENSE or NUMBER

Babbling drift: a hypothesis that babbling changes to resemble the language to which the infant is exposed (Brown 1958; Locke, 1983)

Basic level term: a lexical unit which refers to an item at the most neutral level of taxonomy and which has the greatest communicative value, e.g., "dog" rather than either "Fido" or "animal"

Bootstrapping: the mechanism by which a learner initiates new learning on the basis of an initial absence of knowledge; generally refers to what the learner would "hang on to" in this case, e.g., semantic or syntactic or prosodic boot-strapping

Branching Direction: a general property of language grammars distinguishing languages like Japanese or Sinhala from those like English in terms of their recursion direction, e.g., position of subordinate material to the right or left. See Principal Branching Direction

C$_{HL}$ (Computation for Human Language): Chomsky's (1995) term for the essential computation which underlies knowledge of language

Canonical: having regular structure which is adhered to, e.g., canonical babbling, or canonical syllables

Case role: a semantic role played by a term in a sentence, e.g., as instrument, goal, agent, or patient or theme

C-I (Conceptual-Intentional): a formalization of the interface between the computational system and systems of conceptual structure and language use

Coarticulation: the overlapping articulation of speech sounds

Cognitive Architecture: "the fundamental design specifications of an information-processing system are called its architecture" (Simon and Kaplan 1989)

Commissure: band of nerve tissue connecting hemispheres

Commissurotomy: severing or removing commissure connection between hemispheres

Comprehension strategy: a regular way of responding when interpreting language, e.g., in an experiment

Connectionism: a form of cognitive modeling where simulated networks of simple neuron-like processing units are used to understand human cognition. With this system, input and output units are connected, and the strengths of these connections may be modified through learning

Criterial invariants: properties of the speech stream that would regularly and consistently serve to indicate specific units

Deduction: drawing conclusions by reasoning from general principles; may be independent of experience

Deixis: type of use of words or expressions which rely on context, e.g., "Bring me that"

Dichotic Listening Task: involves simultaneous presentation of stimuli to two ears; measures REA (right ear advantage) or LEA (left ear advantage).

Displacement (syntactic): movement of elements from a basic position (see also Semantic Displacement)

Dissociation: different abilities can be dissociated if one is shown to be still present while another is shown to be absent; usually given damage to a particular brain area

Duplex Perception: the phenomenon in which an auditory pattern is perceived as both auditory form (non-speech) and as phonetic impression (speech). Generated by the dichotic presentation of different digitally synthesized acoustic components

Dyslexia: reading, writing and spelling are selectively impaired

E-language: external reflection of language

Electrical Stimulation Mapping: cortical function is altered by direct electrical stimulation during surgical procedures, often those requiring removal of brain areas in the treatment of epilepsy, often for the purpose of diagnosis of functionally critical cortical areas before resection (Penfield and Roberts 1959; Ojemann 1983)

Ellipsis: omission of elements, e.g., "Mary did too"

Epenthesis: a rule which breaks up clusters of consonants or vowels; process by which successive sounds are separated by the insertion of an intervening sound

Epistemology: a subfield of philosophy that concerns the nature of knowledge

ERP: Event Related Brain Potential: measures electrical fields of activity from cortical neurons in response to a cognitive, motor or sensory stimulus, through recordings from the scalp. ERPs are small voltage changes which are measured, even before overt responses have occurred, through electroencephalographic recordings (EEG) of electrical activity within the brain.

Extension: philosophers' term for the range of individuals to which a term applies; e.g., the extension of "flower" includes "rose, daisy, tulip, etc."; contrast with *intension* (Matthews 1997)

Extensional Theory (of language acquisition): refers to properties of the data rather than of the mind

Fast Mapping: a strategy which allows the child to gain at least partial knowledge about a word meaning from quick observation of its use

Feature Theory: theory of word meaning according to which meanings consist of the bundle of features that are present or absent e.g. the term "bird" might consist of [+wings], [+feathers], [−fur]

FMRI: Functional Magnetic Resonance Imaging: measures responses to cognitive or perceptual events in different cerebral tissues when the brain is pulsed with radio waves while under the influence of a strong magnet. Increases in blood oxygenation reflecting increases in blood flow to active brain areas, assumed to reflect neural function correlated with cognitive and perceptual function, are measured in the form of a BOLD (blood oxygen level dependent) signal, analyzed in terms of Voxels (the volume of neural tissue that is activated) (Kandel and Squire 2000, 1118)

Formant: peaks of energy in acoustic analyses of speech

Functionalism (linguistic): theory concerned with the purposive use of language in real situations

Functor (also Function Word or Functional Category): a form which serves to indicate a grammatical relationship within an utterance rather than to convey semantic content

Generative Grammar: a mental system which creates infinite language

Grammatical Mapping: a theory that UG must construct Specific Language Grammars over time during language development

Habituation: decrease in attention to a stimulus over time

Head (of phrase): the core of phrase structure; the head of a phrase identifies its properties, e.g., N for NP, or C for CP

Head Direction: a parameter describing cross-linguistic variation in terms of which side of the phrase heads appear on, either right or left

Hemispherectomy: removal of one hemisphere of the brain

Hertz: a measure of frequency of oscillation of a wave form (cycles per second)

Holophrase: a term used to refer to children's early single word utterances. Generally signifies that children may intend a whole proposition by a single word

Hypernym: a lexical unit whose meaning includes that of another; e.g. "flower" is a hypernym of "daisy." Also see Hyponym

Hypocoristic: like a pet name, e.g., "doggy" for "dog"

Hyponym: a lexical unit whose meaning is included in that of another; e.g., "tulip" and "rose" are hyponyms of "flower." Also see Hypernym

I-language: internal system which creates the language in the mind of an individual (Chomsky 1986)

Induction: deriving a conclusion based on a generalization from specific instances or examples

Initial State: state of the learner before experience begins

Inscrutability of Reference: the complex, non-direct, indeterminate relation between a word and the real thing it labels (Quine 1971, 142)

Intension: the properties that define a word or concept, e.g., the intension of "cat" may include "furry, four-legged, whiskered," etc.; contrast with extension

Intensional Theory (of language acquisition): refers to properties of the mind; contrast with Extensional

IPA: an acronym for the International Phonetic Alphabet which is designed to represent the sounds found in all human languages

LAD: language acquisition device; Chomsky's early (1965) term for a structure hypothesized to exist in the mind which was specialized for language acquisition and biologically programmed

Language Faculty: a general term referring to that cognitive module responsible for language knowledge and acquisition

Lexicon: list of words; the lexicon of a specific language is the full set of words of the language; "Mental lexicon" is the set of words which we know when we know a language, stored in the mind

Logical Form (LF): a level of representation of sentence meaning in terms of its logical characteristics, e.g., predicate, argument and scope of elements

Low Pass Filter: an experimental manipulation of speech which cuts off frequencies above a certain hertz

Markedness: unmarked structures refer to the most natural, most frequent or most easily acquired, while marked structures refer to more unnatural, less frequent, less easily acquired

Maturation: the process by which a biological structure develops, usually through distinct stages, e.g., tadpole to frog, in a predictable way and according to a regular, biologically determined schedule

MEG (Magnetoencephalography): measures changes in magnetic fields generated by the electrical activity of neurons in the brain in response to an external stimulus or event. Superconducting Quantum Interference Devices (SQUIDS) provide sensitive detection of these magnetic fields

Mental Lexicon: see lexicon

Metathesis: transposition of sounds

Minimal word: a prosodic unit to which different prosodic and morphological processes apply

MLU (Mean Length Utterance): an estimate of the average length of children's utterances; computed over a speech sample taken from a child at a specific time (session) by counting the length of each utterance in the sample and then dividing by the total number of utterances in the sample

Modal Verb: an auxiliary verb which occurs with other verbs and may refer to modes of the verb such as necessity or possibility (e.g., "must, shall, will, can, might" . . . in English)

Modularity: organization in systems that follow independent principles and development

Natural kind terms: nouns that have an identity in nature (rather than general or abstract or artefactual terms), e.g., "gold" is a natural kind term whereas "love" is not

Obligatory context: Brown 1973b, 255; contexts in which an inflection or other grammatical device must appear, as opposed to being optional

OCP (Obligatory Contour Principle): in models of generative phonology, this principle disallowed adjacent identical elements in a representation, e.g., in tone languages, HHL (High High Low) tones would be disallowed in favor of HL

Ontological category: a fundamental classification of the world in terms of such notions as "object" or "substance"

Ontology: subfield of philosophy concerned with the nature of existence

Optional Infinitive (OI): A hypothesis that children optionally allow infinitives in main clauses

Ostension: "behavior which makes manifest an intention to make something manifest" (Sperber and Wilson 1986/1995), e.g., showing someone something by picking it up or pointing to it, etc.

Overgeneralization: the process in which learners extend a grammatical feature or rule beyond its use in adult language

Overregularization: the use of regular verb inflection with an irregular form, e.g., adding "ed" to an irregular verb, as in "goed." A particular case of Overgeneralization

Parsing (natural language): the conversion of a surface string of language by analysis of the string into constituent structure in real time; the output is a bracketed sentence

PET: Positron Emission Tomography: Measures and localizes changing blood flow in the brain during cognitive and perceptual operations after the subject is injected with a positron-emitting radioactive isotope (tracer) and asked to perform various operations of interest. Positrons are "ephemeral subatomic particles that rapidly emit gamma radiation, which can be sensed by detectors outside the head" (Posner and Raichle 1994/1997, 18; see also 58–66).

Phone: a single speech sound defined by its phonetic characteristics rather than its ability to signal contrasts in meaning. Represented between brackets, e.g., [p]

Phonetics: the study of how speech sounds are articulated (articulatory phonetics); their physical properties (acoustic phonetics); and how they are perceived (auditory/perceptual phonetics)

Phonology: the study of the sound system of language; how the particular sounds used in each language form an integrated system for encoding information and how such systems differ from one language to another

Pitch: a perceived property of sounds corresponding to frequency of the sounds, resulting from tension or more rapid variation of the vocal cords

Plasticity: the ability of parts of the brain to take over new functions

Pragmatic lead: an experimental device, by which when a sentence is being tested for its comprehension, the researcher initiates it with an initial indication of what the sentence is about, e.g., "This is a story about. . . ."

Primary Language Data (PLD): the actual original language data to which the child is exposed, and from which s/he must map to knowledge of a specific language; a combination of sound and extra-linguistic experience

Principal Branching Direction: formalizes cross-linguistic variation in branching direction in terms of Complementizer heads and type of subordination

Principle of Minimal Falsifiability: a general principle ordering the child's hypotheses about possible grammars in terms of their "ease of falsifiability" (Williams 1973, 30)

Productivity: use of a particular expression in a frequent, creative way. Different ways of measuring productivity exist in speech samples

Pro Drop: a parameter describing cross-linguistic variation in whether or not the language allows arguments to be null, especially subjects

Projection Problem: "the functional relation that exists between . . . early linguistic experience [PLD] . . . and resulting adult intuitions" (Baker 1979)

Prosodic Bootstrapping Hypothesis: the hypothesis that suprasegmental features (prosody) in the speech signal may be initially encoded by the infant and used in subsequent attainment of other grammatical properties of the speech signal. *See* Prosody; Suprasegmental

Prosody: refers collectively to the variations in certain suprasegmental features of speech production (pitch, loudness, tempo and rhythm)

Prototype Theory: "Theory of word meaning according to which meanings are identified, in part at least, by characteristic instances of whatever class of objects, etc., a word denotes. E.g., people think of songbirds, such as a robin, as having more of the central character of a bird than others, such as ducks, falcons, ostriches. In that sense, a robin or the like is a prototypical instance, or prototype, of a bird" (Matthews, 1997)

Recursion/Recursivity: The property of a system that allows its rules to apply to their own output

Reductionism: ". . . the position that holds that theories or things of one sort can exhaustively account for theories of things of another sort" (McCauley 1999, 712)

Reversible sentences: used to refer to sentences where subject and object can be reversed without anomaly, e.g., "Sally likes Mary," versus "Mary likes Sally"; as opposed to "Sally likes ice cream"

Rich interpretation: interpretation of a child's utterance in a natural speech sample by reference to context, even when this interpretation is underdetermined by the exact form of the utterance

Root Infinitive (RI): infinitives which occur in main (root) clauses (or uninflected verbs analyzed as infinitives)

Semantic Bootstrapping Hypothesis: children first observe "real world" situations and then use these observations to formulate word meanings and other aspects of the formal structure of language

Semantic Displacement: meaning which goes beyond the immediate context of the expression, e.g., in time and/or place or event

Semantics: the study of how words and sentences are related to their meanings

SLI (Specific Language Impairment): a deficit and/or delay in language development which involves specifically linguistic impairments, and may involve no other general cognitive impairments

Spectrogram: output of spectrograph

Spectrograph: provides a visible representation of acoustic properties of speech sounds as a function of *time*, *frequency* and *amplitude*

Speech: sounds performed as oral language

Speech Act: the general behavior in which an utterance occurs and the communicative function it is intended to convey, e.g., declaration, command, question

Strong Continuity Hypothesis: proposes that UG continuously constrains language acquisition over the time course of language development

Suponym: a lexical unit whose meaning includes that of another, e.g., "flower" is a suponym of "daisy." See also hypernym

Suprasegmental: "A vocal effect which extends over more than one sound segment in an utterance, such as pitch, stress, or juncture pattern" (Crystal; 1997a, 171–175; 1997c)

Syntax: Combination of words – and the phrasal units to which words relate – to create sentences; the system of principles, rules, parameters and constraints involved in this

Telegraphic speech: term used to refer to children's early two- or three-word utterances, where functional categories may be missing

Token (versus Type): The actual occurrences of a particular type, e.g., number of times that the verb "run" appears would constitute the number of tokens of this verb

Trigger: a property of the data which links to parameter setting for a language in a direct way

Universal Grammar (UG): (1) the principles that underlie the grammars for all languages and can thus be called "universal"; (2) the theory of the Language Faculty, an innate system of principles that constitute the Initial State of the language learner (Noam Chomsky)

U-shaped developmental curve: describes a course of development which initiates with good performance, then shows decrease in success, followed again later by good performance

Utterance: an individual behavior with speech at a specific time; concrete behaviors (as opposed to sentences, which are linguistic units)

Vegetative Sounds: sounds related to bodily functions, e.g, burping, sucking

Voice Onset Time (VOT): time "between the release of the lips and the onset of vocal cord vibration" (Crystal 1992, 147; 1997)

References

Abbi, A. (1992). *Reduplication in South Asian Languages: an Areal, Typological, and Historical Study*. New Delhi, India: Allied Publishers Ltd.

(2001). *A Manual of Linguistic Field Work and Structures of Indian Languages*. Munich: LINCOM Europa.

Abraham, W., S. Epstein, H. Thräinsson and C. J.-W. Zwart (eds.) (1996). *Minimal Ideas, Syntactic Studies in the Minimalistic Framework*. Amsterdam; Philadelphia: Benjamins.

Adger, D. (2004). *Core Syntax: A Minimalist Approach*. Oxford; New York: Oxford University Press.

Aitchison, J. (1994). *Words in the Mind: An Introduction to the Mental Lexicon*. Oxford; New York: Basil Blackwell.

(1998). *The Articulate Mammal: An Introduction to Psycholinguistics*. London; New York: Routledge.

(2003a). *A Glossary of Language and Mind*. Oxford; New York: Oxford University Press.

Aitchison, J. (2003b). *Linguistics. An Introduction*. London: Hodder and Stoughton.

Aitchison, J. and M. Straf (1982). Lexical Storage and Retrieval: A Developing Skill? In A. Cutler (ed.), *Slips of the Tongue*. Berlin; New York: Mouton de Gruyter.

Akhtar, N. and M. Tomasello (1996). "Two-Year-Olds Learn Words for Absent Objects and Actions." *British Journal of Developmental Psychology* **14**(Pt. 1): 79–93.

Akhtar, N., J. Jipson and M. A. Callahan (2001). "Learning words through overhearing." *Child Development* **72**(2): 416–430.

Akmajian, A. (2001). *Linguistics: An Introduction to Language and Communication*. Cambridge, MA: MIT Press.

Akmajian, A., R. A. Demers, A. K. Farmers and R. M. Harnish (2001). *Linguistics: an introduction to language and communication*. Cambridge, MA: MIT Press.

Allen, G. D. and S. Hawkins (1980). Phonological Rhythm: Definition and Development. In G. Yeni-Komshian, J. F. Kavanagh and C. A. Ferguson (eds.), *Child Phonology*. New York: Academic Press. **1:** 227–256.

Allen, S. E. M. (1994). "Acquisition of some Mechanisms of Transitivity Alternation in Arctic Quebec Inukititut." Ph.D. dissertation. Montreal: McGill University.

(1996). *Aspects of Argument Structure Acquisition in Inuktitut*. Amsterdam; Philadelphia: John Benjamins.

Allen, S. E. M. and M. B. Crago (1993a). The Acquisition of Passives and Unaccusatives in Inuktitut. In J. Matthews and L. White (eds.), *McGill Working Papers in Linguistics*. **9:** 1–29.

(1993b). "Early Acquisition of Passive Morphology in Inuktitut." *Twenty-Fourth Annual Child Language Research Forum*. Stanford, CA: CSLI Publications.

Anderson, S. R. (1985). *Phonology in the Twentieth Century: Theories of Rules and Theories of Representations*. Chicago: University of Chicago Press.

Anderson, S. R. and D. W. Lightfoot (2002). *The Language Organ: Linguistics as Cognitive Physiology*. Cambridge, UK; New York: Cambridge University Press.

Anglin, J. M. (1977). *Word, Object and Conceptual Development*. New York: Norton.

(1993). "Vocabulary Development: A Morphological Analysis." *Monographs of the Society for Research in Child Development* **58**(10 (238)): 1–166.

Angluin, D. (1980). "Inductive Inference of Formal Languages for Positive Data." *Information and Control* **45**(2): 117–135.

Aram, D., B. Ekleman and H. Whitaker (1986). "Spoken Syntax in Children with Acquired Unilateral Hemisphere Lesions." *Brain and Language* **27**: 75–100.

Archibald, J. (1995). Introduction: Phonological Competence. *Phonological acquisition and Phonological Theory*. Hillsdale, NJ: Lawrence Erlbaum Associates: xiii–xxi.

Arlman-Rupp, A. J. L., D. V. N. De Haan and M. van den Sandt-Koenderman (1976). "Brown's Early Stages: Some Evidence from Dutch." *Journal of Child Language* **3**(2): 267–274.

Armitage, S., B. A. Baldwin and M. A. Vince (1980). "The Fetal Sound Environment of Sheep." *Science* **208**(4448): 1173–1174.

Armon-Lotem, S. (1998). Mommy Sock in a Minimalist Eye: On the Acquisition of DP in Hebrew. In N. Ditmer and Z. Penner (eds.), *Issues in the Theory of Language Acquisition*. Bern: Peter Lang.

Armstrong, S., L. Gleitman and H. Gleitman (1983). "What Some Concepts Might Not Be." *Cognition* **13**(3): 263–308.

Asher, J. and R. Garcia (1969). "The Optimal Age to Learn a Foreign Language." *Modern Language Journal* **53**: 334–341.

Aslin, R. N. (1987). Visual and Auditory Development in Infancy. In J. Osofsky (ed.), *Handbook of Infant Development*. New York: J. Wiley and Sons.

Aslin, R. N. (1993). Segmentation of Fluent Speech into Words: Learning Models and the Role of Maternal Input. In B. de Boysson-Bardies (ed.), *Developmental Neurocognition: Speech and Face Processing in the First Year of Life*. Dordrecht; Boston: Kluwer Academic: 305–316.

Aslin, R. N., P. W. Jusczyk and D. B. Pisoni (1998). Speech and Auditory Processing During Infancy: Constraints on Precursors to Language. In W. Damon (ed.), *Cognition, Perception and Language*. New York: J. Wiley and Sons. **2**: 147–198.

Aslin, R. N., D. B. Pisoni and P. W. Jusczyk (1983). Auditory Development and Speech Perception in Infancy. In M. Haith and J. Campos (eds.), *Carmichael's Handbook of Child Psychology: Infancy and Developmental Psychobiology*. New York: Wiley. **2**: 573–670.

Aslin, R. N., D. B. Pisoni, B. L. Hennessy and A. J. Perey (1981). "Discrimination of Voice Onset Time by Human Infants: New Findings and Implications for the Effects of Early Experience." *Child Development* **52**(4): 1135–1145.

Astington, J. W. and J. M. Jenkins (1999). "A Longitudinal Study of the Relation between Language and Theory-of-Mind Development." *Developmental Psychobiology* **35**(5): 1311–20.

Atkinson, M. (1992). *Children's Syntax: An Introduction to Principles and Parameters Theory*. Oxford; Cambridge, MA: Basil Blackwell.

Au, T. K. F. (1983). "Chinese and English Counterfactuals: the Sapir-Whorf Hypothesis Revisited." *Cognition* **15**(1–3): 155–187.

Au, T. K. F. and M. Glusman (1990). "The Principle of Mutual Exclusivity in Word Learning: To Honor or Not to Honor?" *Child Development* **61**(5): 1474–1490.

Au, T. K. F., L. M. Knightly, S. A. Jun and J. S. Oh (2002). "Overhearing a Language During Childhood." *Psychological Science* **13**(3): 238–243.

Austin, J. (2001). *Language Differentiation and the Development of Morphosyntax in Bilingual Children Acquiring Basque and Spanish*. Ithaca, NY: Cornell University.

Austin, J., M. Blume, D. Parkinson, Z. Nuñez del Prado, R. Proman and B. Lust (1996). Current Challenges to the Parameter-Setting Paradigm: The Pro-Drop Parameter. In C. Koster and F. Wijnen (eds.), *Proceedings of the Groningen Assembly on Language Acquisition, 1995*. 87–97.

(1997). The Acquisition of Spanish Null and Overt Pronouns: Pragmatic and Syntactic Factors. In S. Somashekar, K. Yamakoshi, M. Blume and C. Foley (eds.), *Papers on Language Acquisition: Cornell Working Papers in Linguistics*. **15:** 160–177.

Austin, J., M. Blume, D. Parkinson, Z. Nuñez del Prado and B. Lust (1998). Interactions Between Pragmatic and Syntactic Knowledge in the First Language Acquisition of Spanish Null and Overt Pronominals. In J. Lema and E. Trevino (eds.), *Theoretical Analyses of Romance Languages*. Amsterdam; Philadelphia: John Benjamins: 35–51.

Austin, J., M. Blume, D. Parkinson, Z. Nuñez del Prado, R. Proman and B. Lust (1997). The Status of Pro-Drop in the Initial State: Results from New Analyses of Spanish. In A. Perez-Leroux and W. Glass (eds.), *Contemporary Perspectives on the Acquisition of Spanish*. Vol. I: *Developing Grammars*. Boston: Cascadilla Press. **1:** 37–54.

Badecker, W. and A. Caramazza (1989). "A Lexical Distinction Between Inflection and Derivation." *Linguistic Inquiry* **20**: 108–116.

Bahrick, L. E. and J. N. Pickens (1988). "Classification of Bimodal English and Spanish Language Passages by Infants." *Infant Behavior and Development* **11**(3): 277–296.

Bai, Lakshmi (1983, 1984). "Case Relations and Case Forms in Child Language." *Osmania Papers in Linguistics*. Vols. 9, 10. Nirmala Memorial Volume. Hyderabad: Department of Linguistics. Osmania University. 73–101.

(1989, 1984). "Dative in Dravidian-A Perspective from Child Language." *Psycho-Lingua* **XIV**(2): 135–144.

(1996–1997). "Inflection, Split or Not? Evidence from Tamil-Telugu Children." *Osmania Papers in Linguistics* **22–23**: 29–43.

Bai, Lakshmi and C. Nirmala (1978). "Assimilatory Processes in Child Language." *Osmania Papers in Linguistics* **4**: 9–22.

Baird, R. (1972). "On the Rule of Chance in Imitation-Comprehension-Production Test Results." *Journal of Verbal Learning and Verbal Behavior* **11**(4): 474–477.

Baker, C. L. (1979). "Syntactic Theory and the Projection Problem." *Linguistic Inquiry* **10**(4): 533–581.

Baker, M. C. (2001). *The Atoms of Language*. New York: Basic Books.

(2003). *Lexical Categories: Verbs, Nouns, and Adjectives*. Cambridge; New York: Cambridge University Press.

Baker, P., M. Post and H. van der Voort (1995). TMA Particles and Auxiliaries. In J. Arends, P. Muysken and N. Smith (eds.), *Pidgins and Creoles*. Amsterdam; Philadelphia: John Benjamins. 247–258.

Balaban, M. T. and S. R. Waxman (1997). "Do Word Labels Facilitate Categorization in 9-month-old Infants?" *Journal of Experimental Child Psychology* **64**: 3–26.

Baldwin, D. A. (1991). "Infants' Contribution to the Achievement of Joint Reference." *Child Development* **62**(5): 875–890.

(1993a). "Early Referential Understanding: Young Children's Ability to Recognize Referential Acts for What They Are." *Developmental Psychology* **29**(5): 832–843.

(1993b). "Infants' Ability to Consult the Speaker for Clues to Word Reference." *Journal of Child Language* **20**(2): 395–418.

Baldwin, D. A. and E. M. Markman (1989). "Establishing Word-Object Relations: A First Step." *Child Development* **60**(2): 381–398.

Baldwin, D. A., E. M. Markman, B. Bill, R. N. Desjardins, J. M. Irwin and G. Tidball (1996). "Infants' Reliance on a Social Criterion for Establishing Word-Object Relations." *Child Development* **67**(6): 3135–3153.

Banich, M. (1997). *Neuropsychology*. Boston, MA: Houghton Mifflin.

Banich, M. T. and W. Heller (1998). "Evolving Perspectives on Lateralization of Function." *Current Directions in Psychological Science* **7**: 1–2.

Baraniga, M. (1997). "New Imaging Methods Provide a Better View into the Brain." *Science* **276**: 1974–1976.

Barbier, I. (1995). Configuration and Movement: Studies of the First Language Acquisition of Dutch Word Order. Ph.D. Dissertation, Cornell University.

(1996). The Head-Direction of Dutch VPs: Evidence from L1 acquisition. *Proceedings from the Groningen Assembly on Language Acquisition*, Groningen.

Barbosa, P., D. Fox, P. Hagstrom, M. McGinnis and D. Pesetsky (eds.) (1998). *Is the Best Good Enough?* Cambridge, MA: MIT Press.

Barrett, M. (ed.) (1999). *The Development of Language*. Hove, East Sussex: Psychology Press.

Barrett, M. D. (1978). "Lexical Development and Overextension in Child Language." *Journal of Child Language* **5**(2): 205–219.

Bartlett, E. J. (1978). The Acquisition of the Meaning of Color Terms: A Study of Lexical Development. In R. Campbell and P. T. Smith (eds.), *Recent Advances in the Psychology of Language*. New York: Plenum Press. **1**: 89–108.

Bates, E. (1979). *The Emergence of Symbols: Cognition and Communication in Infancy*. New York: Academic Press.

Bates, E. and J. Elman (1996). "Learning Rediscovered." *Science* **274**: 1849–1850.

Bates, E. A. and B. MacWhinney (1987). Competition, Variation and Language Learning. In B. MacWhinney (ed.), *Mechanisms of Language Acquisition*. Hillsdale, NJ: Lawrence Erlbaum Associates. 157–194.

(1989). Functionalism and the Competition Model. In B. MacWhinney and E. A. Bates (eds.), *The cross-linguistic study of sentence processing*. Cambridge, UK; New York: Cambridge University Press. 3–73.

Bates, E. A., I. Bretherton and L. Snyder (1988). *From First Words to Grammar: Individual Differences and Dissociable Mechanisms*. Cambridge; New York: Cambridge University Press.

Bates, E. A., L. Snyder, I. Bretherton and V. Volterra (1979). "First Words in Language and Action: Similarities and Differences." *Stanford Child Language Research Forum*, Stanford, CA.

Bates, E., D. Thal and J. Janowsky (1992). Early Language Development and its Neural Correlates. In I. Rapin and S. Segalowitz (eds.), *Handbook of Neuropsychology*. Amsterdam: Elsevier.

Bates, M., R. J. Bobrow and R. M. Weischedel (1993). Critical Challenges for Natural Language Processing.

Baynes, K. and M. Gazzaniga (1988). Right Hemisphere Language: Insights into Normal Language Mechanisms. In F. Plum (ed.), *Language, Communication and the Brain*. New York: Raven Press.

    (2000). Consciousness, Introspection, and the Split-Brain: The Two Minds/One Body Problem. In Gazzaniga. 1355–1363.

Baynes, K., J. Eliassen, H. Lutsep and M. Gazzaniga (1998). "Modular Organization of Cognitive Systems Masked by Interhemispheric Integration." *Science* **280**: 902–905.

Baynes, K., C. Wessinger, R. Fendrich and M. Gazzaniga (1995). "The Emergence of the Capacity to Name Left Visual Field Stimuli in a Callosotomy Patient: Implications for Functional Plasticity." *Neuropsychologia* **33**(10): 1225–1242.

Beardsley, M. C. (ed.) (1960). *The European Philosophers from Descartes to Nietzsche*. New York: Modern Library.

Beckwith, R., E. Tinker and L. Bloom (1989). The Acquisition of Nonbasic Sentences. *4th Annual Boston University Conference on Language Development*, Boston, MA.

Beeman, M. (1993). "Semantic Processing in the Right Hemisphere May Contribute to Drawing Inferences During Comprehension." *Brain and Language* **44**: 80–120.

Beeman, M. and C. Chiarello (1998). *Right Hemisphere Language Comprehension: Perspectives from Cognitive Neuroscience*. Mahwah, NJ: Lawrence Erlbaum Associates.

Beeman, M., E. Bowden and M. A. Gernsbacher (2000). "Right and Left Hemisphere Cooperation for Drawing Predictive and Coherence Inferences during Normal Story Comprehension." *Brain and Language* **71**: 310–336.

Beers, M. (1995). *The Phonology of Normally Developing and Language Disordered Children*. Amsterdam: University of Amsterdam.

Beilin, H. (ed.) (1975). *Studies in the Cognitive Basis of Language Development*. New York, Academic Press.

Bellugi, U. (1988). The Acquisition of a Spatial Language. In R. Brown and F. S. Kessel (eds.), *The Development of Language and Language Researchers: Essays in Honor of Roger Brown*. Hillsdale, NJ: Lawrence Erlbaum Associates. 153–186.

Bellugi, U., A. Bihrle, H. Neville, S. Doherty and T. Jernigan (1992). Language, Cognition and Brain Organization in a Neurodevelopmental Disorder. In M. R. Gunnan and C. A. Nelson (eds.), *Developmental Behavioral Neuroscience: The Minnesota Symposia on Child Psychology*. **24:** 201–231.

Benedict, H. (1979). "Early Lexical Development: Comprehension and Production." *Journal of Child Language* **6**(2): 183–200.

Berk, S. (1996). What Does Why What Trigger? Ithaca, NY: Cornell University. Unpublished Honors Thesis.

(2002). Why "Why" is different. *BUCLD Proceedings*, Cascadilla Press.

Berk, Stephanie and B. Lust (1999). "Early Knowledge of Inversion in Yes/No Questions, New Evidence from Children's Natural Speech." Paper presented at the Linguistic Society of America Annual Meeting, Los Angeles, CA.

Berko, J. (1958). "The Child's Learning of English Morphology." *Word* **17**(2–3): 150–177. Republished in Lust and Foley 2004.

Berko Gleason, J. and N. Ratner (eds.) (1993a). *Instructor's Manual to Accompany Psycholinguistics*. Fort Worth, TX: Harcourt Brace Jovanovich.

(1993b). *Psycholinguistics*. Fort Worth, TX: Harcourt Brace Jovanovich.

Berlin, B. and P. Kay (1969). *Basic Color Terms: their Universality and Evolution*. Berkeley; Los Angeles: University of California Press.

Berman, R. A. and E. Clark (1989). "Learning to Use Compounds for Contrast: Data from Hebrew." *First Language* **9**(3(27)): 247–270.

Berthoud-Papandropoulou, I. (1978). An Experimental Study of Children's Ideas about Language. In A. Sinclair, R. Jarvella and W. Levelt (eds.), *The Child's Conception of Language*. Berlin: Springer-Verlag. **2**: 55–64.

Bertoncini, J., R. Bijeljac-Babic, P. Jusczyk, L. Kennedy and J. Mehler (1987). "Discrimination in Neonates of Very Short CVs." *Journal of the Acoustical Society of America* **82**(1): 31–37.

(1988). "An Investigation of Young Infants' Perceptual Representations of Speech Sounds." *Journal of Experimental Psychology: General* **117**: 21–33.

Bertoncini, J., R. Morais, R. Bijeljac-Babic, S. MacAdams, I. Peeretz and J. Mehler (1989). "Dichotic Perception and Laterality in Neonates." *Brain Cognition* **37**: 591–605.

Berwick, R. C. (1985). *The Acquisition of Syntactic Knowledge*. Cambridge, MA: MIT Press.

Best, C. T. (1988). The Emergence of Cerebral Asymmetries in Early Human Development: A Literature Review and a Neuroembryological Model. In D. L. Molfese and S. J. Segalowitz (eds.), *Brain Lateralization in Children: Developmental Implications*. New York: Guilford Press.

(1993). Emergence of Language-Specific Constraints in Perception of Native and Non-Native Speech: A Window on Early Phonological Development. In B. de Boysson-Bardies, S. De Schonen, P. Justczyk, P. MacNeilage and J. Morton (eds.), *Developmental Neurocognition: Speech and Face Processing in the First Year of Life*. Dordrecht; Boston: Kluwer Academic.

(1994). The Emergence of Native-Language Phonological Influences in Infants: A Perceptual Assimilation Model. In J. C. Goodman and H. C. Nusbaum (eds.), *The Development of Speech Perception: the Transition from Speech Sounds to Spoken Words*. Cambridge, MA: MIT Press.

(1995). Learning to Perceive the Sound Patterns of English. In C. Rovee-Collier and L. Lipsett (eds.), *Advances in Infancy Research*. Norwood, NJ: Ablex.

Best, C. T., G. McRoberts and N. Sithole (1988a). "Examination of Perceptual Reorganization for Nonnative Speech Contrasts: Zulu Click Discrimination by English-Speaking Adults and Infants." *Journal of Experimental Psychology: Human Perception and Performance* **14**: 345–360.

(1988). "The Phonological Basis of Perceptual Loss for Nonnative Contrasts: Maintenance of Discrimination among Zulu Clicks by English-Speaking Adults and

Infants." *Journal of Experimental Psychology: Human Perception and Performance* **14** 345–360.

Bever, T. (1975). Psychologically Real Grammar Emerges because of its Role in Language Acquisition. In D. Dato (ed.), *Developmental Psycholinguistics: Theory and Applications*. Washington, DC: Georgetown University Press.

(1992). The Logical and Extrinsic Sources of Modularity. In M. Gunnar and M. Maratsos (eds.), *Modularity and Constraints in Language and Cognition*. Hillsdale, NJ: Lawrence Erlbaum Associates. 179–212.

Bever, T. G., J. J. Katz and D. T. Langendoen (eds.) (1976). *An Integrated Theory of Linguistic Ability*. The Language & Thought Series. New York: Crowell.

Bhatia Tej and W. Ritchie (2004). *The Handbook of Bilingualism*. London: Blackwell Publishing.

Bialystok, E. and K. Hakuta (1994). *In Other Words*. New York: Basic Books.

Biber, D., S. Conrad and R. Reppen (1998). *Corpus Linguistics*. Cambridge; New York: Cambridge University Press.

Bickerton, D. (1999). How to Acquire Language Without Positive Evidence: What Acquisitionists Can Learn from Creoles. In M. DeGraff (ed.), *Language Creation and Language Change; Creolization, Diachrony, and Development*. Cambridge, MA: MIT Press. x, 573.

Bijeljac-Babic, R., J. Bertoncini and J. F. Mehler (1993). "How Do Four Day Old Infants Categorize Multisyllabic Utterances?" *Developmental Psychology* **29**(4): 711–724.

Binder, J. and C. Price (2001). Functional Neuroimaging of Language. In R. Cabeza and A. Kingstone (eds.), *Handbook of Functional Neuroimaging of Cognition*. Cambridge, MA: MIT Press. 186–251.

Bird, S. and G. Simons (2003). "Seven Dimensions of Portability for Language Documentation and Description." *Language* **79**(3): 557–582.

Birdsong, D. (1992). "Ultimate Attainment in Second Language Acquisition." *Language* **68**: 706–755.

Birdsong, D. (1999). *Second Language Acquisition and the Critical Period Hypothesis*. Mahwah, NJ: L. Erlbaum Associates.

Bishop, D. (1997). *Uncommon Understanding: Development and Disorders of Comprehension in Children*. Hove, East Sussex: Psychology Press.

Bishop, D. V. M. (1988). Language Development in Children with Abnormal Structure or Function of the Speech Apparatus. In D. V. M. Bishop and K. Mogford-Bevan (eds.), *Language Development in Exceptional Circumstances*. London: Livingston. 220–238.

Blake, J. (2000). *Routes to Child Language: Evolutionary and Developmental Precursors*. Cambridge; New York: Cambridge University Press.

Blake, J. and B. de Boysson-Bardies (1992). "Patterns in Babbling: A Cross-Linguistic Study." *Journal of Child Language* **19**(1): 51–74.

Blake, J. and R. Fink (1987). "Sound–Meaning Correspondences in Babbling." *Journal of Child Language* **14**(2): 229–253.

Blake, J. and G. Quartaro (1990). *Manual for Recording, Transcribing and Analyzing Speech Samples of Preschool Children*. Toronto, Canada: York University.

Blake, J., G. Quartaro and S. Onorati (1993). "Evaluating Quantitative Measures of Grammatical Complexity in Spontaneous Speech Samples." *Journal of Child Language* **20**(1): 139–152.

Blank, M., M. Gessner and A. Esposito (1979). "Language Without Communication: A Case Study." *Journal of Child Language* **6**(2): 329–352.

Bleser, R. D., J. Faiss and M. Schwartz (1995). "Rapid Recovery of Aphasia and Deep Dyslexia after Cerebrovascular Left-Hemisphere Damage in Childhood." *Journal of Neurolinguistics* **9**(1): 22.

Bloom, L. (1970a). *Language Development: Form and Function in Emerging Grammars*. Cambridge, MA: MIT Press.

(1970b). The Reduction Transformation and Constraints on Sentence Length. In L. Bloom (ed.), *Language Development: Form and Function in Emerging Grammar*. Cambridge, MA: MIT Press. 135–169.

(1974). Talking, Understanding, and Thinking. In R. L. Schiefelbusch and L. L. Lloyd (eds.), *Language Perspectives – Acquisition, Retardation, and Intervention*. Baltimore, MD: University Park Press. 285–312.

(1993). *The Transition from Infancy to Language: Acquiring the Power of Expression*. Cambridge; New York: Cambridge University Press.

Bloom, L. and M. Lahey (1978). Deviant Language Development: A Definition of Language Disorders. In L. Bloom and M. Lahey (eds.), *Language Development and Language Disorders*. New York: J. Wiley and Sons. 289–303.

Bloom, L., L. Hood and P. Lightbown (1974). "Imitation in Language Development. If, When and Why?" *Cognitive Psychology* **6**(3): 380–420.

Bloom, L., K. Lifter and J. Hafitz (1980). "The Semantics of Verbs and the Development of Verb Inflections in Child Language." *Language* **56**(2): 386–412.

Bloom, L., E. Tinker and C. Margulis (1993). "The Words Children Learn: Evidence Against a Noun Bias in Early Vocabularies." *Cognitive Development* **8**(4): 431–450.

Bloom, P. (1990). "Subjectless Sentences in Child Language." *Linguistic Inquiry* **21**(4): 491–504.

(1994). "Possible Names: The Role of Syntax-Semantics Mapping in the Acquisition of Nominals." *Lingua* **92**: 297–329.

(1994). Syntax-Semantics Mappings as an Explanation for Some Transitions in Language Development. In L. Levy (ed.), *Other Children, Other Languages: Theoretical Issues in Language Development*. Hillsdale, NJ: Lawrence Erlbaum Associates.

(1996). *Language Acquisition: Core Readings*. Cambridge, MA: MIT Press.

(1999). The Role of Semantics in Solving the Bootstrapping Problem. In R. Jackendoff, P. Bloom and K. Wynn (eds.), *Language, Logic and Concepts: Essays in Memory of John Macnamara*. Cambridge, MA: MIT Press.

(2000). *How Children Learn the Meanings of Words*. Cambridge, MA: MIT Press.

(2001). "Precis of How Children Learn the Meanings of Words." *Behavioral and Brain Sciences* **24**(6): 1095–1134.

Bloom, P. and L. Gleitman (1999). Word Meaning, Acquisition of. In R. A. Wilson and F. C. Keil (eds.), *The MIT Encyclopedia of the Cognitive Sciences*. Cambridge, MA: MIT Press. 856–858.

Bloom, P. and L. Markson (1998). "Capacities underlying word learning." *Trends in Cognitive Sciences* **2**(2(11)): 67–73.

Bloom, R., L. Borod, K. Obler, C. Santschi-Hayward and L. Pick (1996). "Right and Left Hemispheric Contributions to Discourse Coherence and Cohesion." *International Journal of Neuroscience* **88**: 125–140.

Bloomfield, L. (1933). *Language*. New York: Holt, Rinehart and Winston.

Blume, M. (2002). Discourse-Morphosyntax Interface in Spanish Non-Finite Verbs: A Comparison Between Adult and Child Grammars. Unpublished dissertation. Ithaca, NY, Cornell University.

Bohannon, J. and L. Stanowicz (1988). "The Issue of Negative Evidence: Adult Responses to Children's Language Errors." *Developmental Psychology* **24**: 684–689.

Bohannon, J. N., B. MacWhinney and C. Snow (1990). "No Negative Evidence Revisited: Beyond Learnability or Who to Prove What to Whom." *Developmental Psychology* **24**: 221–226.

Bonvillian, J. D., A. M. Garber and S. B. Dell (1997). "Language Origin Accounts: Was the Gesture in the Beginning?" *First Language* **17**(3): 219–239.

Borden, G., K. Harris and L. Raphael (1994). *Speech Science Primer*. Baltimore, MD: Williams and Wilkins.

Borer, H. and B. Rohrbacher (1997). Features and Projections: Arguments for the Full Competence Hypothesis. In E. Hughes, M. Hughes and A. Greenhill (eds.), *Proceedings of the 21st Annual Boston University Conference on Language Development*. Somerville, MA: Cascadilla Press. 24–35.

(2002). "Minding the Absent: Arguments for the Full Competence Hypothesis." *Language Acquisition* **10**(2): 123–175.

Borer, H. and K. Wexler (1987). The Maturation of Syntax. In T. Roeper and E. Williams (eds.), *Parameter Setting*. Dordrecht; Boston: D. Reidel.

Boring, E. G. (1950). *A History of Experimental Psychology*. New York: Appleton-Century Crofts.

Bornstein, M. H. (1975). "Qualities of Color Vision in Infancy." *Journal of Experimental Child Psychology* **19**(3): 410–419.

Bornstein, M., O. M. Haynes, K. Painter and J. Genevro (2000). "Child Language with Mothers and with Strangers at Home and in the Laboratory: a Methodological Study." *Journal of Child Language* **27**.

Bornstein, M., J. Tal, C. Rahn, C. Galperin, M. Lamour, M. Oginop, M-G. Pecheux, S. Toda, H. Azuma and C. Tamis-LeMonda (1992a). "Functional Analysis of the Contents of Maternal Speech to Infants of 5 and 13 Months in Four Cultures: Argentina, France, Japan, and the United States." *Developmental Psychology* **28** (4): 593–603.

Bornstein, M., C. Tamis-LeMonda, J. Tal, P. Ludemann, S. Toda, C. Rahn, M.-G. Pecheux, H. Azuma and D. Vardi (1992b). "Maternal Responsiveness to Infants in Three Societies: The United States, France and Japan." *Child Development* **63**: 808–821.

Boroditsky, L. (2001). "Does Language Shape Thought? Mandarin and English Speakers' Conceptions of Time." *Cognitive Psychology* **43**(1): 1–22.

Bosch, L. and N. Sebastian-Galles (1997). "Native-Language Recognition Abilities in 4-Month-Old Infants From Monolingual and Bilingual Environments." *Cognition* **65**(1): 33–69.

Boser, K. (1989). The First Language Acquisition of German Word Order. Honor's thesis. Ithaca: Cornell University.

(1992). Early Knowledge of Verb Position in Children's Acquisition of German: An Argument for Continuity of Universal Grammar. Master's thesis. Ithaca, NY: Cornell University.

(1995). Verb Initial Utterances in Early Child German: A Study of the Interaction of Grammar and Pragmatics. *Proceedings of the 27th Stanford Child Language Forum.* Stanford, CA: CSLI Publications.

(1997a). The Acquisition of Word Order Knowledge in Early Child German: Interactions Between Syntax and Pragmatics. Ph.D. dissertation. Ithaca, NY: Cornell University.

(1997b) "A New Null Auxiliary Proposal for Strong Continuity in Early Child German: Converging Evidence from Crossectional and Longitudinal Data." In Shamitha Somashekar, Kyoko Yamakoshi, Maria Blume and Claire Foley (eds.), *Cornell Working Papers in Linguistics.* Vol. 15. *Papers on Language Acquisition.* Ithaca: Cornell University. 178–199.

Boser, K., B. Lust, L. Santelmann and J. Whitman (1991). The Theoretical Significance of Auxiliaries in Early Child German. *Proceedings of the 16th Annual Boston University Conference on Language Development.* Boston, MA: Cascadilla Press.

(1992). The syntax of CP and V-2 in Early German Child Grammar: The Strong Continuity Hypothesis. *Proceedings of the North Eastern Linguistics Association.* Vol. 22. Amherst: University of Massachusetts. 51–66.

Boser, K., L. Santelmann, I. Barbier and B. Lust (1995). Grammatical Mapping from UG to Language Specific Grammars: Deriving Variation in the Acquisition of German, Dutch and Swedish. *Proceedings of the 19th Annual Boston University Conference on Language Development.* Boston, MA: Cascadilla Press.

Bourgeois, J. P., P. S. Goldman-Rakic and P. Rakic (1994). "Synaptogenesis in the Prefrontal Cortex of Rhesus Monkeys." *Cereb Cortex* **4**: 76.

Bowerman, M. (1973). *Early Syntactic Development: A Cross-Linguistic Study with Special Reference to Finnish.* London: Cambridge University Press.

(1978). The Acquisition of Word Meaning: An Investigation of Some Current Conflicts. In N. Waterson and C. E. Snow (eds.), *The Development of Communication.* New York: J. Wiley and Sons. 263–287.

(1982a). "Evaluating Competing Linguistic Models with Language Acquisition Data: Implications of Developmental Errors with Causative Verbs." *Quaderni di Semantica* **3**: 5–66.

(1982b). Reorganizational Processes in Lexical and Syntactic Development. In E. Wanner and L. Gleitman (eds.), *Language Acquisition: The State of the Art.* New York: Cambridge University Press.

(1987). Commentary: Mechanisms of Language Acquisition. In B. MacWhinney (ed.), *The Mechanisms of Language Acquisition.* Hillsdale, NJ: Lawrence Erlbaum Associates. 443–466.

(1988). The "No Negative Evidence" Problem: How Do Children Avoid Construction an Overly General Grammar? In J. A. Hawkins (ed.), *Explaining Language Universals.* Oxford; New York: Basil Blackwell. 73–104.

Bowerman, M. (1989). Learning a Semantic System: What Role do Cognitive Predispositions Play? In M. Rice and R. L. Schiefelbusch (eds.), *The Teachability of Language.* Baltimore, MD: Paul H. Brookes.

(1990). "Mapping Thematic Roles Onto Syntactic Functions: Are Children Helped by Innate 'Linking Rules'?" *Linguistics* **28**: 1253–1289.

(1996). The Origins of Children's Spatial Semantic Categories: Cognitive vs. Linguistic Determinants. In Gumpertz and Levinson (eds.).

Bowerman, M. and S. Levinson (2001). *Language Acquisition and Conceptual Development*. Cambridge; New York: Cambridge University Press.

Boysson-Bardies, B. de (1999). *How Language Comes to Children: From Birth to Two Years*. Cambridge, MA: MIT Press.

Boysson-Bardies, B. de, B. Vihman and M. M. Vihman (1991). "Adaptation to Language: Evidence from Babbling and First Words in Four Languages." *Language* **67**(2): 297–319.

Boysson-Bardies, B. de, L. Sagart and C. Durand (1984). "Discernible Differences in the Babbling of Infants According to Target Language." *Journal of Child Language* **11**(1): 1–15.

(1989). "A Crosslinguistic Investigation of Vowel Formants in Babbling." *Journal of Child Language* **16**(1): 1–17.

Brainard, M. and A. Doupe (2002). "What Songbirds Teach Us About Learning." *Nature* **417**: 351–358.

Braine, M. D. S. (1971). On Two Types of Models of the Internalization of Grammars. In D. Slobin (ed.), *The Ontogenesis of Grammar: A Theoretical Symposium*. New York: Academic Press. 153–186.

Braine, M. D. S. (1974). "On What Might Constitute Learnable Phonology." *Language* **50**(2): 27–299.

(1976). "Review Article: Smith, 1973." *Language* **52**(2): 489–498.

Brent, M. and J. M. Siskind (2001). "The Role of Exposure to Isolated Words in Early Vocabulary Development." *Cognition* **81**(2): B33–B34.

Brent, M., A. Gafos and T. Cartwright (1994). "Phonotactics and the Lexicon: Beyond Bootstrapping." In E. Clark (ed.), *Proceedings of the 1994 Stanford Child Language Research Forum*. Cambridge, UK: Cambridge University Press.

Brill, E. and S. Kapur (1997). An Information-Theoretic Solution to Parameter Setting. In S. Somashekar, K. Yamakoshi, M. Blume and C. Foley (eds.), *Cornell Working Papers in Linguistics*. **15**: 200–216.

Brinkman, U., K. F. Drozd and I. Krämer (1996). Physical Individuation as a Prerequisite for Children's Symmetrical Interpretations. Paper presented at the Proceedings of the 20th Annual Boston University Conference on Language Development, Boston, MA.

Bromberger, S. and M. Halle (2000). The Ontology of Phonology. In N. Burton-Clements, P. Carr and G. Docherty (eds.), *Phonological Knowledge: Conceptual and Empirical Issues*. Oxford; New York: Oxford University Press.

Brown, C. and P. Hagoort (eds.) (1999). *The Neurocognition of Language*. Oxford University Press.

Brown, E. and C. Hanlon (1970). Derivational Theory and Order of Acquisition in Child Speech. In J. Hayes (ed.), *Cognition and the Development in Language*. New York: J. Wiley and Sons.

Brown, K. (1999). "Grammar's Secret Skeleton." *Science* **283**(5403): 774–775.

Brown, R. (1957). "Linguistic Determinism and the Parts of Speech." *Journal of Abnormal and Social Psychology* **55**(1): 1–5.

(1958). *Words and Things*. Glencoe, IL: Free Press.

(1970). The First Sentences of Child and Chimpanzee. *Psycholinguistics: Selected Papers*. New York: Free Press.

(1973a). Characterization of the Data and Telegraphic Speech. In R. Brown, *A First Language*. Cambridge, MA: Harvard University Press. 74–90.

(1973b). A First Language: The Early Stages. In R. Brown. *A First Language.*

(1973c). The Study of Adam, Eve and Sarah. In R. Brown. *A First Language.* 51–58.

Brown, R. (1977). Introduction. In C. E. Snow and C. A. Ferguson (eds.), *Talking to Children: Language Input and Acquisition.* Cambridge; New York: Cambridge University Press. 1–30.

Brownell, H. and A. Stringfellow (1999). "Making Requests: Illustrations of How Right-Hemisphere Brain Damage Can Affect Discourse Production." *Brain and Language.* **68**(3): 442–466.

Brownell, H., H. Potter, A. Bihrle and H. Gardner (1986). "Inference Deficits in Right Brain-Damaged Patients." *Brain and Language* **27**: 310–321.

Bruce, D. (1964). "The Analysis of Word Sounds." *British Journal of Educational Psychology* **34**(2): 158–170.

(1994). "Lashley and the Problem of Serial Order." *American Psychologist* **49**(2): 93–103.

Bruner, J. (1964). "The Course of Cognitive Growth." *American Psychologist* **19**(1): 1–15.

Butt, M., T. H. King and G. Ranchard (1994). *Theoretical Perspectives in Word Order in South Asian Languages.* Stanford: CSLI Publications.

Cairns, H. S., D. McDaniel and J. R. Hsu (1993). "A Reply to 'Children are in Control.'" *Cognition* **48**(2): 193–194.

Cairns, H. S., D. McDaniel, J. R. Hsu and M. Rapp (1994). "A Longitudinal Study of Principles of Control and Pronominal Reference in Child English." *Language* **70**(2): 260–288.

Calvin, W. and G. Ojemann (1994). *Conversations with Neil's Brain: The Neural Nature of Thought and Language.* Reading, MA: Addison-Wesley.

Camaioni, L., E. Longobardi, P. Venut and M. H. Bornstein (1998). "Maternal Speech to 1-Year-Old Children in Two Italian Cultural Contexts." *Early Development and Parenting* **7**(1): 9–17.

Campbell, R. and R. Grieve (1982). "Royal Investigations of the Origin of Language." *Historiographia Linguistica* **9**(1–2): 43–74.

Caplan, D. (1992). *Language: Structure, Processing and Disorders.* Cambridge, MA: MIT Press.

(1995). "Issues Arising in Contemporary Studies of Disorders of Syntactic Processing in Sentence Comprehension in Agrammatic Patients." *Brain and Language* **50**: 325–338.

Caplan, P. and M. Kinsbourne (1976). "Baby Drops the Rattle: Asymmetry of Duration of Grasp by Infants." *Child Development* **47**: 532–534.

Caramazza, A. (1997a). Brain and Language. In M. Gazzaniga (ed.), *Conversations in the Cognitive Neurosciences.* Cambridge, MA: MIT Press.

(1997b). "How Many Levels of Processing are There in Lexical Access?" *Cognitive Neuropsychology* **14**(1): 177–208.

Caramazza, A., C. Papagno and W. Ruml (2000). "The Selective Impairment of Phonological Processing in Speech Production." *Brain and Language* **75**: 428–450.

Carden, G. (1986). Blocked Forward Conference. In B. Lust (ed.), *Studies in Acquisition of Anaphora.* Dordrecht: Riedel.

Carey, S. (1978). The Child as a Word Learner. In M. Halle, J. Bresnan and G. Miller (eds.), *Linguistic Theory and Psychological Reality*. Cambridge, MA: MIT Press.

(1985). *Conceptual Change in Childhood*. Cambridge, MA: MIT Press.

Carey, S. and E. J. Bartlett (1978). "Acquiring a Single New Word." *Papers and Reports on Child Language Development* **15**: 17–29.

Carpenter, K. (1991). "Later Rather Than Sooner: Extralinguistic Categories in the Acquisition of Thai Classifiers." *Journal of Child Language* **18**(1): 93–113.

Carpenter, M., K. Nagell and M. Tomasello (1998). "Social Cognition, Joint Attention, and Communicative Competence from 9 to 15 Months of Age." *Monographs of the Society for Research in Child Development* **63**(4): 225.

Carroll, L. (1964). *Through the Looking Glass*. New York: Parents' Magazine Press.

(1998). *Alice's Adventures in Wonderland*. New York: Dutton Children's Books.

Carston, R. (1997). "Enrichment and Loosening: Complementary Processes in Deriving the Proposition Expressed?" *Linguistische Berichte* **8**(Special Issue on Pragmatics): 103–127.

(2002). *Thoughts and Utterances: The Pragmatics of Explicit Communication*. Oxford; Cambridge, MA: Basil Blackwell.

Casasola, M. and L. Cohen (2000). "Infants' Association of Linguistic Labels with Causal Actions." *Developmental Psychology* **36**(2): 155–168.

(2002). "Infant Categorization of Containment, Support, and Tight-Fit Spatial Relationships." *Developmental Science* **5**(2): 247–264.

Casasola, M., L. Cohen and E. Chiarello (2003). "Six-month-old infants' categorization of containment spatial relations." *Child Development* **74**(3): 679–693.

Casasola, M., M. Parramore and S. Yang (forthcoming). "Can English-learning toddlers acquire and generalize a novel spatial word?" *First Language*.

Casey, B. J. (2002). "Windows into the Human Brain." *Science* **296**: 1408–1409.

Cattell, N. R. (2000). *Children's Language: Consensus and Controversy*. London; New York: Cassell.

Cazden, C. (1968). "The Acquisition of Noun and Verb Inflections." *Child Development* **39**(2): 433–448.

(1972). *Child Language and Education*. New York: Holt, Rinehart and Winston.

Chambers, K., K. Onishi and C. Fischer (2003). "Infants Learn Phonotactic Regularities from Brief Auditory Experience." *Cognition* **87**: 869–77.

Chandler, D. (2002). *Semiotics: The Basics*. London; New York: Routledge.

Chapman, R. S. and J. F. Miller (1973). Word Order in Early Two and Three Word Utterances: Does Production Precede Comprehension? *Proceedings of the Fifth Annual Child Language Research Forum*. Stanford, CA: Stanford University.

Charmon, T. and S. Baron-Cohen (1992). "Understanding Drawings and Beliefs: A Further Test of the Metarepresentation Theory of Autism." *Journal of Child Psychology and Psychiatry and Allied Disciplines* **33**(6): 1105–1112.

Chee, M., N. Hon, H. L. Lee and C. S. Soon (2001). "Relative Language Proficiency Modulates Bold Signal Change When Bilinguals Perform Semantic Judgments." *Neuroimaging* **13**: 1155–1163.

Cheng, L. and R. Sybesma (1998). "Yi-wan Tang, Yi-ge Tang: Classifiers and Massifiers." *The Tsing Hua Journal of Chinese Studies, New Series* **28**(3): 385–412.

Chi, J. G., E. Dooling and F. H. Gilles (1977). "Gyral Development of the Human Brain." *Annals of Neurology* **1**(86).

Chien, Y.-C. (1994). Structural Determinants of Quantifier Scope: An Experimental Study of Chinese First Language Acquisition. In B. Lust, G. Hermon and J. Kornfilt (eds.), *Syntactic Theory and First Language Acquisition: Cross Linguistic Persepectives.* Vol II. *Binding Dependencies and Learnability.* Hillsdale, NJ: Lawrence Erlbaum Associates. **2**: 391–415.

Chien, Y.-C. and Y. H. A. Li (1998). The Subject-Orientation Requirement and Chinese Children's Acquisition of Reflexives and Pronouns. *Studia Linguistica Serica.* Hong Kong: City Polytechnic of Hong Kong. 209–224.

Chien, Y.-C. and B. Lust (1985). "The Concepts of Topic and Subject in First Language Acquisition of Mandarin Chinese." *Child Development* **56**(6): 1359–1375.

(forthcoming). Chinese Children's Acquisition of Binding Principles. In P. Li et al. (eds.), *Handbook of East Asian Psycholinguistics.*

Chien, Y.-C. and K. Wexler (1987a). "A Comparison Between Chinese-Speaking and English-Speaking Children's Acquisition of Reflexives and Pronouns." Paper Presented at the 12th Annual Boston University Conference on Language Development, Boston, MA.

(1987b). Children's Acquisition of the Locality Condition for Reflexives and Pronouns. *Papers and Reports on Child Language Development* **26**: 30–39.

(1990). "Children's Knowledge of Locality Conditions in Binding as Evidence for the Modularity of Syntax and Pragmatics." *Language Acquisition* **1**(3): 225–295.

Chien, Y.-C., B. Lust and C.-P. Chiang (2003). "Chinese Children's Acquisition of Classifiers and Measure Words." *Journal of East Asian Linguistics* **12**(2): 91–120.

Chien, Y.-C., B. Lust and S. Flynn (1999). Testing Universal Grammar in Second Language Acquisition: A Study of Chinese ESL High School Students' Interpretation of English Pronouns. 1999 Biennial Meeting of the Society of Research in Child Development, Albuquerque, NM.

Chien, Y.-C., K. Wexler and H.-W. Chang (1993). "Children's Development of Long-Distance Binding in Chinese." *Journal of East Asian Linguistics* **2**: 229–259.

(1995). *Children's Acquisition of the Subject-Orientation Property of the Chinese Reflexive Ziji'.* Sixth North American Conference on Chinese Linguistics. Los Angeles, CA: University of Southern California, Los Angeles.

Chierchia, G. and S. McConnell-Ginet (1990). *Meaning and Grammar.* Cambridge, MA: MIT Press.

Choi, S. (2000). "Caregiver Input in English and Korean: Use of Nouns and Verbs in Book-Reading and Toy-Play Contexts." *Journal of Child Language* **27**(1): 69–96.

Choi, S. and A. Gopnik (1993). Nouns are Not Always Learned Before Verbs: An Early Verb Spurt in Korean. *Proceedings of the Twenty-Fifth Annual Child Language Research Forum.* Stanford, CA: Child Language Research Forum.

(1995). "Early Acquisition of Verbs in Korean: A Cross-Linguistic Study." *Journal of Child Language* **22**(3): 497–529.

Chomsky, C. (1969). *The Acquisition of Syntax in Children from 5 to 10.* Cambridge, MA: MIT Press.

(1986). "Analytic Study of the Tadoma Method: Language Abilities of Three Deaf-Blind Subjects." *Journal of Speech and Hearing Research* **29**(3): 332–347.

Chomsky, N. (1959). "Review of B. F. Skinner's 'Verbal Behavior'." *Language* **35**(1): 26–58.

(1964). Formal Discussion. *The Acquisition of Language*. In U. Bellugi and R. Brown (eds.), *Monographs of the Society for Research in Child Development*, serial no. 92, vol. 29, no. 1: 35–42.

(1965). *Aspects of a Theory of Syntax*. Cambridge, MA: MIT Press.

(1972). *Language and Mind*. New York: Harcourt Brace Jovanovich.

(1975a). *Reflections on Language*. New York: Pantheon Books.

(1975b). *The Logical Structure of Linguistic Theory*. New York: Plenum Press.

(1980). *Rules and Representations*. New York: Columbia University Press.

(1981a). *Lectures on Government and Binding*. Dordrecht, Holland: Foris.

(1981b). "On the Representation of Form and Function." *The Linguistic Review* **1**(1): 3–40.

(1984). *Modular Approaches to the Study of the Mind*. San Diego, CA: San Diego State University Press.

(1986). *Knowledge of Language: Its Nature, Origin and Use*. New York: Praeger.

(1987). *The Chomsky Reader*. New York: Pantheon Books.

(1988a). *Language and Problems of Knowledge*. Cambridge, MA: MIT Press.

(1988b). *Language in a Psychological Setting*. Japan: Sophia University.

(1991a). Linguistics and Adjacent Fields: A Personal View. In A. Kasher (ed.), *The Chomsky Turn*. Oxford; Cambridge, MA: Basil Blackwell. 3–25.

(1991b). Linguistics and Cognitive Science: Problems and Mysteries. In A. Kasher (ed.), *The Chomsky Turn*. Oxford; Cambridge, MA: Basil Blackwell. 26–55.

(1992). *The Minimalist Program for Linguistic Theory*. Cambridge, MA, MIT Press.

(1993a). From Orwell's Problem to Plato's Problem. In E. Reuland and W. Abraham, (eds.), *Knowledge and Language*. Dordrecht/Boston: Kluwer Academic. **1**.

(1993b). *Language and Thought*. Wakefield, RI; London: Moyer Bell.

(1993c). A minimalist program for linguistic theory. In K. Hale and S. J. Keyser (eds.), *The View from Building 20: Essays in Linguistics in honor of Sylvain Bromberger*. Cambridge, MA: MIT Press. 1–52.

(1996). *The Minimalist Program*. Cambridge, MA: MIT Press.

(1999). On the Nature, Use, and Acquisition of Language. In W. C. Ritchie and T. K. Bhatia (eds.), *Handbook of Child Language Acquisition*. San Diego, CA: Academic Press. 33–54.

(2000). *New Horizons in the Study of Language and Mind*. Cambridge; New York: Cambridge University Press.

(2002). *On Nature and Language*. Cambridge; New York: Cambridge University Press.

Chomsky, N. and M. Halle (1968). *The Sound Pattern of English*. New York: Harper and Row.

Chomsky, N. and H. Lasnik (1996). The Theory of Principles and Parameters. In N. Chomsky (ed.), *The Minimalist Program*. Cambridge, MA: MIT Press. 13–128.

Christophe, A., E. Dupoux, J. Bertonicini and J. F. Mehler (1994). "Do Infants Perceive Word Boundaries? An Empirical Study of the Bootstrapping of Lexical Acquisition." *Journal of the Acoustical Society of America* **95**(3): 1570–1580.

Christophe, A., M. Nespor, M. Guasti and B. V. Ooyen (1997). Reflections on Phonological Bootstrapping: its Role in Lexical and Syntactic Acquisition. In G. Altmann (ed.),

Cognitive Models of Speech Processing. A Special issue of *Language and Cognitive Processes.*

Chugani, H. T., M. E. Phelps and J. C. Mazziotta (1987). "Positron Emission Tomography Study of Human Brain Functional Development." *Annals of Neurology* **22**: 487–497.

Cipollone, N., S. Hartman Keiser and Shravan Vasishth (1998). *Language Files.* Columbus: Ohio State University Press, Columbus, Dept of Linguistics.

Clahsen, H. (1982). *Spracherwerb in der Kindheit. Eine Untersuchung zur Entwicklung der Syntax bei Kleinkindern.* Tübingen: Narr.

(1999). "Lexical Entries and Rules of Language: A Multidisciplinary Study of German Inflection." *Behavioral and Brain Sciences* **22**(6): 991–1062.

Clark, E. (1973a). "Nonlinguistic Strategies and the Acquisition of Word Meanings." *Cognition* **2**(2): 161–182.

(1973b). What's in a Word? On the Child's Acquisition of Semantics in His First Language. In T. E. Moore (ed.), *Cognitive Development and the Acquisition of Language.* New York: Academic Press. 65–110.

(1977). Universal Categories: On the Semantics of Classifiers and Children's Early Word Meanings. In A. Juilland (ed.), *Linguistic Studies Offered to Joseph Greenberg.* Saratoga, CA: Amma Libri.

(1978). "Strategies for Communicating." *Child Development* **49**(4): 953–959. Reprinted in Lust and Foley (2004). 423–431.

(1982). The Young Word Maker: A Case Study of Innovation in the Child's Lexicon. In E. Wanner and L. Gleitman (eds.), *Language Acquisition: The State of the Art.* Cambridge; New York: Cambridge University Press. 390–425. Reprinted in Lust and Foley (2004). 396–422.

(1983). Meanings and Concepts. In J. Flavell and E. M. Markman (eds.), *Handbook of Child Psychology: formerly Carmichael's Manual of Child Psychology.* New York: J. Wiley and Sons. **3**: 787–840.

(1985). The Acquisition of Romance with Special Reference to French. In D. Slobin (ed.), *The Cross-Linguistic Study of Language Acquisition.* Hillsdale, NJ: Lawerence Erlbaum Associates. **1**: 687–782.

(1988). "On the Logic of Contrast." *Journal of Child Language* **15**: 317–335.

(1993). *The Lexicon in Acquisition.* Cambridge; New York: Cambridge University Press.

(1997). "Conceptual Perspective and Lexical Choice in Acquisition." *Cognition* **64**(1): 1–37.

(2003). *First Language Acquisition.* Cambridge; New York: Cambridge University Press.

Clark, E. and E. S. Andersen (1979). "Spontaneous Repairs: Awareness in the Process of Acquiring Language." *Papers and Reports on Child Language Development* **16**.

Clark, E., S. A. Gelman and N. Lane (1985). "Compound Nouns and Category Structure in Young children." *Child Development* **56**(1): 81–91.

Clark, E. and J. Grossman (1998). "Pragmatic Directions and Children's Word Learning." *Journal of Child Language* **25**(1): 1–18.

Clark, E. and T. Svaib (1997). "Speaker Perspective and Reference in Young Children." *First Language* **17**(1(49)): 57–74.

Clark, H. (1999). Psycholinguistics. In R. A. Wilson and F. C. Keil (eds.), *The MIT encyclopedia of the cognitive sciences.* Cambridge, MA: MIT Press. 688–690.

Clark, H. and E. Clark (1977). *Psychology and Language.* New York: Harcourt, Brace, Jovanovich.

Clark, R. (1994). Finitude, Boundedness and Complexity: Learnability and the Study of First Language. In B. Lust, G. Hermon and J. Kornfilt (eds.), *Syntactic Theory and First Language Acquisition: Cross-Linguistic Perspectives*. Hillsdale, NJ: Lawrence Erlbaum Associates. **2**: 473–490.

Clements, G. N. (1999a). The Geometry of Phonological Features (1985). In J. A. Goldsmith (ed.), *Phonological Theory. The Essential Readings*. Oxford; Cambridge, MA: Basil Blackwell.

Clements, G. N. (1999b). Phonology. In R. A. Wilson and F. C. Keil (eds.), *The MIT Encyclopedia of the Cognitive Sciences*. Cambridge, MA: MIT Press. 639–641.

Clements, G. N. and S. J. Keyser (1983). *CV Phonology: A Generative Theory of the Syllable*. Cambridge, MA: MIT Press.

Clifford, T. (1984). Acquisition of Pronouns in the First Language Acquisition of English: A Study of Natural Speech. Unpublished Master's thesis. Ithaca, NY: Cornell University.

Cohen Sherman, J. (1983). The Acquisition of Control in Complement Sentences. The Role of Structural and Lexical Factors. Unpublished Ph.D. dissertation. Ithaca, NY: Cornell University.

Cohen Sherman, J. and B. Lust (1986). Syntactic and Lexical Constraints on the Acquisition of Control in Complement Sentences. In B. Lust (ed.), *Studies in the Acquisition of Anaphora. Defining the Constraints*. Dordrecht; Boston: D. Reidel. **I**: 279–310.

(1993a). "Children are in Control." *Cognition* **46**: 1–51.

(1993b). "A Note on Continuity of Universal Grammar: Response to Cairns, McDaniel and Hsu." *Cognition* **48**(2): 195–197.

Cole, R. A. and J. Jakinik (1980). A Model of Speech Perception. In R. Cole (ed.), *Perception and Production of Fluent Speech*. Hillsdale, NJ: Lawrence Erlbaum Associates. 133–163.

Cole, P., G. Hermon and C.-T. J. Huang (2001). Introduction. Long-Distance Reflexives: the State of the Art. In P. Cole, G. Hermon and C.-T. J. Huang (eds.), *Syntax and Semantics*. Vol. XXXIII. *Long-Distance Reflexives*. San Diego, CA: Academic Press.

Cole, P., G. Hermon and L.-M. Sung (1990). "Principles and Parameters of Long-Distance Reflexives." *Linguistic Enquiry* **21**: 22.

Colombo, J. and R. Bundy (1983). "Infant Response to Auditory Familiarity and Novelty." *Infant Behavior and Development* **6**(3): 305–311.

Comrie, B. (1981). *Language Universals and Linguistic Typology*. Chicago: University of Chicago Press.

Comrie, B. (ed.) (1987). *The World's Major Languages*. Oxford; New York: Oxford University Press.

Comrie, B., S. Matthews and M. Polinsky (eds.) (1996). *The Atlas of Languages*. New York: Facts on File, Inc.

Conant, S. (1987). "The Relationship Between Age and MLU in Young Children: A Second Look at Klee and Fitzgerald's Data." *Journal of Child Language* **14**(1): 169–173.

Connelly, M. (1984). *Basotho Children's Acquisition of Noun Morphology*. Colchester: University of Essex.

Cook, V. (1988). *Chomsky's Universal Grammar. An Introduction*. Oxford: Blackwell.

(1994). *Chomsky's Universal Grammar*. Oxford: Blackwell.

Cook, V. and M. Newson (1996). *Chomsky's Universal Grammar.* London: Blackwell.

Cooper, F. S., P. C. Delattre, A. M. Liberman, J. M. Borst and L. J. Gerstman (1952). "Some Experiments on the Perception of Synthetic Speech Sounds." *Journal of the Acoustical Society of America* **24**(6): 597–606.

Cooper, R. P., J. Abraham, J. Berman and M. Staska (1997). "The Development of Infants' Preference for Motherese." *Infant Behavior and Development* **20**(4): 477–488.

Cooper, R. P. and R. N. Aslin (1990). "Preference for Infant Directed Speech in the First Month After Birth." *Child Development* **61**(5): 1584–1595.

Cooper, W. and J. Paccia-Cooper (1980). *Syntax and Speech.* Cambridge, MA: Harvard University Press.

Cooper, W. and E. Walker (1979). *Sentence Processing: Psycholinguistic Studies. Presented to Merrill Garrett.* Hillsdale, NJ: Lawrence Erlbaum Associates.

Corbalis, M. (1991). *The Lopsided Ape: Evolution of the Generative Mind.* New York: Oxford University Press.

Corrigan, R. (1978). "Language Development as Related to Stage 6 Object Permanence." *Journal of Child Language* **5**: 173–189.

Couper-Kuhlen, E. (1993). *English Speech Rhythm: Form and Function in Everyday Verbal Interaction.* Amsterdam; Philadelphia: John Benjamins.

Cowan, N. (ed.) (1997). *The Development of Memory in Childhood.* Hove, East Sussex: Psychology Press.

Crain, S. (1991). "Language Acquisition in the Absence of Experience." *Behavioral and Brain Sciences* **14**(4): 597–650.

  (1999). Semantics, Acquisition of. In R. A. Wilson and F. C. Keil (eds.), *The MIT Encyclopedia of the Cognitive Sciences.* Cambridge, MA: MIT Press. 742–743.

Crain, S. and J. D. Fodor (1985). How Can Grammars Help Parsers? In D. R. Dowty, L. Karttunen and Z. Zwicky (eds.), *Natural Language Parsing: Psychological, Computational and Theoretical Perspectives.* Cambridge; New York: Cambridge University Press.

Crain, S. and D. Lillo-Martin (1999). *An Introduction to Linguistic Theory and Language Acquisition.* Malden, MA: Basil Blackwell.

Crain, S. and C. McKee (1985). Acquisition of Structural Restrictions on Anaphors. *Proceedings of the Sixteenth Annual Meeting of the North Eastern Linguistics Society (NELS).* Montreal: McGill University. 94–110.

Crain, S. and M. J. J. Nakayama (1987). "Structure Dependence in Grammar Formation." *Language* **63**: 522–543.

Crain, S. and P. Pietroski (2002). "Why Language Acquisition is a Snap." *Linguistic Review* **19**(1–2): 163–184.

Crain, S. and R. Thornton (1998). *Investigations in Universal Grammar: A Guide to Experiments on the Acquisition of Syntax and Semantics.* Cambridge, MA: MIT Press.

Crain, W. and K. Wexler (1999). Methodology in the Study of Language Acquisition: A Modular Approach. In W. C. Ritchie and T. K. Bhatia (eds.), *Handbook of Child Language Acquisition.* San Diego, CA: Academic Press. 387–426.

Crain, S., L. Conway and R. Thornton (1994). D-Quantification in Child Language. *Proceedings of the Eastern States Conference on Linguistics.* Ithaca, NY: Cornell University Department of Linguistics.

Crain, S., D. Shankweiler, P. Marcuso and E. Bar-Shalom (1990). *Working Memory and Comprehension of Spoken Sentences: Investigations of Children with Reading Disorders. Neurophysical Disorders of Short-Term Memory*. Cambridge: Cambridge University Press.

Crain, S., R. Thornton, C. Boster, L. Conway, D. Lillo-Martin and E. Woodams (1996). "Quantification without Qualification." *Language Acquisition* **5**: 83–153.

Crelin, E. S. (1969). *Anatomy of the Newborn: An Atlas*. Philadelphia: Lea and Febiger.

Cromer, R. (1987). "Language Growth with Experience without Feedback." *Journal of Psycholinguistic Research* **16**(3). Reprinted in Bloom (1994). 411–420.

(1988). The Cognition Hypothesis Revisited. In F. S. Kessel (ed.), *The Development of Language and Language Researchers: Essays in Honor of Roger Brown*. Hillsdale, NJ: Lawrence Erlbaum Associates. 223–248.

(1994). A Case Study of Dissociations Between Language and Cognition. In H. Tager-Flusberg (ed.), *Constraints on Language Acquisition: Studies of Atypical Children*. Hillsdale, NJ: Erlbaum. 141–153.

Cruttendon, A. (1974). "An Experiment Involving Comprehension of Intonation in Children from 7 to 10." *Journal of Child Language* **1**(2): 221–31.

Crystal, D. (1979). Prosodic Development. In P. Fletcher and M. Garman (eds.), *Language Acquisition*. Cambridge; New York: Cambridge University Press. 33–48.

(1986). Prosodic Development. In P. Fletcher and M. Garman (eds.), *Language Acquisition*. 2nd edn. Cambridge; New York: Cambridge University Press. 174–197.

(1992). *Encyclopedic Dictionary of Language and Languages*. Oxford; Cambridge, MA: Basil Blackwell.

(1997a). *The Cambridge Encyclopedia of Language*. Cambridge; New York: Cambridge University Press.

(1997b). Language and Thought. *Cambridge Encyclopedia of Linguistics*. Cambridge University Press. 14–16.

(1997c). *A Dictionary of Linguistics and Phonetics*. 4th edition. London: Blackwell Publishers.

Crystal, D., P. Fletcher and M. Garman (1976). *The Grammatical Analysis of Language Disability: a Procedure for Assessment and Remediation*. New York: Elsevi.

Curtiss, S. (1977). *Genie: A Psycholinguistic Study of a Modern Day "Wild Child"*. New York: Academic Press.

(1988). Abnormal Language Acquisition and the Modularity of Language. In F. Newmyer (ed.), *Linguistics: The Cambridge Survey*. Vol. II. *Linguistic Theory: Extensions and Implications*. Cambridge: Cambridge University Press. 96–116.

Curtiss, S. and J. Schaeffer (1997). Syntactic Development in Children with Hemispherectomy: The Infl-System. *Proceedings of Boston University Child Language Development* **21**.

Curtiss, S. and P. Tallal (1991). On the Nature of the Impairment in Language-Impaired Children. In J. F. Miller (ed.), *Research on Child Language Disorders: A Decade of Progress*. Austin, TX: Pro-Ed.

Curtiss, S., S. de Bode and G. Mathern (2001). "Spoken Language Outcomes After Hemispherectomy: Factoring in Etiology." *Brain and Language* **79**(3): 379–396.

Curtiss, S., V. Fromkin, S. Krashen, D. Rigler and M. Rigler (1974). "The Linguistic Development of Genie." *Language* **50**(3): 528–554.

Cutler, A. (1994). "The Perception of Rhythm in Language." *Cognition* **50**: 79–81.

Cutler, A. and D. Carter (1987). "The Predominance of Strong Initial Syllables in the English Vocabulary." *Computer Speech and Language* **2**(3–4): 133–142.

Cutler, A. and D. Swinney (1980). Development of the Comprehension of Semantic Focus in Young Children. *Presented at the Fifth Annual Boston University Conference on Language Development*, Boston, MA.

Cutler, A., J. Mehler, D. Nons and J. Segni (1983). "A Language Specific Comprehension Strategy." *Nature* **304**: 159–160.

(1986). "The Syllable's Differeng Role in the Segmentation of French and English." *Journal of Memory and Language* **25**(4): 385–400.

(1992). "The Monolingual Nature of Speech Segmentation by Bilinguals." *Cognitive Psychology* **24**(3): 381–410.

Dale, P. S. (1976). *Language Development: Structure and Function*. New York: Holt Rinehart and Winston.

Dale, P. S. and C. Crain-Thornson (1993). "Pronoun Reversals: Who, When and Why?" *Journal of Child Language* **20**(3): 573–589.

Damasio, A. and H. Damasio (1993). Brain and Language. In A. Goldman (ed.), *Readings in Philosophy and Cognitive Science*. Cambridge, MA: MIT Press. 585–595.

Damasio, A. R. and D. Tranel (1993). "Nouns and verbs are retrieved with differently distributed neural systems." Proceedings of the National Academy of Sciences of the USA **90**, 4957–4960.

Damasio, A., U. Bellugi, H. Damasio, H. Poizner and J. V. Gilder (1986). "Sign Language Aphasia During Left-Hemisphere Amytal Injection." *Nature* **322**: 363–365.

Danesi, M. (1994). "The Neuroscientific Perspective in Second Language Acquisition Research: A Critical Synopsis." *International Review of Applied Linguistics in Language Teaching* **32**(3): 201–228.

Davidoff, J., I. Davies and D. Robertson (1999). "Colour Categories in a Stone Age Tribe." *Nature* **398**: 203–204.

Davis, D. and J. Wimbish (1994). *The Linguist's SHOEBOX*. Waxhaw, NC: Summer Institute of Linguistics.

Davis, K. (1995). "Phonetic and Phonological Contrasts in the Acquisition of Voicing: Voice Onset Time Production in Hindi and English." *Journal of Child Language* **22**(2): 275–305.

Davison, A. (2004). "Structural Case, Lexical Case and the Verbal Projection Problem." In V. Dayal and A. Mahajan (eds.), *Clause Structure in South Asian Languages*. Dordrecht: Kluwer, 199–225.

De Bleser, R., J. Faiss and M. Schwartz (1995). "Rapid Recovery of Aphasia and Deep Dyslexia after Cerebrovascular Left-Hemisphere Damage in Childhood." *Journal of Neurolinguistics* **9**(1): 9–22.

DeCasper, A. and W. P. Fifer (1980). "Of Human Bonding: Newborns Prefer their Mothers' Voices." *Science* **208**(4448): 1174–1176.

DeCasper, A. and M. Spence (1986). "Prenatal Maternal Speech Influences Newborns' Perception of Speech Sounds." *Infant Behavior and Development* **9**(2): 133–150.

DeGraff, M. (ed.) (1999). *Language Creation and Language Change. Learning, Development, and Conceptual Change*. Cambridge, MA: MIT Press.

Dehaene-Lambertz, G. (2000). "Cerebral Specialization for Speech and Non-Speech Stimuli in Infants." *Journal of Cognitive Neuroscience* **12**(3): 449–460.

Dehaene-Lambertz, G. and S. Dehaene (1994). "Speed and Cerebral Correlates of Syllable Discrimination in Infants." *Nature* **370**: 292.

Dehaene-Lambertz, G., S. Dehaene and L. Hertz-Pannier (2002). "Functional Neuroimaging of Speech Perception in Infants." *Science* **298**(5600): 2013–2015.

Delattre, P. C., A. M. Liberman and F. S. Cooper (1955). "Acoustic Loci and Transitional Cues for Consonants." *Journal of the Acoustical Society of America* **27**(4): 769–773.

DeLoache, J. (1995). Early Symbol Understanding and Use. In D. Medin (ed.), *The Psychology of Learning and Motivation: Advances in Research and Theory*. Orlando, FL: Academic Press. **33**: 65–114.

Demetras, M. J., K. N. Post and C. F. Snow (1986). "Feedback to First Language Learners: The Role of Repetitions and Clarification Questions." *Journal of Child Language* **13**: 275–292.

Demorny, L. and E. Mckenzie (1999). "Rhythm in Early Infancy." *Nature* **266**: 718–719.

Demuth, K. (1987). Acquisition of Impersonal Passives: A Matter of Case. *Proceedings of the Boston University Conference on Language Development*. Boston: Boston University.

(1988). Noun Classes and Agreement in Sesotho Acquisition. In M. Barlow and C. A. Ferguson (eds.), *Agreement in Natural Language: Approaches, Theories, Descriptions*. Stanford, CA: Center for the Study of Language and Information.

(1990). Relative Clauses, Cleft Constructions and Functional Categories in Sesotho Acquisition. Paper Presented at the 5th Child Language Congress, Budapest.

(1992). Interactions at the Morpho-Syntax Interface. In J. Meisel (ed.), *The Acquisition of Verb Placement: Functional Categories and V2 Phenomena in Language Development*. Dordrecht: Kluwer Academic Publishers. 83–107.

(1994). On the Underspecification of Functional Categories in Early Grammars. In B. Lust, M. Suñer and J. Whitman (eds.), *Syntactic Theory and First Language Acquisition: Cross Linguistic Perspectives*. Vol 1. *Heads, Projections and Learnability*. 119–134.

(1995). Problems in the Acquisition of Tonal Systems. In J. Archibald (ed.), *Phonological Acquisition and Phonological Theory*. Hillsdale, NJ: Lawrence Erlbaum Associates.

(1996a). Collecting Spontaneous Production Data. In D. McDaniel, C. McKee and H. Cairns (eds.), *Methods for Assessing Children's Syntax*. Cambridge, MA: MIT Press: 3–22.

(1996b). Alignment, Stress and Parsing in Early Phonological Words. *Proceedings of the UBC International Conference on Phonological Acquisition*. Somerville, MA: Cascadilla Press.

(1996c). The Prosodic Structure of Early Words. In J. L. Morgan and K. Demuth (eds.), *Signal to Syntax*. Hillsdale, NJ: Lawrence Erlbaum Associates.

(1997). Multiple Optimal Outputs in Acquisition. *University Of Maryland Working Papers in Linguistics* **5**: 53–71.

(2001). Prosodic Constraints on Morphological Development. In J. Weissenborn and B. Hohle (eds.), *Approaches to Bootstrapping: Phonological, Syntactic and Neurophysiological Aspects of Early Language Acquisition*. Amsterdam; Philadelphia: John Benjamins.

Demuth, K. and S. Suzman (1997). "Language Impairment in Zulu." BUCLD **21**: 1224–1235.

Dennett, D. C. (1978). *Brainstorms: Philosophical Essays on Mind and Psychology*. Cambrige, MA: Bradford Books, MIT Press.

(1996). *Kinds of Minds: Toward an Understanding of Consciousness*. New York: Basic Books.

Dennis, M. (1980). "Capacity and Strategy for Syntactic Comprehension after Left or Right Hemidecortication." *Brain and Language* **10**: 287–317.

(1983). Syntax in Brain-Injured Children. In M. Studdert-Kennedy (ed.), *Psychobiology of Language*. Cambridge, MA: MIT Press. 195–202.

Dennis, M. and B. Kohn (1975). "Comprehension of Syntax in Infantile Hemiplegics after Cerebral Hemidecortication: Left-Hemisphere Superiority." *Brain and Language* **2**: 472–482.

Dennis, M. and H. Whitaker (1976). "Language Acquisition Following Hemidecortication: Linguistic Superiority of the Left over the Right Hemisphere." *Brain and Language* **3**: 404–433.

(1977). Hemispheric Equipotentiality and Language Acquisition. In S. Segalowitz and F. Gruber (eds.), *Language Development and Neurological Theory*. New York: Academic Press. 93–106.

Dennis, M., M. Lovett and C. A. Wiegel-Crump (1981). "Written Language Acquisition after Left or Right Hemidecortication in Infancy." *Brain and Language* **12**: 54–91.

Dennis, M., J. Sugar and H. A. Whitaker (1982). "The Acquisition of Tag Questions." *Child Development* **53**(5): 1254–1257.

Deprez, V. and Amy Pierce (1993). "Negation and Functional Projections in Early Grammar." *Linguistic Inquiry* **24**: 25–67.

De Saussure, Ferdinand (1959). *Course in General Linguistics*. New York: Philosophical Library.

Deutsch, W., C. Koster and J. Koster (1986). "What Can We Learn from Children's Errors of Understanding Anaphora?" *Linguistics* **24**: 203–225.

Deutscher, G. (2002). "On the Misuse of the Notion of 'Abduction' in Linguistics." *Journal of Linguistics* **38**(3): 469–485.

DeVilliers, J. (1995a). Empty Categories and Complex Sentences: The Case of Wh-Questions. In P. Fletcher and B. MacWhinney (eds.), *Handbook of Language Acquisition*. Cambridge, MA: Basil Blackwell.

DeVilliers, J. (1995b). "Introduction to the Special Issue on the Acquisition of Wh-Questions." *Language Acquisition* **4**(1&2): 1–4.

DeVilliers, J. and P. DeVilliers (1978). From Sound to Meaning. In *Language Acquisition*. Cambridge, MA: Harvard University Press. 6–30.

(2000). Linguistic Determinism and the Understanding of False Beliefs. In M. Mitchell and K. Riggs (eds.), *Children's Reasoning and the Mind*. Hove: Psychology Press.

DeVilliers, J., T. Roeper and A. Vainikka (1990). The Acquisition of Long-Distance Rules. In L. Frazier and J. DeVilliers (eds.), *Language Processing and Language Acquisition*. Dordrecht: Kluwer. 257–298.

Devitt, M. (1999). Reference, Theories of. In R. A. Wilson and F. C. Keil (eds.), *The MIT Encyclopedia of the Cognitive Sciences*. Cambridge, MA: MIT Press. 714–715.

Di Sciullo, A. M. and E. Williams (1987). *On the Definition of Word. Linguistic Inquiry Monograph Fourteen*. Cambridge, MA: MIT Press.

Dittmar, N. and Z. Penner (eds.) (1998). *Issues in the Theory of Language Acquisition. Essays in Honor of Jurgen Weissenborn*. Bern: PeterLang.

Dockrell, J. and R. Campbell (1986). Lexical Acquisition Strategies in the Preschool Child. In S. A. Kuczaj and M. D. Barrett (eds.), *The Development of Word Meaning: Progress in Cognitive Development Research*. New York: Springer-Verlag.

Donahue, M. (1984). "Learning Disabled Children's Comprehension and Production of Syntactic Devices for Marking Given vs. New Information." *Applied Psycholinguistics* **5**: 101–116.

Drachman, G. and A. Malkouti-Drachman (1973). Studies in the Acquisition of Greek as a Native Language: 1. Some Preliminary Findings on Phonology. *Ohio State University Working Papers on Linguistics.* 99–114.

Dresher, B. E. (1999). "Charting the Learning Path: Cues to Parameter Setting." *Linguistic Inquiry* **30**(1): 26–67.

Dresher, B. E. and J. D. Kaye (1990). "A Computational Learning Model for Metrical Phonology." *Cognition* **34**(2): 137–195.

Dromi, E. (1987). *Early Lexical Development.* Cambridge; New York: Cambridge University Press.

Dromi, E. and R. Berman (1982). "A Morphemic Measure of Early Language Development: Data from Modern Hebrew." *Journal of Child Language* **9**: 403–424.

Dromi, E., L. B. Leonard, G. Adam and S. Zadoneisky Erlich (1999). "Verb Agreement Morphology in Hebrew-Speaking Children with Specific Language Impairment." *Journal of Speech, Language and Hearing Research* **42** (6): 1414–1431.

Dronkers, N. (1996). "A New Brain Region for Coordinating Speech Articulation." *Nature* **384**: 159–161.

Dronkers, N., S. Pinker and A. Damasio (2000). Language, Thought, Mood and Learning and Memory. In Kandel, Schwartz and Jessell. 1169–1187.

Drozd, K. (2004). "Learnability and Linguistic Performance. A Review of Crain, S. and Thornton, R. 1998. Investigations in Universal Grammar. Cambridge, MIT." *Journal of Child Language* **31**(2): 431–458.

Dye, C. 2004. Optional Infinitives or Silent auxes? New Evidence from Romance Languages and Linguistic Theory 2002. In R. Bok-Bennema, B. Hollebrandse, B. Kampers-Manhe and P. Sleeman (eds.), *Selected Papers from "Going Romance"* 2002. Groningen 28–30 November. Amsterdam: John Benjamins.

(2005a). Identifying Auxiliaries in First Language Acquisition: Evidence from a New Child French Corpus. Unpublished doctoral dissertation. Cornell University. Ithaca.

(2005b). The Status of Ostensibly Nonfinite Matrix Verbs in Child French: Results from a New Corpus. In A. Brugos, M. R. Clark-Cotton and S. Ha. (eds.), *Proceedings of the 29th Boston University Conference on Language Development.* Boston: Cascadilla Press.

Dye, C., C. Foley, M. Blume and B. Lust (2004). *The Acquisition of Verb Morphosyntax: Evidence for the Grammatical Mapping Paradigm.* Linguistic Society of America Annual Meeting, Boston, MA.

Dye, C., C. Foley and B. Lust (2002). *Dissociating Finiteness from Morphology: New Evidence from the Acquisition of Verbal Inflection in French.* Paper Presented at the 32nd Linguistic Symposium on Romance Language, Toronto, April 19–21.

(in preparation). On the Universal Dissociation of Finiteness and Morphology. Evidence from the Acquisition of Verbal Inflection in French. Cornell University.

Dye, C., C. Foley, M. Blume and B. Lust (2004). Mismatches between Morphology and Syntax in First Language Acquisition Suggest a "Syntax First" Model. In *Online Proceedings of the 28th Boston University Conference on Language Development.* Boston: Cascadilla Press.

Eblen, R. (1982). "A Study of the Acquisition of Fricatives by Three-Year-Old Children Learning Mexican Spanish." *Language and Speech* **25**(3): 201–220.

Echols, C. (1993). "A Perceptually-Based Model of Children's Earliest Productions." *Cognition* **46**: 245–296.

Echols, C. H. and E. L. Newport (1992). "The Role of Stress and Position in Determining First Words." *Language Acquisition* **2**(3): 189–220.

Eckert, M., L. Lobardino and C. Leonard (2001). "Planar Asymmetry Tips the Phonological Playground and Environment Raises the Bar." *Child Development* **72**(4): 988–1002.

Edwards, J. (1992a). Transcription of discourse. In W. Bright. (ed.), *International Encyclopedia of Linguistics*. Oxford: Oxford University Press: 367–370.

Edwards, J. (1992b). "Computer Methods in Child Language Research: Four Principles for the Use of Archived Data." *Journal of Child Language* **19**: 435–458.

Edwards, J. and M. Lampert (eds.) (1993). *Talking Data: Transcription and Coding in Discourse Research*. Hillsdale, NJ: Lawrence Erlbaum Associates.

Egido, C. (1983). "The Functional Role of the Closed Class Vocabulary in Children's Language Processing." Unpublished Ph.D. dissertation. Cambridge, MA: MIT.

Eimas, P. D. and J. L. Miller (1992). "Organization in the Perception of Speech by Young Infants." *Psychological Science* **3**: 340–345.

Eimas, P., J. Miller and P. Jusczyk (1987). On Infant Speech Perception and the Acquisition of Language. In S. Harnad (ed.), *Categorical Perception: the Groundwork of Cognition*. Cambridge; New York: Cambridge University Press. 161–195.

Eimas, P., E. Siqueland, P. Jusczyk and J. Vigorito (1971). "Speech Perception in Infants." *Science* **171**: 303–306.

Eisele, J. (1988). Meaning and Form in Children's Judgments about Language: A Study of the Truth-Value Judgment Test. Unpublished Master's thesis. Ithaca, NY: Cornell University.

Eisele, J. and D. Aram (1993a). "Differential Effects of Early Hemisphere Damage on Lexical Comprehension and Production." *Aphasiology*.

    (1993b). "Comprehension and Imitation of Syntax Following Early Hemisphere Damage." *Brain and Language* **46**: 212–231.

    (1995). "Lexical and Grammatical Development in Children with Early Hemisphere Damage: A Cross-Sectional View from Birth to Adolescence." In P. Fletcher and B. MacWhinney (eds.), *The Handbook of Child Language*. Oxford; Cambridge, MA: Blackwell: 664–689.

Eisele, J. and B. Lust (1996). "Knowledge about Pronouns: A Developmental Study Using a Truth-Value Judgment Task." *Child Development* **67**(6): 3086–3100.

Eisele, J., B. Lust and D. Aram (1998). "Presupposition and Implication of Truth: Linguistic Deficits Following Early Brain Lesions." *Brain and Language* **61**: 376–394.

Eisenberg, R. B. (1976). *Auditory Competence in Early Life*. Baltimore, MD: University Park Press.

Elman, J. L. and E. A. Bates (1997). "Response to 'Little Statisticians'." *Science* **276**(5315): 1161–1300.

Elman, J. L., E. A. Bates, M. Johnson, A. Karmiloff-Smith, D. Parisi and K. Plunkett (1996). *Rethinking Innateness: A Connectionist Perspective on Development*. Cambridge, MA: MIT Press.

Entus, A. (1977). Hemispheric Asymmetry in Processing of Dichotically Presented Speech and Nonspeech Stimuli by Infants. In S. Segalowitz and F. Gruber (eds.), *Language Development and Neurological Theory*. New York: Academic Press. 64–74.

Epstein, S., H. Thráinsson and C. Jan-Wonther Zwart (1996). Introduction. In W. Abraham, S. Epstein, H. Thráinsson and C. Jan-Wouther Zwart (eds.), *Minimal Ideas: Syntactic Studies in the Minimalist Framework*. Amsterdam; Philadelphia, PA: John Benjamins.

Epstein, S., S. Flynn and G. Martohardjono (1996). "Second Language Acquisition: Theoretical and Experimental Issues in Contemporary Research." *Behavioral and Brain Sciences* **19**: 677–758.

Epstein, W. (1961). "The Influence of Syntactic Structure on Learning." *American Journal of Psychology* **74**: 80–85.

Erbaugh, M. S. (1986). Taking Stock: The Development of Chinese Noun Classifiers Historically and in Young Children. In C. Craig (ed.), *Noun Classes and Categorization*. Amsterdam: John Benjamins. 399–436.

Erreich, A. (1984). "Learning How to Ask: Patterns of Inversion in Yes–No and Wh-Questions." *Journal of Child Language* **2**: 579–602.

Ervin-Tripp, S. (1964). Imitation and Structural Change in Children's Language. In E. H. Lenneberg (ed.), *New Directions in the Study of Language*. Cambridge, MA: MIT Press. 163–189. Reprinted in C. Ferguson and D. Slobin (eds.) *Studies of Child Language Development*. New York: Holt, Rinehart and Winston. (1973).

Evers, A. and J. van Kampen (1995). Do-Insertion and LF in Child Language. In J. Don, B. Schoten and W. Zonneveld (eds), *O.T.S. Yearbook 1994*. Research Institute for Language and Speech (OTS) of the Utrecht University.

Fabbro, F. (1999). *Neurolinguistics of Bilingualism: An Introduction*. Hove: Psychology Press.

Fabbro, F. and M. Paradis (1995). Acquired Aphasia in a Bilingual Child. In M. Paradis (ed.), *Aspects of Bilingual Aphasia*. Tarrytown, NY: Pergamon. 67–84.

Fee, J. (1995). Segments and Syllables in Early Acquisition. In J. Archibald (ed.), *Phonological Acquisition and Phonological Theory*. Hillsdale, NJ: Lawrence Erlbaum Associates.

Fee, J. and D. Ingram (1980). "Reduplication as a Strategy of Phonological Development." *Journal of Child Language* **9**: 41–54.

Feldman, H., S. Goldin-Meadow and L. Gleitman (1978). "Beyond Herodotus: The Creation of Language by Linguistically Deprived Deaf Children." In A. Lock (ed.), *Action, Gesture, and Symbol: The Emergence of Language*. London: Academic Press. 351–414.

Fenson, L., P. S. Dale, J. S. Reznik, E. A. Bates, D. J. Thal and S. J. Pethick (1994). "Variability in Early Communicative Development." *Monographs of the Society for Research in Child Development* **59**(5(242)): 1–173.

Ferguson, C. A. (1977). Baby Talk as a Simplified Register. In C. E. Snow and C. A. Ferguson (eds.), *Talking to Children: Language Input and Acquisition*. Cambridge; New York: Cambridge University Press.

(1978). Talking to Children: A Search for Universals. In J. Greenberg, C. A. Ferguson and E. Moravcsik (eds.), *Universals of Human Language*. Vol. 1. Stanford, CA: Stanford University Press. Reprinted in Lust and Foley (2004). 176–189.

(1986). Discovering Sound Units and Constructing Sound Systems: It's Child's Play. In J. S. Perkell, D. H. Klatt and K. N. Stevens (eds.), *Invariance and Variability in Speech Processes*. Hillsdale, NJ: Lawrence Erlbaum Associates. 36–57.

Ferguson, C. A. and Farwell (1975). "Words and sounds in early language acquisition." *Language* **51**: 419–39.

Ferguson, C. A., L. Menn and C. Stoel-Gammon (1992). *Phonological Development Models, Research, Implications*. Timomium, MD: York Press.

Fernald, A. (1985). "Four-Month-Old Infants Prefer to Listen to Motherese." *Infant Behavior and Development* **8**(2): 181–195.

Fernald, C. (1972). "Control of grammar in imitation, comprehension and production." *Journal of Verbal Learning and Verbal Behavior* **11**: 606–613.

Fernald, A. and H. Morikawa (1993). "Common Themes and Cultural Variations in Japanese and America Mothers' Speech to Infants." *Child Development* **64**(3): 637–656.

Ferreiro, E. (1971). *Les Relations temporelles dans le langage de l'enfant*. Geneva; Paris: Librairie Droz.

(1978). "What is Written in a Written Sentence? A Developmental Answer." *Journal of Education* **4**: 25–39.

Ferreiro, E. and H. Sinclair (1971). "Temporal Relationships in Language." *International Journal of Psychology* **6**(1): 39–47.

Ferreiro, E., C. Othenin-Girard, H. Chipman and H. Sinclair (1976). "How Do Children Handle Relative Clauses? A Study in Comparative Developmental Psycholinguistics." *Archives of Psychology* **172**: 229.

Fey, M. and J. Gandour (1982). "Rule Discovery in Phonological Acquisition." *Journal of Child Language* **9**(1): 71–82.

Fifer, W. P. and C. Moon (1989). Auditory Experience in the Fetus. In W. P. Smotherman and S. R. Robinson (eds.), *Behavior of the Fetus*. Caldwell, NJ: Telford Press. 175–188.

Fikkert, P. (1994). *On the Acquisition of Prosodic Structure*. The Hague: University of Leiden.

(1998). The Acquisition of Dutch Phonology. In S. Gillis and A. De Houwer (eds.), *The Acquisition of Dutch*. Amsterdam; Philadelphia: John Benjamins. 163–223.

(2000). Acquisition of Phonology. In L. Cheng and R. Sybesma (eds.), *The First GLOT International State-of-the-Article Book*. Berlin; New York: Mouton de Gruyter.

Fischbach, G. (1992). "Mind and Brain." *Scientific American* **267**(3): 48–57. Reprinted as Fischbach (1993).

Fischbach, G. (1993). Mind and Brain. In *Mind and Brain: Readings from Scientific American*. New York: W. H. Freeman. 1–14.

Fisher, C. (2002). "The Role of Abstract Syntactic Knowledge in Language Acquisition: A Reply to Tomasello (2000)." *Cognition* **82**(3): 259–278.

Fisher, C., D. G. Hall, S. Rakowitz and L. Gleitman (1994). When is it Better to Receive than to Give: Syntactic and Conceptual Constraints on Vocabulary Growth. In L. Gleitman and B. Landau (eds.), *The Acquisition of the Lexicon*. Cambridge, MA: MIT Press. 333–375.

Fisher, S., F. Vargha-Khadem, K. Watkins, A. Monaca and M. Pembrey (1998). "Localisation of a Gene Implicated in a Severe Speech and Language Disorder." *Nature Genetics* **18**(2): 168–170.

Flege, J. E. (1995). Second Language Speech Learning: Theory, Findings, and Problems. In W. Strange (ed.), *Speech Perception and Linguistic Experience: Theoretical and Methodological Issues*. Timonium, MD: York Press.

Flynn, S. (1987). *A Parameter Setting Model of L2 Acquisition*. Dordrecht: Reidel.

Flynn, S. (1996). A Parameter-Setting Approach to Second Language Acquisition. In W. Ritchie and T. Bhatia (eds.), *Handbook of Second Language Acquisition*. Hillsdale, NJ: Lawrence Erlbaum Associates. 121–158.

Flynn, S. and B. Lust (2002). A Minimalist Approach to L2 Solves a Dilemma of UG. In V. Cook (ed.), *Portraits of the L2 User*. Clevedon: Multilingual Matters. 93–120.

Flynn, S. and S. Manuel (1991). Age Dependent Effects in Language Acquisition: An Evaluation of "Critical Period" Hypotheses. In L. Eubank (ed.), *Point Counterpoint – UG in the Second Language*. Amsterdam; Philadelphia: John Benjamins.

Flynn, S. and G. Martohardjono (1994). Mapping from the Initial State to the Final State: The Separation of Universal Principles and Language Specific Principles. In B. Lust, M. Suñer and J. Whitman (eds.), *Syntactic Theory and First Language Acquisition: Cross Linguistic Perspectives*. Hillsdale, NJ: Lawrence Erlbaum Associates.

Flynn, S., C. Foley and B. Lust (2000). "Evidence for Grammatical Mapping from Second Language Acquisition." Linguistic Society of America Annual Meeting, Chicago, IL.

Flynn, S. and B. Lust (2002). A Minimalist Approach to 12 Solves a Dilemma of UG in Acquisition. *Portraits of the L2 User*. Clevedon, UK: Multilingual Matters, 93–120.

Fodor, J. A. (1975). *The Language of Thought*. New York: Crowell.

Fodor, J. A. (1983). *The Modularity of Mind: An Essay on Faculty Psychology*. Cambridge, MA: MIT Press.

(1994). How to Obey the Subset Principle: Binding and Locality. In B. Lust, G. Hermon and J. Kornfilt (eds.), *Syntactic Theory and First Language Acquisition: Cross-Linguistic Perspectives*. Hillsdale, NJ: Lawrence Erlbaum Associates. **2:** 429–452.

Fodor, J. A. (1998). *Concepts*. Oxford: Clarendon Press.

Fodor, J., T. Bever and M. Garrett (1974). *The Psychology of Language: An Introduction To Psycholinguistics and Generative Grammar*. New York: McGraw Hill.

Fodor, J. and Z. Pylyshyn (1988). "Connectionism and Cognitive Architecture: A Critical Analysis." *Cognition* **28**(1–2): 3–71.

Fodor, J. A. and Z. W. Pylyshyn (1988). Connectionism and Cognitive Architecture: A Critical Analysis. In S. Pinker and J. F. Mehler (eds.), *Connections and symbols*. Cambridge, MA, MIT Press: 255.

Fodor, J. D. (1998a). "Unambiguous Triggers." *Linguistic Inquiry* **29**(1): 1–36.

(1998b). "Learning to Parse." *Journal of Psycholinguistic Research* **27**: 285–319.

(1998c). "Parsing to Learn." *Journal of Psycholinguistic Research* **27**: 339–375.

Foley, C. (1996). Knowledge of the Syntax of Operators in the Initial State. Unpublished Ph.D. dissertation. Ithaca: Cornell University.

Foley, C., J. Pactovis and B. Lust (submitted). "The Significance of Verb Inflection in First Language Acquisition of VP Ellipsis: Linking LF and PF." Ithaca, NY: Cornell University Press.

Foley, C., Z. Nuñez del Prado, I. Barbier and B. Lust (1997). Operator Variable Binding in the Initial State: An Argument from VP Ellipsis. In S. Somashekar (ed.), *Cornell Working Papers in Linguistics*. Ithaca, NY: Cornell University. **15:** 1–19.

(2003). "Knowledge of Variable Binding in VP Ellipsis: Language Acquisition Research and Theory Converge." *Syntax* **6**(1): 52–83.

Foley, C., B. Lust, D. Battin, A. Koehne and K. White (2000). On the Acquisition of an Indefinite Determiner: Evidence for Unselective Binding. In C. Howell, S. Fish and T. Keith-Lucas (eds.), *Proceedings of 24th Boston University Conference on Language Development*. Boston, MA: Cascadilla Press.

Fortescue, M. (1984/5). "Learning to Speak Greenlandic: A Case Study of a Two-Year-Old's Morphology in a Polysynthetic Language." *First Language* **5**: 101–114.

Fortescue, M. and L. L. Olsen (1992). The Acquisition of West Greenlandic. In D. Slobin (ed.), *The Crosslinguistic Study of Language Acquisition*. Hillsdale, NJ: Lawrence Erlbaum Associates. **3**: 111–219.

Foss, D. and D. Hakes (1978). Linguistic Diversity and Cognitive Categories. In D. Foss (ed.), *Psycholinguistics. An Introduction to the Psychology of Language*. Englewood Cliffs, NJ: Prentice-Hall. 381–397.

Foster-Cohen, S. (1990). *The Communicative Competence of Young Children: A Modular Approach*. London: Longman.

(1994). "Exploring the Boundary Between Syntax and Pragmatics: Relevance and the Binding of Pronouns." *Journal of Child Language* **21**: 237–55.

(1996). "Modularity and Principles and Parameters: Avoiding the 'Cognitively Ugly.'" *First Language* **16**(1(46)): 1–19.

(1999). *An Introduction to Child Language Development*. New York: Longman.

(2000a). "Relevance Theory and Language Acquisition: A Productive Paradigm Shift?" *Child Language Bulletin* **20**(1): 5–19.

(2000b). "Review article of Sperber, D. and Wilson, D. (second edition: 1995) Relevance: Communication and Cognition." *Second Language Research* **16**: 77–92.

Fowler, C. A. (1977). *Timing Control in Speech Production*. Indianapolis: Indiana University Linguistics Club.

Frank, R. (1991). Formal Grammar and the Acquisition of Complex Sentences. *Eighth Eastern States Conference on Linguistics*, Baltimore, University of Maryland.

Frank, R. and S. Kapur (1996). "On the Use of Triggers in Parameter Setting." *Linguistic Inquiry* **27**(4): 623–660.

Fraser, C., U. Bellugi and R. Brown (1963). "Control of Grammar in Imitation, Comprehension, and Production." *Journal of Verbal Learning and Verbal Behavior* **2**: 121–135.

Frazier, L. (1999). Modularity and Language. In Wilson and Keil. 557–558.

Frazier, L. and K. Rayner (1988). Parameterizing the Language Processing System: Left- Versus Right-Branching Within and Across Languages. In J. A. Hawkins (ed.), *Explaining Language Universals*. Oxford; New York: Basil Blackwell. 247–279.

Freedle, R., T. Keeney and N. Smith (1970). "Effects of Mean Depth and Grammaticality on Children's Imitations of Sentences." *Journal of Verbal Learning and Verbal Behavior* **9**: 149–154.

Fremgen, A. and D. Fay (1980). "Overextensions in Production and Comprehension: A Methodological Clarification." *Journal of Child Language* **7**(1): 205–211.

Friederici, A. D. (1995). "The Time Course of Syntactic Activation during Language Processing: A Model Based on Neuropsychological and Neurophysiological Data." *Brain and Language* **50**: 259–281.

Friederici, A. (2002). "Towards a Neural Basis of Auditory Sentence Processing." *Trends in Cognitive Sciences* **6**(2): 78–84.

Friederici, A. and A. Hahne (2001). Development Patterns of Brain Activity Reflecting Semantic and Syntactic Processes. In J. Weissenborn and B. Hohle (eds.), *Approaches to Bootstrapping: Phonological, Lexical, Syntactic and Neurophysiological Aspects of Early Language Acquisition*. Amsterdam: John Benjamins.

Friederici, A. and J. Wessels (1993). "Phonotactic Knowledge and its Use in Infant Speech Perception." *Perception and Psychophysics* **54**: 287–295.

Fromkin, V. (2000). *Linguistics: An Introduction to Linguistic Theory*. Malden, MA; Oxford: Blackwell.

Fromkin, V. and R. Rodman (1998). *An Introduction to Language*. New York: Holt and Rinehart.

Gair, J. (1998). *Studies in South Asian Linguistics* (Selected and edited by B. Lust). Oxford: Oxford University Press.

Gair, J., B. Lust, K. V. Subbarao and K. Wali (2000). Introduction to Lexical Anaphors and Pronouns in some South Asian Languages. In B. Lust, K. Wali, J. Gair & K. V. Subbarao (eds.), *Lexical Anaphors and Pronouns in some South Asian Languages*. Mouton. 1–46.

Gair, J. B. Lust, L. Sumangala and M. Rodrigo (1989). Acquisition of Null Subjects and Control in some Sinhala Adverbial Clauses. In *Papers and Reports on Child Language Development*. Los Angeles, CA: Stanford University. **28**: 97–106.

(1998). Acquisition of Null Subjects and Control in some Sinhala Adverbial Clauses. In J. Gair (ed.), *Studies in South Asian Linguistics: Sinhala and Other South Asian Languages*. Oxford: Oxford University Press, 271–285.

Gair, J., B. Lust, T. Bhatia, V. Sharma and J. Khare (1998). A Parameter-setting Paradox: Children's Acquisition of Hindi Anaphora in "Jab" Clauses. *Studies in South Asian Linguistics: Sinhala and Other South Asian Languages*. J. Gair. Oxford: Oxford University Press: 286–304.

Gair, J. W. (1988). Kinds of Markedness. In S. Flynn and W. O'Neill (eds.), *Linguistic Theory in Second Language Acquisition*. Dordrecht; Boston: Kluwer Academic: 225–251.

(1998). *Studies in South Asian Linguistics: Sinhala and other South Asian Languages*. Oxford; New York: Oxford University Press.

(1998). Subjects, Case and INFL in Sinhala (1991). In *Studies in South Asian Linguistics*. Oxford: Oxford University Press.

Galaburda, A. (1995). Anatomic Basis of Cerebral Dominance. In R. Davidson and K. Hugdahl (ed.), *Brain Asymmetry*. Cambridge, MA: MIT Press. 51–74.

Galaburda, A., G., Sherman and N. Geschwind (1985). Cerebral Lateralization: Historical Note on Animal Studies. In S. Glick (ed.), *Cerebral Lateralization in Nonhuman Species*. Orlando FL: Academic Press. 1–11.

Gallistel, C. R. (1990). *The Organization of Learning*. Cambridge, MA: MIT Press.

(1997). Neurons and Memory. *Conversations in the Cognitive Neurosciences*. In M. Gazzaniga. Cambridge, MA: MIT Press. 71–90.

Gannon, P., R. Holloway, D. Broadfield and A. Braun (1998). "Asymmetry of Chimpanzee Planum Temporale: Humanlike Pattern of Wernicke's Brain Language Area Homolog." *Science* **279**: 220–222.

Gardner, H. (1985). *The Mind's New Science: A History of the Cognitive Revolution*. New York: Basic Books.

Garfield, J., C. C. Peterson and T. Perry (2001). "Social Cognition, Language Acquisition and the Development of the Theory of Mind." *Mind and Language* **16**(5): 494–541.

Garman, M. (1974). "On the Acquisition of Two Complex Syntactic Constructions in Tamil." *Journal of Child Language* **19**(1–2): 163–184.

(1990). *Psycholinguistics*. Cambridge: Cambridge University Press.

Garnica, O. (1973). The Development of Phonemic Speech Perception. In T. E. Moore (ed.), *Cognitive Development and the Acquisition of Language*. New York: Academic Press: 215–222.

(1975). *Some Prosodic Characteristics of Speech to Young Children*. Stanford, CA: Stanford University.

Garrett, M. (1990). Sentence Processing. In D. Osherson and H. Lasknik (eds.), *An Invitation to Cognitive Science*. Cambridge, MA: MIT Press. **1**.

Gathercole, S. (1999). "Cognitive Approaches to the Development of Short-Term Memory." *Trends in Cognitive Sciences* **3**(11): 410–419.

Gathercole, S. and A. Baddeley (1989). "Evaluation of the Role of Phonological STM in the Development of Vocabulary in Children: A Longitudinal Study." *Journal of Memory and Language* **28**: 200–213.

Gathercole, V. C. (1986). "The Acquisition of the Present Perfect: Explaining Differences in the Speech of Scottish and American Children." *Journal of Child Language* **13**(3): 537–560.

Gathercole, V. C., C. Mueller and H. Min (1997). "Word Meaning Biases or Language-Specific Effects? Evidence from English, Spanish and Korean." *First Language* **17**: 31–56.

Gathercole, V. C., E. Sebastian and P. Soto (1999). "The Early Acquisition of Spanish Verbal Morphology: Across-the-Board or Piecemeal Knowledge?" *International Journal of Bilingualism* **3**(2–3): 133–182.

Gazdar, G., E. Klein and G. Pullum (1983). *Order, Case and Constituency*. Dordrecht: Foris Publications.

Gazzaniga, M. (1977). *Consistency and Diversity in Brain Organization*. New York: New York Academy of Sciences.

(1983). "Right Hemisphere Language Following Brain Bisection. A 20-year perspective." *American Psychologist* **38**(5): 525–536.

(1988). The Dynamics of Cerebral Specialization and Modular Interactions. In L. Weiskrantz (ed.), *Thought without Language*. Oxford: Clarendon Press. 430–450.

(1989). "Organization of the Human Brain." *Science* **245**: 947–952.

(1995b). Consciousness and the Cerebral Hemispheres. In *The New Cognitive Neurosciences*. Cambridge, MA: MIT Press. 1391–1400.

(1997). *Conversations in the Cognitive Neurosciences*. Cambridge, MA: MIT Press.

(1998). "The Split Brain Revisited." *Scientific American* **279**(1): 50–55.

Gazzaniga, M. (ed.) (1995a). *The Cognitive Neurosciences*. Cambridge, MA: A Bradford Book.

(2000). *The New Cognitive Neurosciences*. Cambridge, MA: MIT Press.

Gelman, R. and R. Baillargeon (1983). A Review of Some Piagetian Concepts. In P. H. Mussen (ed.), *Handbook of Child Psychology: formerly Carmichael's Manual of Child Psychology*. New York: J. Wiley and Sons. **3**: 167–230.

Gelman, S. and G. Gottfried (1993). The Child's Theory of Living Things. *Proceedings of the Meeting of the Society for Research in Child Development*, New Orleans.

Gelman, S., S. Wilcox and E. Clark (1989). "Conceptual and Lexical Hierarchies in Young Children." *Cognitive Development* **4**: 309–326.

Gelman, S. A. and J. D. Coley (1990). "The importance of knowing a Dodo is a bird: categories and inferences in 2-year-old children." *Developmental Psychology* **26**(5): 796–804.

Gelman, S. A. and E. M. Markman (1987). "Young Children's Inductions from Natural Kinds: The Role of Categories and Appearances." *Child Development* **58**(6): 1532–1541.

Gelman, S. A. and M. Taylor (1984). "How Two-Year-Old Children Interpret Proper and Common Names for Unfamiliar Objects." *Child Development* **55**(4): 1535–1540.

Gelman, S. A., W. Croft, P. Fu, T. Clausner and G. Gottfried (1998). "Why is a Pomegranate an Apple? The Role of Shape, Taxonomic Relatedness, and Prior Lexical Knowledge in Children's Overextensions of 'Apple' and 'Dog.'" *Journal of Child Language* **25**(2): 267–291.

Genesee, F. (2002). Portrait of the Bilingual Child. In V. Cook (ed.), *Portraits of the L2 User*. Clevedon: Multilingual Matters Ltd. 167–196.

Genesee, P. A. (1997). "On Continuity and the Emergence of Functional Categories in Bilingual First-Language Acquisition." *Language Acquisition* **6**: 91–124.

Gennari, S. and K. Demuth (1997). Syllable Omission in the Acquisition of Spanish. *Proceedings of the 21st Boston University Conference in Language Development*. Boston, MA: Cascadilla Press.

Gentner, D. (1982). Why Nouns are Learned Before Verbs: Linguistic Relativity Versus Natural Partitioning. In S. A. Kuczaj (ed.), *Language Development*. Hillsdale, NJ: Lawrence Erlbaum Associates. **2**: 301–334.

Gerken, L. (1994a). Child Phonology: Past Research, Present Questions, Future Directions. A. Gernsbacher (ed.), *Handbook of Psycholinguistics*. San Diego, CA: Academic Press. 781–820.

(1994b). "A Metrical Template Account of Children's Weak Syllable Omissions from Multisyllabic Words." *Journal of Child Language* **21**: 565–584.

Gerken, L. (1996a). Phonological and Distributional Information in Syntax Acquisition. In J. L. Morgan and K. Demuth (eds.), *Signal to Syntax: Bootstrapping from Speech to Grammar in Early Acquisition*. 411–425.

(1996b). "Prosodic Structure in Young Children's Language Production." *Language* **72**(4): 683–712.

(1996c). "Prosody's Role in Language Acquisition and Adult Parsing." *Journal of Psycholinguistic Research* **25**(2): 345–356.

Gerken, L. A. and B. J. McIntosh (1993). "The Interplay of Function Morphemes and Prosody in Early Language." *Developmental Psychology* **29**: 448–457.

Gerken, L. A., B. Landau and R. Remez (1990). "Function Morphemes in Young Children's Speech Perception and Production." *Developmental Psychology* **26**: 204–216.

Gerken, L. A., P. Jusczyk and D. Mandel (1994). "When Prosody fails to Cue Syntactic Structure: Nine-Months-Olds' Sensitivity to Phonological vs. Syntactic Phrases." *Cognition* **51**: 237–265.

Gernsbacher, M. A. (1994). *Handbook of Psycholinguistics*. San Diego, CA: Academic Press.

Gershkoff-Stowe, L. and L. B. Smith (1997). "A Curvilinear Trend in Naming Errors as a Function of Early Vocabulary Growth." *Cognitive Psychology* **34**(1): 37–71.

Geschwind, N. (1972). "Language and the Brain." *Scientific American* **226**(4): 76–83.

Geschwind, N. and A. Galaburda (1987). *Cerebral Lateralization: Biological Mechanisms, Associations and Pathology*. Cambridge, MA: MIT Press.

Gevins, A., B. Cutillo and M. E. Smith (1995). "Regional Modulation of High Resolution Evoked Potentials during Verbal and Non-Verbal Matching Tasks." *Electroencephalography and Clinical Neuroscience* **94**: 129–147.

Gibbons, A. (1995) "Languages' Last Words." *Science* (March).

Gibson, E. and K. Wexler (1994). "Triggers." *Linguistic Inquiry* **25**(3): 407–454.

Gillette, J., H. Gleitman, L. Gleitman and A. Lederer (1999). "Human Simulations of Vocabulary Learning." *Cognition* **73**(2): 135–176.

Gleitman, L. (1990). "The Structural Sources of Verb Meanings." *Language Acquisition* **1**(1): 3–55.

(1994). "The Structural Sources of Verb Meanings." In P. Bloom (ed.), *Language Acquisition: Core Readings*. Cambridge, MA: MIT Press. 174–221.

Gleitman, L. and J. Gillette (1999). The Role of Syntax in Verb Learning. In W. Ritchie and T. Bhatia (eds.), *Handbook of Child Language Acquisition*. San Diego: Academic Press. 280–298.

Gleitman, L. and H. Gleitman (1991). Language. *Psychology*. H. Gleitman. New York: Norton. 333–390.

(1994). A Picture is Worth a Thousand Words, But That's the Problem: The Role of Syntax in Vocabulary Acquisition. In B. Lust, M. Suñer and J. Whitman (eds.), *Syntactic Theory and First Language Acquisition: Cross-Linguistic Perspectives*. Vol. 1: *Heads, Projections and Learnability*. Hillsdale, NJ: Lawrence Erlbaum Associates. 291–300.

Gleitman, L. and M. Liberman (1995). Language. In D. Osherson (ed.), *An Invitation to Cognitive Science* (second edition). Cambridge, MA: Bradford Books. **1**.

Gleitman, L. and E. Wanner (1982). *Language Acquisition: The State of the Art*. Cambridge: Cambridge University Press.

Gleitman, L., H. Gleitman and E. Shipley (1972). The Emergence of the Child as Grammarian. *Journal of Child Language* **1**: 137–164.

Gleitman, L., E. L. Newport and H. Gleitman (1984). "The Current Status of the Motherese Hypothesis." *Journal of Child Language* **11**(1): 43–79.

Gleitman, L., E. Shipley and E. Smith (1978). "Old and New Ways Not to Study Comprehension: Comments on Petric and Tweney's 1977 Experimental Review of Shipley, Smith and Gleitman." *Journal of Child Language* **5**: 501–520.

Gleitman, L., H. Gleitman, B. Landau and E. Wanner (1988). Where Learning Begins: Initial Representations for Language Learning. In F. Newmyer (ed.), *Linguistics: The Cambridge Survey*. Cambridge: Cambridge University Press. **3**: 150–193.

Gleitman, L. and B. Landau (eds.) (1995). *The Acquisition of the Lexicon*. Cambridge, MA: MIT Press.

Gold, E. M. (1967). "Language Identification in the Limit." *Information and Control* **10**: 447–474.

Goldfield, B. (2000). Are Verbs Hard to Understand? Continuity vs. Discontinuity in Early Lexical Development. *Proceedings of 24th Annual Boston University Conference on Language Development*. Boston, MA: Cascadilla Press.

Goldfield, B. and S. Reznick (1990). "Early Lexical Acquisition: Rate, Content, and the Vocabulary Spart." *Journal of Child Language* **17** (1): 171–184.

Goldin-Meadow, S. (1982). The Resilience of Recursion: A Study of a Communication System Developed Without a Conventional Language Model. In E. Wanner and L. Gleitman (eds.), *Language Acquisition: The State of the Art*. Cambridge, UK; New York: Cambridge University Press.

  (1987). Underlying Redundancy and its Reduction in a Language Developed Without a Language Model: Constraint Imposed by Conventional Linguistic Input. In B. Lust (ed.), *Studies in the Acquisition of Anaphora*. Dordrecht; Boston. **2**: 135–170.

Goldin-Meadow, S. (2003). *The Resilience of Language: What Gesture Creation in Deaf Children Can Tell Us About How All Children Learn Language*. New York: Psychology Press.

Goldin-Meadow, S., C. Butcher, C. Mylander and M. Dodge (1994). "Nouns and Verbs in a Self-Styled Gesture System: What's in a Name?" *Cognitive Psychology* **27**(3): 259–319.

Goldin-Meadow, S. and H. Feldman (1977). "The Development of Language Like Communication Without a Language Model." *Science* **197**(4301): 401–403.

Goldin-Meadow, S. and C. Mylander (1983). "Gestural Communication in Deaf Children: Noneffect of Parental Input on Language Development." *Science* **221**(4608): 372–374.

  (1990a). "Beyond the Input Given: The Child's Role in the Acquisition of Language." *Language* **66**(2): 323–355.

  (1990b). "The Role of Parental Input in the Development of a Morphological System." *Journal of Child Language* **17**(3): 527–563.

  (1998). "Spontaneous Sign Systems Created by Deaf Children in Two Cultures." *Nature* **91**: 279–281.

Goldin-Meadow, S., C. Mylander and C. Butcher (1995). "The Resilience of Combinatorial Structure at the Word Level: Morphology in Self-Styled Gesture Systems." *Cognition* **56**(3): 195–262.

Goldin-Meadow, S., E. Yalabik and L. Gershkoff-Stowe (2000). The Resilience of Ergative Structure in Language Created by Children and by Adults. *Proceedings of 24th Boston University Conference on Language Development*. Boston, MA: Cascadilla Press. 343–353.

Goldsmith, J. (1990). *Autosegmental and Metrical Phonology*. Oxford: Basil Blackwell.

  (1995). *Handbook of Phonological Theory*. Cambridge, MA: Blackwell.

  (1999). *Phonological Theory: The Essential Readings*. Cambridge, MA: Blackwell.

Golinkoff, R., K. Hirsh-Pasek, K. Cauley and L. Gordon (1987). "The Eyes Have It: Lexical and Syntactic Comprehension in a New Paradigm." *Journal of Child Language* **14**(1): 23–45.

Golinkoff, R. M., R. C. Jacquet, K. Hirsh-Pasek and R. Nandakumar (1996). "Lexical Principles May Underlie the Learning of Verbs." *Child Development* **67**(6): 3101–3119.

Golinkoff, R., K. Hirsh-Pasek, C. Mervis and W. Frawley (1995). Lexical Principles can be Extended to the Acquisition of Verbs. In M. Tomasello and W. Merriman (eds.), *Beyond Names for Things: Young Children's Acquisition of Verbs.* Hillsdale, NJ: Lawrence Erlbaum Associates. 185–221.

Golinkoff, R. M., K. Hirsh-Pasek, L. Bloom, L. B. Smith, A. L. Woodward and N. Akhtar (2000). *Becoming a Word Learner.* Oxford; New York: Oxford University Press.

Gomez, R. L. and L. Gerken (1999). "Artificial Grammar Learning by 1-Year-Olds Leads to Specific and Abstract Knowledge." *Cognition* **70**(2): 109–135.

(2000). "Infant Artificial Language Learning and Language Acquisition." *Trends in Cognitive Sciences* **4**(5(38)): 178–186.

Goodglass, H. (1993). *Understanding Aphasia.* San Diego: Academic Press.

Goodluck, H. (1991). *Language Acquisition: A Linguistic Introduction.* Oxford, UK; Cambridge, MA: Basil Blackwell.

(1996). The Act Out Task. In D. McDaniel, C. McKee and H. Cairns (eds.), *Methods for Assessing Children's Syntax.* Cambridge, MA: MIT Press. 147–162.

Goodluck, H. and S. Tavakolian (1982). "Competence and Processing in Children's Grammar of Relative Clauses." *Cognition* **11**: 1–27.

Goodsitt, J., J. Morgan and P. Kuhl (1993). "Perceptual Strategies in Prelingual Speech Segmentation." *Journal of Child Language* **20**: 229–252.

Goodsitt, J., P. Morse, J. V. Hoove and N. Cowan (1984). "Infants' Speech Perception in Multisyllabic Contexts." *Child Development* **55**: 903–910.

Gopnik, A. and S. Choi (1990). "Do Linguistic Differences Lead to Cognitive Differences? A Cross-Linguistic Study of Semantic and Cognitive Development." *First Language* **10**: 199–215.

(1995). Names, Relational Words, and Cognitive Development in English and Korean Speakers: Nouns are Not Always Learned Before Verbs. In M. Tomasello and W. Merriman (eds.), *Beyond Names for Things: Young Children's Acquisition of Verbs.* Hillsdale, NJ: Lawrence Erlbaum Associates.

Gopnik, M. (1994). "Impairments of Tense in a Familial Language Disorder." *Journal of Neurolinguistics* **8**(2): 109–133.

Gopnik, M. and M. Crago (1991). "Familial Aggregation of a Developmental Language Disorder." *Cognition* **39**(1): 1–50.

Gordon, P. (1985). "Evaluating the Semantic Categories Hypothesis: The Case of the Mass/Count Distinction." *Cognition* **20**: 209–242.

(1986). "Level-Ordering in Lexical Development." *Cognition* **21**(2): 73–93.

(1996). The Truth-Value Judgment Task. In D. McDaniel, C. McKee and H. S. Cairns (eds.), *Methods for Assessing Children's Syntax.* Cambridge, MA: MIT Press. 211–232.

Goswami, U. and P. Bryant (1990). *Phonological Skills and Learning to Read.* Hove: Lawrence Erlbaum Associates.

Gould, J. L. and P. Marler (1987). "Learning by Instinct." *Scientific American* **255**(1): 74–85.

Gould, S. J. (2001). "Humbled by the Genome's Mysteries." *New York Times.* New York: A-21.

Grimes, B. (1992) Ethnologue: Languages of the World. Dallas, TX: Summer Institute of Linguistics.

Grimshaw, G., A. Adelstein, M. Bryden and G. MacKinnon (1998). "First-Language Acquisition in Adolescence: Evidence for a Critical Period of Verbal Language Development." *Brain and Language* **63**: 237–255.

Grimshaw, J. (1981). Form, Function and the Language Acquisition Device. In C. L. Baker and J. McCarthy (eds.), *The Logical Problem of Language Acquisition*. Cambridge, MA: MIT Press. 163–182.

Grimshaw, J. (1994). Minimal Projection and Clause Structure. In Lust, Suñer and Whitman. 75–84.

Grimshaw, J. and S. T. Rosen (1990). "Knowledge and Obedience: The Developmental Status of the Binding Theory." *Linguistic Inquiry* **21**: 187–222.

Grodzinsky, Y. (1990). *Theoretical Perspectives on Language Deficits*. Cambridge, MA: MIT Press.

Gruber, H. and J. J. Vonèche (1977). *The Essential Piaget*. New York: Basic Books.

Gruber, J. (1969). "Topicalization in Child Language." In D. Reibel and S. Schane (eds.), *Modern Studies in English*. Englewood Cliffs, NJ: Prentice Hall. 422–447.

Grubin, D. (2002). *The Secret Life of the Brain*. PBS, Home Video. WWW.pbs.org.

Guasti, M. (2002). *Language Acquisition: The Growth of Grammar.* Cambridge, MA: Bradford Books, MIT Press.

Guasti, M. T. and G. Chierchia (1999/2000). "Backward Versus Forward Anaphora: Reconstruction in Child Grammar." *Language Acquisition* **8**(2): 129–170.

Guasti, M. and L. Rizzi (1996). Null Aux and the Acquisition of Residual V2. In A. Stringfellow, D. Cahana-Amitay, E. Hughes and A. Zukowsly (eds.), *Proceedings of the 20th Boston University Conference on Language Development*, Somerville, MA: Cascadilla Press.

Guasti, M., M. Nespor, A. Christophe and B. Van Ooyen (2001). Pre-Lexical Setting of the Head-Complement Parameter through Prosody. In B. Höhle and J. Weissenborn (eds.), *Approaches to Bootstrapping*. Amsterdam: John Benjamins.

Guilfoyle, E., H. Hung and L. Travis (1989). "Spec of IP, Spec of VP, and the Notion of 'Subject'." *West Coast Conference on formal Linguistics* **8**: 110–123.

Gumpertz, J. and S. Levinson (1996). *Rethinking Linguistic Relativity*. Cambridge: Cambridge University Press.

Guo, F., C. Foley, Y.-C. Chien, B. Lust and C. P. Chiang (1996). "Operator-Variable Binding in the Initial State: A Cross-Linguistic Study of VP Ellipsis Structures in Chinese and English." *Cahiers de Linguistique Asie Orientale* **25**(1): 3–34.

Guo, F., C. Foley, Y.-C. Chien, C.-P. Chiang and B. Lust (1997). A Cross Linguistic Study of Chinese and English Children's First Language Acquisition of VP Ellipsis Structures. In S. Somashekar *et al.* (eds.), *Papers on Language Acquisition: Cornell Working Papers in Linguistics*. Ithaca, NY: Cornell University, Department of Linguistics. **15**: 20–38.

Haegeman, L. (1991). *Government and Binding Theory*. Oxford: Blackwell.

Hahne, A. and A. Friederici (1999). Rule-Application During Language Comprehension in the Adult and the Child. In A. Friederici and R. Menzel (eds.), *Learning: Rule Extraction and Representation*. Berlin; New York: Walter de Gruyter.

Hale, K. (1994). "On Endangered Languages and the Safeguarding of Diversity." *Language* **68**(1): 1–3.

Hale, M. and C. Reiss (1998). "Formal and Empirical Arguments Concerning Phonological Acquisition." *Linguistic Inquiry* **29**(4): 656–683.

Hall, D., S. Geoffrey, S. Waxman, S. Bredart and A.-C. Nicolay (2003). "Preschoolers' Use of Form Class Cues to Learn Descriptive Proper Names." *Child Development* **74**(5): 1547–1560.

Hall, W., W. Nagy and R. Lin (1984). *Spoken Words: Effects of Situation and Social Group on Oral Word Usage and Frequency*. Hillsdale, NJ: Lawrence Erlbaum Associates.

Halle, M. (1978). Knowledge Unlearned and Untaught: What Speakers Know about the Sounds of their Language. In M. Halle, J. Bresnan and G. Miller (eds.), *Linguistic Theory and Psychological Reality*. Cambridge, MA: MIT Press. 294.

(1997). "Some Consequences of the Representation of Words in Memory." *Lingua* **100**: 91–100.

Halle, M. and N. Clements (1983). *Problem Book in Phonology*. Cambridge, MA: MIT Press.

Halle, P. A. and B. de Boysson-Bardies (1994). "Emergence of an Early Receptive Lexicon: Infants' Recognition of Words." *Infant Behavior and Development* **17**(2): 119–129.

Hamburger, H. (1980). "A Deletion Ahead of Its Time." *Cognition* **8**: 389–416.

Hamburger, H. and S. Crain (1982). Relative Acquisition. In S. A. Kuczaj (ed.), *Language Development: Syntax and Semantics*. Hillsdale, NJ: Lawrence Erlbaum Associates.

Hampton, J. (1999). Concepts. In R. A. Wilson and F. C. Keil (eds.), *The MIT Encyclopedia of the Cognitive Sciences*. Cambridge, MA: MIT Press. 176–179.

Hanlon, C. (1988). The Emergence of Set-Relational Quantifiers in Early Childhood. In Kessel. 65–78.

Harlow, H. F. and M. K. Harlow (1965). The Affectional Systems. In H. F. Harlow, E. M. Schrier and F. Stollnitz (eds.), *Behavior of Nonhuman Primates*. New York: Academic. **1**: 287–334.

Harnad, S. (ed.) (1987). *Categorical Perception. The Groundwork of Cognition*. Cambridge; New York: Cambridge University Press.

Harris, P. L. (1982). "Cognitive Prerequisites to Language?" *British Journal of Psychology* **73**(2): 187–195.

Harris, Z. S. (1955). "From Phoneme to Morpheme." *Language* **31**(2): 190–222.

Hatano, G. R., K. Siegler, R. Imagake and N. Wax (1993). "The Development of Biological Knowledge. A Multi-National Study." *Cognitive Development* **8**: 47–62.

Hatford, G., M. Maybery, A. O. Hare and P. Grant (1994). "The Development of Memory and Processing Capacity." *Child Development* **65**: 1338–1356.

Hauser, M., N. Chomsky and W. Fitch (2002). "The Faculty of Language: What is it, Who has it, and How did it Evolve." *Science* **298**: 1569–1579.

Hauser, M. D. (1997). *The Evolution of Communication*. Cambridge, MA: MIT Press.

Hawn, P. R. and L. J. Harris (1979 published 1983). Hand Asymmetries in Grasp Duration and Reaching in Two and Five-Month-Old Infants. *The Biennial meeting of the SRCD*, San Francisco.

Hecaen, H. (1983). "Acquired Aphasia in Children: Revisited." *Neuropsychologia* **21**(6): 581–587.

Heibeck, T. H. and E. M. Markman (1987). "Word Learning in Children: An Examination of Fast Mapping." *Child Development* **58**(4): 1021–1034.

Heine, B. (1992). African Languages. In W. Bright (ed.), *International Encyclopedia of Linguistics*. New York: Oxford University Press. **1**: 31–35.

Hendelman, W. J. (2000). *Atlas of Functional Neuroanatomy*. Boca Raton, FL: CRC Press.

Henzi, V. (1975). "Acquisition of Grammatical Gender in Czech." *Papers and Reports on Child Language Development* **9**: 188–198.

Hermann, D. (1998). *Helen Keller*. New York: A. Knopf.

Hernandez, A., A. Martinez and K. Kohnert (2000). "In Search of the Language Switch: An FMRI Study of Picture Naming in Spanish–English Bilinguals." *Brain and Language* **73**: 421–431.

Hernandez, A., J. Dapretto, J. Mazziotta and S. Brookheimer (2001). "Language Switching and Language Representation in Spanish–English Bilinguals: An FMRI study." *Neuroimage* **14**: 510–520.

Hesketh, S., A. Christophe and G. Dehaene-Lambert (1997). "Non-Nutritive Sucking and Sentence Processing." *Infant Behavior and Development* **20**(2): 263–269.

Hickey, T. (1991). "Mean Length of Utterance and the Acquisition of Irish." *Journal of Child Language* **18**: 553–569.

Hickok, G., U. Bellugi and E. Klima (1996). "The Neurobiology of Sign Language and its Implications for the Neural Basis of Language." *Nature* **381**: 699–702.

(2001). "Sign Language in the Brain." *Scientific American* **284**(6): 58–65.

Hickok, G., M. Wilson, K. Clark, E. Klima, M. Kritchevsky and U. Bellugi (1999). "Discourse Deficits Following Right Hemisphere Damage in Deaf Signers." *Brain and Language* **66**: 233–248.

Hillis, A. and A. Caramazza (1991). "Category-Specific Naming and Comprehension Impairment: A Double Dissociation." *Brain* **114**: 2081–2094.

Hinofotis, F. B. (1976). An Initial Stage in a Child's Acquisition of Greek as his Native Language. In *Workpapers in Teaching English as a Second Language*. Los Angeles: University of California. **11**: 85–96.

Hinton, G. E. (1992). "How Neural Networks Learn from Experience." *Scientific American* **267**(3): 145–151.

Hirsch, J., D. Rodriguez-Moreno and K. Kim (2001). "Interconnected Large-Scale Systems for Three Fundamental Cognitive Tasks Revealed by Functional MRI." *Journal of Cognitive Neuroscience* **13**(3): 389–405.

Hirsch, J., M. Ruge, K. Kim, D. Correa, J. Victor and N. Relkin (2000). "An Integrated Functional Magnetic Resonance Imaging Procedure for Preoperative Mapping of Cortical Areas Associated with Tactile, Motor, Language and Visual Functions." *Neurosurgery* **47**(3): 711–722.

Hirsh-Pasek, K. and R. M. Golinkoff (1993). Skeletal Supports for Grammatical Learning: What the Infant Brings to the Language Learning Task. In C. K. Rovee-Collier and L. P. Lipsitt (eds.), *Advances In Infancy Research*. Norwood, NJ: Ablex. **8**.

(1996). The Intermodal Preferential Looking Paradigm: A Window onto Emerging Language Comprehension. In D. McDaniel and C. McKee (eds.), *Methods for Assessing Children's Syntax: Language, Speech, and Communication*. Cambridge, MA: MIT Press. 105–124.

Hirsh-Pasek, K. and R. M. Golinkoff (1996a). *The Origins of Grammar*. Cambridge, MA: MIT Press.

(1996b). Two Varieties of Language Acquisition Theories: Sketches of a Field. In *The Origins of Grammar*. Cambridge, MA: MIT Press. 16–41.

Hirsh-Pasek, K., L. Gleitman and H. Gleitman (1978). What did the Brain Say to the Mind? A Study of the Detection and Report of Ambiguity of Young Children. In A. Sinclair, R. Jarvella and W. J. Levelt (eds.), *The Child's Conception of Language*. Berlin: Springer-Verlag.

Hirsh-Pasek, K., D. Kemler-Nelson, P. Jusczyk, K. Wright-Cassidy, B. Druss and L. Kennedy (1987). "Clauses are Perceptual Units for Young Children." *Cognition* **26**: 269–286.

Hirsh-Pasek, K., R. Treiman and M. Schneiderman (1984). "Brown and Hanlon Revisited: Mothers' Sensitivity to Ungrammatical Forms." *Journal of Child Language* **11**: 81–88.

Hirsh-Pasek, K., M. Tucker and R. Golinkoff (1996). Dynamic Systems Theory: Reinterpreting "Prosodic Bootstrapping" and its Role in Language Acquisition. In J. L. Morgan and K. Demuth (eds.), *Signal to Syntax*. Mahwah, NJ: Lawrence Erlbaum Associates.

Hiscock, M. and M. Kinsbourne (1995). Phylogeny and Ontogeny of Cerebral Lateralization. In R. Davidson and K. Hugdahl (eds.), *Brain Asymmetry*. Cambridge, MA: MIT Press. 535–578.

Hock, H. (1991). *Principles of Historical Linguistics*. Berlin; New York: Mouton de Gruyter.

Hockett, C. (1955). *A Manual of Phonology: International Journal of American Linguistics*. Chicago IL: University of Chicago Press.

(1958). *A Course in Modern Linguistics*. New York: Macmillan.

(1960). "The Origin of Speech." *Scientific American* **203**(3): 89–96.

(1961). "Linguistic Elements and Their Relations." *Language* **37**: 29–53.

(1977). *The View from Language: Selected Essays 1948–74*. Athens, GA: University of Georgia Press.

Hoek, D., D. Ingram and D. Gibson (1986). "Some Possible Causes of Children's Early Word Overextensions." *Journal of Child Language* **13**(3): 477–494.

Hoekstra, T. (2000). The Function of Functional Categories. In L. Cheng and R. Sybesma (eds.), *The First Glot International State of the Article Book*. Berlin; New York: Mouton de Gruyter. (*Studies in Generative Grammar* **48**. Harry van der Hulst, Jan Koster and Henk van Riemsdijk (eds.).)

Hohne, E. A., M. Jusczyk and N. J. Redanz (1994). Do Infants Remember Words from Stories? Paper presented at a Meeting of the Acoustical Society of America, Cambridge, MA.

Holden, C. (1998) "No Last Word on Language Origins." *Science* **282** (5393): 1455–1458.

Hollebrandse, B. and T. Roeper (1996). The Concept of DO-insertion and the Theory of Infl in Acquisition. In C. Koster and F. Wijnen (eds.). *Proceedings of the Groningen Assembly on Language Acquisition*. Netherlands, Center Language and Cognition Groningen. 261–271.

Holowka, S. and L. Pettito (2002). "Left hemisphere cerebral specialization for babies while babbling." *Science* **297**: 1515.

Holyoak, K. (1999). Introduction: Psychology. In R. A. Wilson and F. C. Keil (eds.), *MITECS*. Cambridge, MA: MIT Press. xxxviii–xlix.

Hornstein, N. and D. W. Lightfoot (eds.) (1981). *Explanation in Linguistics: The Logical Problem of Language Acquisition*. Longman Linguistics Library no. 25. London; New York: Longman.

Hsu, J. R., H. S. Cairns and R. W. Fiengo (1985). "The Development of Grammars Underlying Children's Interpretation of Complex Sentences." *Cognition* **20**(1): 25–48.

Hu, Q. (1993). The Acquisition of Chinese Classifiers by Young Mandarin-Speaking Children. Unpublished Ph.D. dissertation. Boston, MA: Boston University.

Huang, James (1984). "On the Distribution and Resemblance of Empty Pronouns." *Linguistic Inquiry* **15**(4): 531–574.

Hubel, D. (1979). "The Brain." *Scientific American* **241**(3): 44–53.

Huttenlocher, J. (1974). The Origin of Language Comprehension. In R. L. Solo (ed.), *Theories in Cognitive Psychology: the Loyola Symposium*. Hillsdale, NJ: Lawrence Erlbaum Associates.

Huttenlocher, J. and S. Strauss (1968). "Comprehension and a Statement's Relation to the Situation it Describes." *Journal of Verbal Learning and Verbal Behavior* **7**(2): 300–304.

Huttenlocher, J., M. Vasilyeva, E. Cymerman and S. Levine (2002). "Language Input and Child Syntax." *Cognitive Psychology* **45**(3): 337–374.

Huttenlocher, J. and S. Weiner (1971). "Comprehension of Instructions in Varying Contexts." *Cognitive Psychology* **2**: 369–385.

Huttenlocher, J., K. Eisenberg and S. Strauss (1968). "Comprehension: Relation Between Perceived Actor and Logical Subject." *Journal of Verbal Learning and Verbal Behavior* **7**: 527–530.

Huttenlocher, P. (1990). "Morphometric Study of Human Cerebral Cortex Development." *Neuropsychologia* **28**(6): 517–527.

　(1993). Morphometric Study of Human Cerebral Cortex Development. In M. Johnson. 112–124.

　(1997). Syntaptogenesis, Synapse Elimination, and Neural Plasticity in Human Cerebral Cortex. In C. A. Nelson (ed.), *Threats to Optimal Development. Integrating Biological, Psychological and Social Risk Factors*. Hillsdale, NJ: Lawrence Erlbaum Associates. **27**: 35–54.

Hyams, N. M. (1984). "Semantically Based Child Grammars: Some Empirical Inadequacies." *Papers and Reports on Child Language Development* **23**: 58–65.

　(1986). *Language Acquisition and the Theory of Parameters*. Dordrecht; Boston: D. Reidel.

　(1987). The Theory of Parameters and Syntactic Development. In T. Roeper and E. Williams (eds.), *Parameter Setting*. Dordrecht; Boston: D. Reidel. 1–22.

　(1992). The Genesis of Clausal Structure. In J. Meisel (ed.), *The Acquisition of Verb Placement: Functional Categories and V2 Phenomena in Language Acquisition*. Dordrecht; Boston: Kluwer Academic.

　(1994). Commentary: Null Subjects in Child Language and the Implications of Cross-Linguistic Variation. In Lust, Hermon and Kornfilt (eds.). 287–300.

Hyams, N. M. and K. Wexler (1993). "On the Grammatical Basis of Null Subjects in Child Language." *Linguistic Inquiry* **24**(3): 421–459.

Iaccino, J. (1993). *Left Brain-Right Brain Differences*. Hillsdale, NJ: Lawrence Erlbaum Associates.

Ihns, M. and L. Leonard (1988). "Syntactic Categories in Early Child Language: Some Additional Data." *Journal of Child Language* **15**(3): 673–678.

Imai, M. and D. Gentner (1997). "A Crosslinguistic Study on Constraints on Early Word Meaning: Linguistic Input vs. Universal Ontology." *Cognition* **62**: 169–200.

Ingram, D. (1976). *Phonological Disability in Children*. London: Arnold.

(1981/2). "The Emerging Phonological System of an Italian–English Bilingual Child." *Journal of Italian Linguistics* **2**: 95–113.

(1988). "The Acquisition of Word Initial." *Language and Speech* **31**(1): 77–85.

(1989). *First Language Acquisition: Method, Description, and Explanation*. Cambridge: Cambridge University Press.

(1991). "An Historical Observation on 'Why "Mama" and "Papa"?'" *Journal of Child Language* **18**(3): 711–713.

(1992). Early Phonological Acquisition: A Cross-Linguistic Perspective. In C. Ferguson, L. Menn and C. Stoel-Gammon (eds.), *Phonological Development: Models, Research, Implications*. Timonium, MD: York Press. 423–435.

(1995). "The Cultural Basis of Prosodic Modifications to Infants and Children: A Response to Fernald's Universalist Theory." *Journal of Child Language* **22**(1): 223–233.

Ingram, D. and W. Thompson (1996). "Early Syntactic Acquisition in German: Evidence for the Modal Hypothesis." *Language* **72**(1): 97–120.

Inhelder, B. and J. Piaget (1964). *The Early Growth of Logic in the Child*. New York; London: W.W. Norton & Co.

Inkelas, S. and D. Zec (eds.) (1990). *The Phonology–Syntax Connection*. Chicago, IL: University of Chicago Press.

Isagaki, K. and G. Hatano (1993). "Young Children's Understanding of the Mind-Body Distinction." *Child Development*.

Isagaki, K. and G. Hatano (2003). Conceptual and Linguistic Factors in Inductive Projection. How do Young Children Recognize Commonalities between Animals and Plants? In D. Gentner and S. Goldin-Meadow (eds.), *Language in Mind*. A Bradford Book. Cambridge, MA: MIT Press. 313–334.

Ito, T. (1988). Sentence Production: From Before to After the Period of Syntactic Structure. In Y. Otsu (ed.), *MITA Working Papers in Psycholinguistics*. Tokyo: Keio University. **1**: 51–56.

Jackendoff, R. (1994). *Patterns in the Mind: Language and Human Nature*. New York: Basic Books.

(1997). *The Architecture of the Language Faculty*. Cambridge, MA: MIT Press.

(2002). *Foundations of Language*. Oxford: Oxford University Press.

Jakobson, R. (1941/1968). *Child Language, Aphasia and Phonological Universals*. The Hague: Mouton.

(1971/2004). The Sound Laws of Child Language and their Place in General Phonology. In *Studies on Child Language and Aphasia*. (Reprinted in Lust and Foley 2004.) The Hague: Mouton. 285–293.

(1980). *Brain and Language*. (With the assistance of Kathy Santilli.) Colombus, OH: Slavica Publishers Inc.

(1960/1990). Why "Mama" and "Papa?" Reprinted in L. R. Waugh and M. Monville-Burston (eds.), *On Language: Roman Jakobson*. Cambridge, MA: Harvard University Press: 305–311.

Jakubowicz, C. (1984). "On Markedness and Binding Principles." *North Eastern Linguistic Society. Proceedings of NELS* **14**.

(1993). Linguistic Theory and Language Acquisition Facts: Reformulation, Maturation or Invariance of Binding Principles. In E. Reuland and W. Abraham (eds.), *Knowledge and Language*. Dordrecht: Kluwer Academic Publishers. **1**: 157–184.

(1994b). Reflexives in French and Danish: Morphology, Syntax, and Acquisition. In Lust, Hermon and Kornfilt. 115–144.

Jezzard, P., P. Matthews and S. Smith (eds.) (2001). *Functional MRI: An Introduction to Methods*. Oxford; New York: Oxford University Press.

Joanette, Y., P. Goulet and D. Hannequin (1990). *Right Hemisphere and Verbal Communication*. New York: Springer-Verlag.

Johnson, C. and M. Maratsos (1977). "Early Comprehension of Mental Verbs: Think and Know." *Child Development* **48**(4): 1743–1747.

Johnson, C. and H. M. Wellman (1982). "Children's Developing Conceptions of the Mind and Brain." *Child Development* **53**(1): 222–234.

Johnson, E. and P. W. Jusczyk (2001). "Word Segmentation by 8-Month-Olds: When Speech Cues Count More Than Statistics." *Journal of Memory and Language* **44**(4): 548–567.

Johnson, J. S., L. B. Lewis and J. C. Hogan (1997). "A Production Limitation in Syllable Number: A Longitudinal Study of One Child's Early Vocabulary." *Journal of Child Language* **24**: 327–49.

Johnson, M. (1993). *Brain Development and Cognition. A Reader*. Oxford; Cambridge, MA: Blackwell.

Joshi, A. (1994). Commentary: Some Remarks on the Subset Principle. In B. Lust, G. Hermon and J. Kornfilt (eds.), *Syntactic Theory and First Language Acquisition: Cross-Linguistic Perspectives*. Hillsdale, NJ: Lawrence Erlbaum Associates. **2:** 509–514.

Jusczyk, P. (1997a). *The Discovery of Spoken Language*. Cambridge, MA: MIT Press.

(1997b). Categorical Perception. In *The Discovery of Spoken Language*. Cambridge, MA: MIT Press. 45–56.

(1997c). Learning about the Prosodic Organization of the Native Language. In *The Discovery of Spoken Language*. Cambridge, MA: MIT Press: 90–93.

(1997d). "Finding and Remembering Words: Some Beginnings by English-Learning Infants." *Current Directions in Psychological Science* **6**(6): 170–174.

(1999a). "How Infants Begin to Extract Words from Speech." *Trends in Cognitive Sciences* **3**(9): 323–328.

(1999b). "Narrowing the Distance to Language: One Step at a Time." *Journal of Communication Disorders* **32**: 207–222.

Jusczyk, P. and L. Gerken (1996). Syntactic Units, Prosody, Psychological Reality During Infancy. In Morgan and Demuth. 389–410.

Jusczyk, P. and C. Krumhansl (1993). "Pitch and Rhythmic Patterns and Infants' Sensitivity to Musical Phrase Structure." *Journal of Human Perception and Performance* **19**: 611–640.

Jusczyk, P., E. Hohne and A. Bauman (1999). "Infants' Sensitivity to Allophonic Cues for Word Segmentation." *Perception and Psychophysics* **61**: 1465–1476.

Jusczyk, P., D. Houston and M. Newsome (1999). "The Beginnings of Word Segmentation in English-Learning Infants." *Cognitive Psychology* **39**: 159–207.

Jusczyk, P., A. Friederici, J. Wessels, V. Svenkerud and A. Jusczyk (1993). "Infants' Sensitivity to the Sound Patterns of Native Language Words." *Journal of Memory and Language* **32**: 402–420.

Jusczyk, P., R. Mazuka, D. Mandel, S. Kiritani and A. Hayashi (1993). A Cross-Linguistic Study of American and Japanese Infants' Perception of Acoustic Correlates to Clausal Units. *Biennial Meeting of the Society for Research in Child Development*. New Orleans, LA.

Jusczyk, P., K. Hirsh-Pasek, D. G. K. Nelson, L. Kennedy, A. Woodward and J. Piwoz (1992). "Perception of Acoustic Correlates of Major Phrasal Units to Young Infants." *Cognitive Psychology* **24**: 252–293.

Jusczyk, P. W. (1989). *Perception of Cues to Clausal Units in Native and Non-Native Languages*. Society for Research in Child Development, Kansas City.

Jusczyk, P. W. (1993). Sometimes it Pays to Look Back Before You Look Ahead. In B. de Boysson-Bardies (ed.), *Developmental Neurocognition: Speech and Face Processing in the First Year of Life*. Dordrecht; Boston: Kluwer Academic. 227–236.

Jusczyk, P. W. and R. N. Aslin (1995). "Infants' Detection of Sound Patterns of Words in Fluent Speech." *Cognitive Psychology* **29**(1): 1–23.

Jusczyk, P. W. and J. Bertoncini (1988). "Viewing the Development of Speech Perception as an Innately Guided Learning Process." *Language and Speech* **31**(3): 217–238.

Jusczyk, P. W. and E. A. Hohne (1997). "Infants' Memory for Spoken Words." *Science* **277**(5334): 1984–1986.

Jusczyk, P. W. and D. Houston (1999). "The Beginnings of Word Segmentation in English-Learning Infants." *Cognitive Psychology* **39**(3–4): 159–207.

Jusczyk, P. W., A. Cutler and N. Redanz (1993). "Preference for the Predominant Stress Patterns of English Words." *Child Development* **64**: 675–687.

Jusczyk, P. W., L. A. Gerken and D. K. Nelson (2002). The Beginning of Cross-Sentence Structural Comparison by 9-Month-Olds. Minneapolis, MN: ICIS.

Jusczyk, P. W., P. A. Luce and Charles Luce (1994). "Infants' Sensitivity to Phonotactic Patterns in the Native Language." *Journal of Memory and Language* **33**(5): 630–645.

Kail, R. (1997). "Phonological Skill and Articulation Time Independently Contribute to the Development of Memory Span." *Journal of Experimental Child Psychology* **67**: 57–68.

Kandel, E. and L. Squire (2000). "Neuroscience: Breaking Down Scientific Barriers to the Study of Brain and Mind." *Science* **290**: 1113–1120.

Kandel, E., J. Schwartz and T. Jessell (2000). *Principles of Neural Science*. New York: McGraw Hill.

Kang, H.-K. (2001). "Quantifier Spreading: Linguistic and Pragmatic Considerations." *Lingua* **111**(8): 591–627.

Kappa, I. (2001). "Alignment and Consonant Harmony: Evidence from Greek." Proceedings of the BUCLD 25. Somerville: Cascadilla Press.

Kapur, S. (1994). Some Applications of Formal Learning Theory Results to Natural Language Acquisition. In B. Lust, M. Suñer and J. Whitman (eds.), *Syntactic Theory and First Language Acquisition: Cross-Linguistic Perspectives*. Hillsdale, NJ: Lawrence Erlbaum Associates. **2**: 491–508.

Kapur, S. and G. Bilardi (1992a). Language Learning Without Overgeneralization. *Ninth Symposium on Theoretical Aspects of Computer Science*. New York: Springer-Verlag. 245–256.

(1992b). Language Learning from Stochastic Input. *Fifth Conference on Computational Learning Theory*. San Mateo, CA: Morgan-Kaufman.

Kapur, S., B. Lust and G. Martohardjono (in preparation) On the Language Faculty and Learnability Theory. Intensional and Extensional Principles in the Representation and Acquisition of Binding Domains.

Kapur, S., B. Lust, W. Harbert and G. Martohardjono (1992). "Universal Grammar and Learnability Theory: The Case of Binding Domains and the Subset Principle." In E. Reuland and W. Abraham (eds.), *Knowledge and Language*. Dordrecht; Boston, MA: Kluwer Academic. **3:** 185–216.

Karmiloff-Smith, A. (1979). *A Functional Approach to Child Language: A Study of Determiners and Reference*. Cambridge Studies in Linguistics. Cambridge; New York: Cambridge University Press.

Karmiloff-Smith, A. (1992). *Beyond Modularity*. Cambridge: MIT Press.

Katz, N., E. Baker and J. Macnamara (1974). "What's in a Name? A Study of How Children Learn Common and Proper Names." *Child Development* **45**(2): 469–473.

Kaufman, D. (1994). Grammatical or Pragmatic: Will the Real Principle B Please Stand Up? In B. Lust, G. Hermon and J. Kornfilt (eds.), *Syntactic Theory and First Language Acquisition: Cross-Linguistic Perspectives*. Vol. 2. *Binding, Dependencies, and Learnability*. Hillsdale, NJ: Lawrence Erlbaum Associates. **2:** 177–200.

Kay, D. A. and J. M. Anglin (1982). "Overextension and Underextension in the Child's Expressive and Receptive Speech." *Journal of Child Language* **9**(1): 83–98.

Kayne, R. (1994a). *The Antisymmetry of Syntax*. Cambridge MA: MIT Press.

Kedar, Y., M. Casasola and B. Lust (2004). 18 and 24 Month Olds Rely on Syntactic Knowledge of Functional Categories for Determining Meaning and Reference. *Boston University Conference on Language Development*. Boston, MA: Cascadilla Press.

Kedar, Y. and J. Schaeffer (in preparation). "The Acquisition Of Argumenthood: Missing Articles In Early Hebrew." New York: Cornell University; Haifa: Ben-Gurion University.

Kegl, J. (1994). "The Nicaraguan Sign Language Project: An Overview." *Signpost* **7**(1): 24–31.

Kegl, J., A. Senghas and M. Coppola (1999). Creation Through Contact: Sign Language Emergence and Sign Language Change in Nicaragua. In M. DeGraff (ed.), *Language Creation and Language Change: Creolization, Diachrony, and Development*. Cambridge, MA: MIT Press.

Kehoe, M. and C. Stoel-Gammon (1997). "The Acquisition of Prosodic Structure: An Investigation of Current Accounts of Children's Prosodic Development." *Language* **73**(1): 113–144.

Keil, F. C. (1979). *Semantic and Conceptual Development: An Ontological Perspective*. Cambridge, MA: Harvard University Press.

(1986). The Acquisition of Natural Kind and Artifact Terms. In W. Demopoulos and A. Marras (eds.), *Language Learning and Concept Acquisition: Foundational Issues*. Norwood, NJ: Ablex.

(1989). *Concepts, Kinds and Cognitive Development*. Cambridge, MA: MIT Press.

(1992). The Origins of an Autonomous Biology. In M. M. R. Gunnar (ed.), *Modularity and Constraints in Language and Cognition. The Minnesota Symposium on Child Psychology*. Hillsdale, NJ: Lawrence Erlbaum Associates. **25:** 103–137.

(1994). Explanation, Association, and the Acquisition of Word Meaning. In L. Gleitman and B. Landau (eds.), *The Acquisition of the Lexicon*. Cambridge, MA: MIT Press. 169–196.

(1999). Conceptual change. In R. A. Wilson and F. C. Keil (eds.), *The MIT Encyclopedia of the Cognitive Sciences*. Cambridge, MA: MIT Press. 179–182.

Keil, F. C. and N. Batterman (1984). "A Characteristic-to-Defining Shift in the Development of Word Meaning." *Journal of Verbal Learning and Verbal Behavior* **23**(2): 221–236.

Keil, F. C. and J. J. Carroll (1980). "The Child's Acquisition of 'Tall': Implications for an Alternative View of Semantic Development." *Papers and Reports on Child Language Development* **19**: 21–28.

Keil, F. C., W. C. Smith, D. Simons and D. Levin (1998). "Two Dogmas of Conceptual Empiricism: Implications for Hybrid Models of the Structure of Knowledge." *Cognition* **65**(2–3): 103–135.

Keller, H. (1999) The Day Language Came into my Life. In S. Hirschberg and T. Hirschberg (eds.), *Reflections on Language*. Oxford: Oxford University Press.

Kemler Nelson, D., P. Jusczyk, D. R. Mandel, J. Myers, A. Turk and L. A. Gerken (1995). "The Head-Turn Preference Procedure for Testing Auditory Perception." *Infant Behavior and Development* **18**: 111–116.

Kempermann, G. and F. Gage (1999). "New Nerve Cells for the Adult Brain." *Scientific American* (May): 48–53.

Kempson, R. (ed.) (1988). *Mental Representations. The Interface Between Language and Reality*. Cambridge: Cambridge University Press.

Kenstowicz, M. (1994). *Phonology in Generative Grammar*. Cambridge, MA: Blackwell.

Kent, R. D. (1981). Articulatory-Acoustic Perspectives on Speech Development. In R. Stark (ed.), *Language Behavior in Infancy and Early Childhood*. New York; Amsterdam: Elsevier: 105–126.

Kessel, F. S. (ed.) (1988). *The Development of Language and Language Researchers: Essays in Honor of Roger Brown*. Hillsdale, NJ: Lawrence Erlbaum Associates.

Keurs, M. T., C. M. Brown, P. Hagoort and D. F. Stegeman (1999). " Electrophysiological Manifestations of Open- and Closed-Class Words in Patients with Broca's Aphasia with Agrammatic Comprehension: An Event-Related Brain Potential Study." *Brain* **122**: 839–854.

Kim, J. J., G. F. Marcus, S. Pinker, M. Hollander and M. Coppola (1994). "Sensitivity of Children's Inflection to Grammatical Structure." *Journal of Child Language* **21**(1): 173–209.

Kim, K. H., N. R. Relkin, K.-M. Lee and J. Hirsch (1997). "Distinct Cortical Areas Associated with Native and Second Languages." *Nature* **388**(6638): 171–174.

Kimura, D. (1992). "Sex Differences in the Brain." *Scientific American*: 119–125.

Kiparsky, P. and L. Menn (1977). On the Acquisition of Phonology. In J. Macnamara (ed.), *Language, Learning and Thought*. New York: Academic Press.

Kisilevsky, B. S., S. Hains, K. Lee, X. Xie, H. Huang and H. H. Ye (2003). "Effects of Experience on Fetal Voice Recognition." *Psychological Review* **14**(3): 220–224.

Klatt, D. H. (1989). Review of Selected Models of Speech Perception. In W. Marslen-Wilson (ed.), *Lexical Representation and Process*. Cambridge, MA: MIT Press.

Klee, T. and M. Fitzgerald (1985). "The Relation Between Grammatical Development and Mean Length of Utterance in Morphemes." *Journal of Child Language* **12**: 251–269.

Klee, T. M. and R. Paul (1981). A Comparison of Six Structural Analysis Procedures: A Case Study. In J. F. Miller (ed.), *Assessing Language Production in Children: Experimental Procedures*. Baltimore, MD: University Park Press.

Klein, D., R. Zattore, B. Milner, E. Meyer and A. C. Evans (1997). The Neural Substrates of Bilingual Language Processing: Evidence from Position Emission Tomography. In M. Paradis (ed.), *Aspects of Bilingual Aphasia*. Pergamon Press.

Klein, W. (1998). Assertion and Finiteness. In N. Dittmar and Z. Penner (eds.), *Issues in the Theory of Language Acquisition*. Bern: Peter Lang. 225–245.

Klima, E. S. and U. Bellugi (1966). Syntactic Regularities in the Speech of Children. In J. Lyons and R. Wales (eds.), *Psycholinguistic Papers*. Edinburgh: Edinburgh University Press. 183–219.

Kobayashi, H. (1998). "How 2-year-old children learn novel part names of unfamiliar objects." *Cognition* **68**(2): B41–B51.

Koerner, K. and M. Tajima (1986). *Noam Chomsky: A Personal Bibliography, 1951–1986*. Amsterdam; Philadelphia: John Benjamins.

Kolata, G. (1987). "Association or Rules in Learning Language?" *Science* **237**(4811): 133–134.

Kolk, H. (2000). "Multiple Route Plasticity." *Brain and Language.* **71**: 129–131.

Koopmans Van Beinum, F. J. and J. M. Van der Stelt (1979). Early Stages in the Development of Speech Movements. In B. Lindblom and R. Zetterstrom (eds.), *Precursors of Early Speech.* New York: Stockton.

(1998). Early Speech Development in Children Acquiring Dutch: Mastering General Basic Elements. In S. Gillis and A. De Houwer (eds.), *The Acquisition of Dutch*. Amsterdam; Philadelphia: John Benjamins. 101–162.

Kornfilt, J. (1994). Some Remarks on the Interaction of Case and Word Order in Turkish: Implications for Acquisition. In B. Lust, M. Suñer and J. Whitman (eds.), *Syntactic Theory and First Language Acquisition: Cross Linguistic Perspectives.* Vol. 1.: *Heads, Projections and Learnability*. Lawrence Erlbaum Associates.

Koster, C. (1993). *Errors in Anaphora Acquisition. Faculteit Letteren Universiteit Utrecht. Onderzoeksinstituut voor Taal en Spraak*. Utrecht: University of Utrecht.

(1994). Problems with Pronoun Acquisition. In Lust, Hermon and Kornfilt. 201–226.

Krumhausl, C. and P. Jusczyk (1990). "Infants' Perception of Phrase Structure in Music." *Psychological Science* 1: 70–73.

Kuhl, P. (1976). Speech Perception in Early Infancy: The Acquisition of Speech-Sound Categories. In S. K. Hirsh, D. H. Eldridge, I. J. Hirsh and S. R. Silverman (eds.), *Hearing and Davis: Essays Honoring Hallowell Davis*. St. Louis: Washington University Press.

(1987). Perception of Speech and Sound in Early Infancy. In P. Salapatek and L. Cohen (eds.), *Handbook of Infant Perception*. New York: Academic. **11**: 274–382.

Kuhl, P. and A. Meltzoff (1982). "Discrimination of Auditory Target Dimensions in the Presence or Absence of Variation in a Second Dimension by Infants." *Perception and Psychophysics* **31**(3): 279–292.

(1984). "The Intermodal Representation of Speech in Infants." *Infant Behaviour and Development* **7**: 361–381.

Kuhl, P. K. (1985). Methods in the Study of Infant Speech Perception. In G. Gottlieb and N. Krasnegor (eds.), *Measurement of Audition and Vision in the First Year of Postnatal Life: A Methodological Overview*. Norwood, NJ: Ablex.

(1993). Innate Predispositions and the Effects of Experience in Speech Perception: The Native Language Magnet Theory. In B. de Boysson-Bardies (ed.), *Developmental Neurocognition: Speech and Face Processing in the First Year of Life.* Dordrecht; Boston: Kluwer Academic.

Kuhl, P. K., K. A. Williams, F. Lacerda, K. N. Stevens and B. Lind bolm (1992). "Linguistic Experiences Alter Phonetic Perception in Infants by 6 Months of Age." *Science* (255): 606–608.

Kuhl, P. K., J. E. Andruski, I. Chistovich, L. Chistovich, E. Kozhevnikova and V. Ryskina (1997). "Cross-Language Analysis of Phonetic Units in Language Addressed to Infants." *Science* **277**(5326): 684–686.

Kulikowski, S. (1981). "Possible Worlds Semantics for Early Syntax." *Journal of Child Language* **8**(3): 633–639.

Kunnari, S. (2002). "Word Length in Syllables: Evidence from Early Word Production in Finnish." *First Language* **22**: 119–135.

Kuno, S., T. Ken-ichi and Y. Wu (1999). "Quantifier Scope in English, Chinese and Japanese." *Language* **75** (1): 63–111.

Kushnir, C. and J. Blake (1996). "The Nature of the Cognitive Deficit in Specific Language Impairment." *First Language* **16**: 21–40.

Labov, W. and T. Labov (1978). "The Phonetics of 'Cat' and 'Mama'." *Language* **54**(4): 816–852.

Lachter, J. and T. G. Bever (1989). "The Relation Between Linguistic Structure and Associative Theories of Language Learning: A Constructive Critique of Some Connectionist Learning Models." *Cognition* **28**(1–2): 195–247.

Ladefoged, P. (1993). *A Course in Phonetics.* New York: Harcourt Brace Jovanovich, Inc.

(1996). *Elements of acoustic phonetics.* Chicago, IL: University of Chicago Press.

(1997) Paper presented to Annual Meeting of AAAS, Anaheim, CA.

(2001). *Vowels and Consonants.* Malden, MA: Blackwell.

Laenzlinger, C. (1998). *Comparative Studies in Word Order Variation: Adverbs, Pronouns, and Clause Structure in Romance and Germanic.* Amsterdam; Philadelphia: John Benjamins.

Lai, C., S. Fisher, J. Hurst, F. Vargha-Khadem and A. Monaco (2001). "A Forkhead-Domain Gene is Mutated in a Severe Speech and Language Disorder." *Nature* **413**: 519–523.

Lakshmanan, U. (1994). *Universal Grammar in Child Second Language Acquisition.* Amsterdam; Philadelphia: John Benjamins.

(1995). "Child Second Language Acquisition of Syntax." *Studies in Second Language Acquisition* **17**(3): 301–329.

(2000a). Clause Structure in Child Second Language Grammars. *Proceedings of Generative Approaches to Second Language Acquisition.* Pittsburgh, PA: University of Pittsburgh.

(2000b). "Root Infinitives in Child First Language Acquisition and Child Second Language Acquisition." Paper Presented at Indiana University, Bloomington, Indiana.

Lakshmi, V. S. and A. U. Rani (1993). "Retroflexion in Plural Formation: An Experimental Study with Telugu Children." *Osmania Papers in Linguistics* **19**: 43–58.

Landau, B. and L. Gleitman (1985). *Language and Experience: Evidence from the Blind Child.* Cambridge, MA: Harvard University Press.

Landau, B., L. B. Smith and S. Jones (1988). "The Importance of Shape in Early Lexical Learning." *Cognitive Development* **3**(3): 299–321.

Larson, R. and G. Segal (1995). *Knowledge of Meaning*. Cambridge, MA: MIT Press.

Larson, R., D. Warren, J. F. Silva and L. Sagonis (1995). *Syntactica*. Cambridge, MA: MIT Press.

Lashley, K. (1960 [1948/1951]). The Problem of Serial Order in Behavior. In F. Beach, D. Hebb, C. Morgan and H. Nissen (eds.), *The Neuropsychology of Lashley. Selected Papers of K. S. Lashley*. New York: McGraw Hill. Reprinted in Lust and Foley (2004).

Lasky, R. E., A. Syrdal-Lasky and R. E. Klein (1975). "VOT Discrimination by Four to Six and a Half Month Infants from Spanish Environments." *Journal of Experimental Child Psychology* **20**: 215–225.

Lasnik, H. (1990). On Certain Substitutes for Negative Data. In H. Lasnik (ed.), *Essays on Restrictiveness and Learnability*. Dordrecht: Kluwer Academic. 184–197.

    (2002). "The Minimalist Program in Syntax." *Trends in Cognitive Sciences* **6**(10): 432–437.

Lasnik, H., M. Depiante and A. Steparoy (eds.) (2000). *Syntactic Structures Revisited: Contemporary Lectures on Classic Transformational Theory*. Cambridge, MA: MIT Press.

Lebeaux, D. (1990). The Grammatical Nature of the Acquisition Sequences: Adjoin-Alpha and the Formation of Relative Clauses. In L. Frazier and J. DeVilliers (eds.), *Language Processing and Language Acquisition*. Dordrecht: Kluwer. 13–82.

Lecanuet, J. P. and C. Granier-Deferre (1993). Speech Stimuli in the Fetal Environment. In B. de Boysson-Bardies (ed.), *Developmental Neurocognition: Speech and Face Processing in the First Year of Life*. Dordrecht; Boston: Kluwer Academic: 237–248.

Lee, Kwee-Ock (1991). *On the First Language Acquisition of Relative Clauses in Korean: The Universal Structure of COMP*. South Korea: Hanshin Publishing Co. Also Ph.D. dissertation. Ithaca, NY: Cornell University.

    (1997). *The Acquisition of Korean Numeral Classifiers*. Workshop on First Language Acquisition of East Asian Languages. Linguistic Society of America Annual Meeting, Ithaca, NY: Cornell University.

Lee, K.-O., B. Lust and J. Whitman (1990). On Functional Categories in Korean: A Study of the First Language Acquisition of Korean Relative Clauses. In E.-J. Baek (ed.), *Papers from the Seventh International Conference on Korean Linguistics*. Toronto: University of Toronto Press. 312–333.

Legendre, G. and P. Smolensky (forthcoming). Towards a Calculus of the Mind/Brain: Neural Network Theory. In *Optimality and Universal Grammar*.

Lenneberg, E. (1964a). A Biological Perspective of Language. In *New Directions in the Study of Language*. Cambridge, MA: MIT Press. 65–88.

    (1964b). The Capacity for Language Acquisition. In J. Fodor and J. Katz (eds.), *The Structure of Language*. Englewood Cliffs, NJ: Prentice Hall Inc.

    (1966). The Natural History of Language. In F. Smith and E. Miller (eds.), *The Genesis of Language*. Cambridge, MA: MIT Press. 219–252.

    (1967). *Biological Foundations of Language*. New York: J. Wiley and Sons.

    (1975). In Search of a Dynamic Theory of Aphasia. In E. L. and E. Lenneberg (eds.), *Foundations of Language Development. A Multidisciplinary Approach*. San Diego, CA: Academic Press. **2:** 1–20.

Leonard, L. (1998). *Children with Specific Language Impairment*. Cambridge, MA: MIT Press.

Leonard, L. and E. Dromi (1994). "The Use of Hebrew Verb Morphology by Children with Specific Language Impairment and Children Developing Language Normally." *First Language* **42**: 283–305.

Leonard, L. and K. McGregor (1991). "Unusual Phonological Patterns and Their Underlying Representations: A Case Study." *Journal of Child Language* **18**: 261–271.

Leonard, L., R. Schwartz, J. K. Folger, M. Newhoff and M. Wilcox (1979). "Children's Imitation of Lexical Items." *Child Development* **50**: 19–27.

Leopold, W. F. (1949). *Speech Development of a Bilingual Child: A Linguist's Record*. New York: AMS Press. Reprinted in Leopold 1970.

   (1970). *Speech Development of a Bilingual Child: A Linguist's Record*. Evanston, IL: AMS.

Lepore E. and Z. Pylyshyn (eds.) (1999). *What is Cognitive Science?* Oxford: Blackwell.

Levelt, W. J. M. (1974). *Formal Grammars in Linguistics and Psycholinguistics*. The Hague: Mouton.

Levelt, W. J. M. (ed.) (1991). *Lexical Access in Speech Production. A Cognition Special Issue*. Oxford; Cambridge, MA: Blackwell.

Levitt, A. (1993). The Acquisition of Prosody: Evidence from French- and English-Learning Infants. In B. de Boysson-Bardies, S. D. Schonen, P. Jusczyk, P. McNeilage and J. Morton (eds.), *Developmental Neurocognition: Speech and Face Processing in the First Year of Life*. Dordrecht; Boston: Kluwer Academic. 185–398.

Levitt, A. and J. Aydelott Utman (1992). "From Babbling Towards the Sound Systems of English and French: A Longitudinal Two-Case Study." *Journal of Child Language* **19**: 19–49.

Levy, Y. (1983a). "The Acquisition of Hebrew Plurals: The Case of Missing Gender Category." *Journal of Child Language* **10**(1): 107–121.

   (1983b). "It's Frogs All the Way Down." *Cognition* **15**(1–3): 75–93.

   (1996). "Modularity of Language Reconsidered." *Brain and Language* **55**: 240–263.

   (1997). "Autonomous Linguistic Systems in the Language of Young Children." *Journal of Child Language* **24**(3): 651–672.

Li, P. and L. Gleitman (2002). "Turning the Table: Language and Spatial Reasoning." *Cognition* **83**(3): 265–294.

Li, P. and Y. Shirai (2000). *The Acquisition of Lexical and Grammatical Aspect*. Berlin; New York: Mouton de Gruyter.

Li, P., L. H. Tan, E. Bates and T. Zeng (eds.) (forthcoming). *Handbook of East Asian Psycholinguistics: Chinese*. Cambridge: Cambridge University Press.

Liberman, A. M. (1970). "The Grammars of Speech and Language." *Cognitive Psychology* **1**.

   (1996). *Speech: A Special Code*. Cambridge, MA: MIT Press.

Liberman, I., D. Shankweiler, A. Liberman, C. Fowler and F. Fischer (1977). Phonetic Segmentation and Recoding in the Beginning Reader: The Proceedings of the CUNY Conference. In A. Reber and D. Scarborough (eds.), *Toward a Psychology of Reading*. Hillsdale, NJ: Lawrence Erlbaum Associates. Distributed by the Halsted Press.

Lieberman, P. (1963). "Some Effects of Semantic and Grammatical Context on the Production of Speech." *Language and Speech* **6**: 172–179.

(1968). *Intonation, Perception, and Language. Research Monograph no. 38.* Cambridge, MA: MIT Press.

(1973). "On the Evolution of Human Language: a Unified View." *Cognition* **2**.

(1975). *On the Origins of Language: An Introduction to the Evolution of Human Speech.* New York: Macmillan.

(1992) "Could an Autonomous Syntax Model have Evolved?" *Brain and Language* **43**: 768, 774.

(1996). Some Biological Constraints on the Analysis of Prosody. In Morgan and Demuth. 55–66.

Lightfoot, D. W. (1989). "The Child's Trigger Experience: Degree-0 Learnability." *Behavioral and Brain Sciences* **12**(2): 321–334.

(1991). *How to Set Parameters: Arguments from Language Change.* Cambridge, MA: MIT Press.

(1994). Degree-0 Learnability. In B. Lust, G. Hermon and J. Kornfilt (eds.), *Syntactic Theory and First Language Acquisition: Cross-Linguistic Perspectives.* Hillsdale, NJ: Lawrence Erlbaum Associates. **2**: 453–473.

Lillo-Martin, D. (1999). Modality Effects and Modularity in Language Acquisition: The Acquisition of American Sign Language. In W. Ritchie and T. Bhatia (eds.), *Handbook of Child Language Acquisition.* San Diego, CA: Academic Press: 531–568.

Limber, J. (1973). The Genesis of Complex Sentences. In T. Moore (ed.), *Cognitive Development and the Acquisition of Language.* San Diego; CA: Academic Press: 171–185.

Linebarger, M. (1995). "Agrammatism as Evidence about Grammar." *Brain and Language* **50**: 52–91.

Lisker, L. and A. Abramson (1970). The Voicing Dimension: Some Experiments in Comparative Phonetics. *Sixth International Congress of Phonetic Sciences.* Prague: Academia.

Locke, J. (1968). *An Essay Concerning Human Understanding.* Cleveland, OH: World Publishing.

Locke, J. L. (1983). *Phonological Acquisition and Change.* New York: Academic Press.

(1993). *The Child's Path to Spoken Language.* Cambridge, MA: Harvard University Press.

Locke, J. L. and D. Pearson (1990). "Linguistic Significance of Babbling: Evidence from a Tracheostomized Infant." *Journal of Child Language* **17**(1): 1–16.

Loke, K. K. (1991). A Semantic Analysis of Young Children's Use of Mandarin Shape Classifiers. In A. Kwan-Terry (ed.), *Child Language Development in Singapore and Malaysia.* Singapore: Singapore University Press: 98–116.

Lorsbach, T. C., G. A. Katz and A. J. Cupak (1998). "Development Differences in the Ability to Inhibit the Initial Misinterpretation of Garden Path Sentences." *Journal of Experimental Child Psychology* **71**: 275–296.

Loveland, K. A. (1984). "Learning About Points of View: Spatial Perspective and the Acquisition of 'I/You'." *Journal of Child Language* **11**(3): 535–556.

Lucy, J. A. (1992a). *Grammatical Categories and Cognition: a Case Study of the Linguistic Relativity Hypothesis.* Cambridge University Press.

(1992b). *Language Diversity and Thought: A Reformulation of the Linguistic Relativity Hypothesis.* Cambridge; New York: Cambridge University Press.

Lum, C., R. Cox, J. Kilgour, J. Morris and R. Tobin (1999). "Patsy: A Multimedia Distributed Web-Base Resource for Aphasiologists in Research and Education." *Aphasiology* **13** (7): 573–579.

Lust, B. (1977). "Conjunction Reduction in Child Language." *Journal of Child Language* **4**(2): 257–297.

(1981) Constraint on Anaphora in English Language. A Prediction for a Universal. In S. Tavakolin (ed.), *Linguistic Theory and First Language Acquisition*. Boston, MA: MIT Press.

(1986b). Introduction. In *Studies in the Acquisition of Anaphora. Defining the Constraints.* Dordrecht: Reidel Press. **I**: 3–106.

(1986c). Remarks on the Psychological Reality of the Subset Principle: Its Relation to Universal Grammar as a Model of the Initial State. In C. Clifton (ed.), *Proceedings of the Eighth Annual Conference of the Cognitive Science Society*. Hillsdale, NJ: Lawrence Erlbaum Associates. 420–431.

(1986d). *Studies in the Acquisition of Anaphora*. Volume 1. *Defining the Constraints*. Dordrecht: Reidel.

(1999). Universal Grammar: The Strong Continuity Hypothesis in First Language Acquisition. In W. Ritchie and T. Bhatia (eds.), *Handbook of Child Language Acquisition*. New York: Academic Press. 111–156.

(in preparation). *Universal Grammar and the Initial State: Cross-Linguistic Studies of Directionality*. Cambridge, MA: Bradford Books/MIT Press.

Lust, B. and Y. Chien (1984). "The Structure of Coordination in First Language Acquisition of Mandarin Chinese." *Cognition* **17**: 49–83.

Lust, B. and T. Clifford (1986). The 3-D Study: Effects of Depth Distance and Directionality on Children's Acquisition of Anaphora: Comparison of Prepositional Phrase and Subordinate Clause Embedding. In B. Lust (ed.), *Studies of Acquisition of Anaphora: Defining the Constraints*. Dordecht: Reidel Press. **I**: 203–244.

Lust, B. and L. Mangione (1983). The Principle Branching Direction Parameter Constraint in First Language Acquisition of Anaphora. In P. Sells and C. Jones (eds.), *Proceedings of the 13th Annual Meeting of the North Eastern Linguistic Society*. Amherst, MA: University of Massachusetts. 145–160.

Lust, B. and R. Mazuka (1989). "Cross-Linguistic Studies of Directionality in First Language Acquisition: The Japanese Data (Response to O'Grady, Suzuki-Wei and Cho 1986)." *Journal of Child Language* **16**: 665–684.

Lust, B. and C. A. Mervis (1980). "Coordination in the Natural Speech of Young Children." *Journal of Child Language* **7**(2): 279–304.

Lust, B. and T. K. Wakayama (1979). "The Structure of Coordination in Young Children's Acquisition of Japanese." In F. R. Eckman and A. J. Hastings (eds.), *Studies in First and Second Language Acquisition*. Rawley, MA: Newbury House Publishers. 134–152.

(1981). "Word Order in Japanese First Language Acquisition." In P. Dale and D. Ingram (eds.), *Child Language: An International Perspective*. Baltimore, MD: University Park Press. 73–90.

Lust, B., M. Blume and T. Ogden (in preparation). *Cornell University Virtual Linguistics Lab (VLL) Research Methods Manual: Scientific Methods for Study of Language Acquisition*. Ithaca, NY: Cornell University.

Lust, B., Gair, J. Bhatia and T. Sharma (1986a). Children's Hypotheses on Empty Categories: Acquisition of Hindi Anaphora. *South Asia Linguistics Association.* Urbana, IL.

Lust, B., G. Hermon and J. Kornfilt (1994). *Syntactic Theory and First Language Acquisition: Cross-Linguistic Perspectives.* Vol. 2: *Binding Dependencies and Learnability.* Hillsdale, NJ: Lawrence Erlbaum Associates.

Lust, B., Y.-C. Chien and S. Flynn (1987). What Children Know: Comparison of Experimental Methods for the Study of First Language Acquisition. In B. Lust (ed.), *Studies in the Acquisition of Anaphora* Vol. 2. *Applying the Constraints.* **2**: 271–356.

Lust, B., J. Eisele and R. Mazuka (1992c). "The Binding Theory Module: Evidence from First Language Acquisition for Principle C." *Language* **68**(2): 333–358.

Lust, B., S. Flynn and C. Foley (1996). What Children know about What They Say – Elicited Imitation as a Research Method. In C. McDaniel, C. McKee and H. Cairns (eds.), *Methods for Assessing Children's Syntax.* Cambridge, MA: MIT Press.

Lust, B., K. A. Loveland and R. Karret (1980). "The Development of Anaphora in First Language: Syntactic and Pragmatic Constraints." *Linguistic Analysis* **6**(2): 217–249.

Lust, B., L. Mangione and Y.-C. Chien (1984). The Determination of Empty Categories in First Language Acquisition of Chinese. In W. Harbert (ed.), *Cornell University Working Papers in Linguistics.* Ithaca, New York. **6**: 151–165.

Lust, B., Y.-C. Chien, C.-P. Chiang and J. Eisele (1996). "Chinese Pronominals in Universal Grammar: A Study of Linear Precedence and Command in Chinese and English Children's First Language Acquisition." *Journal of East Asian Linguistics* **5**(1): 1–47.

Lust, B., R. Mazuka, G. Martohardjono and J.-M. Yoon (1989). On Parameter Setting in first Language Acquisition: The Case of the Binding Theory. Paper presented at GLOW conference, Utrecht.

Lust, B., L. Solan, S. Flynn, C. Cross and E. Schultz (1986). A Comparison of Null and Pronoun Anaphora in First Language Acquisition. In B. Lust (ed.), *Studies in the Acquisition of Anaphora. Defining the Constraints.* Dordrecht: Reidel Press. **1**: 245–278.

Lust, B., T. Bhatia, J. Gair, V. Sharma and J. Khare (1995). Children's Acquisition of Hindi Anaphora: A Parameter-setting Paradox. In Vijay Ghambir (ed.), *Teaching and Acquisition of South Asian Languages.* Penn Press. 172–189.

Lust, B., T. Wakayama, W. Snyder, Shin Oshima and K. Otani (1985). *Configurational Factors in Japanese Anaphora: Evidence from Acquisition.* Paper Presented at LSA Winter 1985 Meeting.

Lust, B., J. Kornfilt, J. Hermon, C. Foley, Z. Nuñez del Prado and S. Kapur (1994). Introduction: Constraining Binding, Dependencies and Learnability: Principles or Parameters. In B. Lust, G. Hermon and J. Kornfilt (eds.), *Syntactic Theory and First Language Acquisition: Cross-Linguistic Perspectives.* Vol. II: *Binding Dependencies and Learnability.* Hillsdale, NJ: Lawrence Erlbaum Associates. **2**: 1–37.

Lust, B. and C. Foley (eds.), (2004). *First Language Acquisition. The Essential Readings.* Blackwell Publishing.

Lust, B., Kashi Wali, J. Gair and K. Subbarao (eds.) (1999). *Lexical Anaphors and Pronouns in Selected South Asian Languages: A Principled Typology.* Berlin; New York: Mouton de Gruyter.

Macaulay, R. (1977). "The Myth of Female Superiority in Language." *Journal of Child Language* **5**: 353–363.

MacKain, K. S. (1982). "Assessing the Role of Experience on Infants' Speech Discrimination." *Journal of Child Language* **9**: 527–542.

MacKain, K. S., M. Studdert-Kennedy, S. Spieker and D. Stern (1983). "Infant Intermodal Speech Perception is a Left Hemisphere Function." *Science* **219**: 1347–1349.

Macken, J. A. and D. Barton (1980). "The Acquisition of the Voicing Contrast in Spanish: A Phonetic and Phonological Study of Word-Initial Stop Consonants." *Journal of Child Language* **7**: 433–458.

Macken, M. (1980). Aspects of the Acquisition of Stop Systems: A Cross-Linguistic Perspective. In G. Yeni-Komshian, J. Kavanagh and C. Ferguson (eds.), *Child Phonology*. Vol 1. *Production*. New York: Academic Press. 143–168.

  (1986). Phonological Development: A Crosslinguistic Perspective. In P. Fletcher and M. Garman (eds.), *Language Acquisition: Studies in First Language Development*. Cambridge; New York: Cambridge University Press. 251–268.

  (1995). Phonological Acquisition. In J. Goldsmith (ed.), *The Handbook of Phonological Theory*. Cambridge, MA: Blackwell. 671–696.

Macken, M. A. (1979). "Developmental Reorganization of Phonology: A Hierarchy of Basic Units of Acquisition." *Lingua* **49**(1): 11–49.

  (1992). Where's Phonology? In C. A. Ferguson, L. Menn and C. Stoel-Gammon (eds.), *Phonological Development: Models, Research, and Implications*. Timonium, MD: New York Press.

Macken, M. and C. Ferguson (1981). "Phonological Universals in Language Acquisition." *Annals of the New York Academy of Sciences* **379**: 110–129.

  (1983). Cognitive Aspects of Phonological Development: Models, Evidence and Issues. In K. Nelson (ed.), *Children's Language*. **4**: 256–282.

MacNamara, J. (1972). "Cognitive Basis of Language Learning in Infants." *Psychological Review* **79**(1): 1–13.

  (1982). *Names for Things: A Study of Human Learning*. Cambridge, MA: MIT Press.

MacWhinney, B. (1989) Competition and connectionism. In B. MacWhinney and E. Bates (eds.), *Crosslinguistic Study of Sentence Processing*. New York: Cambridge University Press.

  (1991). *The CHILDES Project: Tools for Analyzing Talk*. Hillsdale, NJ: Lawrence Erlbaum Associates.

MacWhinney, B. and E. Bates (1989). *The Crosslinguistic Study of Sentence Processing*. New York: Cambridge University Press.

MacWhinney, B. and C. Snow (1985). "The Child Language Data Exchange System." *Journal of Child Language* **12**: 271–296.

  (1990). "The Child Language Data Exchange System: An Update." *Journal of Child Language* **17**: 457–472.

  (1992). "The Wheat and the Chaff: Or Four Confusions Regarding CHILDES." *Journal of Child Language* **19**: 459–471.

Mandel, D. R., P. W. Jusczyk and D. Pisoni (1995). "Infants' Recognition of the Sound Patterns of their own Names." *Psychological Science* **6**: 315–318.

Mandel, D. R., P. W. Jusczyk and D. G. Kemler-Nelson (1994). "Does Sentential Prosody Help Infants to Organize and Remember Speech Information?" *Cognition* **53**(2): 155–180.

Mandel, D. R., D. G. Kemler-Nelson and P. W. Jusczyk (1996). "Infants Remember the Order of Words in a Spoken Sentence." *Cognitive Development* **11**(2): 181–196.

Mangione, L., Y.-C. Chien and B. Lust (in preparation). The Representation of Sentential Complements in First Language Acquisition of Mandarin Chinese: A Study of Natural Speech.

Manzini, R. M. and K. Wexler (1987). "Parameters, Binding Theory and Learnability." *Linguistic Inquiry* **18**(3): 413–444.

Marantz, A. (1982). "On the Acquisition of Grammatical Relations." *Linguistische Berichte* **80/82**: 32–69.

Maratsos, M. (1982). The Child's Construction of Grammatical Categories. In L. Gleitman and E. Wanner (eds.), *Language Acquisition: The State of the Art*. Cambridge; New York: Cambridge University Press: 240–266.

Maratsos, M. and M. A. Chalkley (1981). The Internal Language of Children's Syntax: The Ontogenesis and Representation of Syntactic Categories. In K. Nelson (ed.), *Children's Language*. New York: Gardner Press. **2**.

Marchman, V. A., K. Plunkett and J. C. Goodman (1997). "Overregularization in English Plural and Past Tense Inflectional Morphology: A Response to Marcus (1995)." *Journal of Child Language* **24**(3): 767–779.

Marcus, G. (2004). *The Birth of the Mind*. Basic Books.

Marcus, G. F. (1995). "Children's Overregularization of English Plurals: A Quantitative Analysis." *Journal of Child Language* **22**(2): 447–459.

(1998). "Can Connectionism Save Constructivism?" *Cognition* **66**(2): 153–182.

Marcus, G. F., U. Brinkmann, H. Clahsen, R. Wiese and S. Pinker (1995). "German Inflection: The Exception that Proves the Rule." *Cognitive Psychology* **29**(3): 189–256.

Marcus, G. F., S. Pinker, M. Ullman, M. Hollander, T. J. Rosen and F. Xu (1992). "Overregularization in Language Acquisition." *Monographs of the Society for Research in Child Development* **57**(4(228)): 1–182.

Marcus, G. F., S. Vijayan, S. B. Rao and P. M. Vishton (1999). "Rule Learning by Seven-Month-Old Infants." *Science* **283**(5398): 77–80.

Markman, E. (1987). How Children Constrain the Possible Meanings of Words. In U. Neisser (ed.), *Concepts and Conceptual Development: Ecological and Intellectual Factors in Categorization*. Cambridge: Cambridge University Press.

Markman, E. M. (1989). *Categorization and Naming in Children: Problems of Induction*. Cambridge, MA: MIT Press.

(1994). Constraints Children Place on Word Meanings. In P. Bloom (ed.), *Language Acquisition: Core Readings*. Cambridge, MA: MIT Press. **14**: 154–173.

Markman, E. M. and J. E. Hutchinson (1984). "Children's Sensitivity to Constraints on Word Meaning: Taxonomic vs. Thematic Relations." *Cognitive Psychology* **16**(1): 1–27.

Markman, E. M. and G. F. Wachtel (1998). "Children's Use of Mutual Exclusivity to Constrain the Meaning of Words." *Cognitive Psychology* **20**: 121–157.

Markson, L. and P. Bloom (1997). "Evidence Against a Dedicated System for Word Learning in Children." *Nature Publishing Group* **385**(6619): 813–815.

Marler, P. (1987). Sensitive Periods and the Roles of Specific and General Sensory Stimulation in Birdsong Learning. In J. Rauschecker and P. Marler (eds.), *Imprinting and Cortical Plasticity*. New York: J. Wiley & Sons. 100–135.

(1991a). Differences in Behavioural Development in Closely Related Species: Bird-song. In P. Bateson (ed.), *The Development and Integration of Behaviour. Essays in Honour of Robert Hinde*. Cambridge: Cambridge University Press. 41–70.

(1991b). The Instinct to Learn. In S. Carey and R. Gelman (eds.), *The Epigenesis of Mind: Essays on Biology and Cognition*. Hillsdale, NJ: Lawrence Erlbaum Associates.

(1997). "Three Models of Song Learning: Evidence from Behavior." *Journal of Neurobiology* **33**(5): 501–516.

(1998). Animal Communication and Human Language. In N. Jablonski and L. Aiello (eds.), *The Origin and Diversification of Language*. San Francisco, CA: Academy of Sciences. 1–19.

(1999a). Nature, Nurture and the Instinct to Learn. In N. Adams and R. Slotow (eds.), *Proceedings of the XXII International Ornithological Congress*. 2353–2355.

(1999b). "Review of *Apes, Language, and the Human Mind* by S. Savage Rumbaugh, G. Shanker, and T. Taylor." *American Anthropologist*. **101**: 432–436.

Martohardjono, G. (1993). *Wh-Movement in the Aquisition of a Second Language: A Cross-Linguistic Study of Three Languages with and without Movement*. Ithaca, NY: Cornell University.

Massaro, D. and D. Stork (1998). "Speech Recognition and Sensory Integration." *American Scientist* **86**(3): 236.

Matsumoto, Y. (1985). Acquisition of Some Japanese Numeral Classifiers: The Search for Convention. In *Papers and Reports in Child Language Development*. **24**: 79–86.

(1987). Order of Acquisition in the Lexicon: Implication from Japanese Numeral Classifiers. In K. E. Nelson and A. Kleeck (eds.), *Children's Language*. Hillsdale, NJ: Lawrence Erlbaum Associates. **7**: 229–260.

Matthei, E. and T. Roeper (1983). *Understanding and Producing Speech*. Bungay: The Chaucer Press.

Matthews, P. (1997). *The Concise Oxford Dictionary of Linguistics*. New York: Oxford University Press.

Matthews, R. (1991). Psychological Reality of Grammars. In A. Kasher (ed.), *The Chomskyan Turn*. Cambridge, MA: Basil Blackwell. 182–199.

Mattys, S. L. and P. W. Jusczyk (2001). "Phonotactic Cues for Segmentation of Fluent Speech by Infants." *Cognition* **78**(2): 91–121.

Mauner, F. (1995). "Examining the Empirical and Linguistic Bases of Current Theories of Agrammatism." *Brain and Language* **50**: 339–368.

May, R. (1999). Logical Form in Linguistics. In R. A. Wilson and F. C. Keil (eds.), *The MIT Encyclopedia of the Cognitive Sciences*. Cambridge, MA: MIT Press: 486–488.

Mayberry, R. (1993). "First-Language Acquisition after Childhood Differs from Second-Language Acquisition: The Case of American Sign Language." *Journal of Speech and Hearing Research* **36**: 1258–1270.

Mayberry, R., E. Lock and H. Kazmi (2002). "Linguistic Ability and Early Language Exposure." *Nature* **417**.

Maye, J. and L. A. Gerken (2001). Learning Phonemes: How Far Can the Input Take Us? *Proceedings of the 25th Annual Boston University Conference on Language Development*. Boston, MA: Cascadilla Press. 480–490.

Mayeux, R. and E. Kandel (2000). Natural Language, Disorders of Language and Other Localizable Disorders of Cognitive Functioning. In E. Kandel, J. Schwartz and T. Jessell (eds.), *Principles of Neuroscience*. 688–703.

Mazuka, R. (1990). Japanese and English Children's Processing of Complex Sentences: An Experimental Comparison. Doctoral dissertation. Ithaca, NY: Cornell University.

(1996). Can a Grammatical Parameter be Set Before the First Word? Prosodic Contributions to Early Setting of a Grammatical Parameter. In J. L. Morgan and K. Demuth (eds.), *Signal to Syntax: Bootstrapping from Speech to Grammar in Early Acquisition*. Hillsdale, NJ: Lawrence Erlbaum Associates. 313–330.

(1998). *The Development of Language Processing Strategies: A Cross-Linguistic Study Between Japanese and English*. Hillsdale, NJ: Lawrence Erlbaum Associates.

Mazuka, R. and R. Friedman(2000). "Linguistic Relativity in Japanese and English: Is Language the Primary Determinant in Object Classification?" *Journal of East Asian Linguistics* **9**: 353–377.

Mazuka, R. and B. Lust (1990). On Parameter Setting and Parsing: Predictions for Cross-Linguistic Differences in Adult and Child Processing. In L. Frazier and J. De Villiers (eds.), *Language Processing and Language Acquisition*. Dordrecht: Kluwer Academic Publishers. 163–207.

(1994). When is an Anaphor Not an Anaphor? A Study of Japanese "Zibun." In B. Lust, G. Hermon and J. Kornfilt (eds.), *Syntactic Theory and First Language Acquisition: Cross-Linguistic Perspectives*. Hillsdale, NJ: Lawerence Erlbaum Associates. **2**: 145–175.

Mazuka, R., B. Lust, W. Snyder and T. Wakayama (1995). "Null Subject Grammar" and Phrase Structure in Early Syntax Acquisition: A Cross Linguistic Study of Japanese and English. In C. Jakubowicz (ed.), *Recherches Linguistiques de Vincennes*. Vincennes: Presses Universitaires de Vincennes. **24**: 55–81.

Mazuka, R., B. Lust, T. Wakayama and W. Snyder (1986). Distinguishing Effects of Parameters in Early Syntax Acquisition: A Cross-Linguistic Study of Japanese and English. In *Papers and Reports on Child Language Development*. Stanford, CA: Stanford University. **25**: 73–82.

McCauley, R. (1997). "Three Models of Song Learning: Evidence from Behavior." *Journal of Neurobiology* **33**(5): 501–516.

(1999). Reductionism. In Wilson and Keil (eds.), 712–714.

McClelland, J. (2000). Cognitive Modeling, Connectionist. In F. C. Keil and R. A. Wilson (eds.), *Explanation and Cognition*. Cambridge, MA: MIT Press: 137–141.

McDaniel, D. (1986). Conditions on Wh-chains. Ph.D. Dissertation, City University of New York.

McDaniel, D., C. McKee and H. S. Cairns (eds.) (1996). *Methods for Assessing Children's Syntax*. Cambridge, MA: MIT Press.

McGilvray, J. A. (1999). *Chomsky: Language, Mind, and Politics*. Malden, MA: Basil Blackwell.

McGurk and MacDonald (1976). Hearing Lips and Seeing Voices. *Nature* **264**: 746–748.

McKee, C. (1994). What You See Isn't Always What You Get. In B. Lust, M. Suñer and J. Whitman (eds.), *Heads, Projections, and Learnability*. Lawrence Erlbaum Associates: 201–212.

McShane, J. (1979). "The Development of Naming." *Linguistics* **17**(9–10): 879–905.

Meara, P. and A. Ellis (1982). The Psychological Reality of Deep and Surface Phonological Representations: Evidence from Speech Errors in Welsh. In A. Cutler (ed.), *Slips of the Tongue and Language Production*. Berlin; New York: Mouton de Gruyter. 797–804.

Mehler, J. and E. DuPoux (1994). *What Infants Know: The New Cognitive Science of Early Development*. Cambridge, MA: Blackwell.

Mehler, J. F., J. Bertoncini, M. Barriere and D. Jassik-Gerschenfeld (1978). "Infant Recognition of Mother's Voice." *Perception* **7**(5): 491–497.

Mehler, J. F., E. Dupoux, T. Nazzi and G. Dehaene-Lambertz (1996). Coping with Linguistic Diversity: The Infant's Viewpoint. In J. L. Morgan and K. Demuth (eds.), *Signal to Syntax: Bootstrapping from Speech to Grammar in Early Acquisition*. Hillsdale, NJ: Lawrence Erlbaum Associates: 101–116.

Mehler, J. F., P. Jusczyk, G. Lambertz, N. Halsted, J. Bertoncini and C. Amiel-Tison (1988). "A Precursor of Language Acquisition in Young Infants." *Cognition* **29**(2): 143–178.

Meier, R. P. (1991). "Language Acquisition by Deaf Children." *American Scientist* **79**(1): 60–70.

Meier, R. P. and E. Newport (1990). Out of the Hands of Babes: On a Possible Sign Advantage. *Language* **66**(1): 1–23.

Meisel, J. M. (ed.) (1992). *The Acquisition of Verb Placement: Functional Categories and V2 Phenomena in Language Development*. Dordrecht: Kluwer.

Meltzoff, A. N. and M. K. Moore (1977). "Imitation of Facial and Manual Gestures by Human Neonates." *Science* **198**: 75–78.

(1983). "Newborn Infants Imitate Adult Facial Gestures." *Child Development* **54**: 702–709.

Menn, L. (1975). "Counter Example to 'Fronting' as a Universal of Child Psychology." *Journal of Child Language* **2**(2): 293–296.

(1976). "Evidence for an Interactionist-Discovery Theory of Child Phonology." *Papers and Reports on Child Language Development*. Stanford, CA: Stanford University. **12**: 169–177.

(1980). "Phonological Theory and Child Phonology." In G. Yeni-Komshian, J. F. Kavanagh and C. A. Ferguson (eds.), *Child Phonology*. New York: Academic Press. **1**: 23–41.

Menn, L. and E. Matthei (1992). The "Two-Lexicon" Account of Child Phonology: Looking Back and Looking Ahead. In C. A. Ferguson, L. Menn and C. Stoel-Gammon (eds.), *Phonological Development: Models, Research, Implications*. Timonium, MD: York Press.

Menn, L. and N. B. Ratner (eds.) (2000). *Methods for Studying Language Production*. Hillsdale, NJ: Lawrence Erlbaum Associates.

Menyuk, P. and L. Menn (1979). Early Strategies for the Perception and Production of Words and Sounds. In P. Fletcher and M. Garman (eds.), *Studies in Language Acquisition*. Cambridge: Cambridge University Press.

Merriman, W. and L. Bowman (1989). "The Mutual Exclusivity Bias in Children's Word Learning." *Monographs of the Society for Research in Child Development* **54**(3–4(220)): 1–123.

Mervis, C. B. (1987). Child-Basic Object Categories and Early Lexical Development. In U. Neisser (ed.), *Concepts and Conceptual Development: Ecological and Intellectual Factors in Categorization*. Cambridge: Cambridge University Press. 201–203.

Mervis, C. B. and K. Canada (1983). "On the Existence of Competence Errors in Early Comprehension: A Reply to Fremgen and Fay and Chapman and Thomson." *Journal of Child Language* **10**(2): 431–440.

Mervis, C. B., R. M. Golinkoff and J. Bertrand (1994). "Two-year-olds Readily Learn Multiple Labels for the Same Basic-Level Category." *Child Development* **65**(4): 1163–1177.

Mikes, M. (1967). "Acquisition des catégories grammaticales dans le langage de l'enfant." *Enfance* **20**: 289–298.

Miller, G. (1978). Semantic Relations Among Words. In M. Halle, J. Bresnan and G. Miller (eds.), *Linguistic Theory and Psychological Reality*. Cambridge; New York: Cambridge University Press. 60–118.

(1981). *Language and Speech*. San Francisco, CA: W. H. Freeman.

(1996). *The Science of Words*. New York: W. H. Freeman.

Miller, G. and P. Johnson-Laird (1976). *Language and Perception*. Cambridge, MA: Harvard University Press.

Miller, J. (1981). *Assessing Language Production in Children. Experimental Procedures*. Baltimore MD: University Park Press.

Miller, J. and R. Chapman (1981). "The Relation Between Age and Mean Length of Utterance in Morphemes." *Journal of Speech and Hearing Research* **24**: 154–161.

(1983). *SALT: Systemic Analysis of Language Transcripts, User's Manual*. Madison: WI: University of Wisconsin Press.

Mills, A. (1985). The Acquisition of German. In Slobin.

Mills, D., S. Coffey-Corina, et al. (1997). "Language Acquisition and Cerebral Specialization in 20-month-old Infants." *Journal of Cognitive Neuroscience* **5**(3): 317–334.

Milner, B. (1958). Psychological Defects Produced by Temporal Lobe Excisions. *Proceedings of the Association for Research in Nervous and Mental Disease* **36**: 244–257.

Mitchell, P. (1996). *Acquiring a Conception of Mind*. Hove, East Sussex: Psychology Press.

Mithun, M. (1989). "The Acquisition of Polysynthesis." *Journal of Child Language* **16**: 285–312.

Miyahara, K. (1974). "The Acquisition of Japanese Particles." *Journal of Child Language* **1**(2): 283–286.

Miyata, H. (1993). The Performance of the Japanese Case Particles in Children's Speech: With Special Reference to "Ga" and "O." In Y. Otsu (ed.), *MITA Psycholinguistics Circle*. Tokyo: Keio University.

Moerk, E. L. (1980). "Relationships Between Parental Input Frequencies and Children's Language Acquisition: A Reanalysis of Brown's Data." *Journal of Child Language* **7**: 105–118.

Moffitt, A. R. (1971). "Consonant Cue Perception by Twenty- to Twenty-Four-Week-Old Infants." *Child Development* **42**: 717–731.

Mogford-Bevan, K. (1988). Oral Language Acquisition in the Prelinguistically Deaf. In D. V. M. Bishop and K. Mogford-Bevan (eds.). 110–131.

Mogford-Bevan, K. and D. V. M. Bishop (1988). "Language Development in Unexceptional Circumstances." In D. V. M. Bishop and K. Mogford-Bevan (eds.), *Language Development in Exceptional Circumstances*. Edinburgh; New York, Churchill Livingstone: 10–28.

Mohanty, P. (nd). *The Acquisition of Oriya Phonology: A Case Study*. Hyderabad: Center for ALTS. Hyderabad 5001324: University of Hyderabad.

Molfese, D. L., R. B. Freeman, Jr. and D. S. Palermo (1975). "The Ontogeny of Brain Lateralization for Speech and Nonspeech Sounds." *Brain and Language*. **2**: 356–368.

Molfese, D., D. Narter, A. Van Matre, M. Elletson and M. Madglin (2001). Language Development during Infancy and Early Childhood: Electrophysiological Correlates. In J. Weissenborn and B. Hohle (eds.), *Approaches to Bootstrapping: Phonological, Lexical, Syntactic and Neurophysiological Aspects of Early Language Acquisition*. Amsterdam; Philadelphia: John Benjamins. 181–230.

Moon, C., T. G. Bever and W. P. Fifer (1992). "Canonical and Non-Canonical Syllable Discrimination by Two-Day-Old Infants." *Journal of Child Language* **19**(1): 1–17.

Moon, C., R. P. Cooper and W. P. Fifer (1993). "Two Day Olds Prefer Their Native Language." *Infant Behavior and Development* **16**(4): 495–500.

Morford, J. and S. Goldin-Meadow (1997). "From Here and Now to There and Then: The Development of Displaced Reference in Homesign and English." *Child Development* **68**(3): 420–435.

Morford, J., J. Singleton and S. Goldin-Meadow (1995). From Homesign to ASL: Identifying the Influences of a Self-Generated Childhood Gesture System Upon Language Proficiency in Adulthood. *Proceedings of Boston University Conference on Language Development*. Boston, MA: Cascadilla Press.

Morgan, J. (1994). "Converging Measures of Speech Segmentation in Preverbal Infants." *Infant Behavior and Development* **17**: 389–403.

(1996). "A Rhythmic Bias in Preverbal Speech Segementation." *Journal of Memory and Language* **35**: 666–688.

Morgan, J. and K. Demuth (eds.) (1996). *Signal to Syntax: Bootstrapping from Speech to Grammar in Early Acquisition*. Mahwah, NJ: Lawrence Erlbaum Associates.

Morgan, J. and J. Saffran (1995). "Emerging Integration of Sequential and Suprasegmental Information in Preverbal Speech Segementation." *Child Development* **66**: 911–936.

Morgan, J. and L. Travis (1989). "Limits on Negative Information in Language Input." *Journal of Child Language* **16**(3): 531–552.

Morgan, J., D. Swingley and K. Miritai (1993). Infants Listen Longer to Speech with Extraneous Noises Inserted at Clause Boundaries. Paper Presented at the Biennial Meeting of the Society of Research in Child Development, New Orleans, LA.

Morgan, J. L. (1986). *From Simple Input to Complex Grammar*. Cambridge, MA: MIT Press.

Morgan, J. L., R. P. Meier and E. L. Newport (1987). "Structural Packaging in the Input to Language Learning: Contributions of Prosodic and Morphological Marking of Phrases to the Acquisition of Language." *Cognitive Psychology* **19**: 498–550.

Morse, P. A. (1972). "The Discrimination of Speech and Nonspeech Stimuli in Early Infancy." *Journal of Experimental Child Psychology* **14**(3): 477–492.

Muir, D. and J. Field (1979). "Newborn Infants Orient to Sounds." *Child Development* **50**(2): 431–436.

Mulford, R. (1985). "Comprehension of Icelandic Pronoun Gender: Semantic versus Formal Factors." *Journal of Child Language* **12**(2): 443–454.

Muller, R. A., R. D. Rothermel, M. E. Behan, O. Muznik, T. J. Mangner and P. K. Chakraborty (1998). "Brain Organization of Language after Early Unilateral Lesion: A PET Study." *Brain and Language* **62**: 422–451.

Naigles, L. (1998). "Children Use Syntax to Learn Verb Meaning." *Journal of Child Language* **17**: 357–374.

Naigles, L. and S. A. Gelman (1995). "Overextensions in Comprehension and Production Revisited: Preferential-Looking in a Study of Dog, Cat and Cow." *Journal of Child Language* **22**(1): 19–46.

Naigles, L., H. Gleitman and L. Gleitman (1993). Children Acquire Word Meaning Components from Syntactic Evidence. In E. Dromi (ed.), *Language and Development*. Norwood, NJ: Ablex.

Naigles, L. and E. Kako (1993). "First Contact in Verb Acquisition: Defining a Role for Syntax." *Child Development* **64**: 1665–1687.

Naigles, L. R. (1998). Developmental Changes in the Use of Structure in Verb Learning: Evidence from Preferential Looking. In C. Rovee-Collier, L. P. Lipsett and H. Hayne (eds.), *Advances in Infancy Research* Vol. 12. Stamford, CT: Ablex. 298–318.

Nair, S. (1991). "Monosyllabic English or Disyllabic Hindi? Language Acquisition in a Bilingual Child." *Indian Linguistics: Indian Institute of Technology* **52** (1–4): 51–90.

Nakayama, J., R. Mazuka, Y. Shirai and P. Li (eds.) (forthcoming). *Handbook of East Asian Psycholinguistics: Japanese*. Cambridge: Cambridge University Press.

Nazzi, T., J. Bertoncini, et al. (1998). "Language Discrimination by Newborns: Toward an Understanding of the Role of Rhythm." *Journal of Experimental Psychology: Human Perception and Performance* **24**(3): 756–766.

Neeleman, A. and F. Weerman (1997). "L1 and L2 Word Order Acquisition." *Language Acquisition*: 125–170.

Nelson, K. (1974). "Concept, Word and Sentence: Interrelations in Acquisition and Development." *Psychological Review* **81**(4): 267–286.

Nelson, K., J. Hampson and J. Shaw (1993). "Nouns in early lexicons: evidence, explanations and implications." *Journal of Child Language* **20**(1): 61–84.

Nelson, K. E. and J. D. Bonvillian (1973). "Concepts and Words in the 18-month-old: Acquiring Concept Names under Controlled Conditions." *Cognition* **2**(4): 435–450.

Nelson, C. and M. Luciana (eds.) (2001). *Handbook of Developmental Cognitive Neuroscience*. Cambridge, MA: MIT Press.

Nespor, M. and I. Vogel (1986). *Prosodic Phonology*. Dordrecht: Floris.

Neville, H. and D. Bavelier (2000). Specificity and Plasticity in Neurocognitive Development in Humans. In M. Gazzaniga (ed.), *Cognitive Neuroscience: A Reader*. Malden, MA: Blackwell. 83–98.

Neville, H. and D. Mills (1997). "Epigenesis of Language." *Mental Retardation and Developmental Disabilities Research Reviews* **3**(4): 282–292.

Neville, H., J. Nicol, A. Barss, K. I. Forster and M. Garrett (1991). "Syntactically Based Sentence Processing Classes: Evidence from Event-Related Brain Potentials." *Journal of Cognitive Neuropsychology*: 155–170.

Newport, E. (1990). "Maturational Constraints on Language Learning." *Cognitive Science* **14**: 11–28.

Newport, E. L., H. Gleitman and L. Gleitman (1977). "Mother, I'd Rather Do It Myself": Some Effects and Non-Effects of Maternal Speech Style. In C. E. Snow and C. A. Ferguson (eds.), *Talking to Children: Language Input and Acquisition*. Cambridge, UK; New York: Cambridge University Press. 109–150.

Nicol, J. (ed.) (2001). *One Mind, Two Languages: Bilingual Language Processing*. *Explaining Linguistics*. Malden, MA: Basil Blackwell.

Ninio, A. and C. Snow (1999). The Development of Pragmatics: Learning to Use Language Appropriately. In W. Ritchie and T. Bhatia (eds.), *Handbook of Language Acquisition*. New York: Academic Press. 347–383.

Nirmala, C. (1981). "Medial Consonant Cluster Acquisition by Telugu children." *Journal of Child Language* **8**(1): 63–73.

 (1982). *First Language (Telugu) Development in Children. A Short Descriptive Study*. Hyderabad: Osmania University.

Nuñez del Prado, Z., C. Foley and B. Lust (1993). The Significance of CP to the Pro-Drop Parameter: An Experimental Study of Spanish–English Comparison. In E. Clark (ed.), *The Proceedings of the Twenty-Fifth Child Language Research Forum*. Stanford University: CSLI. 146–157.

O'Grady, W. (1997). *Syntactic Development*. Chicago IL: University of Chicago Press.

O'Grady, W., Y. Suzuki-Wei, and S. Cho (1986). "Directionality Preferences in the Interpretation of Anaphora: Data from Korean and Japanese." *Journal of Child Language* **13**: 409–420.

O'Grady, W., M. Dobrovolsky and H. Aronoff (1997). *Contemporary Linguistics: An Introduction*. New York: St. Martin's Press.

Obler, L. and K. Gjerlow (1999). *Language and the Brain*. Cambridge: Cambridge University Press.

Obler, L. and S. Hannigan (1996). Neurolinguistics of Second Language Acquisition and Use. In W. Ritchie and T. Bhatia (eds.), *Handbook of Second Language Acquisition*. San Diego, CA: Academic Press. 509–526.

Ochs, E. (1979). Transcription as Theory. In E. Ochs and B. Schieffelin (eds.), *Developmental Pragmatics*. New York: Academic Press.

 (1982). "Ergativity and Word Order in Samoan Child Language." *Language* **58**(3): 646–671.

Ojemann, G. (1983). "Brain Organization for Language from the Perspective of Electrical Stimulation Mapping." *Behavioral and Brain Science* **2**: 189–203.

 (1991). "Cortical Organization of Language." *Journal of Neuroscience* **11**(8): 2281–2287.

Ojemann, G., J. Ojemann, E. Lettich and M. Berger (1989). "Cortical Language Localization in Left Dominant Hemisphere." *Journal of Neurosurgery* **71**: 316–326.

Oller, D. (1980). The Emergence of Speech Sounds in Infancy. In G. H. Yeni-Komshian, J. Kavanagh and C. Ferguson (eds.), *Child Phonology*. New York: Academic Press.

 (1981). Infant Vocalizations. Exploration and Reflexivity. In R. E. Stark (ed.), *Language Behaviour in Infancy and Early Childhood*. Amsterdam: Elsevier. 85–104.

Oller, D. and R. Eilers (1988). "The Role of Audition in Infant Babbling." *Child Development* **59**(2): 441–449.

Oller, D., L. Wieman W. Doyle and C. Ross (1976). "Infant Babbling and Speech." *Journal of Child Language* **3**: 1–12.

Opper, S. (1977). Concept Development in Thai Urban and Rural Children. In P. R. Wosen (ed.), *Piagetian Psychology: Cross-Cultural Contributions*. New York: Gardner Press.

Osherson D. (ed.) (1995). *An Invitation to Cognitive Science*. Cambridge, MA: MIT Press.

Oshima, S. and B. Lust (1997). "Remarks on Anaphora in Japanese Adverbial Clauses."
    In S. Somashekar, K. Yamakoshi, M. Blume and C. Foley (eds.), *Papers on Language
    Acquisition: Cornell University Working Papers in Linguistics*. Ithaca, NY: Cornell
    University, Department of Linguistics. **15**: 88–100.

Otsu, Y. (1994). Case Marking Particles and Phrase Structure in Early Japanese Acquisi-
    tion. In B. Lust, M. Suñer and J. Whitman (eds.), *Syntactic Theory and First Language
    Acquisition: Cross-Linguistic Perspectives*. B. Lust, M. Suner and J. Whitman. Hills-
    dale, NJ: Lawrence Erlbaum Associates. **1**: 159–170.

Ouhalla, J. (1991). *Functional Categories and Parametric Variation*. London; New York:
    Routledge.

Oviatt, S. L. (1980). "The Emerging Ability to Comprehend Language: An Experimental
    Approach." *Child Development* **51**(1): 97–106.

    (1982). "Inferring what Words Mean: Early Development in Infants' Comprehension
    of Common Object Names." *Child Development* **53**(1): 274–277.

Padilla, J. (1990). *On the Definition of Binding Domains in Spanish: Evidence from Child
    Language*. Dordrecht; Boston: Kluwer Academic.

Papafragou, A. (1998). "The Acquisition of Modality: Implications for Theories of Seman-
    tic Representation." *Mind and Language* **13**(3): 370–399.

    (2002). "Mind Reading and Verbal Communication." *Mind and Language* **17**(1–2):
    55–67.

Papandropoulou, I. and H. Sinclair (1974). "What is a Word? An Experimental Study of
    Children's Ideas on Grammar." *Human Development* **17**: 241–258.

Paradis, M. (1990). "Language Lateralization in Bilinguals: Enough Already!" *Brain and
    Language*. **39**: 576–586.

    (1995). *Aspects of Bilingual Aphasia*. Oxford; Tarrytown, NY: Elsevier Science.

    (2003). Differential Use of Cerebral Mechanisms in Bilinguals. In M. Banich and M.
    Mack (eds.), *Mind, Brain and Language*. Hillsdale, NJ: Lawrence Erlbaum Asso-
    ciates: 351–370.

Paradis, J. and F. Genesee (1997). "On continuity and the emergence of functional cate-
    gories in bilingual first language acquisition." *Language Acquisition* **6**: 911–924.

Parkinson, D. J. (1997). The Acquisition of Phonology in an Optimality Theoretic Frame-
    work. In S. Somashekar (ed.), *Cornell Working Papers in Linguistics* (eds.), **15**:
    282–308.

    (1999). "The Interaction of Syntax and Morphology in the Acquisition of Noun Incorpo-
    ration in Inuktitut (Northwest Territories)." Ph.D. Dissertation. Ithaca, NY: Cornell.

Partee, B. (1999). Semantics. In R. A. Wilson and F. C. Keil (eds.), *The MIT Encyclopedia
    of the Cognitive Sciences*. Cambridge, MA: MIT Press. 739–742.

Peiper, A. (1963). *Cerebral Function in Infancy and Childhood*. New York: Consultants
    Bureau.

Peirce, C. S. (1955). *Philosophical Writings of Peirce*. New York: Dover.

Penfield, W. and L. Roberts (1959). *Speech and Brain Mechanisms*. Princeton, NJ: Prince-
    ton University Press.

Penner, A. and J. Weissenborn (1996). Strong Continuity, Parameter Setting and the
    Trigger Hierarchy: On the Acquisition of the DP in Bernese Swiss German and
    High German. In H. Clahsen (ed.), *Generative Perspectives on Language Acquisi-
    tion. Empirical Findings, Theoretical Considerations, Crosslinguistic Comparison*.
    Amsterdam: John Benjamins.

Penner, S. (1987). "Parental Responses to Grammatical and Ungrammatical Child Utterances." *Child Development* **58**: 376–384.

Penner, Z. and J. Weissenborn (1995). Strong Continuity, Parameter Setting, and the Trigger Hierarchy. In H. Clahsen (ed.), *Generative Perspectives in Language Acquisition*. Amsterdam: John Benjamins.

Pennisi, E. (1999). "Are our Primate Cousins 'Conscious?'" *Science* **284**(June 25): 2073–2076.

Perani, D., S. Dehaene, F. Grassi, L. Cohen, S. Cappa and E. Dupoux (1996). "Brain Processing of Native and Foreign Languages." *NeuroReport* **7**: 2439–2444.

Perani, D., E. Paulesu, N. S. Galles, E. Dupoux, S. Dahaene and V. Bettinardi (1998). "The Bilingual Brain: Proficiency and Age of Acquisition of the Second Language." *Brain* **121**: 1841–1852.

Peters, A. (1976). "Language Learning Strategies: Does the Whole Equal the Sum of the Parts?" *Papers and Reports on Child Language Development* **12**: 178–188.

Peters, A. and L. Menn (1993). "False Starts and Filler Syllables: Ways to Learn Grammatical Morphemes." *Language* **69**(4): 742–777.

Peters, A. and S. Stromquist (1996). The Role of Prosody in the Acquisition of Grammatical Morphemes. In Morgan and Demuth. 215–232.

Peters, M. (1995). Handedness and its Relation to Other Indices of Cerebral Lateralization. In R. Davidson and K. Hugdahl (eds.), *Brain Asymmetry*. Cambridge, MA: MIT Press. 183–214.

Peters, S. (1972). The Projection Problem: How is a Grammar to be Selected? In S. Peters (ed.), *Goals of Linguistic Theory*. Englewood Cliffs, NJ: Prentice Hall.

Peterson, C. C. (2002). "Drawing Insight from Pictures: The Development of Concepts of False Drawing and False Belief in Children with Deafness, Normal Hearing, and Autism." *Child Development* **73**(5): 1442–1459.

Petitto, L. A. (1987). "On the Autonomy of Language and Gesture: Evidence from the Acquisition of Personal Pronouns in American Sign Language." *Cognition* **27**(1): 1–52.

  (1988). "Language" in the Prelinguistic Child. In R. Brown and F. Kessel (eds.), *The Development of Language and Language Researchers: Essays in Honor of Roger Brown*. Hillsdale, NJ: Lawrence Erlbaum Associates: 187–222.

Petitto, L. and P. Marentette (1991). "Babbling in the Manual Mode: Evidence for the Ontogeny of Language." *Science* **251**: 1493–1496.

Petitto, L., M. Katerelos, B. Levy, K. Gauna, K. Tretault and V. Ferraro (2001). "Bilingual Signed and Spoken Language Acquisition from Birth: Implications for the Mechanisms Underlying Early Bilingual Language Acquisition." *Journal of Child Language* **28**: 453–496.

Philip, W. (1995). Event Quantification in the Acquisition of Universal Quantification. Ph.D. Dissertation. Amherst: University of Massachusetts.

Philip, W. and M. Takahashi (1991). Quantifier Spreading in the Acquisition of "Every." In T. Maxfield and B. Plunkett (eds.), *Papers in the Acquisition of WH*. Amherst, MA: GLSA: 283–301.

Phillips, C. (1995). Syntax at Age Two: Cross-Linguistic Differences. In *MIT Working Papers in Linguistics*. Cambridge, MA: MIT Press. **26**.

Piaget, J. (1959). *The Language and Thought of the Child*. London: Routledge and Kegan Paul.

(1962(1945/1951)). *Play, Dreams and Imitation in Childhood*. New York: Norton.

(1980). Opening the Debate. In M. Piattelli-Palmarini (ed.), *Language and Learning: The Debate Between Jean Piaget and Noam Chomsky*. Cambridge, MA: Harvard University Press. 23–34, 163–167. Reprinted in part in Lust and Foley (2004).

(1983). Piaget on Piaget. In P. H. Mussen (ed.), *Cognitive Development*. New York: John Wiley & Sons. **3**.

Piaget, J. and B. Inhelder (1969). *The Psychology of the Child*. New York: Basic Books. (First Published in French, 1966 *La Psychologie de l'enfant*. Paris: Presses Universitaires de France.)

(1973). *Memory and Intelligence*. New York: Basic Books.

Piattelli-Palmarini, M. (ed.) (1980). *Language and Learning: The Debate Between Jean Piaget and Noam Chomsky*. Cambridge, MA, Harvard University Press.

Pienemann, M. (1991). "COALA: A Computational System for Interlanguage Analysis." *LARC Occasional Papers* **1**(September 1991): 1–26.

Pierce, A. (1992). *Language Acquisition and Syntactic Theory*. Dordrecht: Kluwer.

Pilon, R. (1981). "Segmentation of Speech in a Foreign Language." *Journal of Psycholinguistic Research* **10**: 113–121.

Pine, J. and E. Lieven (1997). "Slot and Frame Patterns in the Development of The Determiner Category." *Applied Psycholinguistics* **18**(2): 123–138.

Pinker, S. (1981). "On the Acquisition of Grammatical Morphemes." *Journal of Child Language* 8: 477–484.

(1984). *Language Learnability and Language Development*. Cambridge, MA: Harvard University Press.

(1987). The Bootstrapping Problem in Language Acquisition. In B. MacWhinney (ed.), *Mechanisms of Language Acquisition*. Hillsdale, NJ: Lawrence Erlbaum Associates. 399–442.

(1989a). *Learnability and Cognition. The Acquisition of Argument Structure*. Cambridge, MA: MIT Press.

(1989b). Markedness and Language Development. In R. Matthews and W. Demopoulos (eds.), *Learnability and Linguistic Theory*. Dordrecht: Kluwer Academic. 107–127.

(1991). "Rules of Language." *Science* **253**(5019): 530–535.

(1994). *The Language Instinct*. New York: W. W. Morrow and Co.

(1994b). Words, Words, Words. In Pinker (1994) New York: W. W. Morrow and Co. 126–153.

(1999). "Out of the Minds of Babes." *Science* **283**(5398): 40–41.

(2001). "Talk of Genetics and Vice Versa." *Nature* **413**: 465–466.

(2002). *The Blank Slate: the Modern Denial of Human Nature*. New York: Viking Press.

Pinker, S. and A. Prince (1988a). "On Language and Connectionism: Analysis of a Parallel Distributed Processing Model of Language Acquisition." *Cognition* **23**: 73.

(1988b). *On Language and Connectionism: Analysis of a Parallel Distributed Processing Model of Language Acquisition*. Cambridge, MA: MIT Press.

Pisoni, D. B., S. E. Lively and J. S. Logar (1994). Perceptual Learning of Nonnative Speech Contrasts: Implications for Theories of Speech Perception. In J. C. Goodman and H. C. Nusbaum (eds.), *The Development of Speech Perception: The Transition from Speech Sounds to Spoken Words*. Cambridge, MA; MIT Press: 121–166.

Pizzuto, E. and M. C. Caselli (1992). "The Acquisition of Italian Morphology: Implications for Models of Language Development." *Journal of Child Language* **19**(3): 491–557.

Plunkett, K. (1996). Connectionist Approaches to Language Acquisition. In P. Fletcher and B. MacWhinney (eds.), *The Handbook of Child Language*. Oxford; Cambridge, MA: Blackwell. 36–72.

Poeppel, D. and K. Wexler (1993). "The Full Competence Hypothesis of Clause Structure in Early German." *Language* **69**(1): 1–33.

Polka, L. and J. Werker (1994). "Developmental Changes in Perception of Nonnative Vowel Contrasts." *Journal of Experimental Psychology* **20**(2): 421–435.

Pollack, I. and J. M. Pickett (1964). "The Intelligibility of Excerpts from Conversation." *Language and Speech* **6**: 161–171.

Posner, M. (1995). "Modulation by Instruction." *Nature* **373**: 198–199.

(1997). "Neuroimaging of Cognitive Processes." *Cognitive Psychology* **33**: 2–4.

Posner, M. and M. Raichle (1994/1997). *Images of Mind*. New York: Scientific American Library.

Posner, M., S. Petersen, P. Fox and M. Raichle (1988). "Localization of Cognitive Operations in the Human Brain." *Science* **240**: 1627–1631.

Posner, M., M. Rothbart, M. Farah and J. Bruer (2001). "Special Issue: The Developing Human Brain." *Developmental Science* **4**(3).

Potts, M., P. Carlson and R. Cocking (1979). *Structure and Development in Child Language: The Preschool Years*. Ithaca, NY: Cornell University Press.

Powers, S. (1995). *The Acquisition of Case in Dutch*. Dutch–German Colloquium on Language Acquisition, Publikatie nummer 66, Universiteit van Amsterdam. Instituut voor Algemene Taalwetenschap.

Powers, S. and D. Lebeaux (1998). More Data on DP Acquisition. In N. Dittmar and Z. Penner (eds.), *Issues in the Theory of Language Acquisition*. Bern: Peter Lang.

Price, C. (2000). "The Anatomy of Language: Contributions from Functional Neuroimaging." *Journal of Anatomy* **197**(3): 335–339.

Prince, A. and S. Pinker (1988). "Rules and Connections in Human Language." *Trends in Neurosciences* **11**(5): 195–207.

Prince, A. and P. Smolensky (1997). "Optimality: From Neural Networks to Universal Grammar." *Science* **275**: 1604–1610.

Pullum, G. and W. Ladusaw (1986). *Phonetic Symbol Guide*. Chicago, IL: University of Chicago Press.

Pullum, G. K. and B. C. Scholz (2002). "Empirical Assessment of Stimulus Poverty Arguments." *Linguistic Review* **19**(1–2): 9–50.

Putnam, H. (1975). The Meaning of Meaning. In H. Putnam (ed.), *Mind, Language and Reality*. Cambridge; New York: Cambridge University Press. 215–271.

Pye, C. (1980). The Acquisition of Grammatical Morphemes in Quiché Mayan. Ph.D. Dissertation. Pittsburgh, PA: University of Pittsburgh.

(1983). "Mayan Telegraphese." *Language* **59**(3): 583–604.

(1986). "Quiché Mayan Speech to Children." *Journal of Child Language* **13**(1): 85–100.

(1992). The Acquisition of K'iché Maya. In D. Slobin (ed.), *The Cross-Linguistic Study of Language Acquisition*. Hillsdale, NJ: Lawrence Erlbaum Associates. **3**: 221–308.

(1994). "Review of 'The CHILDES Project: Tools for Analyzing Talk' by Brian MacWhinney, LEA, 1991." *Language* **70**(1): 156–159.

Pye, C., D. Ingram and H. List (1987). A Comparison of Initial Consonant Acquisition in English and Quiché. In K. Nelson and A. Van Kleeck (eds.), *Children's Language*. Hillsdale, NJ: Lawrence Erlbaum Associates. **6**: 175–190.

Pylyshyn, Z. (1980). "Computation and Cognition: Issues in the Foundations of Cognitive Science." *The Behavioral and Brain Sciences* **3**: 111–169.

(1991). Rules and Representations: Chomsky and Representational Realism. In A. Kasher (ed.), *The Chomskyan Turn*. Cambridge, MA: Basil Blackwell: 231–251.

(1999). What's in Your Mind? In E. Lepore and Z. Pylyshyn (eds.), *What is Cognitive Science?* Malden, MA: Blackwell. 1–25.

(1986). *Computation and Cognition: Toward A Foundation for Cognitive Science*. Cambridge, MA: MIT Press.

Quine, W. V. (1973). *The Roots of Reference*. La Salle, IL: Open Court.

(1960). *Word and Object*. Cambridge, MA: Technology Press of MIT.

(1971). The Inscrutability of Reference. In D. Steinberg and L. Jakobovits (eds.), *Semantics*. Cambridge; New York: Cambridge University Press: 142–156.

Radford, A. (1990). *Syntactic Theory and the Acquisition of English Syntax: The Nature of Early Child Grammars of English*. Oxford, England/Cambridge, MA, Basil Blackwell.

(1994a). "The Syntax of Questions in Child English." *Journal of Child Language* **21**(1): 211–236.

(1994b). Tense and Agreement Variability in Child Grammars of English. In Lust, Suner and Whitman. 135–158.

(2004). *Minimalist Syntax*. Cambridge: Cambridge University Press.

Raghavendra, P. and L. Leonard (1989). "The Acquisition of Agglutinating Languages: Converging Evidence from Tamil." *Journal of Child Lang* **16**: 313–322.

Rakic, P. (1986). "Concurrent Overproduction of Synapses in Diverse Regions of the Primate Cerebral Cortex." *Science* **232**: 232–235.

(1988). "Specification of Cerebral Cortical Areas." *Science* **241**: 170–176.

(1993). Intrinsic and Extrinsic Determinants of Neocortical Parcellation: A Radial Unit Model. In M. Johnson (ed.), *Brain Development and Cognition. A Reader*. Oxford: Blackwell. 93–111.

Ramsey, W. (2000). Connectionism: Philosophical Issues. In F. C. Keil and R. A. Wilson (eds.), *Explanation and Cognition*. Cambridge, MA: MIT Press. 186–188.

Ramus, F., M. Hauser, C. Miller, D. Morris and J. Mehler (2000). "Language Discrimination by Human Newborns and by Cotton-Top Tamarin Monkeys." *Science* **288**(5464): 349–351.

Ramus, F., Nespor, M. and Mehler, J. (1999). "Correlates of Linguistic Rhythm in the Speech Signal." *Cognition* **73**: 265–292.

Randall, J. (1990). "Catapults and Pendulums: The Mechanics of Language Acquisition." *Linguistics* **28**(6): 1381–1406.

(1992). The Catapult Hypothesis: An Approach to Unlearning. In J. Weissenborn, H. Goodluck and T. Roeper (eds.), *Theoretical Issues in Language Acquisition. Continuity and Change in Development*. Hillsdale, NJ: Lawrence Erlbaum Associates: 93–138.

Rani, A. U. (1999). Productivity of the Dative in Telugu Children's Speech. *Proceedings of 20th Conference of South Asian Languages Analysis Round Table*. Urbana Champaign, IL.

Read, C., Y. Zhang, H. Nie and B. Ding (1986). "The Ability to Manipulate Speech Sounds Depends on Knowing Alphabetic Spelling." *Cognition* **24**: 31–44.

Rees, N. S. (1978). Pragmatics of Language: Applications to Normal and Disordered Language Development. In R. L. Schiefelbusch, R. Hoyt and M. Barket (eds.), *Bases of Language Intervention*. Baltimore, MD: University Park Press.

Reich, P. (1976). "The Early Acquisition of Word Meaning." *Journal of Child Language* **3**(1): 117–123.

Reilly, J., E. Klima and U. Bellugi (1990). "Once More with Feeling: Affect and Language in Atypical Populations." *Development and Psychopathology* **2**: 367–391.

Reinhart, T. (1983). *Anaphora and Semantic Interpretation*. London and Canberra: Croom Helm.

(1986). Center and Periphery in the Grammar of Anaphora. In B. Lust (ed.), *Studies in the Acquisition of Anaphora*. Dordrecht; Boston: D. Reidel: 123–50.

Remez, R., P. Rubin, S. Burns, J. Pardo and J. Lang (1994). "On the Perceptual Organization of Speech." *Psychological Review* **101**: 129–156.

Rescorla, L. (1980). "Overextension in Early Language Development." *Journal of Child Language* **7**(2): 321–335.

Restak, R. (2001). *The Secret Life of the Brain*. Washington, DC: Joseph Henry (National Academy Press).

Reznick, J. S. (1990). "Visual Preference as a Test of Infant Word Comprehension. *Applied Psycholinguistics.* **11**: 145–165.

Rice, M. (1996). *Towards a Genetics of Language*. Mahwah, NJ: Lawrence Erlbaum Associates.

Rice, M. and K. Wexler (1996). Toward Tense as a Clinical Marker of Specific Language Impairment in English-Speaking Children. *Journal of Speech and Hearing Research* **39**: 1239–1257.

Rispoli, M. (1995). Factors Contributing to the Frequency of Pronoun Case Overextension. *Twenty-Seventh Annual Child Language Research Forum*. Stanford, CA: Stanford Linguistics Association.

Ritchie, W. and T. Bhatia (eds.) (1996). *Handbook of Second Language Acquisition*. San Diego, CA: Academic Press.

(1999). *Handbook of Child Language Acquisition*. San Diego, CA: Academic Press.

Ritter, N. A. (2002). "Introduction." *The Linguistic Review* **19**(1–2): 1–8.

Roberts, L. (1989). "Are Neural Nets like the Human Brain?" *Science* **243**(4890): 481–482.

Roeper, T. (1991). How a Marked Parameter is Chosen: Adverbs and Do-Insertion in the IP of Child Grammar. In T. Maxfield and B. Plunkett (eds.), *University of Massachusetts Occasional Papers, Special Edition. Papers in the Acquisition of WH: Proceedings of University of Massachusetts Round Table, May 1990*. Amherst, MA: University of Massachusetts. 175–202.

(1993). The "Least Effort" Principle in Child Grammar: Choosing a Marked Parameter. In Reuland and Abraham. **1**: 71–104.

Roeper, T. and J. deVilliers (1994). Lexical Links in the Wh-Chain. In B. Lust, J. Hermon and J. Kornfilt (eds.), *Syntactic Theory and First Language Acquisition: Cross-Linguistic Perspectives*. Vol. 2. *Binding, Dependencies, and Learnability*. Hillsdale, NJ: Lawrence Erlbaum Associates. 357–390.

Rosch, E. (1973). On the Internal Structure of Perceptual and Semantic Categories. In T. E. Moore (ed.), *Cognitive Development and the Acquisition of Language*. New York: Academic Press.

Rosch, E. and C. B. Mervis (1975). "Family Resemblances: Studies in the Internal Structure of Categories." *Cognitive Psychology* **7**(4): 573–605.

Rovee-Collier, C. (1997). "Dissociations in Infant Memory: Rethinking the Development of Implicit and Explicit Memory." *Psychological Review* **104**: 467–498.

(1999). "The Development of Infant Memory." *Current Directions in Psychological Science* **8**(3): 80–85.

Rovee-Collier, C. and P. Gerhardstein (1997). The Development of Infant Memory. In N. Cowan (ed.), *The Development of Memory in Children*. Sussex: Psychology Press. 5–39.

Rovee-Collier, C., K. Hartshorn and M. Di Rubbo (2003). "Long Term Maintenance of Infant Memory." *Developmental Psychology* **29**: 701–710.

Rowland, C. F. and J. M. Pine (2000). "Subject–Auxiliary Inversion Errors and Wh-Question Acquisition: What Children do Know?" *Journal of Child Language* **27**: 157–181.

Ruke-Dravina, V. (1973). On the Emergence of Inflection in Child Language: A Contribution Based on Latvian Speech Data. In C. A. Ferguson and D. Slobin (eds.), *Studies of Child Language Development*. New York: Holt, Rinehart and Winston. 252–267.

Rumelhart, D. and J. McClelland (1986). On Learning the Past Tenses of English Verbs. In J. McClelland and D. Rumelhart (eds.), *Parallel Distributed Processing: Explorations in the Microstructure of Cognition*. Cambridge, MA: MIT Press. **2**.

Ryle, G. (1979). *On Thinking*. Totowa, NJ: Rowman and Littlefield.

Sabbagh, M. A. and M. A. Callanan (1998). "Metarepresentation in Action: 3-, 4-, and 5-Year-Olds' Developing Theories of Mind in Parent–Child Conversations." *Developmental Psychology* **34**(3): 491–502.

Saffran, J., R. N. Aslin and E. Newport (1996). "Statistical Learning by 8-Month-Old Infants." *Science* **274**(5294): 1926–1928.

Saito, M. and N. Fukui (1998). "Order in Phrase Structure and Movement." *Linguistic Inquiry* **29**(3): 439–474.

Salidis, J. and J. S. Johnson (1997). "The Production of Minimal Words: A Longitudinal Case Study of Phonological Development." *Language Acquisition* **6**(1): 1–36.

Samarin, W. J. (1967). *Field Linguistics: A Guide to Linguistic Field Work*. New York: Holt, Rinehart and Winston.

Sanches, M. (1977). Language Acquisition and Language Change: Japanese Numeral Classifiers. In M. Sanches and B. Blount (eds.), *Sociocultural Dimensions of Language Change*. New York: Academic Press.

Santelmann, L. (1995). "The Acquisition of Verb Second Grammar in Child Swedish: Continuity of Universal Grammar in Wh-Questions, Topicalization and Verb Raising." Ph.D. dissertation. Ithaca, NY: Cornell University.

Santelmann, L. and P. Jusczyk (1998). "Sensitivity to Discontinuous Dependencies in Language Learners: Evidence for Limitations in Processing Space." *Cognition* **69**: 105–134.

Santelmann, L., S. Berk, and B. Lust (2000). Assessing the Strong Continuity Hypothesis in the Development of English Inflection: Arguments for the Grammatical Mapping Paradigm. In R. Billery (ed.), *Proceedings of the XIX West Coast Conference on Formal Linguistics*. Medford, MA: Cascadilla Press. **19:** 439–452.

Santelmann, L., S. Berk, S. Somashekar, J. Austin and B. Lust (2002). "Continuity and Development in the Acquisition of Inversion in Yes/No Questions: Dissociating Movement and Inflection." *Journal of Child Language* **29**(4): 813–842.

Sapir, E. (1921). *Language*. New York: Harcourt, Brace and Co.

(1925). "Sound Patterns in Language." *Language* **1**: 37–51.

Satz, P. (1979). "A Test of Some Models of Hemispheric Speech Organization in the Left- and Right-Handed." *Science* **203**: 1131–1133.

Savage-Rumbaugh, E. S., S. Shanker, and T. Taylor (1998). *Apes, Language and the Human Mind*. New York: Oxford University Press.

Schacter, J. (1990). "On the Issue of Completeness in Second Language Acquisition." *Second Language Research* **6**: 93–124.

Schaeffer, J. (1997). *Direct Object Scrambling in Dutch and Italian Child Language*. Ph.D. dissertation. Los Angeles, CA: University of California, Los Angeles.

Schaeffer, J. and M. Tajima (2000). *The Acquisition of Direct Object Scrambling and Clitic Placement: Syntax and Pragmatics*. Amsterdam; Philadephia: John Benjamins.

Schafer, G. and K. Plunkett (1998). "Rapid Word Learning by Fifteen-Month-Olds Under Tightly Controlled Conditions." *Child Development* **69**(2): 309–320.

Schick, B. (2000). Language Experience Effects in ASL and Manual Pointing. Paper presented at AAAS, Washington, DC.

Schieffelin, B. (1979). Getting It Together: An Ethnographic Approach to the Study of the Development of Communicative Competence. In E. Ochs and B. Schieffelin (eds.), *Developmental Pragmatics*. New York: Academic Press.

Schlaggar, B., T. Brown, H. Lugar, K. Visscher, F. Miezin and S. Petersen (2002). "Functional Neuroanatomical Differences between Adults and School-Age Children in the Processing of Single Words." *Science* **296**: 1476–1479.

Schutze, C. (1997). "INFL in Child and Adult Language: Agreement, Case and Licensing." Ph.D. dissertation. Cambridge, MA: MIT.

Schutze, C. T. (1996). *The Empirical Base of Linguistics: Grammaticality Judgments and Linguistic Methodology*. Chicago, IL: University of Chicago Press.

Schvachkin, N. K. (1973). The Development of Phonemic Speech Perception in Early Childhood. English translation by Elena Dernbach. In C. A. Ferguson and D. I. Slobin (eds.), *Studies of Child Language*. **13**: 101–132.

Schwartz, R. and L. Leonard (1982). "Do Children Pick and Choose? An Examination of Phonological Selection and Avoidance in Early Lexical Acquisition." *Journal of Child Language* **9**(2): 319–36.

Sebastian-Galles, N. and S. Soto-Faraco (1999). "Online Processing of Native and Non-Native Phonemic Contrasts in Early Bilinguals." *Cognition* **72**(2): 111–123.

Segalowitz, S. and B. Berge (1995). Functional Asymmetries in Infancy and Early Childhood: A Review of Electrophysiologic Studies and their Implications. In R. Davidson and K. Hugdahl (eds.), *Brain Asymmetry*. Cambridge, MA: MIT Press. 579–616.

Segalowitz, S. and F. Gruber (1977). *Language Development and Neurological Theory*. New York: Academic Press.

Seidenberg, M. (1994). "Language and Connectionism: The Developing Interface." *Cognition* **50**(1–3): 385–401.

Seliger, H. W., S. Krashen and P. Ladefoged (1975). "Maturational Constraints in the Acquisition of Second Language Accents." *Language Sciences* **36**: 20–22.

Selkirk, E. O. (1984). *Phonology and Syntax. The Relation between Sound and Structure.* Cambridge, MA: MIT Press.

Senghas, A. (1995a). *Children's Contribution to the Birth of Nicaraguan Sign Language.* Cambridge, MA: MIT Press.

(1995b). The Development of Nicaraguan Sign Language via the Language Acquisition Process. *In Proceedings of 19th Annual Boston University Conference on Language Development.* Boston, MA: Cascadilla Press.

Senghas, A. and M. Coppola (2001). "Children Creating Language: How Nicaraguan Sign Language Acquired a Spatial Grammar." *Psychological Science* **12**(4): 323–328.

Serra, Miquel, E. Serrat and R. Sole (2000). *La Adquisicion de Lenguaje (Language Acquisition).* Barcelona: Ariel.

Seuss, Dr. (1957). *The Cat in the Hat.* New York: Random House, Inc.

(1963). *Hop on Pop.* New York: Beginner Books.

(1965). *Fox in Socks.* New York: Beginner Books.

(1979). *Oh Say Can You Say?* New York: Beginner Books.

Shady, M. (1996). "Infants' Sensitivity to Function Morphemes." Ph.D. dissertation. Buffalo: State University of New York at Buffalo.

Shady, M., L. Gerken and P. Jusczyk (1995). "Prosody Serves as a Linguistic Marker to Local Co-Occurrence Patterns in Ten-Month-Olds." In D. MacLaughlin and S. McEwen (eds.), *19th Annual Boston University Conference on Language Development.* D. Boston MA: Cascadilla Press. **2**: 553–562.

Shafer, V., M. Morr, J. Kreuzer and D. Kurtzberg (2000). "Maturation of Mismatch Negativity in School-Age Children." *Ear and Hearing.* Lippincott Williams and Wilkins: 242–251.

Shafer, V., D. Shucard, J. L. Shuchard and L. Gerken (1998). "An Electrophysiological Study of Infants' Sensitivity to the Sound Patterns of English." *Journal of Speech, Language, and Hearing Research* **41**: 874–886.

Sharma, V. (1973). *A Linguistic Study of Speech Development in Early Childhood,* Ph.D. dissertation. Agra University.

Shatz, M. (1978). "Children's Comprehension of Question-Directives." *Journal of Child Language* **5**: 39–46.

Shatz, M., E. Hoff-Ginsberg, and D. Maciver (1989). "Induction and the Acquisition of English Auxiliaries: the Effects of Differentially Enriched Input." *Journal of Child Language* **16**(1): 121–140.

Shaywitz, B. A., S. E. Shaywitz, K. R. Pugh, R. T. Constable, P. Studlarksi and R. K. Fulbright (1995). "Sex Differences in the Functional Organization of the Brain for Language." *Nature* **373**: 607–609.

Shi, R., J. Werker and J. Morgan (1999). "Newborn Infants' Sensitivity to Perceptual Cues to Lexical and Grammatical Words." *Cognition* **72**: B11-B21.

Shipley, E., C. Smith and L. Gleitman (1969). "A Study in the Acquistion of Syntax: Free Responses to Verbal Commands." *Language* **45**: 322–342.

Shirai, Y. (1997). "Is Regularization Determined by Semantics, or Grammar, or Both? Comments on Kim, Marcus, Pinker, Hollander and Coppola (1994)." *Journal of Child Language* **24**(2): 495–501.

Shirai, Y. and R. Anderson (1995). "The Acquisition of Tense-Aspect Morphology." *Language* **71**: 743–762.

Shvachkin, N. (1948/1973). "The Development of Phonemic Speech Perception." In C. Ferguson and D. Slobin (eds.), *Studies of Child Language Development*. New York: Holt, Rinehart and Winston: 91–127.

Simon, H. and C. Kaplan (1989). Foundations of Cognitive Science. In M. Posner (ed.), *Foundations of Cognitive Science*. Cambridge, MA: MIT Press.

Simons, D. and F. C. Keil (1995). "An Abstract to Concrete Shift in the Development of Biological Thought: The Insides Story." *Cognition* **56**(2): 129–163.

Simons, G. and S. Bird (2003a). "Building an Open Language Archives Community on the OAI foundation." *Library Hi Tech* **21**(2): 210–218.

(2003b). "The Open Language Archives Community: An Infrastructure for Distributed Archiving of Language Resources." *Literary and Linguistic Computing* **18**: 117–128.

Sinclair, A., R. J. Jarvella and W. J. M. Levelt (eds.) (1978). *The Child's Conception of Language*. Springer Series in Language and Communication. Berlin; Heidelberg; New York: Springer-Verlag.

Sinclair, H. (1967). *Acquisition du langage et développement de la pensée*. Paris.

(1973). Language Acquisition and Cognitive Development. In T. E. Moore (ed.), *Cognitive Development and the Acquisition of Language*. New York: Academic Press.

(1995). "Language Acquisition and Cognitive Development." In R. Arzapalo and Y. Lastra (eds.), *Comparative Linguistics and Language Acquisition*. Geneva; Mexico: University of Geneva: 98–100.

Sinclair, H. (2004a). Comparative Linguistics and Language Acquisition. In Lust and Foley (eds.). 98–100.

Sinclair, H. (2004b). Language Acquisition and Cognitive Development. In Lust and Foley (eds.). 239.

Singleton, D. (1989). *Language Acquisition: The Age Factor*. Clevedon, OH: Multilingual Matters.

Singleton, J. and E. Newport (1993). "When learners surpass their models." Urbana-Illinois: University of Illinois Department of Psychology.

Singleton, J. L., J. P. Morford, and S. Goldin-Meadow (1993). "Once is Not Enough: Standards of Well-Formedness in Manual Communication Created Over Three Different Timespans." *Language* **69**(4): 683–715.

Skinner, B. F. (1957). *Verbal Behaviour*. New York: Appleton-Century-Crafts.

Skuse, D. H. (1988). Extreme Deprivation in Early Childhood. In D. V. M. Bishop and K. Mogford-Bevan (eds.), *Language Development in Exceptional Circumstances*. Edinburgh; New York: Churchill Livingstone. 29–46.

Slavoff, G. and J. Johnson (1995). "The Effects of Age on the Rate of Learning a Second Language." *Studies in Second Language Acquisition* **17**: 1–16.

Slobin, D. (1973). Cognitive Prerequisites for the Development of Grammar. In C. Ferguson and D. Slobin (eds.), *Studies of Child Language Development*. New York: Holt, Rinehart and Winston. (Reprinted in Lust and Foley 2004: 240–250.)

Slobin, D. (1996). From "Thought and Language" to "Thinking for Speaking". In J. Gumperz and S. Levinson (eds.), *Rethinking Linguistic Relativity*. Cambridge: Cambridge University Press. 70–96.

Slobin, D. (ed.) (1985). *The Crosslinguistic Study of Language Acquisition*. Hillsdale, NJ: Lawrence Erlbaum Associates.

Slobin, D., L. Dasinger, et al. (1999). Native Language Reacquisition in Early Childhood. In *Twenty-fourth Annual Child Language Research Forum*. Stanford, CA: Stanford Linguistics Association.

Slobin, D. and C. Welsh (1973). Elicited Imitation as a Research Tool in Developmental Psycholinguistics. In C. Ferguson and D. Slobin (eds.), *Studies of Child Language Development*. New York: Holt, Rinehart and Winston: 485–497.

Smith, B. L. and D. Oller (1981). "A comparative study of pre-meaningful vocalizations produced by normally developing and Down's Syndrome infants." *Journal of Speech and Hearing Disorders*. **46**: 46–51.

Smith, C. S. (1970). "An Experimental Approach to Children's Linguistic Competence." In J. Hayes (ed.), *Cognition and the Development of Language*. New York: J. Wiley and Sons. 109–135.

Smith, I. (1999/2001). *The Phonetics Tutor*. Toronto: York University.

Smith, L. B. (1984). "Young Children's Understanding of Attributes and Dimensions: A Comparison of Conceptual and Linguistic Measures." *Child Development* **55**(2): 363–380.

Smith, M. D. and J. L. Locke (eds.) (1988). *The Emergent Lexicon from a Phonetic Perspective*. San Diego, CA: Academic Press.

Smith, N. (1973). *The Acquisition of Phonology*. Cambridge; New York: Cambridge University Press.

(1982). *Mutual Knowledge*. New York: Academic Press.

(1987). Universals and Typology. In S. Modgil and C. Modgil (eds.), *Noam Chomsky: Consensus and Controversy*. New York: Falmer Press: 57–66.

(1989). *The Twitter Machine: Reflections on Language*. Oxford; Cambridge, MA: Basil Blackwell.

(1990). "Can Pragmatics Fix Parameters?" In I. Roca (ed.), *Logical Issues in Language Acquisition*. Providence, RI: Foris: 277–289.

(1997). "Structural Eccentricities." *Glot International* **2**(8): 7.

(1999). "Bonobos." *Glot International* **4**(3): 9.

(1999 republished 2004). *Chomsky: Ideas and Ideals*. Cambridge; New York: Cambridge University Press.

(2002a). *Language, Bananas, and Bonobos: Linguistic Problems, Puzzles, and Polemics*. Oxford; Cambridge, MA: Basil Blackwell.

(2002b). "Modules, Modals, Maths and the Mind." *Glot International* **6**(2): 248–250.

(2003). Dissociation and Modularity: Reflections on Language and Mind. In M. Banich and M. Mack (eds.), *Mind, Brain and Language*. Hillsdale, NJ: Lawrence Erlbaum Associates.

Smith, N. and I. M. Tsimpli (1995). *The Mind of a Savant. Language Learning and Modularity*. Oxford; Cambridge, MA: Basil Blackwell.

Smolensky, P. (1991). Connectionism, Constituency, and the Language of Thought. In B. Loewer and G. Rey (eds.), *Meaning in Mind: Fodor and His Critics*. Oxford; Cambridge, MA: Basil Blackwell. 201–228.

(1996). "On the Comprehension/Production Dilemma in Child Language." *Linguistic Inquiry* **27**(4): 720–735.

Snow, C. and C. Ferguson (1977). *Talking to Children: Language Input and Acquisition*. Cambridge; New York: Cambridge University Press.

Snow, C. and M. Hoefnagel-Hohle (1978). Age Difference in Second Language Acquisition. In E. Hatch (ed.), *Second Language Acquisition*. Rowley, Newbury House. 333–344.

Snow, C. E. (1972). "Mothers' Speech to Children Learning Language." *Journal of Society for Research in Child Development* **43**(4): 549–565.

Snyder, L., E. A. Bates, et al. (1981). "Content and Context in Early Lexical Development." *Journal of Child Language* **8**(3): 565–582.

So, L. and B. Dodd (1995). "The Acquisition of Phonology by Cantonese-Speaking Children." *Journal of Child Language* **22**(3): 473–495.

Sober, E. (1975). *Simplicity*. Oxford: Clarendon Press.

Soderstrom, M., P. Jusczyk and D. K. Nelson (2000). Evidence for Use of Phrasal Packaging by English-Learning 9-Month-Olds. In *Proceedings of 24th Annual Boston University Conference on Language Development*. Somerville, MA: Cascadilla Press.

Soja, N. N. (1986). "Color Word Acquisition: Conceptual or Linguistic Challenge." *Papers and Reports on Child Language Development* **25**: 104–113.

Soja N. N., S. Carey and E. S. Spelke (1991). "Ontological Categories Guide Young Children's Inductions of Word Meanings: Object Terms and Substance Terms." *Cognition* **38**: 179–211.

— (1992). "Perception, ontology and word meaning." *Cognition* **45**(1): 101–107.

Somashekar, S. (1995). Indian Children's Acquisition of Pronominals in Hindi "Jab" Clauses: Experimental Study of Comprehension. M.A. thesis. Ithaca, NY: Cornell University.

— (1999). Developmental Trends in the Acquisition of Relative Clauses: Cross-Linguistic Experimental Study of Tulu. Ph.D. dissertation. Ithaca, NY, Cornell University.

Somashekar, S., B. Lust, J. Gair, T. Bhatia, V. Sharma and J. Khare (1997). "Principles of Pronominal Interpretation in Hindi Jab Clauses: Experimental Test of Children's Comprehension." In S. Somashekar, K. Yamakoshi, M. Blume and C. Foley (eds.). 65–88.

Somashekar, S., K. Yamakoshi, M. Blume and C. Foley (eds.) (1997). *Cornell Working Papers in Linguistics*. Ithaca, NY: Cornell University. **15**.

Souweidane, M. M., K. H. S. Kim, R. McDowell, M. I. Ruge, E. Lis and G. Krol (1999). "Brain Mapping in Sedated Infants and Young Children with Passive-Functional Magnetic Resonance Imaging." *Pediatric Neurosurgery* **30**: 86–91.

Spelke, E. S., R. Kestenbaum, D. Simons and D. Wein (1995). "Spatiotemporal Continuity, Smoothness of Motion and Object Identity in Infancy." *British Journal of Developmental Psychology* **13**(Pt 1): 113–142.

Spelke, E. S. and S. Tsivkin (2001). Initial Knowledge and Conceptual Change: Space and Number. In M. Bowerman and S. Levinson (eds.), *Language Acquisition and Conceptual Development*. Cambridge; New York: Cambridge University Press.

Spencer, A. (1986). "Towards a Theory of Phonological Development." *Lingua* **68**(1): 3–38.

Sperber, D. and D. Wilson (1995/1986). *Relevance: Communication and Cognition*. Oxford; Cambridge, MA: Basil Blackwell.

— (1998). The Mapping Between the Mental and the Public Lexicon. In P. Carruthers and J. Boucher (eds.), *Language and Thought*. Cambridge: Cambridge University Press: 184–200.

Sperry, R., M. Gazzaniga and J. Bogen (1969). In P. J. Vinken and G. Bruyn (eds.), *Handbook of Clinical Neurology*. New York: Wiley. **4**: 273–290.

Sperry, R. W. (1961). "Cerebral Organization and Behavior." *Science* **133**: 1749–1757.

Sperry, R. W. (1968). Mental Unity Following Surgical Disconnection of the Cerebral Hemispheres. *The Harvey Lecture Series 62*. New York: Academic Press. 292–323.

Springer, K. and F. C. Keil (1991). "Early Differentiation of Causal Mechanisms Appropriate to Biological and Nonbiological Kinds." *Child Development* **62**: 767–781.

Springer, S. and G. Deutsch (1993). *Left Brain, Right Brain*. New York: W. H. Freeman and Co.

Srinivas, N. C. and P. Mohanty (1995). The First Fifty Words: A Case Study of a Telugu-Speaking Normal Child. Dissertation. University of Hyderabad.

Srivastava, G. P. (1974). "A Child's Acquisition of Hindi Consonants." *Indian Linguistics* **35**(2): 112–118.

St. George, M. and D. L. Mills (2001). Electrophysiological Studies of Language Development. In J. Weissenborn and B. Hohle (eds.), *Approaches to Bootstrapping: Phonological, Lexical, Syntactic and Neurophysiological Aspects of Early Language Acquisition*. Amsterdam: John Benjamins.

St. James-Roberts, I. (1981). "A Reinterpretation of Hemispherectomy Data without Functional Plasticity of the Brain." *Brain and Language* **13**: 31–53.

Stager, C. L. and J. F. Werker (1997). "Infants Listen for More Phonetic Detail in Speech Perception than in Word-Learning Tasks." *Nature* **388**(6640): 381–382.

Stambak, M. and H. Sinclair (1990). *Le Jeux de fiction entre enfants de 3 ans*. Paris: Presses Universitaires de France.

Stampe, D. (1969). The Acquisition of Phonemic Representation. *Proceedings of the 5th Regular Meeting of the Chicago Linguistic Society*. Chicago, IL: Chicago Linguistic Society. (Reprinted in Lust and Foley 2004. 307–315.)

Stanley, J. (1999). "Logical form, Origins of." In R. A. Wilson and F. C. Keil (eds.), *The MIT Encyclopedia of the Cognitive Sciences*. Cambridge, MA: MIT Press. 488–489.

Stark, R. (1978). "Features of Infant Sounds: The Emergence of Cooing." *Journal of Child Language* **5**: 379–390.

Stark, R., K. Bleile, J. Brandt, J. Freeman and E. Vining (1995). "Speech-Language Outcomes of Hemispherectomy in Children and Young Adults." *Brain and Language* **51**: 406–421.

Stark, R. (ed.) (1981). *Language Behaviour in Infancy and Early Childhood*. North-Holland: Elsevier.

Sterelny, K. and M. Devitt (1999). Language of Thought. In M. Devitt (ed.), *Language and Reality: An Introduction to the Philosophy of Language*. Cambridge, MA: MIT Press. 451–453.

Stiles, J. (1998). "The Effect of Early Focal Brain Injury on Lateralization of Cognitive Function." *Current Directions in Psychological Science*: 21–26.

Stoel, C. M. (1974). The Acquisition of Liquids in Spanish. Dissertation. Stanford, CA: Stanford University.

Streeter, L. A. (1976). "Language Perception of 2-Month-Old Infants Shows Effects of Both Innate Mechanisms and Experience." *Nature* **259**: 39–41.

Stromswald, K. (1990). Learnability and the Acquisition of Auxiliaries. Ph.D. dissertation. Cambridge, MA: MIT.

(1996). "Analyzing Children's Spontaneous Speech." In D. McDaniel, C. McKee and H. Cairns (eds.), *Methods for Assessing Children's Syntax*. Cambridge, MA: MIT Press. 23–53.

(1998). "The Genetics of Spoken Language Disorders." *Human Biology* **70**: 297–324.

(2000). The Cognitive Neuroscience of Language Acquisition. In M. Gazzaniga (ed.), *The New Cognitive Neurosciences*. Cambridge, MA: MIT Press. 909–932.

(2001). "The Heritability of Language: A Review of Metaanalysis of Twin, Adoption, and Linkage Studies." *Language* **77**(4): 647–723.

Supalla, T., J. L. Singleton, S. Supalla, D. Metlay and G. Coulter (1993). *Test Battery for American Sign Language Morphology and Syntax*. Burtonsville, MD: Linstok Press.

Suzman, S. (1980). "Acquisition of the Noun Class System in Zulu." *Papers and Reports on Child Language Development* **19**: 45–52.

Swingley, D. and R. Aslin (2000). "Spoken Word Recognition and Lexical Representations in Very Young Children." *Cognition* **76**: 147–166.

Tallal, P., S. L. Miller, G. Bedi, G. Byma, X. Wang and S. S. Nagarajan (1996). "Language Comprehension in Language-Learning Impaired Children Improved with Acoustically Modified Speech." *Science* **271**: 81–84.

Tardif, T. (1996). "Nouns Are Not Always Learned Before Verbs: Evidence From Mandarin Speakers' Early Vocabularies." *Developmental Psychology* **32**(3): 492–504.

Tardif, T., S. Gelman and F. Xu (1999). "Putting the 'Noun Bias' in Context: A Comparison of English and Mandarin." *Child Development* **70**(3): 620–635.

Temple, E. (2002). "Brain Mechanisms in Normal and Dyslexic Readers." *Current Opinion in Neurobiology* **12**: 178–183.

Temple, E., G. Deutsch, R. Poldrack, S. Miller, P. Tallal and M. Merzenich (2004). "Neural Deficits in Children with Dyslexia Ameliorated by Behavioral Remediation: Evidence from Functional MRI." *PNAS* **100**(5).

Terrace, H., L. Petitto, R. Sanders and T. Bever (1980). On the Grammatical Capacity of Apes. In K. Nelson (ed.), *Children's Language*. Gardner Press. **2**: 371–443.

Tesan, G. (2003). To Be or Not To Be – an Affix: Inflectional Development in Child Language. *Proceedings of 28th Annual Boston University Conference on Language Development*. Boston, MA: Cascadilla Press.

Tesar, B. (1998). "An Iterative Strategy for Language Learning." *Lingua* **104**(2): 131–145.

Tesar, B. and P. Smolensky (1998). "Learnability in Optimality Theory." *Linguistic Inquiry* **29**(2): 229–268.

(2000). *Learnability in Optimality Theory*. Cambridge, MA: MIT Press.

Thatcher, R. W., R. A. Walker and S. Guidice (1987). "Human Cerebral Hemispheres Develop at Different Rates and Ages." *Science* **236**: 1110–1113.

Thomas, M. (2002). "Development of the Concept of 'The Poverty of the Stimulus'." *The Linguistic Review* **19**(1–2): 51–72.

Thomason, S. G. and T. Kaufman (1988). *Language Contact, Creolization, and Genetic Linguistics*. Berkeley, CA: University of California Press.

Thompson, J. and R. Chapman (1977). "'Who is Daddy?' revisited: The Status of Two-Year-Olds' Over-Extended Words in Use and Comprehension." *Journal of Child Language* **4**: 359–375.

Thornton, R. (1990). Adventures in Long-Distance Moving: The Acquisition of Complex Wh- Questions. Dissertation. Storrs, CT: University of Connecticut.

(1995). "Referentiality and Wh- Movement in Child English: Juvenile Delinquency." *Language Acquisition* **4**(1): 139–175.

(1996). Elicited Production. In D. McDaniel, C. McKee and H. S. Cairns (eds.), *Methods for Assessing Children's Syntax*. Cambridge, MA: MIT Press: 77–102.

(2002). "Let's Change the Subject: Focus Movement in Early Grammar." *Language Acquisition* **10**(3): 229–271.

Thornton, R. and S. Crain (1999). "Levels of Representation in Child Grammar." *Linguistic Review* **16**(1): 81–123.

Thornton, R. and K. Wexler (1999). *Principle B, VP Ellipsis, and Interpretation in Child Grammar*. Cambridge, MA: MIT Press.

Thrainsson, H. (1996). On the (Non-) Universality of Functional Categories. In W. Abraham, S. Epstein, H. Thrainsson and J.-W. Zwart (eds.), *Minimal Ideas*. Philadelphia, PA: John Benjamins: 253–281.

Tincoff, R. and P. W. Jusczyk (1999). "Some Beginnings of Word Comprehension in 6-Month-Olds." *Psychological Science* **10**(2): 172–175.

Toga, A. and J. Mazziotta (1996). *Brain Mapping: The Methods*. San Diego, CA: Academic Press.

Tomasello, M. (1992). *First Verbs. A Case Study of Early Grammatical Development*. Cambridge: Cambridge University Press.

(1995). Pragmatic Contexts for Early Verb Learning. In M. Tomasello and W. Merriman (eds.), *Beyond Names for Things: Young Children's Acquisition of Verbs*. Hillsdale, NJ: Lawrence Erlbaum Associates.

(2000a). *The Cultural Origins of Human Cognition*. Cambridge, MA: Harvard University Press.

(2000b). "Do Young Children Have Adult Syntactic Competence?" *Cognition* **74**: 209–253.

(2000c). "The Item-Based Nature of Children's Early Syntactic Development." *Trends in Cognitive Sciences* **4**(4): 156–163.

Tomasello, M. and M. Barton (1994). "Learning Words in Nonostensive Contexts." *Developmental Psychology* **30**: 639–650.

Tomasello, M. and P. Brooks (1998). "Young Children's Earliest Transitive and Intransitive Constructions." *Cognitive Linguistics* **9**(4): 379–395.

Tomasello, M. and A. Kruger (1992). "Acquiring Verbs in Ostensive and Non-Ostensive Contexts." *Journal of Child Language* **19**(2): 311–33.

Tomasello, M. and W. E. Merriman (1995). *Beyond Names for Things*. Mahwah, NJ: Lawrence Erlbaum Associates.

Tomasello, M., R. Strosberg and N. Akhtar (1996). "Eighteen Month Old Children Learn Words in Non-Ostensive Contexts." *Journal of Child Language* **23**: 157–176.

Tomblin, J. (1999). Paper presented to AAAS Annual Meeting.

Trehub, S. E. (1976). "The Discrimination of Foreign Speech Contrasts by Infants and Adults." *Child Development* **47**: 466–472.

Trehub, S. E. and H.-W. Chang (1977). "Speech as Reinforcing Stimulation for Infants." *Developmental Psychology* **13**(2): 170–171.

Trehub, S. and E. Schneider (1985). "Recent Advances in the Behavioral Study of Infant Audition." In S. E. Gerber (eds.), *Development of Auditory Behavior*. New York: Grune and Stratton.

Trueswell, J., I. Sekerina, N. Hill and M. Logrip (1999). "The Kindergarten-Path Effect: Studying On-Line Sentence Processing in Young Children." *Cognition* **73**(2): 89–134.

Tucker, M., A. M. Jusczyk and P. W. Jusczyk (1997). American Infant Discrimination of Dutch and French Word Lists. *Proceedings of Boston University Conference on Language Development*. Boston, MA: Cascadilla Press.

Turk, A. E., P. W. Jusczyk and L. Gerken (1995). "Do English-Learning Infants Use Syllable Weight to Determine Stress?" *Language and Speech* **38**(2): 143–158.

Tyler, L. K. and W. D. Marslen Wilson (1978). "Some Developmental Aspects of Sentence Processing and Memory." *Journal of Child Language* **5**(1): 113–129.

(1981). "Children's Processing of Spoken Language." *Journal of Verbal Learning and Verbal Behavior* **20**(4): 400–416.

Uriagereka, J. (1998). *Rhyme and Reason: An Introduction to Minimalist Syntax*. Cambridge, MA: MIT Press.

Uttal, W. (2001). *The New Phrenology: The Limits of Localizing Cognitive Processes in the Brain*. Cambridge, MA: MIT Press.

Vaid, J. and G. Hall (1991). Neuropsychological Perspectives on Bilingualism: Right, Left, and Center. In A. G. Reynold (ed.), *Bilingualism, Multiculturalism, and Second Language Learning*. Hillsdale, NJ: Lawrence Erlbaum Associates. 81–112.

Vainikka, A. (1993). "Case in the Development of English Syntax." *Language Acquisition* **3**(3): 257–325.

Valian, V. (1986). "Syntactic Categories in the Speech of Young Children." *Developmental Psychology* **22**(4): 562–579.

(1990). Logical and Psychological Constraints on the Acquistion of Syntax. In L. Frazier and J. DeVilliers (eds.), *Language Processing and Language Acquisition*. Dordrecht; Boston, MA: Kluwer Academic.

(1991). "Syntactic Subjects in the Early Speech of American and Italian Children." *Cognition* **40**(2): 21–49.

(1992). Categories of First Syntax: Be, Be+ing, and Nothingness. In Meisel (1992). 401–422.

(1993). "Discussion. Parser Failure and Grammar Change." *Cognition* **46**: 195–202.

(1994). Children's Postulation of Null Subjects: Parameter Setting and Language Acquisition. In Lust, Hermon and Kornfilt (eds.). 273–286.

(1999). "Input and Language Acquisition." In W. C. Ritchie and T. K. Bhatia (eds.), *Handbook of Child Language Acquisition*. San Diego, CA: Academic Press. 497–530.

Van de Weijer, J. (2001). "Vowels in Infant- and Adult- Directed Speech." *Lund University Working Papers in Linguistics* **49**: 172–175.

van der Hulst, H. and N. Smith (1982). *The Structure of Phonological Representations: Part 1*. Dordrecht: Foris.

Van der Lely, H. K. J. (1998). "SLI in Children: Movement, Economy and Deficits in the Computational-Syntactic System." *Language Acquisition* **7**(2–4): 161–192.

Van Valin, R. D. (1992). An Overview of Ergative Phenomena and Their Implications for Language Acquisition. In D. Slobin (ed.), *The Cross-Linguistic Study of Language Acquisition*. Hillsdale, NJ: Lawrence Erlbaum Associates. **3**: 15–38.

Vargha-Khadem, F. and M. Corballis (1979). "Cerebral Asymmetry in Infants." *Brain and Language* **8**: 1–9.

Vargha-Khadem, F., E. Isaacs, H. Papaleloudi, C. Polkey and J. Wilson (1991). "Development of Language in Six Hemispherectomized Patients." *Brain* **114**: 473–496.

Vargha-Khadem, F., L. Carr, E. Isaacs, E. Brett, C. Adams and M. Mishkin (1997). "Onset of Speech after Left Hemispherectomy in a Nine-Year-Old Boy." *Brain* **120**: 159–182.

Varley, R. and M. Siegal (2000). "Evidence for Cognition Without Grammar from Causal Reasoning and 'Theory of Mind' in an Agrammatic Aphasic Patient." *Current Biology* **10**: 723–726.

Varma, T. L. (1979). "Stage 1 of a Hindi-Speaking Child." *Journal of Child Language* **6**(1): 167–173.

Velton, H. (1943). "The Growth of Phonemic and Lexical Patterns in Infant Speech." *Language* **19**(4): 281–292.

Verma, M. and K. P. Mohanan (1990). Introduction to the Experiencer Subject Construction. In M. Verma and K. P. Mohanan (eds.), *Experiencer Subjects in South Asian Languages*. Stanford, CA: Stanford Linguistics Association Center for the Study of Language and Information, Stanford University.

Vihman, M. (1982). "A Note on Children's Lexical Representations." *Journal of Child Language* **8**(239–264).

Vihman, M. and S. Velleman (2000). Phonetics and the Origins of Phonology. In N. Burton-Roberts, P. Carr and G. Docherty (eds.), *Phonological Knowledge: Conceptual and Empirical Issues*. New York: Oxford University Press.

Vihman, M., R. DePaolis and B. Davis (1998). "Is There a 'Trochaic Bias' in Early Word Learning? Evidence from Infant Production in English and French." *Child Development* **69**(4): 935–949.

Vihman, M., M. Macken, R. Miller, H. Simmons and J. Miller (1985). "From Babbling to Speech: A Re-Assessment of the Continuity Issue." *Language* **61**: 395–443.

Vihman, M. M. (1996). *Phonological Development: The Origins of Language in the Child*. Cambridge, MA: Blackwell.

Vinnitskaya, I., C. Foley and S. Flynn (2001). *Grammatical Mapping in the Acquisition of a Third Language*. Linguistic Society of America Annual Meeting.

Vogel, I. (1975). "One System or Two: An Analysis of a Two-Year-Old Romanian–English Bilingual's Phonology." *Papers and Reports on Child Language Development* **9**: 43–62.

Vogel, P. M. and B. Comrie (eds.) (2000). *Approaches to the Typology of Word Classes. (Empirical Approaches to Language Typology*. Vol. 23.). Berlin: de Gruyter.

Volterra, V., O. Capirci, G. Pezzini, L. Sabbadini and S. Vicri (1996). "Linguistic Abilities in Italian Children with Williams Syndrome." *Cortex* **32**: 663–677.

Von Frisch, K. (1967). *The Dance Language and Orientation of Bees*. Ithaca, NY: Cornell University Press.

Vygotsky, L. S. (1962). *Thought and Language*. Cambridge, MA: MIT Press.

Wagner, L. (2002). "The Heritability of Language." *Trends in Cognitive Sciences* **6**(5): 198.

Wakefield, J. R., E. G. Doughtie and L. Yorn (1974). "Identification of Structural Components of an Unknown Language." *Journal of Psycholinguistic Research* **3**: 262–269.

Wapner, W., S. Hamby and H. Gardner (1981). "The Role of the Right Hemisphere in the Apprehension of Complex Linguistic Materials." *Brain and Language* **14**: 5–33.

Waterson, N. (1971). "Child Phonology: a Prosodic View." *Journal of Linguistics* **7**(2): 179–211.

Waugh, L. R. and M. Monville-Burston (eds.) (1990). *On Language: Roman Jakobson*. Cambridge, MA: Harvard University Press.

Waxman, S. R. (1999). "Specifying the Scope of 13-Month-Olds' Expectations of the Scope of Novel Words." *Cognition* **70**(3): B35–B50.

Waxman, S. R. and A. E. Booth (2000). "Principles that are Invoked in the Acquisition of Words, but not Facts." *Cognition* **77**(2): B35–B43.

Waxman, S. R. and T. Hatch (1992). "Beyond the Basics: Preschool Children Label Objects Flexibly at Multiple Hierarchical Levels." *Journal of Child Language* **19**(2): 217–242.

Waxman, S. R. and D. Markow (1995). "Words as Invitations to Form Categories: Evidence from 12- to 13-Month-Old Infants." *Cognitive Psychology* **29**(3): 257–302.

Weber-Fox, C. and H. Neville (1996). "Maturational Constraints on Functional Specializations for Language Processing: ERP and Behavioral Evidence in Bilingual Speakers." *Journal of Cognitive Neuroscience* **8**(3): 231–256.

Weir, R. H. (1970). *Language in the Crib*. The Hague: Mouton de Gruyter.

Weisler, S. and S. Milekic (2000). *Theory of Language*. Cambridge, MA: MIT Press.

Weissenborn, J. (1990). "Functional Categories and Verb Movement: The Acquisition of German Syntax Reconsidered." *Linguistische Berichte (Special Issue)* **3**: 190–224.

Weissenborn, J. and B. Höhle (2001). *Approaches to Bootstrapping: Phonological, Lexical, Syntactic and Neurophysiological Aspects of Early Language Acquisition*. Amsterdam: John Benjamins.

Weist, R. (1983). "The Word Order Myth." *Journal of Child Language* **10**: 97–106.

Wellman, H. M. (1990). *The Child's Theory of Mind*. Cambridge, MA: MIT Press.

Werker, J. (1994). Cross-Language Speech Perception: Developmental Change Does Not Involve Loss. In J. Goodman and H. Nusbaum (eds.), *The Development of Speech Perception: The Transition from Speech Sounds to Spoken Words*. Cambridge, MA: MIT Press: 93–120.

Werker, J. and J. Pegg (1992). "Speech Perception and Phonological Acquisition." In C. Ferguson, L. Menn and C. Stoel-Gammon (eds.), *Phonological Development: Models, Research and Implications*. Parkton, MD: York Press.

Werker, J. F. and R. C. Tees (1983). "Developmental Changes across Childhood in the Perception of Non-Native Speech Sounds." *Canadian Journal of Psychology* **37**(2): 178–286.

Werker, J. F. and A. Vouloumanos (2000). "Who's Got Rhythm?" *Science* **288**(5464): 280–281.

Werker, J. and R. Tees (1984a). "Cross-Language Speech Perception: Evidence for Perceptual Reorganization During the First Year of Life." *Infants' Behavior and Development* **7**: 49–63.

   (1984b). "Phonemic and Phonetic Factors in Adult Cross-Language Speech Perception." *Journal of the Acoustic Society of America* **75**: 1866–78.

   (1999). "Influences on Infant Speech Processing: Toward a New Synthesis." *Ann. Rev. Psychol.* **50**: 509–535.

Werker, J., J. Gikilbert, K. Humphrey and R. Tees (1981). "Developmental Aspects of Cross-Language Speech Perception." *Child Development* **52**: 249–355.

Werker, J. F., L. Cohen, J. L. Lloyd, M. Casasola and C. L. Stager (1998). "Acquisition of Word-Object Associations by 14-Month-Old Infants." *Developmental Psychology* **34**(6): 1289–1309.

Wetstone H. and G. Friedlander (1973). The Effect of Word Order on Young Children's Responses to Simple Questions and Commands. Paper presented at Annual Meeting of the Society of Research in Child Development.

Wexler, K. (1990). "Innateness and Maturation in Linguistic Development." *Developmental Psychobiology* **23**: 645–660.

(1993). The Subset Principle is an Intensional Principle. In E. Reuland and W. Abraham (eds.), *Knowledge and Language*. Dordrecht; Boston: Kluwer Academic. **1**. 217–239.

(1994). Optional Infinitives, Head Movement and the Economy of Derivations. In D. Lightfoot and N. Hornstein (eds.), *Verb Movement*. Cambridge: Cambridge University Press. 305–382.

(1999). Maturation and Growth of Grammar. In W. C. Ritchie and T. K. Bhatia (eds.), *Handbook of Child Language Acquisition*. San Diego, CA: Academic Press. 55–110.

Wexler, K. and Y.-C. Chien (1985). "The Development of Lexical Anaphors and Pronouns." *Papers and Reports on Child Language Development* **24**: 138–149.

Wexler, K. and P. Culicover (1980). *Formal Principles of Language Acquisition*. Cambridge, MA: MIT Press.

Wexler, K. and R. M. Manzini (1987). "Parameters and Learnability in Binding Theory." In T. Roeper and E. Williams (eds.), *Parameter Setting*. Dordrecht; Boston: D. Reidel. 153–166.

Whalen, D., A. Levitt and Qi Wang (1991). "Intonational Differences Between the Reduplicative Babbling of French- and English-Learning Infants." *Journal of Child Language* **18**: 501–516.

White, K., J. Morgan and L. Wier (2004). "Is a 'dar' a car? Effects of mispronunciation and context on sound-meaning mappings." Poster presented at 29th Annual Boston University Conference on Language Development. Boston.

White, L. (1996). Universal Grammar and Second Language Acquisition: Current Trends and New Directions. In Ritchie and Bhatia (eds.). 85–120.

White, L. and F. Genesee (1992). "How Native is a Near Native Speaker?" Paper Presented at the Boston University Conference on Language Development.

Whitman, J., K-O. Lee and B. Lust (1991). Continuity of the Principles of Universal Grammar in First Language Acquisition: The Issue of Functional Categories. *NELS Proceedings of the North Eastern Linguistics Society Annual Meeting, 21*. Amherst: University of Quebec at Montreal, University of Massachusetts. 383–397.

Whorf, B. L. (1956). *Language, Mind and Reality: Selected Writings of Benjamin Lee Whorf*. Cambridge, MA: MIT Press.

Wilkinson, K. M. and S. A. Stanford (1996). Mechanisms of Fast Mapping in Preschool Children. In *Proceedings of 20th Annual Boston University Conference on Language Development*. Boston, MA: Cascadilla Press.

Williams, E. (1981a). Language Acquisition, Markedness and Phrase Structure. In S. Tavakolian (eds.), *Language Acquisiton and Linguistic Theory*. Cambridge, MA: MIT Press. 8–34.

(1981b). "On the Notions 'Lexically Related' and 'Head of a Word'." *Linguistic Inquiry* **12**: 245–274.

Wilson, R. (1999). Introduction: Philosophy. In. R. Wilson and F. Keil (eds.), *MIT Encyclopedia of the Cognitive Sciences*. Amherst: MIT Press. xv–xxxvii.

Wilson, R. A. and F. C. Keil (eds.) (1999). *The MIT Encyclopedia of the Cognitive Sciences*. Cambridge, MA: MIT Press.

Wimbish, J. S. (1989). *SHOEBOX: A Data Management Program for the Field*. Dallas, TX: Summer Institute of Linguistics Academic Computing.

Wimmer, H. and J. Perner (1983). "Beliefs about Beliefs: Representation and Constraining Function of Wrong Beliefs in Young Children's Understanding of Deception." *Cognition* **13**(1): 103–128.

Winjen, F., E. Krikhaar and E. den Os (1994). "The (Non) Realization of Unstressed Elements in Children's Utterances: Evidence for a Rhythmic Constraint." *Journal of Child Language* **21**(1): 59–83.

Wisniewski, E. and D. Medin (1994). "On the Interaction of Theory and Data in Concept Learning." *Cognitive Science* **18**(2): 221–281.

Witelson, S. F. (1977). Early Hemisphere Specialization and Interhemispheric Plasticity: An Empirical and Theoretical Review. In S. J. Segalowitz and F. Gruber (eds.), *Language Development and Neurological Theory.* New York: Academic Press. 213–289.

Witelson, S. F. and D. L. Kigar (1988). "Anatomical Development of the Corpus Callosum in Humans: A Review with Reference to Sex and Cognition. In J. Segalowitz (ed.), *Brain Lateralization in Children: Developmental Implications.* New York: Guilford. 35–57.

Woods, B. T. and S. Carey (1979). "Language Deficits after Apparent Clinical Recovery from Childhood Aphasia." *Annals of Neurology* **6**(5): 405–409.

Woods, B. T. and H. L. Teuber (1978). "Changing Patterns of Childhood Aphasia." *Annals of Neurology* **3**: 273–280.

Woodward, A. L. and E. M. Markman (1991). "Constraints on Learning as Default Assumptions: Comments on Merriman and Bowman's 'The Mutual Exclusivity Bias in Children's Word Learning'." *Developmental Review* **11**(2): 137–163.

(1998). Early Word Learning. In W. Damon, D. Kuhn and R. S. Siegler (eds.), *Cognition, Perception and Language.* New York: J. Wiley and Sons. **2**: 371–420.

Woodward, A. L., E. M. Markman and C. M. Fitzsimmons (1994). "Rapid Word Learning in 13- and 18-Month-Olds." *Developmental Psychology* **30**(4): 553–566.

Xu, F. (2002). "The Role of Language in Acquiring Object Kind Concepts in Infancy." *Cognition* **85**(3): 223–250.

Xu, F. and S. Carey (1995). Do Children's First Object Kind Names Map onto Adult-Like Conceptual Representations?" In *Proceedings of 19th Annual Boston University Conference on Language Development.* Boston, MA: Cascadilla Press.

Xu, F., S. Carey, K. Raphaeldis and A. Ginzbursky (1995). Twelve-month-olds have the conceptual resources to support the acquisition of count nouns. In *Proceedings of 26th Stanford Child Language Research Forum.* Stanford, CA.

Yamada, J. (1990). *Laura: A Case for the Modularity of Language.* Cambridge, MA: MIT Press.

Yamamoto, K. and F. C. Keil (2000). "The Acquisition of Japanese Numeral Classifiers." *Dissertation Abstracts International Section A: Humanities and Social Sciences* **61**(1): 159.

Zaidel, D. (1994). "Worlds Apart: Pictorial Semantics in the Left and Right Cerebral Hemispheres: Current Directions in Psychological Science." *American Psychological Society* **3**(1): 5–8.

Zurif, E. (1980). "Language Mechanisms: A Neuropsychological Perspective." *American Scientist* **68**: 305–311.

Zurif, E. (1983). Aspects of Sentence Processing in Aphasia. In M. Studdert-Kennedy (ed.), *Psychobiology of Language.* Cambridge, MA: MIT Press.

Author index

Subject index